M000285578

Alabama Baptists

Southern Baptists in the Heart of Dixie

RELIGION AND AMERICAN CULTURE

Series Editors
David Edwin Harrell
Wayne Flynt
Edith L. Blumhofer

Alabama Baptists

Southern Baptists
in the Heart
of Dixie

Wayne Flynt

The University of Alabama Press
Tuscaloosa and London

Copyright © 1998
The University of Alabama Press
Tuscaloosa, Alabama 35487-0380
All rights reserved
Manufactured in the United States of America

1 2 3 4 5 6 7 8 9 • 06 05 04 03 02 01 00 99 98

Publication of this book has been made possible in part by a
subvention from the Alabama Baptist Historical Commission.

∞

The paper on which this book is printed meets the minimum requirements of
American National Standard for Information Science-Permanence of Paper for
Printed Library Materials, ANSI Z39.48-1984.

Library of Congress Cataloging-in-Publication Data

Flynt, J. Wayne, 1940–
    Alabama Baptists : Southern Baptists in the heart of Dixie / Wayne
Flynt.
      p.   cm. — (Religion and American culture)
    Includes bibliographical references and index.
    ISBN 0–8173–0927–6 (cloth : alk. paper)
    1. Alabama Baptist State Convention—History. 2. Baptists—
Alabama—History. 3. Alabama—Church history. I. Title.
II. Series: Religion and American Culture (Tuscaloosa, Ala.)
BX6462.4.A2F57   1998
286′.1761—dc21
                                         97–44003

British Library Cataloguing-in-Publication data available

For Alabama Baptists

Contents

Preface

The purpose for writing this book was simple: to explain Baptists to themselves and to explain them to others, with a focus on the people who called themselves Alabama Baptists. Who were they? What did they believe? How did they relate to their society? What institutions did they create to sustain their work?

Writing the history of a denomination in an era widely described as postdenominational seems strange. Baby boomers and post boomers supposedly join congregations, not denominations. And pentecostals have eclipsed evangelicals as the most rapidly growing Christian groups. The evidence from Alabama certainly supports these hypotheses. As the twentieth century waned, Alabama Baptists experienced little growth. Congregational loyalty and theological belief count for more than fidelity to denomination. But this book is about people who lived in the nineteenth and twentieth centuries, not in the twenty-first. Even if denominations are becoming anachronistic—a highly dubious assumption—Baptists continue to dominate Alabama as few religious groups do in any state. One in four Alabamians and nearly two of three church members belong to churches of the Alabama Baptist State Convention (ABSC), the highest percentage of Southern Baptist Convention (SBC) dominance of any state. Every aspect of the state's life—its politics, commerce, and education—is interwoven with the ABSC.

Although denominational history is one of the oldest and most venerated ways of making sense of American religion, it is not static. A recent book edited by Robert Bruce Mullin and Russell E. Richey entitled *Reimagining Denominationalism* (1994) describes how denominational history has changed. Early histories of religious groups were usually written by someone from within the group to preserve basic information about its origins and to defend and extol its beliefs. Since the 1930s, denominational history has shifted toward the intellectual and social context in which the denomination functioned.

Denominational history has at least two audiences: the community of like-minded believers (in this case, Alabama Baptists); and those outside the denomination who seek to understand it. This fact makes the work of the denominational historian difficult. Writing about people in the pews (women, African Americans, ethnics), about social status and power relationships, or about the way culture or more accurately various subcultures shaped the denomination may please academics who read the book. But ignoring white males who provided the denomination's leadership, or condemning their defense of conservative values, strikes people within the faith community as the worst kind of presentism, of projecting the values of our time back into the past. The best denominational histories, in my view, pay attention both to the values of the faith community and to the broader secular society in which such values operated. To explain the values of believers requires appropriate attention to doctrine, ritual, belief, practice, and ethical behavior. To explain the relation of believers to their society requires appropriate attention to politics, to economics, and above all else in Alabama, to race.

Compounding the problems of this requisite double vision is the changing nature of the Southern Baptist Convention (and most other denominations as well). Once upon a time the SBC was one of the most self-contained of all denominations. In recent years the story has become much more complex. A congregation may still be officially connected to the SBC but choose to give its mission contributions to the more moderate Cooperative Baptist Fellowship. Or it may feel alienated from the state convention, which it considers insufficiently conservative, and give its money directly to the SBC. Fundamentalist Alabama Baptists proclaim that they feel more comfortable with like-minded Presbyterians than with "denominational loyalist," "moderate," or "liberal" Baptists. Those varieties of Baptists sometimes explain that Jews come closer to their historic Baptist views on separation of church and state than do their fundamentalist Baptist brothers and sisters.

The organizational structure of the ABSC is more traditionally loyal and intact than virtually any other state Baptist convention. But even among Alabama Baptists strains have appeared. Perhaps the proper analogy for the relationship of 3,000 individual congregations to the ABSC is that of a spider web with complex linkages and fragile elements. Churches are linked at many points—some to transdenominational fundamentalist or pentecostal groups and leaders (Jerry Falwell and Moral Majority, Pat Robertson and Christian Coalition); others to ecumenical and community social agencies and main-line denominations. Some eschew all external links and remain loyal only to the SBC regardless of who leads it or what they believe. All these strands are fragile and hard to reconstruct once broken. If one can argue that Alabama probably has more congregations still solidly tied to the ABSC and Southern Baptist Convention than other states, it is probably safe to add that the connecting strands have seldom been so tenuous.

This fact underlines the importance of careful examination of congregation and individual leadership as well as denominational structure. While not ignoring ABSC institutions, this history focuses on individual Baptists, their congregations, and how they were related to the denomination.

Another issue to be considered in writing denominational history is the role of authorship. Is it best to have an insider or an outsider write it? Insiders belong to the faith community about which they write. This association gives them certain advantages. They have intuitive insights not available to others. They understand certain complex issues from a lifetime of common cultural identity and participation. They have made their own faith commitment to the common values of the group.

The down side of such history is the loss of objectivity. Insiders share too much of the common faith and become uncritical about compromises and inconsistencies. They refuse to ask hard questions or subject their own group to the careful and critical scrutiny they impose on others. The "good guys" become missionary Southern Baptists; the "bad guys" are Primitive Baptists, foot-washing Baptists, or Landmark Baptists.

To this time, every general history of Alabama Baptists has been written by an insider, namely by a white, male, ordained Alabama Baptist preacher. And each one has been excellent in its own way. Alabama Baptists have proven unusually historically minded. Only thirteen years after the first state convention met, they commissioned one of their own, Hosea Holcombe, to collect histories of all congregations and compile a history of the denomination's origins. The result, Holcombe's *History of the Rise and Progress of the Baptists in Alabama,* published in 1840, remains a classic. One of the earliest state histories written by a man who is arguably the state's first historian, it set a standard of rigor that was admirable for its time. Even though Holcombe's history is a triumphal celebration of the denomination's origins (and is often unkind to dissenters), it is also self-critical and thoroughly grounded in original research.

The organization of the Alabama Baptist Historical Society in 1893 led to publication of the second history, B. F. Riley's *History of the Baptists of Alabama,* two years later. As a well-educated representative of New South values of industrial progress and racial moderation, Riley was the ideal spokesman to describe a rapidly maturing denomination. No longer focused on its primitive pioneer origins, Riley emphasized Baptist growth, power, and sophistication. The revival of the Alabama Baptist Historical Society in 1903 (led by such luminaries as John R. Tyson, the chief justice of the state supreme court) led to a special centennial celebration of Alabama Baptist life in 1923 and the publication of Riley's updated *A Memorial History of the Baptists of Alabama.*

The history society became moribund for the second time after 1923 and was not revived for a decade. In 1933 the state convention created a committee on the preservation of Alabama Baptist history and designated the Howard College library depository for historical records. A new history society was formed in 1936 with more than a hundred members. Under the indefatigable leadership of Howard College religion professor James H. Chapman, the collection of Baptist history began in earnest.

Subsequent histories by denominational leaders covered mainly their own spheres of influence or times (denominational chief executive officers George Bagley and A. Earl Potts both wrote memoirs, for instance). Two exceptions were Hermione Jackson, who wrote a splendid history of Alabama Woman's Missionary Union (WMU), and A. Hamilton Reid, who wrote a general denominational history bringing the story of Alabama Baptists to the mid-1960s. What united these histories was their focus on institutions and their narrow denominational context. At least in the case of the Jackson volume, however, there is a surprisingly strong element of criticism of the male hierarchy and its attempt to dominate Baptist women.

The present volume will try to build upon the strengths of the earlier attempts without repeating their mistakes. Like any history, it will have different strengths and weaknesses. I am an "insider" in the sense that I have shared a common Baptist faith for nearly half a century. I grew up in Alabama Baptist churches. My world view was shaped by the people about whom I write. But I was also trained as a professional historian. The canons of my profession are dispassionate objectivity and self-criticism. However, I am under no illusions about the purity of such standards. Historians are people also—they have political beliefs and religious ideals; they cast their lots with certain sides in controversies like everyone else. In that sense, they continue to struggle with objectivity whether they write as insiders or outsiders.

I have made every effort to overcome the liabilities of insider history.

Where possible I try to let parties to a controversy speak for themselves. I have attempted to be fair to the losing side of denominational controversies as well as to winners. Most particularly I have avoided making fun of deeply held beliefs that I do not share. It is easy enough to consider distant ancestors benighted and backward from the perspective of our own enlightened hindsight—but it is uncharitable to them and unfair of us. We should be as sensitive to the context of their times as we hope historians a hundred years from now will be generous to us. Our standards cannot be imposed on them. But neither can we overlook their foibles and inconsistencies. We must let them speak their beliefs, even when those beliefs shock and embarrass those of us who are their spiritual descendants. Perhaps their absolute certainty about matters we now universally consider wrongminded will, at the very least, make us more humble, never a bad thing for religious people to experience.

As we judge distant ancestors, we would do well to remember that no denomination does all things equally well. If the primary focus of a religious people is on evangelism and church growth, they are often less gifted at developing internal spirituality and external social ethics. To some extent then, one must judge Alabama Baptists by their own values and priorities.

At the same time, one must note the roads not taken and hold them accountable for their own decisions. It may be true that the best way to transform society is not by the social gospel but by converting individuals and letting them change race relations for the better. But any fair observer, examining the influence of white Alabama Baptists on racial justice within their society, must hold the denomination to its own standards of measurement. How much did "born-again" individuals alter Alabama's racial structure for the better? And how much was racial justice imposed from the outside by secular politics, courts, and culture? Are Alabama Baptist churches as racially accepting as the state's secular college football teams, universities, or National Guard units? If Scripture is inerrant, as many Baptists believe, how could they so fundamentally misunderstand its intent when they almost universally used it to defend slavery, segregation, or the rejection of women as voters? These are not "politically correct" questions growing from historical presentism. They are questions of consistency applied to the self-proclaimed values of a people.

In a sense, self-criticism is easier now than it was for Holcombe, Riley, and Reid. Internal disagreements were so intense by the late twentieth century that Baptists disagreed with each other more fiercely than they did with other denominations or even for a time with the secular culture all around them. The collapse of consensus has made Baptists more aware of their differences, which in many ways is the theme of this book.

The premises from which I have worked are simple. Believing that religion can be viewed from various perspectives, I have sought to understand Alabama Baptists on three levels. Being an Alabama Baptist involved individual experience between a person and God. At this level, conversion, spiritual growth, discipleship, and personal ethics are central.

I also examine Alabama Baptists as a congregational experience. A group of like-minded people unite in commitment to Christ. At this level, the centrality of family, friends, neighbors, and community emerges. Local organizations (Sunday school, Woman's Missionary Union, deacons, pastors, church discipline) are paramount.

Finally, I focus on Alabama Baptists as a denominational experience: a group of relatively like-minded congregations committed to common theology and polity. To facilitate their mission in the world, churches deemphasized their differences in order to construct institutions, train leaders, and work cooperatively and efficiently. Not everyone begins with the cultural assumptions of Southern Baptists. But few religious groups have been as single-minded or as intense in implementing their ideology.

I have organized the book chronologically. In each time span, I have looked at Alabama Baptists internally and externally. What did the church mean internally to its own communicants? What did belief, baptism, fellowship, discipline, the rituals and symbols of worship mean to them? Externally, how did the church help people relate to the world around them? How did changes in the secular world alter both external practice and internal meaning?

Viewed in this way, Alabama Baptist history is less like a sturdy organ, reliably predictable if sometimes a little monotonous, than a more responsive and adaptable accordion, expanding and contracting with each new requirement. Between 1823 and 1845 many hyper-Calvinists left Alabama Baptist ranks for the Primitive Baptists. Still the denomination grew. Between 1865 and 1874 nearly half of all Alabama Baptists left to form black Baptist churches. Still the denomination grew. A decade later, many white Baptists deserted missionary congregations to join pentecostal and holiness churches. Still the denomination grew. In the 1960s Alabama Baptists lost racial and political moderates to more liberal denominations and fundamentalists to independent Baptist congregations. Still the denomination grew. Throughout all these crises, the denomination continued to grow by preempting the conservative, middle-class, white center of Alabama society. By its own measurements of victory—church growth, numbers of baptisms, influence on its culture—the denomination was hugely successful.

My first research on this book began in 1966 as a newly arrived faculty member at my alma mater, Howard College. As a Baptist ministerial student unhappy with my denomination's stand on race, I had decided upon graduating in 1961 to pursue a doctorate in history rather than a problematical pulpit in a denomination convulsed by racial conflict. No less committed to ministry, I became institutionally engaged in Alabama Baptist churches as a Sunday school teacher, Baptist Training Union director, deacon, and occasionally as a supply preacher. Years later, as chairman of the Southern Baptist and Alabama Baptist historical commissions, I had a chance to practice what I had long preached, namely a new kind of professional, thoroughly researched, contextually rich Baptist history. A quarter century after I began research for this new kind of Baptist history, historian Marlene H. Rikard (then chair of the Alabama Baptist Historical Commission) asked me to formalize the project as a new history of Alabama Baptists for the 175th anniversary of the state convention. That request began an intense, decade-long sprint to finish a project that ultimately stretched across a third of a century.

Without the work of earlier generations of faithful Baptists who gathered and wrote history, the task would have been overwhelming. Hosea Holcombe, Benjamin F. Riley, Davis C. Woolley, James H. Chapman, Hermione Jackson, Lee N. Allen, A. Hamilton Reid, and others made an impossible job merely a difficult and demanding one. Frances Hamilton and the late John Loftis, directors of the Alabama Baptist Historical Commission, were uniformly helpful and encouraging.

Numerous graduate students at both Samford University and Auburn University produced high-quality theses and dissertations that filled gaps in our knowledge. Notable among them were Robert F. Crider, Cynthia A. Wise, John H. Burrows, Kate Campbell, Karen Stone, Susan Hunt Ray, Robert E. Praytor, and Carol Ann Vaughn.

Cooperative denominational officials were essential. Although they knew they would not agree with all my arguments or conclusions, they trusted me to be fair. Their trust and confidence speaks volumes about how respect for individual freedom of conscience and intellect still survives among Alabama Baptists. Men and women who called themselves "fundamentalist" in theology did not look over the shoulder of a self-confessed "moderate" nor in any way seek to control this project or dictate its outcome. A. Earl Potts, Troy L. Morrison, and Hortense Barnes deserve my particular thanks.

So kind and cooperative were they that I regret having to use terms like "fundamentalist," "moderate," and "liberal," which in recent times have become weapons with which to inflict wounds rather than terms of objective analysis. The nomenclature of the historical profession requires the use of such terms to place historical discourse in a commonly understood language. But the reader should understand (and certainly will if he or she reads to the end) that such terms completely fail to capture the temperament of combatants. Theological "liberals" in this book can be and often are racist and intolerant, arrogant in their own knowledge, and condescending toward Baptist folk traditions. Conversely, theological "fundamentalists" can often be racially open, even prophetically courageous. They can also be kind and accepting of differences. Although I consider myself a product of 1930s and 1940s neo-orthodox, moderate theological influences, my personal sympathies in this book tend to be with hard-pressed bivocational ministers who often knew too little theology to think or act ideologically. For them, the call to proclaim the gospel and minister to people much like themselves while earning a living by the sweat of their brows in coal mines or textile mills, on farms or in factories, left them little time for extended theological debate.

If the page of dedication afforded sufficient space, I would dedicate this book to John H. Thomas and Charles C. Worthy, who ushered me into the Christian faith; to B. Locke Davis, C. Otis Brooks, and John H. Jeffers, who were my long-time pastors; to W. Albert Smith, my father-in-law and a model of nondogmatic fundamentalism; and to William T. Edwards, my freshman college teacher of Old and New Testament, later my friend and colleague, whose theology was more critical and liberal than the others. What these mentors had in common was a fervent commitment to being Baptist and a warm personal faith. They were all white males. One would hope that the next generation of denominational historians will be touched just as deeply by nurturing female Baptists, for they have often sustained churches when males failed and have often been the most faithful envoys of Christian witness. What did *not* distinguish these early influences on me was a common theology. The ones I mention as formative in my own Christian pilgrimage were fundamentalist, conservative, moderate, and liberal.

I also owe an enormous debt of gratitude to archivists. Elizabeth C. Wells and Shirley L. Hutchens at Samford University went well beyond the normal duties of their office, suggesting collections I should examine, revealing anecdotes they discovered, and tracking down the most obscure material, sometimes in collections they had not even inventoried. Bill F. Sumners, my former student and archivist at the Southern Baptist Historical Archives in Nashville, and his boss, the late Lynn May Jr., put up with my annual summer research trips for nearly a decade.

Harmon Straiton at Auburn University Library sympathized with anyone forced to read every issue of the *Alabama Baptist* from 1843 until 1998. During my multiyear hibernation in his sanctuary, Harmon finally grew so concerned that he set me up with my own microfilm reader in a precious carrel normally reserved for distinguished visiting professors. When I managed to trap myself inside the carrel late one Friday evening due to a malfunctioning door lock, Harmon was ready the next Monday with a red ribboned basket labeled "Carrel Survival Kit," which contained a box of crackers and a liter of water. Such good humor from librarians and archivists across the South made the years pass agreeably if not rapidly.

I owe a particular debt of gratitude to friends who read the book in manuscript and corrected numerous factual errors. Charles H. Lippy, Samuel S. Hill Jr., Bill J. Leonard, Lee N. Allen, Frances Hamilton, Marlene Rikard, Elizabeth Wells, Shirley Hutchens, and Earl Potts are due more gratitude than mere friendship can provide. So is Nicole Mitchell, editor in chief of The University of Alabama Press, who shepherded this project to completion. The Alabama Baptist Historical Commission also provided generous support to keep this lengthy book within the financial range of ordinary Baptist people who wish to purchase it.

Finally, I thank Wickham Henkels, Peggy Mason, and Dorothy Flynt. Wickham is my faithful editorial assistant, who has an uncanny eye for infelicity of word and phrase and who is sufficiently my friend to tell me the unvarnished truth when no other person than my wife, Dorothy, is so reckless. Peggy Mason typed this manuscript, surprised that someone in this computer age still writes with fountain pen on legal pad. If Baptists are correct and there is a heaven, Peggy will certainly have a special reward for having so efficiently and promptly deciphered my scratchings. Not since archaeologists tackled the Rosetta Stone has a human being been confronted with such a daunting task. That she was able to accomplish this task in two pressure-packed months should convince any skeptic that miracles still do happen. Dorothy is my best friend and soul mate, whose faithful ministries as a WMU director, as an English language teacher of internationals, and in a variety of other offices never lets me forget the pivotal role of Baptist women.

As for the inscription on the dedicatory page, it reflects my deepest gratitude to the people who are the subjects of this study. Usually kind and earnest, funny and entertaining, hospitable and sincere, Alabama Baptists can also be cantankerous, infuriating, irascible, contradictory, and hypo-critical. Which is to say they are a good cross section of the human species and a lot like the rest of humanity. But they are never uninteresting, which is no small matter when one spends a third of a century studying them.

Alabama Baptist Chronology

October 2, 1808	Flint River Baptist Church established
June 3, 1809	Enon Baptist Church (Huntsville First Baptist Church) established, first permanent ABSC church
October 28, 1823	Alabama Baptist State Convention (ABSC) met for first time at Salem Baptist Church near Greensboro
1838	Judson College established in Marion
1841	Howard College established in Marion
1843	*Alabama Baptist* begins in Marion
1844	ABSC passes the Alabama Resolutions affirming right of slaveholders to serve as missionaries and rejecting jurisdiction of Baptist Home Mission Society. Led to establishment of Southern Baptist Convention.
1845	Southern Baptist Convention established
1845	the Board of Domestic Missions (SBC) located in Marion
1847	Eliza Sexton Shuck appointed missionary to China, first Alabama Baptist foreign missionary
1861–1865	Civil War
1865–1874	division of Alabama Baptist churches into white and black congregations
1879	women's central mission's committee for Alabama announced (beginning of Woman's Missionary Union)
1882	Home Mission Board (SBC) moves from Marion to Atlanta
1886	Washington B. Crumpton becomes executive secretary of state mission board, a position he will hold for a quarter century (1886–1895, 1899–1915)
1887	ABSC votes to move Howard College from Marion to Birmingham
1888	WMU (SBC) organized

1889	Alabama WMU organized
1890–1896	Populist Party uprising in Alabama
1891	Alabama Baptist Children's Home founded
1913	Women allowed to attend ABSC as messengers
1917–1918	U.S. involvement in World War I
1919	the Seventy-Five Million Dollar Campaign is launched
1919	L. L. Gwaltney becomes editor of *Alabama Baptist*
1920	Mentone Springs acquired as convention assembly ground
1921	WMU relocates its national headquarters from Baltimore to Birmingham
1925	the Cooperative Program (SBC) begins
1928	Alabama Baptists divide over the presidential candidacy of Democrat Al Smith
1929	stock market crash marks beginning of the Great Depression nationally
1936	Alabama Baptist Historical Society reestablished and becomes permanent custodian of denomination's records and history
1941	World War II begins
1947	Shocco Springs assembly grounds purchased
1947	Howard College extension department established
1950	Southside Baptist Church in Birmingham becomes first church in Alabama to broadcast a worship service on television
1950	Leon Macon replaces L. L. Gwaltney as editor of *Alabama Baptist*
1954	U.S. Supreme Court rules "separate but equal" schools for African Americans to be unconstitutional
1954	Mary Essie Stephens begins thirty-year career as executive director of Alabama WMU
1960	Alabama Baptists split again over a Catholic presidential candidate, John F. Kennedy
1961	Mobile College opens
1963	SBC revises 1925 Baptist Faith and Message
1963	ABSC headquarters moves into new offices on southern bypass in Montgomery
1965	Howard College changes name to Samford University

1972	ABSC elects first woman vice-president
1976	SBC launches "Bold Mission Thrust" as a quarter-century growth strategy
1979	Biblical inerrantists win control of SBC
1983	Women in Ministry (SBC) established
1990	Cooperative Baptist Fellowship established by denominational moderates
1990	Ralph Waldo Beeson bequeaths Samford University a sum that ultimately reaches $55 million, one of the largest contributions in the history of U.S. higher education
1993	Mobile College changes name to University of Mobile
1998	ABSC celebrates its 175th birthday

Alabama Baptists

Southern Baptists in the Heart of Dixie

1

Confronting the Frontier, 1800–1845

". . . a living spectacle of ignorance, superstition, and crime."

arly on a Saturday morning in 1820, a solitary figure hurried toward the schoolhouse at Bellville in Conecuh County. From his farm four miles south of Evergreen, Rev. Alexander Travis had a fifteen-mile walk to his newly organized Murder Creek Baptist Church. Travis, always neatly dressed on his long Saturday stroll, made a striking appearance at more than six feet tall. The journey to his once-a-month preaching station would have been quicker had he used his horse. But that animal had to plow from Monday through Friday and needed rest. The leisure that Travis allowed his plow horse, he denied himself. Saturday afternoon and Sunday morning he devoted to his Murder Creek congregation. The next three weekends would take him in opposite directions to each of three different congregations (to Mars Hill, Warden Creek, and Salem churches). Although he would pastor the Murder Creek congregation until his death in 1852, other pastorates during his thirty-four-year ministry in Alabama stretched across south-central Alabama from Claiborne on the Alabama River to Damascus on the Florida border.[1] As the only ordained Baptist preacher in Conecuh County, Travis felt keenly the awesome burden of the gospel.

The frontier that Travis encountered when he moved to Big Pond in

1818 (a year before Alabama became a state) was as wild a region as the Southeast had to offer. The curious name of his church, Murder Creek, captured harsh frontier realities. The denominational newspaper that he read in later years recorded many cases of violence. Just before Christmas in 1844, a dozen men with blackened faces burst open the door of the Burgess family on a farm near Cahawba in Dallas County. They had come to deliver a petition declaring the family to be undesirable and demanding they move. The mob was armed and intended to enforce its demand by seizing and paddling the father, mother, son, and two adult daughters. Instead, the family, forewarned of the intrusion, fired into the mob, killing two attackers and wounding others. In the ensuing melee, Burgess was stabbed to death and one of his daughters was killed by a shotgun blast. The other females engaged in hand-to-hand combat with knives. Members of the mob who could still do so fled the county. The Baptist editor dutifully reported the bad reputation of the family but vigorously defended their resistance, asking his readers what they would do differently if an armed band kicked open their door in the dead of night. Even at the state's highest seat of learning, the University of Alabama, a shooting occurred the same year as the Burgess affair. And during the following year, students angered by a speech by the Baptist preacher-president, Basil Manly Sr., broke windows in the chapel and tore up the pulpit Bible.[2]

When not perplexed by the excesses of human beings, Alabama pioneers encountered the vagaries of nature. Less than a decade before Travis arrived in Conecuh County, a series of tremors rumbled across the Southeast. The New Madrid earthquake in 1811 was estimated by geologists to have measured 8.2 on the Richter scale, making it the largest in North America since before the time of Christ. Jets of sulphur and water erupted from fissures in the earth, huge lakes and falls were formed in Tennessee, and the Mississippi River briefly reversed course. For weeks, aftershocks drove nervous families out of their houses. To Muskogee Native Americans (called "Creeks" by whites), these events came as a judgment against their apostasy. They had taken up white men's ways, adapted to agriculture, begun to drink alcohol, converted to Christianity, and worn European-style clothes. The ensuing nativist religious revival culminated in a bitter war.[3] Among white settlers, the earthquakes quickened the camp meeting revivalism that had begun at Cane Ridge, Kentucky, in 1801 and had spread from there across the southern frontier.

After Andrew Jackson defeated the Creek uprising, the Treaty of Fort Jackson in August 1814 opened Creek land west of the Coosa River. The restoration of peace beckoned to men such as Alexander Travis to come to

Alabama, God's "clearing in the thicket," where they could carve an earthly paradise out of the wilderness.

For those brave enough or sufficiently foolhardy to settle the newly opened lands, taming the wilderness was no easy matter. Minutes of the 1827 Alabama Baptist State Convention mentioned their discouragement: "The wilderness is all before you, behind you, around you; the inhabitants of the waste places are in the midst of you and before your eyes, a living spectacle of ignorance, superstition, and crime."[4]

Those brave souls undaunted by earthquakes, Indians, wars, and wilderness were often brought low by human mortality. In the Old Beulah Cemetery in Conecuh County, seven miles south of Evergreen, the bones of Alexander Travis, his wife, and his son rest in peace behind one of the innumerable churches he founded. Although Travis lived a long life by the reckoning of his times (sixty-two years) and pastored Beulah Church for three decades, Eliza M. Payne, whose remains lie nearby, was not so fortunate. Born two years before the great earthquakes began, she died in July 1828, only nineteen years old. If ordinary mortals needed any reminding, H. L. Horn's tombstone in the Clairmont Baptist Church cemetery conveyed a macabre message: "Please remember man, as you pass by, As you are now, once was I. As I am now, you must be. Prepare for death and follow me."[5]

In a way hardly comprehensible to succeeding generations, life was a perilous journey. This world was not their home. They were quickly passing through.

For those who shared a span of years equal to that of Alexander Travis, Alabama's frontier offered unrelenting toil. The physical exertion required to clear forests, break new land, build log houses, and cultivate crops left little energy or money for institution building. Schools and churches had to wait, and colleges were only a distant dream. Nearly all Alabamians (except those who inhabited a thin thread of land along the coast at Mobile or an occasional clearing along the river at Huntsville, Tuscaloosa, Montgomery, or Selma) took their living from the soil. And for all the agricultural bounty of the western Alabama canebrake or the alluvial Tennessee Valley, Alabama could be a stingy earth mother. South of the valley, high mountains broke farm plots into small corn patches and cut Tennessee River towns off from commerce or communication with south Alabama. In the southeastern corner of the state, tall pine forests provided a canopy over poor sandy soil that nourished a nutritious wiregrass, suitable for herds of pigs and cattle but inadequate to sustain commercial agriculture. Though affluent planters would emerge in time in the Black Belt and Tennessee

Valley, most white settlers would remain small yeoman farmers. They lived out their years in hard struggle with the land, treasuring those rare moments after lay-by time in July when the religious among them could attend a camp meeting or when the profane could engage in more worldly amusements. Even among the religious, impassable trails and grinding labor limited church attendance to once a month or less. Throughout the nineteenth century, many rural Baptist churches met not at all during winter and spring.

Obstacles so formidable make even more significant the blossoming of evangelical religion on the Alabama frontier. Whether as talisman against earthquake, flood, or drought, or as hope for life to come, evangelical Christianity sprang from Alabama's soil as prolifically as corn or cotton.

Although the expression of their faith was altered in time by the graft of a new frontier culture, the seed they planted was doctrinally ancient and uniform. A few families or individuals gathered at a home or schoolhouse. They consented to join together in rituals of baptism and communion. They selected a name. They wrote a statement of principles, variously called a confession, articles or abstracts of faith, or a constitution (but never a "creed," which evoked memories of papist autocracy or Anglican hierarchy). The principles were straightforward, generally Calvinistic in theology and Baptist in tradition. They made it clear that humankind lived in two worlds: the world of the spirit, where God saw and knew all, reigned in power, and held majestic and frightening sway over the universe; and the world of the local community, where people tried to live together in order and decency. As trinitarians, they believed in God the Father, Jesus the Son, and the Holy Ghost. The Bible was their guidebook, contained the words of God, and constituted their only rule of faith and practice. Reflecting Baptist Calvinism, they affirmed the doctrine of election, that the sovereign God's foreknowledge resulted in the election of the chosen-in-Christ before the foundations of the world. Baptists believed humanity was also plagued by the sin of Adam and Eve translated to modern man and woman through all generations. In the presence of so great a propensity to sin, man's righteousness was as nothing and he could not by his own nature and free will recover from his original condition. But Christ's righteousness redeemed, justified, and sanctified fallen humanity. Once saved, the saints would persevere in grace and never fall away. Jesus had established two ordinances for his followers: baptism by complete immersion and the Lord's Supper. Only regularly baptized, called, and properly ordained ministers could administer these ordinances. Beyond this world of tears was an eternal world not seen by eyes to which the redeemed would fly in the resurrection and general judgment to come. In that kingdom, eternal punishment awaited the wicked and eternal joy the righteous.[6]

Occasionally these principles contained qualifications, elaborations, or warnings more related to the complex workings of this world than to the divine. Both the Enon Baptist Church in Huntsville (later First Baptist) and the Eufaula Baptist Church affirmed the Lord's Day or "Christian Sabbath" as a day of abstaining from secular work and recreation. The Huntsville congregation also endorsed the visible church as a congregation of faithful Christians who had agreed "to keep up a Godly discipline, according to the rules of the gospel." The Mount Hebron church, formed near Leeds while Alabama's constitutional convention met in August 1819, also solemnly covenanted to "keep the unity of the spirit in bonds of peace," to meet together at "convenient seasons," to "sympathize with each other and to pray with and for each other." Eufaula Baptists covenanted to "walk together in church relationship with brotherly love," to pray for each other, to bear each other's burdens, support the poor, and to rear families in the "nurture and admonition of the Lord." They pledged to win others to faith in Jesus and to live circumspectly in the world. They acknowledged that new life in Christ imposed "a special obligation . . . to lead a new and holy life." This little congregation in Barbour County (which was to produce more Alabama governors than any other county) even added an article on government. Because civil officials were divinely appointed to maintain an orderly society, church members should pray for, honor, and obey magistrates ("except in things opposed to the will of our Lord Jesus Christ, who is the only Lord of the conscience, and prince of the kings of the earth"). The Big Creek Baptist Church in Jefferson County censured "obnoxious ardent spirits" and vowed not to tolerate members who made or used alcohol, "unless in medicine and where advisable against diseases."[7]

Eufaula Baptists carefully qualified their "declaration of faith." They noted that the articles were merely declaratory, that they had no authority to bind the conscience. Holy Scripture was the only authoritative rule governing faith and practice. Though the articles reflected the opinion of most churches, Baptists had no creed "as a bond of union and communion." The articles merely informed those seeking entrance to the congregation about "the faith requisite to fellowship" and the congregation's scriptural beliefs about which Christians might disagree.[8]

Legendary frontier preacher and Baptist historian Hosea Holcombe emphasized that Baptists recognized no external power and no general standard. The "whole apparatus" of Catholicism and the Church of England—"catechisms, creeds, and books of prayer," "laws and formularies"—designed to control individual Christian conscience was regarded by Baptists as an "unhallowed innovation on the moral and intellectual property of man."[9]

In addition to a statement of theological principles and a covenant, most congregations acknowledged human frailties in rules of decorum to govern church conferences. Usually held on the Saturday before monthly preaching on Sunday, the conference handled all church business. These rules established the offices of moderator and church clerk, who would preside and record proceedings. They established democratic procedures for debate, allowed the moderator to maintain order and end discussion after both sides had been heard, prohibited interrupting speakers ("unless they departed from the subject"), and provided for unanimous consent for receiving or dismissing members and a majority vote on other matters.[10] Most congregations required male members to attend all services; if they missed a specified number of church conferences without cause, they faced exclusion from the congregation.

Exactly where and when the first Baptist church on Alabama soil began is a hotly disputed matter. Mobile Baptists speculate that the Shiloh church (or Eight Mile Creek Church as it was originally called) may date from as early as 1803.[11] If so, these early Baptists left no record to support their claim. The distinction of first Alabama Baptist church goes to Flint River church, constituted in the home of James Deaton with eleven or twelve members on October 2, 1808. This congregation later sided with antimissionary forces and became a Primitive Baptist church. So the honor of being the first documented, continuously operating, missionary Baptist congregation belonged to Huntsville First Baptist Church. Originally named West Fork of Flint River church and later called Enon, the congregation began on June 3, 1809.[12] It seems entirely appropriate that Alabama's initial missionary Baptist church should have been called Flint, an extremely hard, fine-grained form of quartz that gives off a spark of fire when struck. The founders no doubt had in mind their location on Brier Fork of the Flint River, but their name evokes the flinty nature of the people called Alabama Baptists.

The basis for naming churches varied as did much else about American Christianity. Early churches in Europe and even some in America had been named for saints. But as ordinary people asserted control over their own institutions, they democratized names of churches as well. They named congregations after geographical features, doctrinal beliefs, or biblical sites. Among early Alabama Baptist churches in the Muscle Shoals Association were place names such as Mill Creek, Little and Big Cypress,

Russell's Valley; theological terms like New Hope; and biblical names like Bethel, Carmel, Hepzibah, and Macedonia. In other associations, Shiloh, Salem, Ebenezer, and Enon were popular.

As soon as a handful of churches had been established, they sought fraternal relations with like-minded folk. The one hundred twenty or so churches that had been formed by 1823 belonged primarily to seven associations that were formed according to geographic considerations. They straddled rivers, were formed between them, or developed along three major federal roads that crisscrossed the state. Lines separating them were never hard and fast. On the eastern end of the Tennessee River, the Flint River Association (anchored by Huntsville) organized churches from Tennessee to just south of the river. To the west, the Muscle Shoals Association spread from the shoals of the Tennessee River at Florence south into the mountains. To the southeast, the Mount Zion Association included churches organized between the Coosa and Warrior Rivers, a region that would later become Birmingham. The huge Cahawba Association straddled the Cahaba River and stretched beyond the Warrior, dominating central Alabama and including most of the Black Belt. To the southwest, Montgomery anchored the Alabama Association. Southwest of Montgomery, the Bethel Association lay in the fork of the Alabama and Tombigbee Rivers. To the east of Bethel and dominating south-central Alabama was Alexander Travis's Beckbe Association.[13]

After being established in private homes, congregations usually expanded into some larger public building, perhaps a school or courthouse. Next came a crude log building, often without floors or windows. Four logs laid oblong established the foundation. On top of these, members stacked smaller notched logs to reach whatever height they desired. On the dirt floor they placed benches of split logs with legs attached to the bottom side. Early pulpits consisted of two poles driven into the ground with wood pieces nailed up as a breast covering, then finer boards nailed on top where the minister could lay Bible and sermon notes, if he had any. The floor of the pulpit area might be raised by wood slabs laid across two logs. A short split log on four legs allowed the preacher to sit when other parts of the service commenced. When the weather became oppressively hot, pastors often led their congregations outside where they could sit more comfortably under a shade tree.[14]

On one occasion patriarch Alexander Travis walked into a new pulpit built especially for him. Unfortunately, the carpenter, impressed with Travis's height of six feet two inches, had constructed so huge a pulpit that the breast board came to the preacher's chin. To walk from behind the

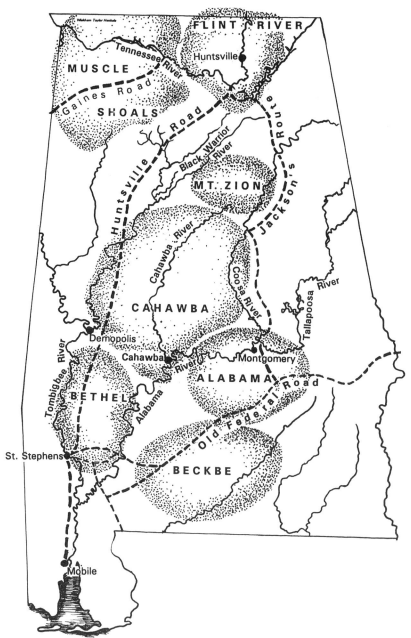

This map of Alabama shows the approximate locations of the seven Baptist associations when the Alabama Baptist State Convention was established in 1823. (Map drawn by Wickham Taylor Henkels)

Pine Torch Church and Cemetery, in what is presently the Bankhead National Forest, was a pioneer Baptist log church that became a Primitive Baptist congregation. (Courtesy of Samford University Archives)

pulpit and preach from its side would have offended the congregation and embarrassed the carpenter. So, Travis pulled the pastor's bench up to the pulpit, climbed on top of it, stared down at his congregation now fully able to see him, and began to preach.[15]

By the 1830s and 1840s, increasing prosperity allowed many churches to erect more permanent buildings. Siloam church in Marion erected an $8,000 structure in 1837 to replace a building that had cost only $600. By 1849 the church boasted a $10,000 brick sanctuary. Although buildings usually remained square, boxlike structures, seats, windows, and stoves were often added, enhancing the comfort of worshipers. Log buildings gave way to double-story brick structures built in Greek Revival style with balconies that stretched across the back and halfway down each side. In the late 1840s, Auburn First Baptist Church erected a building that seated two hundred, with a front porch and two entrances, one for women, the other for men. The boxlike pulpit had steps on either end and doors to close the preacher inside. Some churches financed such construction by selling pews. Although free seats had some advantages, they did tend to divide families. With rented pews, families generally sat together. With free pews, men usually sat on one side of the church, and women, girls, and young boys sat on the other. Although many churches had separate doors for men and women, Baptist leaders were by no means of one mind on gender separation. The editor of the *Alabama Baptist* complained in 1844 that such seating arrangements separated brothers from sisters and often led to children disrupting services. If custom ordained the separation of the sexes, he preferred that fathers should take sons of all ages to sit with them, and mothers should sit with daughters.[16]

The functioning of such a church was as simple as its construction. Church officers included a part-time pastor, clerk, deacons, and elders. Churches generally met once a month for conference and preaching. As late as the 1840s, the twenty-three churches in Montgomery, Lowndes, Dallas, Macon, and Autauga Counties that constituted the Alabama Association had only two churches that conducted services each Sunday.[17]

Associations prospered as the number of churches increased. Although this voluntary grouping of churches initially tended to follow geographical features, the rise of antimission sentiment soon divided associations along theological lines as well. Associational meetings usually occurred in the fall and lasted from Friday through Saturday or Sunday. Any church desiring to participate elected one or more representatives and sent a letter detailing the statistical record of the church. Meetings opened with a sermon preached by a minister selected the previous year. Such exposure often promoted the preacher to the status of minor celebrity in his locale. Next the association elected a moderator and clerk. Ministers and laymen sometimes became fixtures in their roles as moderators, winning reelection each year for decades. The business meeting determined the various benevolent causes to be supported with contributions and often degenerated into furious theological battles over Calvinism and missions. Churches also sent questions about various theological and ethical matters to be resolved by the collective wisdom of the brethren. Delegates sometimes declared their position on contemporary issues, but the fierce independence of each congregation minimized the authority of such resolutions.[18]

Most associational meetings included a few "corresponding members," delegates from other associations who attended but could not vote. This exchange of delegates and associational minutes provided an important medium for maintaining harmony and unity within the fledgling denomination. Through the association, independent people and churches found ways to cooperate and to make their work more efficient.

The chief issue at associational meetings was contained in a circular distributed by mail. At each meeting someone was appointed to draft the letter for the next gathering. Sometimes the association designated the topic; at other times the choice was left to the writer. Topics ranged from doctrines to missions to benevolence and often provoked lively debate. The circular was replaced in time by the annual doctrinal sermon, which was supplemented by a denominational newspaper that often featured articles on doctrine.[19] In 1843 the Alabama Association published a circular on "strict communion." The doctrinal exposition argued that more than conversion was necessary to participate in communion. Baptism, sound faith, and obedience to Scripture were all important.[20]

The Alabama Association dominated state Baptist life. After antimission churches withdrew, the association was a strong supporter of missions and provided six of Alabama's fourteen delegates to the 1845 Augusta meeting where the Southern Baptist Convention was begun.

Bethel Association, which met every three months in 1844 rather than annually, debated foot washing, temperance, Sunday school, and ministerial duties at its June meeting. While delegates debated such weighty matters inside the Hebron church in Perry County, two ministers preached to slaves in a nearby grove.[21]

By 1840 Baptists had established a firm outpost on the Alabama frontier. At statehood in 1819, there were no more than fifty Baptist churches in the state, most of them very small. Twenty years later, Holcombe estimated that there were thirty associations with 500 churches, 300 ministers, and 25,000 members.[22]

Preachers, Worship, and Proclamation

What lay behind the striking results about which Holcombe boasted was more than a frontier filled with peril. Such conditions merely provided fertile soil for the gospel. But that ground was contested by many theories and denominations. The success of Baptists was due to the message they proclaimed and the remarkable men and women who proclaimed it. Although only men stood in the forefront and received popular adulation, much of the success resulted from women who quietly and ardently converted their husbands and children and built the infrastructure of churches, which were overwhelmingly female in membership.

Worship services in nineteenth-century Alabama Baptist churches were simple and infrequent. There was no Sunday school until late in the century except in urban churches and the most progressive rural congregations.[23] Sunday services were usually casual. Folklore from Russellville First Baptist Church recalls the informality of a crowded worship service in pioneer days. An elderly woman, unable to find a place to sit, yelled: "Fetch me a chair from the wagon, babe." A person in the church offered her a seat, to which she replied loudly: "I've got a seat [but] nowheres to put it." Even Basil Manly Sr., perhaps the state's most erudite Baptist minister, sometimes encountered problems with such informality. Arriving in Huntsville to preach at Enon in 1846, he discovered that the church had no pulpit Bible. He could not remember all his text, so he had to change it. The brick floor was covered with several inches of straw, and the few benches were askew. The scene reminded Manly more of a barn than a sanctuary. One woman carried a hymnbook in her pocket, allowing the service to commence. But when Manly stood in the pulpit, the book board was low and only three inches wide, not even large enough for his notes (perhaps reflecting a widespread Baptist belief that preachers should not use them). Despite these distractions, Manly plowed ahead with his sermon until an elderly deaf man mounted the pulpit beside him and stuck his ear as close to the preacher's mouth as possible. Not satisfied merely to listen, the old man sometimes groaned in disappointment. Finally, he despaired of hearing altogether and began to read Manly's notes. The preacher's summary of his effort was predictably discouraging: "The Devil had place, preacher, and all. . . . I drew up my glasses, took my notes, read from them as well as I could, and brought matters to a conclusion. . . . I had a wretched time of it."[24]

Hymnody was as informal as the rest of worship. Preachers often avoided Manly's embarrassment by carrying both Bible and hymnals in their saddlebags because both were rare in pulpits. Collections of hymns by Watts, Dorsey, Ripon, and Cluster were favorites, though Hosea Holcombe compiled his own collection, adding some hymns that he wrote. Basil Manly Sr. and his son also compiled a *Church Psalmody.* Most of these collections grouped hymns by topics, but they often were in the same meter and became monotonous. Shaped-note or "Fa So La" music made up in timbre and power what it lacked in variety.

Because few individuals in a worship service had a hymnbook, the leader "lined out" songs (usually two lines at a time) to the congregation. The singing was usually animated and loud, although confusion sometimes resulted from lining out the verses. Some could not remember the words and mumbled their own version. And the leader had to be careful what he said before a congregation accustomed to repeating his every word. One piece of religious folklore from northwestern Alabama recalls a hapless pastor who announced that he would line out the words to "On

Jordan's Stormy Banks I Stand." He reached for his glasses, but did not have them. Facing the congregation, he explained, "My eyes are dim, I cannot see; I left my specs at home." The congregation dutifully sang his words, which fit the hymn's meter.[25]

Mishaps with music caused little disruption because services focused on the word, on hearing and speaking. Art and architecture occupied lowly positions. So did communion, at least relative to Catholic and Anglican churches. Usually confined to quarterly or even semiannual observance, this central act of worship in liturgical churches was so infrequent among Baptists as to constitute a discernible break in the rhythm of congregational life. Rather than cultivate a sense of awe and mystery in the presence of God, services focused on converting the lost, urging the burden of soul winning and missions on the saved, and denouncing private unrighteousness. Even the spatial arrangement of the church suggested the priorities of the word. Choirs, where they existed, were seated behind the pulpit. The church was not altar- but pulpit-centered, from which the word was proclaimed. The sermon sought to evoke a sense of urgency and individual responsibility in listeners.[26]

Preachers who proclaimed the message of repentance and new life did so from a strong sense of calling. Most ministers could provide a vivid account of their personal summons to preach. No one pondered more deeply or wrote more persuasively about the ministerial call than Hosea Holcombe. He urged that no man enter the ministry who did not feel the apostle Paul's sense of compulsion. If called, preachers "should feel the word as a fire burning in their bones." A man who sensed such a message from God should not act rashly. He should examine "every corner of his own heart," should study Scripture and pray, should satisfy himself that he sought only the love of God and to convert sinners.

Once called, Holcombe urged ministers to cultivate private as well as public piety. The preacher must be as committed to entering "the dwelling of the poor and obscure to warn and console them" as he was to making converts among the influential in "great assemblies." Many preachers appeared zealous and preached eloquently, Holcombe warned. They won applause and flattery; they thrived on the life of itinerant preaching. But it was far easier "to find a good preacher than a good pastor." For this reason churches were urged to be cautious about granting ordination. Holcombe believed that no single congregation could ordain a man and that there was no New Testament authority for a church licensing ministers. The biblical pattern of ordination was the imposition of hands by a presbytery of ministers gathered to evaluate the applicant's character, mental qualifications, and doctrinal soundness.[27] Only after such careful scrutiny should a preacher be ordained and authorized to proclaim the gospel in Baptist churches.

That not all preachers spent enough time in self-analysis and personal reflection or that all churches were sufficiently cautious about ordination was demonstrated by a series of embarrassing incidents and uninspiring sermons. Hosea Holcombe recorded the sad fate of Limestone Baptist Church, founded in 1812, and its pastor, Thomas O'Banion. The congregation excluded O'Banion for drunkenness and dissipation, and early in the twentieth century the church became extinct. Holcombe was equally critical of Ezekiel Craft, a Revolutionary War veteran and pastor of Meridian Line Baptist Church in the Flint River Association. Craft, according to Holcombe, "cannot preach, neither can he be considered an orderly man." His church ceased to exist in the early 1830s. In 1829, Linden church excluded its pastor for adultery, but at least the church survived.[28]

Elder Obadiah Echols, first pastor of the Auburn First Baptist Church in 1838, had no recorded moral lapses but apparently was less than spectacular in the pulpit. A memorial recalled Echols as a preacher "without much method, but earnest, always entertaining, quaint, and at times somewhat tedious." A deliberate speaker who was often emotional, Echols "would have been effective" except for a habit "of taking after a side thought at times." He was "quite useful whenever his mind became deeply interested in his subject and when engaged in revival meetings."[29] Seldom was praise offered with more qualifications.

In 1844 the editor of the denominational newspaper offered a perceptive critique of factors that led to ineffective preaching. He listed a poor library (which inhibited sermon preparation), low salaries (which required ministers to take secular jobs), uncomfortable houses of worship, and lack of personal devotion (ministers spent too much time in visiting, gossiping, and reading newspapers instead of devoting at least four hours a day to prayer, study, and meditation).[30]

The core of the ministerial problem was bivocationalism. Most nineteenth-century Baptist preachers either preferred to earn their livelihood in a secular occupation or were forced to do so by the strict biblicism of parishioners who constantly reminded them that Paul earned his living at tent making and nowhere did the New Testament record Jesus as receiving a salary. Occasionally such arguments were sincerely held and biblically based. More often they reflected frontier notions of democracy, fear of a professional clergy class, or plain stinginess among subsistence farmers who participated in a barter economy and seldom had cash to give the church.

Occasionally preachers treated lay resistance to adequate salaries with sardonic humor. Daniel P. Bestor—a distinguished Black Belt minister, teacher, and state legislator—chose not to demand a salary and give up his plantation for fear the churches he pastored would renege on their pledges and leave him destitute. Once, while dining with an affluent member of the Black Belt's renowned "canebrake" society, Bestor was surprised by the man's admonition that the pastor ought to preach more often. "If I had your talents," his friend reprimanded, "I would ride up and down all over the State and set it afire." "Very well, Brother," Bestor countered. "I will make you a fair proposition. You ought to be as much concerned about the salvation of the people as I. I understand you have an income of twenty thousand dollars a year. Your family is about the size of mine. I know you can live comfortably on ten thousand. Just give me the other ten and I will give myself wholly to preaching."[31]

Other preachers learned to be less pious and more pragmatic about their salaries as well. When Fellowship church in Wilcox County renewed the call of its founding pastor Kedar Hawthorne in 1842, he agreed on condition that the church would "sustain him" adequately. In 1844 the Eutaw church sent forth a pathetic plea for someone to serve as pastor. The people were poor and had no money to pay a salary. The former minister had preached once a month but had stopped coming. Since then, the church had conducted no regular services and had twice skipped the season of protracted meetings for lack of a preacher.[32]

The negative effect of bivocationalism was perpetual financial worry among those who neglected secular jobs and perpetual guilt among those who neglected ministerial duties. Their churches could expect little more than minimal service: preaching once a month, officiating at marriages and funerals when convenient, counsel during times of trouble.

Bivocationalism had its positive side as well. Ministers shared the life experiences (droughts, fluctuating prices for crops, political squabbles) of parishioners. They belonged to the community in ways that a professional minister never could. The very characteristics many considered liabilities (lack of education, lack of deference, low pay) integrated them into democratic frontier society. Their closeness to the people, the egalitarian way they were called, licensed, and ordained, the ease with which barely literate young men could begin preaching, all these factors assured them a respectful hearing and provided Baptists a steady supply of ministers. This abundance of raw talent confounded the more restrictive Presbyterians and

Episcopalians, who established high educational standards and paid decent salaries but had problems finding enough qualified candidates to fill their pulpits.

The preachers of this first generation were not of one piece. They were self-educated, bivocational farmers and splendidly educated bivocational university presidents. Some were stem-winding, emotional evangelists who eschewed notes and preached as the spirit moved them. A few were renowned for their careful organization, thoughtful analysis, and gracefully written manuscript sermons.

Not surprisingly, the unlettered substantially outnumbered the erudite. George G. McLendon as a boy settled with his family in Pike County during the winter of 1824. He was ordained by the Salem church near Brundidge in 1840 after serving his church as deacon and clerk. When he began to preach, he had no formal education and could barely read the Bible. By enormous exertion he educated himself and during the early 1840s organized and pastored churches in Dale and Pike Counties. He also farmed, operated a general merchandise store, served as a census taker, and became a Master Mason. Later, while pastor of the Ramer Baptist Church, McLendon baptized the parents of Dr. John R. Sampey, who in that church began a distinguished career that made him one of the South's most distinguished ministers and president of Southern Baptist Theological Seminary.[33]

McLendon's life experiences were typical of the first generation of frontier Baptist preachers. Nathan Slay (who organized the Seale Baptist Church about 1833 and preached across west Alabama from Citronelle to Livingston) was taught to read and write by his wife after they married. Robert Carson, who moved to Lowndes County in 1837, was a poorly educated farmer-minister who barely earned enough to feed and clothe his family. Jacob H. Schroebel was a poorly educated Catholic tanner and shoemaker in Claiborne (Monroe County) when he was converted under the preaching of Alexander Travis. Despite his lack of education, he became known as one of the most eloquent preachers in south Alabama and ended his career as pastor of the Saint Anthony Street Baptist Church in Mobile.[34]

William McCain, who pastored in the Coosa River Association, was also an uneducated man known for "unction and power that lifted his hearers far above all his imperfections of style and delivery." He also possessed the folk wisdom and wit held in high regard by generations of rustic, unsophisticated pioneers. On one occasion he took eight new Christians to be baptized in a creek in Jefferson County. As the service progressed, seven boys frolicked on a tree that had fallen across the

stream. The boys disrupted the solemn
service and ridiculed McCain. Just as the
preacher finished immersing the last candidate and was walking up the bank, the
log gave way, tumbling the boys into the
water. McCain laughed, then announced
to the assembled congregation: "Brethren,
we have beat the devil today; we have
baptized eight while he has only baptized
seven!"[35]

Not all early Alabama preachers were
cut from rough cloth. Legendary preacher
Eldred B. Teague was a graduate of the
University of Alabama, a favorite student
of Basil Manly Jr., and became president
of a college in Tuskegee. Daniel P. Bestor
was also a well-educated preacher-educa-
tor who founded Lafayette Female Academy, a Baptist school in Greensboro, and
served as a trustee of both Howard College and the University of Alabama. As
a preacher, contemporaries said that he
was without peer "intellectually or orator-
ically." Dr. William Fluker was a Virginia
aristocrat of excellent education and cultural refinement who built a large plantation near Moscow after settling there in

Jacob H. Schroebel, a poorly educated tan-
ner and shoemaker in Claiborne (Monroe
County), was converted by the preaching of
Alexander Travis. Later Schroebel became
an eloquent preacher and pastor of Saint
Anthony Street Baptist Church in Mobile.
(Courtesy of Samford University Archives)

1833. He pastored many churches in west Alabama. D. H. Gillette was a
native New Yorker, the son of a physician, and an honors graduate of Hamilton Theological Institute. He pastored Baptist churches in New Jersey and
Charlottesville, Virginia, before coming to Saint Anthony Street Baptist
Church in Mobile in 1843 after J. H. Schroebel died. His erudition was quite
a contrast to his predecessor's untutored but passionate sermons. Joshua
Hill Foster—planter, preacher, and professor of physics and astronomy at
the University of Alabama—descended from the famous Baptist family at
Foster's Settlement on the Warrior River. The Foster family furnished a
daughter, Martha Foster Crawford, who became a renowned missionary to
China, and an array of county and state officials.[36]

One scholar has carefully analyzed the preaching of eight of Alabama's
best-known frontier Baptist preachers. The eight men—William Carey

Crane (1836–1885), Jabez Lafayette Monroe Curry (1825–1903), James Harvey DeVotie (1813–1892), Basil Manly Sr. (1798–1868), Basil Manly Jr. (1825–1892), John Jefferson Deyambert Renfroe (1803–1888), Hardin Edwards Taliaferro (1825–1902), and Isaac Taylor Tichenor (1825–1902)—came from a variety of backgrounds. Some common features united them. All were dedicated to missions, favored education, were pro-South, proslavery, pro-Confederate, and all wrote at least some sermons in manuscript form. All used biblical texts for their sermons. All were pious and orthodox in their personal beliefs. They rejected rationalism. Basil Manly Jr. wrote the Abstract of Principles for Southern Baptist Theological Seminary, penned an apologetic for biblical inspiration, and was the driving force in organizing the SBC Sunday School Board, with the Bible as its primary textbook. All labored over their sermons, both in preparation and in delivery. All used poignant, compelling illustrations in the great oral tradition of southern story telling. All were evangelistic. Although none spent a ministry devoted primarily to camp meeting revivals or protracted meetings, all urged gospel demands for repentance and conversion. Carey Crane estimated converts under his preaching at 2,500. DeVotie baptized at least 1,500. Renfroe baptized hundreds in two years as a Civil War chaplain.[37]

Despite so many similarities, the eight followed different paths into the ministry, possessed different personalities and temperaments, and exercised their gifts of ministry in quite different ways.

James H. DeVotie became one of the denomination's most respected preachers at three influential churches: Montgomery First Baptist, Tuscaloosa First Baptist, and Siloam in Marion. After a brief stint as a student at Furman University, the twenty-year-old was called to pastor the Montgomery congregation in 1834. Two years later he became pastor in Tuscaloosa. In both places DeVotie proved to be a fractious, opinionated man whose pastorates were both stormy and generally successful. His personality first emerged at Furman, where he withdrew during his first year after writing insulting letters to one of the professors. The Board of Agents of the South Carolina Baptist Convention denounced his arrogance and insolence. Under his tutelage, the Montgomery church began weekly preaching, one of only two congregations in the Alabama Association to do so. But his hard-headedness alienated members of the congregation. He married a non-Baptist woman whom some members considered vain, worldly, and "devoted to fashion." At a called meeting in May 1835, members voted to terminate the youthful minister. They also invited five ministers to help resolve their differences with DeVotie. The only one of the five who responded was Alexander Travis, who made his way to Montgomery to try to unify the two hostile camps. In order to maintain neutrality, he refused to stay in the homes of either group, registering instead at a hotel. After each faction had its say separately, Travis called a general prayer meeting. DeVotie at first refused to attend but later hid behind a door to listen. Travis prayed a passionate prayer for contrition, repentance, and unity that so moved DeVotie that he walked down the aisle in tears to pray for a restoration of fellowship.[38]

DeVotie's Tuscaloosa pastorate was equally stormy. Despite his zeal, eloquence, and enterprise (plus two marvelous revivals during his four-year pastorate), some well-educated University of Alabama officials in the congregation criticized his lack of scholarly credentials. Influential educator-pastor E. B. Teague conceded DeVotie's eloquence but dismissed his sermons as "eloquent nothings."[39]

In time DeVotie transcended his youthful immaturity. As pastor of Siloam church in Marion, he helped establish Howard College, became the first chairman of its trustees, moderated the Cahawba Association, became corresponding secretary of the state convention, and served as president of the Alabama Baptist Bible Society and the Southern Baptist Domestic Board of Missions. He also helped establish and edit the *Alabama Baptist,* which he briefly owned.[40] As passing years mellowed bruised egos, DeVotie was remembered as one of the most beloved pioneer Baptist preachers.

The path of Basil Manly Sr. often crossed DeVotie's. Both had South Carolina connections; both pastored congregations in Montgomery and Tuscaloosa; both became prominent figures in the Alabama and Southern Baptist conventions. But there the similarities ended. Valedictorian of his graduating class at South Carolina College and former pastor of the prestigious First Baptist Church of Charleston, South Carolina, Manly became president of the University of Alabama in 1837, a position he occupied for eighteen years. Almost immediately he began to criticize DeVotie and Tuscaloosa First Baptist Church for lack of vision and energy. The congregation needed a new building but could not raise the money to construct it. Revival meetings had a negative effect on Tuscaloosa and "injured the public mind." Members resisted pastoral labor and seemed to believe that a "row once a year answers all purposes in religion." Such harping criticism may have been a factor in DeVotie's resignation as pastor in 1839. Manly often supplied the pulpit in the interim between pastors.[41]

What the Tuscaloosa congregation got in place of DeVotie was one of the most important "gentleman theologians" of the antebellum South.[42] Manly played a role in establishing the Alabama Hospital for the Insane, the Southern Baptist Theological Seminary, the Alabama Historical Society,

Basil Manly Sr., Baptist preacher and president of the University of Alabama, was one of the state's most erudite and respected ministers. (Courtesy of Samford University Archives)

Furman University, and the Southern Baptist Convention. A native of North Carolina, he was converted by the ministrations of a slave. After Manly's distinguished career in South Carolina, he became a bridge between the more settled, sophisticated Baptist world of the Atlantic seaboard and the raucous denominational life of the Southeast.[43]

Manly's Alabama career as president of the state university (1837–1855), state Baptist evangelist (some called him the "Baptist Bishop of Alabama"), and pastor of Montgomery's First Baptist Church (1859–1864) was broken by a four-year interlude as pastor back in Charleston. As the most prominent member of the Tuscaloosa church, he personally recruited most of the seven pastors whose terms overlapped his, usually without consulting the church. Despite his role in recruiting them, he seldom had a good word to say on their behalf. Yet Manly was widely beloved by the congregation and rejoined it in his twilight years while his son Charles served as pastor.[44]

A strict Calvinist in theology, Manly produced no extensive theological writings. But he did influence John Leadley Dagg and James P. Boyce, the first systematic theologians produced by Southern Baptists. And his son Basil Jr. produced one of the most important Baptist defenses of Scripture in the nineteenth century.[45]

As a preacher, Manly's sermons were practical, simple, dignified, and earnest. He utilized a large and precise vocabulary and was not overly emotional. At one camp meeting he preached, some of the sisters began to shout. Though not critical of their emotionalism, he confessed: "I might have shouted a time or two myself; but I find I do not know how." Samuel Henderson, a contemporary minister who knew him well and often heard him preach, wrote that Manly could melt an audience to tears in a moment: "You were almost lifted off your seat. A glow from the Throne seemed to come down." But Manly did not approve of "calling people up" or other forms of psychological manipulation that might short-circuit "real enquiry."[46]

As a pastor, Manly combined high standards with compassion. On one hand, he cheered the exclusion of two women from his congregation, one for attending services by a Mormon preacher and the other for refusing to pay rent on her pew. But he also opposed the exclusion of a woman who gave birth to a child out of wedlock. When he preached the funeral of the infant nine months after its birth, he pitied the penitent mother and pronounced that "Christ will receive such though [she is] scorned by a guilty world."[47]

Like Manly, Hardin Edwards Taliaferro was a North Carolinian, but there the similarities ended. Taliaferro or "Skitt," as he was nicknamed as a boy, was born in Surry County where as late as 1850 one-third the adult men and more than one-half the adult women were illiterate. As a young man he moved to Tennessee with his brother, attended an academy briefly, surrendered to the ministry, and married. In 1835 he moved to a farm one mile from the little town of Talladega, Alabama, where he lived for twenty years. A tanner by trade, he also farmed a small plot of land and preached for nine or ten churches in a fifty-mile circuit that stretched along the Coosa River. Though occasionally criticized as "sometimes a little too frank and outspoken," he had a successful pastorate (1838–1839) at Talladega Baptist Church and was called to serve the church again (1847–1853). During this second pastorate, Taliaferro suffered "perplexing doubts and fears" and a sense of God's remoteness. Several years later, Taliaferro wrote a book, *The Grace of God Magnified: An Experimental Tract,* which described his "torture of the soul." Basil Manly Sr. introduced the book, which circulated widely in the South. One contemporary called it unsurpassed "by any book of confessions in our language."[48]

Whatever anguish Taliaferro experienced, he apparently hid it from his congregations. A tall man of more than six feet, erect, with profuse hair and beard, he was as emotional as Manly was restrained. When deeply moved, he often wept in the pulpit. A planter who frequently heard him preach in 1844–1845 recorded his impressions. An April 1844 sermon and communion service at the Talladega church left members joyful and strengthened. In July Taliaferro delivered a "delightful and comforting discourse." Later that month he and his brother-in-law, Samuel Henderson, preached a camp meeting. They both "seemed to be full of the Grace of God, dispensing the word to a large and attentive congregation." "Numbers of sinners" bowed down before the "throne of Grace, asking the forgiveness for their sins."[49]

After his crisis of faith, Taliaferro returned for a third tour of duty at the Talladega Baptist Church, helped organize Sunday schools and the Coosa River Book Society to distribute Bibles and tracts, and became active in the Masons. He later moved to Tuskegee, where he edited the *Alabama Baptist* with his brother-in-law and pastored four small Macon County churches. He also began submitting humorous articles to the *Southern Literary Messenger* in Virginia. In 1859 his articles were published anonymously under the title *Fisher's River-Folks and Scenes by Skitt, Who Has Been Thar,* which (after his identity as author was revealed following his death) established him as a major literary figure among the southwestern humorists. Combining farming, preaching, and his tannery with writing was no easy task. Yet he excelled at all. After the Civil War he edited a secular paper, the *Tuskegee News*, became a missionary to blacks under appointment of the American Home Mission Board, and pastored several black churches.[50]

Neither Hosea Holcombe nor Alexander Travis left manuscript sermons to be analyzed. Yet they were arguably the two most influential Alabama Baptists between 1819 and 1845. Had Baptists named bishops, Holcombe undoubtedly would have been the bishop of north Alabama and Travis the bishop of the south.

Travis crisscrossed southern Alabama from his base in Conecuh County. In addition to assisting in the establishment of numerous churches, he was elected for twenty consecutive years moderator of the Beckbe (later Bethlehem) Association. In 1823 at the initial meeting of the Alabama Baptist State Convention, delegates elected Travis their first domestic missionary. He furnished his own outfit, paid his own expenses, and received a salary of a dollar a day when he was itinerating. His mission field was southern and southeastern Alabama. He would "lay by" his crops about the first of July, turn his farm chores over to his sons and slaves, then tour his circuit, preaching camp meetings wherever he traveled. The tour would usually consume a month and was repeated after fall harvests. So time-consuming were his ministerial duties that he finally hired one of his converts, Kedar Hawthorne (soon to become a famous preacher in his own right), for $300 a year to manage his farm. So great was his reputation as a preacher that one poor woman without a horse or mule reputedly once walked twenty miles to hear him preach.[51]

Like many of his contemporaries, Travis's world was perhaps nearer the world of Christ's than it was the twentieth century. Signs, wonders, and dreams constantly infringed on reason. In autumn 1828, Elder John Ellis, pastor of the Claiborne Baptist Church, died. For some months afterward, this important Alabama River town had no Baptist services. Travis showed no interest in the job because the town was forty miles from his home, making a visit even once a month difficult. But early in 1829 he dreamed that he received a ticket to a ball in Claiborne. He recognized the names on the invitation as members of the Baptist church there. When he awoke, he related the dream to his wife and explained that it meant that he would be called to pastor the church. Days later he received a letter from the church inviting him to preach and signed by the exact same persons who had sent the invitation in his dream. The dream convinced him "that the Lord had called him to preach the gospel unto them." In February 1829 he began a revival that continued on and off for two years. One of his many converts was Catholic tanner Jacob Schroebel, who later preached so effectively in south Alabama and Mobile.[52]

The same year that Travis settled just south of Evergreen, Hosea Holcombe brought his family to farm at Jonesboro in Jefferson County. Holcombe was full of paradoxes. Though he complained that worldly affairs
diminished the work of pastors, he farmed 600 acres of land and was sued
for a debt he owed in 1836. The man whom Alabama historian A. J. Pickett
called the "pioneer Alabama historian" and author of "the first distinc-
tively historical volume published in the state" (*History of the Rise and Progress of the Baptists in Alabama*, 1840) had almost no formal education. Although largely self-educated, in time he accumulated an extensive private
library. Soon after arriving in the state, he was called as pastor of the Enon
church (Jefferson County), but his fame came as a church starter. In 1819
he helped establish Ruhama and Mount Hebron churches, in 1822 Rock
Creek, in 1827 Rupe's Valley (all in Jefferson County), and in 1833 Union
(in Shelby County). He was also zealous in creating mission and temperance societies (calling temperance the "handmaid of religion"), circulating
Baptist literature, and writing and publishing hymns and pamphlets. In
1822 as moderator of the Cahawba Association, Holcombe helped plan the
first state Baptist convention and attended as representative of the Jonesboro Ladies' Society. For six consecutive years delegates elected him president of the state convention.[53]

Like Basil Manly Sr., Holcombe was a strict Calvinist who often
preached doctrinal sermons. Six feet tall, ungainly in bearing, and with
swarthy complexion and bald head, Holcombe's round shoulders stooped
and he became red-faced when he preached. One contemporary remembered the sincerity and clarity of his sermons, though he was "far from
showy." Another recalled his ardor in the pulpit, his voice rising "by uniform steps to a high pitch" but never engaging in "sudden bursts of emotion." In younger years his energy and fervor could hold congregations
spellbound for two hours. In his twilight years, his sermons became "tender, tearful, and short."[54]

Although elders (who were ordained but did not pastor) and pastors
dominated early Baptist churches, deacons played key roles as well. The
tradition of universal priesthood of believers enhanced the role of laity and
produced numerous lay preachers, many of whom in time became licensed
or ordained. Others retained the status of laymen, and the diaconate was
the universal lay leadership role in Baptist churches. The duties of deacons
in early nineteenth-century Alabama churches generally included keeping
records of all members, soliciting money, admonishing those who did not
pay their pledges, and circulating a subscription list within the community

so that friends of the church who might not actually belong to it could still contribute.[55]

Beliefs and Doctrines

Whether laity or clergy, Alabama Baptists struggled during the early decades of the nineteenth century with fundamental and defining issues of doctrine and belief. About the authority of the Bible, there was little disagreement. Although they did not use words fashionable in later years (such as "literal" or "inerrant"), they certainly traced their authority directly to the Bible. Preachers carefully cited texts from it and extolled Scripture as the antidote to rationalism. In 1844 the editor of the *Alabama Baptist* admonished readers to give Scripture careful attention, read it in context, commit it to memory, and omit nothing that could change its meaning. Hosea Holcombe put the matter succinctly: "Give us the Bible and let us alone."[56]

Despite such surface unity, divisions became heated when conversation turned to the meaning and interpretation of Scripture. On that issue there seemed to be as many opinions as there were Baptists. It is tempting to dismiss most of these disputes as petty. Some critics alleged that the first mention of Baptists in the Bible was in Genesis 13:9: "If thou wilt take the left hand, then I will go to the right; or if thou depart to the right hand, then I will go to the left." Despite an obvious propensity for controversy, early conflicts among Alabama Baptists were no laughing matter.

Perhaps the best frontier example of how devoted Bible-believers could differ on the meaning of Scripture involved the practice of foot washing. The Bible seemed clear enough on the issue. John 13:14 admonished Jesus' disciples: "If I then, your Lord and Master, have washed your feet, ye also ought to wash one another's feet." Furthermore, in the history of the first-century church, common practice seems to have been for women to "wash the saints' feet" (I Timothy 5:10).

That seems to be the way frontier Alabama Baptists often understood the Bible. In the records of Huntsville's Enon church, the matter of foot washing was brought up on November 1, 1809, at a Saturday church conference. When members could not resolve the issue, it was "laid over" until March 1810. At that time members decided they had a duty to "wash the saints' feet." Oxford First Baptist had no such debate. The church's 1836 Abstract of Principles included an article that affirmed belief "that as our Lord and Master washed His disciples' feet so we ought to wash one another's." The first major dissension in Wetumpka First Baptist occurred at a March 1823 conference over foot washing. One faction wanted to abandon the practice, but the majority insisted that it was a biblical mandate. Five years later the issue threatened to split the church, and members compromised. The church retained the practice but reduced its frequency from once a month to twice a year. Gradually the practice fell into disuse and was finally discontinued altogether.[57]

No biblical dispute shaped early Alabama Baptists so profoundly as Calvinism. Some recent historians have overemphasized the role of emotion and revivalism in the South. A case can be made that biblicism and Calvinism played at least as large a role. The doctrine of Calvinism has been so widely cited to explain every aspect of southern culture that its precise theological meaning has been obscured. At one level such emphasis seems to explain the legendary fatalism of southerners. Faced with seemingly inexorable forces of both nature and history, Baptists simply acquiesced to events as "God's will." Such fatalism was in fact an entirely logical and appropriate response to a world of powerlessness, of farmers who could not control the capricious forces of nature, of mothers who had no access to physicians or hospitals for their children. But as knowledge and resources increased, southerners were still resistant to control of their lives. They often neglected their own safety and health, reasoning that when "your number is up, your number is up!"

Such stereotypes of Calvinist influence are both simplistic and distorting. The debate over John Calvin's theology originated in Europe, where it centered on issues of God's sovereignty, goodness, and rationality. So-called five-point Calvinism came to the southern frontier in more precise form as doctrines of total human depravity, the perseverance of the saints (popularized as "once saved, always saved"), and predestination (some were predestined by God to be saved, others to be damned).[58] Although Baptists were Calvinists in the general sense of that term, they modified the doctrine.

Strict Calvinism tended to dominate Baptist thought in Charleston, South Carolina, which produced Basil Manly Sr. and many other early Alabama preachers. In 1844 Manly prepared the annual circular of the Tuscaloosa Association on article three of its Abstract of Principles: "We believe in the doctrine of election; and that God chose his people in Christ, before the foundation of the world." He provided numerous scriptural references to support his careful deductive logic. God was sovereign in his power. His foreknowledge was perfect. He knew who would be lost and who saved. His design for the moral universe was election. This design provided assurance to sinners who had no right to claim salvation. As sovereign God, he could bestow the gift of salvation on whomever he selected.

Next came the qualifications. In Manly's mind, the doctrine of election did not contradict individual exertion. Individuals still must conduct themselves "precisely . . . as if there were no purpose of God." No one knew he was not elected. A possibility therefore existed that any particular individual might be saved, and such a possibility demanded ardent exertion. People were still free agents, atonement for sin had still occurred, salvation was still freely extended, and all who willed to do so could still come to Christ.[59] To call such logic the reasoning of a "strict Calvinist" takes liberty with the term. It better reflects the constant modification typical of frontier influence on doctrine imported from a European environment.

Manly's emphasis upon human exertion and individual response reflected the powerful influence of revivalism on early Alabama Baptist thought. If Charleston, South Carolina, provides the clearest ancestry for Calvinism, Sandy Creek, North Carolina, lays firmest claim to the revival tradition. Ardent, charismatic, emotional, independent, biblicist, the Sandy Creek tradition merged elements of both Calvinism and Arminianism.[60]

Arminians waged holy war with Calvinists from the seventeenth century forward. They repudiated predestination as a rejection of free grace and free will as well as a contradiction of God's goodness. To Arminians, the Calvinist God was "arbitrary, capricious, and unreasonable." Doctrinally, Arminianism became most firmly established among Methodists.[61]

Among Alabama Baptists, the erudite Daniel P. Bestor and the fervent Sion Blythe best represent the Arminian strain. Bestor brought from his native Connecticut a strict Calvinist theology, believing that "the elect were virtually justified from everlasting." But gradually his theology changed as he performed the functions of minister on the Alabama frontier. By the end of his life, one Calvinist friend accused Bestor of "verging on Arminianism."[62] Blythe was one of Alabama's most successful revivalists, described as "tender, urgent, vehement." But his Calvinist contemporary, E. B. Teague, also noted what was said about many of the Sandy Creek preachers: he possessed little analytical ability, was better at winning sinners to faith in Christ than in training them in doctrine, and was "somewhat of an Arminian."[63]

Patriarch Hosea Holcombe was a strict Calvinist, but also tolerant and broad-minded toward deviation from what he considered orthodoxy. He believed that most first-generation Alabama preachers took a "middle ground" view of Calvinism. There was also much confusion in the state. What some called "Calvinism . . . is denominated Arminianism with others; and a misunderstanding sometimes occurs from a different manner of expression." Nonetheless, Holcombe did grieve over a "considerable number of ministers in Alabama" who had departed from "the old Baptist foundation" and "from the Scriptures" in their doctrine and preaching. In general, he still believed that such preachers "advance good doctrine"; but he warned churches to be more cautious whom they ordained. Nor should presbyteries lay hands on those "who are not established in the truth." Many young preachers, he warned, "dreaded" the doctrines of predestination and election and could not reconcile those doctrines to their evangelistic belief in the agency and accountability of humanity.[64]

Although Holcombe and Blythe maintained their friendship despite disagreements about predestination and election, not all theological disputes ended so amicably. Frequent essays in the *Alabama Baptist* (especially during 1844) on "Election," "Justification," "Perseverance," and "Free Will" made it clear that doctrinal wars raged among Baptists. Two incidents revealed the tension.

In the fall of 1835, E. B. Teague attended the Mulberry Association in Autauga County. Traveling from Tuskegee required a two-day journey through nearly unbroken forest. When he emerged from the woods, Teague encountered a spacious brush arbor that had been prepared for the meeting. No sooner had he climbed out of his saddle than he sensed the tension among his brethren. A venerated pastor, Isaac Suttle, reputedly an Arminian, was scheduled to preach the doctrinal sermon. Several younger preachers (including some converted by the venerable Suttle) had adopted a hyper-Calvinist position and now opposed their former spiritual shepherd. At least on this occasion Suttle carried the day with what Teague called an "extraordinarily well delivered" sermon that was "a complete triumph, chaining the vast audience for more than an hour and satisfying the most skeptical."[65]

The other incident took longer to resolve. In 1832, Bethel church in Tuscaloosa split. Elder David Andrews, pastor of the congregation, which had been established in 1818, advocated Arminianism, and a bare majority of strict Calvinists excluded him along with nearly half the congregation. An associational committee sustained the majority and some churches branded the seceders "schismatics and heretics." Andrews formed a new congregation and prospered. In time he moved to the Salem Church, where a majority adopted his Arminian views and excluded thirty-four strict Calvinists. Andrews converted enough Baptist churches to Arminianism that he was able to organize them into the North River Baptist Association.

As years passed, some of the iconoclasts admitted their errors and sought reconciliation with former churches. Churches of the Tuscaloosa Association set two conditions for reconciliation: all the seceders must be restored to fellowship by their original churches and be rebaptized. The seceders refused, arguing that the conditions were unreasonable. Finally in 1849, a council was appointed, and Basil Manly Sr. was asked to prepare a sermon on the subject of sovereign grace and free will. Manly's sermon, entitled "Divine Efficiency Consistent with Human Activity," was a masterful compromise. Usually preachers forced listeners to choose between God's sovereignty and human freedom, but Manly argued that man worked out his own salvation because God worked inside man's will to accomplish his purposes. So brilliantly did Manly resolve the theological conflict between Calvinists and Arminians that the sermon was published and widely circulated in Alabama. The North River Association incorporated this theology in a new Abstract of Principles, ending the long division.[66]

Although strict Calvinists and Arminians usually found ways to work cooperatively, compromise with hyper-Calvinists proved impossible. Convinced that if God wanted people converted he need rely upon no human agent, hyper-Calvinists rejected revivalism, missions, denominational bureaucracies, and benevolent organizations. Although Calvinist doctrine lay at the root of this divisive confrontation, Baptist benevolence was its most obvious expression. Whereas moderate Calvinists and Arminians might disagree about predestination, election, or free will, they generally agreed on benevolence.

Some historians have interpreted benevolences (such as Sunday school and missionary, tract, Bible, and temperance societies) as efforts by self-serving conservative religious elites to control poorer folks. This argument is not convincing. Such religious groups hardly felt their power eroding in the flush years of the Great Awakening that swept the South after 1800. Furthermore, their efforts at uplift were consistent with traditions of self-abnegation and concern for others that gave rise to both women's rights and abolition movements in the northeast.[67]

Benevolence societies proliferated in the United States after 1812 in the form of the American Bible Society, the American Tract Society, the American Sunday School Union, as well as through various denominational agencies. They met resistance in the South for a variety of reasons. Some poor southerners resented benevolence societies as patronizing organizations that singled them out from more affluent neighbors. Others resisted what they considered to be reforms emanating from New England and upstate New York, a region also identified with such radicalism as women's rights and abolitionism. Actually, resistance to benevolence societies in Alabama seems to have been confined mainly to hyper-Calvinist Baptists. Others were surprisingly supportive, especially given the northern origins of organized benevolence.[68]

What made benevolence organizations palatable to most Baptists was the incredible level of destitution on the early Alabama frontier. Although the word "destitution" correctly suggests that most recipients of such assistance were indigent, it carried a more precise meaning in the early nineteenth century. It referred to people who lacked Bibles, religious reading matter, or religious institutions. In the mid-1820s, a survey by the Tuscaloosa County tax collector found that nearly one out of three families had no Bibles. Baptist minister Willis Burns, a missionary for the Tuscaloosa Association, visited 224 families in the 1840s and found 99 of them "Roman Catholics or fatal errorists," 70 habitually neglecting evangelical preaching, and 37 without Bibles. In 1845 a colporteur (an itinerant minister who raised money from the affluent in order to give Bibles and tracts to the poor, or at least sell them cheaply) encountered two women dressed in rags and living in a squalid cabin. Although one woman was a former Baptist and the other previously a Methodist, both had married poorly—one had married a drunkard, the other a "lazy huntsman." Now they each had a child, lived in poverty, had not seen or heard a minister in years, and had no Bible.[69]

Such conditions created support for benevolence from a wide range of Baptists. Constantly confronted with such conditions in the rural areas where he preached, strict Calvinist Basil Manly Sr. endorsed benevolence societies. Fellow Tuscaloosa preacher and University of Alabama faculty member Joshua Hill Foster (who served as corresponding secretary of a benevolence, the Alabama Central Sunday School Union) endorsed Sunday schools because they encouraged order (they produced an exemplary "class of citizens thoroughly trained in the great principles which constitute the groundwork of all correct moral and civil law, thus preventing crime, and operating as a conservative agent in promoting . . . our political institutions, amid all the discordant elements rapidly concentrating in our country"). Women who formed Tuscaloosa's Female Baptist Missionary Society, established in 1824, endorsed benevolence societies because they believed such organizations elevated the status of women. The Alabama Baptist State Convention regularly passed resolutions between 1844 and 1857 praising them (although the praise ended abruptly when the mainly northern societies began attacking slavery).[70]

No less a Calvinist than Hosea Holcombe was also an advocate of benevolence societies. He scolded Alabama Baptists who prayed for the coming of Christ's kingdom when in fact the means for the conversion of the world was already in their hands. Holcombe followed this admonition with a litany of worthy causes that Baptists should support: missions, temperance, Bible societies, and the crusade against tobacco.[71]

Among the earliest Alabama Baptist benevolence organizations was the Alabama Baptist Bible Society, organized in 1836. James H. DeVotie served as its president until 1856, when I. T. Tichenor succeeded him. In addition to dispatching many colporteurs under auspices of the Alabama Baptist State Convention, the society also established a depository (or bookstore) in Selma in 1855. Benevolence also involved pioneer Baptists in a broadly ecumenical effort through the Alabama Bible Society, which had been formed a dozen years before the Baptist Bible society.[72]

For a denomination long renowned for its animosity to the use or manufacture of alcoholic beverages, Alabama Baptists waged surprisingly heated battles over the issue between 1819 and the 1840s. Many churches, like Oxford First Baptist, used wine in communion services and commissioned a respected deacon or elder to grow the grapes and make the wine. South Alabama patriarch Alexander Travis was a teetotaler himself, though two deacons in one of his churches drank whiskey in moderation. Travis brought the matter before the church conference when the two men began to drink heavily. The deacons and their wives turned the tables on Travis, moving to expel him for reporting their drunkenness without first talking to them privately as required by Scripture. Travis, who could not attend the conference, was expelled. He demanded another trial because of his absence, and as word spread through the community, a large crowd of Methodists and non-Christians showed up to watch the Baptists fight. Persuaded by the powerful preacher to reinstate him, church members then expelled the two deacons, who subsequently joined an antimission church.[73] As this case makes clear, Baptist church discipline was often ambiguous on the use of alcohol. Members were usually charged and excluded for drunkenness or the abuse of alcohol, seldom simply for its use.

As the decades unfolded, Baptist policy on alcohol became increasingly strict. Local temperance societies were established in Marion, Tuscaloosa, and elsewhere. During the 1840s the *Alabama Baptist* published dozens of temperance editorials, some of them calling on the Alabama legislature to prohibit the retail sale of liquor. Temperance essays denounced alcohol use by deacons and church leaders, blaming it for pauperism, high taxes, crime, poverty, death, and the declining influence of religion. And if such offenders were wealthy, the editorials complained, churches hardly ever excluded them.[74]

Hyper-Calvinists greeted these frenzied efforts to reform human society with mounting scorn. Although theology was at the heart of the battle over benevolent societies, many social forces intensified the conflict. The authority of associational and state organizations impinged on local church authority. Well-meaning benevolent societies seemed to run roughshod over frontier individualism. The deleterious social consequences of alcohol abuse seemed more obvious and urgent in towns and cities than in rural areas. Poorly educated yeoman farmers disagreed with affluent planters and townspeople over the importance of ministerial education and salaried clergy. Some historians have depicted the antimission movement as a conflict of class and folk cultures, of poor white farmers primarily in the hills and piney woods versus planters and townspeople.[75] But this explanation seems unconvincing in Alabama where antimission sentiment was strong in all sections of the state.

The institutional expression of hyper-Calvinism was the antimission movement, which gave rise to Primitive Baptist churches. Many of the oldest churches and associations (including the Flint River Baptist Association, the state's first) were dominated by antimissionary forces, who retained control of the institutions and forced missionary Baptists to withdraw and form new associations. Some tensions over missions and benevolence existed between Calvinists, Arminians, and hyper-Calvinists from the formation of the first Baptist churches in Alabama. But conflict accelerated at about the time the first state convention was held in 1823.

As early as 1818, the Flint River Association refused to cooperate with the Board of Foreign Missions. By the early 1820s, nine churches in Lawrence, Franklin, Morgan, and Lauderdale Counties were divided over missions. The battle reached its zenith in the 1830s and 1840s. The 1837 state convention listed twenty-one associations statewide, twelve of them deeply divided over missions. Four opposed missions and only three were clearly in favor.[76]

Antimission forces seemed strongest in the Tennessee Valley and the hill country to the south. In 1836 Holcombe visited the Flint River Association as state convention historian and as a correspondent of his home Canaan Association. The state convention had consistently supported missions, and when it met with the Canaan Association in 1829, delegates adopted a resolution praising Bible and tract societies as well as Sunday schools. So when Holcombe arrived at the Flint River meeting, he was not received cordially. His letter of correspondence was first laid on the table; then the association declined any correspondence with Canaan. Two years later the Flint River Association received an inquiry from the Kelly's Creek Baptist Church about whether missionary societies were scriptural. No, the delegates responded; and to add insult to injury, they also adopted a "non-fellowship resolution," severing all contact with missionary societies and all who belonged to them. The association resolved that the "merits of Christ alone" were sufficient for salvation, "unaided by human effort." That same year (1838), missionary churches in the area formed Liberty Association (later the Madison Association). By 1840 these churches (Enon, Poplar Creek, and Athens) had been expelled from the Flint River Association, finalizing the split in north Alabama.[77]

In the south-central portions of the state, the Alabama Association experienced sharp divisions. When antimission forces offered a resolution against Sunday schools and temperance, tract, and missionary societies, Elder Lewis C. Davis, the association's moderator, declared his support of religious liberty and vowed never to be bound by such resolutions. The eccentric Davis was a corpulent carpenter-preacher who later became a planter as well and was known for his simple, rough preaching style, which earned him the nickname of "Club Axe Davis." He was influential enough to defeat the antimission resolution, but by the late 1820s every church in the association except Montgomery First Baptist contained significant antimission influence. Promission preachers even stopped using words such as "missions," "societies," "money," and "heathen" and substituted "itinerant" for activities designed to spread the gospel. In 1838 the association elected Elder David Moor (a hyper-Calvinist) as moderator and David Lee (an advocate of missions) as clerk. The mission forces prevailed by only two votes on key resolutions. As a result, seventeen antimission churches withdrew and formed the Ebenezer Association, while twenty-three missionary churches remained in the Alabama Association. Though it was probably the most promission association in the state, only two or three of the twenty-three remaining churches were thoroughly committed to missions. Neither association had strong leadership. Missionary leaders alleged that hyper-Calvinist Elder Moor, who served for nearly two decades as moderator of the Ebenezar Association, became an alcoholic. And they conceded that their own moderator in 1843, Elder T. D. Armstrong, possessed little originality, read infrequently, shamelessly plagiarized the sermons of others, and was a "first class ranter" who, on calm evenings, could be heard preaching two miles away. On one occasion, when he preached in Tuscaloosa before an audience of University of Alabama officials, legislators, and other distinguished persons, Armstrong determined to remain dignified. But before long he had reverted to preaching "country fashion," began to whoop and gesture, knocked candles over, and brought much of the canine population of Tuscaloosa to the meeting barking at him.[78]

To the south, the Conecuh River Association split in 1839, with thirty-two of forty churches opposed to missions. The Bethlehem Association lost its most popular young schoolteacher-minister, James A. Butler. Converted by the legendary Alexander Travis, Butler was considered the most talented young preacher in the association. But he was also quite belligerent, according to his critics. He railed against "pedobaptism" and Arminianism and, when asked to write the association's circular in 1829, drafted a hyper-Calvinist document on "Special Redemption." The association rejected the letter, alienating Butler so deeply that he stormed out of the meeting with another man's hat. So extreme a Calvinist was he that he once said that God would take him away the instant he had completed the work for which he had been ordained. To that assertion, a missionary leader in Conecuh County replied: "I hope he will for if he lets you live another day, you will get into mischief." The association excluded Butler on charges of heresy.[79]

Although differences in doctrine stood at the center of the antimission controversy, small farmer resentment of the wealthy was not entirely absent. E. B. Teague recalled a friend who was chided because he contributed a dollar to the American Bible Society. He defended his action by claiming his right to contribute his own money to any cause he chose. Not so, his critics responded. After a heated argument, one of them ended the discussion by saying: "We have no use for the rich."[80]

In time hyper-Calvinists called themselves Primitive Baptists, and their missionary foes referred to them as "Hardshell," "foot-washing," or just "antimission" Baptists. Their zealous preachers suffered from lack of salary and too little time for education or preparation. Lack of outreach left them heavily dependent on the natural increase of their families. They retained strong folkways and a deep commitment to their communities, but they did not grow much. Although missionary Baptists claimed the victory, the denomination remained crippled by the dispute until near the end of the century, especially in north Alabama.[81]

By 1845 missionary Baptists had survived the frontier and disputes with each other. But the weary task of building religious institutions had just begun.

2

Taming the Frontier, 1800–1845

"The seed has been sown that will bring forth much fruit."

central concern of the first generation of Alabama Baptists was order. How could they instill order on the frontier, foster discipline amid chaos, define roles for all within a fractured and dangerous society? Organizing a society is a complicated process not given to neat categories. At one level, the frontier church operated in such a way as to establish and maintain white male hierarchy. At a more subtle level, church discipline defined the boundaries of sacred community in ways more liberating to women and blacks than the surrounding secular society. Chronology made a difference as well. In the early stages of religious formation, egalitarian relationships, localism, and individualism thrived.[1] In later years, hierarchical values, emphasis on education and a professional clergy, and ecclesiastical centralization became more common. Women, children, and blacks found appropriate slots within a white, male-oriented society. Churches were dominated by ministers, elders, and deacons, all white males, who composed only a minority of total church membership.

The conventional interpretation of southern evangelicalism is that it sought little more than personal conversion and enthroned an exaggerated sense of individualism. But another core value of the antebellum South was that all live orderly lives within a stable society. Missionary Baptists believed that the path of prideful individualism, like the road of hyper-Calvinism, led to chaos and disaster. Far from lone individuals adrift in an isolated frontier society, members of early antebellum Baptist churches participated in a disciplined group within an increasingly orderly society. In this way Baptists were not so much captives of their culture as they were its shapers.[2]

Hosea Holcombe clearly understood that the greatest danger to his infant denomination was not hyper-Calvinism or even atheism. It was disorder. He admonished fellow believers about the chaotic conditions of pioneer Baptist churches. Baptists flooded onto newly opened Alabama land from more than half the settled states, bringing heterodox religious ideas with them. Many squatted on land to which they had no legal claim, established churches, then had to move on after their land was legally surveyed and sold to others. This constant upheaval played havoc with early churches. Ministers, elders, and deacons refused to impose discipline upon unruly congregations, and churches adopted rules of conduct to the taste of members. As Holcombe phrased it, "A number of Baptists contend for a lax discipline, believing men are of such a texture that they cannot be bound by rigid, or strict rules."[3]

Church Discipline

It is easy to make light of church discipline by citing specific cases to illustrate how intolerant early Baptists were of perceived misconduct. Such flippancy obscures the heart of the social function of frontier religion. It aimed not so much at punishing wanderers as recalling them to faith and full fellowship within a sacred community. Bound together in the wonder of Christ's redeeming love, Baptists believed that the sins of a brother or sister inflicted pain and disapprobation upon the entire family. Congregational discipline closely resembled parental constraint of a child: the intent was not to exclude one's offspring but to clarify the boundaries of accepted conduct, to forewarn that if the child valued the safety, nurture, and support of the family, then it must adhere to certain standards.

Like the punishment of a child, the discipline of church members ranged from mild "rebuke" or "admonition," to "exclusion," "excommunication," "expulsion," or "cutting off." These words were important symbols. When a congregation "cited" a member, it also appointed a committee (almost always male) to investigate and bring the wayward person before the next church conference. If the person could not appear in person to explain the alleged misconduct, or if the committee investigation was incomplete, action could be delayed to some future meeting. Usually the offending person "gave satisfaction" to the congregation and the charges were dismissed. Or the person "acknowledged" the offense and repented. Even the most grievous sins (drunkenness, adultery, fornication, illegitimacy, theft, heresy) were promptly forgiven if the accused demonstrated remorse. Only when the indicted member refused to appear, would not deny the charges, or would not repent did the congregation act. The threatened "expulsion" or "cutting off" of a person from a valued place within a supportive community was a powerful stimulus to reform. Most either energetically and promptly denied the charge or contritely confessed the sin and begged forgiveness. Even when expulsion occurred, members often returned to the fold during some future camp meeting or revival when the spirit convicted them of their sin.

Although the most frequent discipline charges involved disorderly conduct (drunkenness was the most frequently cited offense, followed by absence from services without excuse, activities with another denomination or even with another variety of Baptist, fighting, stealing, profane language, cheating), less obvious sins also threatened the evangelical community. Some congregations strongly opposed membership in secret societies. In later years, as Baptists became more affluent and influential, no fraternal organization was more popular than the Masonic order. But in these initial years of low status, many churches expelled members who joined the Masons.[4]

Two incidents in the mid-1840s demonstrate the complexity of issues confronting those who tried to establish moral order on the Alabama frontier. After a disastrous fire burned their building and many members departed, the Wetumpka Baptist Church called Philip H. Lundy of Georgia as pastor in 1844. His brief pastorate was beset with rumors of his wife's adultery. Several months after he resigned as pastor, he returned to the church to lodge charges of spreading malicious rumors about his wife. The committee enlarged its charge to include not only allegations of gossip but also the alleged misconduct of Lundy's wife. So serious were the charges that the church committee was augmented with members from five other churches. The extensive investigation involved numerous witnesses and resulted in a report to the church that was thorough, balanced, and fair. The charge that Mrs. Lundy was unkind to her husband seemed well substantiated. But whether their obvious marital unhappiness was exclusively her fault, the committee could not determine. She had certainly conducted herself in an imprudent way that "excited suspicion in the community," and the committee recommended her expulsion based on this misconduct. But on the more serious charge of adultery, it could find no convincing evidence.[5]

Even more spectacular charges were lodged against Jonathan Davis, pastor of the Eufaula Baptist Church during the mid-1840s. A committee of seven was charged with investigating rumors that the pastor engaged in "immoral intimacy" with a slave woman named Leacy, who was also a member of the church. The official report charged that Davis secretly walked down a dark, deserted road at night with Leacy despite "knowledge of the fact that bad reports had been and still were circulating among the blacks and some whites" about his improper conduct. Davis defended himself in writing, denying all charges except his conversation with Leacy, which he conceded was a "great imprudence" on his part. For this breach of church order, he apologized profusely.

The committee was not satisfied with Davis's explanation and enlarged its membership to include ministers from Tuskegee, Montgomery, and Georgia. Its report found no evidence of adultery but did cite him for "imprudence and indiscretion" and recommended that he be excluded. Church members who supported Davis rejected this recommendation, and after affording him opportunity for "acknowledgments and explanations verbally," voted to retain him. The committee, however, voted to suspend him temporarily from the ministry, and his family was granted letters of dismissal from the church.

As the case dragged into 1848, petitions arrived from other churches asking the Eufaula congregation to restore Davis to the ministry so that they might hear the popular minister preach. Eufaula negotiated with one of these churches, which Davis had joined, but in the end refused to rescind its action.

Meanwhile, the black church conference heard charges from Leacy's master accusing her of fornication and voted to exclude her from fellowship. In these proceedings, her master detailed the conduct between Leacy and Davis that had been the basis for charges against him. According to the pastor's explanation of events, Leacy was trying to seduce him. She even told him that two Eufaula white men had accused her of rejecting their sexual advances because she was "too intimate with Jonathan Davis." Following her expulsion, the committee found additional evidence against Davis. Similar charges of fornication with a slave woman and member of his church in Georgia had been lodged against him. This additional evidence caused the committee of ministers to reject Davis's request to be restored to the ministry. With this decision, the affair that had dragged on for two years finally came to an end.[6]

These two cases demonstrate the complex relationship of Christianity, gender, and race. In neither case was there a female or a black on the investigating committee. Yet in each case white male committee members went to great length to rule fairly and were dubious about the testimony of a fellow white male pastor.

Furthermore, discipline cases demonstrate that women and blacks often exercised considerable influence over church proceedings even when they did not directly participate. In fact, religious boundaries that did exist were less restrictive to them than secular boundaries within the larger society.

The rise of women's consciousness in nineteenth-century America owed much to the church. The second Great Awakening (1800–1840), the rise of female mission societies, and the temperance crusade later in the century were particularly important episodes for women. To some degree, women shaped their religious culture by resistance to male authority and masculine culture. They believed that men often drank too much, squandered family resources on alcohol and gambling, abused or neglected them and their children. They concluded also that male church members neglected missions and contributed too little to support and sustain pastors and church programs. Some historians claim that "women's culture" developed more slowly in the South because southern religion reenforced ties to kin and community rather than to other women. The southern church propounded hierarchical male values that affirmed equal partnership in theory but denied it in practice. Only after the Civil War, historians argue, did southern women build collective identity both inside and outside the church. Other historians emphasize the liberating role of the antebellum church, which allowed women to assert themselves in new ways and resist male oppression. Born-again women used their new relationship with Christ to carve out psychological and social space from worldly husbands. They were brought together in a public body that often allowed them to speak and occasionally even to vote. Women's opinion, however expressed, mattered in a church where an average of two-thirds the members were women. Churches, in fact, became the chief means by which Alabama women established a public life. [7]

By no means was there a single, uniform pattern of church conduct or discipline involving women. As decades passed, churches tended to become more restrictive for both female and black members. But in the early days, considerable variety existed. The Wetumpka church experienced controversy in 1823 over who could vote to call a pastor. The church finally agreed to "give all persons who [were] members a voice in the choice" (apparently including both women and slave members). The 1838 Uniontown church rules of decorum provided that "the sisters shall be entitled to vote on the reception and exclusion of members and choice of pastor." At the Mount Hebron church in February 1830 a female was appointed to cite a woman member being brought before the church on discipline charges.[8]

Disciplinary proceedings during the nineteenth century at Mount Hebron church near Leeds reveal the feminization of the congregation. From the initial discipline incident in 1826 until the last in 1904, church minutes record 242 cases. Of these, 181 charged men (172 citations were against whites, 7 against slaves, and 2 against free blacks); 61 cases were lodged against women (58 whites, 2 slaves, 1 free black). So in a church that was 65 percent female, women accounted for only 25 percent of the alleged ethical and religious violations of church order. The 35 percent minority of men committed 75 percent of the breaches of acceptable conduct.

Types of offenses reveal even more clearly the gender differences in discipline. Although women held no church offices and could not vote at church conferences, they helped define the boundaries of male conduct. The charge most frequently cited in discipline cases was alcohol abuse. But excessive drinking also factored into a number of other activities that threatened family and community standards: fighting, gambling, wife and child abuse, adultery, and other "disorderly" conduct. Of the fifty-four cases of "excessive drinking," "too much drinking," "intoxication," and "whiskey-making," all involved males and all but one were lodged against white males. All eighteen cases of swearing involved white males. Gambling, card playing, unlawful use of public funds, swindling, overcharging, and Sabbath violation were also exclusively male sins. Charges of quarreling, fighting, and anger affected twenty-three men but only one woman. The church also excluded one man for wife abuse. Conversely, some "sins" seemed unique to women. Charges of heresy were lodged against three women but never against a male.

Men and women seemed to be equal partners in other categories of transgression. The church cited thirty-two men and twenty women for dancing, six women and five men for falsehood/slander, eight men and four women for nonattendance, fifteen men and thirteen women for joining another denomination, and four men and two women (one of them a free black woman) for immorality/adultery. Most of the charges leveled against women came after 1845, when Baptists achieved higher status and worried more about relatively trivial issues like dancing than more substantial moral lapses that threatened family or community.

Discipline meted out by the Mount Hebron church clearly served to curb disorderly conduct by males and to protect women and children from the harshest aspects of frontier society, to socialize and civilize males in a way defined by females. Women's influence over men who did vote mitigates their absence from most discipline committees or as voters at church conferences.

Another curiosity at Mount Hebron was the frequency with which women rejected the jurisdiction of the church over their private conduct or when they were forced to engage in actions offensive to the church because of their husbands. The clearest example was when a husband compelled his wife to join another denomination. Some wives moved their church membership when their husbands were excluded from fellowship. More intriguing is the large number of wives who refused to do so. Forced to choose between solidarity with their embarrassed husbands or loyalty to Christ and his church, they usually chose the latter course, perhaps privately believing that their husbands had received the punishment due them.[9]

The Cahawba Association officially recognized gender and race as factors in the exercise of church discipline in 1826. The association responded to an inquiry about the duty of churches toward members who moved away without requesting letters of dismission. The association pondered the matter, then recommended excluding such members from fellowship unless they were "wives or slaves whom the church considers to be restrained," in which case "tender forbearance should be exercized."[10]

If the central function of the frontier church was preaching (from which women were excluded) and the primary task of deacons was fund raising and maintaining the church building in good order, women needed a role in the church structure. They usually found it through female mission societies. As churches developed a more complex educational structure later in the century, female roles greatly expanded.

By the mid-1840s the irregular patterns of female participation in Baptist churches apparently began to embarrass denominational leaders, and the *Alabama Baptist* published a series of articles defining women's roles. In July 1843 an article reminded women that their finest attribute was piety. A year later the paper featured a debate about whether women should be allowed to vote in church conference. The article deemed it prudent not to allow women to vote because it would violate the biblical injunction that women "shall not speak nor usurp authority" over men. But it did urge churches to allow women to vote for pastors because women usually raised most of the money to pay them. Lest there be any misunderstanding about the limits of females' gospel freedom, however, the paper printed an essay two months later quoting Ephesians as urging wives to submit to their husbands in "filial fear." The husband was the lord of his family but should not reign like a tyrant. Christian men should express love for their wives, paternal affection for their children, and mercy for their slaves.[11]

The inclusion of slaves with women and children demonstrated their inferior status in the antebellum church. At the core of the legal defense of slavery was the constitutional proposition that slaves were property and might be disposed of however their owners determined. At the core of the theological defense of slavery was the proposition that God had ordained and sustained the institution. For friend and foe of slavery alike, the peril rested in the interpretation. Just as justices differed over the meaning of the Constitution, black and white Christians disagreed about how slaves should function within the church.

Traditionally, historians have deplored the ethical inconsistency of evangelical Christians owning slaves, together with the sorts of potential abuses apparent in the Eufaula Baptist Church incident. The defense offered by southern churchmen was that slavery was little enough price to pay for salvation of slave souls through all eternity. But that argument is more convincing if one is a master rather than a slave.

In recent years historical attention has focused on the ways black and white forms of Christianity interacted, creating mixed elements in Christianity like the ones that characterized southern music, cuisine, and folklore. So thoroughly were African and Western elements combined that one recent history of race and religion in Mississippi was entitled "a mingled yarn." Whites taught blacks Christianity. Blacks taught whites spirituality. In the years prior to the 1840s, blacks and whites typically worshiped together, perhaps with slaves in the back rows, but at least in the same buildings. Spatial separation became more customary after 1840, with slaves sitting in the balcony or even attending separate services. Blacks and whites interpreted rituals, hymns, and Scripture differently. Life over Jordan might mean heaven to whites but freedom from slavery to blacks. Exodus from bondage in Egypt might be a remote historical allusion to whites but a hopeful future expectation to blacks. Images of a suffering servant represented Christ to whites but might be a description of a slave's current condition.

Worship to many whites must be planned, sermons written out, rational, somber, serious, and focused. To most blacks, worship should be joyous, vital, emotional, spontaneous, an end in itself. Blacks might worship the same God, but they interjected many African conceptions of spirit and soul-travels, trances, and possession experiences. The spiritual journey (which blacks called "trabelin") had an African antecedent. The Baptist term "elder" (which designated a chosen leader in the church) paralleled the African tribal meaning.[12]

Later, when blacks were free to form their own churches and select their own leaders, whites would interpret many of their worship forms as pagan superstitions. But during the early years of the Republic, Baptists had little respectability to lose by consorting with blacks. They were a radical sect, despised and consisting largely of poor, disinherited people. Many of the rituals they extended to blacks (the hand of fellowship when blacks joined the church, baptism with whites in the same creeks and rivers, shared communion services, and even foot washings) conveyed an egalitarian gospel.

Many Baptists before 1820 were abolitionists who had no economic stake in the slave system. Hosea Holcombe gave servants inherited from his mother's estate to his half-brother because he did not believe he should own slaves. Lee and Susanna Compere, English missionaries who came to Alabama by way of Jamaica, South Carolina, and Georgia, were even more pronounced in their racial iconoclasm. In Jamaica, they had become abolitionists, and as missionaries to the Creek Indians at Tuckabatchee on the Tallapoosa River, they befriended Creeks against white incursions and the black slaves of Creeks against their Indian masters. Neither action endeared them to white members at the Montgomery First Baptist Church, which Compere served as first pastor. But he did survive long enough to be elected president of the Alabama Baptist State Convention in 1829 before migrating to Arkansas. Perhaps those who elected him did not know about his abolitionism. Or, perhaps in the 1820s such views did not matter much. In 1820, a Shelby County Baptist farmer, John Teague, expressed "scruples about holding African slaves." And even so prominent a state leader as E. B. Teague as late as 1840 was not "clear as to the perpetuation of the curse pronounced on Canaan." No race, he believed, was created for the perpetual service of another race.[13]

Such misgivings about slavery soon passed. As Baptists prospered on plantations, they extolled the positive benefits of slavery. Strict Calvinists, many of whom owned slaves themselves, led the assault on the antislavery forces. Antimissionary Baptists, following the lead of Alexander Campbell and Barton Stone, opposed slavery until the 1840s, a fact that only heightened the flight of missionary Baptists from their fellowship.

The chief weapon in the Baptist proslavery arsenal was the Bible, especially Pauline admonitions for slaves to accept their lot in life and Genesis 9, which contains an account of Noah and his three sons, Ham, Shem, and Japheth. In this account, Noah drank too much wine and fell asleep naked inside his tent. When Ham saw his father's nakedness and went outside to tell his brothers, Noah cursed Ham's son, Canaan, and condemned him to be "a servant of servants . . . unto his brethren." Thus, went the proslavery argument, did God create the black race and condemn Africans to perpetual slavery. Thereafter, as abolitionist Theodore Weld wrote in 1838, slaveholders "never venture abroad without [the curse of Noah]; it is a pocketpiece for sudden occasion, a keepsake to dote over, a charm to spell-bind opposition, and a magnet to draw around their standard 'whatsoever worketh abomination or maketh a lie.' "[14]

Despite such interpretations of Scripture, day-to-day Baptist church life offered blacks more equality than they received elsewhere in southern society. Most white Baptists believed blacks had souls and were persons of worth—not a universal opinion even among southern intellectuals. Baptists sometimes allowed blacks to offer testimony against whites, as in the Eufaula discipline case, a right blacks did not have in Alabama civil courts.[15]

Many Alabama Baptist churches allowed black members a considerable role in their own religious lives. In the Wetumpka church, not only could blacks vote for pastor, but a committee of elderly black men was appointed to oversee the behavior of black members and cite them when necessary. Until 1844 the church conducted integrated services, but that year blacks began to worship separately, and they were no longer invited to church conference. In 1846 the church selected six black deacons and licensed two black preachers after clearing one of charges of unsound doctrine. They preached to the separate black congregation, which thrived. The Eufaula church had a separate black conference to discipline blacks. At the Montgomery church blacks voted in church conference the same way whites did until 1840, although they had separate communion and baptismal services. But in 1840 Stephney, a slave belonging to Peyton Bibb, was charged with keeping a house of ill repute, lying, and working on the Sabbath. When the conference considered a motion to excommunicate Stephney, he was acquitted by a vote of 8 to 14. Whites voted 7 to 5 to exclude him, but blacks cast 9 votes to acquit and only 1 to convict. This was the first occasion when the black vote thwarted the majority will of whites. And it was the last. White members created a separate black congregation, with their names on a separate roll, that met in the afternoon after white worship ended. They also conducted their own business in a separate conference.[16]

In Talladega, planter James Mallory recorded in his diary various accounts of black fellow Baptists. In April 1845 he rejoiced at a revival that had broken out among slaves but wondered about the sincerity of their professed conversions. Later he attended services at the newly created African church, which was apparently a branch of the Talladega Baptist congregation. Some slaves seemed interested in the sermon preached by the church's white pastor, but "they would greatly prefer to be always preached to by one of their own colour however ignorant."[17]

Across the state in Tuscaloosa, the Baptist church also spawned a black congregation after many years of united worship. In 1824, 1825, and 1826, Billy, a black man, was elected to represent the church as a delegate to the Cahawba Association. William Martin (a black minister in the church and perhaps the same person earlier identified only as Billy) was elected the following two years. But the association did not accept him as a delegate. Although whites did not always ordain blacks when black members requested such action, in the mid-1840s the church authorized black ministers to conduct funerals and marriages and also appoint six "exhorters" from their ranks. This action, however, conflicted with Alabama law, which required white attendance when more than five slaves assembled.[18]

Judged by the number of black Baptist preachers ordained by antebellum churches, there was ample opportunity for African Americans to hear preaching by one of their own race, even if the occasion was closely supervised by whites. Talladega planter James Mallory saw nothing strange about his visit to the Mount Ashby church in March 1844. When the white pastor did not arrive, a "Black brother" preached with "much force," drawing "from nature to sustain the power and divinity of God." And sometimes a black preacher became so popular that he was sought after by whites as well as blacks.

Caesar Blackwell, the slave of John Blackwell, joined the Antioch church at Mount Meigs in 1821 by experience and baptism. Two years later the church licensed him to preach. In 1828 the congregation tried to buy his freedom, but his master refused. The Alabama Association took up the cause and purchased him as a preaching assistant to the associational missionary, who also owned Caesar's wife and child. Caesar preached freely (keeping the money he received) until 1835, when rising tensions over abolitionism caused the association to restrict his activities and require him to return all funds above his actual expenses. By this time the slave preacher had an extensive library, had imbibed Calvinist theology, and enjoyed debating the doctrines of election, grace, and the perseverance of saints. So popular a preacher was Blackwell that churches clamored for his services, and, when he preached at the annual associational meeting, standing-room-only crowds of whites and blacks thronged to hear him. He was a tall man with a melodious voice and wonderful elocution who insisted on a decorous worship service. If a parishioner began to shout, he would pause and gently chide: "My brethren and sisters, when your cup is full, let it run over, but don't tilt it any." In 1844, despite ill health, he baptized ninety-nine.[19] Among his converts were Nathan Ashby and Jacob Belser, who would play key roles in the formation of Alabama's black Baptist convention during Reconstruction.

One reason for Blackwell's popularity with antebellum whites was his attempt to purge black Christianity of its African spiritualism. In 1844 an editor for a Baptist paper in New York heard Blackwell conduct a service for blacks at the Montgomery church. At the church conference that followed, the white pastor and clerk joined Blackwell to examine candidates for baptism, though the black man did most of the questioning. He warned the new Christians against "dreams, visions, voices, and such like." Instead, he urged them to "let us know how you have regarded yourselves and how your character appeared before God. Then tell us how you were led to hope and on what you rely." After the testimonials, Blackwell led the congregation in singing "spirited songs" through the streets of Montgomery on their way to the creek to be baptized.[20]

The sudden shift in attitude toward Caesar Blackwell in 1835 reflected changes both in Alabama civil law and in the mood of white Baptists in the aftermath of slave insurrections in South Carolina and Virginia. In 1832 the Alabama legislature banned education for blacks and assemblies of more than five slaves off their master's plantation and prohibited them from testifying in court. Three years later the state Baptist convention took its first definitive stand on slavery, condemning northern abolitionists for seeking to alienate blacks from whites, arming assassins, and threatening relations between masters and slaves.[21]

Mount Hebron Baptist Church tended toward the liberal end of the Baptist spectrum on race. Of 376 names recorded on the church roll between 1819 and 1865, 51 were names of slaves and 2 were free blacks. Their names were listed chronologically among whites in the order that they joined, not separately by race as was common. Many slaves joined when their master did. Others joined long before their masters or despite the fact that their masters never became members. Although church records referred to slaves by only their first names, they accorded free blacks family names as well. Over the years, seven male slaves and two females stood before the church accused of unacceptable conduct. Two were excluded for quarreling, two for fighting, one for lying, another for nonattendance, and one for Sabbath violation. The two black females committed the most grievous offenses. One ran away from her master and was excluded. In a later case (1858) the church appointed Mary's master, who had brought a charge of "unchristian conduct," to investigate and report to the church conference. Normally the church allowed members personally to answer charges against them. But in this case, Mary's master made her reply and predictably she was excluded. Before this case, black members had always appeared to defend themselves.

Perhaps the most revealing discipline case in Mount Hebron's history occurred in 1855 and demonstrates the way Christian fellowship blurred racial distinctions. The charges alleged that some white members had attended a Christmas party in the slave quarters of the Shepherd plantation and had danced with blacks. At least eleven slaves on the plantation were members of the church. The five white males who investigated the case confirmed that six white church members had indeed visited slaves in their cabins and that one or two of them had engaged in "fiddling and dancing." Three of the whites "gave satisfaction" and were retained; the other three failed to exonerate themselves and were excluded.

Four months after the resolution of the interracial Christmas dance, the church cited Sister Audea Harris for visiting the slave quarters of the Shepherd plantation. She spiritedly defended her visit as official business and disapproved such conduct. The church accepted her explanation.[22] The length of each investigation and the seriousness afforded the two incidents revealed the racial tensions at Mount Hebron. Having brought the two races together in sacred community (to worship together, take communion together, be baptized together), white members now scrambled to define the limits of fraternity. Whites and blacks might share hymns, preaching, discipline, and the right hand of fellowship, but they must not share the slave quarters, fiddling, or dancing. The specter of six white males dancing with black women at a Christmas party was bad enough; but a white female member frequenting a slave cabin alone raised even greater questions of propriety. Mount Hebron Baptist Church, having first blurred racial distinctions in the process of defining religious community, now desperately tried to reorder and redefine those distinctions within a larger secular society that absolutely would not tolerate social race mixing.

Most interesting in the complex mixture of religion and race on the Alabama frontier was the existence of several independent black Baptist churches that belonged to regular Baptist associations. In fact, one of these churches claimed to be the oldest Baptist church in Alabama.

According to local lore, the Stone Street Baptist Church was established under a brush arbor in Mobile in 1806, nearly thirty years before the first white Baptist congregation in the city. In 1841 the Saint Anthony Street

Stone Street Baptist Church, Mobile, an African American congregation, which claimed origins in 1806, nearly thirty years before the first white Baptist congregation was established in the port city. (Courtesy of Samford University Archives)

Baptist Church formed an African branch and invited blacks to join. Apparently, this semiautonomous branch merged with the older Stone Street church, making the latter a legal appendage of the white congregation. As the white church declined, the black branch grew, until black members refused to "submit themselves to the rules and regulations of the church." In 1845 a new white congregation, the Saint Francis Street Baptist Church (later Mobile First Baptist), became sponsor of the largely autonomous black congregation. The Cahawba Association accepted the African branch church, as it was then called, provided its pastor was white and an orthodox Baptist. Also, only white men could represent the church as associational delegates. A split in the black church led to formation of a second independent black congregation with a white pastor in 1859, and the original Stone Street church reclaimed its name and called a black pastor.[23]

At the other end of the state, blacks organized two independent congregations. The African Huntsville Church was organized in 1808 and had 432 members by 1849. It joined the Flint River Association, which allowed black delegates to represent the congregation. African Baptist Church Cottonport, founded in the mid-1820s, also joined the Flint River Association. When both churches sent delegates to association meetings, blacks made up more than one-seventh of the delegates.

Fraternal relations between African Huntsville and the Flint River Association were so strong that when antimissionary sentiment swept the association and caused missionary churches to withdraw, the black church remained. Perhaps the abolitionist views of Alexander Campbell and Barton Stone influenced the decision, or perhaps black leaders had developed hyper-Calvinist views themselves. For whatever reason, the church became a Primitive Baptist congregation and remained actively involved in the Flint River Association until after the Civil War. Curiously, the African Cottonport Church remained true to missionary doctrine and dropped out of the association in 1840.[24]

Revivalism

Church discipline was one way to tame a disorderly frontier. Revivalism was another, as revivals became the chief vehicle for conversion. Few converts were made in the infrequent monthly worship services, but seasons of revival swept communities after lay-by time in July when isolated farmers deserted their fields for camp meetings.

The great revival that broke out in Kentucky in 1800 set the stage for three decades of southern revivalism. Services usually began with a prayer meeting at sunrise, then continued through two rounds of sermons before lunch, a third in the afternoon, and a fourth at night. Some services lasted four or five hours, and when the spirit of God was especially active, exhausted worshipers might not retire until after midnight. Participants constructed sheds, stands, brush arbors, and even tents at campgrounds such as Parks, three miles from Scottsboro, or Flat Rock on Sand Mountain, or Thompson near Princeton.[25] Numerous ministers of several denominations preached, but doctrine took second place to calls for repentance and acceptance of Christ as savior. Such ecumenical revivals gave rise to what one historian has called "the Southern church," which agreed on central Christian issues: humanity's sinfulness, the imperative of salvation, the destiny of persons to be damned to hell or rewarded in heaven, and the necessity of individual response.

In a sense, these revivals also severed American evangelicalism from

European emphasis on sacraments, communion, reason, theology, written sermons, and aristocratic trappings. Here on the frontier, with no other setting than nature, poorly educated preachers proclaimed a simple gospel, emotion swept reason aside, social equality reigned among the throngs of ordinary people, and the urgency of Christian faith became obvious to all. Words such as *decide, follow, commit, yield, surrender, give,* and *sacrifice* reinforced southern individualism by making clear that each person had to initiate the new birth by a specific action or response to God's offer of grace. Revivalism thus "Arminianized" Calvinist theology by emphasizing free will, individual choice, and salvation to all who sought it.[26]

By the 1830s sectarian differences had eroded the influence of camp meetings, and the more denominational protracted meeting replaced them. Lasting from four to sixteen days, such meetings might still occur at a campground, but they tended to feature preachers of a single denomination and to be more orderly. They continued the frontier tradition of associating conversion with a special period of revival rather than with the regular worship of a congregation.

Whatever called, these special seasons of revival won converts and changed lives. E. B. Teague described the greatest revival he witnessed in nearly seven decades of preaching. During the summer of 1832 he attended a protracted meeting at the Bethesda Baptist Church in the Coosa River Valley. Five Baptist preachers began services in the church but to no effect. Finally they moved to a brush arbor where they seemed infused by the Holy Ghost. People came forward, sometimes fifty in a single service. Strong men "fell upon the ground apparently helpless, lying there for hours, so powerful was the reaction of soul upon body. When they began to hope in Christ, they would rise and often soberly join in the singing."[27]

Hosea Holcombe also remembered 1832 as the greatest outpouring of redemption he ever witnessed. He recalled a revival that began in October 1831 and lasted for more than a year. It began among twelve or fifteen families tenting on a campground: "The groans and cries of repenting sinners, the songs and prayers, the shouts and praises of Christians, formed an awful, yet delightful harmony." During the year following this outbreak, three or four churches baptized nearly 500 new converts. During the cold winter in 1831–1832, Holcombe baptized more than 150 persons himself. An 1834 revival in the Cahawba Association resulted in 110 conversions.[28]

Not all revivals were successful. James Mallory attended a camp meeting in September 1843 near Talladega at which the preachers "ably despensed the word to an orderly . . . assembly, but it seemed not to be the Lord's time to bless—the meeting broke up without any additions. . . . I truly hope the seed has been sown that will bring forth much fruit." A five-day meeting by nine preachers a year later was more successful, winning eight or ten conversions. Mallory recorded in his diary the centrality of such events. On September 4, 1846, Mallory's family left their plantation and "our thoughts from the cares of the world to pay some days of homage to him who made us." The revival, preached by Basil Manly Sr., resulted in twenty-four conversions.[29]

By the 1840s increasing worldly status and success eroded the emotional fervor of Baptist revivalism. Intense debate erupted over the efficacy of camp revivals and protracted meetings because of the excesses often associated with them. Youthful courting, gambling, horse trading, family visiting, and other worldly activities swirled around the fringes of the meetings. In the services themselves, the emotional conduct that Hosea Holcombe described embarrassed better-educated Baptists. By 1840 Holcombe conceded that many churches disapproved of the meetings with their "screams, cries, groans, shouts, notes of grief, and notes of joy, all heard at the same time," which "made much confusion, a sort of indescribable concert." Oftentimes preachers would speak at the same time, some in exhortation, others in prayer, still others in disagreement. During one such cacophonous service, an elderly minister filling the pulpit stopped preaching and stared at his competitors. Finally a brother inquired: "Why do you not unite and pray with us?" The preacher responded: "I have been endeavouring to pray for some time that the Lord would be pleased to forgive you for your disorderly conduct." Despite the excesses, Holcombe believed such meetings produced "much good wheat" among "a considerable quantity of chaff."[30]

The debate spilled over into the pages of the *Alabama Baptist* in 1844. The editor acknowledged excesses but agreed with Holcombe that such meetings on the whole were a useful tool of evangelism. To avoid problems, he advised, churches should select preachers who would preach doctrinal sermons on depravity, the necessity of salvation, atonement, and justification by faith alone. They should avoid "popular preachers" as well as those "too cultivated in manners and taste." Popular preachers were too much inclined to "hortatory preaching, mere exhortation, exhibiting almost nothing of the Bible and addressed to the passions and feelings alone and often degenerating into rant and boisterous, empty declaration." Exhorters often applied pressure that was "highly reprehensible." Nor was the noise, excitement, and confusion conducive to "deep religious feeling." James De-Votie also expressed negative opinions about such revivals. While attending one camp meeting, he saw young men trading horses on the edge of the clearing. After accepting an offer to share a meal, the first item offered him was a bottle of brandy.[31]

The attack on such meetings drew a strong rebuttal that defended the zeal, emotion, and energetic preaching. Shouts and crying were entirely appropriate in the circumstances of conviction and repentance even if depicted as a sad spectacle of "animal excitement, noise, confusion, and disorder." Even if a tornado brought salvation, the writer argued, "let us invoke the presence of the tornado."[32]

When revivalistic entreaties failed to tame the frontier by voluntary conversion, Alabama Baptists turned to politics. At first glance, nothing seems more incongruous than revivals and politics, the one summoning sinners to voluntary newness of life as a way of establishing order in society, the other seeking to compel order by legislative action. And no audience seems less likely for fierce political partisanship than supposedly otherworldly Baptists who sought their vindication not in this world but in the world to come.

Yet, camp meeting revivals and mass political meetings emerged from common egalitarian assumptions. Both were features of Jacksonian democracy or, as one historian called them, "disorderly displays of popular power" against the established order. Each sparked debate between raucous frontier masses and more genteel elites about the role of common folks in religion and politics. Both mass political rallies and camp meetings celebrated the personal power and freedom of choice of ordinary people. Both preferred emotional harangue to educated and intellectual discourse.[33]

Such political enthusiasm is less surprising to those familiar with the Baptist heritage in Virginia and the Carolinas, whence so many Alabama Baptists came. The aristocracy along the Atlantic seaboard was appalled by the free mingling of social classes (of slaves, free blacks, and whites) in their camp meetings and ridiculed their "ignorant enthusiasm." Baptists, in turn, denounced finery of dress, horse racing and gambling, fiddling and dancing, as well as oppressive state churches to which many aristocrats belonged. The world of the Baptist preacher was an egalitarian world of "humble men seeking their own ultimate meanings according to their own lights."[34]

Even after Baptists moved from the fringes of society as disturbers of the social peace into the new elite of planters and merchants, they retained a commitment to republicanism and democratic institutions. Although evangelical politics did not endorse the most radical social reforms (abolitionism or women's rights, for instance), it did develop a more "mature social ethic," becoming involved in benevolent causes such as education and care for the poor and reforms for the insane, seamen, and other "neglected classes."[35]

Alabama Baptists followed this pattern. Joah Lawler, a largely self-educated preacher, served as land registrar when the Creek territory was opened to settlement, as a Shelby County judge, in both houses of the legislature, and two terms in Congress. Baptist preacher and domestic missionary John Ellis Sumners was the first probate judge in Bibb County and represented Bibb in the state legislature during the 1830s. Thomas Chilton was a lawyer-preacher in Talladega, where he pastored the Baptist church, developed a lucrative law practice, and became active in Democratic Party politics. Before coming to the frontier, he had served as both a Democratic and a Whig congressman in Kentucky. His brother served as a Baptist deacon, president of the Alabama Baptist State Convention, and as chief justice of the state supreme court. Jefferson Falkner, a largely self-taught sawmiller, studied law and the Bible, pastored churches in Lafayette and Chambers Counties, was elected county judge in Randolph County and to the state senate from Randolph and Tallapoosa Counties.[36]

Daniel P. Bestor, Baptist preacher and Whig member of the state legislature, founded several female academies and introduced the first bill in the Alabama legislature to create a state system of public schools. (Courtesy of Samford University Archives)

The most influential and respected Alabama Baptist preacher-politician was Daniel P. Bestor. Originally from Connecticut, Bestor began female academies in LaGrange (near Athens) and Greensboro in addition to tending a plantation and preaching. He relished political life and once countered E. B. Teague's gentle chiding that he was too involved in politics by responding, "I am no priest." On another occasion, while stumping for the Whig presidential candidate, the Democratic governor of Mississippi was in his audience. The esteemed politician sent the preacher a message that he respected Bestor in his "proper place" but would not consent to "hear a man preach on Sunday who has been dabbling in politics all the week." To that remark, Bestor replied: "Tell [the governor] there is no room in the house for him [anyway]." As a Whig legislator from Greene County, Bestor chaired a special committee on public education. He introduced the first bill to establish a system of public schools in Alabama, though his bill was tabled.[37]

Evidence that such political enthusiasm was not confined to a few leaders is abundant. During legislative sessions in the 1840s, the *Alabama Baptist* carried weekly reports on the progress of bills, published governors' messages to the legislature, and editorialized about bills it did not approve.[38]

A particularly divisive conflict between Democrats and Whigs in 1844 even soured the season of protracted revivals. One meeting broke up just before statewide elections in August because citizens became so engrossed with politics. The editor of the denominational paper used the occasion to scold a society that placed religion second to politics. James Mallory attended the protracted meeting at Talasahatchie in June 1844 and recorded in his diary that "the people seemed to be more engaged in politicks than the cause of our Lord and master." Like Bestor, Mallory was a planter and a Whig, but many of their fellow Baptists were ardent Democrats.[39]

After the Whig Party declined because of internal dissension over slavery, a new American or Know-Nothing Party arose in its place. Mallory joined the nativist party because of his opposition to Catholics and Mormons. His decision reflected a growing wave of anti-Catholicism that swept Alabama in the 1840s. Although seldom mentioned earlier, Catholics were accused in the *Alabama Baptist* of subverting American institutions, owing allegiance to the pope, and sexual perversion.[40]

Education

Although nativism won support among Alabama Baptists, so did public education. Not only did Daniel Bestor first propose a statewide system of public schools, but Milo P. Jewett, the president of Judson College, wrote one of the most persuasive essays in favor of Alabama public schools in 1844. Next to the education of one's own children, Jewett argued, nothing was more important than the education of the entire community. Either Alabama must educate "THE WHOLE PEOPLE" or fall behind other states.[41]

Like Jewett, James DeVotie was from the Northeast and valued public education. Recalling the public schools he attended in New York, DeVotie praised their development of "mental capital," the way they extended to "all classes an opportunity to rise from ignorance to a good degree of intellectual culture." The blessings that they conferred on him made DeVotie

"an advocate of their establishment for others; none should be overlooked."
Like Jewett and Bestor, DeVotie spent his entire career in Alabama promoting public education.[42] In higher education, Baptist preachers served as the first two presidents of the University of Alabama (Alva Woods and Basil Manly Sr.) and Daniel Bestor served as a trustee.

Nor did Baptists neglect education within their own denomination. Although they have been accused of anti-intellectualism, this constituted only one strain of Baptist culture. It is true that many uneducated Baptists feared education as destructive to piety and resented fastidious, educated ministers. Such attitudes may even have predominated during the early frontier stage. But it is also true that no sooner had early Baptists established churches than many of them began schools. Baptists near Gorgas built a church in 1824 and a log cabin school next to it in 1840. The school charged each pupil a fee of one dollar a term but offered free tuition to children whose parents could not pay. James DeVotie began the Athenaeum School in Tuscaloosa shortly after settling there. Daniel Bestor, an excellent scholar of natural history and entomology, started girls' schools wherever he settled.[43]

Alabama Baptist interest in higher education stemmed from several sources. Many New England and New York Baptist migrants to the Black Belt had profited from fine educations unavailable in Alabama. As their sympathies on the slavery question shifted toward their own plantation interests, they were increasingly reluctant to send their children to New England colleges where they might be tainted by abolitionism. Another factor was the Baptist missions movement begun at the end of the eighteenth century. Adoniram and Ann Hasseltine Judson of Burma and their coworker in the United States, Luther Rice, spawned a missionary movement that energized Baptists. Rice believed that the most effective way to serve the cause of missions was to establish schools where Baptist leaders could be educated. Education was also part of a "culture of aspiration" by which ministers sought higher status and was the chief benevolence of southern evangelicals before the Civil War.

These patterns in Baptist life converged on the small town of Marion in Perry County. In 1840 Marion was a flourishing village of twelve hundred inhabitants and an important hub for a substantial agricultural hinterland. As the center of the northwestern edge of the Black Belt, it served as home for numerous wealthy planters, while others gained wealth in mercantile and real estate businesses. Its citizens (many originally from the Northeast) were as highly regarded for their culture and hospitality as for their wealth. So many of the prominent families were Baptist that a writer from Richmond, Virginia, who visited Marion in 1844 called the town "the Baptist Capital of Alabama."[44] Centered at Siloam Baptist Church in Marion, local Baptists established Judson College in 1838, Howard College in 1841, and the *Alabama Baptist* in 1843. In 1845, the Southern Baptist Convention located its domestic mission board in Marion as well.

When Baptists began to plan a college in 1834, Marion and Greensboro (towns only miles apart in the Black Belt) became chief contenders for it. Both offered substantial bonuses for the prize, but Marion already had a Presbyterian school nearby, so attention turned to its neighbor.

Baptists intended the new institution to be a manual labor school then enjoying considerable vogue. The plan was simple. Buy a farm, construct a few buildings, purchase farm equipment, and invite students who would study their books in the forenoon and farm in the afternoon. Products of the farm would feed students and faculty, and the surplus sold on the market would generate sufficient income to pay for instruction and administration. Students would learn to respect physical as much as literary culture, an important lesson on the egalitarian Alabama frontier.

The Alabama Baptist State Convention appointed a committee of Lee Compere, Alexander Travis, and A. J. Holcombe in 1832 to plan an institution "for the education of indigent young men called to the ministry." Two years later the convention changed its instructions to include a literary program along with theology and requested Greensboro preacher Daniel Bestor to present theological lectures until a permanent professor could be hired. Trustees bought a tract of 355 acres one mile from Greensboro and began classes in January 1836.

From the beginning the project floundered. Baptists subscribed too little money to pay off debt on the land. Income from the farm never met expenses. The national panic of 1837 dried up contributions. Students opted for the literary course of study, mathematics, and science but not for theology. In April 1837, just as the time arrived to plant crops for its second agricultural season, dissension among the faculty caused trustees to suspend classes. Attempts to pay off debts were unsuccessful, and the school closed permanently. The convention appointed a new education committee in 1838 and vowed to try again.[45]

Creation of Judson College was a much more satisfying and successful undertaking. Such ventures for female education had only just begun, with a new Methodist Woman's College in Macon, Georgia, chartered in 1836, claiming to be the first women's college in America. Perhaps this information inspired Edwin D. King (a wealthy Baptist layman and trustee of the University of Alabama) to ask Julia Barron to invite a group of interested

Julia Ann Tarrant Barron, prosperous Marion businesswoman and planter, was a cofounder of both Judson and Howard Colleges. She was their major early benefactor and co-owner of the *Alabama Baptist*. (Courtesy of Samford University Archives)

Marion Baptists to her home for a discussion of women's education. Particularly supportive of the idea was Barron's pastor at Siloam church, James DeVotie. Although the group reached no conclusion, Barron kept the dream alive. She invited Milo P. Jewett to visit her and talk about a new school. Barron then rented the first building used by Judson and lodged the Jewetts when they moved to Marion. She also opened her large home to two Judson teachers, who lived with her for a year. Her contribution of cash was one of the largest made to construct the first brick building in 1841. The school was named for Ann Hasseltine Judson, a missionary whom Barron greatly admired, and Barron's son Tom became one of three male students in the first class of the Judson Female Institute in 1839. Later Barron became a founder of Howard College as well and made the first major financial gift to the male Baptist college. She and her son both contributed land for the new campus. About the same time she became a co-owner of the *Alabama Baptist*.[46]

Julia Ann Tarrant Barron was born in South Carolina in 1805. The Tarrant family moved to Perry County about 1820, where Julia's father opened a store. Eight years later Julia married William Barron, but her husband died four years later, leaving her a wealthy young widow. Her brother and sister became prosperous citizens as well, and her sister subsequently married Henry Talbird, who was president of Howard College at the time. In addition to contributing the land on which Siloam church was built and her other philanthropies, Barron was a successful businesswoman. She owned thirty-five slaves, twenty-nine of whom she worked on her plantation. Although she did not continue her husband's mercantile business, she purchased lots in Marion, co-owned the state denominational newspaper, and multiplied her wealth during the 1850s. Her fortunes declined precipitously after 1865. Her physician son died in 1868 and his wife in 1875, leaving the elderly Barron to raise two granddaughters. She was forced to sell her house and died in 1890 at age eighty-four, impoverished and largely forgotten by the Baptists who owed her such a huge debt.[47]

Many of Barron's colleagues in the founding of Judson played prominent roles in establishing Howard College in 1841. In December of that year, DeVotie and Jewett offered Samuel S. Sherman the use of a building for an "English Classical School." Sherman, a native of Bennington County, Vermont, may have been acquainted with Jewett, who was also a Vermont Baptist. Sherman had come to Tuscaloosa where he opened a private preparatory school and had taught ancient languages at the University of Alabama. He accepted DeVotie's offer and moved to Marion in 1842. Julia Barron provided the initial money, a $4,000 house and lot. DeVotie, who was selected president of the board of trustees, suggested that the college be named for British prison reformer and philanthropist John Howard. Howard had received favorable mention in the *Alabama Baptist* for his efforts to help the poor, and the use of his name is a testimony to how deeply the reform impulse had taken root among some early Alabama Baptist leaders.[48] The twenty-six-year-old Samuel Sherman was chosen president, and the school opened in January 1842 with nine boys.

Howard College began primarily as a literary college, but plans began immediately to recruit a professor of theology "for the purpose of giving instruction to pious young men who bring evidence of their call to the ministry from the churches to which they belong." DeVotie set about raising funds for the theological chair and soon had $20,000 for that purpose.[49]

In January 1844 a new professor of theology arrived—Jesse Hartwell. Born in Massachusetts and educated at Brown University in Rhode Island, Hartwell had moved in 1836 to Alabama where he pastored the church in Carlowville and quickly rose in Baptist ranks. In 1839 he was elected president of the state convention, and while living in Marion he became president of the Board of Domestic Missions. When he took charge of the theology program, four young ministers awaited his tutelage, though all were judged academically inadequate and were shifted to the literary department to correct their deficiencies.[50]

The manual labor school's guiding principle of labor and religion was replaced by Howard College's emphasis on learning and religion, and the college curriculum emphasized liberal arts. Knowledge of Greek and Latin were requisites for admission, as were English, history, and mathematics. A preparatory school to teach such skills began in 1842 and lasted for half a century.[51]

Sherman and Hartwell were accustomed to the New England pattern of training ministers in which they prepared broadly in the classics and mingled freely with students from a variety of backgrounds and interests. But many pioneer Alabama Baptists had different ideas about how to educate ministers. They needed more preachers immediately; that had been their goal in creating the manual labor school and Howard. Less than two years after Howard opened, some were already disillusioned with Yankees Sherman and Hartwell. An essay on "Educating of the Ministry" observed in December 1844 that Alabama Baptists were divided on whether God needed educated preachers. If he did, the ones attending Howard might be influenced by Hartwell's "unfortunate views" on "justification." Hartwell required his ministerial students to write down their ideas, which they then read "page after page until the dry mess is finished." The essayist believed that preachers should leave their sermon manuscripts in their pockets and preach as men did in the primitive church. Preachers who sought a strict separation of ministerial students from those in other curricula finally forced Sherman and Hartwell to leave. Sherman was a classicist, not a theologian, and Hartwell's theological and homiletical views obviously did not match those of many Alabama Baptists. The choice of minister Henry Talbird to replace educator Sherman was a clear victory for Baptists who had founded the college mainly to train ministers. Despite these changes, few ministerial students attended. At no time did more than twenty enroll during a single term before the Civil War. Explanations for this low enrollment vary. Frontier Alabama preachers needed no college preparation to gain a pulpit. Antieducation sentiment ran high. And young ministers often came from families too poor to pay Howard's tuition.[52]

Whatever their misgivings, many Baptists welcomed the creation of Judson and Howard. In 1843 the *Alabama Baptist* editor rejoiced at growing interest in education for women. That same year a Baptist preacher from Talladega wrote DeVotie that though he could not contribute to Howard College, he rejoiced at its creation. It was hard to overcome the poverty of the Alabama frontier, he wrote, and when people did so, they often developed a "mania for wealth" even more destructive than their earlier poverty. Many Baptists now blessed with wealth had "been reared without having their minds cultivated" and were insensitive to the advantages of religious education. But "men cannot instruct others until they are informed themselves," and he looked forward to the day when Howard would greatly improve the educational standard of Baptist ministers. That was the dream of Howard's founders and of its early leaders.[53]

The *Alabama Baptist*

Next to the colleges, no institution was more important to the emerging denomination than the *Alabama Baptist*. The paper communicated news, provided a forum for debate, publicized associational meetings and state conventions, and generally welded disparate Baptists into a well-informed, cooperative unit. Milo Jewett, James DeVotie, and Julia Barron began the *Alabama Baptist* in 1843 after several earlier attempts to launch a paper had failed. Jewett initially served as the editor, though DeVotie became sole proprietor four years later and finally turned the journal into a viable financial undertaking. As with Howard College, Baptists promoted the paper out of sectional loyalty and state pride. The editors listed its functions in

February 1844 as discussing doctrine, defending the principles of "Regular Baptist churches," exposing heresy, sustaining morality, rebuking sin "whether . . . in high places or low," distributing Christian literature, promoting Christian education, informing readers about missions, and advocating "total abstinence" from the use of alcohol. A regular farm column carried the latest news about soil chemistry, crops, and livestock. All this information came to eager readers for only six dollars a year (owners cut the price in half in February 1845).[54] Under a variety of names and owners, the paper served its constituency faithfully until shut down by Federal troops in 1865.

The Alabama Baptist State Convention

The catalyst for the flourish of institution building was the Alabama Baptist State Convention (ABSC). Although individual churches and associations did yeoman duty spreading the gospel, building and sustaining colleges and denominational papers required a coordinated, statewide effort. Creating a statewide organization was no easy task. Geographical barriers divided Alabama into different regions. Communication and transportation between regions were difficult under the best of circumstances and impossible under the worst. No navigable river ran between the Tennessee Valley and south Alabama. Roads were primitive and often impassable. No north-south railroads existed prior to the Civil War that afforded passage through the mountains of north Alabama. As a consequence, social, economic, and political differences sharply divided residents of the two major regions. North of Shelby County and south of the Tennessee River, plantations and slaves were rare, subsistence white farmers flourished, and Democratic politics predominated. In the Tennessee Valley and Black Belt, planters reigned supreme, slaves outnumbered whites, and Whigs often held sway. As a consequence of these divisions, not one but many conventions arose in Alabama. Although the Alabama Baptist State Convention that began in 1823 is the best known and the only one to survive, other conventions were organized as well: the General Association of Middle Tennessee and North Alabama (1841), the East Alabama Baptist Convention (1856), and the postwar General Association of South Eastern Alabama.[55]

Only two southern states had organized Baptist conventions prior to Alabama (South Carolina in 1821 and Georgia in 1822), and both of those states furnished many pastors to the state. It seems likely that some of them inspired Alabama Baptists to act in 1823. Another factor in starting the state convention was the desperate need to coordinate mission and educational efforts in the face of rising antimission opposition.[56]

The immediate source of the 1823 meeting at Greensboro was correspondence by James A. Ranaldson, a Baptist preacher living at Claiborne in Monroe County. He invited missionary societies to elect delegates to a state convention and summoned them to meet at Salem Baptist Church near Greensboro on October 28. The details of this meeting are obscure. Twenty delegates were elected, but only fifteen attended. Whether the others were antimission people or simply unable to attend is uncertain. Delegates were elected from seven missionary societies. Missionary societies in Perry, Greene, and Conecuh Counties sent eleven of the delegates, and ladies' societies in Jonesboro and Greensboro also elected representatives.[57]

Women were not listed as delegates to the convention, but at least one attended and others played key roles. Nancy Lea accompanied her husband, who represented the Perry County Missionary Society. Some records list her as elected along with her husband, but the official minutes list only him. Hosea Holcombe attended as a representative of the Jonesboro Ladies Society, in which his wife, Cassandra ("Cassey") Jackson Holcombe, was an active member despite the responsibilities of tending nine children. Her society sent one of the largest mission offerings to the new convention: $20.50. Harriet Harrison and Cassey Holcombe (who both used their given names, not their husbands' first names as was common at the time) sent a message with their contributions: the women of their society believed in the importance of missions and desired to share in this new enterprise. Christ's admonition that the poor widow should share her resources inspired their charity, as did the example of Phoebe: "as Phebe [sic] was bearer of the epistle of Paul to the Romans, and Priscilla and Chloe were helpers, so would we also reach forth a helping hand, and assist in carrying into effect your laudable design." Seven other women's societies sent money, most of them from among the seventeen identifiable ladies' societies south of the mountains.[58]

The convention elected Charles Crow first president and James Ranaldson secretary, drafted a constitution and a message to state Baptists, appointed fifteen domestic missionaries to work six weeks each for a dollar a day, and encouraged education. The constitution determined methods for participation in the state convention (delegates from missionary societies, churches, and associations that regularly contributed to convention causes), listed the officers to be elected, and specified the objectives of the convention as promoting missions and religious education. The address to Baptists affirmed the scriptural authority of missions and urged an end to discord over the matter. Alabama, just emerging from a "waste howling wilderness," needed the efforts of missionaries. So did the Creek Indians within the state's borders and Burma and Africa overseas.[59]

This labor so enthusiastically begun in 1823 soon floundered. Some of the fifteen domestic missionaries appointed by the convention turned out to be strongly antimission in sentiment. A resolution continuing ministerial scholarships was tabled at the 1827 convention. Trouble arose among domestic missionaries who spent too much time in well-supplied areas of the state and too little in destitute regions. In 1829 some missionaries received no salary for lack of contributions. The 1835 convention was perplexed with a multitude of problems. Churches refused to pay their pastors, "emissaries of Papish darkness" threatened American institutions, and northern abolitionists attacked southern institutions. The 1844 convention barely avoided "collision or schism" when "in things not absolutely essential" each side had compromised.[60]

Regional differences complicated all these problems. Baptists in the northern part of the state complained that their compatriots in the south controlled the convention. In fact, during the first half century of its life, the ABSC did hold forty-two sessions in south Alabama and only eight in north. Both colleges and the state Baptist newspaper were located in the south. But then most of the wealth and contributions came from that area as well. So localized was the convention that when it met at Tuscaloosa in 1833 only four delegates attended from outside the vicinity. And few delegates attended from any area. The 1834 convention, the largest to that time, enrolled only fifty delegates.[61]

Alabama Baptists had confronted the wilderness and they had tamed it. But in a sense they stood poised at the edge of a huge precipice in 1845. Their denomination was about to split along sectional lines. The state convention was so poorly attended that it seemed to serve little function as a representative denominational body and was in fact a weaker institution than some of the large associations. Its academies, colleges, and denominational newspaper were newly begun and financially fragile. Internally, Baptists were divided along a number of lines: theologically, between hyper-Calvinists, strict Calvinists, and Arminians; by class, between affluent planters and merchants on one side and struggling yeoman farmers on the other; by region, between north and south Alabama; by political party, between Democrat and Whig; by institutions, between antimission and mis-

sionary; by temperament, between individualists who recognized no constraints or collective responsibilities and connectionalists who believed
that communities as well as individuals had to be redeemed. Perhaps it was
the end of the beginning. But the challenges to a people newly emerging
from the frontier still seemed formidable.

3

The Work of the Gospel, 1845–1860

"If we don't hunt our meat, we will perish."

O n a hot day in late August 1846 a throng of Baptists descended into a valley at Greensboro, passed through a neat board fence, and filed into some 700 or 800 seats. Before them was a pond supplied by three springs. A turf-covered island in the middle of the pond contained a summer cabin connected by a bridge to a larger house on shore. Candidates for baptism changed clothes in the large house, then proceeded across the bridge, down a flight of stairs, and into the pond where they sank beneath the cool waters, symbolically dying to old life and rising to new.[1]

This 1846 baptism at Greensboro must certainly have been the most elaborate, well-designed service performed in antebellum Alabama. No other written accounts even approach it. But whether a simple service in a creek or this memorable ceremony initiated one into new life, baptism was at the heart of the Baptist mission. Convert sinners. Baptize them. Train them for wholesome living.

Converting Sinners

Judged by their growth between 1845 and 1860, Baptists performed the tasks of conversion and baptism well. Although most antebellum southerners were not church members, the rate of church growth was faster than population increase. Whereas only one southerner in eight belonged to a church in 1840, one in four did so twenty years later. In 1845, 37,000 Alabama Baptists were organized into 653 churches and 38 associations. They were led by 267 ordained ministers, who baptized some 2,700 new Christians that year in services similar to the one at Greensboro. By 1860 their ranks had increased more than six times to 237,000 and their churches to 805. In numbers both of converts and of churches, Baptists had finally overtaken their Methodist rivals and were the largest religious denomination in Alabama.[2]

Protracted revivals and camp meetings continued to be the medium for most conversions. Baptist spokesmen were increasingly ambivalent about such meetings, admitting that there were emotional excesses along with the conversions. In 1845 the *Alabama Baptist* praised a protracted meeting at the Hopewell church that was conducted with "order and propriety." Preachers made no attempt to force sinners to the mourners' bench, yet eleven whites and four blacks were converted. E. B. Teague preached such a service in 1848 at Beulah church in Greene County. As he hitched his horse and walked toward the church with his saddlebag, "the air seemed electric with love." The pastor greeted him with a proposal to share revival duties. Teague was a renowned preacher, clearly superior to him. But the pastor believed that he was unmatched as an exhorter. Teague could preach and he would exhort. The combination produced at least one and sometimes a half dozen conversions every service for a week. Not even torrential rains and high waters could prevent a revival at Liberty church in Tallapoosa County in 1849. Men simply cut down trees, dropped them across the creeks, and forded the streams. The revival netted thirteen conversions.[3]

Associational missionaries continued to ride circuit during revival season (July to October), preaching dozens of protracted meetings. John Tolbert of Marengo County, missionary for the Bethel Association, preached revivals for thirty-three days in 1850. Mostly he preached in churches. In all, the congregations where he labored added thirty-two new members. During the three years he served as missionary for the Alabama Association, Mathew Bishop traveled an estimated 4,000 miles, conducted thirty protracted meetings, preached 335 sermons, baptized 100, and helped constitute five new churches.[4]

Such efforts reaped huge harvests for the associations. During 1851 the Alabama Association reported 288 baptisms. That same year, the Liberty

Association counted 399, the Coosa River Association 268, and the Union Association 130.[5]

Notwithstanding such successes, protracted meetings drew their share of criticism. Even John Tolbert, who was a successful revivalist, believed protracted meetings had mixed effect. At their best, they stirred lukewarm Christians, reclaimed the backslidden, and added large numbers of new converts to the church. At their worst, they created disciples who were full of emotion but possessed little sense of duty and did not grow between the annual meetings. The moral standards of such disciples seldom matched their initial enthusiasm. Other critics complained that protracted meetings emphasized the extraordinary phenomena of Christianity while ignoring the routine means of grace. There was a vast difference, one critic wrote, between preaching Christ crucified and the "vapid and empty declamation with which meetings of this character are often distinguished." Revival theology seemed to be: "get religion, and that speedily, [or] . . . be inevitably damned." The doctrine of grace received scarcely any attention. S. D. Worthington perfectly captured the ambiguity of his generation about protracted meetings with a memorable metaphor: "He that is born in a storm will require a storm to keep him awake." But, most Baptists reasoned, better to be born in a storm than not to be born at all.[6]

Opinion was less divided about camp meetings. Judson College president Milo Jewett recorded his impression of such an event near Woodville in Perry County during August 1845. Although one preacher impressed him, another was poorly regarded in the community. Still another missed no opportunity to mount his "theological war-horse" from which he directed attacks on Presbyterians and Baptists. The meeting degenerated into much noise and confusion in violation of the New Testament admonition for decency and order. Blacks sang, prayed, shouted, and screamed until after midnight. Jewett concluded that the density of settlement by 1845 made such meetings unnecessary.[7]

Despite widely held reservations, not all Baptists were willing to abandon a revered frontier tradition. The Bethlehem Association passed a resolution urging churches to combine their efforts on a single camp meeting. Although most of the association's churches held protracted meetings during 1846, not one camp meeting was held. One advocate preferred them because they required people to leave their routine surroundings and travel to a place with fewer diversions. Slaves could also accompany masters. Fewer preachers were needed. Nor did he believe that camp meetings were too disorderly.[8]

Grant's Creek Baptist Church at Foster's Settlement, Tuscaloosa County, was the home church of longtime China missionary Martha Foster Crawford and influential pastor Joshua Hill Foster. (Courtesy of Samford University Archives)

Workers in the Harvest

This advocate of camp meetings made at least one important point. The growth in numbers of Baptist ministers had not kept pace with the rapid gain in membership. One reason associational missionaries had to engage in exhausting itineraries was that there were too few preachers to conduct all the protracted meetings being scheduled. This lack of manpower resulted from numerous sources: low pay, exhausting work, and bivocationalism that required many ministers to hold down two or three jobs. An additional factor was increasing standards for preachers, which proved another source of controversy among Alabama Baptists.

In theory the call to preach was as democratic as ever. God bade a man proclaim the gospel. God's call came to the bold and the timid, to blacks and whites, to rich and poor, to educated and illiterate. Baptists welcomed them all. But increasingly denominational leaders recognized that more complex factors were at work. Although they imposed no specific guidelines or standards (any effort to do so would have been futile anyway given the autonomy of each congregation), they did warn against hasty ordination. One leader advised churches to look for evidence of a call—and the evidence should consist of more than emotion. Otherwise some "ignorant enthusiast might adhere to his notion of a divine call" and try to thrust himself on the church, while an intelligent disciple who was shy and diffident might be restrained.[9]

Although Alabama Baptists tended to deify these early ministers because of their courage in the face of adversity, in fact they experienced misgivings and hardships common to all ministers. When adversity occurred, even so eminent a divine as I. T. Tichenor doubted his call. On his twenty-fifth birthday, Tichenor confided to his diary that he had lived half his allotted years "and yet how little have I done for God. Nearly four years since I entered the ministry and how little have I accomplished." Sin continued to plague his "impure nature."[10]

Nor did the denominational editor believe that such doubts disqualified a minister. In fact such misgivings about one's piety might reflect the importance and holiness he attached to the ministry. The evidences of a sincere call included a desire

Joshua Hill Foster, tutor in physics at the University of Alabama, was a distinguished pastor of many churches in Alabama. (Courtesy of Samford University Archives)

for the hard work of ministry despite difficulties and costs, constancy, and personal spirituality. Doubts were inevitable for most serious young ministers.[11]

Evidence indicates that churches took seriously warnings to be more careful about ordination. The educational level of ministers obviously improved. In January 1852 Auburn First Baptist Church ordained William Williams as its new pastor. The presbytery grilled Williams carefully about his Christian experience, call to ministry, and doctrinal views. Williams had studied law before his call but had decided he wanted to devote full time to preaching. Grant's Creek Baptist Church in Tuscaloosa County was equally careful in ordaining Joshua Hill Foster the following month. Foster, a graduate of the University of Alabama where he was then a tutor in physics, became pastor of Tuscaloosa First Baptist Church. The Wetumpka church refused to ordain Ned Atkins in 1855. Although he was an exemplary member of the church, members declined to ordain him because he could not read.[12]

Of course, mistakes did occur. Samuel Henderson remembered a dispute in a presbytery concerning the ordination of a Tuskegee man. Henderson opposed the ordination but another minister begged him to consent in order to satisfy the church seeking ordination. Henderson finally consented against his better judgment, a decision he later regretted when the minister was excluded for "grossly immoral conduct."[13]

The decision of the Wetumpka church not to ordain Ned Atkins because of his illiteracy reflects the increasing value that Alabama Baptists placed on ministerial education. Although historians have often depicted frontier Baptists as anti-intellectual common folk who disdained an educated clergy, the truth is much more complex. As Baptists in towns and plantation districts acquired more wealth and education, they preferred educated pastors. In 1845 the editor of the denominational paper printed a lengthy list of books that every minister ought to own. His recommendations included not only books on the Bible and systematic theology but also books on history and science. He particularly extolled histories of the United States, England, and Scotland by George Bancroft and David Hume. Of seventy-four books on the recommended list, the editor/minister personally had read seventy-two, including the Latin Vulgate Bible, the Septuagint in Greek, Cruden's *Concordance,* the Greek New Testament, and a Greek grammar.[14]

Four years later the editor reiterated that ministers should be men of intelligence who could read Scripture in the original languages and who understood its historical context. The Bible was "a highly metaphorical book" filled with "tropes and metaphors." Sometimes one could easily understand the meaning of Scripture; at other times understanding required the "skill of the sage." Repeating the same advice three years later, the editor acknowledged that "designing and wicked men" had damaged biblical truth by their learning, but "undesigning and good men have done the same for want of greater knowledge." In a series of articles on what ministers should know, the editor added philosophy to the lengthening list.[15]

In 1854 Joseph Walker dispensed similar advice to theology students at Howard College. A preacher's usefulness depended on his intellectual ability, Walker believed. Personal conversion and a divine call came first; but when God called a man, he called the entire person, including the mind. One did not have to possess the highest mental powers, and many men of ordinary intellectual capacity filled pulpits splendidly. But Walker challenged students to develop their mental powers because a minister continually had to "replenish his stock of information. Ideas have wings" and must constantly be replaced with new ones.[16]

Such advice did not sit well with many Alabama Baptists. Even the editor of the denominational paper warned in 1853 of a huge shortage of Baptist ministers. Many young men of "natural endowments" had no financial means with which to acquire education. Churches should fund a "good country school" education for such men and furnish them a few books. If a minister could not afford theological education, then let him apprentice himself to a pastor who could instruct him. College education was fine, but colleges could not supply an adequate number of ministers. And many of the best Alabama pastors were men of common sense, native eloquence, endurance, and spiritual mindedness unpolished by a college degree.[17]

Other Alabama Baptists were more forthrightly anti-intellectual. "Jose" wrote the state Baptist paper that too many pastors tried to please their congregations by "literary displays" when the real function of preaching was "to use plainness of speech, to inforce truth in its simplest form, so as to meet the capacity of the ignorant." Another writer agreed, complaining about Baptist preachers who employed "gorgeous language" to describe sin "as a sort of unfortunate evil." To substitute reason for revelation or intellect for passion was to invite infidelity. Another writer advised that personal piety, doctrinal soundness, energy, and devotion counted for more than education. Many urban and college churches preferred educated preachers because they were fastidious. But such churches paid a price: "The sacrificing at the shrine of popular applause is killing the orthodox spirit of many congregations. The poor leave the church unfed; and when God's poor leave a church, orthodoxy and piety will soon follow."[18]

Even so trivial a matter as ministerial titles reflected similar divisions. In 1854 the editor of the *South-Western Baptist* opposed the use of "reverend," "parson," and especially "Dr." when referring to Baptist ministers. "Away with all these honorary titles and all clerical assumptions," he admonished. Use only humble biblical titles such as bishop, elder, and deacon. An anonymous doctor of divinity did not take kindly to such assaults on his species. These attacks, he wrote, arose from petty jealousy and had triggered a backlash among educated Baptists. He predicted that "D.D.'s will multiply as crickets in August."[19]

Most Alabama Baptists in the 1850s were probably somewhere between these two extreme positions. Education was useful but not superior to sincere if untutored piety and gospel ardor. A Kingston resident admonished educated ministers not to patronize uneducated ministers. Given the inadequate public schools of Alabama, an educated ministry was unlikely. The reason many uneducated ministers were so highly regarded was that they did not pretend to be superior to common folk; they were equals and mingled with the "masses of people." But he also scolded uneducated ministers for their jealousy of learned preachers, which was often the motive for their criticism.[20]

Given the emphasis on God's call and the popular preference for spontaneity and naturalness in the ministry, Baptist preachers dispensed an amazing amount of practical advice to ministerial neophytes on everything from sermon preparation to the kinds of clothes to wear. Ministers should not aim at "elegant composition and brilliant tropes" so much as simple, correct speech properly enunciated. When preparing sermons, preachers should select Scripture appropriate to the occasion and congregation, read an exposition on it, study, and explain the meaning of each important term.[21] The editor of the *Alabama Baptist* criticized a minister who began a revival with a "labored disquisition on the existence of God," which might have been appropriate for another occasion but was ineffective in a revival setting. Refined and intellectual congregations should not have to listen to "careless and uncultivated" sermons, nor should unlettered congregations be bored by "tawdry and pompous eloquence"; "rhetorical flourishes, metaphysical distinctions and niceties" were "illy suited to enlighten a congregation of blacks." The editor condescendingly advised preachers to address "Negroes and children" in monosyllables if possible.[22]

When advice turned to the sermon itself, Baptists once again divided sharply. Many leading ministers wrote manuscript sermons, and the *Alabama Baptist* often published their texts. Nor did such a practice seem to distract from their effectiveness. William L. Yancey, regarded by many as the most eloquent American orator of the 1850s, often heard I. T. Tichenor preach in Montgomery and called him one of the most impressive preachers of his time. Tichenor's sermons were topical, simple, and contained only brief analysis. He was a careful student of rhetoric who often preached extemporaneously though from elaborate study notes. Basil Manly Sr. used manuscript notes in his sermons.[23]

Criticism often focused on the sermon manuscript. In addition to occasional charges of plagiarism in such sermons, many laymen and preachers criticized ministers for reading boring manuscripts from the pulpit. The Liberty Association passed a resolution in 1846 against the increasing practice of reading sermons and urged preachers to speak extemporaneously. One bored layman entered the fray on behalf of a more animated old-time style of preaching. He liked educated preachers but preferred "not so much science as the cross." If preachers insisted on writing out their manuscript, let them memorize it. If any minister read a sermon to him again, he promised to stretch out on the pew and take a nap. "Orion" agreed, arguing that if the goal of a sermon was to instruct a congregation, extemporaneous sermons were superior to manuscripts. Either kind of sermon could be cold and lifeless, he added, but written sermons could be of no other type.[24]

Some leaders tried to find middle ground. An anonymous essayist in 1853 concurred that extemporaneous sermons were generally more effective, but a sermon had to be tailored to circumstances. In towns where "people will be fastidious" and where parishioners were accustomed to lyceum speakers who read from prepared manuscripts, reading written sermons might be appropriate. Suggestions that preachers need do nothing more than preach "Christ and him crucified," which required only "a gushing warmth," ignored the "deep things of God" that could be revealed only by careful study. Distinguished professional men were too well educated for extemporaneous sermons. Another anonymous writer agreed. He argued that every minister had to develop his own style. Preachers who found spontaneous inspiration should preach that way, although they still should prepare carefully beforehand. Those who wrote manuscript sermons should memorize them if they could, but read them if they could not. Another layman recalled a pastor in southern Alabama who read all of his sermons to an attentive congregation and baptized a new convert nearly every month.[25]

The role of emotion in sermons also attracted attention. Many firsthand accounts of antebellum sermons describe high levels of emotion, including the preacher's profuse weeping. One minister wrote that the Greek words for preaching meant to persuade and declare. Sorrow for sin and repentance could only be obtained by preaching at the heart in order to reach the head, not the other way around. The gospel was a declaration of "tender compassion" rather than "a dogma to be disputed over." Another writer reminded that Christ wept over Jerusalem, and all regenerate people must weep over depravity.[26]

Nor should sermons be too long. "Whenever weariness begins, edification terminates," one experienced pastor advised. No sermon ought to extend beyond forty-five minutes, nor should the entire worship service last more than an hour and a half. Preachers should not call attention to themselves with flashy clothes or white handkerchiefs. "Orion" again demurred, warning that while sermons should not be judged by a watch, many sermons went too long.[27]

Other preachers offered more general advice. Focus on pastoral duties, they advised, not "worldly matters." Do not take sides in church disputes. Avoid "promiscuous conversation" on the streets or in stores as well
as "professional cant." Do not answer "every malicious scribbler who cen-
sures you through the newspaper," D. P. Bestor advised, and be cautious
when writing books. There were too many books already. If one wrote po-
etry, publish it only after marriage lest someone consider the minister trivial and romantic. Basil Manly Sr. advised a young minister not to seek
popularity and to attend theological school if possible, but if not, to study,
pray, and write at least an hour every day.[28]

Such meticulous attention to detail qualified a Baptist minister for a
church call and perhaps even a modest salary. The decision on calling a
pastor began in the ethereal world of piety but usually ended in the practical world of finance. The *South-Western Baptist* offered advice to churches
seeking a pastor: pray for guidance; seek a pastor who was pious and orthodox; establish a bond between pastor and church; support "adequately
the man God gives them"; select him for an indefinite period, not for a single year.[29]

By the mid-1840s some larger churches had ended the practice of calling a pastor annually in favor of indefinite service. In 1846 the Greensboro
church elected Thomas Chilton "pastor for life" to congratulations by the
denominational paper. Such practice, the editor noted, allowed the pastor
dignity and stability and reduced the "sycophantic deference to the members" that characterized annual calls.[30] Subsequent years produced dozens
of letters and editorials pleading with churches to adopt this practice and
to pay pastors adequately so they could devote full time to the ministry. The
Union Association joined the chorus in 1849, and a ministers' convention
in Montgomery did likewise in 1853.[31]

Despite such fervent appeals, the vast majority of Alabama Baptist
preachers received less than a living wage when they received any salary
at all. A. T. M. Handey pastored six Macon County churches in 1856; two
paid him nothing, one provided $300 a year, the other three paid $250, $190,
and $159—a total of slightly less than $900. And preachers had come to
expect such conditions. Basil Manly Sr. chided a young pastor who, after
accepting the pastorate of the Tuscaloosa church, had gotten married. Such
action without the approval of church members who had offered to board
and feed him was unfair because his hosts now had two persons to feed:
"No minister ought even to go courting without leave first . . . from all his
congregation. And if allowed to be married, he should never have any child

born to him at all. Paul talks about 'leading about *a wife;*' he does not say child."[32]

As urban churches began to extend
indefinite calls and pay adequate salaries,
they had to find new ways of raising
money. One innovative practice, used by
the Greensboro and Eufaula churches,
was to assess each member's property according to its value, then levy appropriations for the church based on ability to
pay. After losing a pastor because of low
pay in 1850, future governor John Gill
Shorter (a deacon in the Eufaula church)
proposed a change from deacons managing church funds to the use of a finance
committee. Each church member had to
report to the committee the net value of
his or her estate at the beginning of each
year. Then the committee would assess
each member a pro rata amount and collect funds sufficient to pay the pastor and
other expenses. If a member refused to
submit an estimate of value, the committee was authorized to make an evaluation
based on its own judgment.[33] Apparently
this program worked because the church
used it throughout the decade. As competition for skilled ministers became more
intense, every dollar was important.

James Harvey DeVotie, influential and irascible pastor of Montgomery, Tuscaloosa,
and Marion churches, was editor of the *Alabama Baptist* and president of the state Baptist Bible Society. (Courtesy of Samford University Archives)

One of the few documented cases of salary negotiation involved James
Harvey DeVotie, one of the four or five most respected antebellum Baptist
ministers. In 1853 DeVotie was at the peak of his influence. He was editor
of the denominational newspaper, trustee of the denominational college,
president of the denominational Bible Society, and an official of the new
SBC Board of Domestic Missions. After threatening to resign his Marion
pastorate in 1853, offers began to roll in, and he soon had a number of
churches in a bidding war. A Greenville, South Carolina, church originally
offered him a salary of $1,000 but soon increased it to $1,200 plus his moving expenses. The church also offered indefinite tenure at the pleasure of

pastor and congregation, a minimum six-month notice before termination, and quarterly payment of his salary. With other offers in hand from churches in LaGrange, Georgia, Hopewell, Alabama, and New Orleans, Louisiana, DeVotie played a tough game with his suitors. He asked the Greenville church for a salary of $1,500, or $1,200 plus scholarships for his three sons to Furman University. Had the LaGrange church offered $1,500 and been willing to build a larger house of worship, he probably would have accepted that offer. After first accepting, then declining the Greenville offer, he finally accepted $1,500 from Hopewell, which was located only a few miles from Marion. Although DeVotie discerned the "leadership of God's allwise Providence" in the move, his correspondence makes clear that one sign of that providence was the salary offer.[34]

DeVotie was the rare exception in a state whose Baptist pastors generally went begging. More typical was the case of "W. C. D.," a poor man who worked hard on his farm, had no money with which to purchase Bible commentaries, and who wrote the editor of the denominational paper with questions about church practice and history. An aged minister whose wife and children were deceased, who had cancer, and who had mortgaged all his property to sustain his ministry, complained: "I am left to pine in negligence and want. Alas! Is this the genius of the gospel of good will?"[35]

Given the preponderance of poor churches, it is no surprise that Alabama experienced a chronic shortage of ministers. In 1853 the editor of the *South-Western Baptist* attended three associations, and in every one churches went begging for pastors. By 1859 the editor noted that membership had nearly doubled since 1844, but the number of Baptist ministers apparently had declined because of low pay and indefinite call.[36]

Doctrine

At the heart of preaching was doctrine. During these formative years, doctrinal sermons played a major role in religious life, perhaps explaining why so few conversions were recorded in regular Sunday services. Doctrine also played an important role in associational meetings and state conventions. Only in the fervent atmosphere of the camp meeting or protracted revival was doctrine largely ignored.

The *Alabama Baptist* filled its pages with doctrinal sermons and essays. Individual series sometimes continued for months. Between April and June 1849, the paper featured front-page doctrinal essays on atonement, the Holy Spirit, the new birth, sanctification, perseverance of the saints, election, judgment, and future punishment. Essays on free will, election, predestination, and fatalism constituted an 1856 series. In addition, the editor frequently answered doctrinal queries from churches, answers that constituted a sort of mini-Baptist catechism.[37]

As doctrinal convictions became stronger, creedalism became a concern. In 1846 Alabama Baptists vigorously debated the advisability of creeds. The dispute began in the Coosa River Association in July when delegates debated the question of whether a church ought to be constituted without a creed or confession of faith. The answer (argued in an essay read to the delegates) was that such documents were "human instruments" used to distinguish sects. They "divided Christians into factions" and therefore should not be used in constituting a church. Men created creeds to suppress heresy; but instead of suppressing heresy, creeds reduced the authority of Scripture, the "only instrument upon which a Christian church should be constituted." Both Scripture and the authority of Christ opposed creeds and confessions of faith, which originated with the "son of perdition" and had led to more martyrdom than had paganism.[38]

"H" (presumably Jesse Hartwell, professor of theology at Howard College) replied to this attack by admitting that creeds could be misused. But creed was nothing more than a "general summary of Bible truth" used for ages among Baptists to differentiate their beliefs. To progress, a church had to be united on belief and practice. Each person had a creed or belief about the meaning of Scripture. Nevertheless, he agreed that creedal Baptist churches should not criticize noncreedal ones.[39] In a sense, these two conflicting positions remained central to Alabama Baptists for 150 years and were no closer to being reconciled at the end of the twentieth century than in the middle of the nineteenth.

The same could be said for biblical authority. If creed was not to be the glue holding Baptists together, what bonding did serve that function? The answer seemed obvious: the Bible. Discussing the alleged sovereignty and independence of Baptist churches, a series of essays in 1858 reminded that the Bible was "law" in Baptist churches and overruled congregational autonomy.[40] James DeVotie epitomized an entire generation of preachers in a sermon entitled "Scripture the Inspiration of God." Although DeVotie did not use the words *literal* or *inerrant*, he certainly espoused the central authority of Scripture.[41]

Essays on hermeneutics (the theory/science of biblical interpretation) in the *Alabama Baptist* suggested some benchmarks for biblical interpretation. There were both literary and moral standards for interpreting Scripture. Literary qualifications included knowledge of the original languages in which the Bible had been written, rhetoric and logic, analysis of the arguments and reasoning of biblical writers in order to detect and reconcile "apparent discrepancies," and historical context (the history, religion, manners, customs, and geography of the times). Without all these skills, preachers would have "an imperfect and confused knowledge of the Bible." Another article on the same subject insisted that the only true meaning of words was their grammatical meaning. The literal meaning of words was preferable to their figurative meaning (unless the meaning was clearly metaphorical, as when Christ referred to himself as the "living bread" to be "eaten"). Nor should poetic language be taken literally, as when the Bible predicted that in heaven people from East and West would "sit down" with Abraham (people would have no physical existence in heaven and thus to describe them as sitting down was to use a "trope," a word used in a figurative rather than in a literal way).[42]

Although all Baptists seemed to hold the Bible in high esteem and regard it as the standard for faith and practice, they agreed on little else. Some read the Bible literally, interpreted the "days" of Genesis 1 as periods of twenty-four hours, and believed the earth to be recently formed. Others (notably the influential revivalist/pastor E. B. Teague) insisted that the Mosaic days were "equivalent to lengthened periods" of time and that the flood was local and not universal. He saw no conflict between these views and the authority of Scripture. In a commencement address at the University of Alabama, Teague argued that the point of the flood story was humanity's wickedness and God's punishment. At that particular time, humankind occupied only a limited territory; hence human beings could be wiped out without a universal flood. Tuscaloosa seemed to spawn iconoclasm. The pastor of the church there, Thomas F. Curtis, was pronounced one of "the freshest, most original and fertile of the preachers of the time." He later taught theology at Howard College and often preached at the state convention. He wrote that the Jewish belief in a special relationship with God was a product of national vanity and believed human beings had inhabited the earth 100,000 years before Adam.[43]

When such conflicts in interpretation occurred, how should Baptists resolve them? In a series of essays, the denominational paper suggested that where differences existed about the meaning of Scripture, the congregation should defer to the pastor because of his lifetime study of the Bible. The writer did not advise blind obedience to preachers but proclaimed that "we should be very sure that we are right before we undertake to oppose God's ministers in any way."[44]

If Baptist lay people recognized the authority of the Bible when they understood it and their pastor's opinion when they did not, it is amazing that they battled so fiercely over a variety of beliefs. Obviously the individualism and frontier independence of Baptists made them highly suspicious of authority. Equally obvious were the fierce differences of their pastoral leaders. The assumption that Baptist pastors who had carefully studied Scripture would agree on its meaning was mistaken, as a series of biblical controversies made clear.

Even deciding which translation of Scripture to read created an uproar. To the generation of Baptists occupying Alabama before 1845, venerating the Bible meant the King James Version (KJV). Debate over new translations of the Bible began in 1851 and raged for half a decade. The editor of the *South-Western Baptist* at first took no position on the matter, opening his pages to advocates of each side. But in April 1851 he declared his opposition to a proposed revised version as serving no useful purpose. The editor gave his critics space for rebuttal, admitting that he was only a fallible man and that he might be wrong. "W. C. C." penned essays on the other side of the issue, arguing that changes in words and meanings since the KJV made it obsolete. Resistance to new scientific and philosophical ideas had made an "ignoramus" of the church during Galileo's time and threatened to do so again.[45]

Subsequent years produced every conceivable argument on both sides of the issue. Proponents of the revised version argued that the KJV was the flawed product of hierarchical Anglicans. Opponents blamed the impetus for the revised version on the disciples of Alexander Campbell. The Tuskegee Association passed resolutions opposing the revision in 1852 and again the following year, calling it "unwise in its inception, imprudent in its prosecution, and disastrous in its consequences." Convinced that the monstrosity had begun with so-called "reformers, better known among us by the name of Campbellites," the increasingly sectarian Tuskegee Baptists feared the complicity of "northern, western, and south western Baptists" as well. The tension over the revision spilled over into the 1855 state convention despite the efforts of officials to keep it out. They encouraged Baptist advocates of revision to hold a separate meeting in Montgomery where they could endorse such reforms to their hearts' content.[46]

Alabama Baptists did not need a new version of Scripture to divide them; they were divided enough about the meaning of the KJV. They could not even agree on the efficacy of foot washing. The primitive practice did not comport well with newfound Baptist affluence and education and was increasingly relegated to the rural fringes of the denomination. The Cahawba Association boasted that all its churches had abandoned foot washing by 1845. This news infuriated one writer who deplored churches neglecting a practice specifically commanded by Christ on the night he was betrayed.[47]

All these debates remained secondary to the dispute over Calvinism. Although by 1845 most churches and associations had already split over missions, and the Primitive Baptists were rapidly constituting a separate denomination, argument still raged between strict Calvinists, hyper-Calvinists, and Arminians.

At the heart of evangelical Christianity is the belief that human beings cannot save themselves. They respond to God's offer of grace precisely because they cannot save themselves. But how is God's grace extended? To all who seek it by a free act of will? Only to those preordained by God? Most antebellum Baptist pastors believed human beings could act freely only insofar as the Holy Spirit moved them toward the salvation God had already ordained.[48]

The so-called covenant theology spawned by Calvinism meant different things to different people. To James Watt of Russell County it meant nothing more than the unfolding revelation of God that led to salvation. To H. E. Taliaferro of Talladega County it meant America as a new Zion, the fulfillment of God's ancient covenant with "our fathers." Covenant theology certainly did not support Primitive Baptists (whom Taliaferro called the "antinomian predestination" group, those "croaking babblers of that gloomy school").[49]

Thomas F. Curtis (professor of theology and moral science at Howard College) probably did the best job of translating Calvinist issues into ideas comprehensible to the average lay person. Using Acts 27 as his text, Curtis reminded his listeners of the way Paul survived a shipwreck. God's purpose was that all should be saved from the storm. But despite God's repeated promise of salvation, Paul admonished the sailors to make every effort possible, as if God had promised nothing. Had the sailors and Paul not exerted themselves to the fullest, they might have drowned. It was true, he concluded, that God had chosen his people from all eternity. Yet the salvation clear to God was contingent and conditional upon the elect's repentance and faith, as if God had not elected them at all.[50]

However awkward this straddling of Calvinism might make Baptists appear, it also provided them firm footing between hyper-Calvinist Primitive Baptists on one side and Arminian Methodists on the other. By the 1850s, virtually all their preachers defended the same ground. A sermon by C. F. Sturgis condemned the "religious one ideaism" of the antinomian hyper-Calvinists and the free will excesses of the Arminians. Not at all charitable to either group, Sturgis concluded that there was "strong family likeness" in this "baptized heathenism." One sprang from the other as "an active pestilence springs from a stagnant marsh." Baptists blended human and divine agency into just the proper mixture. "Crispus" praised such doctrinal discussions as essential if Arminianism was to be defeated. And it must be defeated because from it sprang every kind of heresy: "Romanism, Puseyism, Universalism, Campbellism, Methodism and Episcopalianism."[51]

An effect of such sectarian Calvinism was conflict with other denominations. One reason camp meetings fell out of favor was the interdenominational preaching typical of such gatherings. Basil Manly Sr. complained that when he resigned as president of the University of Alabama, his Methodist successor and the "pedobaptist" faculty refused to hire Baptists. "Kappa" added a class element to the argument. Methodists were "a little on the grand order [and] the Episcopalians even more." In Marion conflict swirled around Presbyterians who allegedly accused Baptists of polygamy and questioning the virgin birth of Jesus. Baptists responded with an aggressive offensive against infant baptism. Attacks on the "Campbellites" (followers of Alexander Campbell) hardly ever abated during the antebellum years. When immigrants poured into Alabama during the 1850s, these intramural contests became even more exotic. One Baptist preacher recalled a steamboat trip down the Alabama River to Mobile in 1855. While stuck on a sandbar with swearing, smoking, whiskey-drinking "rabble," he thought the trip a complete loss. But then he met both a Catholic and a German immigrant, who was a rationalist. He had heard that such people existed but never before had he actually talked with them.[52]

Not all Baptists were so sectarian. Country areas experienced such a shortage of preachers that they devised a pragmatic ecumenism. One Sunday Baptists worshiped at their own church, another Sunday with the Methodists, the next with Presbyterians. In such frontier conditions the practical necessities of getting along with one another softened the theological differences of their leaders.

A second result of Calvinist theology was more personal than social. Baptists learned to rely on the providence of God. If God had a plan for all his chosen before the foundations of the world, humanity's proper role was to find and accept that destiny. Twenty-year-old Amanda C. Edwards received the comfort of Calvinism when her nine-day-old daughter died and she became grievously ill. At first Edwards was extremely anxious and fearful. But as her faith took over, she became "transformed and content." She died the following morning. When the thirteen-year-old daughter of James Graham of Lowndes County contracted scarlet fever while attending the female college in Auburn, the disease spread to her father and brother. Both daughter and son died, prompting a Baptist leader to comment: "Inscrutable are the ways of Providence! Yet remember fond parents that 'the Judge of all the earth will do right.' " When a drought threatened crops in 1855, the editor of the denominational paper wrote: "We have no fellowship for the religion which ignores the providence of God in supplying the common blessings of life." When Basil Manly Sr. survived a terrible yellow fever season in Charleston, South Carolina, the editor concluded "surely the Lord has some important work for his servant yet to do, seeing he has shielded him thus amid such dangers."[53]

Dispensational, apocalyptic, and millennial theology established only a tiny beachhead on the wide shore of Calvinism. As early as 1854 the *South-Western Baptist* carried an article dividing Christian history into certain epochs or dispensations. The author named four cycles of God's revelation: the patriarchs, law and prophets, gospel, and last times. "J. S. B." wrote in 1855 that popery and infidelity were thriving, heaven and hell were marshaling forces for the final conflict, and the antichrist had grasped the pillars of the church. But most Baptists were apparently too busy making money during the cotton boom of those years to rush the end times, and J. S. B.'s prophecy received a cool reception.[54] The fact that one finds so few sermons on the subject reflects the buoyant optimism of the times.

As for the origins of later controversies, one finds hardly a clue. Baptists generally showed a preference for continuity, conservatism, and tradition over change, liberalism, and modernity, but they discussed these issues more in terms of class and education than of theology. The editor of the *South-Western Baptist* wrote in 1852 that change was inevitable and often good. But it could also injure the church. Infidelity might appear in the garb of traditional Christianity, though it often manifested itself in the "horribly distorted" shape of liberalism. It appealed especially to "learned" people because of its "literary pretensions" and claims of rationality. A few years later the editor denounced words such as *conservative* and *orthodox* as "humbugging words" that meant nothing. Oftentimes, H. E. Taliaferro wrote, it was conservatives who insisted that he use gentle terms for "factionalists, fanatics, abolitionists, and bandy courtly epithets with errorists of religion."[55] Such equivocation was not his style nor conservatism his cause.

The most obvious legacy of Calvinism was the continuing debate over missions. Although permanent division of Baptists was well under way before 1845, the process continued throughout the middle of the century. In 1847 the agent employed by the state convention failed in his efforts to raise money for missions because few pastors had the courage to collect a Sunday mission offering. E. B. Teague faced opposition everywhere he solicited for missions, even within his own association, where some objected to his sermon on missions. In Huntsville, antimission sentiment blighted Baptist work for years. In eastern Alabama, the newly formed Lebanon church split when the pastor and a group of followers joined the antimission cause. At the Big Springs church in Randolph County, the congregation warred over the same subject until a female member ended the abstract theological discussion with a simple frontier aphorism: "If we don't hunt our meat, we will perish."[56]

As the antimission controversy continued, a new battle erupted that was based more on ecclesiology (church practices) than Calvinist theology. Landmarkism began in Tennessee and Kentucky with James M. Pendleton, Amos C. Dayton, and James R. Graves (who were sometimes called the "Nashville triumvirate"). Meeting in 1851 in Cotton Grove, Tennessee, Graves's followers repudiated the authority of non-Baptist churches, ministers, and ordinances. Assuming the primacy of the local church, Graves wrote that only Baptists correctly practiced the ancient rituals of the church and could rightly claim the authority of Christ. Unless an authorized Baptist preacher performed baptism by immersion, it was improperly conducted. Christ had established a visible kingdom of true Baptist churches that had a continuous existence from the first century to modern times. All other churches were impostors. Because each church administered its own discipline, only it could administer communion to members, excluding even those who belonged to other Baptist churches (hence, "closed communion"). The same logic extended to organizations not authorized by the Bible (such as mission boards). Although Graves's followers did not separate from the SBC until 1905 (when they organized the General Association of Landmark Baptists), they left a trail of controversy across the South.

Debates concerning closed communion broke out in Alabama in 1849 and soon merged into the larger Landmark controversy. J. B. Hawthorn accused the Landmarkers of intolerance for assuming that "all truth and virtue" belonged to Baptists. J. H. DeVotie preached a sermon on prejudice, urging Baptists to be more tolerant of one another.[57]

These jousts were preliminary to the main bout, featuring Samuel Henderson and J. R. Graves. Henderson was a native of Tennessee whose father had established the first newspaper in Talladega. Henderson became pastor of the Good Hope Baptist Church before moving to Tuskegee in 1845 where he helped organize the Tuskegee Baptist Association and the East Alabama Female College. From 1852 until 1859 he served as editor of the *South-West-*

ern Baptist, which became more militant and confrontational under his editorship. After lengthy service in the state convention, he was elected vice-president in 1858. Henderson launched his offensive against Graves in the pages of the *South-Western Baptist* in 1857. For the next thirty-one months, virtually every issue of the paper contained an attack: Graves was a native of Vermont who had lived in Ohio and whose support for slavery was suspect; Graves plagiarized the writings of others; Graves defended an article advocating polygamy.

From the pages of the *Tennessee Baptist,* which he edited, Graves answered volley for volley. Denying that he was an abolitionist, Graves wrote that in fact he owned slaves. He accused Henderson of participating in an ecumenical communion service at a schoolhouse on Hatchett Creek in Clay County.[58]

Not even the revered Basil Manly Sr. escaped censure. When the state convention brought Manly back from South Carolina as general evangelist at an annual salary of $3,000, "Vox Populi" strenuously objected. Accusing Manly of being a closet anti-Landmarker and fearful that he would become the "diocesan bishop" of Alabama, he warned that the "growing host of Landmark Baptists in Alabama" would fight any attempt to erode the authority of pastors. Apparently Manly did use his influence to block selection of a Landmark pastor at the Ash Creek church in Tuscaloosa County, writing a deacon that Landmarkism would "eat out the spirit of peaceful, productive piety" and produce a "bitter unchristian hostility to every liberal-minded person that does not think as they do." D. P. Bestor came to Manly's defense, arguing that his only offense was his independence of thought and refusal to join the Landmark faction: "This miserable vice is borrowed from the political arena, where I trust, the Baptists of Alabama, will suffer it to remain." So divisive did the Landmark debate become that it dominated the 1858 state convention.[59]

As the 1850s ended, Baptist leaders pleaded with their people not to make Landmarkism a test of fellowship. Brethren with widely different views could work harmoniously on many other issues.[60] The Civil War put an end to the most obstreperous phase of the dispute, but Landmark beliefs put down deep roots in Alabama. Many churches retained belief in closed communion and continuous succession throughout the twentieth century.

As Manly's communication with a deacon of the Ash Creek church made clear, the role of deacons became increasingly prominent as education and wealth raised the consciousness of laymen. In Eufaula First Baptist Church men such as future governor John Gill Shorter assumed responsibility for organizing and managing church finances. In 1849 the *Alabama*

Baptist discussed at length the qualifications for deacons. A deacon had to be a man of "unquestionable piety," "honest report," sound in faith, well read in Scriptures, a man of wisdom, prudence, energy, and zeal. The duties of deacons included relieving the pastor of temporal cares such as raising money and paying bills, caring for widows, orphans, and the poor, visiting members and reporting their needs, promoting peace and harmony, and reconciling petty differences between members. They were restricted from preaching the gospel, administering the ordinances of the church, or governing the church at conference. Some churches added other restrictions. First Baptist Tuscaloosa would not ordain a deacon until he married.[61]

Institution Building

Increasing wealth and status encouraged Baptists to new efforts on behalf of denominational education. With public education nonexistent or regarded as defective, Baptists turned to their own academies and colleges. Montgomery Baptists hired a teacher in 1851 and began an academy with sixty pupils. That same year, the Coosa River Association's committee on education proposed establishing a Talladega male high school. Female schools in Lafayette and Tuskegee thrived. In 1856 the Liberty Association moved its military academy from Fredonia to Lafayette.[62]

At the unofficial Baptist capital of Alabama in Marion, both Judson and Howard Colleges reaped the benefits of Black Belt affluence. Augmented by the acquisition of the *Alabama Baptist* in 1843 and the domestic mission board of the SBC two years later, Marion Baptists were exuberant and tremendously supportive of education. Both colleges enrolled students in preparatory and college classes, and the annual springtime examinations became major social events in the Black Belt. Crowds came by buggy from throughout southern Alabama and eastern Mississippi for the week of public examinations, recitations, and graduation ceremonies. Judson students (dressed in their pink and white dress uniforms) and Howard cadets answered questions, read original literary compositions, presented vocal and instrumental music, delivered orations on contemporary events, and received awards. Milo Jewett's decision in 1855 to leave Alabama and resettle in Poughkeepsie, New York (where he established Vassar College) was a substantial blow to Judson. Jewett's emphasis on writing, mathematics, foreign languages, and history, as well as his insistence that the fine arts be treated as serious academic disciplines rather than social graces, set the college apart from many female academies.[63]

Howard College also flourished, despite the initial opposition of Basil

Manly Sr. Manly feared that competition from Howard would weaken the University of Alabama. But Jesse Hartwell and other pastors quietly urged state leaders to ignore Manly's concerns. Baptists, Hartwell advised, needed to "draw off the mind from cotton growing to the cultivation of the intellect." Ironically, denominational leaders later (in 1850 and again in 1858) tried to recruit Manly to become president of the new Baptist school.[64]

By 1846 the editor of the *Alabama Baptist* pronounced Judson and Howard the most important agencies of the denomination. Howard was particularly critical to the enlightenment of a state so poorly served by public schools. The influence of the denomination depended upon "keeping pace with the intellectual advancement of other churches." Accomplishing this task depended on an educated clergy such as Howard would produce. Ministerial education should center on theology rather than general education but required cultivation of both intellect and spirit. Preachers must learn proper grammar, refinement, oratorical skills, and mental discipline so as not to offend educated lay people.[65]

Howard College appointed a distinguished minister, Samuel S. Sherman, president. Its curriculum was similar to that of the University of Alabama and its ministerial enrollment remained low (six ministerial students studied theology in 1849). In 1846 a four-story brick structure opened, with chapel, laboratory, and offices on the lower two floors and dormitory rooms on the top two. An architectural flaw neglected fire escapes other than inside stairways. This omission proved fatal in the fall of 1854 when a midnight fire erupted, trapping students on the top floors. A faithful slave of President Henry Talbird known only as Harry lost his life trying to arouse sleeping students, many of whom were burned or badly injured when they jumped from upper-floor windows.[66]

James DeVotie assumed primary responsibility for rebuilding the college at the urging of Marion citizens and the Cahawba Association. He traveled more than 5,000 miles during the next fourteen months and raised $40,000. At the end of that time, the college's $80,000 endowment was four-fifths of what was required to make the school self-supporting. One of the gifts established fifty scholarships of $250 annually for poor men seeking to enter the ministry.[67]

Howard College's Marion neighbor, the *Alabama Baptist*, also underwent considerable change. In 1849 Alexander W. Chambliss, a native of South Carolina, became editor and changed the name to the *Alabama Baptist Advocate*. A year later, Chambliss acquired the subscription lists of the defunct *South-Western Baptist Chronicle* of New Orleans and renamed his paper the *South-Western Baptist*, under which name the paper functioned for a decade and a half.[68] Two years later, in 1852, Chambliss resigned, and Albert Williams and Samuel Henderson became editors. They moved the paper briefly to Montgomery, then to Tuskegee, where Henderson pastored the Baptist church. Chambliss had increased subscribers from 600 to 1,600, but the number fluctuated depending on how zealously the editor tried to collect the three-dollar annual fee. By 1858 Henderson's combative editorials on slavery, abolitionism, and Landmarkism had generated nearly 4,000 subscribers, enough to allow purchase of the most modern new steam-powered printing press. Henderson employed his brother-in-law, gifted humorist H. E. Taliaferro, as associate editor in 1856 and turned the paper over to him three years later.[69]

Institution building within the church continued to focus on church discipline. So important was this matter that the denominational paper frequently answered queries from churches about specific cases and ran long series about the theology of church discipline (one series in 1860 continued for thirteen weeks).[70]

A. W. Chambliss (then of Tuskegee), the future editor of the *Alabama Baptist*, explained the purpose and function of discipline in an 1845 sermon. He drew a distinction between private and public disputes. Private differences should be resolved between the parties only, Chambliss argued; public offenses required corporate resolution to prevent the rise of heresy and slander of the church. Although Scripture recognized no distinctions between persons, conditions varied. Slaves and wives had fewer opportunities than masters and husbands, as did illiterate members compared to educated ones. Discipline must consider opportunity as well as offense. The severity of the offense depended on whether it was specifically forbidden by the Bible (murder, fighting, lying, stealing, drunkenness, or adultery) or merely discouraged for the good order of the church (attending dances, theater, or circuses or playing a violin). Also, Chambliss added, the church must not forget that the purpose of discipline was to reprove and correct and should be applied with tenderness. Discipline must also be impartial. There must be no favoritism toward rich or poor, male or female, black or white.[71]

Although discipline continued from earlier days, the nature of discipline changed to reflect improved economic circumstances. In Marion, a dispute arose in 1856 between a member of Siloam church and pastor James DeVotie and the church building committee. The church had invited bids for a new building, and the member accused the committee of rejecting his low bid and rigging the process against him. The church allowed each party to the dispute to select four members of a discipline committee that heard the charges, and the eight members elected a ninth. The committee ruled that the aggrieved member had refused attempts at reconciliation, had made his unjustified charges in public, and should apologize. He refused and was excluded.[72]

Class and racial concerns also intruded on church discipline. The editor of the denominational paper complained in 1845 that wealthy members who took advantage of others in trade and commerce, charged exorbitant profits, or loaned money at usurious rates of interest often escaped censure because of their money and influence. Affluent planter church members who allowed their slaves to go hungry or inadequately clothed were "worse than an infidel."[73] "Tau" wrote in 1859 that urban churches did not accept the discipline of country congregations because they believed country people incapable of rendering wise decisions. Country people retaliated by accusing their city brethren of "living in fine mansions and worshipping in a brick meeting-house." "Tau" advised both country and urban churches to mind their own business when it came to matters of church discipline.[74]

As discipline became more complicated, the church organization became more complex. Following years of sporadic Sunday morning preaching, town churches began to conduct weekly services and to organize Sunday schools, prayer meetings, and missionary societies. In 1850 the Eufaula church began a Sabbath school and a Monday night prayer meeting. The Wetumpka church had begun a Sunday school at least as early as 1842 and established a library of theology books and Bible commentaries for use by its teachers in 1859. In 1851 Joshua Hill Foster helped organize the Alabama Central Sunday School Union to encourage the organization of Sunday schools in western Alabama.[75]

Another aspect of change from rural frontier to urban settlement appeared in music. In earlier decades, pastors had lined out hymns that congregations repeated. But as urban churches grew, robust congregational singing gave way to choirs. A series of articles in the *South-Western Baptist* in 1857 sought to provide a biblical rationale for the use of music in worship. The lyric should be evangelical in nature but also dignified, solemn, and devotional. Each congregation should determine whether singing should be done by the entire congregation or by only a choir.[76]

On this last point, Baptists vigorously disagreed as they did on so many other matters. A correspondent to the denominational newspaper in 1859 deplored the tendency of choirs to do all the singing in Baptist churches. He traced this malady to singing schools, where ambitious teachers sought to exhibit their pupils and thereby advertise their own ability. Naturally, parents were delighted to see their children and youth sing; so, choirs replaced congregational singing and singing masters began to rival preachers for public attention. The correspondent complained that God intended *all* disciples to sing, not just the ones in choirs.[77]

According to contemporary accounts, the premier music in Alabama Baptist churches could be found in Mobile's Saint Francis Street church, which had a large choir led by a "superior singer." What made the church so unusual for the times was its combination of choir and congregational singing. Every seat in the church had a hymnbook and Bible, and everyone sang. The effect, according to visitors, was delightful.[78]

When members of such churches attended associational meetings, they brought new standards of professionalism as well. Usually embracing a number of counties (the Coosa River Association in 1845 included Calhoun, Talladega, Saint Clair, Shelby, Coosa, and Tallapoosa Counties), associations received annual reports from churches, passed resolutions on various doctrinal and public issues, collected and dispensed missions offerings, and employed missionaries. The Salem Association employed two missionaries in 1849, one for ten months, the other for five and a half. One traveled 2,000 miles, preached 219 sermons, and constituted six churches. The other traveled more than 1,200 miles, preached 139 sermons, baptized forty-four, and constituted two churches. Thanks partly to their efforts, churches within the association gained 555 members and eight new churches. The editor of the *Alabama Baptist* made it clear that old haphazard standards of recording and distributing records would not do in a modern age. He criticized the printed report of the Bethel Association for errors in grammar, capitalization, and punctuation (the "commas look as if they were sprinkled on the page out of a pepper box!"). The report was printed on poor-quality paper by worn-out type. Everything was "in bad taste." For only a bit more, associations could have their reports printed professionally so as to impress the reader. Even more revealing was the phenomenal circulation of Bethel's report. The association published 1,200 copies to distribute to other associations and churches, a circulation twice that of the state denominational newspaper at the time.[79]

The state convention followed the path of associations toward more elaborate programs and more complex organization. As late as 1847 E. B. Teague described the convention as spontaneous. There was no program except for a few committee reports on missions and temperance. There were no prearranged speeches. Anyone who felt led to speak did so. Delegates sometimes forgot important matters, and the proceedings included long intervals without any activity at all.[80]

Two years later the state convention appointed temperance, education, Sunday school, and domestic and foreign missions committees to report each year. There followed a steady improvement in mission offerings and decorum. By 1850 total mission offerings exceeded $20,000, and the 133 delegates (53 of them ministers) represented fifty-nine churches, associations, and societies.[81]

Creation of the Southern Baptist Convention in 1845 added yet another layer of bureaucracy to the rising edifice of Alabama Baptist life. State Baptists were delighted when the SBC located its Board of Domestic Missions at Marion. One reason for creation of the convention was the long-standing complaint of Baptists in the South that the American Baptist Home Mission Society had neglected the lower Mississippi Valley. The choice of Marion seemed logical to them because the Siloam church was often considered the strongest Baptist congregation west of Georgia and east of the Mississippi River. On other SBC matters, rank-and-file Alabama Baptists had misgivings. Joseph Morris of Clinton complained that requiring a church to contribute $100 annually for three years in order to send a messenger to the SBC would exclude most Alabama churches that were too poor to do so. The system threatened to replace a republican system with an aristocratic one. Jesse Hartwell disagreed, arguing that several churches could unite if necessary to raise the money. Others complained that the convention undermined the authority of local churches and associations. Defenders pointed out that no church was bound in any way by actions of the SBC. Every church remained "a sovereign and independent body."[82]

Few Baptist preachers could afford to attend the SBC except when it met in Alabama (during the antebellum era, it met in the state only once). E. B. Teague attended his first SBC in Nashville in 1851. He traveled nearly three hundred miles by stagecoach, then returned by steamboat down the Cumberland, Ohio, and Mississippi Rivers, thence by railroad and stagecoach home. The trip cost him more than $100, a tenth of the average annual salary of pastors of even the most affluent Baptist churches. And most churches paid none of their pastor's expenses to the meeting. As a consequence, the 1851 Nashville meeting registered only 175 delegates.[83]

An activity made possible by the new convention was the commissioning of missionaries to foreign fields. One speaker at the 1845 SBC in Augusta was a missionary to China, J. Lewis Shuck. His wife had died in China, and Shuck had returned with his children and one of his Chinese converts. Alabama Baptist messengers to the convention persuaded Shuck to bring his convert to Alabama, and during 1846 they spoke fourteen times in the state. One of their presentations was in the Grant's Creek church at

Foster's Settlement, where Martha Foster was a member. Another was at Judson College. So moving was the appeal that James DeVotie advised Alabama Baptists to travel fifty miles if they had to in order to hear Shuck and Yong See Sarng, his convert.[84]

Eliza Gable Sexton did not have to travel at all. Although a native of Pennsylvania, she was teaching music, art, and foreign languages at Judson when Shuck arrived in the summer of 1846. His brief stay there netted him the most generous contribution of his southern tour, $500 from students and another $200 or $300 from townspeople. More important, it netted him a bride. Milo Jewett performed the wedding ceremony for Shuck and Sexton before the entire student body, and the newlyweds were soon on their way to Shanghai. Shuck had been appointed earlier as the first Baptist missionary to China; but when the SBC was established, the native Virginian resigned his earlier

Martha Foster Crawford was a Baptist teacher/missionary in China, 1852–1909. (Courtesy of Photo Library, Foreign Mission Board, Southern Baptist Convention)

appointment and sought commissioning as the first missionary of the new convention. His wife was the first missionary from Alabama to be appointed. Through subsequent years until her death in childbirth in 1851, Eliza Sexton Shuck received faithful support from the Ann Hasseltine Judson Missionary Society at Judson.[85]

Eliza Sexton's brief career at Judson barely qualifies her as Alabama's first foreign missionary. By right of true residence, that honor probably belongs to Martha Foster. Descended from one of Alabama's most distinguished families, Martha Foster attended the Baptist girls' school in Lafayette, then began to teach for an old family friend, E. B. Teague. A series of failed romances left Foster disillusioned with men and contributed to a growing sense of call to China. She asked Teague to write the newly established Foreign Mission Board on her behalf in 1851, but officials explained that the board did not appoint single women and preferred not to send single men. About the same time, an unmarried preacher, Tarleton P. Crawford, also applied. The board official showed Teague's letter to Crawford and suggested the young woman from Alabama might be the answer to his prayers. Crawford departed immediately for Alabama and, after much hunting, tracked down Martha Foster. Following a brief, extremely practical courtship of several weeks, the couple was married and set sail for China, where Martha Foster Crawford labored for more than a half century. Although their marriage was as stormy as their long sea voyage to China, it weathered missionary conflicts, her husband's split with the Foreign Mission Board, creation of his new Gospel Mission, and a host of other problems. Martha Foster Crawford sent regular reports on China that were published in the *Alabama Baptist*. She probably did more to inspire interest in missions than any single person in the nineteenth century. Had it not been for her husband's eccentricities, she might well have emerged as the patron saint of Southern Baptist foreign missions rather than her younger recruit and best friend, Lottie Moon.[86]

Baptists Confront Their Culture

As the remarkable life of Martha Foster Crawford makes clear, Alabama Baptists confronted God's plan for them in a complex tangle of gender, race, secular politics, and sectional animosities. All around their tiny patches of Christian enlightenment was a seemingly unbroken forest of religious destitution.

Despite the dawning of an affluent age for much of Alabama, reports pouring in from Baptist colporteurs revealed the coexistence of two societies. In cities like Mobile, Montgomery, Huntsville, and Eufaula, and in rural areas of the Black Belt and Tennessee Valley, increasing wealth and education made possible an ecclesiastical sophistication rivaling that of Presbyterians and Methodists. Only miles away, abject poverty, illiteracy, and deprivation reigned supreme. A colporteur in Bibb County reported that though he happened upon a log cabin every three or four miles, he saw only one school as he crossed the county. A woman told him there had been only one sermon preached in her vicinity during the previous ten months. Her daughter had died proclaiming that "Jesus died for poor folks"; but if true, there was little evidence of it in Bibb County. That same year J. R. Haggard reported on four days of travel during which he encountered thirty-five families, twenty-three of them destitute of religious knowledge. In many families, no one could read. Five families he visited one day contained twelve members over age twelve who could not read. One illiterate woman belonged to a Baptist church whose pastor had resigned from lack of interest. The colporteur wondered in his report, "When will our legislature do something for the education of the people?" Two colporteurs in Jefferson County visited twenty-eight families that year, nineteen of them without Bibles.[87]

Poverty evoked an outpouring of concern that was manifested both in growing support for the Alabama Baptist Bible Society and in greater benevolence within churches. Nearly all rural congregations and not a few urban ones contained poor people, especially among their slave members. As a result, care for widows, orphans, and the poor was more than a formal responsibility of deacons; it was an urgent necessity. In October 1853 the Eufaula church appointed a committee to help poor members. The committee reported that anyone "at all conversant with the requirements of their Lord . . . well know that the duty of affording relief to the poor among us cannot be neglected without guilt attaching to those who have the means and yet disregard this duty." The committee proposed quarterly subscriptions of funds for the poor. In February 1854 such funds made possible the burial of two indigent members of the church. James DeVotie preached a powerful sermon on the poor, whom he considered special objects of God's care. Christ himself was born in a manger into the family of a carpenter, DeVotie explained, and spent his entire ministry identifying with the poor. Most of his disciples were poor people.[88]

Despite such efforts, the poor often fell through the cracks of this voluntary system of benevolence, especially if they belonged to no church. One correspondent to the denominational paper reported the fate of a ninety-year-old couple, the man a veteran of the Revolutionary War. The man could not read, his wife was nearly blind, and both were bound for the county poorhouse. It was not so, the correspondent wrote, in the first century when Christians cared for their brethren and disciples "had all things in common": "Surely there is a fault somewhere when the Lord's poor are allowed to end their days under such gloomy and depressing circumstances."[89]

In Mobile, Baptists translated such concerns into a unique seamen's ministry in 1859. They anchored a ship thirty miles south of Mobile near Grant's Pass, where some fifty to seventy-five ships often anchored. The Bethel ship ministry contained a chapel, a hospital, and quarters for a minister/physician and his family and servants. During the shipping season, the bay contained a permanent population of some 2,000, as well as 20,000 seamen who passed through, many of them ill or injured. The Seamen's Friend Society employed a minister/physician who both preached and tended to the medical needs of the poor.[90]

Alleviating poverty was not the only or even the most important way

Baptists sought to change society. They also tried to regulate personal conduct. During the first decades of the nineteenth century, the temperance movement was stronger in the North than in the South. Southerners resisted reform movements, partly because abolitionism and feminism were elements of the reformism rippling through the Northeast. Temperance strength was also greatest among the middle class and in towns, whereas the South was poorer and more agrarian and rural than the North. Also, in mountainous areas of the South, many subsistence farmers needed to market corn in the form of whiskey in order to earn cash income.[91]

As the nineteenth century unfolded, Baptists and Methodists soon made up for their slow start. They formed temperance societies, passed resolutions against the sale of alcohol, and excluded church members for drunkenness or for making and selling "ardent spirits." In a litany that would be oft repeated over the following century and a half, the editor of the *South-Western Baptist* in 1853 claimed to "eschew all connection with politics" and vowed to "carefully avoid all interference with elections." But this vow did not keep him from political efforts to restrict the liquor traffic, which he defined as a moral issue.[92]

Not all Baptists agreed on the theology or the best strategy for restricting alcohol use. In 1849 the Liberty Association rejected the membership application of the Rechab church because it was a "total abstinence church." Making abstinence a test of Christian fellowship might divide the association where some churches were "not prepared for the measure." Although the association longed for a time when all churches would agree with the position of the Rechab church, "for the present . . . until light shall have been more generally disseminated," such action would only create division. In 1853 an anonymous writer argued against prohibition, though he believed alcohol use to be harmful. He feared that legal action to compel prohibition enlarged government power at the expense of individual freedom, liberty, and independence. He concluded that the state was not bound to improve the morals of its citizens.[93]

Many Baptists also believed that personal recreation should be regulated. Although Baptists endorsed good reading and some forms of physical exertion, they condemned card playing, attending the theater, and dancing. Dancing was less a sin per se than an expression of frivolity and lightheartedness. Such entertainments diverted attention from more pious and important pursuits. The denominational paper printed a set of criteria by which to judge all recreation. Godly recreation should not awaken "evil passions," depend on chance, produce lassitude or weariness, or be too exciting.[94]

On the persistent question of Masonry, an emerging consensus judged that membership should be left to the individual. Basil Manly Sr. was not a Mason but defended the right to join. The pastor of the Saint Francis Street church in Mobile deplored petty disputes over Masonry that divided churches. H. E. Taliaferro, editor of the *South-Western Baptist,* concurred in this view. The Bible contained no teaching on the subject, and the right to belong to the Masons was the privilege of any free citizen. He believed that attempts by churches to abridge such rights only brought the church into disrespect.[95]

Dueling, though a matter of honor to some aristocrats, was "a reproach to a Christian nation," according to most Alabama Baptists. Even so prominent a citizen as William L. Yancey could not escape censure. The editor of the denominational paper was not impressed when Yancey refused to fire in a duel despite widespread public praise for his "chivalrous" conduct. The editor did not believe willingness to be murdered was scriptural and denounced dueling as "a wanton and sinful exposure of life, highly offensive in the sight of the creator." Yancey was sufficiently chagrined by the criticism to write a lengthy defense of his actions. Fifteen years later, a different editor of the same paper called dueling a "heathenish practice" that should be "banished from civilized countries."[96]

Although Baptists differed over how much they should attempt to impose their beliefs on others, they vigorously championed public education. In 1845 the editor of the *Alabama Baptist* deplored the fact that only a third of the estimated white school-age population attended school. Nearly a decade later, a different editor affirmed the importance of moral education. He believed that fundamental principles of Christian morality could be incorporated in public schools without infringing on the freedom of any sect, though he conceded that Catholics and unbelievers disagreed.[97]

During 1854 legislative debates about creating Alabama's first statewide system of public schools, the editor wrote a series of four editorials favoring such action. Education, he wrote, was the birthright of all Americans. It was also a matter of public utility because the true wealth of any state was the intellect of its people. Prosperity could only be accomplished by extending common schools to every child, which "would be the most profitable investment the state has ever made in any enterprise." Most leading reformers who pushed through the 1854 public school law were either Baptist or Methodist. Three years after this legislation passed, the editor of the *South-Western Baptist* rejoiced at the change it had wrought. The number of pupils in public schools had nearly doubled.[98]

Nor did Alabama Baptists ignore other aspects of cultural and eco-

nomic modernization. Tuscaloosa pastor/professor Joshua Hill Foster
played a key role in organizing the Alabama Historical Society in 1850 and
served as its first secretary. Two years later, A. J. Pickett, Alabama's most
distinguished mid–nineteenth century historian, was baptized into membership of Montgomery First Baptist Church amid considerable statewide
publicity.[99]

Although ordinary Baptists were as likely to be farmers as their secular
neighbors, their denominational newspaper increasingly sided with industrial interests that sought to diversify the state's economy. Editor H. E.
Taliaferro promoted railroad construction and urged Baptists to invest in
Shelby Iron Works. One of his readers concurred in 1860, arguing that capital was necessary to develop the state's resources. He condemned political
demagogues who excited laboring class prejudices against capital.[100] As the
state perched on the edge of the Civil War, more and more citizens became
alarmed about the serious lack of industry, especially in a state with abundant natural resources.

Forces of modernization not only transformed ideas about education
and the economy but also generated debate about proper relations between
the sexes. Women had played a marginal role in pioneer Alabama churches,
often unable to speak before mixed-sex gatherings or even attend monthly
conferences. Changing attitudes after 1845 as well as financial necessity
combined to enlarge the role of women. Simply put, women were obviously
better at raising money than men. When donations proved inadequate to
build a church in Selma in 1849, women sponsored a fair to raise money.
They used the same strategy a half decade later to pay off the church debt
when the men failed to do so. Wetumpka women also bailed out their men
when they could not raise sufficient funds to rebuild the church after it
burned in 1845. Men had unsuccessfully tried to solicit donations. When
women switched to fund-raising events, they were able to complete the
rebuilding. Women in the Tuskegee church furnished the inside of their
new building in 1859 the same way. They sold items made by their sewing
societies as well as tickets to organ, violin, guitar, and piano concerts. In
Marion, the Female Benevolent Society at Siloam church provided clothes
and board for a ministerial student attending Howard College. Male Baptists often disapproved of women's money-making efforts, viewing them
as too secular. Men preferred private solicitation or assessment while
women chose more collective and social forms of fund raising. But when
men could not raise the money to build, equip, or decorate their churches
or fund missions, they did not hesitate to ask women to help. [101]

Women also played a role in revivalism, albeit a more private one. During a three-week meeting in New Bern in 1857, women conducted a prayer meeting every afternoon to which they invited their female friends. They sang and prayed, and the thirty-one baptisms that resulted from the revival more than doubled the white membership of the church.[102]

Alabama Baptists took a surprisingly enlightened view of education for women, though oftentimes with predictable reservations about the roles such education should equip women to perform. The *Alabama Baptist* frequently called attention to the importance of educating women and extolled the merits of Judson College and the East Alabama Female College. In 1853 the editor visited the latter institution, which enrolled 115 females, and praised the students' excellent recitation of mathematical rules and concepts. The editor looked forward to the time when education for women would produce enough teachers, authors, and publishers to eliminate all northern influence in the South. In 1857 the editor noted that women had long since proved their intellectual capacity in foreign languages and science. As a result they should lay aside "frivolous literature" and study languages, science, history, and classical literature (anything "worthy of the mind God has given you") so they could take their rightful intellectual place beside men.[103]

Such expansive visions of women's lives were usually qualified in one way or another. The editor of the denomination's newspaper wrote a series on education in which he deplored the frivolous courses that made women "better suited for pretty toys than for housewives." Women's schools produced too many "novel readers" and "ball-room belles" and too few housewives with "motherly skills." A woman who identified herself only as "a Baptist mother" extolled education for women and the recognition of equal intellectual capacity between the sexes. Women could rise above "mere household drudges" to become "sympathizing, understanding friends" of men. But even a woman with such compassionate concepts of gender relations rejected women as voters, officeholders, or "sitting in the president's chair." Women should exercise such influence through men and their sons.[104]

Future missionary Martha Foster wrote in 1850 that northern women were obsessed with women's rights conventions where they resolved not to submit to male rule. Such female radicalism made Foster "blush for my sex." She did not deny that women suffered discrimination. But the reform of such conditions would result from equal education opportunities. She expected such reform "as I expect the millennium." Evidence for her optimism came from the admission of a woman to a medical college in Philadelphia, an event that made her "heart swell with joy and gratitude."[105]

Other Baptists also noted differences between southern and northern women. In 1845 the editor of the *Alabama Baptist* cited a case in which a woman in the North was charged with a crime in court. In the South, "a female, who has any respect for herself, would sooner throw herself into the fire" than appear in court. "We look for the standard of morality among our females," he added, "and if it is low there, we feel that we are plunging into a depth of degradation too vile for reflection, too deep [for] utterance." In another essay, the editor condemned northern women for serving on juries and bringing suit in courts, where they would hear "sounds which should not fall upon a woman's ear." In such ways, woman (who had been intended as a check "upon man's inclination to evil") became "lost to modesty."[106]

Nonetheless, women could play a role in the reform of private and public morality. Saral A. Newson publicly criticized women for using snuff. In church discipline cases, private female conduct was more carefully monitored than male. The Big Creek church in Jefferson County (which did not allow women to speak in church) excluded a single woman for giving birth to an illegitimate child. But a search of thousands of church minutes revealed no equivalent dismissal of a single man for fathering a child out of wedlock.[107]

During the 1853 legislative sessions, Baptists launched a petition campaign in every county on behalf of prohibition. The same newspaper that urged southern women to eschew jury duty and courts, lest they be offended by vile politics, urged women to circulate temperance petitions. If there was any question of social and moral reform that was appropriate to women and on which they should be heard, the editor wrote, it was temperance.[108]

James DeVotie epitomized Victorian male ambivalence about women. In a sermon, DeVotie pronounced woman's nature to be sinful. Because she was "first in the transgression" (sinning before Adam), she suffered universal degradation in "heathen countries" where her fate revealed the importance of God's salvation. But from such poor material God had constructed a person "kindred to the holy angels." The characteristics of a redeemed woman were modesty, meekness, an even temper, cheerful spirit, patience, and benevolent works. Women occupied a sphere separate from men. The deeds of men were open to public scrutiny, but "the sphere and labor of women are measurably unseen and would be unknown were it not for their results." Women constituted a majority in churches and benevolent organizations and served courageously as missionaries. But a wife grew wise "by the discourse of her husband and the husband good

humored by the conversation of the wife." She made him amiable, he made
her esteemed, and their virtues were blended in the family.[109]

Antebellum Baptists and Race

Growing racial tensions left Alabama Baptists less ambivalent about
African Americans. Several trends accelerated after 1845. White Baptists
expressed greater commitment to the active evangelization of slaves, often
as a form of social control to make them obedient and subservient. More
black congregations requested to be allowed to worship separately from
whites. Increasing northern attacks on the morality of slavery led to the
creation of the Southern Baptist Convention. When this division did not
end sectional animosities, Alabama Baptists sought biblical and theological
justification for secession from the Union as well as from northern Baptists.

The opportunity God had provided Baptists to convert African Americans became a central justification for slavery. This fact, in turn, compelled
masters to tend to their slaves' spiritual welfare. Slavery might or might not
be a positive good, but it certainly was a spiritual opportunity. Many white
Baptists were only too aware that slavery promoted white arrogance, sexual
abuse, and needless violence. But they interpreted these conditions as
merely another burden that God had imposed upon fallen humanity. Although they did not stray far from popular white racial assumptions, they
universally accepted the unitary nature of the human race (blacks were
human and possessed immortal souls). Their expanding interest in the religious instruction of slaves between 1845 and 1860 paralleled the nationwide Protestant reform movement as well as the growth of southern nationalism. The most enlightened and reform-minded planters were the ones
most likely to express concern for their slaves' welfare and to endorse scientific agriculture, African colonization, temperance, public education, and
foreign missions. Although evangelization of slaves was part of a national,
religiously inspired reform movement, it was also carefully supervised and
motivated by a desire to maintain order and ensure a profitable utilization
of slave labor. Whereas northern evangelicals made the Bible a liberating
document of freedom, proslavery preachers turned it into a literalistic defense of human bondage. [110]

In 1846 northern-born Howard College theology professor Jesse Hartwell (writing under the pseudonym "H") penned a lengthy essay on the
religious instruction of slaves. Masters could force slaves to attend services,
he wrote, but compulsion served no useful purpose. The souls of slaves
were of infinite value to God because he was no respecter of persons. Mas-

ters and ministers bore primary responsibility for the spiritual welfare of
slaves. The reluctance of slaves to listen and respond to the gospel did not
lessen the responsibilities of whites who had enslaved them. Religious instruction must be tailored expressly for them.[111]

Apparently this admonition struck home because the 1846 state convention adopted a catechism to aid the religious education and conversion
of blacks. Prepared by A. W. Chambliss of Marion, the *Catechitical Interpreter*
was widely circulated and extensively used by Alabama Baptists. The 1847
convention augmented the catechism with a three-part plan to evangelize
blacks. The plan placed the burden of responsibility on the master, who
was urged to guarantee religious instruction to slaves even if he had to employ a missionary for that purpose. The second recommendation was that
churches should assemble blacks at least one day a month to teach the catechism, hymns, and Scripture. The third part of the plan required black
members to meet once a month for church conference to conduct their business under the direction of the pastor or some experienced white member.[112]

Unfortunately, enthusiasm for this task ebbed and flowed throughout
the antebellum period. In 1854 an essayist deplored the neglect of slaves'
spiritual welfare. The ignorance, superstition, and low morals of blacks did
not surprise him because they had few opportunities to learn. Whites devoted little care and attention to the moral education of slaves, conducted
irregular worship for them, excluded them from family devotionals, forced
slaves to care for them on Sunday, and would be held accountable for these
failures. Even those who demurred because teaching slaves to read and
write violated Alabama law could not excuse their conduct. He advised
that every association select a person to visit plantations and preach to
slaves.[113]

Such chiding had an effect. Urged on by admonitions that there was
no more laudable employment than preaching the gospel to the poor and
enslaved, many ministers responded. An 1846 revival for slaves in Marion
met every night for two weeks. The evangelist described the meetings as
emotional but orderly. Even the most "intelligent and refined" whites could
not have exceeded the propriety and comprehension of the slaves, fifty of
whom were baptized. A Mobile pastor reported similar results in Sunday
afternoon meetings for blacks.[114]

The number of black converts was a major reason for the doubling
of Baptist church membership between 1845 and 1860. In 1847 the Alabama Association had 3,573 members, 1,790 of them black. First Baptist
Montgomery, the premier church of the association, had 411 members, only

96 of them white. The second largest associational church at Mount Meigs had 297 members, only 26 of them white. In 1853 only two of the fifteen churches in the Bigbe Association had more white than black members.[115]

These successes did not result from the purest of motives. At best, white Baptists treated their black brothers and sisters paternalistically. In 1856 the Central Association passed a resolution describing the dependent relationship between master and slave as similar to the one between parent and child. Masters should take their slaves to church as they did their children "and see that they behave themselves while there, and in going to and from church . . . that their owners leave them not to their own choices, but see that each servant is decently prepared in time to go . . . or send an overseer and require a similar observance of good order and subordination, as he does with his children."[116]

At its worst, this religious concern was cynical and manipulative. When the Bethel Association (centered in the Black Belt between Demopolis and Cahawba) petitioned masters to provide for the religious education of slaves, it quoted a leading Alabamian as saying that such instruction was "the truest economy, the only efficient police, and . . . the greatest utility." Conversion of slaves reduced violence, drunkenness, and disorder and thereby added to the value of a master's property by 10 to 12 percent. In 1854 W. H. Carroll reported on a year's preaching to slaves with the permission of three owners and their overseers, resulting in forty-eight baptisms. He later headed a church committee that interviewed the overseers about changes in slave conduct. The overseers reported that slave conduct had markedly improved. Thus, masters who cared for their slaves' spiritual welfare would reap rewards in heaven (praise from God) and on earth (improved performance and efficiency by their labor force).[117]

Baptists also observed the restrictions imposed on slaves both by Alabama law and by custom. The Cahawba Association passed a resolution in 1845 appointing a missionary to preach to slaves "in cases where the owners . . . shall signify their assent and make suitable arrangements." The following year the association recommended that masters allow servants to assemble to read Scripture and pray so long as a white layman was there to supervise instruction. Pastor J. C. Wright of New Bern preached revivals for blacks on a nearby plantation only when two other whites were present to preserve "quiet or order." E. B. Teague preached a revival for slaves in 1852 but allowed only those with written permission from their owners or overseers to attend. The permission attested to the character of the slave. If a convert had a "vicious reputation," Teague delayed baptism until the person demonstrated changed conduct. Although Teague scolded whites for being too suspicious of blacks ("baring their extraordinary excitability, a thing common to all uncultivated people," he wrote, "and their inferior self-respect, they are to be relied on as much as white persons"), he accepted the restrictions placed on him by their distrust.[118]

Once persons were converted, white-black church relations followed no common pattern. Often both races were confused about the boundaries of sacred community. E. B. Teague noted in 1845 that the Eutaw church consisted of seventeen members "exclusive of some half dozen colored persons who account themselves of us, but whose relationship are not yet well determined." At the Big Springs church in Randolph County, slaves were allowed to worship with whites but were not admitted to full church membership. When a white Baptist inquired in 1851 of the denominational newspaper whether a church conference should accept the testimony of a slave against a white person, the editor replied that the testimony of "every man should be received in testimony where it is attended with proper marks of credibility." Not race but veracity, intelligence, and facts should determine the credibility of a witness. Otherwise many crimes of white men would go unreported because they often sinned only in the presence of blacks.[119]

Perhaps because of confusion over the roles of black members, perhaps because of white disapproval of black conduct in worship, perhaps because of black resentment at white paternalism and manipulation, separation of black and white Baptists became more common as the years passed. Although technically blacks remained members of a church with whites, they increasingly were likely to have separate baptisms, communions, church conferences, and worship services. Initiative for this special separation within a technically integrated congregation remains unclear. In some cases whites began it; in other cases blacks sought it. Undoubtedly, white restrictions played a part in the initiative. I. T. Tichenor recorded in his diary in November 1850 contempt for a slave minister whom he heard preach the funeral of black infants ("a most miserable pack of nonsense," Tichenor called the sermon; "I am fearful Bro. Willis does much injury by his preaching"). Three weeks later Tichenor stopped Willis from preaching and began to address the black congregation himself.[120]

Blacks no doubt resented such high-handed treatment and sought as much autonomy as whites would allow them. A writer to the denominational paper in 1857 dismissed restrictive state laws on separate slave religious meetings, arguing that if whites feared that such occasions might foment slave rebellions, then masters or overseers ought to attend slave services. Increasingly that became the norm. The New Bern church conducted a white conference once a month on Saturday morning and a black conference that afternoon. In 1844 blacks at the Wetumpka church began separate baptismal and worship services as well as separate church conferences. In 1846 the church selected a board of black deacons. Seven years later whites appointed five white men to attend black services, an inconvenience so resented by whites that they petitioned the legislature to repeal laws requiring whites to be present at slave meetings. The Tuskegee church grew weary of what white members considered excessive "noise" that slaves made in worship services and, when they occupied a new brick building in 1858, gave their old wooden structure to slaves to use for worship.[121]

The most complete definition of the limits of spatial separation can be found in the First African Church of Tuscaloosa. In 1857 the Tuscaloosa First Baptist Church voted to allow blacks separate administration of their affairs on a different day from whites. A committee of whites defined the new relationship. The black conference would meet twice a month but could not select its own leader. Whites must confirm all membership decisions made by blacks. Blacks could not teach, and any night meetings must be supervised by the white pastor or someone he designated. Any meetings of the black congregation other than the ones specifically designated would be considered illegal.[122]

By 1860 separate services had become routine however much they might strain Alabama law. A railroad manager supervising a crew of two hundred slaves building a line across eastern Alabama allowed them to hold weekly services under the supervision of a black preacher whom he called "a man of fine appearance and good sense." Whites from the Tuskegee church sometimes visited to make sure no mischief was under way, but the editor of the denominational paper considered the slaves so well treated and behaved that he recommended they collect an offering to evangelize abolitionists and "the poor, naked, starving 'free niggers' at the North." The editor also noted that slaves worshiped separately in most town and village churches.[123]

Where they worshiped separately, blacks not only preached and sang differently from whites but also contributed to different causes. They preferred to contribute to missionaries in Africa or to fellow slaves in the South. The September 1859 offering at Eufaula Baptist Church contained twelve dollars for African missions donated by "colored members."[124]

Few tasks are more difficult than unraveling the complex biracial relationship of antebellum Baptists from the viewpoint of blacks. African Americans were seldom candid and were almost always deferential to

whites. But there were clues, most of them retrospective impressions recorded during Reconstruction. Two such memories are especially revealing.

I. T. Tichenor ordained Nathan Ashby, who became the first black pastor of Montgomery's slave congregation. Considered by whites to be "pious
and good mannered," he was in fact a man of many moods. Born in Virginia in 1810, he was raised by his grandmother until he was sold to an
Alabama planter at the age of sixteen. The day he departed for Alabama,
his master told him he was only helping start horses on their way south.
Some miles away from home, he was told that he was part of the stock that
had been purchased. Knowing he would never see his beloved grandmother again, he wept bitterly until an elderly black woman comforted
him. She read his palm, predicting good fortune for him: "Don't cry, for
you are born for good luck. The man who will buy you will be more a
brother than a master," she predicted. "Fear God and be obedient, and you
will do well." Ashby took heart and stopped his weeping. After growing
up in Monroe County, he began preaching in 1845, three years after purchasing his freedom for $900. He married a free woman of color, earned a
substantial income as a carpenter and real estate dealer, and became first
pastor of the black congregation in Montgomery. He interpreted the for-
tune-teller's prediction to have been fulfilled. [125]

Charles Octavius Boothe was also born in Virginia, where he attended
a rural Baptist church in which whites and blacks "sat together to com-
mune and wash each other's feet." Sold with his mother when he was six,
they were taken to Mobile where their treatment was more harsh. A preco-
cious boy who learned to read at age three, he was drawn inexorably to the
Bible. But that book communicated to him a different message from the one
whites received:

> From the days of my earliest recollection, freedom's shadow forms moved
> before the eyes of the Southern slave. He felt . . . the touch and visage of ap-
> proaching liberty. In subdued tones it was whispered upon ears that could
> be trusted, that slavery, with all its accompanying horrors, was soon to be a
> thing of the past. Praying bands were organized and met in distant groves
> to pray for liberty. Gathered beneath the sighing trees and nightly skies,
> they whispered their agonies upon the ears of the almighty—whispered
> lowly, lest the passing winds should bear their petitions to the ears of the
> overseer or master. And often—as with Daniel and his companions in
> Babylon—the God who reveals secrets to them that love him, uncovered
> before our minds coming events, which caused us to laugh and cry. But we

kept these things in our hearts, and it was a wonder to all around that the slave could sing in his furnace of hot afflictions. God in unfolding hope, was with us in the fire, and so we were sustained.[126]

The meaning that Boothe derived from the Bible was the stuff of revolution, both violent ones like Nat Turner's and passive ones where slaves simply disrupted white worship services with emotion and noise. Even as whites sat monitoring the worship of their slaves, something incendiary and liberating was transpiring quite beyond their comprehension.

What whites did know was that meddling Yankee abolitionists (including an increasing number of their northern Baptist brethren) were openly challenging the morality of slavery. Whites could not allow this virus to reach slaves lest an epidemic of emancipation spread across the South. But stopping the idea of freedom was easier said than done. And in repelling the threat to their Christian community, they would sever themselves first from northern Baptists and then from the nation.

Northern criticism of slavery reached an unacceptable crescendo in the mid-1840s. The editor of the denomination's paper spent much of his time in 1844–1845 refuting accounts of southern brutality against slaves. Although he admitted that barbaric conduct sometimes occurred, pious slaveholders condemned such excesses. Southern churches rejected cruelty toward blacks, the traffic in African slaves, buying and selling slaves as an occupation, or separation of families by sale. They also acknowledged their duty to preach to slaves and treat them humanely.[127]

Regrettably such pronouncements carried no weight beyond moral suasion with individual masters, even Baptist ones. The family papers of A. P. Montague (a future president of Howard College) depict a complex pattern of race relations.

In 1869 Lotsey White wrote Howard Montague, an elder in an Essex County, Virginia, Baptist church, praising his kindness to her when she was his slave and a member of his church. Unfortunately, the same could not be said of his brother, Phillip. In Virginia, she had been the wife of Carter Braxton, the servant of Montague's father, who was also a Baptist preacher. When her mother died, Phillip Montague had inherited the Braxton couple and had sold the wife in 1857 to a slave trader from Huntsville. After a time in Alabama, she was sold to a Mississippi planter. Though never properly divorced from her husband in Virginia (from whom she had been forcibly separated), she remarried in Mississippi and was in 1869 a tenant farmer's wife and member of the Mount Zion Baptist Church. She was searching desperately for her relatives. Her parents had also been sold, as had her six siblings, but she had no idea where they lived. "Will you please tell me what has become of them?" she wrote pleadingly to Montague.[128]

When northerners criticized such inhumanity, the denominational editor became defensive. Northerners were hypocrites, he wrote, who allowed women to engage in conduct such as serving on juries that besmirched their purity. Northerners had once owned slaves themselves and many now lived off the proceeds of their sale. By 1845 the editor quoted Abram's reply to Lot against those who were disposed "to cast us out among the moles and the bats because we will not succumb to their whines. . . . 'Is not the whole land before thee? Separate thyself . . . from me; if thou wilt take the left hand, then I will go to the right; or if thou depart to the right hand, then I will go to the left.' "[129]

Alabama Baptists actually initiated the split in the denomination. Weary of years of conflict, the 1844 state convention took up the question of slavery. The incident that precipitated this crisis was a decision in August by the executive board of the Home Mission Society to deny the application of a Georgia slaveholder to be a missionary. Coming only months before the Alabama state convention, this egregious affront was much on the minds of delegates when they gathered for the November state convention. Basil Manly Sr. preached, urging masters to provide religious instruction to their slaves but also arguing that the Bible authorized slavery. The convention appointed a committee to implement Manly's suggestions about providing religious education to slaves. It also passed a resolution on slavery. When one party to a relationship constantly attacked the other, such conduct became disagreeable. Slave owners had contributed money to Baptist mission societies and should therefore enjoy every privilege of service. Only local churches had the right to determine the qualifications of an applicant for missionary appointment. If slaveholders were ineligible to serve, Baptists in Alabama should withhold their contributions to missions. They also sent what became known as the Alabama Resolutions to all Baptist state conventions in the slaveholding states as well as to appropriate mission societies in the North.[130]

Praise poured in from southern conventions as did criticism from the North. Moderates in both regions were swept aside. The Baptist Board of Foreign Missions based in Boston assured that slaveholders were entitled to the same privileges as nonslaveholders but refused to appoint missionaries based on church contributions. The board also vowed not to appoint a missionary who continued to own slaves because such conduct disqualified him from moral and theological fitness for mission service. If Alabama

Baptists would cooperate on these terms, fraternal relations could be maintained; "if they cannot, painful to us as will be their withdrawal, yet we shall submit to it as neither sought nor caused by us." Jesse Hartwell (president of the Alabama convention at the time) considered this reply unsatisfactory, as did many other southern state conventions.[131]

Plans began almost immediately for a meeting of Baptists in Augusta, Georgia, during May. The editor of the *Alabama Baptist* endorsed the meeting because of the northern spirit of "disunion and intoleration towards us." In April 1845 delegates from a number of churches in eastern Alabama met at Lafayette to elect five delegates to the Augusta meeting. The association also denounced the reply of the Boston board. The state designated its officers and directors as delegates, and various associations provided money for their expenses. Of the 293 accredited delegates who attended the Augusta meeting, only fourteen came from Alabama. But among those fourteen were the most distinguished Baptists of their generation: Jesse Hartwell, Basil Manly Sr., E. D. King, Daniel P. Bestor, J. H. DeVotie, Henry Talbird, A. W. Chambliss, David Lee, and Alexander Travis.[132]

Although most Alabama Baptists welcomed the creation of the SBC, a prominent member of the Eufaula church regretted the establishment of a separate southern denomination, arguing that it would waste resources, duplicate programs, and deepen sectional divisions. But his reservations were overwhelmed by enthusiasm for the new organization.[133]

Although issues of ecclesiology and theology certainly drove wedges between Baptists living in different sections of the United States, the central issue in formation of the SBC was slavery.[134] In subsequent decades Alabama Baptists insisted that slavery was only a secondary factor in the split; but their writings between 1845 and 1860 do not support this claim.

The Bible clearly authorized and sanctioned slavery, they believed. Southern slaves were the "best provided, the best ordered, and the best contented laboring population" in the world; though they were poor, the Bible recognized that the poor would always exist under any economic system. Before slavery in America, Africans had enslaved each other, and the black race was incapable of "great moral elevation."[135]

Although a number of Alabama Baptists supported the American Colonization Society (which proposed emancipation and relocation of freed slaves to Africa), even they accepted the biblical inferiority of blacks. The editor of the *Alabama Baptist* in 1850 assumed that eventually slaves would be free—but they must never be free while remaining in America "unless by some bleaching process [their] ebony hue can be transformed." God had marked slaves with their color. While not necessarily a mark of degradation

because African Americans were not naturally inferior to whites, racial differences must be preserved.[136]

The Bethel Association resolved in 1850 that the relationship of slave
to master resulted from God's providence. Calvinism explained the slave's
predicament quite well: "Why, against our will, and in spite of the earnest
protestations of our Southern colonies, was it allowed that they should be
forced upon us and placed under our control?" Obviously the answer to
this question was God's intent to convert Africans by arranging for their
enslavement.[137]

The state's denominational paper vigorously defended slavery throughout the 1850s under a variety of editors. In 1850 the editor insisted that
translators of the new revision of the Bible should make clear that "Jesus
Christ and his apostles recognized slaveholders as men of faith." Fidelity
to the word of God required such recognition. After a brief debate over comments by a Baptist who denied that God made some of his creation for the
service of others, the editor insisted that both Old and New Testaments
recognized slavery and neither denounced it: "As a question of morals, it
is between us and God—whose word does not condemn it—and as a question of political economy, it is with us alone, as free and independent
states." Samuel Henderson (Tuskegee pastor and editor of the paper during
most of the 1850s) was a proslavery Whig who regularly defended the
South during national debates over slavery. He believed slavery to be biblically ordained. He urged northern clergymen to forswear antislavery agitation, which he defined as a political issue inappropriate for ministers. But
he did not follow his own advice, defending slavery during every sectional
crisis.[138]

As sectional feelings intensified, so did the shrillness of the debate.
In 1856 an essayist for the paper blamed abolitionism on the mistaken assumption that slavery was a moral evil, a view not found in the teachings
of Christ or his apostles. Slavery, he added, was "as much an institution of
Heaven as marriage." A letter to the editor in 1860 dismissed the entire
debate equally glibly: "The best defense of slavery . . . is slavery as it is."[139]

The acrimony between northern and southern Baptists was the re-
hearsal for bitter disputes that precipitated secession in 1860. If Christians
could not maintain fellowship despite their differences, there was little
hope that sections could do so. Pulpits on both sides of the Mason-Dixon
line assumed a moralistic tone of condemnation and absence of restraint
unparalleled in American history. Churches became intensely political although they insisted that the issues before them were moral concerns about
slavery or theological disputes about the Bible. When each side insisted

that its causes were God's causes, compromise became impossible. In time, both sides came to see war as an instrument of God's chastisement. Southern preachers gained status in their interaction with planters and political leaders, with whom they shared similar world views. They helped construct conservative and hierarchical social values. They played the major role in constructing the South's defense of slavery, which they took from the Bible, not from philosophy or metaphysics. Thus, southern clergymen played a major role in formulating a secular secessionist movement, all the while denying that they acted politically.[140]

This political ideology emerged in Alabama in stages, each phase occasioned by a major sectional crisis over slavery. In 1850 the question of admitting California to the Union as a free state (thus disrupting the balance in the U.S. Senate between free and slave states) triggered the debate. Like most Alabamians that year, the editor of the *Alabama Baptist* was not yet ready for secession and used his powerful influence to rein in extremists. Secession, he warned, could not occur without civil war. Baptists should not allow "a few reckless hotspurs" to plunge the nation into war. That same month Rev. T. G. Keen spoke to Howard College literary societies warning against reckless political experiments such as secession.[141]

Four years later amid debate on the admission of Kansas and Nebraska, the editor of the denominational paper initially refused to comment on what he judged to be a political question. But when his silence was interpreted as acquiescence to attacks on southern interests, editor Samuel Henderson entered the fray with a vengeance. He denounced antislavery meetings by "noisy tribes of agitators" as threats to the Union. In 1856 he endorsed the nativist, anti-Catholic Know Nothing Party as the best way to defend southern rights and preserve the Union. He deplored secessionists among Alabama Baptists who preached Stephen A. Douglas (Democratic advocate of the rights of territories to prevent slavery) "and him damned" rather than "Christ and him crucified." He warned that ministers who embroiled themselves in politics would alienate half their parishioners. "Rest assured, brother," he admonished pastors, "your services are not needed. If the Union cannot be saved without them, we doubt very much whether it could be saved with them."[142]

John Brown's raid on Harper's Ferry in 1859 (an attempt to spark armed slave insurrection) made Baptists less certain that war could be avoided. Fanatical appeals to "higher law" undermined the Constitution and threatened mob rule, one minister wrote. "Crackbrained abolitionists" were fomenting treason, and many northern churches obviously supported Brown. "Great God!" Samuel Henderson wrote in the *South-Western Baptist*,

"What must be the complexion of that Christianity which can canonize as saints and crown as martyrs, those who sought to butcher millions of their fellow citizens?"[143]

By 1860 Alabama Baptists were reconciled to secession. They scolded Milo Jewett, once so beloved as president at Judson College. President of Vassar College in New York in 1860, Jewett had called the secessionist speech of a southern congressman a "treasonable harangue." The editor of the *South-Western Baptist* accused Jewett of accumulating a considerable estate from slave labor, then changing his tune when he moved north. As the country confronted an unprecedented crisis, the editor urged that all Christians extend forbearance toward those with whom they differed politically. Southerners should also forget former theological disagreements over Landmarkism and consider only their duties as southerners.[144]

The election of Abraham Lincoln as president in November 1860 precipitated the final crisis. The state convention met at Tuskegee days after the election and urged a day of fasting and prayer. But most Alabama Baptists preferred a more political reaction. "W. R. G." urged the editor of the state journal to "turn your paper politician in some degree" because "not one in fifty cares to read about revivals now. I want to hear you talk coolly about our governmental affairs." The editor gave his constituency what they requested, one editorial after another about the inevitability of secession. He called for state secession conventions before Lincoln took office in March 1861.[145]

When Alabama's secession convention met in January 1861, Baptists played a key role. Baptist Congressman J. L. M. Curry (who had long advocated secession despite the misgivings of most of the counties he represented) resigned from Congress in January. Basil Manly Sr., also a devout secessionist, helped Curry write Alabama's Confederate Constitution. Curry, an active member of the Talladega Baptist Church, was then elected to the new Confederate Congress. James DeVotie voted for secession as well. Tuskegee pastor and longtime editor of the *South-Western Baptist*, Samuel Henderson, was elected as delegate from Macon County to the state secession convention.[146]

Once secession was accomplished, Baptists justified their course in familiar ways. Samuel Henderson turned to the Bible. As Jeroboam and the ten tribes of Israel had rebelled against Rehoboam, so must the South withdraw from the Union. States' rights and southern honor demanded such action because the North proposed a government of "mere majorities" while the South stood for limits and restraints on tyrannical majorities. The Calvinist editor of the *South-Western Baptist* cited God's providence.

Southerners must not quarrel with God's plan for them but act like men, lead the rebellion, and leave the result to God. The American Revolution, he misinterpreted, had produced American Christianity, and this new crisis, like a refiner's fire, would purify it. Nothing so thoroughly developed Christian character, he believed, as adversity. If war came, he predicted, it would pit labor against capital in the North and would be fought on northern soil. A northern invasion of the South was "a simple absurdity. It is the wildest chimera that ever floated in the brain of a modern Don Quixote." "If God be for us," he concluded confidently, "who can be against us?"[147]

4

War and Reunion,
1860–1874

*"He has put a bitter cup to our lips
and he has said we shall drink it."*

hen Basil Manly Sr. began to write a resolution for the 1860 Alabama Baptist State Convention, he mobilized in new ways words previously devoted to God. Manly was more than just a Baptist preacher, state evangelist, and former university president. He was also a man, and a southern man at that. Born into a society that valued personal honor above other traits, he shared the aggressive, manly virtues of his region. His father had served as an officer in the Revolutionary War. Manly defended slavery and states' rights. He despised Abraham Lincoln and the Republican Party.

The words flowed easily as he wrote. Alabama Baptists were subject to "the call of proper authority in defense of the sovereignty and independence of the state of Alabama, and of her sacred right as a sovereignty to withdraw from this union, and to make any arrangement which her people ... may deem best for securing their rights. And in this declaration we are heartily, deliberately, unanimously and solemnly united."[1]

Like resolutions passed by subsequent state Baptist conventions, this one seems to have originated more in the temporal realm of Alabama politics than in the kingdom of God. Attributing heavenly authority to the schemes of men was yet another evidence of the inextricable mixture of Christ and culture.

Perhaps had Manly been a bit younger (he was sixty-two when he penned these words), he would have marched off to war himself. As it was, he did what he could for the cause of southern independence. He ran unsuccessfully for a seat in the Alabama legislature as a secessionist. When his pastor resigned to become a Confederate chaplain, Manly took his place as pastor of Montgomery's influential First Baptist Church. He served as chaplain to the first Confederate Congress, which met in Montgomery, and offered the inaugural prayer when Jefferson Davis was installed as president of the Confederacy.[2] So active was he in secular affairs that he was dubbed "Chaplain of the Confederacy."

Not long after war began, Manly preached one of the most famous sermons of the era, "The Purpose of Calamities." Addressing the question raised by Judges 6:13 ("If the Lord be with us why then is all this befallen us?"), Manly employed his Calvinist theology to argue that the people of God were not exempt from the calamities of history. Faced with the inexorable will of God, Christians had only two options: submit or oppose. If the grand experiment of secession failed, Southerners would fall prey to their enemies and "know the bitter meaning of that sentence: 'they that hated us rode over us.' "[3]

As news from the front turned "dark and uncertain," Manly wrote in his diary that "we are to glorify God in the fires." When his son Richard Fuller marched off to war, Manly prayed for the boy's safety. And when Richard disappeared briefly following the Battle of Petersburg, Manly was distraught ("I am trying not to dishonor God by distrust").[4]

The emotional cycles experienced by Basil Manly Sr. between 1860 and 1865 were typical of the theological roller coaster experienced by most Alabama Baptists. The war began with high resolve and firm confidence in the providence of God to provide military victory. As bloody fighting continued year after year, grim despair replaced giddy enthusiasm, and Alabama Baptists struggled to find the theological meaning of such terrible events. The collapse of the Confederacy spelled the doom of their political hopes. But the theological edifice they erected helped define a distinctive form of Christianity that increasingly diverged from American religion and formed the underpinning of regional southern civilization.

Establishing a New Nation

In the vast new endeavor of sustaining southern nationalism, the first task was mobilization. Southern armies were outnumbered and outgunned, poorly equipped and underpaid. Baptist ministers helped as they

could, first by urging males to enlist and women to sacrifice, then by joining themselves. Shortly after the First Battle of Manassas, the editor of the
South-Western Baptist urged every man who could be spared to enlist in the
army. Other citizens should help organize companies, contribute money,
and pray for the success of southern armies. When Federal troops invaded
the Tennessee Valley, the editor urged women to "aid in rousing up the fires
of patriotism" until the "Goths" were driven from Alabama soil. Alabama
women, the editor wrote, had "no smiles for cowards and drones. If there
is one form of humanity on earth that a noble hearted woman detests . . . ,
it is the man who can, but will not go, to measure arms with a foe that seeks
our ruin." As word of Union depredations spread, the editor wondered if
fellow citizens were "white livered and craven-hearted."[5]

Editor Samuel Henderson not only utilized the pages of his paper to
recruit Confederate manpower but also used his Tuskegee pulpit. In Fast
Day sermons to his congregation, he justified the South's cause. In mass
rallies, he helped raise twelve regiments for the Confederate army.[6]

Others worked equally hard on behalf of the new nation. Rev. I. U.
Wilkes (who pastored a number of quarter-time churches in Perry County)
conducted a special service at the Fellowship church near Plantersville
to present the Brooks Light Infantry with Bibles, blankets, uniforms, flags,
and other provisions. He had baptized many of the men who had enlisted.[7]
Rev. George L. Lee from Conecuh County helped organize the Percy
Walker Rangers from Conecuh and Monroe Counties, a unit in which his
son served. He admonished them: "I want you to do noble deeds—deeds
that will never be forgotten in time or eternity—deeds that will be published in history, and from the judgment seat of Christ—deeds that will
bring glory to God, honor to Christ, happiness to man, confusion to devils,
and to all of old Abe's fanatics, and eternal credit and honor to yourselves."
If male honor was insufficient incentive to bravery, there was always female
admiration, for southern girls waited to marry military heroes.[8]

When the tide of war turned against the South, George Lee did not
despair. In a New Year's greeting to soldiers in 1864, he admonished them
not to become discouraged. God was on their side. If every soldier did his
duty and fought valiantly, there would soon be "a great shaking among the
hosts of . . . enemies, a trembling will seize them and they will flee before
thee." When the enemy did not flee, as at Shiloh, his son could still write
his father with confidence that God had heard their prayers and spared his
life. "My trust is in God," the boy wrote from the battlefield. Finally, in
December 1864, George Lee joined the Confederate army himself.[9]

Lee's decision to join the army was a popular one. Beginning in the summer of 1861, Virginia Baptists began colportage work, preaching and distributing tracts and Bibles in the camps of the Army of Northern Virginia. As the daunting task overwhelmed their resources, Virginia Baptists requested assistance from other states. Montgomery's First Baptist Church took the lead in Alabama, raising money for tracts, Bibles, and religious books and urging other churches to help. Pleas also came from officers, complaining that their regiments had only short-term volunteer chaplains or, in some cases, no chaplains at all. They shamed churches by writing that soldiers deserved full-time chaplains to share their sacrifices and hardships.[10]

Such entreaties were hard to resist, and Baptist ministers joined the army in droves. When H. E. Taliaferro visited Auburn in August 1861 to observe the training of fifteen companies (1,500 men), he discovered that six of the company commanders were Baptists, two of them being preachers. Several lieutenants were also Baptist ministers. Not only did they serve as officers but on Sunday they conducted preaching services. The pastor of Auburn First Baptist Church received a visit from three Methodist soldiers who had converted a comrade. They desired him to baptize the new Christians (presumably by full immersion) in a nearby creek.[11]

Soon pulpits across the state stood deserted as pastors flocked to the Confederate standard. James Boardman Hawthorne (son of legendary Wilcox County Baptist preacher Kedar Hawthorne) was a Howard College graduate and minister who resigned his Mobile pastorate to serve as chaplain of the Twenty-fourth Alabama Infantry Regiment. Washington B. Crumpton (who after the war pastored in Dallas County, headed the Alabama Anti-Saloon League, and served for twenty-five years as state convention secretary) enlisted in the Thirty-seventh Mississippi Regiment, was elected lieutenant late in the war, and was wounded at Vicksburg, Nashville, and Atlanta. Howard College president Henry Talbird, though elderly and in poor health, volunteered. He served as colonel of the Forty-first Alabama Regiment during four fierce battles before poor health forced him to resume academic duties.[12]

Although these pastors survived the war, others were not so lucky. John J. Bullington, a popular pastor and moderator of the Coosa River Association, joined the Thirty-first Alabama Regiment and died of disease in January 1865. Although James Harvey DeVotie refused a chaplain's commission in the army because he believed government pay for a minister was a violation of separation of church and state, his son Noble disagreed on this point. Noble L. DeVotie had attended Howard College two years, then graduated first in his class at the University of Alabama. After three years of study at Princeton Theological Seminary, he returned to Alabama as pastor of Selma First Baptist Church. So many young men in his congregation volunteered that he agreed to serve as their chaplain. His service ended tragically at Fort Morgan, where he fell off a wharf one evening and was swept into Mobile Bay by a strong tide and drowned.[13]

Such tragedies reverberated across the denomination. The 1863 Carey Association report listed twenty-nine deaths of Baptists from wounds or disease while in Confederate service.[14] The editor of the *South-Western Baptist* estimated that at least half the state's active Baptist pastors were in the Confederate army by April 1862. Vast numbers of churches had suspended preaching services. The editor reminded readers of the spiritual gifts described in Romans 12 to indicate the importance of teachers and exhorters in the primitive church. Someone in every church was capable of reading and expounding the word of God and of exhorting members to love each other and engage in good works. Though not ordained, such persons could ensure that Sunday schools continued to meet and that congregations gathered at appointed times for Bible reading, prayer, and singing.[15]

Of the pastors who served the Confederacy, two became legends. When the war began, I. T. Tichenor pastored Montgomery's First Baptist Church, the home congregation of numerous Alabama and Confederate government officials. When many of his members enlisted in the Seventeenth Alabama Regiment, Tichenor joined them as regimental chaplain. Commanded by Colonel Thomas H. Watts (a future Alabama governor), the regiment was assigned first to Pensacola, then to Corinth, Mississippi. While protecting the strategic railroad town of Corinth, the regiment joined other units moving north to intercept Union troops at a landing on the Tennessee River near Shiloh church. When the Seventeenth entered combat on April 6, 1862, it came under withering cross fire that quickly killed or wounded a third of its troops. Tichenor, though slightly wounded himself, took off his hat and waved it in the air while walking up and down the line preaching to his comrades. He reminded them that it was Sunday morning, and at that very hour back in Alabama their families and friends were praying for them. "I called upon them to stand there and die, if need be, for their country," Tichenor recalled in a letter. "The effect was evident. . . . They piled that ground with Yankees slain." Borrowing a weapon, Tichenor functioned as a sharpshooter, reportedly killing a colonel, captain, and four privates with deadly fire. Nor did he express any remorse, boasting that he was fully satisfied with his "labors as chaplain of the 17th," feeling in his heart that "in no other position could I have served the cause of my God or my country so well." The editor of the *South-Western*

Baptist concurred in that estimate: "More than one Federal officer fell under the crack of his rifle. We thank God for such a man."[16]

John Jefferson Deyampert Renfroe earned his fame in less bloody fashion. When the war began, his younger brother, N. D. Renfroe, resigned his pastorate in Jacksonville and joined the Fifth Alabama as a private. While serving in A. P. Hill's division in Virginia, he wrote his brother that it was his "duty to bear a little hardness as a good soldier of Jesus Christ" for the sake of his country's freedom and his religion.[17] In December 1862 N. D. Renfroe was killed in action. Four months after preaching a memorial sermon for his brother in Calhoun County, J. J. D. Renfroe arrived in Fredericksburg, Virginia, to assume the chaplain's duties in the Tenth Alabama (also called Wilcox's Brigade). When he resigned his Talladega church, several members spoke against his leaving. But "three of the sisters" carried the day by remarking that while they esteemed their pastor as highly as anyone, they would cheerfully surrender him to an army in which their sons served (subsequently Renfroe converted two of the three sons and restored the third to church fellowship). From Virginia, Renfroe urged his replacement at the Talladega Baptist Church (J. B. Mays) to come and help preach revivals. Mays at first demurred, explaining that he had never been able to preach simply enough that Negroes and poor whites could understand him. Renfroe brushed aside such excuses, explaining that Wilcox's Brigade included some of the smartest men in Alabama. Mays would have more trouble rising to the intellectual level of his congregation than preaching "down to it."[18]

Renfroe's invitation to Mays came during the great revivals that swept the Confederate army in 1863–1864. There are various sociological explanations for this season of revival. Many of the soldiers were mere teenagers, isolated from their families for the first time and constantly facing death. The revivals began late in the war, after a series of Confederate defeats and heavy casualties. Many soldiers became convinced they would soon be killed. The tedium of camp life, the psychological stress of combat, the unnerving bloodshed of the world's first "modern war" all combined to create a hospitable environment for an outburst of religious fervor. Officers who were initially hostile or indifferent to the religious nurture of their troops became more encouraging as the war dragged on.[19] As soldiers witnessed full-time chaplains sharing their hardships, their respect increased. Although such explanations are useful, they do not fully account for the revivals. For instance, the revivals raged most fiercely through the Army of Virginia and had little impact on northern armies. Whatever the explanation, a spirit of revival swept through the Army of Northern Virginia. A

May 1863 outbreak in the Forty-first Alabama (Henry Talbird's regiment) left Rev. J. G. Nash insufficient time to preach, trying as he did to balance the revival with his regular duties as a Confederate officer.

Renfroe directed the 1863 revival in his own regiment as well as in others bivouacked at Orange Court House near Fredericksburg. During six weeks of rest after the Battles of Chancellorsville and Gettysburg, he preached several times a day. After soldiers read their Bibles, witnessed to each other, and conducted prayer meetings, Renfroe stood at night before what seemed to him a solid acre of men. Sometimes five or six hundred at a time asked him to pray for their salvation. Never before had he experienced such evidence of genuine penitence.[20]

William C. Jordan (son of a Macon County farmer) was a devout Baptist layman and the color sergeant for the Fifteenth Alabama Regiment stationed at Petersburg in 1863. His brigade had no preacher, so he hunted up Renfroe. Despite the five-mile walk to the camp of the Fifteenth Alabama, Renfroe accompanied Jordan and spent several days preaching to the troops. One evening Jordan was awakened by Captain Noah Feagin, who asked Jordan to pray for him. Jordan knelt with him in a ditch and did "the best I could, at the same time feeling very unworthy, and feeling that he was leaning on a very weak rod, but I did my duty the best I could." Two weeks later Feagin went on furlough, joined the church, and was baptized. For those converted by Renfroe's sermons, baptism was a bit more uncomfortable. Jordan and Renfroe broke the ice on a pond and baptized converts in the middle of a swamp.[21]

The chaplain of a Texas regiment who assisted Renfroe during a three-week revival for the Tenth Alabama reported that his friend was exhausted from continuous preaching. But never before had he seen such attention. Throngs of men stood or sat perfectly silent, listening intently to every word Renfroe spoke. Some nights 150 to 200 men asked for prayer. He counted at least seventy-five conversions, and many men came to him trembling and weeping.[22]

Renfroe preached from manuscripts and described the scenes in rich detail. During the six-week revival near Orange Court House after the retreat from Gettysburg, he described the regiment's encampment in an oak grove. Soldiers cut logs for slab seats that were soon filled by the crowds. They used a section of a tree for his pulpit. He preached twice, once in the daytime and again at night. At night, fire stands bathed the pulpit in an eerily incandescent light. Conversions sometimes numbered 150 to 200 at a service, many of them men who were soon killed in action. On one occasion twenty or so of his new converts asked to be baptized as Methodists, so he asked a preacher of that denomination to baptize them. After the sprinkling, the grateful Methodist minister asked Renfroe to pray that they might not backslide into a life of sin. Renfroe, who had been one of J. R. Graves's Landmarkers before the war, had grown more tolerant of other denominations while in the army. But such a request strained even his newfound tolerance. He must somehow utter a prayer celebrating a form of baptism he did not accept (sprinkling) and a theological concept (backsliding) that was anathema to him. Fellow Baptists who attended the baptism and heard his prayer later joked that it "skirmished around in such a way that it did not endorse much of anything."[23]

John Jefferson Deyampert Renfroe, much beloved Confederate chaplain, was pastor of Talladega First Baptist and Southside Baptist in Birmingham. (Courtesy of Samford University Archives)

Early in his chaplaincy, Renfroe's sermons tended to focus on the moral failings of soldiers. To soldiers' persistent complaints about inadequate pay (which they sometimes used to justify theft of property), Renfroe admonished them to be content with their wages. To engage in violence or theft against unarmed civilians as they passed through northern territory was "cowardly and unmanly." The Confederate government was doing its best to pay them an adequate salary, and many soldiers spent their money unwisely. Though he condemned soldiers for stealing pigs, sheep, and horses, he also castigated a Confederate major whom he had seen strike a soldier with his sword (he had never seen the major perform well in combat despite his hard discipline of soldiers). Although Renfroe attributed a similar sermon entitled "The Sin of Stealing" to the sight of soldiers stealing apple butter and cherries in Pennsylvania on their way to Gettysburg, Colonel W. H. Forney (the commander of the Tenth Alabama and later a U.S. congressman from Alabama) joked that what really inspired the sermon was the theft of Renfroe's rations.[24]

After Gettysburg, Renfroe's sermons turned to more cosmic questions. He left a detailed context for one of his sermons, "Royal Business Demands Haste," which he preached just after General A. P. Hill's division (to which the Tenth Alabama was attached) had raided Federal transportation lines near Manassas in the fall of 1863. Hardly had his regiment returned to camp than Renfroe heard Union train whistles on the hastily repaired tracks. For the first time, Renfroe thought to himself (though he told no one else): "What's the use to try it any longer?"[25]

In a sermon preached to his regiment on a Fast Day in August 1863, Renfroe traced war to the "unholy passions of men." War was "a satire upon civilization, a legalized and scientific artifice for the destruction of human life on a mammoth scale." Yet the Bible recounted just wars, and such was their cause. From a human standpoint, their cause seemed lost. But battles went to the righteous, not to the strong. He railed against civilian "speculators, blood-suckers, shylocks, deserters and Tories," who preyed on the poor and undermined Confederate morale. Rich men wagered their property on the outcome of the war, but poor men who owned no slaves wagered the freedom of their children. So the poor had more at stake in maintaining the institution of slavery than the man who owned five hundred slaves. Abolish slavery and the sons of poor whites would take their places as "carriage drivers, body-servants, waiting maids and tenants of the rich." In a sermon that was amazingly prescient, he warned that if the war was lost, the rich would convert their capital to land and force poor whites into tenancy. He urged soldiers to contemplate their offspring a few generations later, "grinding in a factory, scouring a tavern, tilling the soil of the wealthy, and blacking the boots of a dandy," and then "tell me whether the poor have anything to fight for." Contemplate equality with a black man "and then tell me if this is not pre-eminently a poor man's war." Color was the only distinction of classes so long as slavery existed. But economic differences would determine their status if the Confederacy lost. In the South, the wealthy had failed to establish "a controlling aristocracy." In many communities, poor men were as respected as wealthy ones. That was not true in free states where social status was determined by "the weight of the purse." Only in the South had society avoided "free-labor fanaticism" with its class divisions among whites.[26] The sermon was a brilliant exposition of the aristocratic argument for white solidarity against the invading hordes who threatened not only slavery but southern white folkways as well.

A series of Renfroe's sermons attributed the war and particularly southern reverses to sin. God was angry with his people. They had rebelled against him, and their sinful state led to war. Some argued that a merciful God could not be responsible for war or the outcome of battles. The Bible taught otherwise. War occurred according to "the providence of God while

ungodly men are the agents of its accomplishment." God used war to punish evildoers, chastise the wicked, and purge national sins: "He has put a
bitter cup to our lips and he has said we shall drink it." But pure religion
also had a social dimension. Southerners had "woefully neglected" widows
and orphans, the distressed, poor, afflicted, all "objects of our Redeemer's
increasing attention." Southerners must supply temporal as well as spiritual needs of the people.[27]

As the war neared an end and a "great depression" settled over the
army, Renfroe wrote that nearly every man believed he would die. They had
seen so much carnage, so many friends killed and wounded, had received
such numbing bad news from families, were so exhausted by General U. S.
Grant's unrelenting campaign in the Wilderness, that prayer meetings were
held in trenches while soldiers were under bombardment. The people began to murmur, as the Jews had once complained against Moses. After the
brilliant successes of 1861 and 1862 "comes the dark night." The Confederacy had crossed "the sea to freedom only to enter an endless wilderness of
despair." But it was in such ways, he told his weary comrades, that "God
would train Israel up to difficulties." If there was no solace in this world,
then soldiers must seek their vindication in the world to come. Over and
over he preached a sermon on "Heaven" first delivered at the death of his
brother in December 1862. Hell, he reminded them, was as infinitely miserable as heaven was joyous: "Therefore, sinner, turn from the depravity of
your nature and from the evil to come and set your affections upon things
above."[28]

Renfroe's reminiscences of the war dominated the remaining years of
his life. He believed that most converts from his revivals remained true to
their faith, and he illustrated his belief with accounts of men from Wilcox's
Brigade who joined his church in Talladega after the war and served faithfully until their deaths. Indeed, it seems likely that the dramatic church
growth of the late nineteenth century owes much to these conversions.
Many pastors such as William Carey Bledsoe of the East Liberty Association were converted while serving in Virginia during 1863 and 1864.[29]

So compelling were these events for Renfroe that he wrote them into
a manuscript entitled "Campaigns of a Confederate Chaplain." Though
never published, his accounts were riveting. For rapt congregations he
recalled standing on a hill overlooking the wheat fields at Gettysburg
and watching Pickett's division disappear into the smoke of battle. He recounted a sumptuous meal of goose, a lunch interrupted when his brigade
was ordered into action at Petersburg. Two hours after their meal together,
several of his officer companions were struck down in heavy fighting. Be-

fore attending their funeral, he visited wounded Union prisoners of war, some of whom corresponded with him for years after the war ended.[30]

Trying to make sense of these events after the war, Renfroe concluded that the Confederacy lost because of collapsing civilian morale. Newspapers and governors attacked Jefferson Davis and the generals he appointed. Soldiers returned from furloughs with horrible tales of the suffering of their families resulting from the exploitation and neglect of the wealthy. Discouraging letters from wives, mothers, sisters, and daughters begged men to come home. Most women (including his own wife) managed their farms courageously.[31] But other civilians, lacking his family's good fortune or hard work, undermined morale by accounts of their own suffering.

Not all Baptists rendered their service in the army. A surprisingly large number held important political posts. Until his defeat by a peace candidate in 1863, J. L. M. Curry served in the Confederate Congress where he was elected speaker pro tempore of the House of Representatives. After his defeat, he joined the Confederate army as a judicial officer, and he often preached to troops during the Atlanta campaign. Late in the war, he participated in the Battle of Selma and hid in a swamp near the Alabama River when Federal troops overran Confederate defenses. His wife died in April 1865 while he was in service. In 1861, 1862, 1864, and 1865 fellow Baptists elected him president of the state convention, and six months after the end of the war they chose him president of Howard College. One of Curry's colleagues in the Confederate Congress was William P. Chilton, a Baptist deacon from Montgomery. John Gill Shorter, also a deacon, who had served Eufaula First Baptist Church faithfully, presided as governor of Alabama from 1861 until his defeat in 1863. George E. Brewer, pastor of Wetumpka First Baptist Church, served as a member of both houses of the Alabama legislature between 1859 and 1863 before joining a Coosa County infantry company.[32]

The Home Front

For more than a decade before 1861, Alabama Baptists had mobilized for secession. Once the act was accomplished, it was only reasonable for them to help construct a theological foundation for southern nationalism. Confederate nationalism drew almost equally on three intellectual traditions: evangelical Christianity and republican traditions of states' rights and individualism.[33] Clergymen played a key role in the Confederate experiment by endorsing republican traditions, proclaiming God's special providence for the South, defending slavery, demanding justice in the administration of Confederate policy, cleansing the South of sin in order to strengthen its moral standing before God, beseeching God's help through regionwide Fast Days, and providing theological meaning to military defeats.

Hardly had Lincoln been elected president than the editor of the *Baptist Correspondent* (a newly established paper in Marion) made his position clear. Southern rights should be maintained within the Union if possible. But Union or no Union, the rights of the South were paramount. Although he denied any intent to make his paper a political journal, few issues failed to discuss politics. The February 27 edition, for instance, reprinted on the front page the provisional constitution of the Confederate States of America.[34]

The editor of the *South-Western Baptist* disagreed with the Landmark theology espoused by the new denominational paper but not with its southern nationalism. In January 1861 he urged the creation of two confederacies, one slave and the other free, that would compete for supremacy of the American continent. Like his colleague across the state in Marion, the Tuskegee editor insisted that his paper was not a political journal. But comment on politics was not inconsistent with religion. Denying that slavery was the only issue involved in secession, he focused on unfair northern-imposed tariffs and differing theories of government. The North preferred democratic institutions governed by majority vote. The South favored republican institutions intended to limit unrestrained majorities. Better one tyrant, the editor wrote, than eighteen million. The Confederacy sought only liberty and independence and to defend itself. The Union sought to confiscate the property of the South in an offensive war. God himself had implanted the South's values of honor, justice, and equality among whites and would not allow those values to perish. The editor also urged readers to support their own newspapers, magazines, books, and publishing companies.[35]

After denying that slavery was the sole reason for secession, the *South-Western Baptist* spent considerable time and space defending slavery. Calvinism furnished a hospitable theology to justify slavery. Nowhere had slaves so prospered as in the South. Even their own efforts in Africa had not elevated the race to a level equal to their condition under slavery. Southern whites understood "negro character" better than other Americans and were therefore better teachers of Christianity to Negroes. Four million "heathen" had been "thrown on" the South as a "burden of God's providence." As descendants of Ham in Africa, they were the most morally, socially, and physically degraded of all peoples ("Not a solitary change, except for the worse, appears to have passed over this miserable people for three or four thousand years"). God's providence had ordained that blacks be servants. Only as blacks accepted the condition of servitude "to which an allwise Creator has decreed them" could they prosper. Equality of the races was not only a practical absurdity, it was also a violation of the Bible (especially Genesis 9:27).[36]

Hatred was not too strong a word for Baptist attitudes toward northerners. When Abraham Lincoln issued the Emancipation Proclamation, the *South-Western Baptist* condemned it as "another proclamation from King Abraham," the "Washington despot." Contending that emancipation was intended to inspire slave rebellion and the butchery of southern women and children, the editor defined northern war policy as atheistic. When Federal troops invaded the Tennessee Valley, they occupied the plantations of Rev. R. H. Taliaferro, brother of the former editor of the paper, and his son-in-law. They allegedly forced his daughter to cook for Union troops and refused her requests to allow slaves to assist her. It was in the context of such events that Basil Manly Sr. preached to the 1863 Southern Baptist Convention in Augusta. He declared that he never wanted to see his northern brethren again until the righteous of both countries, purified from sin, met in heaven. "I may be called on to bury my son in the struggle," he concluded. "I may be compelled to see the sanctity of my home violated. . . . I myself may be imprisoned, tortured or put to death. Be it so, be it not, I accept all before I will wear the yoke which our enemies are seeking to impose [on] us."[37]

Such belligerence was essential to the mobilization of a Christian population to wage total war. Resort to arms for purposes of defense or to repel invasions was "perfectly consistent with Christian character and duty," the denomination's paper explained. "The question for the Christian soldier . . . is not whether it is his duty to kill his fellow man—but . . . whether the law of self-preservation, the highest interests of society and government—nay, the law of God, do not all unite in commanding him to fight for his brethren, his sons and daughters, his wife and his house." If "the invader should fall in such a contest as this, on whom does the blame rest? He took his own life!"[38] Such theology explains I. T. Tichenor's careful accounting of his kills at Shiloh and the glorification of such actions in Christian journals.

How could Christians doubt the outcome of such holy war? They had not provoked it. They fought in defense of their homes and property. On the other side was an army of "foreign mercenaries, incited only by the lust of plunder." Such a "rabble soldiery" could not conquer ten million proud, free people, even if they were outnumbered three or four to one. The North had repudiated "the God of the Bible" and invented an "anti-slavery God" and an "anti-slavery Bible." Yankees had appealed to the sword, and they would perish by it. The editor "never had the least misgivings as to the final result of this great revolution."[39]

Doubts came soon enough. As more and more soldiers died and defeats piled up, Alabama Baptists contemplated their sins. Responding to periodic calls by Jefferson Davis for Fast Days when all ministers should urge repentance from sins and moral cleansing, pastors renewed their sense of special destiny. In June 1861 Samuel Henderson told his Tuskegee congregation that they must humble themselves before God and repent. The rest of his sermon was a tirade against the doctrine of racial equality. A year later he observed another day of prayer for the Confederacy, this time warning his hearers that without the consolation of religion the war would bring only despair. Fast Days seem to have been universally observed in Baptist churches no matter how small or rural.[40]

As Fast Day observances make clear, theology underwent subtle changes as the war proceeded. At first convinced of the absolute righteousness of their cause, Alabama Baptists engaged in little self-doubt or internal criticism. That perception slowly changed as casualties mounted.

Even at the beginning of the conflict, some Baptists were troubled by the overidentification of Christianity with the Confederacy. To proposals that the cross become the official Confederate flag, the editor of the state Baptist paper objected on the grounds that such a symbol confused religion with politics. Christ's kingdom was "not of this world." Despite his enthusiastic defense of a Christian's right to take life in wartime, he could not bring himself to place southern armies under a Christian banner. After all, the biblical ideal was that nation would not lift up sword against nation. Even though he defended slavery, the editor rejoiced that Alabama and other Confederate states had rejected reopening the "iniquitous" slave trade from Africa. Although he furiously attacked the Emancipation Proclamation for its encouragement of servile insurrection, the editor also rejected extremist southern proposals to kill Union POWs if any butchery of white women and children occurred.[41]

Later the paper condemned various forms of greed and avarice among southerners. Following a series of military defeats in 1862, the editor blasted Confederate congressmen for spending too much time debating their own salaries and too little on saving the South from despotism.[42]

The editor applauded congressional decisions to tax wealthy southerners to fund the war as well as fair conscription laws. Property taxes constituted the most reasonable taxation and should exempt the poor. The passage of a draft law would equalize the burden of waging war. An all-volunteer army had denuded the male population of some parts of Alabama and left others largely untouched. When the Confederate Congress repealed a law allowing wealthy men to hire substitutes for them, the editor praised the law as just.[43]

It was the suffering of the poor that most concerned Alabama Baptists. Federal occupation of the Tennessee Valley, severe drought, taxes on crops, the loss of farm animals, and the absence of all able-bodied white men from many small farms combined to plunge much of Alabama's population into near starvation during 1863. The state Baptist paper urged farmers to plant corn and raise hogs, cattle, mules, and horses in order to feed the population. He denounced those who insisted on growing cotton as interested only in their own gain.[44]

One angry Baptist denounced Alabamians for neglecting the poor. Mechanics had been drafted from their jobs with pledges that those left behind would care for their families. Yet most farmers were speculating on their crops, driving up prices, and depriving poor families of food. While mechanics served in the trenches "to keep the Yanks from getting the property of this heartless speculator," he exploited the "laboring classes." No poor soldier could feed a family on a private's pay of eleven dollars a month. If planters were not willing to sacrifice their cotton profits to feed the families of poor soldiers, the angry Baptist wrote, then the Confederate government should draft crop speculators into the army. A week after running this letter, the editor of the state paper recounted being in the home of a church member when a woman appeared. She had ridden fifteen or twenty miles seeking bread for her children. Her husband was in the army, and though she lived in a wealthy community, the cheapest corn sold for two dollars a bushel. "Now, this is wrong," the editor wrote, "grievously wrong." A week later, the editor warned that the fierce patriotism of the first two years of the war was being extinguished by greed and exploitation. A common spirit of sacrifice had propelled southern armies to victory, but then "this cursed love of money seized our people and what is the result?" Disaster and defeat. Perhaps the solution was a state tax to raise money from wealthy counties in order to feed people in poor ones. The state legislature should also fix the prices of corn, bacon, salt, and other essentials and limit cotton production to individual family consumption. Otherwise, treason and avarice would undermine the Confederacy.[45]

J. J. D. Renfroe confirmed these sentiments in a report from the front. He recalled walking across the Gettysburg battlefield with litter bearers after the fighting ceased. As they picked up the wounded, the most pathetic soldiers were the poor ones who, while dying, worried about what would become of their destitute children.[46] One solution to this problem was offered at the 1863 state convention when delegates passed a resolution endorsing a Baptist orphanage. Various churches and associations endorsed the idea and began raising money for the Orphan Asylum of Alabama.[47]

Catastrophes such as drought and military defeat raised troubling theological questions. If Robert E. Lee's defeat of George McClellan's huge army in the 1862 Peninsula campaign reminded Alabama Baptists of Judah's victory over the vast Assyrian army of Sennacherib, how were they to explain the fall of Vicksburg, Nashville, and Atlanta or bloody defeats at Gettysburg and Franklin, Tennessee?[48] How could individuals explain personal tragedies like the one that befell William Jordan, a Baptist farmer from Macon County? When Jordan left home after a furlough, he kissed his beloved only son, a two-year-old not yet awake. Weeks later on his way to Gettysburg, he received a letter from his wife describing the death of his son from measles. "It completely unhinged and wilted me for about three days," Jordan wrote, but "finally I became submissive to it, as it seemed I was rebelling against God." He reasoned that perhaps the boy would have caused a great deal of trouble had he lived and thus "all things work together for good for those who love God . . . , and these afflictions work out for us a far more exceeding and eternal weight of glory."[49]

The editor of the *South-Western Baptist* also adjusted his theology to events. Early in the war with southern armies on the offensive, he believed a northern victory to be "simply impossible" unless the South surrendered the moral high ground by a spirit of hatred or by atrocities. The editor dismissed anxiety expressed by some that the First Battle of Manassas was the Armageddon predicted in the Bible, a harbinger of the end of the world. He called such a prediction "contrived and silly." Such biblical analogies to contemporary events reminded him of the argument that because both ducks and men had two legs, two eyes, and a mouth, they must be alike. Much interpretation of biblical prophecy, he warned, consisted of flawed reasoning.[50]

As the war progressed and southern morale wavered, Alabama Baptists sought desperately to shore up the cause with appropriate theology. War demanded a higher standard of morality to stem the spread of hatred, revenge, avarice, intemperance, profanity, and licentiousness. The length of the war was related to the gravity of the people's sins. At the 1862 meeting of the East Liberty Association, delegates wrestled over a resolution declaring that "the present civil war which has been inaugurated by our enemies must be regarded as a providential visitation upon us on account of our sins." After heated discussion, delegates amended the motion by inserting behind "war" the words "though entirely justified on our part."[51]

Baptist leaders repeatedly reassured the people that the worst was over. In February 1863 the *South-Western Baptist* proclaimed that the South had crossed over its Red Sea, that its "baptism of blood is well nigh completed." The "shinning [sic] shore of deliverance" was in view. Six months later, after the fall of Vicksburg and the severing of the Confederacy, the paper predicted that southern armies would soon roll back the invaders "with the help of God." After Gettysburg, the paper reminded that King David in his darkest affliction proclaimed renewed hope in God.[52]

The most predictable theological meaning of the war traced it to the beneficial effects of suffering. The war was a "refiner's fire" that purified God's people. Perfection was attained through suffering, and tribulation was the test of authentic character. When I. T. Tichenor preached to the Alabama associational meeting in Lowndes County four months after the Battle of Gettysburg, he chose his text from Hebrews 12:5 ("My son despise not thou the chastening of the Lord"). He admonished his hearers to recognize God's hand "in the adversities of providence." To doubt God's ultimate vindication of the South, the editor of the *South-Western Baptist* warned, was nothing less than infidelity.[53]

Alabama Baptist theologians returned again and again to the deep well of Calvinism to try to water a parched theology. But as before the war, the paradox of God's sovereignty and providence seemed to leave too little room for man's arrogance and human failure. The day before Christmas in 1863, the editor of the *South-Western Baptist* reflected on a year of tragedy and defeat. He did not doubt God's sovereignty over nations nor humanity's duty to submit without complaint to providence. But humankind was also bound to "use all the appointed means" at their disposal to ward off calamities. God might even modify his judgment because of man's reaction. The South's calamities of the past year might have occurred under God's supervision, but they had precise human causes such as bad counsel by the Confederate cabinet and bad generalship.[54]

Whatever theological twist they gave it, southern Protestants provided the cement that held the Confederacy together for four years.[55] Lacking numbers, equipment, money, and allies, southern armies were galvanized not primarily by abstract theories of states' rights or the defense of slavery. Rather, they were energized by resentment against outsiders who threatened their freedom and by a religion that convinced them that their cause was just, that God was on their side, that as a result they could not lose.

Whatever defeats and suffering they endured represented nothing more than a temporary purification that would make their civilization holier when God delivered glorious victory and vindication. But for that Christian assurance, the Civil War would likely have been shorter and far less bloody.

The effect of the war on Baptist institutions was devastating. The denomination's seminary and most of its colleges closed. The publication society and Sunday School Union suspended operations. The Bible Board in Nashville ceased activities when that city fell to Union troops in 1863. The new Foreign Mission Board (FMB) had difficulty distributing money to its missionaries in Africa and China. One couple affected by the funding crisis was Martha Foster Crawford and her husband in far-off Shanghai. Tarleton Crawford had to find work in translating and real estate to pay their expenses, enterprises that entangled him in secular financial affairs that soured his relations with fellow missionaries, alienated some Chinese, and ultimately precipitated a break with the FMB and creation of a rival Baptist mission in China.[56]

The state convention continued to meet, though with new priorities and concerns. The 1861 gathering reaffirmed its support of secession, praised Jefferson Davis for his dependence on God, urged all Baptist churches to observe Fast Days, set aside parts of the program each day to discuss "present conditions of the country," and acknowledged the providence of God in "leading us into our present condition." The convention appointed a superintendent to coordinate Alabama's efforts to minister to its soldiers. Although the convention was larger than expected and harmonious, there was a sharp reduction in mission gifts.[57] J. L. M. Curry was elected president in 1861 and reelected the following year.[58]

The effect of war on associations and churches varied according to location. After a smaller than usual Tuskegee Association meeting in 1861 and sharply lower mission offerings, the 1862 gathering rebounded, doubling its mission gifts (though nearly all the money was designated to army colportage work). Cahaba (Cahawba) Association in central Alabama reported a dearth of revivals at its 1863 meeting, as did Carey Association in the eastern part of the state. Of eighteen churches in the Cahaba Association, all experienced declines in membership after 1860. Seven churches had no baptisms at all in 1861, and that many more reported only one immersion. In 1862 church membership in the association was down by more than 10 percent, and eleven churches reported no baptisms. Only two churches reported revivals that year. Revivals in 1863 resulted in 114 baptisms, the largest number since 1859, and a net gain of sixty-one members.

The following year brought a record 222 baptisms as the religious fervor of the army camps apparently spread back home. In 1863 and 1864, George L. Lee (pastor of the Monroeville Baptist Church) reported more than 175 baptisms each year in revivals he held in Monroe and Butler Counties. The Alabama Association also experienced a large ingathering in 1864 (607 baptisms, 114 of them at Montgomery First Baptist Church).[59]

Few Baptist churches were so successful. The Wetumpka church just north of the capital city had no pastor between 1862 and 1866 and only one deacon remained when all others left for the army. When services were held at all, church elders usually conducted them. Virtually all male members of the Big Springs church in Randolph County served in the army, leaving only women who occasionally met for prayer and foot washing. Because the congregation believed that women should remain silent in church, services were suspended and the building was used as a post office and blacksmith shop. Female members conducted Sunday schools in congregations less restrictive of women, and in some Sunday schools they also taught mathematics and the alphabet after schools closed.[60]

Talladega First Baptist Church was fortunate to have good substitutes for pastor J. J. D. Renfroe while he served in Virginia, but the congregation was reduced to old men and women. They faithfully kept Fast Days, a special concern of one member, planter James Mallory, who had two sons serving in Virginia. Although both survived serious wounds, Mallory filled his diary with theological pondering ("holy God seems angry with us; may we be humble and cause his anger to cease").[61]

Eufaula's First Baptist Church was one of the most influential in the state. Located in the Barbour County seat, the church had employed some of the state's most respected pastors. When the war began, the pastor was W. N. Reeves, a man some called "the handsomest man in Alabama." One Baptist paper wrote that at least women could say they "always looked upon an agreeable object when he was preaching." The church also boasted one of the state's largest Sunday schools. In 1862 Reeves raised a company of infantry, which he served as captain. In July of that year, members requested the pastor to correspond with all church members in Confederate service. In November, members voted to donate the church's carpets to the Confederate army for use as blankets. The following year the church appointed a committee to investigate the moral deportment of members. It scolded members for a variety of sins: Sabbath breaking, profanity, horse racing, card playing, dancing, and drinking. Baptists, the report concluded, had "ever been a peculiar people," their peculiarity being "an unflinching adherence to all the commands and teachings of the word of

God." The church also adopted new articles of faith with stricter discipline, reflecting growing concern about how the declining success of Confederate armies might be related to moral conduct at home. The church also scrupulously observed days of fasting and prayer and contributed substantial amounts to poor families in the vicinity.[62]

Elizabeth Rhodes, a member of the Eufaula church, kept a diary during the war. Pastor Reeves was a frequent dinner guest in the Rhodes home, and Elizabeth and her husband were active in the church. She believed that God had chastened southerners through the calamity of war, but she was also confident that sincere prayer and repentance would result in God's deliverance. She initially rejoiced at God's providence in the Confederate victory at First Manassas. But days later she tried to make theological sense out of the death in that battle of a local physician, who only the year before had graduated from the University of North Carolina Medical College with high honors but who was now "cut off on just entering . . . a long life of usefulness." Again Calvinism supplied a convenient answer ("an overruling Providence has seen fit to remove him and we should not reminisce"). Her diary reflected the theology of her pastor, who only weeks earlier had preached a sermon based on verse two of the Ninety-ninth Psalm ("Clouds and Darkness around Him, righteousness and judgment are the tribulation of His time"). Although God's divine intent might be temporarily obscured, Reeves said, the time would come when his providence would be clear to all. Rhodes did what she could to ameliorate such judgment, faithfully visiting the poor, praying, and assisting in the church's choir and Sunday school.[63]

Other Baptist institutions were as disrupted as churches. The *Baptist Correspondent* in Marion prospered during the final year of peace but published its last issue in November 1861. The *South-Western Baptist* in Tuskegee encountered difficulties in January 1861 when the printer joined the Tuskegee Light Infantry. H. E. Taliaferro had to assume printing as well as editing responsibilities in addition to pastoring four churches and tending his family. These burdens were simply too heavy, and he announced suspension of the paper in March 1862. He explained that all printers were in the army, paper was outrageously expensive, and subscribers owed him $10,000. But in April, former editor Samuel Henderson (pastor of the Tuskegee church) agreed to resume his duties as editor, and many subscribers paid their overdue bills rather than allow the paper to cease operations. Lack of newsprint remained a problem, and by August 1863 the paper was down to two pages of war news and editorial opinion. In November 1863 the paper declined to half a sheet, and in August 1864 the *South-Western*

Baptist announced the conscription of another printer and reduction to bi-weekly publication.[64]

The fate of the paper at the end of the war is uncertain. What is known is that the last issue appeared on April 13, 1865. Accounts differ over the suspension. Henderson claimed that Major General James H. Wilson arrested and then released him under $20,000 bond with strict orders not to publish the paper. Having read the paper, General Wilson considered its editorials political and seditious. From the general's point of view, there were sound reasons for such a conclusion. Henderson had played a key role in promoting and sustaining Confederate nationalism.[65]

Howard College fared even worse than the denominational newspaper. Two tutors and forty of the college's sixty-two students volunteered for the army before or just after the bombardment on Fort Sumter. Most served together in the Marion Light Infantry, which fought many battles as part of the famous Fourth Alabama Regiment. Most remaining pupils were preparatory students too young for military service. Debating societies declined and the literary magazine ceased publication. Trustees abolished the professorship of theology because no theology students enrolled. The president of the board of trustees, Ishaw W. Garrot, was killed in action near Vicksburg in June 1863. The Vicksburg campaign resulted in so many Confederate casualties that the army decided to establish hospitals to the east of the war zone. Marion was a perfect location, and Confederate officials first approached Noah K. Davis, president of Judson College. He vigorously protested, explaining that his college enrolled 250 women while the Howard College campus was largely deserted. The Confederacy's medical inspector approved the shift, and Howard's two dormitories became a hospital. College enrollment dropped to twenty-seven in October 1863, almost all of them Marion residents. Rent from the Confederate government paid the costs of operating the school. A year later trustees suspended instruction except for recovering Confederate soldiers, a program that enrolled 125 disabled patients. Even these classes ended in March 1865, just before Federal troops occupied Marion and transferred Howard's dormitories to freedmen. By war's end, the dormitories were ramshackled and the endowment gone.[66]

Howard's sister institution, Judson College, fared better. Although female students were often reduced to penury status, their education continued largely uninterrupted. Some could not return home for summer vacations because of interruption of rail service, and many lost fathers, brothers, and boyfriends in military service. But combat missed Marion. In fact, the chief "casualties" of the war were two former Judson presidents, Milo

Jewett and Samuel Sherman. Both men lived in the North when war began and neither was friendly to secession. According to Judson tradition, anger against Jewett reached such fever pitch that a Marion woman invaded Jewett Hall to stab the former president's portrait through the heart. Sherman fared somewhat better because he aided Confederate POWs, earning the gratitude of Marion citizens and even a tearful reunion celebration after the war.[67]

Black Separation

Marion's warm reunion with Samuel Sherman was an aberration, an exception to the bitterness sweeping the state. Troubled by financial crises, military occupation, emancipated slaves, and Republican political control, white Baptists entered nearly a decade of Reconstruction that redefined their form of Christianity. Nowhere was the change more obvious than in race relations. When the war ended in 1865, nearly half of all Alabama Baptists were African Americans. By the end of Reconstruction in 1874, few blacks remained in Southern Baptist churches. The change did not occur all at once.

Hardly had the war ended when white Alabamians began redefining the status of freedmen. To the decision of an Alabama jurist that emancipated slaves were unfit to fill any office or even to vote, the editor of the denominational newspaper offered hearty consent. Although Negro education was a "Christian duty," such nurturing must be kept out of the hands of northerners. If working with northern Baptists to educate blacks required southerners to accept social and political equality or acknowledge slavery to have been a sin, then they "must decline the union." E. B. Teague wrote that too much blood had been shed to permit amicable relations between white regional Baptists. Such fraternalism could develop only in a new generation that had been spared sectional animosity and war. The Central Baptist Association at its fall 1868 session rejected a proposal by the northern Baptist Home Mission Society to cooperate in educating blacks for full citizenship. The association called such a proposal "purely political" and contrary to "Christ's Kingdom." It even threatened to withdraw from the SBC unless communication with northern Baptists ended.[68]

Alabama Baptists charged that northern missionaries had intrigued among black Baptists to cause disaffection from their white brothers. The northern emphasis on social equality and political rights largely explained the withdrawal of African American members into all-black churches. Following a brief period of interest in evangelizing blacks, both southern and

Alabama Baptists lost interest. By 1867 there was little mention of evangelizing freedmen, whether in denominational papers or state conventions.
The 1868 convention reported that race relations were rapidly deteriorating. The causes of this decline were obvious. Black Baptists were superstitious and credulous ("no delusions are too absurd to find entrance into
their minds"). Some of their leaders repudiated the Bible as a "white man's
book," and in their separate churches they had fallen under the influence
of "prophets and prophetesses" who led them into "every abominable and
revolting excess of idolatry."[69]

Hardening racial lines resulted in racism and segregation. One 1868
correspondent to the denominational paper argued that though Negroes
had rational and moral faculties, they were in fact subhuman. He believed
that the Hebrew word *nachash* (translated in the Bible as "serpent") should
have been translated "Negro." God's curse of the serpent in the Garden of
Eden had thus been a curse on blacks. As long as Baptists considered Negroes fully human, they had an obligation to them, he reasoned. But if considered subhuman, blacks could be crushed. Rev. A. T. Holmes wrote that
white Baptists should discontinue relations with blacks. If they accepted
equality with blacks at associational meetings and state conventions, then
how could they justify denying Negroes full rights in Baptist churches and
at "white firesides"?[70]

Although such views represented minority opinion, some churches
and associations did exclude black members. Liberty church in Coosa
County and Four Miles church in Shelby County asked Negro members to
withdraw their letters and establish their own churches. Associations rejected the applications of newly formed black Baptist churches. By 1869
Alabama Baptists had largely lost interest in evangelizing or educating African Americans. In 1869 the SBC's renamed Domestic and Indian Mission
Board at Marion employed a missionary to Negroes in Alabama, but despite half a year's work, he baptized not a single black. The state convention
no longer contained reports on Negro evangelism. When the Alabama Colored Baptist State Convention decided to build a theological school for
its ministers, delegates to the Alabama Baptist Convention advised against
doing so. When black members of the Midway Baptist Church withdrew
their membership in 1870, whites no longer allowed them to bury their
dead in the church cemetery. Although some Alabama Baptists (notably
J. L. M. Curry and B. F. Riley) continued to work tirelessly for black advancement, their enthusiasm was not shared by most whites.[71]

Despite pontification to the contrary, neither did blacks receive much
help from northern Baptists. When the war ended, the American Baptist

Home Mission Society (white) and the integrated American Baptist Free Mission Society began to evangelize freedmen. Largely to blunt such efforts, the SBC established a Committee on the Religious Instruction of the Colored People. Southern blacks remained wary of all these groups. The various northern agencies ignored local blacks, refused to help establish a national black Baptist university and seminary, and provided little money to evangelize freedmen. Northern blacks and whites who came to the South as missionaries and teachers neither well understood nor much respected the religious folkways of former slaves. They sometimes reacted to surviving African elements the same way white Alabama Baptists did, referring to them as superstitions and idolatry.[72]

At the core of black-white Baptist relations in Alabama was black self-determination. Had freedmen been willing to accept a role subservient to whites, racially integrated churches would have remained the norm. For a variety of reasons, white Alabama Baptists were not eager for their black members to form separate churches. Some retained real affection for members with whom they had shared fellowship for decades. Others worried whether blacks would remain theologically orthodox once they no longer had white preachers and deacons supervising their worship. Still others feared the influence of northern missionaries who might use black churches to launch Republican political forays. As a result, white Baptists seldom initiated the exclusion of blacks and often entreated them to remain.

Hardly had fighting ended than William P. Chilton of the Tuskegee church introduced a resolution at the 1865 Baptist State Convention. According to his resolution, the altered political status of freedmen did not necessitate any change in church relations. Although blacks certainly had the right to withdraw and form their own churches, the convention resolved that "we . . . believe that their highest good will be subserved by their retaining their present relation to those who know them, who love them, and will labor for their welfare."[73]

Paternalistic as such a pronouncement was, it was sincere, and many white Baptists tried to make the best of the new relationship. Nor were black Baptists quick to reject them. In fact, during the years 1866 to 1870, the racial composition of churches followed an irregular path. Many blacks initially remained in churches dominated by whites. Some newly formed black churches called white pastors, who faithfully served their newly enfranchised parishioners.

H. E. Taliaferro, one of Alabama's most respected preachers and a former editor of the denominational newspaper, was more conciliatory toward blacks than most white Alabama Baptists. He accepted appointment by the American Baptist Home Mission Board and pastored a black church at Mount Meigs. Taliaferro had pastored the church before the war and continued to pastor the black church, baptizing thirty or forty per month in 1866. He boasted of the decorum of his black congregation and of their affection for him despite the efforts of a northern missionary to alienate them. When they elected James Foster (a black man) pastor in 1869, Taliaferro called him a man of "fervent piety and rare ability." Taliaferro continued to pastor other black churches until at least 1872.[74]

White ministers preached revivals for black churches throughout the 1860s. In 1867 two white preachers conducted revivals for Negro churches in Tuscumbia and Mount Pleasant. M. A. Verser, missionary for the Muscle Shoals Association, helped constitute three black churches in 1868, as did two white ministers in Talladega County, who also ordained a black pastor. The Coosa River Association ordained three black preachers during 1868 who pastored a total of six black churches. J. W. D. Parker conducted a special theological institute for black preachers during the spring of 1869. The Negro church at La Place discharged its black minister and called a white, J. J. Cloud, as pastor.[75]

Such biracialism was the exception, not the rule. Blacks precipitated most splits because of their distinctive understanding of Christianity, their sense of community, their desire to assume roles of leadership, and their concerns about black political, economic, and educational welfare. To both white and black Alabama Baptists, the war had brought an apocalypse of judgment. For whites, emancipation was an apocalypse of doom; to blacks, it was a judgment that brought liberation and deliverance. For freedmen, religious separation was merely another dimension of political liberation.[76]

Although some associations reported substantial numbers of black members as late as 1868, separation was well under way by that time. The Salem Baptist Church in Greensboro (host to the first state convention and to five other antebellum meetings of the denomination, more than any other church) was a thriving congregation of 650 members at the onset of war. By 1866 it had disbanded. The church building was sold to Hale County for a courthouse and one-fourth of the proceeds was given to black members, who used the money to build a church. For three decades thereafter, Greensboro had no white Baptist church. An 1869 article in the denominational paper mentioned the "dissolution in almost all our churches of the pleasant and intimate church relations heretofore existing between the whites and blacks."[77]

Although the consequences of separation were the same, the details of racial division varied from congregation to congregation. At the Wetumpka

Salem Baptist Church, Greensboro, Alabama. The original log church outside Greensboro was the site of the establishment of the Alabama Baptist State Convention in 1823. The structure pictured here was built in 1843 and was used for a thriving biracial congregation until 1866 when the church disbanded. The building was used as the Hale County Courthouse (with the wing added) until 1907. The Greensboro Baptist Church was organized in the building in 1894. (Courtesy of Samford University Archives)

church, 80 percent of the membership was black at the end of the war. Freedmen continued to conduct separate services in the church basement, but rumors began to spread in the town, requiring white members to reassure townspeople. White church elders met with the black congregation and attributed the rumors to "slight indiscretions magnified by the political prejudices of the times." The elders also approved the request of black members to permit two blacks to preach to them. During the following four years, black preachers led the church to establish a separate congregation in a different building, though the son of a beloved white Wetumpka minister donated land and materials.[78]

In Tuscaloosa black members requested their own church in 1865. A five-person committee of whites (including Basil Manly Sr., Charles Manly, and Joshua Hill Foster) met with black members. Of the ten black males who met with them, eight favored separation and two preferred continued membership in Tuscaloosa's First Baptist Church. Whites consented to the separation but declined to ordain Prince Murrell, a black man, as pastor or to help in any way. On November 20, one-third of the black church members asked to withdraw their letters, but the church voted to table the matter. Blacks sought to withdraw again in 1866, but instead the church brought charges against Murrell of sassing white leaders who tried to restrain him. He refused to appear to answer the charges and was excluded from membership. By September most blacks had joined Murrell, leaving only a remnant in the mother church. The church licensed one of these blacks, who became the leader of the remaining Negro members. By 1867 their numbers had declined to only sixteen. That year the church excluded all blacks who had joined Murrell's new congregation.[79]

The issue in the Tuscaloosa church (determination of whites to retain control) triggered many splits. The Alabama Association reported in 1867 that its churches should encourage blacks to form their own congregations "under the direction and supervision of their white brethren." A north Alabama association allowed blacks to select their own pastors so long as they were white. A report from Evergreen stated the matter frankly. The future of black churches was not promising because "white people have no power or influence over them." Black preachers, "however ignorant, can command a crowded congregation when our best, most learned white ministers, have no attendance from them." Blacks exercised no discipline over members and accepted any applicant as a member. The white correspondent predicted that black Baptists would soon "relapse into the grossest superstition, idolatry and heathenism." Conversely, the Tuskegee church encouraged its black spin-off congregation because the new pastor was unlike most black preachers. He was not conceited, had no interest in politics, and refused to allow political meetings in his church (unlike the new African Methodist Episcopal Zion Church in Tuskegee).[80]

Separation in Eufaula resulted from a long negotiation. In May 1866, black members applied for their letters in order to constitute a new church. Whites granted their request and allowed them to use the church building until they could build their own. The following month blacks offered to buy the Eufaula church building. Negotiations began that resulted in sale of the old building to blacks in December 1867.[81]

In Talladega, separation was more complex. The black congregation continued to meet separately but with J. J. D. Renfroe as pastor of both white and black congregations. He baptized hundreds of blacks, fifty-six in 1869 alone. Renfroe praised his parishioners for avoiding "the usual [Negro] excesses and bad tendencies." His services produced no shouting or confusion. When whites initiated the subject of separation, blacks declined, although they already conducted their own business conference. When three blacks asked to be ordained, Renfroe decided only one of them was worthy of such action. Suddenly Renfroe's opinion of his black congregation changed. "I tremble for Zion in their hands," he wrote. "They are so careless and lax in receiving members," allowed "very foolish things" in their services, and were more resistent to church discipline than when they were slaves ("Now every one does as he pleases with impunity").[82] A member of the Talladega church, planter James Mallory, agreed with his pastor. Although Mallory interpreted Confederate defeat as a divine mandate for black freedom, he spoke disparagingly of their 1868 protracted meeting. They met day and night with "screams, yells, and distressing cries." Blacks believed, he wrote in his diary, that religion consisted of "feeling happy."[83]

E. B. Teague reported similar excesses at Selma. The pastorium was next to the First Baptist Church, where freedmen conducted services several days a week in the basement. Although he praised the black preacher for his scriptural and eloquent sermons, Teague dismissed much of what he heard as "mere senseless rant." When invited to preach, he told blacks frankly that they would still be servants of whites until the end of time.[84]

By far the most important new black congregation was the Columbus Street church in Montgomery. I. T. Tichenor helped black members of Montgomery's First Baptist Church in whatever ways he could after the war. He wrote letters for illiterate members to help them locate relatives separated by slavery. When they expressed a desire to constitute a separate congregation, he unsuccessfully traveled to the North to help them secure funds. After the failure of that mission, Tichenor helped them borrow money in Montgomery.[85]

Montgomery blacks laid the cornerstone of their new church on Columbus Avenue in 1867 and called Nathan Ashby (who had preached to them before the war) as pastor. It was in this new church building that the Alabama Colored Baptist State Convention was formed in 1868 with Ashby as first president. There also the National Baptist Convention, Incorporated, was established, electing the host pastor as its first president. By turn of century, Columbus Street was reputedly the largest Baptist church in the world, with five thousand members.[86] Expatriot members who moved to Chicago during subsequent black migrations formed a church there mainly from former members of Columbus Street church.[87]

Although many white ministers ridiculed the new black state convention, H. E. Taliaferro attended the organizational meeting. Though all races contained religious demagogues, he observed, and a "few ambitious hotspurs" had shown up in Montgomery, the "best talent" among Alabama's black Baptists had assumed positions of leadership.[88]

Unfortunately, good race relations among Alabama Baptists soon dissolved into a sea of recrimination, political intrigue, and violence. Talladega planter and Baptist layman James Mallory became a fiercely partisan Democrat who helped defeat Republicans. By 1874, the year that Democrats won the governorship and permanently wrested control from the GOP, there was so much political interest within the Talladega First Baptist Church that "not much else is talked about or thought of." When Democrats triumphed in the November elections, Mallory rejoiced at redemption from radical rule.[89] His former black Baptist brothers and sisters across town did not interpret the providence of God in the same way.

The fate of Liberty church near Sumterville was more tragic: during Reconstruction the church was burned. Several stories circulated in the Bigbe Association about the cause of the fire. One attributed it to whites who burned the church after Republicans used it for a meeting. Another rumor attributed its destruction to a furious white man whose wife had sat beside a Negro woman at a church service. Whatever the truth, some members joined the church in Sumterville, some affiliated with other congregations, and the Liberty Baptist Church ceased to exist.[90]

In the summer of 1870 a different kind of congregation met at the Baptist church in the Goshen community of Cherokee County. Ku Klux Klansmen selected a twelve-man execution squad to murder William Luke, a white northern minister who had begun a school for blacks in Calhoun County. Among the death squad was a Baptist preacher as well as farmers and former Confederate soldiers. The night of Luke's murder, they met at another Baptist church and proceeded to Cross Plains, where they carried out the killing.[91]

According to one account, Selma First Baptist Church was nearly the scene of a pitched gun battle between black and white members. Blacks, allegedly incited by carpetbaggers, claimed the church property because they constituted a majority of members. Pastor J. B. Hawthorne learned of the plot and gathered some friends; they armed themselves and confronted blacks on their way to the church. Hawthorne's force raised their weapons and threatened to kill the first man who took another step. The mob quickly dispersed.[92]

Such incidents were not typical. Though white and black Baptists went their separate ways, a residue of kindness remained. In 1867 J. L. M. Curry preached a revival in Marion where the son of one of the largest antebellum Perry County planters was converted. Immediately after his baptism, two elderly Negroes, both former slaves of his father, rushed forward to give him "the right hand of fellowship" and express "in simple but touching language" their thanks to God for his conversion.[93]

In 1870 whites in Carlowville excluded blacks from their church, and Negro members formed the Hopewell Baptist Church. Three years later whites allowed an elderly black woman to take communion with them. As other elderly blacks learned of this incident, they also asked to participate. Finally, the Carlowville church allowed blacks to join them for communion one Sunday afternoon a month under the supervision of the white pastor.[94]

What emerged from the racial separation between 1865 and 1874 was both tragic and liberating. Secular contact between the races produced racial stereotypes and misunderstanding. With contact also severed in the sacred sphere, there was no place for the races to meet in common purpose and mutual affection. Evangelical churches thus accepted racial separation as the basis for postwar race relations.[95] Their proclamations of brotherhood had a hollow ring when white Baptists could not find a way to surmount the barriers of race. The separation also cost Southern Baptists 400,000 black members.[96]

The separation was liberating for black Baptists. Despite the political and economic failures of Reconstruction, it did provide African Americans control over their families and churches. In many ways, black Baptist ministers were like their white colleagues. They stood in the mainstream of revivalistic, emotional, conservative, nineteenth-century Protestantism. Though mainly poor, bivocational, and Calvinistic, like their counterparts, blacks in other ways diverged from white Baptists. Their emphasis upon God creating all races of one blood, their focus on the fatherhood of God and the brotherhood of man, and their affirmation of the worth of the humblest, most illiterate sharecropper deviated in degree if not in substance from whites. And their combination of old-time religion with racial uplift was certainly unique. They combined otherworldly traditional theology with a gospel of social change.[97] They provided their people political and economic leadership, organized the Republican Party, started schools and colleges, then moved on to temperance crusades and in time to cautious but firm opposition to segregation. Ultimately, it would be from black Alabama Baptist churches that they would launch the final assault on segregation.

Hard-Times Religion

Several eras in the history of Alabama Baptists have tested the collective spirit of the people. The Great Depression of the 1930s was such a time, but arguably the most severe challenge occurred between 1865 and 1874. Demoralized, impoverished, internally divided according to both race and theology, whites were obsessed with throwing off Republican rule. The litany of their disasters was Jobian in scale. Of some 127,000 white men aged fifteen to sixty in 1860, between 34,000 and 40,000 were dead five years later. Another 35,000 were disabled. An estimated 130,000 whites were destitute by the end of 1865. For every 1 black who received food rations from the Freedmen's Bureau, 2.3 poor whites received such assistance.[98]

White Alabamians looked to their preachers to make sense of this tragedy. Baptist ministers did their best, recycling arguments they had used to sustain Confederate morale. Tuskegee pastor Samuel Henderson preached a sermon in February 1866 entitled "Adversity the Test of Christian Integrity." In the sermon, he coined the term "adverse providence." An unruffled life, he assured his congregation, had the same effect on character that light reading had on the mind. Conversely, tribulation created patience and hope. It was all well and good to blame the war on national sins. But nations had no souls and could not sin. So national sins were merely the aggregate sins of individual people who must repent if the nation was to be healed.[99]

Former chaplain J. J. D. Renfroe returned to his Talladega congregation in the summer of 1865 to preach to an expanded congregation. A Union garrison occupied the town and many Federal soldiers attended services at the Baptist church. Three of them were among revival converts, and the entire town turned out for the baptismal service in Talladega Creek. Conquered and conqueror went under the waters in spiritual fraternity, and Renfroe rejoiced that "Mason and Dixon's line never did run through the Kingdom of Jesus Christ."[100]

His conclusion was premature. As Reconstruction settled over the state, lines hardened and the local Union presence became more oppressive by the day. In January 1866 Renfroe preached a sermon on "Redeeming the time, because the days are evil." Selecting his text from Ephesians 5:16, he rejoiced that 1865 had ended. For some in his audience (he must have stared pointedly at the uniformed soldiers), it had been a year of triumph. For others, it had been a year of lamentation and poverty. A cause for which most of his members had prayed had proven an utter failure. Four terrible years of war seemed a single season of history—eventful, revolutionary, painful to remember. The legacy of the times was defeat and sorrow, widows and orphans. For him personally, those years marked the "keenest regret" of his life. "Yet to thy mandate I bow and kiss the rod that smote me!" Southerners had repented of their follies and mistakes, and he had sworn an oath of allegiance to the United States and sung a new song, "My Country 'Tis of Thee." But it was hard to sing a new song as he stared into a sea of brass buttons in a background of blue. He had learned the value of discretion, but his mind was free even if his tongue was not. He told the story of a Confederate POW who was instructed by his guards not to disparage the Union though he could think what he pleased. When a guard later asked what was on his mind, the proud Rebel replied: "I am thinking, 'Dam the Yankees.' " In evil times, people must resist temptation. The pastor returned later to write afterthoughts on the pages of his manuscript. Within six months of preaching the sermon, Renfroe's eighteen-month-old daughter died. That loss began a series of calamities that cost him the lives of six children and his wife over the next twenty-one years. As he noted later, "I have had sorrow upon sorrow" that made the tribulation of war seem not so bad after all.[101]

Such despair settled over churches like a pall. The 1868 meeting of the Eufaula Association pronounced the churches within its venue "cold and indifferent." When the pastor of the Wetumpka church visited churches of the Central Association, he found similar destitution and disorganization. There were no Sunday schools or prayer meetings and only occasional Sunday services. Only two churches within the entire association held weekly services, and mission activities had nearly ceased. Even his church was forced from weekly to biweekly services.[102]

The Black Belt was particularly hard hit, as many whites moved west. One pastor reported that Baptist churches in Perry County were more depressed than he had ever seen them. Six rural congregations near Marion had no pastors and were slowly dying. In Wilcox and Monroe Counties, churches were in precarious condition, with declining ethical standards and some Baptists converting to Mormonism. Many churches had too few members to attract ministers. In Tuskegee, the denomination's East Alabama Female College had burned and the local Baptist church had hardly replaced membership losses to death and exclusion. After Samuel Henderson resigned as pastor of the Tuskegee church, it experienced a succession of short-term pastorates like inexperienced E. R. Carswell. The young, fiery, and argumentative preacher locked horns with influential layman John Swanson, who after a heated exchange advised Carswell to "go off to school and learn more and [especially] how to conduct a Baptist church as pastor." Carswell promptly resigned. The fact that the church was virtually bankrupt did not help matters.[103]

Many Baptist churches were particularly vulnerable to such vicissitudes because even in good times their members were poor. In mountainous Randolph County, the Big Springs Baptist Church consisted mainly of tenant farmers and cotton mill workers. So poor were they that they could not maintain their church building, which was used as a blacksmith shop until the congregation was reorganized in the late 1860s.[104] The Tallassee church membership was also mainly textile mill operatives. Composed of what one preacher called an "unsettled population," membership fluctuated according to the prosperity of Tallassee's cotton mills. Because of their long work weeks, members could not attend revivals or midweek services. If mill workers missed a day of labor, they lost their jobs.[105]

There were, of course, compensations for pastors of such churches. H. E. Taliaferro, who pastored the part-time Tallassee church for many years while living in Tuskegee, called the congregation unusual in its willingness to assume responsibility. Members believed in lay preaching and lay working. They loved good preaching and were responsive to his ministry. "Let a man mix with a church of poor, praying, working people," he wrote, and the pastor would "admire the wisdom of Jesus for companionizing with them." E. B. Teague expressed the same opinion. Though poor country people were often emotional, he preferred their enthusiasm to "formal and tame" urban Baptists.[106]

The state convention fared no better than the churches. The 1868 meeting at Marion registered only thirty delegates from beyond the vicinity of the host church. Poverty partly explained the slim attendance, but politics played a role as well. State and national elections had occurred only three days earlier. As a consequence, many whites feared a wave of violence and stayed home to protect their families. One preacher wrote sadly, "We have more of politics . . . than the grace of God . . . , more of the Kingdom of the World than of Jesus." After J. J. D. Renfroe's convention sermon about confidence in God during hard times, delegates spent most of their time discussing conditions in their sections of Alabama. The cotton crop was discouraging; white church members were despondent, impoverished, discouraged, and in debt, and many planned to migrate west. Black members, wrote a columnist for the *Christian Index,* were establishing their own churches where "ignorance is the teacher," "superstition the sad and revolting lesson," and "debasing orgies" the consequence. Black worship contained vestiges "of the old idolatrous practices and notions of Africa, repressed and kept down by the better moral influences to which they were subjected [during slavery], but never wholly eradicated." Rev. G. F. Williams from Mobile concluded that the "boundaries of Zion, in this State, are narrowing rather than widening."[107]

Conventions in the early 1870s fared little better. Only fifteen associations were represented at Eufaula in 1872, indicating a "falling off of interest." The following year the state convention had no money with which to publish the minutes for 1871–1873. Most associations were not represented at the 1874 meeting either, indicating indifference, lack of unity, and refusal to cooperate for missions. One angry correspondent from eastern Alabama denounced the "devil-invented excuse" that hard times justified neglect of duty.[108]

Another reason for slumping attendance at the state convention was massive migration. Between 10 and 15 percent of the white population left Alabama after the war, an exodus exceeded only in South Carolina. Total migrants probably exceeded fifty thousand, with most of them heading west to Texas. Among their numbers were many Baptist preachers. The editor of the denominational paper estimated in 1874 that as many as one-third of Alabama's "effective ministry" had migrated since 1865. An Alabama pastor who had moved to Texas attributed this migration to a number of factors. Some left because of personal ambition, others because they were restless for new challenges, and still others because church members were so poor they could not pay pastors a salary. A preacher who had left for Sardis, Mississippi, urged his friends to join him ("I have no desire to return to Alabama"). Still another correspondent believed most pastors left less because of low salary than because of the exclusivism of state Baptist leaders: persons not native to Alabama were not welcomed or encouraged to participate in denominational life.[109]

Although concerned leaders cited many reasons for the exodus of preachers, salary seems to have been the chief culprit. George Lee (pastor at Monroeville) complained bitterly in his diary about churches with adequate income that paid pastors "a poor wretched pittance," forcing them to farm in order to survive. Then members complained because their preachers' sermons were inadequate and repetitive. Congregations, he wrote, "love their pastor with their lips, but hate him . . . with their purse."[110]

Confederate veteran Thomas B. Espy of Leesburg pastored four churches and farmed during 1867 but made nothing off his few acres of corn and cotton. He survived by pastoring multiple churches (including the Athens Baptist Church) and teaching school. He wanted to devote all his time to preaching, but "unfortunately my brethren won't send me into the harvest, which is ripe." During the previous year, he had consumed only a hundred pounds of bacon and six bushels of corn for the four members of his family and his horse, which he had to ride twenty miles a Sunday to preach. Finally, he joined the migration from Cherokee County, moving to Little Rock, Arkansas, where he pastored the First Baptist Church and became editor of the *Western Baptist*.[111]

The editor of the denominational paper knew of only two pastors in south Alabama (one in Marion, the other in Mobile) whose church salaries afforded them adequate livelihood. The editor of the *Tuscumbia Herald* listed only two others in north Alabama whose churches paid full salaries.[112]

Denominational leaders wrestled with the solution to this problem. Lists of the duties of deacons prominently featured the task of collecting contributions for the pastor's salary. Leaders realized the key to better support was a better educated laity. They urged ministers to preach more on financial stewardship. But they also confronted theological problems, especially in north Alabama, where hyper-Calvinism held sway. In that region, many lay persons still believed pastors should not be paid a salary, that mission money "sticks to the hands of those who direct it," and that if God wanted "heathen" converted, he would miraculously raise up ministers among them.[113]

In such a financial environment, the fate of denominational institutions was predictably grim. The 1865 state convention asked its president, Confederate statesman J. L. M. Curry, to accept the presidency of Howard College. Curry reluctantly agreed, largely because he was a widower and his daughter was a student at Judson. The promised salary of $5,000 was attractive in such slack times. He was also loyal to the state and believed in the value of education. He moved his eight-year-old son Manly to Marion in mid-December and took up his duties in January 1866. Believing that it would strengthen his credibility with preachers, he had himself ordained to preach (a decision he later regretted, feeling no call to pastor a church). Then he began to crisscross the state in search of funds and students. During 1866 alone, he preached 119 sermons, not counting addresses to prayer meetings, Sunday schools, and Baptist associations. Unfortunately, enrollment reached only forty-one students for the year. Trustees could not pay his salary, and in April 1868 he resigned. Convention officials paid part of his back salary from proceeds of the sale of Salem church in Greensboro, but the sum was too little and too late. Curry left for Richmond College, where he taught history and literature before achieving national fame as general agent for the Peabody and Slater Funds in the 1880s (which promoted public education in the South). In 1885 he was appointed ambassador to Spain. Following his death, Alabama bestowed upon him one of its two places in the National Hall of Fame, located in the rotunda of the Capitol in Washington.[114]

Notwithstanding their respect for Curry (delegates reelected him president of the state convention in 1866), the convention could not or would not support Howard College. In 1868 faculty salaries were thousands of dollars in arrears. The college had reduced tuition to $75 a year, and townspeople agreed to board students for $15 a month. Even then too few students enrolled to pay the school's bills. Once Howard ministerial students had filled the larger pulpits of the state; by 1868 this spring of spiritual nourishment was "well-nigh dry." After Curry left, presidents came and went in rapid succession, one lasting a year, another two.[115]

Stability finally returned in the person of James Thomas Murfee. The native Virginian and graduate of Virginia Military Institute was well known in Alabama as a professor of mathematics and commandant of cadets at the University of Alabama. He had served as architect for rebuilding the university until clashes with its collaborationist-Republican administration led to his resignation. After he accepted the presidency of Howard College in 1871, he radically revised the curriculum. He imposed rigorous training in English and mathematics and required each student to do his own scientific experiments and to compose literary compositions to be critiqued by classmates and professors. Each student had to recite his own words and ideas daily. He replaced the standard English-classics curriculum with elective courses. Whether because of the new curriculum, economic improvements in the state, or respect for Murfee, enrollment increased rapidly to 124 students in 1872.[116]

Judson College experienced less turmoil. The school had only one president between 1865 and 1872 and enrolled five times more students than Howard College during the 1865–1866 term.[117]

The fate of the denominational newspaper was more problematic. After Federal troops closed down the *South-Western Baptist* in 1865, publisher Samuel Henderson began negotiations with the Georgia Baptist paper. With the approval of the Alabama state convention in November 1865, the two papers merged. Though published in Atlanta, the *Christian Index and South-Western Baptist* contained an Alabama section edited by Henderson and later by J. J. D. Renfroe.[118]

Josephus Shackelford, the dean of Baptist ministers in north Alabama, launched the *Christian Herald* at Moulton in 1865. He moved the paper to Tuscumbia in 1867 and to Nashville five years later. Although he energetically solicited contributions of news from associations, the state convention never accepted the paper as official voice of the denomination.[119]

Dissatisfied with the lack of an official Baptist paper, the 1873 state convention remedied the problem. It named Marion pastor Edwin T. Winkler (an erudite graduate of Brown University) editor of the *Alabama Baptist*, assisted by E. B. Teague, J. J. D. Renfroe, and D. W. Gwin. The convention retained ownership until 1878, when editorial jealousies and hard financial times caused the convention to transfer title of the paper to Winkler and Rev. John L. West. Although publishers of the *Christian Index* fought creation of the new *Alabama Baptist* and tried to undermine it by merging with Shackelford's paper, the paper survived and slowly forged the unity and communication link that the denomination so desperately needed.[120]

Visions of Springtime

In the midst of Reconstruction despair, the editor of the *Christian Index and South-Western Baptist* wrote in 1867 that Baptists must put aside their gloom. They should recall the fate of the Jews in Babylonian captivity. Their land had been invaded and ravaged. Their men had been slain in battle. Their government had been subverted. Their royal city had been burned. Their population had been enslaved. The task of Alabama Baptists was to seek peace, reconciliation, and national unity. "It could scarcely harm us," he concluded, "to dream of spring for the moment."[121]

The removal of so many pastors by death and migration made way for a new generation of leaders. Some, like E. B. Teague and Samuel Henderson (who served as president of the state convention from Curry's departure in 1868 until 1873), had been active before the war but emerged as luminaries after 1865. Others were promoted into special prominence by the war (J. J. D. Renfroe and I. T. Tichenor). Many were deeply involved in secular politics. Henry Cox Hooten served in the Confederate army, practiced law, preached, and was elected tax assessor in Bullock County. Like many Alabama Baptists, he despised Reconstruction and tried to defeat Republicans. He also ran into trouble with the Freedmen's Bureau, which investigated claims that he had ordered a black family off his farm after they had worked for him all season. A. N. Worthy of Troy led Baptist work in southeastern Alabama, practiced law, and represented Pike County as a Democratic senator in the legislature during Reconstruction. Bailey Bruce, pastor in Jackson and DeKalb Counties and moderator of the DeKalb Association, represented his home district at the 1865 state constitutional convention. As a member of the legislature representing DeKalb County, he led the prohibition forces in north Alabama. His colleague, J. B. Appleton (schoolteacher, DeKalb County superintendent of education, and erudite leader of the Cherokee Baptist Association) served two terms as a Democrat in the Alabama legislature.[122]

Slowly the inertia of early Reconstruction began to wear off. Scattered revivals broke out across the state. A July 1867 meeting in Tallapoosa County baptized thirty-eight. That same month a revival at Second Baptist Church in Montgomery converted forty-five. An 1869 protracted meeting at Montgomery First Baptist Church added forty more.[123]

New mission efforts began. Jonathan L. D. Hillyer determined to establish a Baptist church in the new industrial town of Birmingham. He began services in a store in 1871 that attracted a polyglot audience of merchants, mechanics, and farmers. Methodists, Presbyterians, Episcopalians, and even Catholics had their own edifices, a frustrated Hillyer wrote, but Baptists had erected no building. When the domestic mission board stopped paying his salary in 1872 because of financial difficulties, the indefatigable Hillyer turned down a pastorate in Georgia, worked as a carpenter, sold his household furnishings, and wrote articles for the paper so he could stay in Birmingham. He visited churches in Tuscaloosa, Selma, and Mobile, trying to save his struggling church field. Birmingham deserved a better preacher than he was, Hillyer admitted, but he did what he could because no one else volunteered. When his tour netted only $53 of the $5,000 needed, Hillyer exploded in rage. Saint Frances Street church in Mobile was proposing to add $20,000 in embellishments. If the church would "leave off a few curls in the brackets and a few lines in the frescoing, they can spare us a hundred dollars or two," he wrote in frustration. Whether or not his chiding did any good, by July 1872 he had constituted First Baptist Birmingham with twenty-one members.[124]

The necessity to evangelize a new generation also created enthusiasm for Sunday school. I. T. Tichenor and other leaders held an Alabama Baptist Sabbath School state convention in 1867. The affair became an annual event to publicize Sunday schools. In 1869 thirty delegates organized a South Alabama Sunday School convention. They viewed the organization as a particularly effective vehicle of child evangelism, though few adults attended.[125]

Ministry to Birmingham mechanics and Chinese railroad workers demonstrated how industrialism was beginning to transform Alabama. The key to such change was the railroad. As the Central of Georgia system built westward from Atlanta and the Louisville and Nashville constructed line south from Nashville, railroads transformed churches as well as the economy. Just as the newly reinstituted *Alabama Baptist* unified Baptists through communication, railroads united them by transportation. In 1873 E. B. Teague reminded north Alabama Baptists that they could no longer use the mountain barrier as an excuse for not attending state conventions or supporting Judson and Howard Colleges because these institutions were located in south Alabama. Railroads afforded easy transportation and allowed the state convention to appoint a committee to involve north Alabama Baptists in more cooperative enterprises. Baptists in eastern Alabama had also formed a separate convention because of difficulties with transportation. But new railroad lines allowed Baptists to visit and get to know each other. Associational meetings grew as train travel swelled registration. But not all the changes were positive. When the railroad bypassed the Uchee community east of Tuskegee, the Good Hope Baptist Church began a long decline until at last it closed completely.[126]

In such a chaotic world, Baptists adhered firmly to traditional beliefs despite change whirling all around them. At the core of their world was the word, expounded from the pulpit and read from the Bible. Although virtually all Baptists agreed that preaching was central to their purposes, they disagreed widely about the nature of the proclamation. The excessive emotionalism of black worship that so repelled whites also led to criticism of their own protracted meetings. One correspondent complained in 1869 about people whose Christianity consisted mainly of "periodical religion" instead of regular, routine worship. He sharply condemned what he termed the "spasmodic religion" of revivalism. When describing a four-week protracted meeting at Montgomery First Baptist that same year, the pastor emphasized the "quiet thoughtfulness" of the crowds, which expressed "no undue excitement."[127]

Advice to young preachers about their sermons emphasized careful preparation. E. B. Teague advised them to select a topic or text narrow enough to allow substantive development, focus on the central issues, and apply the theme to the realities of life. The editor of the denominational journal disagreed with Teague's narrow focus, fearing that it produced sermons "too elevated" for the masses, who were too poorly educated to follow elaborate discussion. Better the preacher select a text that he could apply broadly to doctrine or real-life situations. Samuel Henderson pleaded for a more spontaneous style of preaching. Ministers might choose as theme some incident "fresh in the minds of hearers" rather than a scriptural text. They might organize the sermon around a great truth to be im-

Sanctuary of Selma Baptist Church. Every part of the building focused on the pulpit and huge pulpit Bible, symbol of the centrality of the Bible and the sermon in Baptist life. (Courtesy of Samford University Archives)

parted (as Paul had on Mars Hill), rather than around three points. If sermons were conceived as scriptural text followed by divisions and subdivisions, then no such sermon was recorded in the New Testament. Preachers should judge the success of their sermons by souls saved rather than by rules followed or customs that often neutralized the power of the gospel.[128]

In practice, each preacher adapted such advice to his own preference and style. J. J. D. Renfroe wrote out every word, starting with biblical text, moving to broad theme, and ending with concrete application. His sermons were carefully constructed, ran to forty or so pages of tightly written prose, and required careful attention. But they also frequently rose to the level of oratorical eloquence expected by the times. James DeVotie began sermons with a text, studied every word, determined the central doctrine or truth involved, compared the text to other Scriptures to assure conformity with central biblical teachings, read commentaries and sermons about the passage to eliminate possible errors in his own understanding, selected illustrations, then wrote "pretty full notes." Apparently this discipline worked for him. During his three years at Tuscaloosa he baptized an average of thirty-four per year and at Siloam church in Marion, an average of nearly forty-two annually for fourteen years. Among his converts were eleven men who became preachers in Alabama.[129]

J. L. M. Curry, despite his reservations about being ordained, became one of Alabama's most successful and popular preachers. Unlike Renfroe and DeVotie, he preached from only a scrap of paper containing a few notes. Described as an impassioned orator and as a logical thinker who was sound theologically, Curry was considered by denominational leaders to be a blazing meteor in the dark theological sky of Reconstruction ("He speaks to you through every muscle, every feature, every gesture, every movement of the body"). So intent was he to convey his own emotions to others that one observer wrote, "he sweeps you unresistingly along with him, taking captive all your convictions, and you embrace his conclusion before he has announced it."[130]

For Curry as well as for other Alabama Baptists, the Bible was "God's infallible word." But which translation was infallible and what doctrinal meaning one attributed to infallibility were less certain. Some insisted that only the King James Version was infallible. Others welcomed the revised version of 1881 as more accurate. The editor of the *Baptist Correspondent* published passages from Luke's gospel to show readers how well the revised version read. He believed Alabama Baptists would be both "gratified and instructed" by the revision.[131] Some were. Many were not!

Baptists fiercely disputed the meaning of what they read regardless of the version. The *Baptist Correspondent* adhered to the Landmark school of J. R. Graves, blistering Basil Manly Sr. when he returned to Alabama as general evangelist for the state convention. Writers accused the Baptist patriarch of using his position to advance anti-Landmark views and destroy denominational harmony. They also turned their fire on the Howard College president and faculty, blaming them for declining enrollment.[132]

Baptists also squabbled over issues of gender. Theological lines between men and women had always been confusing. Biblical accounts seemed to support the prevalent male belief that women had been first in the Fall and should assume a subservient position in the church. Yet church discipline cases seemed to confirm what most men believed (consciously or subconsciously)—that women were morally superior to men. Women represented purity, goodness, harmony, humility, moderation, cooperation, family, home, and self-control. They were more likely to belong to a church and less likely to violate the ethical standards of that church (at least judged by the frequency of exclusion in discipline cases). Men, on the other hand, lacked self-control, engaged in drinking, swearing, fighting, and gambling, expressed an exaggerated sense of honor in self-destructive conduct like duels and wars and were self-assertive, aggressive, and competitive. Males often fought the demons that tempted them, but they seldom won.[133] Men won the biblical argument. Women won the ethical victory.

Not surprisingly, such conflicting theological assumptions produced differences of opinion about the proper role of women in church and society. The multiple shocks between 1865 and 1874 required that every resource be mobilized, and churches turned more and more to women for help. They had to sustain congregations during the war because most men were absent. After the war they had to assume a larger role in fund raising, especially for missions. When the Selma Baptist Church was without a pastor and could not pay the debt on its parsonage, women raised the $1,000 necessary to avert disaster. When pew rentals failed to provide Eufaula First Baptist Church enough to pay annual expenses in 1869, women held a fair to raise money to build a parsonage. To plan the fair, the church appointed two committees, one male, the other female (apparently the first female committee ever appointed by the congregation). By 1872 the Ladies Benevolent Society of the church met weekly and raised hundreds of dollars annually for church and mission projects. When the church was unable to raise enough money to employ a full-time pastor in 1873, it appointed a committee of women to raise the necessary funds, and the women succeeded where men had failed. When the associational meeting came to Eufaula, it was the women who were asked to arrange for out-of-town delegates, even though church members elected only men to represent them.[134]

When time came to support two new Baptist missionaries in China, state leaders urged women to organize mission groups to be called "Woman's Mission to Woman."[135] Such mission projects began the transformation of Ladies Benevolent Societies (which had previously focused on raising money for the internal use of their congregations) into mission societies (whose funds went largely to causes external to the local church). Although laymen and pastors did not at first realize the full implications of such a change, they caught on quickly. Strapped for funds to operate churches and pay pastors' salaries by the diversion of money to mis-

Eldred B. Teague, educator and preacher, was one of the most influential denominational leaders of the nineteenth century. (Courtesy of Samford University Archives)

sions, males were not keen on this reallocation of resources. During following decades, many of them fiercely opposed the establishment of women's mission societies, some for theological reasons but many for personal reasons as well.

Beloved patriarch E. B. Teague went even further into the quagmire of gender relations. As Martha Foster Crawford's pastor and spiritual adviser, he had intervened on her behalf with the Foreign Mission Board. In 1870 Teague wrote an essay for the denominational paper advocating the election of women deacons. He cited the scriptural precedent of Phoebe and early church history where Roman Christians cited the use of deaconesses. Although these sources did not conclusively prove his case, they strongly intimated such a function for women. Deaconesses could help pastors minister to the poor as well as perform other duties. These "female assistants to deacons and pastors" should be carefully chosen because such an act would increase their dignity by "special endorsement of the church." Teague's proposal received immediate endorsement from an anonymous "Sister in Christ," who bemoaned the failure of deacons to attend to God's business because they were too busy with their own. Paul's advice to the churches about using women as servants had been ignored by men who instead emphasized the apostle's admonition that women keep silent in public. What was surprising was the absence of male criticism to Teague's suggestion. [136]

Evidence that such opinions represented a minority view abounds. Even Martha Foster Crawford disparaged woman suffrage, and temperance leader W. B. Crumpton chastised his own cause for allowing women influential roles. He wrote that women had damaged the temperance cause with "zeal not according to knowledge." And despite women's active role raising money for their church, Mrs. L. A. Hawkins of Eufaula defined a separate sphere for women designed for them by a providential creator. Women should not crave freedom, power, or influence, she wrote. They had neither the physical nor mental power of men, yet they exercised vast influence over the moral development of their husbands and children. The family was her "true sphere," the home her domain. There were exceptions like Queen Elizabeth or Mary of Medici, but such women were "unsexed paragons" who inspired repugnance in Hawkins.[137]

The Civil War and Reconstruction were more theological watersheds of Alabama Baptists than they were pivotal to political and economic conditions. In the long run, not much changed in terms of who exercised political and economic control of Alabama. But religion underwent jarring changes. The role of Baptist clergy became much more political, initially on behalf of secession, mobilization, and sustaining Confederate morale, then later in explaining the theological meaning of the South's defeat, and finally in throwing off Republican rule. Baptists identified the denomination with the Democratic Party and southern separatism. They celebrated the South's distinctive heritage, interpretation of history, and vision of the future (God's special destiny for them). They might have lost a war, but they were determined to win the peace. They cultivated their own religious institutions, rejected reunion with northern Baptists, and created a form of religious separatism that had religious, cultural, and racial dimensions. In religion, they hewed to conversionism, individualism, revivalism, personal piety, strict biblicism, and orthodoxy while rejecting northern "false doctrine" and emphasis on social ethics. Culturally, they tried to lead their congregations toward more urbane and orderly worship, a more centralized and efficient denominational structure, and greater personal discipline over the moral conduct of members. Racially, whites separated from their black brothers and sisters, whom they described in paternalistic and unflattering ways. What blacks interpreted as apocalyptic emancipation, whites viewed as historic tragedy. What blacks valued as the demonstrative, heartfelt moving of God's spirit among his people, whites viewed as superstition and emotional excess. What blacks did to mobilize the Baptist church toward self-help and political control, whites viewed as unbiblical social salvation. Yet, in many ways, their separate Baptist strands traced to a single taproot. Try as they might to impose more decorum on the worship patterns of their people, erudite pastors, both black and white, often failed. Unlettered black and white Baptists preferred exuberant, emotional, joyous, spontaneous, unstructured expressions of God's presence. Their hymns, like their food, blended African and European elements into a spiritual succotash too satisfying to bother sorting out the separate elements. Like their white counterparts, most black preachers were poorly educated, bivocational, poorly paid, and rural minded. Like it or not, rural folkways and primitivism (chanting, singing, praying) dominated the worship of both races of Baptists, as the testimony of an entire generation of visitors from the North made clear.

For all their similarities, after 1865 differences between black and white Alabama Baptists predominated. Whereas northern Baptists divided between evangelical/fundamentalists and liberal/modernists, in the South blacks and whites divided over race and between those who maintained rural folk traditions and those who sought the professionalism and prestige of the rising urban middle class. In the long run, southern differences of race and class mattered as much as northern differences about theology.[138]

After the Civil War, southern evangelicalism bequeathed American Protestantism a legacy of pessimism, despondency, defeat, and despair. When northern Protestantism moved on to engage new forces of industrialism, urbanization, and immigration (adjusting theology and Christian ethics as it went), white southern Baptists preferred to stay as they were, following familiar paths through a threatening forest of dangers.

5

Building a New South, 1875–1890

"Educate, educate, educate in order that our children may perform a worthy part in the new age that dawns upon us."

For people intent on building a new kind of South, the post-Reconstruction era did not get off to a good start. In 1877 J. J. D. Renfroe blasted his fellow Baptists in three essays entitled "Wants of Baptists." They did not support missions, the denominational paper, Baptist colleges and seminaries, or anything else that cost money. As a denomination, Alabama Baptists had little influence on noble causes despite 100,000 white members enrolled in 1,200 churches. At least there was no disunion among them, he added sarcastically, because controversy required the exertion of too much energy.[1]

Confusion and Conflict

Conditions in the state confirmed Renfroe's criticism. Although Alabama contained 621 ordained Baptist ministers in 1875, some counties in western Alabama had none. One pastor of five part-time churches reported that "coldness seems to pervade . . . most of them." In 1880 Decatur Baptists still had not replaced their building, which was burned by Union **157** troops during the war. That same year the Athens church had no regular services, and its membership was declining. The church at Courtland had dwindled to only four members. In Cherokee County one church had been taken over by followers of Alexander Campbell and another by Methodists. The Tuscumbia church had employed no resident pastor for three years and had few members. North of Birmingham only two churches had preaching services every Sunday. Few north Alabama congregations supported missions, education, or any other benevolence cause.[2]

Despite the positive effect of railroads on denominational unity, a legacy of cultural and political sectionalism remained. Central Baptist Association (isolated from other Baptists by the Coosa River to the west and mountainous or hilly terrain on the other three sides) had no town larger than the tiny hamlet of Rockford and participated little in denominational affairs. When the state convention ventured north of the mountains, few attended even among those who lived in north Alabama. A pastor newly arrived from another state chided Alabama Baptists for their destructive north-south intrastate sectionalism.[3] Baptist ineffectiveness stemmed not only from economic problems attributable to war and Reconstruction. It also owed much to internal divisions and doctrinal disputes.

Most rural churches continued to issue an annual call despite opposition from denominational leaders. An expression of local church hegemony and Baptist democracy, the practice made life precarious for ministers and fostered instability. State missions secretary Washington B. Crumpton attacked the practice despite the insistence of its defenders that it was biblical. Crumpton (the longtime secretary-treasurer of the ABSC) warned that "religious tramps and clerical church hunters" thrived on the system. The practice also disrupted congregations annually because factions divided over candidates. Even pastors who retained a bare majority were likely to resign in order to save their churches from division.[4] Nor did such a system encourage prophetic preaching.

Low salaries also continued to plague the denomination. Baptists in north Alabama especially argued that paying regular salaries to their pastors was unscriptural. As a result, one minister in the region received only $25 a year for monthly services at four churches. His wife and children had to work in the fields to survive. Denominational officials pleaded for adequate pay so ministers could devote full time to ministerial duties. They extolled the model of Union Springs Baptist Church, where a committee canvassed all members, determined how much each could contribute, appointed a wealthy member to account for a stipulated sum paid in monthly installments, then elected a pastor for an indefinite tenure based on such pledges.[5]

As a consequence of low pay, most pastors continued to be bivocational. In rural areas especially, pastors performed no function beyond occasional weddings and funerals, presiding at the monthly church conference, and preaching once a month. So, holding other jobs was a simple matter. A pastor in Oxford knew of only three men in his third of the state who could support their families on what churches paid them. They had to supplement their income. J. I. Stockton of Decatur earned his primary living as a carpenter, and even luminaries such as E. B. Teague and B. H. Crumpton had to supplement their salaries by teaching school.[6]

Although preaching remained the primary vehicle for extending the kingdom of God, Baptists reached no consensus over how this proclamation should be accomplished. Many prominent divines (such as E. T. Winkler of the Siloam church in Marion) wrote manuscript sermons that circulated well beyond their local communities. Others condemned written sermons, quoting legendary English Baptist Charles H. Spurgeon, who said he would rather be hanged than write out a sermon.[7]

Arguments over the roles of emotion and intellect also divided Baptists. As preachers obtained better education, they became too scholarly, according to one critic. Instead of simplifying the gospel, they mystified the congregation. A critic cited another Spurgeon witticism: Instead of "feed my lambs," scholarly preachers interpreted their mandate as "feed my Camelopards" because only giraffes had necks long enough to reach food placed so far over their heads.[8]

Other critics deplored the introduction of slang into preaching that debased the gospel. Influenced by popular revivalists, Baptist preachers had begun to use "silly songs, vociferous prayers, senseless appeals, and affected zeal" in order to bring emotions to fever pitch. Then they entreated "mourners in the most 'rousatious' manner." Such services reminded one critic of black worship, which often degenerated into "a wild rave." A eulogy to the distinguished antebellum preacher David Lee recalled his poor education and modest ability as a preacher but praised him for never descending to "the lower plain of ribaldry and slang of pulpit montebanks." It was easy to err on the side of excessive rationalism as well. Pastors do well, the editor of the *Alabama Baptist* advised, to remember a story from Camden. A woman in the Wilcox County town was asked how she liked the sermon by the Baptist preacher. "Very well," she replied, "but it wasn't deep, nothing but the Bible." The pastor took the remark as high praise and advised all Baptist preachers to preach that way.[9]

In addition to arguments about preaching substance and style, Alabama Baptists fought over a variety of denominational matters. A convention decision in the 1880s to move Howard College from Marion to Birmingham ignited a firestorm, as did a decision in 1878 to sell the *Alabama Baptist* to private owners. Subsequently, some readers canceled subscriptions because the owners published advertisements for patent medicines. When owner John L. West sold the paper in 1885 to layman John G. Harris (who moved the paper to Montgomery), the convention again erupted into controversy. But without funds to run the paper itself, the convention had no alternative but to approve the sale.[10]

Conflict between the renamed Home Mission Board SBC and the newly formed state mission board compounded denominational problems. Initially state Baptists fiercely supported the HMB. But when it moved from Marion to Atlanta in 1882, many Alabama Baptists transferred loyalty to their state board. The 1885 state convention produced a lively debate among J. J. D. Renfroe, B. F. Riley, and others about the method for funding missions. Mission money went from churches to the newly created state mission board; from there it was distributed to the home and foreign mission boards of the SBC. The state board kept revenues to fund its mission activities and pay the salary of the corresponding secretary. Samuel Henderson and others defended the state board as necessary to the growth of Baptist work in Alabama, but B. F. Riley proposed reforms that made the state, home, and foreign boards coequal and mandated a cooperative relationship among them. Appointment of a committee to study changes in dispensing mission funds did little to diffuse the conflict, which continued throughout the decade. One pastor even proposed that the HMB be abolished and its duties returned to the states. When I. T. Tichenor and B. F. Riley both refuted him, he accused them of a personal vendetta and of charging him with "crazy crankism."[11]

The debate triggered a soul-searching self-analysis. State missions secretary W. B. Crumpton warned that continued strife over such issues was dividing the denomination. He predicted that Baptist influence had been eclipsed in at least fifty towns because of such rows. Many refused to attend association meetings or the state convention because of the rancor. Baptists needed to behave themselves for a while and settle their differences quietly. J. J. D. Renfroe responded to Crumpton's assessment of Alabama Baptists by agreeing that the denomination had stagnated, but he traced the cause to excessive sensitivity. Every time someone wrote an article about a subject on which Baptists disagreed, "some religious dead beat will fly to pieces like a joint snake and reply with a personal thrust." Some interpreted his comment as a "personal thrust," which did not help matters any. Other correspondents attributed the sour spirit to casual attitudes by churches toward licensing and ordaining ministers, a practice that had lowered the quality of preachers in the state.[12]

As if these impediments were not bad enough, Alabama Baptists continued to disagree on a wide variety of doctrinal questions. They fought over foot washing, although the practice survived primarily as a part of rural folkways. Urban ministers and denominational leaders insisted that the single reference to the practice in John's gospel was not sufficient scriptural authority. Defenders of the practice wondered how many times the Bible had to command an ordinance and the epistles describe it before the practice carried biblical authority.[13]

Antimission sentiment died more slowly than foot washing. In north Alabama hyper-Calvinistic Primitive Baptists contested every congregation and association. In 1877 the Cherokee Association rejected contributions to pay the salary of a state evangelist. Four years later the Carey Association (Clay County) came under antimission control and refused to fund an evangelist. In 1890 an association on Sand Mountain refused to appropriate funds to assist destitute ministers. Critics carried the day by arguing that preachers were called to preach whether or not they were paid. Frustrated denominational leaders predicted that "Hardshell" churches would not disappear until two projected railroads opened inaccessible Sand Mountain to more modern ideas. Other critics subjected Primitive Baptists to withering ridicule. They told a piece of religious folklore about a Primitive Baptist preacher who claimed he could prove that missionary Baptists were swindlers. He had "hearn" that Baptist missionary Adoniram Judson was running a bank with mission funds over in "Burmy." The rustic had decided to investigate the rumor himself, had saddled up his "crittur, and went thare and it was all true."[14]

Although Baptists rejected the hyper-Calvinism of Primitive Baptists, they retreated little from their own Calvinistic theology. They left the matter of election to each Baptist church, and differences usually amounted to little more than arguments over definitions. When the Lincoln Missionary Baptist Church was constituted in Talladega County in 1887, the ninth article of faith affirmed that God's election was consistent with man's free agency. But some universalism crept into the Baptist tent. One correspondent from Conecuh County wrote that infants, the mentally impaired, and "unreached heathen" were "uncontaminated by sin" and hence "outside the Gospel plan of salvation." Belief in "bringing an innocent infant to judgment" was "absurd," and the fate of such souls rested "among the unrevealed things of God."[15]

Along with Calvinism, Landmarkism left perhaps the deepest theological mark on Alabama Baptists. A series of articles in the *Alabama Baptist* in 1876 traced Baptists to the time of Christ, a basic tenet of Landmarkism. J. J. D. Renfroe, author of the series, quoted Charles Spurgeon as writing that Baptists sprang "direct from the loins of Christ." Renfroe believed that modern claims that Baptists descended from the Protestant Reformation constituted a Catholic reading of history. The editor of the paper acknowledged vigorous debate on the origins of Baptists but denied that historical evidence supported either claim.[16]

Gradually some churches began to accept members who had been immersed, even if the baptism had not been performed by a Southern Baptist preacher. This acceptance provoked criticism from Landmark-influenced leaders. E. B. Teague, though accepting women deacons, was adamant about Baptist origins. If temporizing and compromising in the convention did not end, Teague threatened to become "an out and out Landmarker." Delegates to the Mount Carmel Baptist Association voted overwhelmingly in 1883 to rebaptize any Primitive Baptist seeking membership even if the person had been immersed previously. Such a person had not been baptized "for the proper purpose, by a proper administrator."[17]

Landmarkers in Alabama also attacked the spread of "open communion" (allowing members of other churches or denominations to partake communion) in the North and even among Virginia Baptists. Alabama state conventions featured numerous sermons and debates on the subject and frequent references to "our denomination," "sect," or "evangelical denomination."[18]

Part of the resurgence of Landmarkism and especially its popularity in the 1890s can be traced to growing class divisions among Baptists. Landmark ideals took deepest root among rural and poorer people, while urban and affluent churches became more tolerant. Landmarkers were primitivists and anticentralizers in the tradition of nineteenth-century republicanism and 1890s populism.

George S. Anderson (pastor of Wetumpka First Baptist Church) assumed a leading role among Landmarkers and spread his views through a training program for Baptist ministers who lacked seminary education. He held institutes throughout the state and conducted a correspondence course as well. His monthly newsletter (the *Sermonizer*) was sent to all nine hundred Baptist ministers in the state. But his shrill advocacy of Landmark principles gradually alienated denominational loyalists and even middle-class members of his own congregation. In the midst of the controversy, Anderson resigned his pastorate. His defenders denounced "some D.D.s" (doctors of divinity) who had "stretched and widened our Baptist truths until they are almost lost from our day and generation."[19]

New controversies intruded on these familiar disagreements. The advent of Darwinian science after 1850 precipitated a crisis in thinking that was to divide Alabama Baptists for more than a century. Better-educated people within the denomination usually contended that science and religion did not conflict and moved toward a position of theistic evolution. Acknowledging that species did indeed mutate and adapt and that life on earth was of longer duration than previously believed, they nonetheless insisted on God's role in creation and denied the spontaneous origin of life. Poorer, rural, and less-educated Baptists tended to support an antievolutionary stance that pitted truths revealed by religion against the new science. Although class lines generally explain this division, there was much crossing over. Some well-educated denominational leaders rejected evolutionary science, and some poorly educated farmers recognized the process of adaptation and change as a phenomenon they observed daily in their barnyards.

The editors of the *Alabama Baptist* greeted evolutionary science cautiously. Reviewing an 1876 lecture in New York, they noted that no Egyptian, Mesopotamian, or Chinese archaeological artifacts dated from earlier than five thousand years B.C. Editorial accounts of lectures by English biologist Thomas Henry Huxley during his 1876 American tour summarized his evolutionary views without disputing them. But the following year, editor E. T. Winkler warned that when science intruded on religion, it should not be dogmatic. Winkler, a graduate of Rhode Island's Brown University and Newton Theological Seminary in Massachusetts, was one of the denomination's best-educated and most influential pastors (Siloam church at Marion). He believed that Darwinian evolution was not fact but theory (an "ingenious speculation," he called it). The geologic history of America was incompatible with evolution, he wrote. An unsigned 1877 editorial (unlikely by Winkler because the paper had multiple editors at the time and the attack on education is uncharacteristic of him) took a harder stand. The writer had recently preached a sermon claiming that people once called atheists were now called scientists. The editorial called two articles in a recent scientific magazine "openly" and "defiantly infidel." Colleges employed atheistic professors who corrupted the minds of youth. The author warned that a "diploma from a renowned university . . . is dearly purchased by the sacrifice of an immortal soul." Better a generation of unlettered Christians than a "brood of infidel scientists."[20]

After Winkler became owner of the paper in 1878, he tried to find a middle ground on issues of science and religion. They were separate spheres, and trouble arose when one encroached on the other. Theistic evolution was consistent with the systematic progress of nature. Speaking on the "new theology" at the Coosa River Association in 1888, G. A. Nunnally acknowledged tension between old faiths and new scholarship. But such "restlessness" was no cause for alarm. Christians should willingly surrender what new theology and scholarship proved spurious. New discoveries in chemistry and biology changed science just as new discoveries in archaeology changed theology. The old theology contained too much "bone and some of the joints were man-made out of pig iron." The new theology was born in doubt and would either survive close scrutiny or be proved false. Amid such confusion, preachers should preach what they believed the Bible taught. Be honest, be consistent, be earnest and humble in their conclusions, practice what they preached, he admonished, because truth had many sides.[21]

Nunnally's sermon began with the new science but ended with the new theology. And it was from this source that even greater peril seemed to be directed at traditional beliefs. The so-called higher criticism or theological liberalism emanating from German universities was making its way to America and challenging orthodoxy. Liberalism is not easily defined. In Europe, it was born as part of humanism (focus on man rather than God). It modified or rejected the doctrine of original sin. It tended to emphasize the social implications of Christianity over conversion, the unifying aspects of Christianity over sectarianism, the rational aspects of Christianity over faith, Christ as ethical teacher rather than as divine redeemer, Darwinian evolution rather than Christian cosmology, and universal salvation rather than eternal judgment in hell. The tools of liberalism included modern science and criticism of the Bible using the same linguistic, archaeological, historical, and literary canons applied to any other piece of literature. This criticism tended to undermine the authority and supernaturalism of the Bible as well as such doctrines as the trinity, Calvinistic election, and immortality. Modernism took these positions even further into humanism by emphasizing the perfectibility of man and theistic naturalism (nature operated largely without God).

Such generalizations do not hold true for all. A Christ-centered liberalism emerged that differed both from Unitarian liberalism on one hand and from orthodox Calvinism on the other. World War I and the Great Depression also chastened modernists and liberals and gave birth to "realistic theology" or neo-orthodoxy, which reemphasized humanity's sinfulness, the transcendence of God, and the need for divine revelation, albeit with a Bible they continued to subject to historical criticism.[22]

These new theological ideas hardly dominated Alabama's orthodox terrain, but they did establish beachheads. An anonymous correspondent who called himself "Vox" wrote to the *Alabama Baptist* urging that the Bible be studied historically. The language of men was recorded in the Bible, language "not exempt from the necessary laws and limitations of human speech." God's mind was unchangeable, but human beings received the revelation according to their own circumstances and needs. An anonymous writer who identified himself only as "Eufaula" created an uproar in the summer of 1879 by praising his new pastor as a man of broad theological learning. A number of correspondents did not like that description, arguing that the term *theologian* usually described someone whose "exalted genius" was not satisfied with the simple teachings of the Bible. Although theology was not inherently evil, it often shrouded biblical truth in intellectual sophistry. If theology were defined as a system of religious truth taught in the Bible and espoused through the ages by preachers both literate and illiterate, then theology was useful. But as a way of sanctifying great intellects to undermine the Bible, theology was iniquitous. J. J. D. Renfroe attacked "Eufaula" for substituting evolution for separate creation and for reducing the story of Adam and Eve to allegory.[23]

"Eufaula" struck back with humor and satire. He staged a mock surrender in 1879, pledging not to read another book by Calvin, or a "long list of noble worthies whose names and writings never die," or even Baptist articles of faith. He had determined to read nothing but Matthew, Mark, Luke, and John. To Renfroe's claim that he was an evolutionist, he responded that the charge had sent him reeling back to "anti-deluvian [*sic*] oyster beds hunting up his ancestors." To charges that he denied the Genesis creation story, "Eufaula" cited orthodox sources that the biblical flood was not universal and that the "days" cited in Genesis I were indefinite periods of time, not twenty-four-hour days.[24]

Little is known about "Vox" and "Eufaula" except that the latter spent his summers in New York, where his travels may have exposed him to new currents of theology. But the fact that both men chose pseudonyms speaks volumes about the unpopularity of their ideas.

W. N. Reeves of Eufaula was less timid. In a revival at Huntsville First Baptist Church, Reeves tried to harmonize science and religion. According to one listener, he denied the inspiration of the Bible though not its doctrines, flirted with universalism and humanism, and endorsed evolution. J. J. D. Renfroe, who heard Reeves preach a revival in Greenville, pronounced his ideas "milder than infidelity" but not orthodox Calvinism. Reeves rejected predestination, which earned him scorn as an "infidel with regard to much of the Bible" from another correspondent. That such opinion was not universal in Alabama is proven not only by "Vox" and "Eufaula" but also by David G. Lyon, associate editor of the *Alabama Baptist* during the 1870s and 1880s (who went on to Harvard University, where he occupied the chair of Semitic languages and Assyriology and was considered the foremost scholar of Semitic languages in the United States).[25]

Such liberal views were held by a minority of Alabama Baptists. More typical were the growing attacks on doubt, skepticism, unorthodox books, and higher criticism. A series of articles on "linguistic science" (scientific and linguistic study of the Bible) in 1876 opened the debate. E. T. Winkler noted that in some ways southern conservatism was a barrier to progress; but such opinions had also spared the South "ruinous isms which, wave after wave, have swept over the North and West."[26]

E. B. Teague weighed in against higher criticism the same year. He criticized the "mania" to study in Germany and declared German scholars overrated. Such scholarship had carried Christianity into rationalism and to the edge of the abyss. It made theology unintelligible to ordinary Christians when the essential element of scriptural interpretation should be "broad common sense" and a "devout and reverent heart." Ministers needed common sense more than education to save them from "wild speculations."[27]

E. T. Winkler admitted there were not extant copies of the original manuscripts of the Bible, but he insisted on the reliability of the oldest Latin copies. He vigorously defended the Old Testament against a Jewish scholar who discounted David's authorship of the Psalms and Moses' writing of the Pentateuch. If Christians admitted a single error in the Bible, Winkler wrote, that error destroyed the credibility of all biblical claims.[28]

J. J. D. Renfroe defended orthodoxy before ministerial students at Howard College in 1885. He denounced science that claimed that the "lessons of a fossil are superior to the lessons of Moses." Science that questioned the Genesis account of creation or alleged that man's fall from grace was an allegory was mere conjecture. Higher criticism had undermined the credibility of the Bible. But knowledge of the Bible was the highest wisdom a minister could obtain, and Scripture had "God for its Author, salvation for its end, and truth without any mixture of error for its matter." Humanity must have "infallibility" as the basis for faith, and though there had been errors in copying and interpreting the Bible, there had been no original errors.[29]

In the 1870s, Alabama Baptist wrath fell on Crawford H. Toy, professor of Old Testament at Southern Baptist Theological Seminary. A Confederate veteran and native Virginian, Toy had studied theology and Semitic languages for two years in Germany before joining the faculty at his alma mater in 1869. His use of biblical criticism alienated many Baptists and led to his resignation ten years later. He became Hancock Professor of Hebrew and Oriental Languages at Harvard and subsequently achieved international fame for his scholarship.

Toy's conversion to higher criticism was fairly thorough. He translated the "virgin" described in Isaiah as a "young woman," denied that Isaiah passages widely held to predict Christ's birth were messianic, and attributed the book of Ezekiel to Babylonian legends. When Toy was forced to resign in 1879, Winkler praised his character and scholarship but denied his orthodoxy. But even Winkler's criticism reflected the subtle influence of linguistic analysis. Winkler defended the first chapter of Genesis from Toy's argument that the biblical writer believed creation had occurred in six twenty-four-hour days. Not so, replied Winkler. Toy's definition of "day" was too narrow and scientific. The "day" alluded to might be an indefinite period of time and thus harmonize with evolutionary science. The Genesis creation story was "a hymn of the creation chanted and remembered," not a scientific fact. Although Winkler defined such a view as part of the Bible's "infallibility," subsequent generations of Baptists would allege that Winkler's interpretation was as infused with the "poison of rationalism" as Toy's.[30]

Support for Winkler, Renfroe, and other advocates of orthodoxy came from far and near. A New York reader of the *Alabama Baptist* congratulated the editors for "loyal adherence to Bible truth." Such constancy contrasted to the liberalism and doctrinal looseness of northern periodicals, which were undermining northern churches. J. C. Hiden of Eufaula decided to read for himself David Friedrich Strauss, the father of mythical theories of Scripture who taught at the University of Tubingen. Hiden spent the summer of 1889 plowing through two large volumes that debunked supernaturalism and reduced the historical Jesus to a fraud. Strauss, Hiden concluded, was "perfectly wild," as fanciful as "the most illiterate Hard-Shell preacher at a bush meeting." Another correspondent satirized higher criticism by telling his own mythical story of a young seminarian who had just assumed the pulpit at "Gum Spring" Baptist Church. In his first sermon on allegory, the immature pastor insisted that the story of creation, like many other stories in the Old Testament, could not be interpreted literally. An elderly man took the young man aside and asked that the next time he

preached he write out some rules in simple words where allegory and par-
able existed as opposed to where one could find "ginuine, naked truth." If
such instructions were impossible for him, he should not preach any more
about allegory because such sermons robbed people of their beliefs and
hopes. Thereafter the chastened pastor preached "the plain, simple Gospel."[31]

Alabama Baptists were equally adamant in rejecting another tenet of
liberalism, the unity of all churches. At the level of local communities, considerable practical ecumenism existed in Alabama. Because most Baptist
churches met only once a month, members often visited Methodist or Presbyterian churches when their own was not in session. "Union" Sunday
schools were common in small towns like Plantersville, where the Baptist
pastor extolled the merits of a Sabbath school that enrolled Baptists, Methodists, Presbyterians, and Disciples of Christ. Union revivals were common, and some Baptist congregations suspended their own services to attend revivals at Methodist and Presbyterian churches.[32]

Organic union was another matter. Alabama Baptists rejected reunion
with northern Baptists for sectional, racial, and theological reasons. The
only valid basis for union with other evangelical Christians was agreement
on the proper method of baptism and on doctrines such as the priesthood
of the believer, soul liberty, separation of church and state, and other historic Baptist beliefs. The editor of the state paper believed that for all the
problems caused by denominational divisions, church union would create
more.[33]

For all their commitment to Calvinist orthodoxy, Alabama Baptists
seem largely ignorant of English fundamentalism. John Nelson Darby's
dispensational premillennialism (Darby divided history into a number of
distinct eras or "dispensations," predicted Christ's imminent return, and
argued that a secret church existed that blurred denominational lines) did
not take root in the South. Although Alabama Baptists certainly expressed
popular reverence for the Bible and affirmed biblical authority, they produced little systematic theology, and their views were often contradictory,
as in the case of E. T. Winkler's defense of the Genesis creation story. Nor
is there much evidence that emphasis on the Holy Spirit and personal holiness took hold, though "a holiness man" from Missouri split the Cuba
Baptist Church in 1885.[34]

Keeping German infidels and northern heretics at bay proved easier
than convincing Alabama women and blacks that God had ordained subservient roles for them. During the last decades of the nineteenth century,
women in pentecostal, Holiness, and evangelical churches began to assume

more leadership. Biblical roles of submission and piety contradicted their growing influence in missions and fund raising. Evangelical women as well as men found their Christian ideals of self-control and commitment to spiritual values in conflict with the New South corporate order that enshrined aggressive materialism. They felt threatened by a feminized church and a gender system that began to suggest that women's sphere extended beyond home and family to public morality and church. Fraternalism (Masons, Confederate veterans' organizations, Odd Fellows, Knights of Pythias) increasingly dominated the male world. In the 1840s, fewer than one-half million males belonged to such groups. By 1897 five and a half million men (one of every four adult males and a majority of urban white-collar and professional men) belonged. In this sense, the enormous popularity of Masonic membership among Baptist preachers was a symbol of their movement into the middle class (J. J. D. Renfroe was chaplain of his Masonic lodge in Talladega, and William Carey Bledsoe, pastor of churches in the East Liberty Baptist Association, was grand chaplain of Alabama Masons for forty-seven years).[35]

Though Masonic membership united male Alabama Baptists, church dominated the lives of females. The absence, death, or maiming of large numbers of white males during the Civil War forced women to occupy new roles in churches just as it imposed new economic and family responsibilities on them. The chaotic economic fluctuations of Reconstruction compounded these problems. The Burnt Corn Baptist Church was in such desperate condition when war ended that a revival preacher recommended the church dissolve. Years later he reported that a "few faithful sisters resolved to hold on and hope and pray for a brighter day." As a result, a church rose from the ashes, added twelve new members, and thrived again.[36]

Raising money became a central female function. In Birmingham a women's organization calling itself the "Busy Bees" raised money through a strawberry festival to furnish the new parsonage for First Baptist Church. In Talladega the ladies' groups prepared a supper to help fund a new church house. In Wetumpka the pastor appointed a committee of young, single women to raise money for a church bell.[37] Although many churches (especially in towns) utilized female fund raising, some males continued to attack projects such as festivals, fairs, and suppers as unscriptural. Often they simply did not approve collective, social ways of raising money. Because few females of that generation earned money themselves, they could not respond to private solicitation, but they could raise substantial sums in their own ways.

Ladies' aid and benevolent societies dated from antebellum years but flourished in the 1870s. Women organized such a society at Huntsville in 1870 and two years later at Town Creek Baptist Church in Benton. At Town Creek, twelve women pledged one-tenth the salary of a new single missionary to China, Lula Whilden. Although all members were housewives, they put aside a small amount each month for missions. During the first four years of the organization, the women gave $237 to missions. In Greenville, organized women's work began in 1872 under the title of "Willing Workers." At first members met in private homes, but to quiet male criticism they moved their meetings to the church.[38]

China missionaries such as Lula Whilden, Martha Foster Crawford, Lottie Moon, Jumelle Williams, and especially Willie Kelly sparked tremendous interest among Baptist women. So did Mrs. H. P. McCormick, Mrs. E. A. Puthuff, and Mrs. J. W. McCollum who left for Mexico and Brazil with their husbands during the 1880s.

After organizing in churches, women began to push for recognition within associations. In 1885 the president of the Prattville Woman's Missionary Union (WMU) was elected as a delegate to the associational meeting. That year several women from mission societies appeared as delegates. Proposals to create an associational WMU for the East Liberty Association were defeated that same year, but in 1888 Julia Vernon of Cusseta led the effort to recognize WMU against strong opposition from preachers. Decidedly unchivalrous pastors described Vernon as "the little girl with red shoes on just [for] show" and WMU members as their "long haired brethren." Although action by the state convention that year had established a statewide WMU, pastors of the East Liberty Association refused to allow Vernon to read the WMU report. Instead, a sympathetic male pastor (Joe Hunter) read it. In the back of the church Mrs. Crawford Johnson of Dadeville listened while he read. After the delegates had filed out, she greeted Hunter at the pulpit and both wept, he in sympathy, she in "pure anger, for all my Irish blood was at fever heat ready to fight." Julia Vernon hugged Johnson and consoled her: "Don't cry; it is God's work, and he will look after it." Johnson remembered the advice all her life, concluding that she was called only to do the best she could and leave the consequences to God.[39]

D. G. Lyon, associate editor of the denominational paper, advised women to organize mission societies because their support was essential. Women had been reluctant to exert leadership because of "appearing forward," he wrote in 1876. But they must put aside "excessive timidity" on behalf of China missionaries.[40]

Such advice from many male supporters led to the organization of a statewide WMU, but that accomplishment came only after a protracted battle. The 1877 convention constitution had no gender restrictions on who attended. But when the Montevallo Ladies Missionary Society sent two female delegates that year, the subsequent convention voted to exclude representatives of mission societies from the convention.[41]

In 1878 the FMB created women's central committees in each state as auxiliaries of the state convention to help raise money for missions. Mrs. S. F. Prestige of Selma announced the formation of a state WMU in March 1879. But the central committee seems to have become dormant until 1881 when Mrs. E. J. Forrester of Fort Deposit took over. Her husband was strongly supportive and denied that the new organization was a radical innovation. The state board of missions recommended the central committee for women, and Forrester made an eloquent plea for it at the 1881 state convention.[42]

Although the convention accepted Forrester's proposal, opposition was widespread. Rev. W. S. Rogers cited an unfortunate northern precedent. A women's mission society had refused to be bound by a male board and decided to manage its own funds. What assurance did the state mission board have that Alabama women would not do likewise? M. W. E. Lloyd (pastor of Auburn First Baptist Church) raised more fundamental objections. This was yet another example of the "modern movement" against divine order. If women were given a state central committee, they would next want a state convention, a state paper, and their own mission board. To even bring such a question before the convention was to risk "the most unnatural and ruinous division of the denomination the mind of man can conceive."[43] Perhaps. But the minds of women did conceive it, the votes of men did establish it, and somehow the state convention survived.

The function of the new central committee was different from ladies' aid societies. The earlier societies had raised money for a multitude of local church projects; the new mission societies would concentrate all their fund raising on state, home, and foreign missions. The talent of women should be fully developed. Women could serve Christ best, E. J. Forrester believed, by engaging in their own work rather than by acquiescing in what their husbands desired.[44]

Women quickly followed up their victory at the 1881 convention by organizing at the local level. One woman wrote Mrs. Forrester that her mission society had enrolled five little girls who were raising "missionary hens" for sale, and the women had planted two cotton patches, the proceeds of which would be devoted to missions. Another woman wrote for information. She had organized a society with fourteen members, thanks to help from the men of her church. "I am ashamed of my ignorance," she added, "but . . . we live in a muddy country away from railroads and towns, and such a movement was never contemplated in our church until recently."[45]

Not only did women organize; women spoke. Although this seems a small accomplishment, it was often a traumatic undertaking in the 1880s. Many men cited passages of Scripture indicating that women should be silent in church. How seriously they took such advice is hard to determine because most Sunday school teachers were already women. But in the 1880s women were moving well beyond even that sphere. They spoke to Sunday school conventions and associational meetings. Annie B. Andrews told the Newberne Ladies Baptist Missionary Society in 1882 that outside Christianity there were only two classes of women: those necessary to perform menial services for men and those who contributed to men's pleasure. The gospel liberated women and redirected their activities toward duty to themselves, their race, and to God. Women were demanding that old prejudices be swept away. God did not create one-half the human race to provide pleasure and menial services to the other half, she concluded.[46] Despite Andrews's flowery Victorian language, she proclaimed a theology of liberation.

Mrs. William E. Hatcher of Richmond spoke to these issues in an address to the state WMU meeting in 1886. She asked how women could best serve God. Women's role within the SBC was ill defined. In the North, the issue had been resolved by providing women an independent organization. In the South, Baptist women were apparently going to have an organization presided over by male SBC leaders.[47] Though not critical of such an arrangement, she did emphasize the confusion it would cause.

In 1889 Miss C. A. Parker delivered a paper on women's work to the Union Association's Sunday school convention. She began by acknowledging her belief in the biblical principle that women should learn in silence and subjection. Women should not preach, lecture, or "mingle in the dirty cesspool" of politics. Women's sphere was to raise money for charitable purposes. That her lecture before a mixed assembly of males and females seemed to violate God's assigned role of "meek and quiet" submission seemed not to trouble her in the least.[48]

Others (both men and women) were deeply troubled by these shifting roles for women. Throughout the 1880s, they carried on a polite but spirited debate over gender issues. Just the fact that women wrote to the denominational paper, whether routinely reporting women's news or vociferously arguing for expanded roles, was a change from times past. P. T. Henderson weighed into the debate in 1882: Scripture assigned woman a separate but not inferior sphere from man. Her function as mother and her modesty prohibited a public sphere as speaker, voter, or military leader. Man was also better fitted for the ministry. Because she was "first in the transgression which brought sin into the world," woman was assigned the home and the birth and nurturing of children as her sphere.[49]

Jonathan P. Shaffer expressed a different concern. He warned women that Scripture did not sanction WMU to organize or operate outside the church. He mentioned a church where a number of wealthy widows (their husbands killed during the Civil War) decided to separate their mission gifts from church offerings. They sent their money straight to the WMU central committee, bypassing the church. The result was a severe drain on church finances. Such concerns about independence explain otherwise incomprehensible criticisms of missionary societies that met in private homes rather than in church buildings.[50]

A WMU woman responded to Shaffer's concerns. The problem, she wrote, was not the independence of mission societies or the central committee but the "dreadful apprehension" of males that soon they would lose their monopoly on speaking at the state convention. Shaffer defended himself with a vigorous rebuttal. He denied that the issue was separate status for WMU; he only wanted their money to be administered through the church treasurer so that societies were under the control of the local church, not the central committee. As for talking at the state convention, he did not expect that "Southern women . . . will ever forsake the exalted position which they occupy to become mannish on the platform" or desire to talk at state conventions like northern women.[51]

Two women debated these issues in the *Alabama Baptist* during 1887. Mrs. Manly (presumably Mrs. Charles Manly) believed that women should organize mission societies only in cooperation with their pastors and brethren. Their funds should go into the church treasury to be distributed according to action by the entire membership. A Mrs. Davis took the opposite side. Women had a right to organize independent mission societies, control their own funds, and send money directly to the central committee. Female readers chose up sides in subsequent letters.[52]

Two problems precipitated this debate. Women were not allowed to speak or vote in most church conferences. J. J. D. Renfroe admonished women to obey Paul's admonition to keep silent in church. They should ask their husbands at home any questions they had, and they could influence church decisions by such conversation. "Masculine power," he believed, "is doubly powerful when stimulated by the modest and well meant power of women." Like other critics of women speaking in church, he did believe women should be allowed to vote. A Baptist church was a pure democracy, he reasoned, and women and minors had as much right to vote as adult men. Furthermore, there was scriptural precedent for such a procedure. M. G. Hudson agreed with Renfroe's admonition for women to remain silent but disagreed with his reasoning about women voting. "No one whom the Lord has put in such positive subjection can properly exercise, or is entitled to the right of suffrage in the churches—or for that matter out of them either." Citing his own battery of Scriptures, Hudson extolled "the secondary position occupied by women from Adam to Messiah."[53]

The second problem derived from the first one. If females could not vote or speak in conference, then male church members decided how mission money raised by females should be spent. In many cases their decisions to spend the money on a preacher's salary or to pay for church improvements violated the mission priorities of women who had raised the money. Nor was ministerial opposition to independent mission societies entirely scriptural. Given their substandard salaries and desperate financial straits, many pastors did not view charitably the determination of women to divert precious financial resources to missionaries in China and Africa.

Despite such opposition, WMU work was well established in Alabama by the mid-1880s. The untimely death of Mrs. E. J. Forrester shortly after the birth of her daughter in 1883 slowed progress, but other women stepped into the breach. They moved the central committee to Montgomery and urged all mission societies to forward funds they raised directly there. Then the central committee deposited the money with the state mission board. The central committee elected its own officers. In 1885 the state convention made the women's central committee a standing committee of the state convention, although it did not allow women to report directly to the convention lest they violate the scriptural admonition to remain silent.[54]

Another crisis occurred in 1888 when the Woman's Missionary Union was organized in Richmond, Virginia, as an auxiliary of the SBC. The central committee asked permission to represent Alabama but was denied. At the state convention in Talladega two months after the Richmond meeting, angry male delegates tabled the WMU report and abolished the central committee, giving Alabama the dubious distinction of being the only southern state without a women's central committee.[55]

Such opposition resulted from a confluence of crises both local and national. The 1887 state convention voted to move Howard College from Marion to Birmingham, provoking anger and outrage among Baptists in the Black Belt (which had already lost many members and churches). Then in November 1888 Jewett Hall on the Judson campus burned. This financial disaster, coupled with the furor over Howard's move, created a rancorous mood in the convention. Many church leaders believed WMU was a competitor for precious funds to operate such institutions as well as local churches. Some males believed WMU blurred distinctions between sexes, that "mannish" women led such organizations, and that they moved women beyond their submissive and appropriate spheres. As the editor of the *Alabama Baptist* wrote, unless women knew how to sew and cook they had a "defective education." No amount of music, painting, or "ologies" could replace such elementary skills for women. Landmark leaders such as Rev. M. W. E. Lloyd of Auburn argued that a central committee that received funds directly from a local mission society violated the autonomy of local congregations and contributed to a centralized Baptist bureaucracy. Many males also feared that giving women visible leadership positions within the church and denomination would cause them to challenge the entire evangelical ethos that women should be subordinate to men.[56]

That men had good reason to worry was demonstrated by Baptist women themselves. Their annual WMU reports courteously but firmly challenged a variety of widely held male opinions. The report to the 1881 state convention cited the work of Phoebe and Priscilla as deaconesses as precedent for women working for Christ outside their homes. Nor was the work of a local church left exclusively to males. In Asia, WMU leaders explained, homes were closed to male missionaries, requiring the service of females. And if women missionaries were sent, women must help support them. Indeed, the decision of the Foreign Mission Board in the 1870s to appoint single female missionaries seems to have been both a result of and a catalyst to changing roles for women.[57]

The 1882 report, written by Mrs. S. A. Chambers and read to the convention by a male, had a zing to it. Chambers began by discussing the expectation of many male Alabama Baptists that women ought only to "go to meeting, sing, and make pies for the preachers." Fine as such functions were, women were called to "greater sacrifices." They were called not only to serve their local churches but also to advance "the Redeemer's kingdom in the world." Women "must not wait until every church is lighted with an elegant chandelier before we send the lamp of God's word to the nations that sit in darkness." The new, independent women's societies that troubled many opponents of WMU funded nearly one-quarter of all northern Baptist missionaries. "It is woman that must bear the gospel to woman in some heathen lands: and while other states are sending their best and brightest daughters, shall Alabama have no share in the glorious harvest?" Such admonitions probably seemed innocent enough to the women who wrote them but confirmed the worst fears of many males who heard them.[58]

The WMU faced another hostile reception at the 1889 state convention in Selma. The report on women's work was presented by opponents of WMU, and one pastor suggested that if Alabama Baptist women really wanted to help churches, they should bring their hymnbooks to worship and sing loudly during song services. But John W. Stewart, a pastor from Evergreen, proposed a resolution authorizing a women's missionary society in every church. They would contribute funds through the church treasury to a newly formed central committee to be located in Birmingham. The central committee's officers would include Amanda Tupper Hamilton of Southside church in Birmingham (whose father was the executive secretary of the Foreign Mission Board and whose mother was sister to the founder and first president of Southern seminary). Vice-presidents included Sarah Tarrant Bush (a native of Marion whose great-aunt was Julia Barron, the legendary cofounder of Judson, Howard, and the *Alabama Baptist*). Bush's influential husband was president of the Mobile and Birmingham Railroad, a cotton broker, twice mayor of Mobile, and a generous benefactor of Alabama Baptist causes. Another vice-president, Anna Banks Coor Pender Eager, was the wife of the influential pastor of Parker Memorial Baptist Church in Anniston. The new secretary would be Maryann Bestor Brown (daughter of Daniel P. Bestor, Greensboro minister/lawyer/ state legislator who had introduced the first bill to establish a system of public schools in Alabama).[59]

As Stewart read the names of the new officers, it must have dawned on some delegates that these women were not dangerous radicals but the most distinguished products of their own denomination. Whatever the motivation, delegates passed Stewart's resolution, establishing WMU as a permanent part of Alabama Baptist life. In December 1889 the officers met with four pastors and B. F. Riley (then president of Howard College) to chart their course. To continuing male opposition and refusal to allow women to speak at the state convention, Amanda Hamilton reminded women that no great cause had ever failed to arouse opposition. The key to overcoming resentment was kindness and gentleness, which in time would disarm criticism. To placate male critics, women held no state WMU meetings in 1891 or 1892 and consented for men to read their reports to the state convention. Success was measured in other ways. The number of local societies tripled in the first decade of WMU organization, and their contributions funded the new children's home at Evergreen and the salary of China mission volunteer Willie Kelly. In 1890 women contributed nearly $6,000 to missions, joined the South-wide WMU, and began a regular column in the *Alabama Baptist*. In 1893 they held their first state WMU meeting in Greenville.[60]

As men had warned, the involvement of women in mission societies had much broader implications. They began to agitate for prohibition, seemingly a cause that would have won approval from male Baptists. Indeed, the editor of the *Alabama Baptist* criticized educated young women for frittering away their time and talents in card games, dances, and other worldly pleasures. But what he had in mind as an alternative was not political involvement in the Woman's Christian Temperance Union. Some Baptist women in Talladega joined the WCTU, urged men to vote for prohibition, and denied that they sought the right to vote. They only wanted to help decent men eliminate alcohol abuse from their community. Pastor George B. Eager favorably described speeches by an Iowa WCTU leader in Mobile. Although her audiences initially reacted coolly to her call for both prohibition and woman suffrage, by the end of her lectures they extended her prolonged applause. The editor of the *Alabama Baptist* agreed with Eager. He recounted an example of a man's "detestable lordship" over his wife. A "sweet little woman" he knew had signed a temperance petition. When her husband learned of this action, he commanded her to remove her name, explaining: "I intend to rule my house." Such a husband, the editor wrote, "does not deserve the love and care of a noble woman."[61]

When men failed to enact prohibition laws, it was a small step from women's initial rejection of the vote to vigorous demands for it. Alabama Baptist males vociferously rejected this position as both unscriptural and unnatural. Discussing women voters in the Wyoming territory, the editor of the *Alabama Baptist* wrote that only women of the "lowest description" (waitresses, dancers in saloons, and prostitutes) voted. A decade later (1888) another editor condemned the WCTU for advocating woman suffrage. That same year Rev. J. C. L. Holmes told the graduating class at Judson College that life held something better for them than the extreme radicalism proposed by Susan B. Anthony, who had a "passion for notoriety and the platform." Holmes conceded that women's sphere was now larger than the home, and at least Anthony's "extreme views" had challenged women to seek independence, to define themselves no longer as a "toy for man's leisure." Women knew that home life was often filled with boredom and drudgery. Men had constricted the world of women by pretending they "unsex themselves" when they became physicians, lawyers, or business people. Such restrictions had driven women to the extreme "of the rostrum and the public assembly." The challenge was to reconcile women's new and more public life to the traditional responsibilities of the home.[62]

Most troubling of all to males was the prospect that women might include preaching in the enlarged public sphere. Not only did northern women raise the issue, so did female missionaries. Whether they called what they did "preaching," "speaking," or "witnessing," many female missionaries (especially in China, where custom forbade men to speak publicly to women) in fact preached the gospel. Though few if any sought ordination, they accurately reported how they carried out their work. In 1878 Martha Foster Crawford generated a torrent of male criticism with an article in the *Foreign Mission Journal*. In her report, she referred to women "preaching in the chapels, on the streets of villages and market towns, at . . . fairs and by the wayside, as opportunity offered." Both author and editor subsequently denied the conclusion that women occupied unscriptural positions, insisting that the misunderstanding resulted from an error in punctuation. Although female missionaries were more careful in the future, many of them (including single Alabama female missionaries) frankly described their preaching in personal correspondence. Willie Kelly, the most influential Alabama missionary during the years from 1893 to 1943, had herself made a deaconess in her Shanghai church and opened the office to Chinese women as well.[63]

Many ministers condemned female aspirations to preach. Such pretensions, J. J. D. Renfroe wrote, were unscriptural and "inconsistent with her sex." Paul's admonition to women to remain silent in church should end speculation on the matter, stated the editor of the *Alabama Baptist* in 1888. The idea that such advice applied only to the church at Corinth was "preposterous." A woman agreed, responding to the 1888 editorial by wondering who would care for children and the home if women occupied pulpits. Women must avoid the "notoriety and intoxication" of public life in order to reign over the family, to please their husbands and nurture their children.[64]

Although this theoretical debate occurred among Alabama Baptist elites (denominational officials, convention leaders, at colleges, and among well-educated women), the greatest threat to traditional gender roles came at the forks of the creek. Remote from the centers of denominational power and control, individual Baptist women (perhaps influenced by Holiness and pentecostal models) challenged male restrictions.

The Christmas season of 1888 brought a surprise package to Newton in the form of a female Baptist preacher identified only as Mrs. Perry. Elders of the Newton Baptist Church rejected her request to preach as unscriptural despite her claim to have appropriate credentials of ordination. When the Baptist church rejected her, she began preaching twice a day at the Methodist church. Her services created a sensation in the small town, and Baptists could not resist attending. Some of her Baptist sisters came to believe that Perry "must be filled with the Holy Ghost." Perry's credentials may have come from the Elam Baptist Church in Evergreen Association, where she had appeared months earlier. The pastor there had also refused her request to preach, but he was overruled by his curious congregation. He went home, and she began a revival that lasted several days and resulted in a number of conversions. She invited the pastor to baptize them. When he refused, she immersed them herself. The pastor resigned, the congregation split, and the September 1888 session of the Evergreen Association declared the Elam church to be disorderly, booted it out of the association, and appointed "seven discreet brethren" to conduct an inquiry into the affair. Delegates also appointed three men to prepare a circular on the subject of women preachers. A Newton man who reported these strange proceedings to the *Alabama Baptist* believed that whatever apparent good resulted from "such innovations as the woman preacher," the result was demoralizing to the cause of Christ.[65]

Blacks posed many of the same problems as white women. Like Baptist women, blacks aggressively sought to improve their status and redefine their role in southern society. They demanded equal education and control of their own religious institutions. And as with the claims of women, most white male Baptists were not pleased.

Through the 1870s and 1880s, white Alabama Baptists vigorously defended their region from outside criticism. W. B. Crumpton, E. T. Winkler, and a series of *Alabama Baptist* editors denied charges that conservative whites had reestablished Democratic Party control through violence, fraud, and intimidation. Crumpton attributed racial violence to lazy, intemperate, hot-blooded young men of both races.[66]

Baptist leaders also rejected social equality for blacks. In 1876 Marion pastor E. T. Winkler engaged in a lengthy debate with a northern Baptist who had served three years in Alabama as a missionary to freedmen. White Baptists had ostracized him and had themselves done almost nothing to help blacks. Even though the northerner rejected social equality, interracial marriage, and political organizing, Winkler and W. B. Crumpton dismissed his charges as sectional politics.[67]

Winkler particularly denounced interracial marriage though he accepted interracial churches. He recalled the fate of a white preacher who married an African American woman and had three mulatto children. Both races rejected them because the minister had "violated an ineradicable race instinct." On the other hand, Winkler scolded a white deacon for leaving his church when it admitted a black woman and child in 1880. As long as mixed church membership did not lead to miscegenation, he saw no harm in it, although volatile race relations in cities convinced him that the races were happier and safer when separated.[68]

Racial assumptions among white Baptists followed familiar patterns. Whites must demand that blacks rise to their standard. Whites should not embrace black cultural forms of Christianity just as Alabama missionaries to China should not adopt chopsticks or Chinese dress and customs. Each race had its own distinctions, and whites should seek to convert others while retaining their own cultural values. Such assumptions of white cultural superiority were a major cause for the failure of mission efforts in China and for African American alienation.[69]

As in their attitudes toward women, not all Alabama Baptists agreed on racial matters. A chastened E. B. Teague admitted in 1882 that white Alabamians were too extreme in their claims of Negro inferiority. Whites had attempted to defend the racial status quo at the expense of just treatment. A pastor in Furman considered blacks superstitious and corrupt, but he described them as "a kind, respectful people, generous even in their poverty." Conversely, he wrote that whites were often motivated by avarice in their renting of lands to black tenant farmers.[70]

Throughout the era, Baptist leaders also denounced lynching. Extralegal violence, wrote the editor of the *Alabama Baptist*, was leading to anarchy, and few Christians tried to prevent it. Courts that promised a "speedy" trial to prevent lynchings missed the point. Why conduct a trial at all unless the purpose was to obtain justice? In 1889 the editor praised a husband and wife at Pratt Mines who tried to save the black man accused of raping the wife. They asked neighbors not to resort to mob rule. The editor noted that such actions demonstrated "the power that the religion of Jesus can have over one's passions." Even though the woman could not definitely identify the suspect, a mob hanged him.[71]

On the subject of black education, white Baptists were ambivalent. They believed that blacks had limited intellectual ability and needed white supervision. Elementary education that taught blacks to read, write, and cypher sufficed for the vast majority of African Americans. A few blacks could profit from more education, but they were unprepared for theology school. Although blacks could best evangelize their own people because of their imaginative preaching, most black preachers delivered "unmeaning harangues to others as ill-informed as themselves." Nonetheless, the editor of the denominational paper criticized a bill in the 1889 legislature that divided education funds by race in proportion to the taxes paid by each. Such a bill would virtually destroy schools for blacks, who had little wealth and paid few taxes. The editor warned that the bill resulted from prejudice and once enacted might establish precedent for similar distinctions between poor and rich.[72]

Not all white Baptists agreed that black Christians were poorly informed or ineptly led. J. J. D. Renfroe praised the 1876 Alabama Colored Baptist State Convention, which he attended. The officers (many of whom had served in the state legislature) conducted sessions efficiently. Their sermons were characterized by "correct language, good sense, and sound . . . doctrine." An observer at the Enterprise Colored Baptist Association also expressed approval of the way black Baptists conducted business.[73]

Whites conceded that they should assist blacks who had separated from their congregations, though their motives for doing so varied. Some believed that contact between white and black Alabama Baptists would reduce the influence of northern denominations and Republican political organizations. Others helped because they believed black preachers were superstitious and theologically misinformed. Still others acted for idealistic reasons, arguing that blacks had served their families faithfully as slaves, had not harmed them during the war, and deserved assistance to build their own institutions. Charles O. Boothe, the corresponding secretary of the Alabama Colored Baptist State Convention, became the conduit for white assistance. Boothe requested aid from a number of white associations as well as from the white state convention.[74]

In 1880 the white convention agreed to pay half of Boothe's salary. As a part-time ABSC missionary to blacks, Boothe toured the state conducting institutes for black pastors and soliciting help from white churches. Occasionally a white pastor like Nicholas B. Williams of Livingston (recently returned from missionary service in China) assisted Boothe and won the respect of black Baptists. Despite pledges of help, white Baptists contributed little to Boothe's work, and in December 1881 he resigned.[75]

No cooperative work existed during 1882, but the following year black ministers proposed a renewed effort. White Baptists appointed a committee to meet with blacks but promised no money. The 1884 ABSC urged pastors to preach at black churches when invited. A speaker at the 1886 convention emphasized white responsibility to evangelize blacks but suggested this service could best be accomplished indirectly, by helping educate black pastors. Boothe renewed his efforts toward the same end, often speaking to white associations on behalf of black ministerial education. But so suspicious were whites that denominational leaders usually had to publish personal endorsements of black ministers before white Baptists would support them. At best, whites directed only a tiny trickle of resources toward their indigent brethren.[76]

Organization and Church Discipline

One reason whites invested so few resources in converting and helping black Baptists was that they had herculean problems of their own. One way of coping with these problems was creation of a convention structure. Beginning with the organization of a Sunday school board in 1871, the amorphous state convention began to take on concrete form. Through a series of name changes (Board of State Missions and Sunday School Board, State Mission Board, executive board of the Alabama Baptist State Convention) and relocations (Talladega, Selma, Montgomery) the function of the board remained constant. It organized and directed cooperative mission work for the state convention. In 1880 the convention directed that all mission funds (whether designated for state, home, or foreign missions) should be sent to the state mission board for distribution and that the salary of the board's secretary and his office expenses be paid from these funds. In 1886 W. B. Crumpton of Orrville became "secretary" (the title also changed through the years) but he effectively served as chief executive officer of the board.[77]

Maintaining Christian discipline and good order was primarily the task of churches. As the case of the woman preacher at the Elam Baptist Church demonstrated, sometimes associations imposed discipline on wayward congregations. Usually congregations imposed such discipline on men and women church members such as Elam's intrepid Mrs. Perry.

Renewed emphasis on church discipline resulted from a number of factors. Attempts to explain the defeat of the Confederacy centered on moral laxness. Declining moral standards that tend to follow all wars convinced Alabama Baptists that civilization was on the path to ruin. A Mobile layman argued that discipline was to the church what order was to the family. The *Alabama Baptist* reminded Baptists of the scriptural pattern in Matthew 18 for how Christians should deal with questionable conduct by members.[78]

Proscribed sins included obvious ones as well as more obscure offenses. Prostitution (which was openly tolerated in Birmingham, Montgomery, and Mobile) was an obvious target for church action. So were adultery, fornication, gambling, drunkenness, and profanity. Sabbath desecration required a bit more subtlety in enforcement. So many articles critical of dancing flowed into the office of the *Alabama Baptist* that the editor finally declined to publish any more. One preacher recalled a church he pastored where the daughters of a deacon and church clerk had attended a dance despite his admonitions against it. Eight days later one of the girls died. "Satan," the preacher reasoned, "got the advantage of them." In 1882 the president of Judson College had to defend his school from charges that girls danced during a physical education class. He viewed their after-class activities as harmless, healthy exercise removed from a bad environment. But he quickly moved to forbid dancing on his campus after a storm of protests. Licentious, rationalist, popular literature also came under fire, as did chess and checkers.[79]

Divorce proved the most difficult moral issue to define. The scriptural standard for divorce and remarriage was clear, but Christians differed sharply over it. All agreed that Alabama's divorce laws (among the most liberal in the nation) were too lax. Whether divorced persons could remarry or serve as deacons or pastors when divorced even on biblical grounds was hotly disputed. Several editors of the *Alabama Baptist* took a tolerant approach, arguing that such persons could serve in any role that their talent and opportunity afforded. Churches should not censure the innocent party in a case of adultery, divorce, or remarriage.[80]

Salem Baptist Church in the Tuskegee Association demonstrates the strict discipline imposed on late-nineteenth-century Alabama Baptists. In 1881 the church appointed a committee to talk with members who attended dances. The intent of this action was preventive, not punitive. The offending parties were "very penitential," and the case was dismissed. The church did bring charges in February of that year against a member for "willfully killing hogs and refusing to pay for them," a violation against property and a sin roundly condemned in freedmen. Two years later the church brought charges against members who owed debts, citing Scripture that taught Christians to "owe no man anything." In May 1889 the church conference debated whether card playing was evil, a matter considered serious enough that virtually every male member spoke about it in conference. The church unanimously condemned the practice as "an evil" in which members should not indulge. In August of that year, the church condemned a member for operating a still. Two years later the congregation recommended that a young woman be expelled for fornication, but when she expressed "true sorrow" and asked to be forgiven, a layman spoke on her behalf, and she was restored to full fellowship.[81]

These cases reveal much about the church. As in antebellum days, discipline was scripturally applied, was designed to purge, reform, and retain, not to punish. It reflected the moral consensus of the congregation and was intended to preserve the church untainted from the world. Official church discipline was probably no more judgmental than the private scorn and social ostracism that replaced it in dealing with church members who departed from the straight and narrow path. Of course, its public exposure of private sins held members up to ridicule and community censure, which was both a restraint on conduct and often a source of strife within the congregation. Families frequently rushed to the defense of accused members, who often denied charges or pleaded extenuating circumstances. Trouble frequently resulted. For whatever efficacy they provided, every discipline case was a potential land mine waiting to explode and divide churches.

Of the myriad ethical issues swirling through the churches during the last decades of the nineteenth century, Baptists devoted most energy to alcohol. Curiously, they manifested only passing interest during the 1870s, perhaps preoccupied by financial, racial, and political problems. But in 1880 they seized on the issue with a passion.

The key figure in this energized prohibition movement was W. B. Crumpton. A native of Wilcox County and a Civil War veteran, Crumpton was for a quarter century secretary of the state mission board and the first president of the Alabama Anti-Saloon League. His initial trip to the state legislature was to deliver a petition from Dallas County voters asking for a prohibition referendum. At the time, he knew no politicians and had never been actively involved in politics. He later admitted that visit began his career as a "lobbyist" for prohibition. As an evangelist in the Black Belt, he not only preached protracted meetings but also declared that "the liquor barrel was the chief enemy of all good." At the 1880 state convention in Greenville, he led a fight to restore the committee on temperance and instruct it to report annually to the convention. His motion passed despite opposition from preachers who contended that if the convention took such action it should also establish committees on dancing and card playing. The convention declared itself in favor of "the suppression of the sale and drinking of intoxicating liquors" and reestablished the committee. Crumpton thereafter submitted annual reports on prohibition and considered it his chief objective during his long term as secretary of the state mission board. [82]

Although temperance sentiment had long been strong among Baptists (as numerous church discipline cases made clear), many opposed drinking to excess rather than temperate use of alcohol, for which they found no scriptural prohibition. Ironically, members of W. B. Crumpton's churches

This team played a key role in denominational leadership from 1885 to 1915. *Standing:* longtime secretary-treasurer of the Alabama Baptist State Board of Missions, W. B. Crumpton. *Sitting, at left:* B. D. Gray, pastor, Birmingham First Baptist Church; *at right:* A. C. Davidson, pastor, Southside Baptist Church, Birmingham. (Courtesy of Samford University Archives)

in Wilcox and Dallas Counties made scuppernong wine, which they drank and used in fruitcakes. Even Crumpton partook of these delicacies until fellow pastor B. F. Riley convinced him of their harm. One correspondent to the *Alabama Baptist* inquired as to the proper course of conduct when the majority of members of a Baptist church made and sold whiskey (there were many such churches, he assured the editor). Another anonymous reader of the paper was so bold as to challenge the biblical authority of prohibitionists. The sale of alcohol was no more an inherent sin than the sale of revolvers, tobacco, or poisons, he reasoned, all of which could be misused and cause harm. Temperance in all things was praiseworthy, but extremism harmed the church and divided members. Even fierce prohibitionists often opposed making the issue a political cause.[83]

Baptist education and lobbying on the issue began to pay dividends in the 1880s. Although dry forces lost local option elections in Dale, Henry, Talladega, Tallapoosa, Colbert, and Pickens Counties, they won in Calhoun and Jackson.[84]

A chief way of changing opinions about alcohol was the use of Sunday school lessons. In fact, Sunday schools may have been the single most important aspect of Baptist life after they became widely established in Alabama churches. Before the 1880s, Baptist churches typically had only two monthly services: a church conference and a Sunday preaching service. Some urban congregations like the Eufaula and Montgomery churches had thriving Sunday schools by the time of the Civil War, but such congregations were rare exceptions and mostly enrolled children. Only eleven of Alabama's fifty-three associations had even a single church with a Sunday school in 1875.[85] Over the next fifteen years, the zeal to start Sunday schools rivaled enthusiasm for temperance.

Associational and regional Sunday school conventions spread the word. J. J. D. Renfroe became president of a state Sunday school board. In 1878 a layman addressed the state Baptist convention on behalf of a Sunday school in every church, particularly to instruct youth. Such an organization, he assured delegates, "breaks up the marble yard, the fishing gang, the lounging group, the gadding rabble, and other viler associations of the young on the day of the Lord." Sunday schools promoted personal morality, convicted sinners, educated Christians about Scripture, neutralized foreign influences, promoted temperance, and instilled honesty, sobriety, democratic values, and proper attitudes toward cleanliness and work. In 1891 the SBC recognized the centrality of Sunday school by creating the Sunday School Board at its convention in Birmingham's O'Brien Opera House. The establishment of a Southern Baptist publishing division to educate Sunday school members, after four failed attempts to do so, not only was a central event in southern religious sectionalism but also created perhaps the most important agency in SBC life.[86]

Baptists enthusiastically endorsed religious education, but they also supported public and denominational schools. Although denominational leaders had opposed Republican rule of the state and rejoiced at the return of conservative Democrats to power, they were less than impressed when the new political regime cut taxes and reduced revenue for public schools. J. L. M. Curry not only promoted public schools in Alabama but also became a national force in public education as general agent of the Peabody and Slater Funds. These northern philanthropies pumped millions of dollars into white and black public schools in the South. Curry viewed such education as a check against anarchy and as a means of socializing the poor into middle-class values. He trusted the white political oligarchy to fund schools adequately, though in Alabama that was a hard sell. After his selection to head the Peabody Fund in 1881, he often returned to his native state to address the legislature on behalf of better funding for public schools. Both he and the editor of the *Alabama Baptist* endorsed the Blair educational bill in Congress that for the first time proposed federal funds to states in order to eradicate illiteracy (many southerners opposed the bill as a federal violation of states' rights). One reason for this support was the widespread illiteracy of many white Baptists, including not a few preachers. [87]

Their enthusiastic support of public education was not without reservation. Because Baptists perceived public schools as an extension of their own beliefs, they often complained about the prevalence of Darwinian science and infidelity in the science curriculum and denounced the state for forbidding the teaching of religion. A report to the 1884 meeting of the East Liberty Association urged delegates to send their children to Baptist schools because the faculty consisted entirely of Christians, infidelity was not allowed, and the moral influence was superior. When the University of Alabama began searching for a new president in 1879, the *Alabama Baptist* urged that a Baptist be appointed to the job. Baptists constituted the state's largest denomination, had the largest number of voters, and possessed some outstanding candidates. Such chauvinism disgusted George B. Eager, who deplored the growing tendency of Baptist ministers to disparage public education because it did not allow religion to be taught. Religious instruction and denominational attempts to control state colleges violated historic Baptist principles of separation of church and state, he argued.[88]

Baptist schools were established for a variety of reasons. Some founders deplored the creeping secularization of public schools; others preferred a distinctly sectarian education that grounded Baptist children in denominational beliefs. Many considered public schools so academically inadequate that they hesitated to enroll their children. And in some remote mountain areas of north Alabama, there were simply no public schools at all. The venerable Josephus Shackelford of Moulton and Tuscumbia not only established a Baptist paper for north Alabama but began a Baptist mountain school as well. The Mud Creek Association also began an academy in 1886, the Jerry Fountain School, to serve Baptist children.[89]

Increased emphasis on ministerial education was yet another evidence of Baptist modernization and professionalization. Denominational leaders insisted that Baptists would lose influence over an increasingly well-educated population unless they kept up intellectually. Such advice created tensions between folk and elite traditions among Alabama Baptists. J. J. D. Renfroe addressed these conflicts in an 1877 essay: Alabama Baptists placed too little value on ministerial education because they were prejudiced against educated people and because Howard and Judson graduates seldom returned to live in rural communities. Educated preachers avoided isolated rural areas where churches paid too little to support a family. Yet such communities needed to hear educated ministers in order to develop pride and self-esteem. In 1885 the editor of the denominational paper praised the folk tradition of illiterate Baptist pastors who had been "the chief agents in the diffusion and growth of our principles." This passing generation of unlettered warriors had proclaimed the gospel. But times were changing and pulpit culture must stay ahead of pew culture.[90]

Howard College represented the hopes of this new generation of clergy. Denominational leaders struggled mightily to restore the endowment lost in the war in order to provide scholarships to "worthy poor" ministerial students. W. B. Crumpton criticized the college in 1883 for raising tuition so high that poor boys could not attend. He urged churches to fund construction of cottages on campus so poor students could live there and prepare their own meals. Although the college's president assured Crumpton that no ministerial student had been turned away for lack of money, Crumpton retorted that many poor students simply never applied, believing the tuition prohibitive. Other defenders of the college claimed the real problem was the wretched state of Alabama public schools, which produced students unable to cope with course content at Howard.[91]

One such boy was John Evans Barnes, who grew up on a farm near Pleasant Hill in Dallas County. A timid, self-conscious lad who felt called to the ministry, Barnes was talked into enrolling at Howard College by a church friend and fellow preacher, Sidney J. Catts. Catts wrote Howard's president, James T. Murfee, on his behalf. Murfee arranged for his tuition, and the green country boy took his first train ride to Marion to see a college campus. Barnes's academic preparation was so inadequate that he was assigned to the preparatory school, where he encountered Latin, Greek, and algebra for the first time. He thrived in the Philamathic Literary Society, where he overcame his shyness and learned to speak in public. Five years later (in 1892) he graduated fourth in his class. Supported by Selma First Baptist Church, Barnes attended seminary for a year before financial problems forced him to interrupt his studies. He later acquired his degree and for many years pastored churches in Alabama.[92] In the hard days of the late nineteenth century, there were hundreds of similar stories about men, young and old, struggling their way through Howard College in order to take their places among Alabama's new, college-educated ministry.

No single strategy for calling Alabamians away from their indifference, disorganization, and despair proved more effective than revivalism. As in antebellum years, few conversions occurred in regular Sunday services, though Sunday school and worship might soften the conscience and prime the spiritual pump. It was the dam-burst of emotion at revival time that swept most Baptists into the kingdom of God.

Nationally, revivalism underwent subtle changes between 1875 and 1900. Urban tabernacle revivals (conducted in large tents or rented halls by men like Sam Jones or Dwight L. Moody) became popular. But in Alabama (where cities were scarce) traditional camp meetings and protracted revivals were more the style. Although denominational leaders extolled the virtue of education, 15 percent of Alabama's native white population was illiterate in 1900.

Urban revivalism touched Alabama but not profoundly. Although Dwight Moody emphasized God's grace, he also denounced sin and preached a literalistic, orthodox, premillennial gospel. The *Alabama Baptist* criticized him for not identifying with a denomination, and a Conecuh County Baptist denounced him as a pseudo-Baptist who undermined true Baptist beliefs. Sam Jones, a Methodist preacher born in Chambers County, Alabama, was more of a showman. His preaching was a homespun mixture of wit and satirical denunciation of the educated upper classes. Baptist churches often cosponsored Jones's appearances (as in Birmingham in 1893) despite occasional criticisms of his vulgarity. Jones reacted uneasily to Baptists as well, telling a Birmingham audience that he had "never been a success shipping passengers by the water route." Baptist leaders often criticized Jones for his slang and sarcasm, but when Samuel Henderson heard him in person in 1885, he praised Jones's eccentricity as a way of breaking up "those old incrustations of routine and habit which have insensibly grown upon our churches and have emasculated them of their spiritual powers." The proof was in the pudding, Henderson concluded, and Jones reached the unchurched masses, improved the moral condition of Birmingham, and added 109 new members to the rolls of First Baptist Church.[93]

Local revivals remained the stock and trade of Alabama Baptists. In a state where one out of three Baptist churches had no pastor and where only an estimated 20 percent of members attended once-monthly services, protracted meetings served an essential function. From early July until November, evangelists crisscrossed the state. In 1882 a two-week protracted meeting at the Troy Baptist Church resulted in 100 professions of faith and a baptismal service attended by 2,500 (in a town that did not reach 5,000 population until 1910). A few years later James E. Barnard of Anniston's First Baptist Church baptized 200 people in fifty-seven minutes, a phenomenal seven baptisms every two minutes. In Fort Deposit, merchants closed their stores during an 1889 revival. A five-week revival in Tuscaloosa grew so large it had to be moved to a converted livery stable that seated 2,000.[94]

As in earlier times, primary criticism of camp meetings and protracted revivals centered on emotional excesses. The editor of the denominational paper warned in 1875 that such meetings were "degenerating into wild extravagance." Pastors and churches must impose restraints "on professional revivalists," restore reverential singing, and end hand-clapping, footstomping spectacles before they inflicted serious harm on Christianity. Such a revivalist did not contribute "to a growth in spiritual intelligence among his hearers." Emotionally coercive conversions seldom lasted, the editor warned, and modern camp meetings were more recreational than religious events. Such revivals merely deepened the popular indifference to religion. Four ministers sent a letter to the paper in 1881 describing the confusion and excitement of a protracted revival they had attended. The singing, praying, exhorting, shouting, and crying induced many responses that sometimes were manifested in convulsive fits of laughter. Such exercises, they concluded, derived from "animal excitement" and were "not the best way to promote godliness and piety."[95] In this struggle between Baptist folk religion and modernizers, the latter controlled the future, but not without a fierce battle.

Slowly but surely all these efforts to reorganize and reinvigorate Alabama Baptists paid dividends. Declining churches revived. New churches were begun. Souls were saved. During the seven years between 1875 and 1882, the state mission board put into the field thirty-two men who organized forty churches, baptized 2,000, and increased mission funds sixfold. By 1886, sixty-four associations combined 1,377 churches and enrolled 85,000 members and 14,500 Sunday school students. Baptisms that year reached 8,100. Combined with 125,000 black Baptists, the total for the state exceeded 200,000.[96] The SBC honored this progress by bringing the annual convention to Mobile in 1873, Montgomery in 1886, and Birmingham in 1891. Alabama Baptists did their part to increase the church population of the United States from 17.5 percent of the total population in 1870 to 22.2 percent by 1890.

New South Crusaders

Denominational leaders not only crusaded for the salvation of souls, they also sought the redemption of their region. The rigor with which they sought converts, enforced moral discipline, and rejected alien theology was a way of establishing southern cultural distinctiveness in place of the political identity they had lost in the war. Their attempts to define a separate religious community were successful and created a new civil religion in the South. The southern religious way of life (less optimistic, less democratic, less tolerant, more homogeneous and conservative than northern Protestantism) developed its own rituals, institutions, values, theology, symbolism, and mythology. It waged war on liberalism, labor unionism, feminism, racial equality, and demon rum at the same time it endorsed southern economic development, modernization, and industrialization. At the core of its mythology was the "Lost Cause," a heroic moment (though flawed by slavery) when southerners nearly stared down the northern behemoth of progress, centralization, skepticism, and federalism.

Straddling the gulf between sectional pride and national reconciliation was not easy. If the South was to rebuild, industrialize, and prosper, it must attract northern capital. To defend slavery, oppress blacks, and glorify the Confederacy played into the hands of Republicans who dominated their party by reminding voters of the continuing menace from the southeastern corner of the United States. Nor were denominational leaders prepared to forsake regionalism. They were no less suspicious of heretical ideas pouring in from the North than they had been in the 1850s. They found a solution to this dilemma in the New South creed. They encouraged the South to modernize, helped business develop, eulogized entrepreneurs, praised industry, and established Baptist beachheads in industrial New South cities. Baptists helped promote laissez-faire capitalism by nurturing values of frugality, sobriety, punctuality, and hard work among working-class people and by discouraging unions and political radicalism. They also encouraged diversified agriculture and new technology.[97]

One aspect of the New South movement was paying homage to the Lost Cause. *Alabama Baptist* editors during the 1870s regularly accused Republicans of South baiting, sectional demagoguery, and political corruption. They responded to negative editorials in northern papers. They warned Baptist women against joining the Baptist home mission society organized in Chicago because of "a want of mutual good understanding between the sections." They protested northern textbooks that portrayed the Union as a federal empire, states as mere provinces, or the Confederate army as rebels and ruffians.[98]

Baptist preachers also played key roles in the United Confederate Veterans. W. B. Crumpton served as a chaplain for the UCV and promoted public and Baptist education, scientific agriculture, prohibition, clean politics, and better transportation. At the fifty-fifth meeting of the Central Baptist Association in Coosa County, fifty-six elderly Confederate veterans held a reunion in the church before the evening service. After "hearty hand-shaking and a prayer," "old veterans threw their arms around each other as they sang and wept." A similar Confederate reunion occurred in the East Liberty Association in Lee County, where forty-five veterans reminisced and worshiped. The editor of the *Alabama Baptist* noted "how our war service binds us together," though what he meant by "us" is unclear (Alabama Baptists, veterans, southerners, men, all of these?).[99]

Confederate veteran–preachers never forgot their wartime experiences or tired of discussing them in sermons. Nor did audiences weary of them. For some veterans, their pulpit was a hearth with children or grandchildren gathered round. For preachers who fought in the war, their forum was a congregation of dozens or hundreds of neighbors and friends. Both forums strengthened bonds to the South within family, church, and community.

J. H. Curry pastored four quarter-time churches during the late nineteenth century. A twice-wounded Confederate veteran, he often illustrated sermons with war experiences. In a sermon entitled "The Confederate Soldier," he traced the cause of the war to states' rights, namely, the interference of the federal government with the rights of individuals to own property (slaves). He observed that though the South had lost the war, states' rights had triumphed in national politics. As for soldiers, memory of their "heroic daring, unswerving devotion and marvelous achievements should be kept fresh and sacred in the hearts of our children." History furnished no parallel to their endurance, sacrifice, and unfaltering devotion to a cause. Curry closed the sermon with a plea that his audience care for poor and needy veterans.[100]

J. J. D. Renfroe preached an equally famous sermon on the fourth of July, a day no longer celebrated by many southerners after losses at Vicksburg and Gettysburg on that day. Renfroe believed that southern neglect of a day celebrating American independence was wrong. Except for demagogic politicians, such animosity and sectionalism would have ended for citizens as it had already for combatants. God had overruled the South's ambitions during the war and the North's during Reconstruction. God had vindicated a republican form of government and revealed the folly of slavery, secession, and southern independence. But defeat had also ushered in a new era in relations between master and servant, management and labor, production and capital. The 1876 centennial celebration, the reunions of Confederate and Union veterans, and national expositions had spotlighted southern industrial development. In an economic sense, the destruction of the Confederacy had been a victory for the South. Slavery had been an "indefensible burden" and enfranchised blacks had actually strengthened southern influence in the House of Representatives. Racial harmony had returned. The new national synthesis, Renfroe predicted, would preserve what was best in southern civilization (Baptist commitment to religious liberty, separation of church and state) and graft onto it northern traits of energy, industry, and hard work. The merger of "Old South" and "New South" would produce a better region, and ancient southern characteristics would last forever. Although Renfroe reminisced about personal experiences at Gettysburg, the sermon was really about reconciliation and the future, about God's providence in adversity, about the end of divisive sectionalism and the advent of a new blended nationalism based on the strengths of both regions.[101] Atlanta publisher and New South guru Henry Grady could not have said it better.

Henry Grady, chief architect of the New South movement, was more than a subconscious source for such sermons. He was a palpable force, a secular messiah, and a constant inspiration. At his death, the *Alabama Baptist* wrote that no man of his generation wielded greater influence over the South.[102] Evidence for that assertion lay at every hand. In 1875 Alabama Baptists changed the date of their state convention from the traditional month of November (after crops were gathered) to July, because Baptist laymen in larger cities could not afford to neglect their businesses during fall and winter months. Railroads made it possible for Mobile Baptists to attend conventions in Huntsville and Decatur Baptists to attend conventions in Troy.[103]

Denominational leaders extolled Alabama's rich soils, preached agricultural self-sufficiency, and grieved over droughts and bad crops that forced country boys to desert the land and become clerks in cities. If families were to keep children on farms, they warned, farmers must diversify away from cotton monoculture. The denominational paper devoted a column to farm and household during the 1880s that featured articles on topics as diverse as hog raising and the causes of nervousness and loss of sleep. But the section was greatly reduced from the full page of agricultural information that the paper published in the 1870s.[104]

The editor's heart was not really in agriculture anymore. By the 1880s, industry had moved to center stage. Editor E. T. Winkler predicted that the textile industry would win for the South the independence that its armies had failed to achieve. The South must become independent by manufacturing its own farm equipment, furniture, iron, and machinery. The region "must educate, educate, educate in order that our children may perform a worthy part in the new age that dawns upon us." He featured front-page articles on European investment in southern industry and reported in detail north Alabama's industrial boom. Associate editor Samuel Henderson (who as editor in the 1850s had been a leading exponent of sectionalism) urged Alabamians to forsake cotton farming for the state's coal and iron fields (iron and coal would be "the Moses and Aaron that are to lead us out of our gaulding bondage"). Mission board secretary W. B. Crumpton still toured the state on behalf of temperance and winning souls, but his trip notes in the late 1880s rang of civic boosterism and New South optimism. He placed nearly as much faith in railroads as in religious rituals. W. J. Reddick reported from Autaugaville that his village was abuzz with rumors of a branch-line railroad through the village and a dam across Swift Creek to generate electricity. No doubt cotton mills would follow.[105]

Samuel Henderson predicted that as industry grew so would churches. And he was correct. New industries often donated land for churches, and they preferred religious workers. Preachers reciprocated with praise for industrialists and industrial values. George A. Lofton preached a sermon at Talladega First Baptist Church in 1887 entitled "Corner Lots." There was nothing wrong with acquiring wealth, he told his congregation. In fact the Bible encouraged honest, consecrated wealth. Men were not equal in capacity, merit, or possessions. When guided by "brain and enterprise," money could accomplish great good. He did warn against speculation, gambling in agricultural futures, and "scheming syndicates." He also bemoaned the industrial imperialism in Alabama that saw profits flowing north or to Europe. E. T. Winkler concurred with Lofton, arguing that there was no innate conflict between spiritual and temporal affairs. Piety contributed to "financial prosperity and to personal and social enjoyment." If one first sought the kingdom of God, an enriched and adorned life would not be far behind. Business helped religion by encouraging piety and instilling discipline. But business must be conducted justly and humanely, and the wealthy must acquire burdens of charity toward the poor. George B. Eager preached that the existence of both rich and poor was inevitable. Charity protected the rich from selfishness and should never be exercised in such a way as to strip the poor of their self-respect. Nor were all poor people deserving of help. Some were poor because of opium or alcohol use or because of their profligacy or indolence. All healthy and able-bodied people should work. It was no sin to desire wealth, and the poor must not be content with poverty.[106]

When government meddled with business, *Alabama Baptist* associate editor Samuel Henderson responded quickly and critically. Perhaps the intent of federal and state regulation was well-meaning. But the effect was destructive. He criticized Alabama laws that restricted the employment of children below age fourteen because they would remove poor children from their parents' control and their only source of food and clothing. Henderson believed that ages ten to fourteen constituted a critical stage in the lives of children when they should acquire "skill in labor." Limiting labor to children younger than ten was appropriate, but even then the state should first obtain the consent of industrialists. Nor was ten hours a day too long for children to labor, as any farmer knew. Henderson also denounced creation of the Interstate Commerce Commission to regulate abuses by railroads.[107]

If such editorials seem highly political for a denomination devoted to saving souls, that was because the times were changing. During the years from 1875 to 1900, increasing numbers of Alabama Baptists engaged in partisan politics. Although they adhered to conservative theology and scriptural literalism, denominational leaders left no doubt where they stood politically.[108] In 1875 the editor of the *Alabama Baptist* tried to develop a rationale for the growing political involvements of ministers. Preachers were indirectly related to politics, he wrote. They had to become involved in order to counter abuses on the other side. By proclaiming the equality of all humanity, preachers checked despotic abuses. By proclaiming the divine ordinance of ruling powers, they curbed the excesses of democracy. Thus, ministers mediated the extremes of autocracy and anarchy. But they must engage in politics cautiously. They must represent all classes and be neither a "courtier nor a demagogue." Whenever church and state struck an alliance, it usually produced injustice.[109]

As noble as such sentiments of objectivity and nonpartisanship sounded, reality was never so simple. Usually denominational leaders did enter politics on behalf of a class (businessmen and planters), a party (Democrats), and a section (the South). In January 1876 the editor of the state Baptist paper praised the Democratic governor who had redeemed Alabama from Republican Reconstruction rule. The governor had issued a restraining order against disruptive (Republican) elements that would help control "the fanaticism of reformers and the scandals of apostasy." That same presidential election year, the editor blasted the alleged political corruption of national and state Republican officials. To charges in northern papers that the *Alabama Baptist* was excessively political, the editor admitted that he had always been interested in politics but claimed to confine his editorials to the moral issues that were involved in campaigns. He also believed it his duty to vindicate Christianity, law and order, industry, and "Southern civilization."[110] Such an agenda established a wide field for the editor's political expression.

Nor were other Baptist ministers less timid. In 1876 the editor spent a week in the state capital, speaking with many Baptist legislators, the Baptist state superintendent of education, and other Baptist state officials. To a query about whether ministers ought to engage in politics or hold civil office, editor J. J. D. Renfroe issued a definitive opinion. He acknowledged that over the past quarter century more Baptist ministers had served in the Alabama legislature than from any other denomination. Many others had held office as county commissioners, county clerks, tax collectors, tax assessors, and probate judges. Renfroe argued that during Reconstruction lay people expected ministers to provide outspoken political leadership and lost respect for ministers who failed to do so. Democratic officials persuaded ministers to run for office because they were hard to beat, especially when they ran against "demagogues and grog-shop" operators. If ministers were allowed to vote, Renfroe reasoned, why should they not be allowed to hold public office?[111]

Whether in office or not, denominational leaders expressed their opinions on a variety of political issues, usually in support of New South ideology and policies. When Democratic officeholders proposed to cut taxes by leasing state convicts to private companies and closing prisons, the *Alabama Baptist* praised the money-saving innovation, though it warned that the profit motive alone should not drive penal policy. Generally the paper continued to support the lease of convicts so long as industries provided proper treatment and the state realized a financial benefit. Henry Clay Taul, pastor of Wetumpka First Baptist Church, began a ministry at the state penitentiary at Wetumpka and in 1886 was appointed state chaplain to convicts. He pleaded for Bibles, books, and newspapers for prison camp libraries, but Baptists did not provide much help.[112] Abuses of convicts were common, scandals became nationally publicized, and the denomination largely ignored these problems until early in the next century.

The *Alabama Baptist* did become vigilant against labor union radicalism. During a national wave of strikes in 1877, the editor blamed labor upheaval on financial depression and overcrowding in industrial cities. Strikers nearly always lost, became demoralized, and retaliated by destroying private property. By the following year, the paper took a more vigorous position, deploring socialist agitation among workers. A wave of strikes during the following decade left the paper equally opposed to labor anarchy but somewhat more sympathetic to workers. By 1887 associate editor Samuel Henderson expressed concern for laborers who built companies with their bones and muscles, though he had no sympathy for their lawlessness.[113]

As industrial production and problems crept into Alabama, denominational leaders refocused the denomination away from farming and toward urban/industrial areas. With Alabama's vast mineral resources, the state was soon on its way to becoming the most industrial southern state. Alabama Baptists could not long ignore this reality, and they began to discuss how urban populations could be evangelized.[114] There were several different populations to reach, each with different backgrounds and needs. In the country, churches often united whites of different classes (tenants, small subsistence farmers, and planters). But in the cities, Baptist churches from the outset tended to be organized along class lines.

Often companies donated land on which a church or chapel was to be built. Sometimes the primary motive for such contributions was spiritual. At other times, it was more a matter of social control, growing from a belief that Christian workers were more orderly, disciplined, reliable, and less inclined to join unions and strike. At Helena (where six hundred men dug coal for the Eureka and Central coal and iron companies), the president of the latter company, R. W. Cobb, was also a Baptist layman and president of the state senate. He had welcomed the little church at Siluria to relocate in the town in order to evangelize his miners. At East Florence, a land company donated a lot for a Baptist chapel. In Anniston, the First Baptist Church began in 1883 as a congregation of mostly working-class people. Across town the Woodward Iron Company also gave land for Parker Memorial Baptist Church, which enrolled mainly management, business, and professional people. An English stonemason erected a magnificent sanctuary for Parker Memorial in 1891, funded by a prominent banker in honor of his deceased wife and son. The church called as its second pastor George B. Eager, an erudite Virginian who soon was embroiled in controversy with powerful parishioners. He attacked the Calhoun Club (to which many of his socially prominent members belonged) for serving alcohol. His agitation on the liquor question led to such conflict that he subsequently left Anniston. Parker Memorial became one of the most influential and affluent congregations in Alabama (often hosting state conventions and usually ranking among the top congregations in mission offerings). First Baptist operated largely in its shadows.[115]

J. J. D. Renfroe moved to Birmingham to pastor Southside Baptist Church in 1887, a move symbolic of his strong advocacy of the New South movement. When Renfroe arrived, the church met in a temporary barnlike building. Even in this impermanent setting, the church provided cushions for pews until someone with bedbugs attended, at which point the cushions became infested and had to be burned. Renfroe cut a handsome figure for the affluent congregation, with his black beaver hat, frock coat, black ties, plain gold-rimmed glasses, and four-inch-long gray whiskers. His sermons, which tended to be serious and laced with Civil War illustrations, drew as attentive an audience in Birmingham as they had in Talladega.[116]

The proliferation of urban churches with more complex organizations further eroded the office of deacon. In small, quarter-time churches, deacons assumed a quasi-pastoral function that often led them into the ministry. But as churches in towns and cities called full-time pastors and developed elaborate Sunday schools and women's missionary societies, the role of deacons and laymen declined in importance. Deacons spent more time on finances and less on ministry to the poor, widows, and orphans. An anonymous layman wrote the denominational paper in 1879 criticizing the *Alabama Baptist* as a journal of mainly ministerial opinion. Preachers seemed to think that only they should preach and write, that the proper sphere for laymen was growing cotton and corn. A deacon, also choosing anonymity, wrote a few years later that many preachers were hypocrites who did not liberally and systematically support the finances of their churches.[117]

J. H. Joiner (Talladega newspaper publisher, Democratic politician, prominent Mason, and Baptist layman) faithfully served J. J. D. Renfroe's Talladega church. When the pastor was absent, he preached forceful sermons. As a leader of the state Baptist Sunday school movement, he addressed state conventions. The Sunday school superintendent, he explained, should extend the pastor esteem and should infuse pupils with "affectionate veneration" toward him.[118]

One by-product of industrialization was a new labor force. As foreigners poured into the Birmingham district, Baptists pondered the proper response to them. The growing number of missionaries from the state helped inform Alabama Baptists about other people and places, particularly China, which was rapidly becoming the largest Christian mission field. The *Alabama Baptist* consistently advocated a tolerant position toward Chinese immigrants in the United States. Editors deplored the rise of nativism and opposed state or federal restrictions on Chinese immigrants. Chinese were peaceable, industrious, highly civilized people who were materially contributing to the development of the nation. Harsh treatment of them, especially in California, was antirepublican and unchristian. The editor believed that attacks on immigrants largely resulted from the racial hostility of the white working class, which Congress seemed all too willing to placate.[119]

Baptists urged foreigners to come to Alabama and helped establish churches for German immigrants who settled in Cullman County. In 1881 the state convention appointed Rev. Charles Tecklenburg as a missionary to them. That same year he organized the German Baptist Church with eleven members. He quickly added thirty-two additional members and began two mission stations.[120]

Not all aspects of immigration were so positive. One reason for the urgency to convert immigrants was the increasing likelihood that they were Jewish, Eastern Orthodox, or Roman Catholic. Anti-Catholicism spread as rapidly as the tidal wave of new Italian and eastern European immigrants. Baptists were alarmed at the growing influence of Catholics and their advocacy of state funding for parochial schools. A series of articles in 1889 attacked Catholic candidates for mayor of Montgomery and for state superintendent of education. Editors urged Baptists to vote against Catholic candidates for office and teach schoolchildren the perils of Catholic attitudes toward public education. Editors of secular papers attacked the *Alabama*

Marion, the Baptist capital of Alabama, in 1872, with steeple of Siloam Baptist Church in background. The town at that time was home to Siloam Baptist, Judson and Howard Colleges, and the Home Mission Board of the Southern Baptist Convention. (Courtesy of Samford University Archives)

Baptist for its "intolerably secular" and bigoted 1889 series, which ran for more than two months. But Baptist lay people rallied to their paper and applauded the editor's exposé of the Catholic menace.[121] As when debating the use of liquor, Baptists defined anti-Catholicism as a moral, not a political issue.

Baptist Leaders

Three men who led Alabama Baptists during the years 1875 to 1890 accurately reflect the mood of the times. One of the best educated and most influential was Edwin Theodore Winkler. Graduate of Brown University and Newton Theological Seminary, Winkler came to pastor Siloam Baptist Church in Marion after a distinguished career as a Baptist editor, administrator, and pastor in South Carolina and Georgia. Widely acclaimed for his intellectual and oratorical skills, he was nationally sought after as a speaker for special occasions. He delivered the centennial address at Newton seminary in 1876 and addressed the American home missionary society on the education of freedmen. As a former Confederate chaplain under General P. G. T. Beauregard, he was also a close friend of Robert E. Lee and preached the commencement address at Washington and Lee University after Lee's death. He preached the convention sermon at the 1862 SBC and was elected four times as convention vice-president. While pastor of Siloam church after 1872, Winkler was elected president of the Home Mission Board and editor of the *Alabama Baptist*.[122]

This "prince of preachers" not only helped link Alabama Baptists to the Lost Cause but also defended orthodoxy in theology and politics through the pages of the denominational paper and in sermons. In a tract Winkler wrote on internal improvements, he argued that the federal government should assist southern economic development by dredging rivers and harbors and subsidizing railroads. In his 1876 convention sermon to Alabama Baptists, he urged the primacy of education above all other state needs. But he also warned against a single unorthodox professor who could infect an entire generation with skepticism. He feared the advent of violent conflict between labor and management and the leveling influence of communism. The South with its growing proletariat class was no longer safe from such excesses. Democracy was equally threatened by capitalist speculators who sought riches through "fraudulent bankruptcies and purchased legislatures" and the political power wielded by the "idle, thriftless, and vicious poor." Only educated Christian people engaged in public affairs could protect society from the ruin of one or both groups.[123]

Benjamin F. Riley graduated from Erskine College in South Carolina and Crozer Theological Seminary. He returned to Alabama to pastor in the 1870s and also wrote extensively. For five years in the 1880s and 1890s he served as president of Howard College, then accepted a chair of English at the University of Georgia. He left Georgia to pastor First Baptist Church of Houston, Texas, where he also served as president of the state antisaloon league. He helped organize the Southern Negro Anti-Saloon Federation, which he headed from headquarters in Birmingham. In several books about African Americans, he denounced slavery as a monstrous evil and traced whatever moral depravity whites attributed to blacks to their bondage. The so-called Negro problem of these years was in fact a problem created by white injustice. He condemned violence and oppression against African Americans and endorsed education for blacks. Although he believed in social segregation of the races, Riley denounced racial stereotypes and injustice. Among his nine published books were several on Baptist history and race relations.[124]

Perhaps Riley's most influential book was a volume on Alabama economic development. Written as a guide to those who were considering in-

Isaac Taylor Tichenor played a multifaceted role in state Baptist life. He was pastor of Montgomery First Baptist, a Confederate chaplain and hero, a New South industrialist, first president of Auburn University (Alabama's white land-grant university), and head of the Home Mission Board after it relocated from Marion to Atlanta. (Courtesy of Samford University Archives)

vesting in the state, *Alabama As It Is: The Immigrants and Capitalists Guide Book* became a classic New South promotional guide. State officials employed Riley to use his considerable research and writing skills on the project. Published in 1888, the soft-cover edition of 5,000 copies sold out almost immediately. Officials ordered 25,000 additional copies for prospective investors. The impressive volume contained information on everything from average rainfall and temperature to descriptions of geography, towns, manufacturing, schools, and railroads. So successful was Riley's effort at state boosterism that state officials began publishing an annual Alabama handbook to convey updated information.[125] Probably no other publication did more to advance the cause of the New South in Alabama.

Isaac Taylor Tichenor played a similar role. As a Confederate hero, he tied Baptists closely to the Lost Cause. As a paternalist in race relations, he advocated fair treatment and quality education for Negroes. As an industrialist, he managed Montevallo Coal Mining Company, introduced new steam technology to coal mining, and conducted geological surveys of Birmingham-area mineral resources. When the Alabama legislature created a land-grant university for the state in 1872, Baptists immediately began to lobby for the election of Tichenor as its first president. His knowledge of agricultural chemistry, geology, coal mining, and the state's mineral resources qualified him for the job, and his long pastorate of Montgomery First Baptist Church afforded him important political connections. His selection as president made Tichenor to Auburn what Alva Woods and Basil Manly Sr. had been to the University of Alabama (the man who articulated the school's vision and gave it a sense

of moral purpose). Despite Tichenor's constant frustration at the state's underfunding of the Alabama Agricultural and Mechanical College (later
Auburn University), he recruited a faculty and chartered the school's
course. He emphasized agriculture and engineering, chiding "men of letters" for insufficient interest in agriculture and farmers for their prejudice
against "book farming." He also recognized that the majority of Alabama
parents did not desire their children to become farmers, so he emphasized
classical studies. He urged trustees to admit women in 1875, a decade and
a half before they did so. Tichenor emphasized education that supplied the
wants and relieved the toils of ordinary people as opposed to Latin and
Greek as preparation for careers in law or theology. He divided the school
into four courses of study (letters, science, agriculture, and engineering)
thus creating a hybrid college that was neither classically liberal arts nor
strictly land grant. He taught the agricultural courses himself and argued
passionately for crop diversification. He also challenged the school to develop new agricultural technology that would revolutionize cotton cultivation and reduce by half the labor force needed to grow it. Such labor saving
would revolutionize state industry and produce a lasting legacy to the
state's people.[126]

After a decade of service, Tichenor left Auburn for yet another challenge. By the late 1870s, a major battle raged over the future of the Home
Mission Board. Some states had formed their own state agencies and no
longer supported the HMB. Other states cooperated with the northern Baptist board of home missions. At the 1882 SBC, delegates changed the name
of the agency, elected Tichenor secretary, and moved it from Marion to Atlanta. For nearly two decades, Tichenor directed the HMB, opening missions in Appalachia and Cuba, promoting work in the industrial areas he
so well understood, publishing graded Sunday school material, and directing mission work toward the trans-Mississippi west. Supported by his old
friend, E. T. Winkler, who served as president of the HMB in 1882, Tichenor
locked horns with the head of the Home Mission Society of New York.
Tichenor bluntly challenged the right of northern Baptists to operate in the
region, chided southern states that cooperated with them, and precipitated
a controversy that probably did more than any other event to establish the
SBC as the dominant denomination in the South. Many Baptist historians
consider Tichenor the central figure in establishing SBC hegemony over the
South and of defining the sectional nature of the denomination.[127]

Winkler, Riley, and Tichenor formed an impressive trio, defending
southern orthodoxy, promoting southern economic development, and de-

fining southern sectionalism. As reconcilers of Confederate, Old South, agrarian traditions with national, New South, industrial modernity, they had to walk a tight line to hold their denomination together. Many rural Alabama Baptists were not persuaded by their vision of the new world aborning as events would soon make clear.

6

Revolt at the Forks of the Creek, 1890–1900

". . . the next thing to the church of Christ."

amuel M. Adams's fiery temper matched his red hair as he spoke to a Tuscaloosa County farmers' institute in 1889. Defending the Farmers' Alliance, which he served as state president, Adams denounced national banks as "conceived in sin and born in diabolical iniquity." In its moral and educational influence, he added, the alliance was "the next thing to the church of Christ."

Energized by a passionate desire to help downtrodden farmers, Adams had joined the Farmers' Alliance in 1887 and almost immediately had been elected state president. Reelected continuously to this office into the next decade, he worked with Birmingham merchants to regulate railroad rates. At the 1888 Bibb County Democratic convention, fellow alliancemen selected Adams to represent their county in the state legislature. In that office, Adams proved to be a shrewd, pragmatic political leader of agrarian forces and was elected speaker of the house of representatives. As one of five Alabama delegates to the Saint Louis national alliance convention, he argued that delegates should form a third party. So disenchanted had he become with the Democratic Party, he railed later in his career, that he would burn his arm off rather than vote for its nominees. This comment earned him the sobriquet, "Burn His Arm Off Adams." In 1892 Adams was defeated in a bid for a congressional seat by Democrats who accused him **205**

of pandering to the prejudices of the masses. Four years later he was defeated in his reelection bid for a seat in the legislature. But he remained
chairman of the Populist Party state executive committee and editor of a
Populist newspaper, the *People's Reflector,* in Bibb County.[1]

Despite appearances to the contrary, Samuel Adams was not a professional politician. By calling, he was a Baptist preacher. Born in Dallas
County on December 10, 1853, he lost his father in Confederate service.
As the only means of support for his mother, two sisters, and a younger
brother, the teenage boy worked the fields of his family farm to feed and
educate his siblings. He obtained virtually no formal education, though
he studied each night from his limited family library and whatever books
he could borrow. In 1871 he married and six years later joined the Baptist
church. Feeling a call to the ministry, he was ordained in 1881 and began
to preach every Sunday. Aware of his educational deficiencies, he accepted
a ministerial scholarship from the Cahaba Association and enrolled at
Howard College. When financial problems and family duties interrupted
his studies, he resigned from Howard, repaid the scholarship, and returned
to his quarter-time churches, studying at night as best he could. He farmed
ninety acres of land and managed to pay all his bills and stay out of debt.
But he became increasingly agitated over the suffering of his church members who, unable to pay their mortgages, were sinking into cash tenancy
and sharecropping.[2]

Reuben F. Kolb came from a very different background, though he
wound up in the same political party as Adams. Born in Eufaula in 1839,
Kolb's father ran a general store and cotton commission business. His
mother was a member of the Shorter family, which was prominent in Barbour County and state politics. He joined the Eufaula Rifles when war began, rising from sergeant to captain and the command of Kolb's Battery.
His finances declined during Reconstruction, during which time he operated a grocery store and opera house. He failed in a bid to become post-
master. He was more successful in truck farming, at which he won a national reputation in northern markets, especially for a famed watermelon
that he developed and called "Kolb's Gem." He became active in the Democratic Party and in Eufaula First Baptist Church. Selected as commissioner
of agriculture in 1887, Kolb used the office to advocate the interests of small
farmers. He spoke tirelessly at farmers' institutes and was deeply affected
by the poverty he observed. The Farmers' Alliance backed him for the
Democratic gubernatorial nomination, but party conservatives narrowly
defeated him at the 1890 state nominating convention. After his defeat,
Kolb joined the exodus into a third party called Jeffersonian Democrats (or

Populists). Twice he carried the party's banner into gubernatorial campaigns, and twice corruption, chicanery, and fraudulent returns in the Black Belt denied him the governorship. Though he accepted defeat graciously in 1892, the scope of ballot tampering and violence two years later caused him to challenge the results. The same day his opponent was officially sworn in as governor, Kolb staged a shadow ceremony from the back of a wagon a few blocks away, surrounded by two hundred armed supporters.[3]

Samuel Adams and Reuben Kolb, one a Baptist preacher and the other an active Baptist layman, were key actors in one of the nation's most important political dramas. Economic depression, agricultural collapse, and political rebellion split the country, produced a powerful third party, and propelled older parties in directions that produced major reforms for whites and the middle class. For fifteen years, Alabama Baptists engaged in class conflict and teetered on the brink of division. That they remained essentially united despite theological disagreements, the rise of new poor folk churches, class and political differences reveals how deeply they were united institutionally.

Hard-Time Religion

Hard-time religion not only sustains people amid war, death, and reconstruction; it also molds them in special ways during times of economic privation.

Conditions turned especially sour for Alabama farmers in the late 1880s. Cotton prices dropped to between five and six cents a pound, less than the estimated cost of production.[4] Churches filled with subsistence white farmers declined along with the fortunes of their members.

Alarming reports poured in from across the state. From Town Creek in north Alabama, J. B. Huckabee reported that members of his most prosperous church could contribute less than three dollars per month. Another pastor canceled his subscription to the *Alabama Baptist*. "My churches paid me off in promises. I never was in such straits financially in my life," he explained. The paper received so many similar letters in 1895 that it issued a special appeal for help. That year more than two thousand subscribers were in arrears, some of them owing for three years or more. Ministerial students at Howard College could not pay their bills because churches could not pay their pledges for ministerial scholarships. By 1896 Howard's finances were in such dire straits that a Philadelphia company that held the mortgage to the Birmingham campus threatened foreclosure for failure to pay interest. W. B. Crumpton wrote the Foreign Mission Board in 1894 that the state could contribute little to missions because of disastrous cotton crops and prices. The following year he warned that the board had no funds to provide summer employment for ministerial students. He advised students to seek out destitute churches that could not pay them in order to assist the denomination and gain preaching experience. Commenting on the suicide of a Selma businessman whose bank had failed, the editor of the state paper warned Baptists to live within their incomes, borrow no money, raise enough to eat, deal honestly with all, and "strive to get rich slowly."[5] He need not have added the latter advice.

It was into such conditions of rural poverty that John Franklyn Norris was born near Dadeville in 1877. Struggling unsuccessfully to survive on a tenant farm, Norris's father turned to alcohol for consolation. When Norris was eleven, the family moved to Texas where cheap land offered a new beginning. But conditions were little better there. The family lived in a dilapidated, unpainted shack. Warren Norris took his misfortunes out on his son, beating John so badly that he lacerated the boy's skin and broke his nose. Converted to his mother's Baptist religion in a brush arbor revival, young John's faith was strengthened when he survived three bullet wounds from horse thieves, followed by gangrene and inflammatory rheumatism, which left him voiceless and paralyzed for three years.[6] The legacy of rural Alabama poverty helps explain a man (J. Frank Norris) who decades later emerged as one of God's angry men, determined to purge all Baptists who did not believe as he did.

Rural poverty left other kinds of scars as well. There were religious answers to the questions many poor farmers were asking that differed from Baptist opinions. Although many of the leaders of the new Church of God were substantial farmers, most of the members were marginal farmers who left rural Baptist and Methodist churches to join the newly established pentecostal denomination. On Sand Mountain, a black female preacher won a following among blacks and poor whites with claims that she could miraculously heal diseases and call down fire from heaven. She reputedly practiced interracial foot washings in her meetings. In Walker County, a sanctified missionary Baptist minister from Mississippi appeared, preaching a "second work of grace" or Holiness gospel. He won twenty or so followers in the Pleasant Grove Baptist Church. His services sometimes lasted all night with members reportedly standing on benches and shouting or lying prostrate as if slain in the spirit.[7]

Such aberrations among Alabama Baptists were rare. But poverty was not, and a denomination of the common folk had special appeal to people down on their luck. D. M. Ramsey of Tuscaloosa preached to the 1889 state Baptist convention about concern for the poor. "From the lofty place where God sits," he thundered, "the beggar is as high as the rich man." God had chosen a lowly cobbler, William Carey, as the first Baptist missionary and a poor man, Charles Spurgeon, to awaken London. Baptists had always sought to reach the poor and must make special efforts to do so in such a dark time. Furnace Hill Baptist Church in Sheffield served poor workers employed in the town's blast furnaces and appealed for financial help in 1890. The Bessemer Baptist Church also enrolled mainly poor workers from blast furnaces but managed to provide their pastor food and a pittance for a salary. The Dallas Avenue church in Huntsville conducted entertainments and collected dues in order to provide $60 a month to the city's poor (even though only three members of the church, not including the pastor, owned homes).[8]

Baptists took seriously Ramsey's advice to the 1889 state convention. W. B. Crumpton declared that every factory and mining town should have a Baptist church. To help accomplish that goal, he hired Howard College students as summer missionaries to organize work at Blossburg, Cardiff, Brookside, New Castle, Pratt, Cat Mountain, and Wheeling coal mines. The Westside church in Phenix City had a membership consisting mainly of textile workers. Selma First Baptist Church formed a mission for operatives of the Selma Cotton Mill. The pastor of the Coalburg Baptist Church had a Christmas party for the children of immigrant miners in 1892 to demonstrate God's concern for them. W. J. Ruddick worked at a sawmill six days a week to earn a living and preached for three churches that employed many of the mill workers.[9]

Ruddick's ministerial career was typical of the Baptist ministry in Alabama. He was indigent, poorly educated, and bivocational. In theory, denominational leaders agreed that churches should pay their pastors a salary sufficient to allow them to preach full-time. In practice, the poverty of the denomination made that impossible. Of some 1,700 white Alabama Baptist churches in 1898, only 36 had preaching every Sunday. Only 130 of the denomination's 1,017 ministers in 1898 had college or seminary education.[10]

The Politics of Temperance and Agrarianism

Even a church of the people perceives reality from a certain point of view. By the 1880s, Alabama Baptists viewed the world largely through the prism of their hostility to alcohol. That single issue dominated editorial reference in the *Alabama Baptist* and appeared in numerous sermons. Churches and associations drafted resolutions opposing the use or sale of alcoholic beverages. Statewide conventions were held to mobilize prohibition forces. W. B. Crumpton lobbied fiercely in Montgomery. Large numbers of Baptists became single-issue voters, casting their ballots for state legislators solely based on how they stood on liquor issues.

Many concerns drove this passion. Having lost the war, Alabama evangelicals were determined to repent of whatever sins provoked God's judgment on them. Personal morality seemed as good as any starting place. They also perceived newly emancipated African Americans as a threat to their personal safety, especially when blacks were drinking. New immigrants from southern and eastern Europe brought cultural patterns of alcohol use as well as Catholicism. Alcohol abuse was also a serious social problem. Baptists correctly associated excessive drinking with lynching, mob activity, crime, personal feuds, family violence, political corruption, poverty, and other social problems.

At first, Baptists led organized temperance activity, followed closely by Methodists and Presbyterians. Between 1865 and 1880 they focused on banning the sale of liquor around churches, factories, coal mines, and schools.[11] By the 1880s, the prohibition movement had become highly political and focused on state government. Perceived as a social reform by its advocates, prohibition merged easily into broader movements to improve Alabama society and politics.

When a historian of agrarian radicalism tried to unravel Samuel Adams's populism, he could find no compelling explanations.[12] Had he looked beyond politics, he would have found the key in the temperance crusade. In 1884 Adams wrote the *Alabama Baptist* that his Chilton County church was deeply split over the whiskey trade. Only eternity, he warned, would fully reveal the evils of alcohol.[13] That letter began Adams's long journey into third-party politics.

Adams spoke for an entire generation of ministers and denominational leaders. Many ordinary Baptists saw no harm or even scriptural prohibition against moderate use of alcoholic beverages. They believed temperance was a matter of personal moral discipline, not a subject for statewide political action. But the tide swung sharply in the 1880s toward political involvement. For the first time, the entire denomination mobilized its muscle to force the state to enact moral legislation, and a mighty army it became. Once mobilized for political action, the denomination discovered what all religious groups encounter. What one Baptist considered a compelling moral issue, another Baptist considered political meddling that had nothing to do with religion. Tied to old political parties by bonds of tradition, loyalty, and self-interest, Baptists were not easily diverted into single-issue, third-party politics. As Samuel Adams was to discover, Baptists would respect moral rectitude and conviction in their leaders but not necessarily vote as they suggested.

On whiskey matters, Baptists believed they had obtained a consensus. One delegate to the 1890 state convention preached that there were "three things any of us can speak on—swinging loose and going to the zenith—whiskey, the Catholics and the 'niggers.' " Between January 1881 and January 1885, the *Alabama Baptist* published some fifty editorials on temperance, more (the editor believed) than any newspaper he had ever seen.[14]

Many of these articles focused on the social damage that resulted from alcohol use. In 1890 the editor wrote that the surest solution to racial conflict was to abolish the saloon. He could remember not a single race riot or conflict that was not "precipitated either by drunken white or negro men." In the same issue, he wrote that the saloon was the farmer's worst enemy. Each year that a farmer drank made him poorer while purchasing elegant carpets and clothes for the wife and children of saloon keepers. The winning essay for the Howard College commencement medal in 1891 (on the assigned topic: "What Is the Greatest Hindrance to American Progress?") dealt with "the whiskey menace." Abolishing whiskey, the ardent young student reasoned, would free money for education, turn immigrants into useful citizens, and banish socialism, communism, and anarchism.[15]

Mobilizing an entire denomination took a while and occurred at various levels. Individual ministers occupied the lowest but most important rung in the chain of command. Their temperance sermons persuaded reluctant parishioners and infused passion in the already converted. J. H. Curry of Northport preached a temperance sermon to his three charges (the Northport, Bethel, and New Lexington churches). The sale or use of alcohol was "an unmitigated evil, a sin against God and man," he proclaimed. It destroyed the happiness of families while creating paupers and criminals. Christians must vote as they prayed, electing politicians who would end the traffic. That no compromise with such evil was possible became clear as Curry reached the crescendo of his sermon:

> "[Whiskey] represents the most cold-bloodied, heartless and gigantic traffic in blood that the world has ever seen; because it is evil, only evil, and that continually. . . . It is the dead-march of a frightful plague; a calamity indescribable; a loss that is irreparable. . . . It is the serpent and adder, the fiend and fury, the enemy of God and man. . . . Listen to the cry of the or-

phan, whose father was murdered by strong drink. Listen to the heart-bro-
ken lamentations of wailing widows. . . . From every gallows and dungeon
of darkness, from every hearth-stone, blackened and blistered by its ne-
farious power, occurring voices come to brand this business as the worst
enemy of the human race. . . . This business is of hell, comes from the devil,
leads to him, [is] condemned of God and of all good people."[16]

His parishioners might disagree with his opinions. They could not
doubt his ardor.

Properly educated by their pastors, church members circulated prohibition petitions to local politicians. In 1892 the Antioch Baptist Church in
Bibb County petitioned its representative in the legislature not to vote for
a bill repealing prohibition in the county.[17]

The next level of pressure was exerted by associations. By the 1880s,
virtually all associations had active temperance committees that reported
at each annual meeting. The temperance report to the 1890 Tuscaloosa
Association called on Christians to back their prayers with votes. Ministers attending the Cahaba Association that same year voted unanimously
to refuse to pastor any church that tolerated drunkenness. In 1896 the
Montgomery Association blamed nine-tenths of the nation's social problems on the saloon. Compared to the liquor question, delegates resolved,
such passionately debated contemporary issues as the coinage of free silver, tariffs, and immigration policy "dwindle into absolute insignificance."
The solution was to examine every candidate for public office from governor down to local officials and not vote for anyone who drank alcohol. The
resolution also urged every church in the association to set aside one Sunday to discuss temperance issues. The Newton Association concurred in
this resolution. Sometimes unanimity was not so easy. At the 1890 Troy Association, the temperance report placed primary responsibility for prohibition on personal restraint and education by local churches, not on civil law.
This position precipitated a vigorous debate by those who believed legislation afforded the best solution.[18]

At the state level, the transcendent figure in Alabama's prohibition
movement was state mission board secretary W. B. Crumpton. In 1884
Crumpton advertised a temperance convention in Tuscaloosa by refuting
a friend's complaint that men could not be legislated into heaven. Crumpton replied that the Alabama legislature passed laws against gambling, obscene and profane language in public places, and cruelty to animals. So
why not legislate morality concerning the use of alcohol? In 1891 Crumpton outlined a multistage strategy that within two decades would make

Alabama legally dry. First came a statewide temperance meeting for white people (later, he suggested, the white group might cooperate with a parallel black temperance organization). Women should organize an auxiliary to the men's league. All these organizations would distribute temperance literature and conduct lectures. They would enter politics only as individuals. They should start a statewide temperance newspaper and organize down to the county and beat levels.[19]

Calls for "direct, positive, aggressive action" on temperance reverberated through Baptist ranks. Setting a goal of five hundred local prohibition clubs, denominational leaders reassured pastors that such work was nonpartisan and that they "need not enter the political arena." The reality of their experience did not match that prediction. Twice prohibition forces lost in Talladega County because they did not organize politically. When dry forces finally prevailed under the leadership of J. J. D. Renfroe, bars remained open, first clandestinely, then in open defiance of the law. A grand jury refused to indict owners of saloons, which operated exactly as they had before prohibition because politicians and law enforcement officials permitted them to do so. Baptists began to realize that the battle was not won when laws were passed but when politicians enforced laws. Only the determined exercise of political power would bring victory.[20]

Translating an amorphous recognition of the need for temperance reform into concrete political action occurred in a remarkably brief three-year period between 1884 and 1887. Finding the proper political vehicle for the prohibition crusade took much longer.

Venturing into the stream of temperance politics threatened to pull church people into deeper waters and a faster current than they had bargained for. Only a decade away from Reconstruction, party leaders warned that infidelity to the Democratic Party would divide the white vote and usher in neo-Reconstruction rule by black and white Republicans. Baptists argued furiously about whether prohibition or white political solidarity mattered most.

Temperance questions also put Baptists at odds with agents of modernization. Although some New South advocates extolled the virtues of sobriety and a morally disciplined labor force, prohibition was in some ways an attempt by rural people to impose their values on cities with their heterogeneous populations. The "saloon problem" was viewed by most Alabamians as primarily a town-city threat to traditional values and part of a larger struggle between declining rural areas and booming urban centers. As a result, cosmopolitan Baptist leaders entered the prohibition fray cautiously, often scorning single-issue politics and proposing local option pro-

hibition elections in each county and city as preferable to a statewide prohibition amendment.

Between 1884 and 1887, Baptists conducted a spirited theological debate over the politics of prohibition. They created essentially a shadow prohibition party that gradually moved away from the Democratic Party and
into a larger reform movement. This sampling of the waters of reform occurred in stages. Baptists first angrily denounced Democrats who were reluctant to prohibit alcohol, and they organized their forces into a separate
temperance faction. When Democrats attacked them for entering politics,
Baptists developed a carefully thought-out rationale for political organization. Because they found temperance allies in the rural-based Farmers' Alliance faction of the Democratic Party, they quickly waded deeper into the
stream of reform politics within the Democratic Party. When the Democratic hierarchy stoutly resisted reform, the more liberal faction broke away.
In the 1890s, some elements of the Farmers' Alliance plunged head-first
into the rapid currents of third-party, populist politics, and many temperance-minded Baptists went with them. Other temperance-minded Baptists backed away from this extreme action, deciding that racial solidarity,
party harmony, and middle-class business and planter economic interests
mattered more than a whimsical crusade against demon rum. They bided
their time, held their peace, and welcomed a new reform spirit that swept
through a chastened Democratic Party after 1896, which made the party
of their fathers more amenable to prohibition and other humanitarian reforms.

The editor of the *Alabama Baptist* from 1881 to 1884, W. C. Cleveland,
opposed a national or statewide prohibition law as well as creation of a
"political temperance party." He feared that such politicization would split
whites, undermine the Democratic Party, and harm the cause of temperance. Instead, Cleveland urged individual Christians to spurn liquor, and
he urged prohibition leaders to marshal their energy for local option elections. [21]

In 1884 Baptist opinion began to move away from Cleveland's cautious
advice. George E. Brewer (pastor in Lafayette) wrote an essay for the paper
entitled "Christian Voters of 1884," wherein he chided voters for their traditional party loyalty despite the party's disregard for moral issues. Voters,
he wrote, should support no candidate or party that refused to endorse prohibition. The new editor of the *Alabama Baptist* entered the debate, writing
that though he intended to discuss politics only when it intruded on moral
issues, he was disturbed by the tendency to vote for party nominees regardless of their "incompetency or immorality." [22] The battle was now joined.

At the 1884 state convention in July, George E. Brewer delivered the temperance address and W. B. Crumpton presented the temperance report. Brewer urged Baptists to organize on behalf of temperance candidates, to pressure the political process on behalf of prohibition, and to reject advice that evangelical Christians should concentrate on saving souls and avoid politics. Crumpton boldly called for a constitutional amendment prohibiting the manufacture or sale of alcoholic beverages in Alabama. After considerable criticism of his report, Crumpton muted his position a week later, denying that he favored mixing religion and politics. Promoting temperance by voting for it in elections was not mixing the temporal with the spiritual, he explained unconvincingly to his critics. Having followed the year-long prohibition debate, John C. Orr wrote in November that he had decided never again to vote for "any more whiskey guzzlers." Henceforth, he would vote the prohibition ticket.[23]

Baptist forces loyal to the Democratic Party rallied against this nascent rebellion. Spurred on by attacks from the secular press that prohibition politics abridged personal freedom and made prohibitionists like communists (the one abridged personal rights, the other property rights), shaken Baptist leaders began to backtrack. B. F. Riley and the editor of the *Alabama Baptist* denounced Frances Willard and the Woman's Christian Temperance Union for combining prohibition with woman suffrage. Associate editor Samuel Henderson warned that if the national temperance movement endorsed woman suffrage, the South would never support it. He opposed creation of a partisan prohibition party or discussion of such a political question in a house of worship. Although one's convictions on temperance should modify one's ballot, those who bolted the Democratic Party on the basis of a single issue acted unwisely. Responding to heated criticism of his position that prohibition should be kept out of politics, Riley clarified that he meant only that prohibition should not be made a test of party loyalty, or that candidates be required to support it, or that voters desert the Democratic Party for a prohibition party. All that prohibitionists sought was local option, and this objective must be achieved through the Democratic Party in order to avoid "negro rule." "As southern people," the editor wrote in 1888, "we are compelled to see that our safety, morally as well as materially, lies . . . in the success of the democratic party."[24]

The summer of 1886 presented Baptists several occasions to apply these theories. In June a Democratic Party primary in Tuscaloosa featured two men who favored local option against two others who preferred legislative enactment of countywide prohibition. The *Alabama Baptist* endorsed the more conservative course of letting Tuscaloosa voters decide for themselves without legislative action. A month later Crumpton led a statewide prohibition convention in Birmingham that sought to organize temperance forces. Almost immediately the harmony of the convention was disrupted by a group of men who demanded that only those willing to pledge support to a third party should be registered to participate. When a majority of the three hundred participants rejected this position, nearly two dozen men walked out of the meeting and formed the Prohibition Party. The editor of the *Alabama Baptist* attended the meeting, joined the majority opposed to a third party, and endorsed local option. He reasoned that in a state where nine-tenths of state legislators were Democrats, formation of the Prohibition Party made no sense, especially when the new party polled only 600–700 votes in its first try.[25]

This conservative local option course of action, endorsed by Democratic and Baptist leaders, offered no prospect for success, a fact that prohibitionists began to realize. The July convention scolded the state Democratic nominating convention for its discourteous reception of a delegation requesting that the party endorse prohibition by local option. J. J. D. Renfroe declared his loyalty to the Democratic Party but insisted that prohibitionists within the party be given fair treatment. A Baptist correspondent from Gadsden was even more forthright. Although he believed that the Democratic Party could be transformed into the natural vehicle for the prohibition crusade, this goal could be accomplished only by political agitation. Chief among those who argued that prohibition should be kept out of politics, he wrote, were saloon keepers, antiprohibitionists, and "all the red-eyed, purple-nosed politicians."[26]

Other Baptists were less certain that the Democratic Party was an appropriate vehicle for reform. Chief among this group were two Baptist preachers, Samuel Adams of Bibb County and L. C. Coulson of Jackson County. Adams deplored the attempts of Democratic officials to keep prohibition out of party politics even as he applauded the party for its rescue of Alabama from Reconstruction. Many others endorsed Adams's position. Like him, they concluded that prohibition was inherently political and could be achieved only when one party endorsed it and led the effort to enact it. If the Democratic Party adopted the cause, there would be no need for a third party. If it refused, that decision made creation of a third party inevitable. As the Democratic Party dallied, more and more Baptists endorsed the new Prohibition Party.[27]

L. C. Coulson of Scottsboro in mountainous Jackson County combined ardor for prohibition with concern about the poor. Prayers on behalf of poor tenant farmers were worth little, he wrote just before Christmas 1886, unless Baptists shared whatever resources they possessed. Just as Baptists should act as they prayed toward the poor, they should vote as they prayed regarding prohibition. In 1883 he helped organize prohibition forces in Jackson County, where according to his estimate thirty-six saloons operated, more than the number of churches in the county. The cause of this proliferation was the refusal of churches to declare forthrightly that members should not vote for any candidate who drank. Although he considered himself "as good a Republican as ever lived," Coulson refused to vote for any candidate of his party "who would wink at the liquor traffic." Many of his Democratic friends agreed with him on the centrality of prohibition. In 1887 Coulson wrote the *Alabama Baptist* that legislative inaction proved that Alabama's Democratic Party was under the control of "the whisky power." That December he attended the national Prohibition Party convention in Chicago, where he advised delegates to cast aside old parties until national prohibition was accomplished. He had gloried in the overthrow of slavery in 1865 and now he looked forward to the overthrow of liquor. Despite such views, he remained an influential leader in the denomination, writing the Tennessee River Baptist Association report in 1889.[28]

As the 1890 elections approached, Baptist prohibitionists became increasingly agitated at the lack of Democratic support. Prohibition legislators began to tattle on colleagues whom they saw frequenting Montgomery saloons. The editor of the *Alabama Baptist* began praising some legislators by name and denounced one Baptist deacon member of the state house of representatives for allegedly supporting a bill to repeal prohibition in Goodwater in return for a pledge by Republicans not to oppose his reelection. Members of Montgomery's First Baptist Church heard a sermon in 1889 entitled "Christ as an Agitator" that addressed prison reform and legislative attempts to repeal local option. When legislators began to debate prohibition a month later, the denomination staged a "Baptist Congress" in the capital, where 120 preachers gathered to hear sermons on a variety of subjects, especially prohibition.[29]

Many of the legislators they lobbied were members of their own denomination. By 1887 at least twenty-two prominent Baptists served in the house (including at least two preachers and the moderator of the South Bethel Association) and seven in the senate (including at least two preachers).[30] Yet prohibition laws were repeatedly defeated in both legislative bodies.

By the early 1890s, the *Alabama Baptist* took a more political approach to prohibition. Under the ownership of John G. Harris (himself a candidate for state superintendent of education), the paper endorsed by name a number of Democratic candidates. Among the favored were laymen Jim Crook for governor, Harris for superintendent of education, Thomas H. Clark from Montgomery County for the legislature, and Judge Jonathan Haralson for the supreme court. The editor admitted that he had always been interested in politics and had attended the Chilton County Democratic convention to ensure a majority for prohibition forces. He noted that a favorite cry of the whiskey crowd was for preachers to stay out of politics. He responded that "the world needs to learn that it is the preacher's business to help rescue the perishing, and that it is needful sometimes in order to attain this end to spear the sharks that line the way." And spear the sharks Baptists did, electing seven ministers to the lower house in 1890 (making thirty-nine Baptists in all, compared to thirty-one Methodists, who held second place). In the senate, eleven Methodists and six Baptists outnumbered a smattering of members from other denominations.[31] The paper had never before taken such keen interest in the denominational preference of legislators nor been able to cite their numbers so precisely.

Although the denominational paper supported Democratic candidates from local to national levels in 1890, the editor warned the party against coalitions with "the whisky power." The following year the paper became actively involved in Montgomery's mayoral campaign against "whisky men, gamblers, bullies and toughs." When its reform candidate won, the paper received much of the credit. To the north in Birmingham, cleavages in city government also followed ethnic and religious lines rather than economic interest groups. Political conflict in the 1890s swirled around moral issues such as control of saloons, prostitution, gambling, and Sabbath observance. As missions board secretary W. B. Crumpton made clear, Baptists would not vote for "barroom men" just because the Democratic Party nominated them. When a leader of the Democratic Party warned Crumpton that such attitudes threatened to transfer control of the state to Republicans, Crumpton replied that if such a shift occurred it was the fault of the party nominating unacceptable candidates, not of Baptist voters following their consciences.[32]

Crumpton's warning was merely the first volley in what soon became a steady barrage of Baptist criticism of the Democratic Party. By 1894 Crumpton was criticizing newly elected governor William C. Oates for his weak stand on prohibition. B. F. Riley, alarmed that Crumpton's criticism of the new Democratic governor might alter the delicate (and probably fraudulent) majority Democrats had just won over Populist insurgents, talked with Oates. Riley then reported that the governor did not personally drink alcoholic beverages although he did oppose prohibition. He also warned Crumpton that the times were too critical to "impair public esteem for the Chief Executive of Alabama."[33]

Alabama Baptists and Agrarian Radicalism

The spirited debate between Crumpton and Riley grew out of a full-scale Baptist rebellion against the Democratic Party. At one end of the party, Baptist patricians such as B. F. Riley remained loyal, fearing African American political control of the Black Belt and perhaps the entire state should the party split. Many of them also represented New South industrialist and planter interests. Other Baptist leaders (like Crumpton) desperately sought to remain loyal to the white man's party even as its antiprohibition views increasingly alienated them. Still others, like Samuel Adams and L. C. Coulson, were inclined toward a reform third party from the start. Not only did they prefer the forthright prohibition views of the reformers, but they also preferred reformist positions on regulation of corporations, currency questions, and fairer treatment of tenant farmers and industrial laborers.

Some historians have misread ministerial rhetoric and concluded that Southern Baptists believed the task of preachers was to save souls, not to meddle in politics. They interpret such preachers as tools of hegemonic ruling-class interests and bulwarks of the Redeemer Democratic political order. Such ministers fiercely opposed the third-party Populist revolt. Conservative Democrats in turn defended evangelical churches because of their support for Old South myths and New South creeds.[34]

Other historians see in the Farmers' Alliance and Populist Party the imprimatur of evangelical religion. The vocabulary of protest used by farmers to oppose injustice came directly from the Bible. Drawing heavily on Old Testament prophetic writings, agrarian reformers insisted that God sided with oppressed people and that human beings counted for more than money. Although alliancemen never believed that prohibition would solve their economic problems, they agreed that it was a necessary beginning. Evangelical Christianity was a major source of American political radicalism during the nineteenth and twentieth centuries, so it is no surprise that it fueled the reform fires glowing to white heat in Alabama during the 1890s.[35]

Even before the Farmers' Alliance organized, Baptists perceived the serious economic problems besetting farmers. E. T. Winkler heard the head of the Alabama State Grange speak at Auburn in 1874 and praised his discussion of the exploitation of farmers. When independent reformers and

Republicans organized in Clay County in 1888, they elected a preacher, M. M. Driver, chairman. He attacked corruption, "bossism," and the Democratic Party, divided the county over the role of preachers in politics, and accepted the nomination for county tax assessor. Riley M. Honeycutt, a Confederate veteran, farmer, and Baptist preacher, led independent reformers in Chilton County, where he was elected tax collector.[36]

Similar political insurgency began in Limestone County. Religious fervor, according to one historian, was more a factor in the reform agenda of 1,900 members of the county's Farmers' Alliance than either economic or political anxiety. Alliancemen identified God as the inspiration for their organization and the Christian spirit of brotherhood as the force sustaining membership and energy. Members applied alliance lyrics to traditional hymn tunes so that both Christian theology and hymnology appealed to the class interests of rural evangelicals.[37]

Because most Baptist preachers were bivocational farmers, alliance programs that addressed agricultural problems appealed to them. The status that preachers enjoyed in rural society made them natural alliance leaders, and many were chosen to lead local chapters. The editor of the *Alabama Baptist* in 1890 had farmed into his twenties and proudly acknowledged his membership in the organization. He praised alliance newspapers for their balanced treatment of agricultural issues, attended the annual alliance convention, praised the cooperative alliance store, urged farmer solidarity against "combines and trusts," and considered alliancemen the most reliable and fair-minded members of the legislature.[38]

The editor also utilized the language of Zion when extolling the alliance cause. Upon reading its declaration of purposes, he described alliancemen as "sound, humane, and God-fearing." When urging the state Grange to merge with the alliance, he praised its objective to educate farmers about public policy and its campaign against "oppressive corporations" that unjustly discriminated against farmers. He also noted that the alliance enrolled many Alabama Baptist leaders.[39]

P. S. Montgomery of Ashville was one such leader. As a member of the Farmers' Alliance and a Baptist preacher for thirty-four years, Montgomery defended the organization as a benign institution that tried only to avoid lawsuits and eliminate the credit system by buying and selling through farmer-owned stores. The alliance took as guide "the word of God." Rather than detract from ministers' devotion to their churches, Montgomery claimed, membership in the organization made them more aware of the needs of their flocks. Nearly all Baptist preachers he knew were also farmers, and alliance membership allowed them to identify fully with their agrarian congregations.[40]

Montgomery could have added one other reason why Baptists joined the alliance: its strong commitment to prohibition. The *Alabama Baptist* carefully recorded one local alliance after another that adopted resolutions favoring prohibition. Whereas "professional politicians" and lawyers could not be trusted to enforce prohibition laws, "the moral men, the honest men, the debt paying and God fearing men . . . coming into power, thanks to the Alliance movement," would reform the Democratic Party. Whatever progress toward temperance the 1891 legislature achieved, the *Alabama Baptist* attributed to the alliance. Its membership embraced "the bone and sinew of the church and state" and its program had accomplished more political reform than any other organization in Alabama.[41]

So loyal were Baptist alliancemen to their organization that some denominational leaders warned that they were in danger of neglecting spiritual duties for temporal ones. Critics questioned the propriety of using church houses for alliance meetings, especially in cases where distinctions between alliance and church virtually disappeared. In one community, the minister preached, moderated the Saturday church conference, then spent the rest of the day conducting alliance business before his congregation/alliance chapter. Critics also charged that alliances fostered class divisions and were often led by "designing demagogues."[42]

The transition from the benign alliance of the 1880s to the fiercely partisan Populist Party of the 1890s split off many Baptists who would not desert the Democratic Party. But a surprisingly large number moved into the new party, led by their ministers. Important Populist ministers included J. M. Loftin (Bullock County), John L. Stuart (Covington County), A. J. Hearn (Choctaw County), Samuel M. Adams (Bibb and Chilton Counties), and L. C. Coulson (Jackson County).

Coulson emerged as editor of the *Jackson County Hornet,* a colorful Populist paper in northeastern Alabama. Amazingly liberal on racial issues and fiercely devoted to prohibition, Coulson spent much of his time refuting warnings by Democrats that populism threatened white supremacy. He replied that such racial rhetoric might still frighten whites in south Alabama, but in the northern part of the state the Populist-Republican fusion ticket would openly solicit black voters. Referring to a reform leader of the Democratic Party who shared many Populist ideas, Coulson wrote that the man "looked like a turkey, gobbled like a turkey, but was roosting in the wrong place for a turkey."[43]

Samuel M. Adams was at various times editor of a Populist paper, head of the state Farmers' Alliance, state chairman of the Alabama Populist Party, and speaker of the state house of representatives. He believed that neither traditional party could enact substantive reform. As leader of the reform forces in the legislature, Adams introduced legislation to strengthen the state railroad commission to regulate rates. He also forcefully articulated the need for Christians to enter politics, frequently citing Scripture to argue that one served God by serving the people through government. Such biblical rhetoric came easily to Adams, who throughout his political career regularly preached revivals in Baptist churches across the state.[44]

It fell upon Adams to defend the decision of so many of his ministerial colleagues to enter politics. Rev. Charles B. Carter precipitated the debate in March 1892 with a front-page article in the *Alabama Baptist* deploring ministerial involvement in politics. Decrying the fact that an estimated 80 percent of the ministers who were running for office or editing Populist papers were Baptists, Carter chided them for deserting their pulpits. Could they not find souls that needed saving? he wondered.[45] Adams responded in the following issue. Obviously Carter did not understand conditions in rural Alabama, Adams wrote. He compared agricultural conditions in the spring of 1892 to those of Nehemiah 5 (which contained the prophet's criticism of leaders who exploited the people by charging interest, taking the lands of farmers, and enslaving their children).[46]

Although divided on this issue, many Alabama Baptists wrote articles defending Adams's position. W. R. Whatley of Alexander City did not intend to run for office himself but defended the right of preachers to enter politics on behalf of causes that benefited the people. The editor of the paper agreed, noting that issues regarded by Baptists as moral (currency, prohibition, education, honesty in politics, divisions between labor and management, immigration policy) involved politics. "Perhaps we will have to speak our mind without fear," he concluded, "hoping only to please God and save our fellow man." He also noted that whatever reservations Baptists might have about preachers entering politics, they were doing so in every county in Alabama. Many ran for local office to supplement their salaries, he pointed out, and such jobs gave them time to study. They were fully qualified, so he saw no reason to prohibit their political activity. At the 1894 state Baptist convention, J. A. French of Talladega preached on "The Relation of the Pulpit to Politics," arguing that preachers should champion truth and righteousness in public life. The sermon sparked vigorous discussion between A. J. Dickinson of Selma First Baptist Church, who warned of impending political anarchy, and J. B. Hawthorne, formerly pastor of the same church, who replied that if Baptists ignored the ethical principles of the Bible they ignored half the gospel. He specifically mentioned the need to speak out on behalf of temperance and labor-management conflicts.[47]

A. J. Dickinson responded to this debate with a series of sermons ("Christian Civics of the New Testament" and "Honest Elections") in which he warned that partisan politics eroded respect for government and had brought Alabama to the point of anarchy. Political corruption (which many historians believed cost Populists gubernatorial victories in both 1892 and 1894) had become so widespread that he believed the only solution was a constitutional convention to disfranchise blacks so that neither party could manipulate their votes. Other Baptists also condemned political corruption and urged preachers to speak out openly against it. The editor of the *Alabama Baptist* took up the Populist cry for a fair count in 1896, warning that if public officials refused to investigate charges of vote stealing, "public opinion . . . should make it so hot for them that they would resign." And if Populist allegations were false, they should be branded as liars and punished.[48]

Contributing to Baptist sympathy for Populist causes was the gubernatorial candidacy of Reuben F. Kolb. Long active as a layman in the Eufaula First Baptist Church, Kolb had served as a popular commissioner of agriculture and speaker on behalf of agricultural reform at numerous Farmers' Alliance meetings. He used the pages of the *Alabama Baptist* to communicate with farmers, urging them to report corporate price gouging on fertilizer prices or other corporate abuses. The paper's editors regularly praised Kolb for efficient management of his office and for his agricultural reforms. When he was first mentioned as a candidate for governor in 1889 at the Democratic state nominating convention, the Baptist paper praised his qualifications for the office and predicted he would make a fine chief executive.[49] Although the paper did not endorse Kolb after he assumed leadership of Alabama's Populist Party, his involvement certainly muted its criticism of the Populists.

Criticism there was, however—the sort of rancorous political disagreement that dissolved friendships and split churches. At the core of this disharmony was the fear of white Democrats that Populists would divide the white vote and make possible an era of Negro rule. They might agree with the alliance critique of economic injustice, but they believed that differences over prohibition, currency reform, corporate abuses, and labor-management conflict must be resolved within the Democratic Party.

The strongest philosophical opposition to Baptist involvement in politics came from those who were influenced by doctrines such as the spirituality of the church and separation of church and state. The first position maintained that the task of Christianity was to save souls, not influence politics. Even on an issue as urgent as prohibition, they believed the task of the church was to persuade individual members to vote correctly, not to act collectively. Many Baptists interpreted their denomination's historic commitment to separation of church and state to mean that preachers should stay out of politics.

Cary C. Lloyd addressed both issues in a sermon entitled "Separation of Church and State." Lloyd was educated as a physician before the Civil War and had practiced in Greenville and served in the Confederate army. He began preaching after the war. As clerk of his association for a quarter century and as father of a Democratic state legislator from Butler County, he wielded considerable influence. Lloyd preached that the church had no authority to legislate and that preachers who entered politics blended secular and sacred. When they did so, they created confusion, strife, and discord within churches. And when the cause was populism, they severed lifelong ties of Christian fellowship and love. As a result of such activity, the Democratic Party ("that faithful custodian of our liberties") was torn with dissension, ecclesiastical and civil liberties were endangered, and religious intolerance thrived. Church leaders were largely to blame for these divisions, and preachers should "return to their pulpits long prostituted to political ends [and] hold up the banner of Christ now waiting in the mire and filth of political shame and disgrace."[50]

Other ministers conceded the right of Baptist preachers to enter politics on behalf of some causes (prohibition) but not others (populism). They increasingly criticized the class-based antitown and antibusiness rhetoric of the Populists. W. B. Crumpton, who fiercely championed political action on behalf of prohibition, criticized preachers who sowed distrust of merchants, bankers, warehouse owners, or railroad owners. He attributed such attitudes to religious paranoia that branded anyone who disagreed a spy or paid agent of a conspiracy. Such Baptists also tended to oppose denominational boards and newspapers. These attitudes resulted from ignorance (his description of Populists strongly resembles Baptist stereotypes of Primitive and Landmark Baptists as well). Such class-based demagoguery, the editor of the denominational paper warned, threatened to undermine the progress being made by the New South and the businessmen who were its architects. When preachers neglected the gospel to discuss the need for a bimetallic system of currency (a popular Populist cause), they should not expect "much deference from conservative and sensible people."[51]

Furthermore, Baptists who initially praised preachers who ran for office began to criticize them once elected. They little understood the necessity of compromise inherent in political bodies. When preacher/legislators found it necessary to build coalitions by supporting bills they might not have preferred or by voting for imperfect bills as better than no legislation at all, Baptists were quick to criticize.

That was the fate of Samuel Adams. Baptist legislators backed a bill in the 1891 legislature to ban freight and excursion trains from traveling on Sundays. Although Adams (who led Farmers' Alliance forces in the legislature) did not actively lobby to kill the bill, he did vote against it. The *Alabama Baptist* blasted his opposition, blaming him for the bill's defeat. Adams defended himself by arguing that legislating morals had limitations. Furthermore, the bill would have harmed Mobile-area alliancemen who had to ship perishable fish, oysters, and farm products by train to earn a living. Also, employees of railroads had not petitioned him in favor of the legislation even though it was ostensibly designed for their benefit. The editor of the denominational paper was not persuaded. He found it ironic that a Baptist preacher had blocked a measure designed to protect the Sabbath from desecration.[52]

Democrats also deftly counterattacked their Populist-inclined brethren. In 1892 the chairman of the state Democratic campaign committee appealed to Alabama ministers to aid the party. Stable government benefited church and state, he argued, and prevented anarchy. Many Baptists agreed with party policy on tariffs, currency, and other issues as well. A man from Davenport described himself as a Baptist and a Democrat, adding, "I can't understand how a Baptist can be of any other political faith."[53]

With such deep divisions within churches, it is no wonder that reports of church strife poured in from around the state. The editor of the *Alabama Baptist* warned in 1890 that many Baptists seemed more devoted to the alliance than to the church. As a result, some alliancemen in their zeal to enlist fellow church members actually bullied them and divided churches. A rural pastor reported that members of his congregation had become so absorbed in politics that bad feelings had sapped the strength of the church.[54]

The bitter 1892 gubernatorial campaign widened these divisions. W. B. Crumpton grieved at a poorly attended associational meeting in Wilcox County that he blamed on political rallies by Democrat Thomas G. Jones and Populist Reuben F. Kolb. While in the village of Furman, he had visited in a home where a child greeted him with "hurrah for Jones." That evening another child (mistaking him for one of the candidates) had shouted, "Howdy, Mr. Kolb!" Such excitement was demoralizing to the church, he believed, and caused people to be consumed by "blind passion."[55]

The next few months confirmed his opinion. Sunday school classes ignored the Bible for talk of currency questions. Knots of men standing outside churches waiting for worship services to begin became so absorbed in political arguments that they sometimes missed the service. So bitter did the gubernatorial contest become by July that "families are divided, churches disturbed and Christ's work neglected." Nightly political rallies in July and August were so well attended that revivals were postponed or poorly attended. For a year after the election, the Shiloh church in Pike County had no pastor because the "dreadful political excitement" had "almost torn the church to pieces." J. A. French of Talladega tried to quiet emotions by preaching a sermon entitled "How Christians should conduct themselves during a political campaign."[56]

Two years later conditions had improved only marginally. J. A. French tried a preemptive strike, writing "A Word About State Politics" before the summer 1894 gubernatorial election. Ministers should anticipate repetition of the bitter 1892 campaign and try to prevent it. They must avoid partisanship themselves by remaining politically neutral. W. B. Crumpton noted that many pastors ignored French's advice and allowed politics "to well nigh ruin them." Whichever party won, Crumpton reminded, the country would survive and God would remain in command. A Howard College student pastor reported that in his Estaboga church some members had more politics than religion. The pastor of the Lineville Baptist Church regretted that "we are in the midst of political nonsense in this community."[57]

So concerned was the editor of the *Alabama Baptist* at a rash of dismissals of pastors because of their political views or because of declines in contributions, that he feared Baptists had turned from the worship of God "to the Moloch of politics." Country churches especially had been demoralized during the past half dozen years, he wrote, and the "great masses of our people, including the women in many instances," had been consumed with politics. So cautious was the editor that he even condemned the June 1895 Howard College magazine for allowing a discussion of currency questions.[58]

As the 1896 gubernatorial campaign approached, the editor urged pastors to preach from Genesis 13, where Abram pleaded with Lot that they dwell together in unity. Hatred and fanaticism had prevailed in 1892 and 1894, he wrote, disrupting churches, dividing families, and embittering communities. As a result, "the wheels of Zion were clogged, the devil captured the field, and for a time reveled in his spoils. Heaven wept and Zion mourned in her desolation." The ground rules in 1896 must be different. Let every man advocate his personal political views, yet still be considered a brother. Let preachers vote their consciences, but avoid partisanship lest they commit "a form of ministerial suicide." Frequent references to the restoration of peace and harmony in churches began to appear, especially after the revival season. The pastor of Harpersville Baptist Church wrote that "for the first time in years our people are at peace with one another."[59]

The cyclonic fury of populism had abated, and the Democratic Party had prevailed, though with new reformist leaders. Samuel Adams confided to friends that he had wasted six years of his life and vowed to quit politics and devote all his remaining days to preaching. The *Alabama Baptist* rejoiced at this news, though the celebration was short-lived. Adams could not bring himself to disengage from politics and soon plunged back into the fray as an ally of Democratic Party reform governor, Joseph F. Johnson.[60]

Denominational officials began to agitate for prohibition and a constitutional convention that would disfranchise African Americans, thus removing a central bone of contention between Populists and Democrats. But this time they decided on individual action rather than attempting to mobilize the entire denomination. As a chastened W. B. Crumpton admitted, Baptists must deal with prohibition delicately. In an imperfect world, statewide prohibition seemed an unachievable goal, and Baptists settled temporarily for a state dispensary as better than open saloons on every corner. They shied away from the Prohibition Party because it endorsed reforms other than prohibition, thus threatening to reopen all the old wounds of the short-lived Populist crusade.[61] Baptists, in short, had learned a hard lesson. Preachers entered politics at considerable risk to the welfare of their churches and to themselves.

Baptists and Society

Despite much scar tissue from the bruising political battles of the 1890s, Baptists did not disengage from society. The Populist interlude sparked debate over a whole range of public policy matters. Once released, Baptists could find no wizard wise enough to stuff the genie of politics back into its container.

Much of their thinking about Christianity and society followed well-worn paths. Growing support for prohibition was part of a larger movement to regulate the conduct of society. Whereas Alabama Baptists had once been content to use church discipline to enforce their beliefs, they increasingly sought to impose their moral values on Alabama society by law. Not that church discipline had disappeared. Indeed, most rural churches still vigorously regulated the conduct of members even as such practices disappeared in urban congregations. As late as 1899, the *Alabama Baptist* urged the application of discipline for drunkenness, lying, profanity, adultery, corrupt business practices, slander, and "worldliness." The editor wrote that when church discipline exited the front door of a church, the devil entered from the rear to spread disorder and moral looseness.[62]

Although urban churches increasingly dispensed with church discipline, they rigorously championed local and statewide legislation regulating Sunday activities (so-called blue laws prohibiting certain forms of recreation and business activity on Sundays). They called for strict regulation of laws against prostitution and opposed all forms of gambling.[63]

The *Alabama Baptist* constantly campaigned for agricultural reform, especially scientific and diversified agriculture and subsistence farming. A series of editors praised any new agricultural reform initiative, whether planting fruit trees, the organization of a fruit growers' association in Brewton, development of alternative crops like celery or asparagus, or the rising cattle and dairy industries. The chief barrier to agricultural prosperity in the 1890s, according to the denominational paper, was cotton monoculture.[64]

The nearly century-long devotion of Baptists to public schools continued as well. Although Howard College president B. F. Riley proposed a series of six Baptist academies scattered across Alabama to compensate for the state's lack of high schools, most Baptists believed public education should be the highest priority of state government. In an address on "Education, Schools, and School Teachers," J. H. Curry deplored the decline of the school term following Reconstruction. Many of the best teachers had been driven from the classroom by low pay. Alabamians excused their lack of support by citing the poverty of the state; but Curry believed quality education to be the best investment citizens could make. To begrudge tax money spent on schools, he wrote, was "cruel stinginess."[65]

The *Alabama Baptist* regularly called on the legislature to appropriate more money for schools, praised the Alabama Education Association, and endorsed tougher certification standards for teachers. J. L. M. Curry (Baptist preacher and secretary of the Peabody Fund) became the guru of the public school movement in Alabama. Education, he argued in numerous speeches and sermons, was an inalienable, universal right of American children. He refuted what he called the creed of the ruling conservative political hierarchy in Alabama that education would disqualify the working classes from the position of life for which God intended them.[66] The gospel was the "magna carta of the rights of man," which assumed that even the humblest person had sufficient mental capacity to understand profound moral truth. And if the common people could grasp the noblest ethical truths, surely they could comprehend mathematics and literature.[67]

Such matters of social morality increasingly captured the attention of Alabama Baptists. Particularly notable in this growing consciousness was George B. Eager, the forthright pastor of Parker Memorial in Anniston and later Montgomery First Baptist. With degrees from Mississippi College and Southern Baptist Theological Seminary, Eager was well versed in the social thought of late-nineteenth-century American social Christianity. Considered a brilliant orator, Eager was in high demand to address both religious and secular audiences. Furthermore, his Montgomery congregation included a large number of legislators, judges, and other state officials, so his opinions carried unusual weight. He argued passionately for racial fairness, for restrictions on child labor, and for control of alcohol use and gambling. At the 1895 state convention Eager preached on the relationship of religion to social reform. Citing a text in Malachi, Eager noted that intemperance, neglect of the poor, and oppression of wage earners were not new problems. Worker-management conflict, he believed, arose from the mutual selfishness of capital and labor. He forcefully denounced oppression of the poor by the rich but proposed following the Sermon on the Mount, not unionism or political protest, as a solution. A multipart series of sermons on "Christian Civics," preached in 1899, contended that Christians were trustees of the public interest, and ministers had every right to enter politics as individuals on behalf of moral causes. He also endorsed restrictions on voting to eliminate those unworthy of the franchise. Civic literacy (knowledge about the structure and function of government), not the ability to read and write, should be the requirement to vote. Perhaps recalling Democratic Party corruption in 1892 and 1894, he argued that race should not determine who voted because society had less to fear from Negro males than from corrupt white men. Women should not be enfranchised because as wives, mothers, and homemakers, they were too busy "to be burdened with the ballot."[68]

A. J. Dickinson (the influential pastor of the Selma First Baptist Church) shared Eager's interest in the relationship between Christianity and society. Like Eager, he frequently preached and lectured on the subject. The development of sociology in northern universities had transformed the way the church perceived society, and he regretted its slow penetration of southern colleges. He especially praised the *American Journal of Sociology*, published by the University of Chicago. Preachers not only should change society by changing individuals, they also should address corporate social problems as the Hebrew prophets had. Dickinson described Isaiah as a social reformer "unmercifully scathing" of the social evils of his time. So was Christ a social reformer. Only by sealing their "lips to half the word of God" could preachers avoid following his example. In his essay, Dickinson quoted as authority the "Sociology of Christ" by Shailer Mathews, a professor at the University of Chicago and a man quickly emerging as a primary figure in the social gospel movement.[69]

The editor of the *Alabama Baptist* agreed with Eager and Dickinson. Historically, he wrote, Christians had so stressed right thinking (theology) that they had ignored right living (ethics). The modern trend toward ethics and action rather than "pious feelings or the passive acceptance of religious dogma" was an important corrective. Although theology and ethics were inseparable, they must also have a true and proportionate relationship to each other.[70]

From that theological supposition, the newspaper and many individual Baptists began a long odyssey that led them more deeply into social reform. Haltingly at first, then with accelerating speed in the 1890s, they addressed prison conditions, mental health, poverty, labor unrest, corporate abuses and monopolies, urbanization, and immigration.

Prison conditions in Alabama were wretched by any humane standard. Under terms of the convict lease system, the state rented prisoners to industries and plantations where they were often mistreated and abused. Competition for prison labor was fierce, resulting in political corruption. Treatment of convicts was so barbaric that state prison inspectors were often bribed not to report abuses. Young boys guilty of petty offenses were incarcerated with older men who had committed felonies. During the 1890s, Julia Tutwiler conducted investigations of prison conditions that led to substantial improvements.

The *Alabama Baptist* published Tutwiler's 1893 report and endorsed her call for a teenage reformatory. To complaints from legislators that the state had no money for such a facility, the editor admonished readers to consider carefully Tutwiler's exposé, then instruct their legislators about what ought to be done. He reminded readers that some youthful offenders still wore knee pants and needed Christian friends.[71]

The convict lease system involved more complex issues. After initially calling for humane treatment of convicts in 1890, editors took a more benign view during the next few years. A personal visit to Pratt Coal Mine convinced the editor that convicts were treated as well as possible, that food was wholesome, clothing adequate, and corporal punishment rare. Often editors used harsh prison conditions to warn youth against the dangers of gambling, drinking whiskey, and other forms of vice.[72] The denomination remained largely unaware of abuses that soon embarrassed the state as revelations of brutality spread nationwide.

Another conflict involved inadequate tax revenue and inhumane care of Alabama's mental patients. In 1893 the denominational paper summarized the annual report of the superintendent of the state mental hospital. So inadequate was the facility at Tuscaloosa that many mental patients were housed in county jails. Some were tied in huts or locked naked in outhouses and fed through slots in the door. Conditions, the editor wrote, were unworthy of a civilized people, and he demanded that the legislature appropriate $25,000 to enlarge the state mental hospital.[73]

Concerns about just treatment of Native Americans also perplexed Baptists. The Alabama Baptist deplored the relocation of western tribes away from ancestral lands as well as cuts in federal funding for Indian education. It attributed the massacre of Sioux at Wounded Knee in 1890 to the intrusion of whites onto Sioux lands and the rascality of white traders. But the paper also treated Native Americans paternalistically, suggesting that much of their troubles resulted from "heathen" superstitions.[74]

Newly arrived immigrants posed a different problem. Despite vigorous opposition to restrictive legislation aimed at Chinese during the 1880s, Baptist opinion turned sharply nativist in the 1890s. Perhaps the difference was that Baptists had a large number of missionaries in China lobbying against laws aimed at Chinese, legislation that offended China and made missionary work more difficult. Baptists had no missionaries in southern and eastern Europe. Furthermore, Chinese were Buddhist or Taoist in religion, neither well understood by Americans. Southern and eastern European immigrants were Catholics and Jews, both well known to Alabama Baptists. Another problem was prohibition. Whereas American Protestants had become politically militant on this issue, newly arriving Catholics and Jews opposed prohibition. Although anti-immigration sentiment may seem a strange candidate for inclusion in a list of social "reforms," many Alabama Baptists interpreted the issue as compelling them to change government policy in order to restrict immigrants. A leading advocate of the social gospel, Josiah Strong, was also one of the leading spokesmen for restricting immigration. The editor of the Alabama Baptist cited Strong's book, Our Country, for its warning against the perils of mass immigration. Many of these immigrants hated American laws, desecrated the Sabbath, were anarchists, socialists, or nihilists, joined radical labor unions, and committed crimes. The United States had become a "dumping ground" for the nations. In Alabama, the editor added, immigrants formed labor clubs that met on Sunday, led strikes in coal mining regions, and required military intervention to protect law-abiding citizens from anarchy.[75]

Chief among the dangers posed by the new immigrants from southern Europe was the fact that most were Catholics. Although anti-Catholicism had ebbed and flowed in Baptist thought throughout the century, by the 1890s it had become a sustained and major element. Immigrants brought their "religious and irreligious views," the editor of the *Alabama Baptist* wrote in 1893, and "there is danger that we may become foreignized in religion (or irreligion) and morals." Rev. John T. Christian wrote in 1895 that the nation's open door invited "anarchism, Catholicism, and errors too numerous to mention." Christian urged the Home Mission Board to redouble its effort to convert this new generation of immigrants. Meanwhile, all immigration should be suspended for twenty years while the country absorbed them.[76]

The editor of the *Alabama Baptist* used Christian's new book (*Americanism or Romanism, Which?*) as a major source in the debate over immigration. He warned that Catholicism was the religion of the "whisky seller." Fornication and adultery were common among Catholics, who treated the Sabbath more as holiday than holy day. Rum and Romanism went together, as did gambling and other vices. The paper opposed a Catholic who ran for mayor of Mobile and endorsed the American Protective Association, a new anti-Catholic, anti-immigrant organization.[77]

Beyond closing the spigot on the pipeline of Catholic immigration, Alabama Baptists disagreed on how best to deal with Catholics. The *Alabama Baptist* published the thirteen principles of the newly created American Protective Association in 1894, principles that would have sharply limited the religious freedom of Catholics. This publication precipitated a year-long debate. Rev. Tom Henderson of Childersburg shared APA's concerns but deplored its remedy. To respond to religious persecution against Protestants by engaging in persecution of Catholics was "the blindest and most reckless of folly." George Eager of Montgomery agreed. In a negative essay on the APA, Eager urged Baptists to avoid "unchristian and un-Republican methods of warfare even against Romanism." Political discrimination against Catholics, atheists, or anyone else violated Baptist principles as well as the U.S. Constitution.[78]

Many Alabama Baptists took the opposite side of this debate. W. B.

Crumpton defended the APA. Although he deplored its secrecy, Crumpton supported its determination to keep Catholics from holding public office. Eager criticized Crumpton's article, and dozens of correspondents wrote in on both sides of the argument. Most sided with Crumpton and expressed support for the APA.[79]

Opinion about Jews was more tolerant. Partly because many Baptists were millennialists who believed that restoration of a Jewish state ("Zionism") was a fulfillment of biblical prophecy, they deplored the persecution of Jews. In contrast to the editor's opposition to electing a Catholic mayor of Mobile, in 1890 he praised the election of a Jew to the state senate from Wilcox County. When Birmingham businessman Samuel Ullman spoke at Howard College, L. T. Reeves (a ministerial student and member of the Franklin Debating Society) praised the speaker as "a highly educated Jew." Ullman discussed Jewish contributions to history and informed students that his religion anticipated not a religious messiah but a political messiah who would restore the Jewish state in Palestine. Reeves was highly impressed with Ullman and not offended by his messianic theories.[80]

As the 1890s depression ravaged Alabama, Baptists had to deal with a tidal wave of a different kind, an avalanche of poor people begging assistance. Scriptural guidelines regarding obligations toward the poor within a congregation were clear and explicit. The church must assist widows, orphans, and poor members. At an 1894 ordination service for new deacons at the Auburn First Baptist Church, patriarch I. T. Tichenor chose his text from the second chapter of Acts. In the early church, there were so many poor members that wealthier Christians sold their possessions and distributed the proceeds according to need. This model instructed Christians how they must respond when necessity arose. R. P. Whitman, a layman in the Huntsville First Baptist Church, became widely known for his charitable contributions to the poor of that city. The Saint Francis Street Baptist Church in Mobile helped support two orphanages, the Mobile home for the impoverished, the King's Daughters (who visited and financially assisted the sick, poor, and afflicted), and indigent widows. The church believed in "helping the poor who try to help themselves, and not in that senseless expenditure upon them which superinduces vagrancy and tramps."[81] Like most Americans, members of the Saint Francis Street church divided poor people into the deserving and undeserving.

Concern for poor people outside the religious community was more problematical. S. P. West of Anniston appealed for Baptists to help several thousand poor people who resided in county almshouses. They did not attend churches because of bad health, inadequate clothes, or indigence.

They were, in fact, Alabama's forgotten people, with neither family nor church to care for them. West proposed construction of a chapel at each poorhouse, where ministers of various denominations could preach on Sunday. Christ loved the poor as much as the rich, West wrote, but in Alabama the state seemed to care more for their bodies than churches did for their souls.[82]

West's indictment was searing and largely true. But there were glimmers of awakening. J. G. Bow of Eufaula and the women of Eufaula First Baptist Church established a mission church at the city's cotton mill. They conducted a Sunday school and prayer meeting for cotton mill workers and established a free reading room. W. B. Crumpton condemned usury and financial oppression of poor people, although he opposed congressional legislation to solve these problems. J. C. Hiden of Eufaula rejected socialism but concluded that the debate about redistributing property had forced Americans to become more sensitive to social injustice. The editor of the Alabama Baptist praised Josiah Strong's book, The New Era, for its portrayal of poverty among the masses. The editor agreed that the church had been indifferent to their problems.[83]

Applying ethical theories about poor, working-class people to specific situations proved difficult, especially when the poor were Catholic immigrants or striking workers. Between the Chicago general strike of 1886 and the Pullman and Homestead strikes of 1892 and 1894, the nation was swept by a series of desperate, bloody labor-management confrontations. Hundreds died in violence associated with these struggles.

The Alabama Baptist laid out a philosophy in 1886 that most Baptists followed throughout the next few decades. Both capital and labor had legitimate rights. There was a difference, however, between legitimate business and "moneyed monopolies" that were tyrannical, autocratic, and operated as a "ruthless oppressor" of labor. Despite the editor's sympathy for working people, he did not justify lawlessness or the use of force against capital. The application of even-handed justice and arbitration of grievances could resolve disputes between "honest capital" and "honest labor."[84]

Application of these theories to the Alabama coal miners' strike of 1894 positioned Baptists against labor. Even though the Alabama Baptist recognized that miners had legitimate complaints, it condemned them as "sullen, refactory, and desperate." Only the National Guard and Alabama's conservative farm population prevented anarchy. The paper congratulated the governor for sending troops into the Birmingham region to preserve order. The paper also noted the disruption of Baptist churches in the coal camps by the strike.[85]

The *Alabama Baptist* outlined principles to govern such confrontations, and George Eager turned his considerable intellectual talent to the problem as well. The editor wrote that workingmen had a right to organize and strike for higher pay. Corporations had a right to establish whatever salaries they wished and to hire any person who would work for that wage to replace a striker. No corporation should be allowed to pay wages with scrip redeemable only at a company commissary. The state must protect the life and property of both workers and corporations. Eager preached a sermon during the strike admitting that laborers had legitimate grievances and that the wealthy had grown more corrupt and defiant. But neither of these facts justified strikers' lawlessness. Laborers had the right to seek redress for their complaints but only with "due regard for social order." Sympathy for the poor and oppressed was commendable but must not be expressed by torch, rifle, or dynamite.[86]

Those closer to the scene, who pastored workers' churches or mined coal themselves as bivocational preachers, disagreed with some of these conclusions. They understood that many workers were deeply religious. When Southside Baptist Church in Birmingham held special services for railroad workers and the unemployed during the strike, the church was filled night after night. Joshua Hill Foster, pastor of Ruhama Baptist Church, presided over a class-conscious congregation. His church was divided into three cliques: a professional and business group led by a lawyer; a contingent of factory and foundry workers led by a puddler; and a Howard College group consisting of faculty, students, and their families. Members agreed to support him but could not pay his salary because of depression and labor unrest. One day his cow disappeared. A man told him that miners from Pratt City had taken it to slaughter and divide among their starving families. Foster told them they were welcome to the cow if it prevented hunger. But he was happy to leave Ruhama to pastor Parker Memorial Baptist Church in Anniston. While pastor there, he led in establishing missions at Glen Addie for foundry workers and at the Blue Mountain net and twine mill.[87]

Baptists were as ambivalent about corporations as they were about industrial workers. The state had a long history of opposition to banks, industries, and corporations. As rural people who mainly farmed for a living, they interpreted their interests as separate from both capital and labor.

Denominational leaders often endorsed New South goals of industrialization, but even they were not prepared to give corporations a blank check. They bragged when "the leading businessmen of the town" were Baptists and applauded John D. Rockefeller's philanthropy toward his new

A fashionably dressed Rev. and Mrs. Robert M. Hunter pose in front of the South
Avondale Baptist Church pastorium in Birmingham some time between 1890 and
1895. (Courtesy of Samford University Archives)

Baptist university (the University of Chicago). But they also criticized corporations for acting "virtually above the law." "Aggressive capital" had become tyrannical and "soulless," had engaged in conduct that justified the
uprising of small farmers and producers. Corporations must be regulated
and society must find ways to harmonize and balance the rights of individuals and corporations. Nor should farmers teach their children to consider merchants and manufacturers as robbers and thieves because prejudices by one class against another would not solve the nation's economic
problems.[88]

Some of the most severe social problems in the United States resulted
from rapid urbanization. Although Alabama's population remained predominantly rural until nearly halfway through the twentieth century, Baptists were concerned about city life. Immigrants concentrated in cities,
where industries thrived, labor unions were organized, and strikes occurred. Although Alabama Baptists recognized the problem, they offered
few solutions beyond trying to evangelize urban populations.[89] Many
frankly resented the increasing attention and resources that the denomination invested in towns and cities. The editor of the *Alabama Baptist* worried

Mount Hebron Baptist Church near Leeds, late nineteenth century. The church, with its separate doors for men and women and strict discipline, was typical of traditional rural congregations. (Courtesy of Samford University Archives)

that attention paid to prosperous New South cities drained population off depressed farms, widening income disparities between farm and city. Rural people increasingly resisted financial drives to raise money for city missionaries or ministerial education because they believed urbanites were wealthier than they and that their sons, once educated, preferred to pastor affluent urban churches rather than declining rural congregations.[90]

The Continuing "Race Problem"

Race defined southern society more profoundly than any other single issue, and the 1880s and 1890s were decades of hardening racial lines. Attempts to disfranchise black males were successful in the 1901 Alabama Constitution. Worsening economic conditions combined with political upheaval to make the years from 1882 to 1902 the most racially violent in Alabama history; 244 people were lynched, 198 of them African Americans.[91]

Formal relations between black and white Baptists remained proper but not cordial. Whites continued to promise help for Selma University and institutes for black ministers and laymen. But whether because of lack of interest or hard financial times, little money was forthcoming. The state mission board employed highly respected black Baptist preacher W. H. McAlpine to work among his people and urged white ministers to attend institutes for black preachers. McAlpine made little progress, and in 1895 only an estimated 200 of 1,400 ordained African American Baptist preachers had any education.[92] In 1897 the convention discontinued this cooperative effort.

Beneath this modicum of civility was a sea of resentment. White Baptists criticized the black denomination for being too political. The Fifteenth Amendment to the Constitution (which gave African Americans the right to vote) "flew in the face of nature," wrote the editor of the white Baptist paper. It should be repealed and "the Negro problem" turned over to "honest, uncorrupted, and incorruptible white rule" (although, if Populist charges of widespread Democratic vote stealing are to be believed, there is little evidence of this "honest, uncorrupted . . . white rule").[93]

One correspondent to the *Alabama Baptist* wrote that everywhere two races coexisted, one dominated the other. Few blacks had accomplished anything in the professions, he concluded, and the nation would be well served by returning them to Africa and replacing them with European immigrants. Such racial prejudice, he added, was not unique to the South but was universal among humanity. A speaker at the 1892 state convention disagreed with repatriation, arguing that African American laborers protected the South from "the scum and corruption of the old countries." Better a godly Negro who read his Bible than a "Bohemian who only knows how to make bombs."[94]

Segregation sentiment settled over Baptists like a heavy fog. In 1890 the editor of the *Alabama Baptist* negatively viewed George W. Cable's controversial new book, *The Negro Question*. Although Cable was a native of Louisiana, his racial iconoclasm had forced him to move North. Denying Cable's plea for more attention to racial injustice, the editor believed that race had received entirely too much attention already, especially from a "certain class of agitators like Mr. Cable." That same year the state convention had an uproar over the decision of the American Baptist Publication Society to include four African Americans on a list of two hundred authors of articles in the *Baptist Teacher*, which was widely used in Baptist Sunday schools. Only after assurances that the outrage would be corrected did Alabama Baptists agree to continue support of the society. A. J. Dickinson, though socially advanced on many issues, was one with his culture on race. When he attended the 1895 Baptist Young People's Union convention in Baltimore, he rejoiced that few Negroes were present despite efforts by some

Baptists to "further social equality." The African American presence was far less than at recent Southern Baptist conventions, which still attracted substantial numbers of black delegates.[95]

One of the most revealing insights into Baptist attitudes about race occurred in 1891. That year the *Baptist Leader*, official organ of the Alabama Colored Baptist State Convention, discussed an incident that had occurred in a Montgomery store. A male clerk had ignored a black woman and waited on a white customer. When the clerk returned, the black woman used abusive language to protest the insult, whereupon the white clerk slapped her. The *Baptist Leader* editorialized that the woman should have immediately returned the blow. The editor of the *Alabama Baptist* republished the article but reached a different conclusion. In a white establishment, a white clerk should show preference to white customers. In a Negro store, a black clerk should show preference to black customers, in which case the white should promptly leave.[96]

However much they might identify with their culture on race, most Baptists drew the line at violence. The *Alabama Baptist* consistently denounced lynching, although the editor diminished the effect of his abhorrence by blaming it on delays in justice due to lawyers whose appeals postponed trials. In an 1894 editorial the paper attributed most lynchings either to white racial pride or concerns about the safety of women. But no circumstance justified such violence however much one might sympathize with victims of rape or murder. Commenting on a sermon entitled "Mob Rule," the editor called on preachers to speak out against lynching.[97]

The Continuing "Woman Problem"

Almost as troubling as blacks who seemed to forget their "place" in society were white women who seemed confused about their proper sphere. With few exceptions, Alabama Baptists believed in a hierarchical society in which men dominated the public sphere and women had their say in private. Although the *Alabama Baptist* insisted in one editorial that there was no double standard of morality (girls had as much right to drink, swear, curse, and gamble as boys), the lesson to be drawn was that "the moral law is no more binding upon the weaker sex than upon the stronger."[98]

Beyond the sphere of the home, much confusion existed about a woman's proper role. Baptist men (at least the ones who gave their opinion in a public forum) believed that the Bible prohibited women from occupying public space. They should not speak in public, organize groups for service, run for office, or vote. The editor of the *Alabama Baptist* congratu-

Willie Hays Kelly, one of Alabama's most beloved missionaries, was born in Wilcox County. She served as W. B. Crumpton's secretary until she went to China in 1893, where she served until forced to return to Montgomery in 1937. Kelly was a WMU favorite. (Courtesy of Photo Library, Foreign Mission Board, Southern Baptist Convention)

lated southern women in 1892 for largely avoiding "the craze of woman suffrage." J. W. Willis wrote an essay for the paper on the "New Woman." Isaiah described her as haughty, with stretched-forth neck and wanton eyes, walking and mincing as she went. "As for my people," Willis quoted the prophet, "children are their oppressors, and women rule over them." Preachers who opposed the new woman were in danger of being "bloomeranged," he quipped.[99]

Baptist men were equally opposed to a larger role for women in the church. They refused to allow women as delegates to associational and state Baptist conventions and even asked men to read their WMU reports. A professor at Southern Baptist Theological Seminary cited the apostle Paul as authority for not allowing women to speak or pray in public. H. C. Hurley (who pastored Jasper First Baptist Church) was inspired to write a twenty-five-page pamphlet on the subject of "The New Woman and the Church" that provided scriptural support for women's subordination and public silence.[100]

Although the *Alabama Baptist* sometimes referred to the wives of deacons as "assistant deacons" or "deaconesses," it seems that the reference was more to their service than their title. At least some women challenged this barrier, though not always in Alabama. Willie Hays Kelly of Camden (who served as W. B. Crumpton's secretary at the state mission board) volunteered for mission service in China. Because of the national depression, the Foreign Mission Board had no funds to send her, so Alabama's infant state WMU assumed responsibility for her salary. For the next half century as a single woman missionary to Shanghai, Kelly cultivated Alabama support for missions. She was undoubtedly the most beloved missionary of her era to the Alabama WMU and while on furlough frequently spoke at state meetings. But she did not adhere to the subordinate role recommended for women in her homeland. Convinced that male missionaries could not reach Chinese women, she not only preached but also had herself and two other Chinese women made deacons at Old North Gate Baptist Church in Shanghai. Although Alabamians were generally unaware of this fact, it is unlikely that it would have spoiled her relationship with the WMU.[101]

Women preachers worried male denominational leaders even more. As one seminary president explained, when Catholic women wanted to preach, the church sent them to a convent. When Baptist women wanted to preach, the denomination had no idea what to do with them. The editor of the *Alabama Baptist* had a solution. Tell them they were wrong, that God did not want women to preach.[102]

Although Baptist males generally agreed that women should not preach or serve as deacons, they agreed on little else about women's role. Could or should women organize and lead their own meetings? If so, what was the relationship of these societies to the local church? Who should control and administer the money they raised? Should they be allowed to attend and vote at associational meetings and state conventions? Women generally ignored male debates and went about their business.

Within local congregations, women continued to lead ladies' aid societies, which conducted the church's philanthropy toward widows, orphans, shut-ins, the elderly, and the poor. At the Tuskegee Baptist Church, the nineteen members of the society paid for repairs and insurance on the pastorium, supported an invalid former sexton of the church, and conducted benevolence work in the town. When the congregation had two disastrous experiences with pastors, women saved the church. Only a woman would serve as Sunday school superintendent, and women also led prayer and singing and represented the church at associational meetings when men refused to attend. At Bethany Baptist Church in Sumterville, women planned an oyster supper to raise money to heat the church so worship services could be held in winter months.[103]

After their initial victory at the 1889 state convention, women quickly enlarged their mission service. Annie Ashcraft of Florence (who began her mission work as a member of Judson College's Ann Hasseltine Judson Missionary Society) became the first woman to speak before the state convention. WMU officials wanted to appoint a woman organizer in 1890 but had no money. While attending a Methodist mission society meeting, some of their leaders noticed that Methodist women assessed members ten cents each to pay expenses. Baptist women adopted that scheme. But as the first state WMU organizer (Amanda T. Hamilton) recalled, men often took the money that women raised for missions and spent it on local churches. The attitude of "the brethren" seemed to be: "If you do not help to build chapels at home, and hang chandeliers and bells in them, you shan't play in our church yards." Male church leaders even appropriated the mission money raised by Sunbeams (the children's mission group organized by WMU). In later years, Hamilton remembered, men were "converted from [the] error of their way."[104]

The officers of the first WMU central committee appointed by the ABSC in 1889 included Amanda Tupper Hamilton, Annie Eager, and Maryann Bestor Brown. The choices could hardly have been better. Amanda Tupper Hamilton had direct ties to the FMB through her father, its longtime director. She served as the first state organizer and later as WMU state president (1911–1912). Maryann Bestor Brown served as initial state WMU secretary. Her father was a legendary Baptist preacher, state legislator, and author of Alabama's first public school legislation. She married a prominent Sumterville planter and moved to Livingston after the Civil War. Fluent in French and Latin, she taught languages while living in Livingston. After moving to the Birmingham suburb of East Lake, Brown began a seven-year career as WMU state secretary. When she died in 1897, her daughter (Hermione Brown Malone) took her place as secretary.[105] Anna ("Annie") Banks Coor Pender Eager served as first president of the state WMU and was reelected each year until 1897. A native of Utica, Mississippi, Annie Eager lost her father (who was a surgeon in the Confederate army) when she was a child. After graduating from Hillman College, she married George Eager (a friend later wrote that they were "the most perfectly matched couple I have ever known"). In Montgomery she became active in literary clubs and served as president of the Montgomery Infirmary Association and as vice-president of the Public Library Association and of the Boys' Industrial School. She was a charter member of the Alabama Federation of Women's Clubs when it was formed in 1895 and served the organization as vice-president and president. She often presented papers before women's groups and helped begin the official newspaper of the federated women's clubs. During her tenure as state president of the federation, the organization began the boys' industrial school (she was a charter member of its board of control). After her husband left Montgomery to join the Southern seminary faculty, Annie Eager led the campaign to establish a WMU training school in Louisville.[106] She accomplished all these commitments while raising three sons.

Women also made progress at the associational level. Lida B. Robertson was granted a seat at the 1890 Mobile Association and allowed to present a report on behalf of WMU. Apparently some delegates objected to a woman speaking to the association because B. F. Riley read her report the following year. After the 1891 report, the association adopted a resolution urging that women's missionary societies be organized in every church. The first associational WMU meeting occurred in 1893. The following year six women registered at the associational meeting representing churches. In 1896 some males objected to WMU, claiming that mission emphasis should be conducted by churches, not separate women's societies. The women present responded that women often ministered to the sick, poor, dying, and unfortunate with greater care and promptness than men and that the "livest churches" in the association were those with women's missionary societies. By 1902 WMU had become a regular feature of associational life, although men continued to read the report that women wrote.[107]

By the late 1890s, Alabama WMU was well established. Baptist women assumed the primary role for local church benevolence as well as for state, national, and foreign missions. By their fifth statewide convention in December 1897, twenty-one associational WMUs contributed more than $8,000 to missions. The *Alabama Baptist* extolled their "quiet, modest, earnest" service. The editor assured anxious men that WMU women did not seek "to usurp the place of the men, but in an humble way to do the work of the Lord." Every pastor and deacon should encourage WMU organization, which produced "more spirituality, more cooperation, a livelier church membership and larger and more interesting congregations." The problem was, the editor wrote the following year, that some pastors thought "no one ought to do anything in the church but themselves." Pastoral jealousy of women particularly crippled country churches. Interference with the money women raised for missions made it difficult for them even to pay the salary they had pledged to missionary Willie Kelly.[108] This problem they would soon solve by demanding complete autonomy over mission funds they raised.

Old-Time Religion, New-Time Religion

Although new subterranean currents in theology were bubbling to the surface of American religion, the flow reached Alabama slowly. The old-time religion of summer revivals, emotional preaching, and biblical literalism still prevailed. Music continued to play a major role both in protracted meetings and in regular Baptist worship, though the growing professionalism of choirs matched that of ministers. Even country churches began to acquire organs and pay more attention to organized choirs and

A baptism by Rev. Robert M. Hunter in the Choctahatchie River about 1890. Old-time religious revivals still flourished in Alabama despite the political conflict of the times. (Courtesy of Samford University Archives)

congregational singing. The *Alabama Baptist* extolled such singing as the only part of worship in which everyone could participate. But good music programs must have strong leaders and well-practiced choirs. The editor criticized the "mean stubbornness of some members of choirs, who, because they can't dictate, 'kick,' get angry, and pout. Such folk are a nuisance." Uplifting religious music also required a competent director, not some man "who will 'whine-out' in a long drawn-out, doleful way some long-meter tune that will make the people feel as though they were down deep in a lonely valley." "Better have good singing with a poor sermon," the editor concluded, "than a fine sermon with poor singing."[109]

Theological Conflict

Try as they might to preserve unsullied traditional ways, modernity penetrated thickets of theological orthodoxy as easily as new railroad lines ripped through primitive forests. Preserving the peace of Zion from the rumble of distant theological thunder was no easy task.

Although the editor of the *Alabama Baptist* admitted that there was a Christian doctrine of scientific evolution that some good men believed, he wrote in 1891 that the theory of evolution had "seen its best days," and its influence was receding. Other correspondents dismissed evolution entirely as the product of skepticism. Better that Baptists ignore all such theories in favor of the "simple Bible faith" of their forefathers, one correspondent wrote of evolution.[110]

Higher criticism and religious liberalism sparked keener debate. Historical discussion of this conflict has often made two fundamental errors: it parodies orthodoxy as intolerant and uninformed, and it assumes that all Alabama Baptists were of one mind on the subject.

Undoubtedly some uneducated ministers did begin to resemble the creatures they refused to acknowledge as ancestors in their uninformed attacks on evolutionists and liberals. But some extremely well educated preachers also demurred in the new patterns of thought. The editor of the *Alabama Baptist* noted that, in the name of tolerance, liberalism often sought to crush other beliefs as narrow and dishonest. J. H. Curry (pastor at Northport) did not condemn honest and devout criticism of the Bible that might even strengthen personal faith. But he feared that the net effect of higher criticism was to produce more skeptics than mature Christians. Rev. P. T. Hale preached a similar sermon at Southside church in Birmingham entitled "Attacking the Word of God with a Penknife." The sermon was reprinted in the *Alabama Baptist* and widely cited. Like Curry, Hale did not object to historical and literary criticism of the Bible, but such criticism should be done "reverently, in a teachable spirit, and with no preconceived adverse theories." Such a spirit should regard miracles as a possibility, if not a fact. Higher critics were often too skeptical and arbitrary, too willing to accept scientific theory as fact. He had often changed his interpretation of Scripture because of new discoveries in anatomy, geology, and biology and had come to emphasize sociological questions more. In an earlier time, the church had trembled before the Copernican revolution (which proved that the earth was not the center of the universe). But Christianity had survived that earlier scientific revolution and would survive this one as well.[111]

J. C. Wright summarized the positive contributions of higher criticism in an 1899 essay. He defined such criticism as the historical and literary study of the Bible, its authors, chronology, style, and the internal relationship of the writings. Although he pronounced much of higher criticism "fanciful" and some of it even perverted, he also believed it had merit. Not all German higher critics were radicals, though all lowered the status of the Bible to that of any other book and "eviscerated Christianity of God, Christ, Bible, everything divine and supernatural." Such criticism, he concluded, transformed Christianity into the product of natural evolution.[112]

On the other side of the dispute were George Eager of Montgomery First Baptist Church and A. J. Dickinson of Selma First Baptist Church. Eager would soon leave Alabama to study at the University of Chicago and then teach at Southern Baptist Theological Seminary. One of his sermons thoroughly explored the major issues in the debate. Scripture had not been dictated by God, a view he believed "now abandoned by well nigh all." The canon of the Old and New Testaments had not been miraculously determined nor had the Bible been preserved free of error by copyists through the ages. Translators of the revised version had found many such errors and even some deliberate changes and interpolations. He specifically rejected Dwight L. Moody's argument that unless one believed every word and syllable of the Bible, one might as well "make a bonfire of them, and build a monument heaven-high to Voltaire and Paine." Eager suggested his own alternative. The problem was not the Bible but Baptist assumptions about it. Infallibility applied to matters of salvation, not historical issues. The meaning of Scripture was related to the age and people to whom it was addressed. Even when Baptists spoke most emphatically "the words of the Lord," they spoke "as living men among men." Everywhere in Scripture were traces of human personality, and the truth of one age was not automatically applicable to another.[113]

For three decades as Alabama's most outspoken theological liberal, A. J. Dickinson defended higher criticism, scientific history, inductive thinking, evolution, and the University of Chicago. One historian assigns him primary responsibility for preventing fundamentalists from controlling the state convention. As pastor of one of the most important Black Belt churches, associate editor of the *Alabama Baptist,* and a popular and successful revival preacher, Dickinson was highly regarded even by those who did not share his theological opinions. The authority of Scripture, Dickinson wrote in 1894, rested on neither inspiration nor inerrancy, but upon Jesus Christ. Scriptures were "authenticated revelations of the person of Christ."[114] In subsequent articles, Dickinson questioned the Pauline authorship of Hebrews, proposed merger of Howard College and the University of Chicago, and criticized pastors who condemned higher criticism without reading it. Dickinson ardently defended his alma mater, the University of Chicago. To charges that higher critics dominated the faculty, he responded that such ideas were common in all seminaries, including

Southern Baptist Theological Seminary, where he estimated that half the courses included elements of higher criticism. William R. Harper, president of the University of Chicago, wrote in 1894 that Genesis and Babylonian creation stories borrowed from a similar source, and he questioned the historicity of the biblical creation and deluge accounts. Many Alabama Baptists considered Harper's writings heretical. The editor of the *Alabama Baptist* denounced Harper's views, announcing that the paper would "walk in the old paths." Dickinson defended Harper even while he affirmed the "infallibility of the Bible." He believed that Baptist commitment to soul liberty and free thought allowed members to conclude that Genesis was "history idealized in story, selected, arranged and colored by the inspired writer to teach not history or science, but religious and moral truth."[115]

At the other end of the theological spectrum from Dickinson, advocates of Landmarkism tightened their grip on the state. As in the debates over theological liberalism, denominational leaders maintained a remarkable civility. Many writers to the *Alabama Baptist* grieved over increasing tensions between Baptists, Methodists, and Presbyterians because of Landmark insistence that Baptists preserved the only true biblical faith. Christianity that should unite communities instead divided them, the editor wrote remorsefully. Urban ministers especially ignored Landmark doctrines and helped organize interdenominational pastors' unions. Landmarkers responded by calling such efforts "sickly, sentimental catholicity." One wrote that he was disgusted with the practice of calling Methodists and others "brother" when they were not part of the true church, had not been properly baptized, and did not believe in the perseverance of the saints. "This 'brothering,' " he concluded, "is to say the least of it, hypocrisy." Despite such occasional outbursts, the denominational journal still spoke kindly of Landmark pastors and gave them prominent attention in the journal. The editor did not fear that the denomination would split, as many predicted, so long as individual churches did not make such issues a test of fellowship. Landmark doctrines were not vital Baptist principles such as salvation by grace, believers' baptism, religious liberty, missions, and congregational government. As a result, Baptists should be tolerant of differing opinions.[116]

Landmarkers and their opponents squared off most divisively over obscure but important historical documents discovered by Southern seminary president William H. Whitsitt. At the center of the ensuing storm stood Judge Jonathan Haralson. Haralson was a member of A. J. Dickinson's Selma church (as were half a dozen other state Baptist leaders including H. S. D. Mallory, president of the ABSC and legal adviser to its mission board; Mrs. M. L. Woodson, who helped organize the Baptist orphanage; Mrs. Law Lamar Sr., longtime Judson College trustee; and Kathleen Mallory, chief executive of both Alabama and SBC WMU). A graduate of the University of Alabama and Louisiana State University, Haralson practiced law in Selma, served as chairman of the Howard College trustees, and was elected to the Alabama Supreme Court in 1892. He was elected president of the state convention in 1874 and held the office until 1892. From 1888 until 1899 he also served as president of the Southern Baptist Convention, the longest continuous term in the denomination's history. He was also the first layman to hold the office. Renowned for his skills in parliamentary procedure and his fairness when presiding over controversial meetings, Haralson would need every legal and intellectual resource during the Whitsitt controversy. In 1879 Whitsitt began to write a scientific, fully documented history of Baptists. He spent months conducting research at the British Museum and at Oxford and Cambridge Universities. Most controversial among his findings was that Baptists began to immerse new believers only in 1641. Thus, the Baptist denomination with its unique doctrines could not be traced back in a continuous line to 30 A.D. as Landmarkers claimed. Publication of this finding precipitated a three-year controversy with Landmarkers that did not end until Whitsitt's forced resignation as seminary president in 1899 (when he joined what one Baptist historian described as "The Friendless Fraternity of Exiled Professors").[117]

At first Whitsitt's views made little impact on Alabama. When he preached at the 1896 state convention in Huntsville, at Judson and Howard Colleges, and at Southside church in Birmingham, he was well received. Although he affirmed that immersion was the proper scriptural form of baptism, he had found no historical documentation of its use by Baptists earlier than 1641. Joseph Judson Taylor, pastor of First Baptist Church in Mobile, dismissed the controversy as a rural-urban dispute. Both sides passed resolutions, which the editor of the *Alabama Baptist* declined to publish, citing Baptist freedom to believe what they preferred. The editor also urged associations to pass no resolutions until a full, free, and impartial investigation had been completed. The pastor at Thomasville marveled "that so great ado has been made over so small an affair."[118]

When the controversy reached the 1897 SBC in Wilmington, North Carolina, Haralson presided brilliantly to defuse tensions. He met with both sides before the convention, asked for expert opinions about Whitsitt's research to convince himself of its accuracy, and allowed each side to air fully its arguments. Delegates from Alabama generally aligned in defense of Whitsitt and against those demanding his resignation.[119]

Back in Alabama the Wilmington convention had resolved nothing. Z. D. Roby (pastor of Opelika First Baptist Church) in a fit of temper accused Haralson of unfairly presiding to help Whitsitt. He later sent George Eager (Haralson's Montgomery pastor and close friend) a letter of apology that he asked be shared with the judge. Haralson vigorously defended his conduct as presiding officer in a private letter to Eager, which he urged be shown to Roby.[120]

Other Alabama Baptists were not so circumspect. They debated the issues emotionally and publicly. The Central Association passed a resolution asking the state convention to demand Whitsitt's firing. The East Liberty and Carey Associations also called for his resignation. For three weeks before the November state convention, the *Alabama Baptist* printed one attack on Whitsitt after another. At the convention two hundred delegates gathered amid great tension. A committee appointed to handle the affair presented majority and minority reports. The majority report, written by Joshua Hill Foster and L. O. Dawson, asked seminary trustees to examine the dispute impartially and take appropriate action. The minority report, drafted largely by Josephus Shackelford, asked that the president resign or be fired. After three hours of debate, E. B. Teague moved that the entire matter be tabled, which won a large majority. Though Teague was no defender of Whitsitt, he realized the convention was headed for a split as emotions raged out of control. Press representatives had come to observe and report the convention's disintegration. Instead they recorded its reconciliation. After tabling the reports, delegates resolved that whatever their views on Whitsitt, they would not allow them to destroy Baptist fellowship, harm mission work, or be brought before the ABSC again.[121]

Unfortunately this harmony was short-lived. Anti-Whitsitt forces determined to bring the matter before the SBC. Haralson had planned a well-earned retirement from Baptist politics, but from across the convention denominational leaders implored him to accept another term. If he refused, they predicted disaster. A new, inexperienced president would not be able to handle the volatile controversy. J. J. Taylor warned Haralson that even in Alabama some anti-Whitsitt Landmark forces planned to start a new denominational newspaper.[122]

Suddenly in July 1898 Whitsitt announced his resignation, and reactions varied widely. Haralson privately breathed a sigh of relief. He had supported Whitsitt and saw no reason why his ideas should disqualify him as a member of the seminary faculty. But he regretted the way Whitsitt had publicized his views and considered the president only "a great man," not an "indispensable" one. The controversy had distracted the convention for three years and must end. Haralson also seriously considered proposals from some to sever the seminary from the convention for fear that otherwise Landmarkers would gain control. Such control would result in disfranchising any Southern Baptists who favored "progress and enlightenment in the religious world."[123]

A. J. Dickinson deplored the entire affair. He had hoped the SBC would be a pioneer in conservative biblical studies. There had been a ripening scholarship of the finest caliber at SBTS, he wrote, but reactionary attacks on John A. Broadus, James P. Boyce, and Whitsitt had largely destroyed it. Any serious seminary scholar would now have to "report to the denominational executioners by order of the trustees." The South would never produce its own biblical scholars until kindness, courtesy, and a more hospitable intellectual climate prevailed. In his study, Dickinson wrote sermons surrounded by books written by Phillip Schaff, Adolf Harnack, and other higher critics. He pleaded that Baptists be patient with "every young Erasmus God give[s] us, and not dig him up by the roots in wantonness because he does not serve in our harness." Dickinson's article did not sit well with many Alabama Baptists, who deluged the *Alabama Baptist* with criticism of Dickinson for reopening the divisive affair. Some subscribers canceled the paper. Others renewed their pleas for tolerance. The pastor of Ruhama Baptist Church spent an entire worship period summarizing the controversy in hopes of cooling emotions.[124]

As the century ended, missions secretary W. B. Crumpton (ever the optimist) congratulated Alabama Baptists for their relative harmony compared to other state conventions. He speculated on the sources of unity within the denomination. Alabama Baptists disagreed as sharply as Baptists in other states, yet the state convention had avoided a "disgraceful row." The reasons, he wrote, included superb presiding officers (notably Judge Haralson), who had not allowed debate to go on interminably or degenerate into ugly words. Most discord in Alabama happened between state conventions, not at them.[125] It was a good thing. Given the torrid battles of the previous fifteen years over Farmers' Alliance politics, temperance, theological liberalism, Landmarkism, the role of women, and similar matters, had Baptists chosen to discuss their differences fully in a meetinghouse or state convention, there likely would have been no denomination left to save by the time they argued over the fate of W. H. Whitsitt.

7

Progressivism and Baptists, 1900–1920

"I belong to the church military and not the church millinery."

n a magisterial history of the South from 1877 to 1913, C. Vann Woodward wrote that the three major trends in American religion during those years—modernism, ecumenism, and the social gospel—virtually bypassed the South.[1] Despite Woodward's standing as the most influential American historian of the twentieth century, on this judgment he was incorrect. Modernist or liberal theology did carve out a beachhead in the South, though orthodoxy confined it to the periphery of the battlefield and slowly decimated it by purges, firings, and denominational pressure. Most southern theological liberals found their opponents too formidable and in time joined the growing northward exodus of the South's best educated and least orthodox. Ecumenism confronted equally formidable obstacles. Deeply loyal to region and sectional denominations, few southern evangelicals could surmount religious localism on behalf of any transcending theology, whether liberal or fundamentalist. They were religious in their own way, according to the values and assumptions of their region.

Social Christianity was another issue. Although southern evangelicals did not succumb to belief that Christianity was essentially about transforming society (nor, in fact, did most northern advocates of the social gospel believe that concept either), they did seek to apply Christian ethics to society's problems in a way unprecedented either before or after the two decades following 1900. Much of this energy came from the times. The decades that produced Republican president Theodore Roosevelt and Democrat Woodrow Wilson were optimistic ones, bursting with idealism, naiveté, and belief in the capacity to change both humanity and society. However much southerners deviated from these beliefs, many of their brightest and most influential sons and daughters were affected by the virus of social reform, especially those who studied or traveled outside the South. There was no gigantic door at the Mason-Dixon line shutting out new ideas. Southerners were not of one mind nor did they possess a siege mentality. They read. They listened. They thought. And many of them changed their minds about the nature of southern society, seeking to make it more like they believed Christ would have it be.

Woodward essentially raised the wrong issue. The operative question is not, why did the major trends of American Christianity bypass the South? The key issue is, why did movements so favorably begun and endorsed by such influential leaders wither after so short a time?

In 1944 the Alabama Baptist Historical Society sought to identify the most influential denominational leaders of the years between 1900 and 1925. Laymen and pastors responded with hundreds of names. Twenty prominent Alabama Baptist males ranked the list. The sixteen who ranked highest (not surprisingly, all men) were led by W. B. Crumpton, longtime mission board secretary and state temperance leader. Behind him came pastors of prominent churches, more than half of them involved in the social gospel movement. At least half of them also had been influenced by higher criticism, some to a considerable degree. Paul V. Bomar, Alfred J. Dickinson, A. C. Davidson, J. E. Dillard, Lesley L. Gwaltney, Lemuel O. Dawson, John W. Phillips, and Charles A. Stakely represented unorthodox trends by nineteenth-century Alabama Baptist standards.[2] At opposite ends of the theological ranking were Morgan Marion Wood (who ranked number thirteen) and A. J. Dickinson (who stood fifth).

Morgan Wood was born in 1853 in Jefferson County. His education at Ruhama Academy under the tutelage of a Baptist preacher was interrupted by the Civil War, leaving him with scant formal preparation. A brief sojourn at Howard College ended when fire destroyed the family home. Wood taught school briefly before entering the ministry in 1879. In 1883 he began pastoring the Big Creek Baptist Church in Tuscaloosa County and traveling about western Alabama on the revival circuit. Later he pastored numerous half- and quarter-time churches, served as state missionary for northwestern Alabama, then pastored a number of churches in the Birmingham area. He served as officer of the Birmingham Association and as recording secretary of the state convention for the first third of the twentieth century. Renowned as a revival preacher, his meetings were characterized by spiritual fervor that often produced exceptional conversion experiences.[3] Wood demonstrated no trace of modernism.

Alfred J. Dickinson was part of the same generation but the product of very different education and theology. Born on his family's Virginia plantation in 1864, Dickinson attended the University of Richmond and Southern Baptist Theological Seminary, where he compiled a brilliant academic record and was chosen to deliver the 1886 commencement address. Later he attended short courses at Harvard and the University of Chicago. After pastoring the influential Selma First Baptist Church during the 1890s, he was called as pastor of Birmingham's First Baptist Church in 1901. During nearly two decades as pastor in the steel city he became deeply involved in local politics on behalf of temperance and moral reform, served as trustee of Judson and Howard Colleges as well as the state Baptist orphanage, and was a member of the State Mission Board and state convention executive committee. He resigned his pastorate to run for Congress as a labor reform candidate in 1918, then engaged in social work at Camp Sheridan near Montgomery during World War I. After the war he worked for the federal and state departments of health as a lecturer. Never much interested in evangelism (membership at Birmingham First Baptist Church declined toward the end of his pastorate), he wrote before his death in 1923 that social work had brought him out of his "high pulpit where preachers talk of narrow doctrines and faith and vague traditions" and down to earth where ordinary people lived. "I have spent a number of years in the so-called pastoral work," he wrote, "and from a standpoint of good done, my time was worse than wasted."[4]

Dickinson's theology was modernist. He often charged his antagonists with soft-mindedness because they so often criticized what they had not read or understood. Renowned for his wide reading and scholarly preaching (which was often over the heads of his congregations), he once wrote that "a lazy man cannot be a modernist in any age." In defense of evolution, he chastened churches for filling the heads of schoolchildren with traditions on Sunday that modern high school science teachers disproved during the week. A "modernized Baptist," he wrote, was a Christian "with a larger, richer, more workable and efficient Bible than his father possessed." Baptists had always been "modernists" to the age in which they lived, he believed.

Dickinson's daughter remembered her father as the "most deeply religious person" she knew but also as a man who hated sham and humbug, which he took special delight in ridiculing. He was impatient with "noisy conversions and ecclesiastical whoopee." He enjoyed the company of ordinary, even illiterate men because he admired their toughness and lack of pretense. He read Latin to her and spent hours each day studying in his library, especially reading religious sociology and ancient history. Other acquaintances remembered him for the theological liberalism, which they believed reduced his influence among Alabama Baptists.[5]

Orthodox brethren directed sharp fire at what they called Dickinson's "learned, liberal, lucid, logical and loose position." They accused him of defending men "neither noted for personal piety nor friendliness to the Bible." They charged him with propagating the same "radical and destructive criticism" as the higher critics with the "purpose of infusing its poison into the minds of the Baptist people of the state." Dickinson responded to one such critic as "our brother" who "comes forward with an acute case of the disorder we had in mind."[6] Pastors and laymen began to form behind their favorites, and the war was on.

Traditional Religion in Progressive Alabama

Change came fast during these years, so fast that Alabama Baptists could not entirely absorb it. But the swift currents of change bypassed many eddies of orthodoxy. Liberal and social gospel ministers rose to significant positions of denominational influence while self-educated bivocational ministers at the forks of the creeks continued to proclaim a simple gospel of conversion largely oblivious to the flood swirling all around them.

Demsey W. Hodges and Joseph W. Phillips were cut from a more familiar piece of Baptist material than the maverick Dickinson. Hodges was born near Headland in Henry County in 1888. One of thirteen children, he married when he was eighteen and already had a child when he felt called to preach. At age twenty-one he gave up farming, sold his inheritance of forty acres, and enrolled in Newton Baptist Institute (which essentially provided high school work). Later he worked his way through Howard College, clerking in a shoe store and collecting for a hardware store. He found time to participate as a member of Howard's debate team, graduated cum laude, and in 1916 became pastor of the Headland Baptist Church. After two years as an army chaplain in France, he began evangelistic work. Operating from Dothan with a large tent, he preached 396 times in 230 days during 1925 and recorded 385 professions of faith. An active Mason, he continued in evangelism until his retirement in 1949.[7]

Joseph W. Phillips was often confused with John W. Phillips, the famous and modernistic pastor of Mobile First Baptist Church. Other than a common name, they shared few similarities. Joseph Phillips was born in Barbour County in 1859. Ordained in the Salem Baptist Church (Dale County) in his early twenties, he pastored small churches in Barbour, Dale, Pike, and Henry Counties. Educated in local schools but without college or seminary training, he taught school, farmed, and cut timber to pay his bills. He preached from an outline with each section tied to a passage of Scripture.[8]

At the center of their religious world (and that of most other Alabama Baptists) was revivalism. Far away from large cities, in churches like Big Springs Baptist in Randolph County, the cycle of religious life still revolved around the two-week summer revival after crops were laid by. A few elderly sinners and most children who had "reached the age of accountability" (usually reckoned as the sexual awakening brought on by puberty) were converted. Baptism occurred in a pool of Big Springs. Many evangelists were of the "hellfire and brimstone" persuasion, which was probably necessary in a community where one of the most popular games was called "bootleggers and sheriff" (children hid their "liquor"—actually bundles of sticks—in the woods and other children tried to find it). Revivals were effective in evangelizing if not always so successful in changing the conduct of converts. As the local church historian remembered, "at Big Springs if people were not Baptist they were considered somewhat strange."[9]

Even revivalism subtly changed after 1900. Demsey Hodges was typical of the new phase. In the nineteenth century, few men earned a living in full-time evangelism. By 1920 professional revivalists were increasingly popular. Local revivals in towns began to give way to city mass meetings of the type staged by former professional baseball player Billy Sunday. The editor of the *Alabama Baptist* regretted Sunday's slang and acrobatic pulpit performances but rejoiced at his success in reaching the unsaved masses. Although revivalism declined nationwide after 1910, it remained a main course on the religious menu of Alabama Baptists.[10]

Revivalism had been much more effective evangelizing rural people than urban. In 1906 Alabama's 162,000 Southern Baptists were concentrated in rural areas. The 1900 Birmingham city directory listed only ten Baptist churches (compared to seventeen Methodist, sixteen National [black] Baptist, nine Presbyterian, five Episcopal, three Catholic, and two Jewish).

Catholics led all Birmingham denominations in 1906 with 29 percent of church members. National Baptists, white Methodists, Presbyterians, and Southern Baptists followed in order of rank.[11]

The strategy for addressing Baptist weakness in towns and cities was a vigorous campaign to plant new churches. State mission board secretary W. B. Crumpton worried constantly that industrial towns were slipping beyond the reach of Baptists. A major portion of his 1902 report to the state convention dealt with mill and factory workers. These native whites had been mostly faithful members of rural Baptist churches until they moved to town. Then "a spirit of indifference" descended upon them. They would not seek membership in fashionable "up-town" First Baptist churches, nor would they organize their own mill village congregations. Country churches showed little interest in financing mission ventures in new industrial communities because they did not consider such areas deprived. Crumpton's 1912 and 1913 reports returned to the same theme with particular focus on coal mining camps in the northern third of the state. Few of these churches could retain a regular pastor because members were too poor to pay his salary. That left the church fields open "to any religious crank, or sower of heresy who comes along." (The kind of "crank" Crumpton feared was no modernist from the University of Chicago; the "sower of heresy" in coal camps and mill villages was more likely a Holiness or pentecostal preacher.) Crumpton's solution was a full-time evangelist to miners and mill workers.[12]

Efforts to evangelize industrial workers began to pay dividends, aided greatly by mining and cotton mill companies that believed godly workers were more reliable, more conservative, and less likely to join unions, to strike, or otherwise to cause trouble. Companies often donated land for churches, built and owned the church house, constructed a parsonage, paid part or all of the minister's salary, and even ran pipes from the central heating plant to provide warmth in winter.

Two examples from north Alabama coal camps in Palos and Birmingham illustrate the pattern. In Palos, the mine superintendent endorsed the church, which had one of the largest Sunday schools in rural Jefferson County. The superintendent (whom the *Alabama Baptist* praised as a man who "was on the right side of every question that came up") also refused to allow liquor sales in the camp. Red Mountain Baptist Church (also known as Reeder's church) met in a building owned by Tennessee Coal and Iron Company (TCI), the district's largest industry. At Docena, the new Baptist church enrolled mainly coal miners from a TCI mine.[13]

Cotton mill workers at Avondale Mills in Birmingham built Packer Memorial Baptist Church in their mill village in 1900. Pastors were usually mill workers (when the mill closed in 1971, the pastor had worked in the mill for thirty-five years). Two years after Packer Memorial was organized, workers in Sylacauga's Mignon mill village organized the Mignon Baptist Church. The congregation consisted mainly of textile workers (who often perceived the Methodist church as filled with company "stewards and higher-ups"). The company furnished the building, heat, and pastorium until it sold village houses in 1950. W. B. Crumpton reported in 1913 that most of Mignon's members were women and children, but so were most employees because the company worked more child labor than any in the state. On a tour of Shawmut, a mill village in the burgeoning Chatta- hoochee Valley, Crumpton spoke well of the company for partly financing the church. This and other company welfare convinced Crumpton that cor- porations did have souls and were solving disputes with labor.[14]

One important task of such churches was the distribution of charity. They regularly collected and distributed money to poor members, widows, and orphans. A benevolence committee at Ruhama church expended $20 to $100 annually to poor people living in East Lake. Florence First Baptist Church created a committee on the poor to distribute money donated by a wealthy member, but he insisted the church change the name to the "good- will committee" to remove the symbolism of superiority/inferiority sug- gested by the original name. Wetumpka First Baptist Church created a similar committee to aid the poor both inside and outside the church. John W. Stewart (a native of Randolph County and longtime pastor of the Ever- green church in Butler County) doggedly promoted the state Baptist or- phanage that was established in 1891. Appearing at virtually every associa- tional meeting, he recounted stories of abused and abandoned children that often left both speaker and audience in tears. His lifelong advocacy of children earned the traditionalist Stewart a place on the honor roll of most distinguished Baptists of the early twentieth century.[15]

Overseeing such assistance statewide was an increasingly efficient de- nominational bureaucracy. In keeping with the themes of efficiency and data gathering that characterized progressivism, the state convention com- pletely reorganized its structure in 1915. The revisions changed the basis of representation, abolished a number of boards that had appealed sepa- rately to churches for funding, and created in their place a thirty-six-mem- ber state executive board. The board was authorized to hire employees it needed to implement convention work and to submit an annual budget. Among prominent ministers on the original executive board were A. C. Davidson of Birmingham's Southside Baptist Church, Charles Stakely of

Montgomery First Baptist Church, A. J. Dickinson of Birmingham First Baptist Church, and W. F. Yarborough of Anniston's Parker Memorial Baptist Church.[16]

Neither Frank W. Barnett (editor of the *Alabama Baptist*) nor A. J. Dickinson approved what they viewed as centralizing tendencies in both ABSC and SBC. Barnett explained the clash in political terms, of old-line conservatives trying to preserve their power against the democratic masses. He referred to his antagonists as "bosses," "autocrats," "Bourbons," "conservatives," and "Tories." He described the masses as "progressives" and "democrats." Barnett's pastor, A. J. Dickinson, agreed. When a resolution at the state convention proposed to replace elected district representatives on the executive board with direct appointments, Dickinson denounced the proposal as neither scriptural nor "Baptistic."[17]

Leadership of virtually all Baptist institutions changed between 1900 and 1920, some in dramatic ways. Frank Barnett resigned a pastorate in Georgia in 1902 in order to buy the *Alabama Baptist*. He established a new office in Birmingham and transferred the paper to private ownership. After he became assistant editor of the *Birmingham Age-Herald* in 1918, he sold the paper back to the denomination, having doubled subscriptions to more than 10,000. L. L. Gwaltney became the new editor in 1919, beginning three decades of service that would make him Crumpton's successor as the best known and most highly regarded Baptist in the state.[18]

W. B. Crumpton's nearly three-decade term as head of the denomination came to an end in 1916, although the convention twice elected him president until he refused to serve again in 1919 because of age. The convention selected W. F. Yarborough, pastor of Parker Memorial Baptist Church, to replace him, though no one could do so in the affections of Alabama Baptists. Yarborough remained in the position until 1919, long enough to launch the Seventy-Five Million Dollar Campaign in Alabama (a program that essentially replaced single fund drives with the Cooperative Program). In 1919, the first year of the drive, total contributions climbed from $777,000 to $1.15 million.[19]

Financial improvements did not materially help Judson and Howard Colleges, which remained underfunded if competently administered. Paul V. Bomar, president of Judson from 1913 to 1923, was pastor at Siloam church and professor of Bible and psychology before his election as president. A graduate of Wofford College and SBTS as well as a postgraduate student at the University of Chicago, he also made the 1944 list of most important Alabama Baptist leaders. Andrew P. Montague (descendant of a distinguished Virginia family) left the presidency of Furman University for

Howard College in 1902 and served as president for a decade. A classicist who disparaged technical education, he held degrees from the University of Virginia and George Washington University (Ph.D.). Howard made substantial progress under his leadership, both in quality of curriculum and endowment. One of the school's graduates, C. E. Crossland, won a prestigious Rhodes scholarship.[20]

Perhaps most important of all the changes and reorganizations was a simple demographic fact. The center of the denomination was shifting from the Black Belt (centered in Montgomery) to north Alabama. By 1921 three-fifths of the membership and an equal percentage of pledges to the Seventy-Five Million Dollar Campaign came from the northern portion of the state. Of six state conventions between 1914 and 1920, only one was held in south Alabama. Howard College had moved from Marion (as had the Home Mission Board earlier), ending that town's dominance of Baptist life. Barnett also moved the *Alabama Baptist* headquarters to the bustling steel city of Birmingham. Baptists in the northern part of the state began to complain about their underrepresentation on the new executive board and the decision to locate the new Baptist hospital in Selma. They believed that booming coal and steel towns needed more of the convention's financial resources. Rural churches in south Alabama disagreed.[21]

Other traditions changed as well. Although church discipline remained a factor in the life of rural churches, it rapidly disappeared after 1900 in urban congregations. Wetumpka First Baptist Church appointed a discipline committee, but it brought charges against only one person before dissolving. Perhaps one factor in the change was the decline in farmer members and the rapid increase in prominence of professionals and businessmen. Even rural churches used discipline less frequently. Myra Ponder of Hatchett Creek Baptist Church in rural Clay County remembered going to a square dance during these years with a group of young people from her church. When angry church leaders threatened to bring them before the congregation, they threatened to leave the Baptist church and join the more permissive Bethlehem Methodist Church. The charges were dropped.[22]

Uniting urban and rural, liberal and fundamentalist Baptists in this and all epochs were foreign missions. The pathway to China pioneered by Eliza Shuck, Martha Foster Crawford, and Willie Kelly before 1900 became a superhighway after the dawn of the new century. T. W. and Minnie Ayers, Cynthia A. Miller, Lois and A. Y. Napier, Alice Huey, Floy White Adams, Mary Anderson, the Taylor brothers (Richard V. and Adrian S.), and a host of others followed where pioneers had led. T. W. Ayers became the first physician to serve with the FMB on a foreign field. He recruited a host of others, including his physician son, Sanford. Other Alabama Baptists left Alabama for Mexico (Rosa Golden and Jessie Ennis Hatchell), Argentina (Mattie Cox Justice), and Japan (Daisy Pettus Ray). The Alabama WMU mobilized its resources especially for China missions, shipping money and supplies constantly and paying some salaries.[23]

The Battle for the Bible: Round One

If missions most united Alabama Baptists, theology most divided them. At the heart of the conflict was the University of Chicago. By turn of century, higher criticism had become deeply embedded in its faculty. Shailer Mathews (who graduated from the University of Berlin) joined the Chicago faculty in 1894 and pioneered work in social psychology. His first major work, *The Social Teachings of Jesus* (published earlier as essays in the University-sponsored journal, the *American Journal of Sociology*) interpreted Jesus' message as primarily a call to change society. Mathews's theology was critical and experiential (based more on religious experience than biblical authority). He accepted the value of biblical doctrines but not divine inspiration of Scripture. Though respectful of the Bible, he expressed equal admiration for human intellect. The atonement and sacrifice of Jesus became secondary to Jesus' ministry, his incarnation, and his service to humanity. Other Chicago professors contributed to the sociohistorical, social gospel approach to Christianity and the Bible. So did non–University of Chicago theologians, including the famous Baptist pastor in New York City, Walter Rauschenbusch (especially his book, *Theology for the Social Gospel*).[24]

Various Alabama Baptists accepted parts or all of this "new theology." Many of them held degrees from the University of Chicago or attended summer institutes and special seminars there. Paul Bomar, Charles B. Williams (who had a Ph.D. from Chicago and became president of Howard College in 1919), J. C. Stivender (who became pastor of Ruhama Baptist Church in 1919 and had two degrees from Chicago), A. J. Dickinson (who attended theological institutes there), and John W. Phillips (pastor of Mobile First Baptist Church who occasionally lectured at the university) were among Alabamians directly influenced by the institution and its distinguished theology faculty. Many other pastors and laymen came under the school's indirect sway, including A. J. Dickinson's two brothers. J. G. Dickinson attended the University of Richmond and SBTS and pastored at Uniontown, Gallion, Demopolis, Gadsden, and Evergreen. J. V. Dickinson pastored a variety of churches in Alabama and shared his brothers' theological views. Hugo L. Black (later a U.S. senator and influential justice of the U.S. Supreme Court) taught the Baraca Sunday school class at Birmingham First Baptist Church and admired A. J. Dickinson. Frank Barnett disagreed with his pastor about the new theology but remained a close friend. He did share his pastor's enthusiasm for the social gospel.

Many Baptists beyond Dickinson's sphere looked favorably on at least some aspects of modernist theology. James H. Chapman studied at Columbia and Boston Universities and founded the Howard College department of religious education in 1918. He imprinted religious sociology at the core of the curriculum. Ruhama pastor Cecil V. Cook was charged by members of his congregation with being a modernist and resigned after a stormy tenure. H. H. Hibbs of East Lake wrote the *Alabama Baptist* during a debate over the new theology in 1915 that there was value in both higher criticism and orthodoxy.[25]

Many Baptists who rejected modernism affirmed its tradition of unhindered intellectual inquiry. Amid frequent editorial blasts at higher critics, Frank Barnett defended intellectual freedom in Baptist colleges. Extolling the Baptist heritage of soul liberty, he deplored denominational demagoguery that "boasting of its own self-sufficing orthodoxy, becomes the worst of all tyrannies in striving to force its narrow tests upon all who are willing to receive with open minds truth from any source." "Deliver us," he concluded, "from a narrow clericalism and petty Baptist popes."[26]

Doctrinal sermons preached in Alabama between 1900 and 1920 were remarkably free of fundamentalist theology. One list of Baptist "cardinal doctrines" centered on personal faith in Christ, Scripture as the only authority in matters of faith and practice, the autonomy of each congregation, and the necessity for ethical living. A. G. Moseley's sermon on "Sound Doctrines" (preached at Evergreen in 1902, Enterprise in 1907, and Wetumpka in 1913) emphasized the same themes, especially the doctrine of salvation by grace. He also rejected Calvinistic fatalism and liberal de-emphasis on original sin.[27]

At the center of the battle for the new theology in Alabama stood three men, all giants within the denomination. A. J. Dickinson was the most outspoken. His combative articles defending new scholarship by professors at the University of Chicago were unrelenting. Christianity, he wrote in response to Barnett's 1906 criticism of the new theology, contained a complex mixture of truth and error. Many ideas accepted as "truth" in 1906 at some earlier time had been regarded as error. Faith depended on one's personal relationship with Jesus, not on assent to certain doctrines. Throughout his entire ministerial career, Dickinson wrote sardonically, Southern Baptists had been "crying 'wolf, wolf,' but to this writing no wolf has appeared and the flock has been needlessly stampeded. The wolf turns out at most to be only a goat."[28]

In 1913 Dickinson and H. B. Woodward engaged in a spirited debate about the new theology. Dickinson defended modernism for harmonizing Christianity with modern science. Ancient history, literary criticism, geology, and other sciences had delivered Christianity virtually a "new book," one richer and more workable to a "modernized Baptist" even if it was no longer an "infallible guide." Woodward preferred not to be such a Baptist and insisted that most members of the denomination and most biblical scholars disagreed with Dickinson.[29]

John W. Phillips was equally blunt. A native of Kent, England, Phillips had followed his father's trade of carpentry and emigrated to America at the age of fifteen. While working in New York, he had enrolled as a ministerial student at Colgate University. Upon graduation, he had pastored a number of prominent Baptist churches in New York state (including one in a mining area where he attracted a large working-class congregation), baptizing as many as fifty-seven in one year. He became a leader of the state Baptist convention and a popular lecturer on college campuses. Phillips often traveled to Europe to indulge his fascination with ancient history, studying at the British Museum, the University of Berlin, and finally completing his Ph.D. in Egyptology at the University of London. His expertise as an Egyptologist won him fame on the Chautauqua lecture circuit as well as visiting lectureships at Colgate, the University of Chicago, and elsewhere.

In 1911 Phillips retired to Mobile to grow pecans and oranges. The Sunday he visited First Baptist Church, the congregation was without a pastor. The pulpit supply committee asked him to preach the next week. He did so, and the influential congregation called him as pastor. The call was not unanimous; some dissented because he was a "Yankee." Others objected to his unorthodox theology. After his first few sermons, one prominent woman circulated a petition calling for his resignation. Phillips refused to resign and in time became a respected pastor of a united congregation. During the next two decades as pastor, he became, according to Mobile's mayor, the "most loved man in Mobile" (where he was familiarly called "Doctor John"). He was twice chosen to preach the annual state convention sermon and was elected president of the convention as well. In 1931 he delivered the annual keynote sermon at the Southern Baptist Convention. Despite controversy over its modernist theology, he was elected vice-president of the SBC a year later.[30] A kindly disposition, his earlier fraternizing with New York miners, and his personal warmth gave him considerable advantages over the aloof, cool, and combative A. J. Dickinson. But his erudition was equally great and his commitment to modernistic theology just as firm.

L. L. Gwaltney was less specific about theology than Phillips and Dickinson but even more widely read in science. Like many other theological liberals of his day, Gwaltney was a native Virginian and a graduate of the University of Richmond (the state Baptist university and a center of heterodoxy). He took his Greek major on to Union Theological Seminary in Richmond, then to SBTS. When he entered the University of Richmond, he wrote years later, he had accepted the Bible as literally true. But faculty influences there changed his mind. Advocates of capital punishment who cited the Mosaic law as a justification for their views encouraged his intellectual restlessness. He believed they ignored the "higher teaching of Jesus." He also questioned exact dating of the origin of life that traced it back only six to ten thousand years. He tried to straddle the modernist controversy, criticizing humanism, secularism, and atheistic evolution while praising an intellectual spirit of inquiry, the application of Christian ethics to society, and higher criticism. In his sermons, Gwaltney used modern science, anthropology, and biblical archaeology to defend the Bible.[31]

From the time Gwaltney moved to Alabama in 1908 he pastored a series of influential churches at Prattville, Greenville, and Florence. In each place he advocated a spirit of open inquiry and rigorous study of the Bible as well as philosophy and theology. Gwaltney developed a lifelong fascination with science and insisted that it did not conflict with religion. Although the origins of life could be found in God's initiative, other questions were open to exploration. Did the "days" mentioned in Genesis mean periods of twenty-four hours or more? Did the earth exist for millions of years? Under the old theological regime, he told one congregation, merely asking such questions branded a preacher as "an ass braying in a bank of mist." In the new theological climate, the "only abnormal ass is the one that ceases to bray." To him, the nebula hypothesis of gaseous materials cohering at the beginning of creation posed no theological problem whatever. Life on earth, he believed, originated in the seas and evolved through a long process of adaptation to environment. In sermons preached in Prattville and Greenville between 1909 and 1912, Gwaltney frankly shared his evolutionary ideas with his congregations and actually lived to tell about it. Theistic evolution did not diminish God's power, he assured them. Even if humankind descended from a microbe, there had to be an initial "involution or infolding." Although he knew few atheists or skeptics in Prattville, he knew many people who had "honest difficulties and doubts" about the Bible's account of creation.[32] In other ways, Gwaltney was safely orthodox. He defended biblical miracles, preached fervent, evangelistic sermons calling for repentance and spiritual rebirth, and condemned the liquor traffic, prostitution, gambling, and pornography.[33]

By no means did men such as Dickinson, Phillips, and Gwaltney have the field of battle to themselves. Within both the SBC and the state, they came under spirited fire for their views. Victor I. Masters, the preeminent Southern Baptist ethicist of the time and a vigorous champion of applying Christianity to social problems, atttacked theistic evolutionists as timid compromisers who had neither sufficient courage to follow their unproven theories to straight evolution nor adequate faith to accept the simple biblical story of creation. Instead they believed that once apes became "well practiced in stone-throwing and permanently addicted to hind-leg walking," God endowed them with human souls.[34]

Closer to home, opposition came from some unlikely sources. Lemuel Orah (L. O.) Dawson graduated from Howard College and SBTS before attending classes at the University of Berlin. He returned to Alabama to pastor Tuscaloosa First Baptist Church (1892–1924) and later to teach Bible at Howard College. Although he commended the scholarship of Adolph von Harnack and Bernard Weiss, higher critics who taught at Berlin, he described their students as "entirely without enthusiasm" for Christianity. He hoped that German scholarship would soon move in a less damaging direction.[35]

Frank Barnett was even better educated and more widely traveled than Dawson. A native of Barbour County, Barnett studied at the University of Alabama and at Vanderbilt before traveling to Europe, where he attended the Sorbonne, the University of Vienna, and the University of Berlin. He capped off his education with a law degree from New York University and theological study at SBTS and Yale. After briefly practicing law in Eufaula and an equally brief pastorate, Barnett bought the *Alabama Baptist* and made it a financial success. Known as one of the best public speakers in Alabama, he was also renowned for his vanity (while he later edited the *Birmingham Age-Herald,* a colleague counted twenty-seven personal pronouns in a single column).[36]

In light of his splendid education, his membership in A. J. Dickinson's church, their close personal friendship, his strong advocacy of the social gospel, and his championing of a free climate of opinion, one might assume that Barnett would have been a vigorous champion of modernism. That was not the case. Barnett denounced the new theology and urged that its practitioners be driven from the denomination. Tolerance for "Baptist Unitarians" (as he called higher critics) would sow "moral poison" in the denomination and start Southern Baptists on the slope of decline that northern Baptists had already begun. He called one theology professor at the University of Chicago a "dangerous heretic" who threatened Christianity more than an avowed atheist.[37]

Barnett made no effort to reconcile such views with his call for academic freedom or with his close friendship with his pastor, A. J. Dickinson. Had Barnett's advice about purging the denomination been followed, his pastor would have been the first Alabama Baptist expelled. The passing years softened Barnett's opinions and by 1915 muted his opposition to modernism.

Other Alabama Baptists took up the cause that Barnett relinquished. A. J. Preston, selected as one of the sixteen most respected Baptists of the era, wrote that the theory of divine inspiration was inconsistent with higher criticism. Though men had written the Bible, they had actually cowritten it with the spirit of God, which was in charge of word choice. Johnston Myers denounced seminaries for allowing heretical teachings. Jesse A. Cook, who was quite sympathetic to the social gospel, attacked modernism for having "no word for the hungry or broken heart of man, no remedy for sin." As the years passed, he, like Barnett, modified his view. By the 1940s he considered modernism too "this worldly" and fundamentalism too "other worldly." Liberal religion needed the "core truths" of fundamentalism, which in turn needed to adopt the social applications of liberalism.[38]

Ecumenism ranked with higher criticism as a flash point in theological discourse. Interdenominational cooperation struck at the heart of the Landmark theory that only Baptist beliefs and practices represented the orthodox, primitive church. And Landmarkism still prevailed in many rural Alabama churches. In addition, many non-Landmarkers believed interdenominationalism diverted Baptists from their principal task of soul winning and tainted them with liberal influences. Beloved denominational leader W. B. Crumpton opposed all forms of church union, as did Frank Barnett initially.[39]

Barnett underwent a rapid metamorphosis after 1910. By 1911 he began to write favorably about the Men and Religion Forward Movement, one of the major interdenominational laymen's movements of the early century. When the group organized work in Birmingham in 1912, it drew Barnett's praise despite its Methodist leadership.[40]

The most unqualified support for ecumenism predictably came from

A. J. Dickinson. During a lengthy and tempestuous debate in 1919–1920, Dickinson urged Baptists to cooperate in the Interchurch World Movement. Denying they would thereby renounce Baptist beliefs, he instead declared such work to be the only way to promote Christianity throughout an entire community. So vigorous was the response on both sides of this debate that Frank Barnett finally refused to publish any more articles pro or con. As one correspondent wrote, Baptists were far less inclined than in previous decades to believe that their own denomination was the only or even the principal instrument of God's work on earth.[41]

Social Christianity

The almost total lack of support for organic church union among Alabama Baptists provided the single most compelling support for C. Vann Woodward's thesis that the three major trends of early twentieth-century American Christianity passed by Alabama. Strong support for the application of Christian principles to social problems constituted the greatest exception to his argument.

Because historians first investigated the application of Christianity to social problems in the North, the northern way became normative for all American Christianity. Applying the name "social gospel" to this phenomenon made the movement appear more radical than it was, a repudiation of the salvation of individual souls in preference for the salvation of society. Some advocates did in fact carry the social gospel to extremes. Because there was finite time, money, and energy, Christianity in the North did spend less time on evangelism and more on social reconstruction. The forces transforming the United States—industrialism, urbanization, immigration—struck the North with greater force and disruption. The more rural South escaped the worst of this battering and remained a more agrarian and traditional society. Exaggerated historical claims about the radicalism of the social gospel and its rejection of personal salvation and equally inflated views of southern Christianity's resistance to change left two inaccurate stereotypes that well served popular religious culture in each region. In the North, the view that southerners were people who rejected new ideas confirmed the region's backwardness in religion as in other matters of intellect and culture. In the South, the view that northerners were people who followed every new religious fad confirmed that region's essential unrighteousness, apostasy, and heresy. Like most stereotypes, each had some core of truth but was badly flawed in detail.

The discovery of robust Jacksonian, populist, and progressive political traditions forced new historical attention to conflict within southern society and politics. But all of these reform traditions operated differently in the South. The region remained more rural, more agrarian, and more obsessed with race. Its white population and religion were more homogeneous than in other regions. Paternalism (which is an early stage in the development of most social liberalism) seemed to have been frozen in time in the South. In a closely knit community of rural people, where neighborliness had institutional social significance (house raisings, corn shuckings, log rollings, quiltings), private and church charity was not an irrelevant, supernatural, or otherworldly consideration. As southern society became more industrialized and urbanized, private neighborliness and paternalism could no longer resolve problems. There was a lag as rural people came to town and at first rejected institutional and cooperative solutions. Meanwhile, city pastors slowly recognized the need for more corporate approaches to solving urban problems.

In particular, conditions changed in Alabama. Developments in the textile industry made Alabama one of the four leading southern textile states. Development in coal and iron ore mining and the steel industry made Alabama the leading southern mining and manufacturing state. Rapid growth of population throughout the Birmingham district sucked rural people into towns and cities much faster than in neighboring states. Among these newcomers were many immigrants from southern and eastern Europe. All these forces of change required Christianity to adjust to emerging social problems that occurred more slowly in other southern states.

Nor was the social gospel as unacceptable to urban Baptists as first appeared. The application of Christianity to the problems of society owed more to actual firsthand experience with the poor, urban workers, and immigrants than it did to theory. Alabama Protestants could be expected to be among southern pioneers in applying Christianity to reform because their state was a leader in experiencing urban-industrial disruption similar to that in the industrial Northeast and Midwest.

The social gospel was not conceived as some exotic new form of Christianity. Its leaders did not renounce traditional Christian doctrines. Sin, repentance, conversion, salvation, holiness, perfection, new life—all were still vital, even if applied to the social order as well as to individuals. If the South was more rural than the North, then the form social Christianity took focused more on Appalachian mountain schools and the rural church movement and less on immigration and labor-management conflict.

Whether in North or South, conversion was still important. Reforming society was for many social gospelers merely another tool of evangelism, a way of letting a new population see for itself God's love made manifest.

Advocates of the social gospel came in many forms. Evolutionary leaders such as Shailer Mathews favored cautious, gradual change. They were suspicious of socialism, retained a strong commitment to individual conversion, saw the church as an ameliorating force on social injustice, and tended to be paternalistic (middle-class Christians did things *for* the working class through settlement houses and other social ministries).

Revolutionary social gospelers like Walter Rauschenbusch labored *with* the working class through labor unions, strikes, and political clubs. They endorsed socialism, identified with working-class causes, insisted that the church take sides in disputes between labor and capital, and proposed to change drastically the structure of society. Individual conversion came too slowly to make much impact on an unjust society. Many radicals were college or seminary professors who were naively optimistic about the possibilities of social renovation. Within this range of opinion, Alabama Baptist advocates of the social gospel mainly belonged to its evolutionary wing and generally rejected revolutionaries. [42]

Among Southern Baptists, the new currents of thought took root slowly. Despite the widespread rejection of modernist theology and church union, the social gospel attracted adherents because firsthand experience left many Southern Baptists shaken by the extent of poverty, degradation, injustice, and poor health. As in the 1880s and 1890s, their desire for prohibition forced them into political realms they had been reluctant to enter. Baptist women often led the movement for social regeneration. WMU women, often trained in their new school in Louisville, opened Good Will Centers or urban settlement houses. In 1913 the Southern Baptist Convention established a social service committee to address a broad range of social problems. Individual states followed the lead of the SBC by establishing similar committees. Although most of them interpreted social service as merely an alternative form of evangelism, the committees initially addressed a wide range of economic and social issues, including farm tenancy and child labor. At Southern seminary, Edgar Y. Mullins, O. R. Mangum, and Charles S. Gardner became advocates of the social gospel.

Many state Baptist papers and denominational leaders opposed such trends. Rural ministers were often positively hostile to the social reformist ideas of urban, elite Baptist ministers, accusing them of liberalism and even heresy. Nonetheless, many historians interpret the years between 1900 and 1920 as the high tide of social activism, a tide that would ebb quickly after

World War I. Furthermore, social gospelers and progressive Baptists failed to alter in any enduring way the basic conservative vision of Southern Baptists. Ultimately, progressive Southern Baptists retreated to a more conservative, mission-oriented, traditional, evangelical stance in order to remain part of their larger fellowship.[43]

Politics was not a new venture for Alabama Baptists. To accomplish the primary reform of the era (prohibition) required herculean effort. Either recalcitrant legislators had to be converted to the cause or they had to be replaced. By 1900 Baptists were veterans of nearly two decades of legislative lobbying and political organizing. Despite the scars they still bore from the bruising political battles of the populist era, they were spoiling for a fight. And this time, progressive winds were blowing in their favor. New progressive legislators who sought a more rational, efficient, and just economic and social order believed that the sale and use of liquor exacerbated Alabama's formidable social problems. Reform politics and prohibition intersected and paved the way for Baptist progressives to enter a broader reform coalition.

The acknowledged leader of this denominational effort was the legendary W. B. Crumpton. Not only was Crumpton director of the state mission board and president of the state convention during the first two decades of the century, but he was also president of the newly established Alabama Anti-Saloon League, vice-president of the American Anti-Saloon League, and chief strategist for the state's prohibition forces. Even the slogan he adopted for his new organization hinted at political battles that lay ahead: "We are on the trail of the liquor traffic and our camp fires will never go out." Despite opposition from most state newspapers, many of the state's leading lawyers and politicians, and more than a few Baptist laymen, pastors ignored arguments against their involvement in politics. Despite having no patronage to distribute and no political office from which to operate, Crumpton created one of the most powerful political lobbies in Alabama history. Although he never held public office himself (some admirers contended he could have had the governorship for the asking), he made and unmade state officials and helped drive one powerful U.S. senator (Oscar Underwood, who was twice nominated for president of the United States) from office. Often called Alabama's "Great Commoner" in tribute to his similarities to William Jennings Bryan, Crumpton was, according to one biographer, "Alabama's Foremost Citizen."[44]

One advantage progressive Baptists had in legitimating their causes among their fellows was that on the chief religious reform issue of the day, prohibition, nearly all preachers were of one mind. L. L. Gwaltney might be soft on creationism, but he was a tiger on demon rum. In a fiercely partisan sermon series urging the social gospel, Gwaltney reminded listeners that the church was threatened less by external enemies, than it was by its own members who brought reproach upon it by their conduct. Every time a church member entered the liquor business, he was profiting from the suffering of a brother.[45]

A. G. Moseley (who pastored churches at Evergreen and Wetumpka) preached several sermons on the alcohol problem. Total abstinence was the most reasonable rule of Christian conduct. Wine made one forget poverty for a moment but afterwards the poor man was even poorer. The remedy to the liquor traffic, Moseley believed, was in equal parts moral suasion and legislation. At either end of these solutions were extremists (advocates of total national prohibition and those who charged that preachers had no business in politics). The task of Baptists was to pursue a course of firm resolve both to convince and to restrict.[46]

The 1904 organization of the Anti-Saloon League in Birmingham with Crumpton as first president launched Alabama's new era of prohibition politics. Crumpton hired Brooks Lawrence, a Presbyterian minister who had headed the antisaloon league in Ohio, to become superintendent of the Alabama league. He also appealed for all Sunday schools to donate their collections on a specified Sunday to fund it. A speaker's bureau provided temperance lecturers for every county, and a newspaper carried temperance news to the farthest corners of the state. Despite their antiecumenical spirit, the 1903 state convention appointed a committee to work with other denominations to form the league. At the 1904 state convention (where A. J. Dickinson proposed creating a permanent preacher's conference preceding the state convention each year), one of the first topics of the pastors was "The Preacher and Politics."[47]

Crumpton posed the issue in terms of the forces of light and darkness. On one side were progressives who attempted to enact reform, even sometimes to do things regarded as radical. On the other were conservatives who blocked progress. Conservatism had once conveyed the meaning that a person was safe and stood for something. Now "to be conservative . . . is to be hesitating, cautious, cowardly." Strenuous times called for progressives, not conservatives.[48]

Despite their theological disagreements, Crumpton and Dickinson were fellow soldiers in the prohibition army. Dickinson led the discussion on the church and politics at the 1907 pastors' conference. Social righteousness, he argued, usually originated in the church but had to be enacted by the state. The two institutions (church and state) had to work along parallel tracks in their respective spheres. He had been charged, Dickinson wrote unapologetically in 1909, with being a "political parson." This charge was true: "I belong to the church military and not the church millinery. I wear no robes that may not be soiled in the service of humanity. I am not of the cloth, but of the sack cloth. No man or journal will deny me the right to speak to you as a citizen."[49]

Frank Barnett, the chief denominational advocate of the social gospel, shared the temperance enthusiasm of Crumpton and Dickinson. Like them, Barnett insisted that the issue was as much a matter of social welfare as personal morality. Like them also, he defended the right of ministers to become aggressively involved in politics. "Ultra conservative and timid" church members might "elevate their eyebrows and rub their pious hands in deprecation" of such militancy, but he believed "in a Christianity that will make man march up to the polls and vote for the right." Political corruption prevailed because so many respectable Christians were afraid to soil themselves by actively engaging in the political process.[50]

Barnett went much further than Crumpton or Dickinson in connecting prohibition to broader economic concerns. He condemned the link between what he called the "whiskey trust" and "big business." To conservative charges that prohibition was an assault on private property, Barnett wrote that usually the right to own property and human rights were identical, but when they clashed, human rights should always take precedence over property rights. To arguments that workingmen ought to buy whiskey because it carried the union label, Barnett wrote that unionism intended to liberate labor, prevent diseases, provide a living wage, end child labor, and provide a sanitary, safe job environment. All these worthy goals of unionism were undermined by support for liquor. Barnett frequently cited leading progressives like Ida M. Tarbell on the social and economic damage done by alcohol.[51]

Baptist ministers might disagree on theology, social reform, and church union, but on the issue of prohibition they spoke with one voice. Gone were the timid voices of the 1890s who worried that overly critical attacks on conservative Democrats might open the way for a neo-Reconstruction era. With the Negro eliminated from Alabama politics by the new 1901 constitution, Baptists had the luxury of unqualified devotion to a single issue even if it meant toppling the party of their fathers. And most elected Democratic officials quickly saw which way the winds of political reform were blowing. As minister after minister vowed to mobilize his congregation on behalf of prohibition, politicians tacked their sails and drifted with the new breeze.[52]

Never before and not again until the 1980s were Alabama Baptists so politically partisan, however much they might deny it. In 1900 the *Alabama Baptist* openly endorsed the election of William J. Samford of Opelika as governor. Though denying that Baptists agreed on a single political candidate, W. B. Crumpton noted that most white voters were either Baptists or Methodists, and politicians helped their chances of election when they announced their identification with these denominations. In 1902 the *Alabama Baptist* favorably compared gubernatorial candidate W. O. Jelks, who attended a Baptist church, to his Episcopalian opponent. The paper also endorsed its former editor who was running for state superintendent of education.[53]

During the critical legislative battle for statewide prohibition in 1907, Alabama Baptists wielded amazing political power. Associations petitioned legislators from their counties to support statewide prohibition. The Anti-Saloon League established a temperance bureau in Montgomery to mobilize prohibition-voting Christians. The *Alabama Baptist* published names of legislators who endorsed statewide prohibition and alleged that African Americans were actively opposing such efforts. In November 1907 Baptists generated much of the majority to vote Alabama into the column of dry states.[54]

After 1907 Baptists lobbied for strict enforcement of prohibition. W. B. Crumpton combined racial politics with prohibition, describing whiskey bottles "sold only to the brutish negroes" that contained pictures of nude white women. "White men who have wives and daughters should never forget that picture" and should elect legislators bound to enforce the state's new prohibition laws. The Prattville and Union Springs Baptist Churches petitioned U.S. Senator John H. Bankhead to pass legislation preventing the shipment of liquor into dry states. In Samson, Alabama, Baptists formed a constitutional prohibition union and began organizing every beat in the county. In 1910 Baptists rallied around gubernatorial candidate Hugh S. D. Mallory, a longtime prohibitionist, economic progressive, member of Selma First Baptist Church, and five-term state Baptist convention president. The *Alabama Baptist* made little effort at nonpartisanship, especially because Mallory's leading opponent, Emmett O'Neal, was viewed as unreliable on enforcement.[55]

In 1906 Baptists were more successful, rallying behind progressive prohibitionist Richmond P. Hobson for Congress. Hobson (who also favored regulation of monopolies and railroads, direct election of U.S. senators, and woman suffrage) won favorable attention among Baptists both in his successful 1906 congressional race and in his unsuccessful 1914 bid for the

U.S. Senate. His endorsement of direct election of U.S. senators won support from B. F. Riley, who had long endorsed the reform.[56]

In 1920 Baptists mobilized behind yet another prohibitionist/progressive, L. B. Musgrove of Jasper. Musgrove had served as chairman of the committee to enforce prohibition in Alabama, a service that had earned him high marks from Alabama Baptists. He ran against incumbent U.S. Senator Oscar W. Underwood, a longtime opponent of prohibition. Musgrove mobilized labor unionists, woman suffragists, and prohibitionists into a powerful coalition that nearly defeated Underwood in 1920 and drove him into retirement six years later.[57]

Prohibition was the major issue of private morality interjected into Alabama politics but not the only one. Baptists agitated for restrictions on gambling, speculation on cotton, lawlessness, and prostitution as well.[58] These crusades focused on Birmingham, a city as renowned for its sin as for its steel. The 1910 annexation election that created "Greater Birmingham" multiplied the white Protestant population of the city and augmented its political power. Organized into the Anti-Saloon League and the Law and Order League and backed by many working- and middle-class men, this "moral element" became active on behalf of Sunday blue laws and antigambling and antisaloon legislation. The "liberal element" denounced them as dominated by "political parsons" who had no business in politics. A. J. Dickinson became the leader of the element that sided with moral reform and also drifted into anti-Catholic political activism.[59]

Questions regarding Alabama Baptists and the social gospel abound. How broadly did support for enlarged social ministries extend? Were they committed to a true transformation of society by applying the gospel to social conditions, or were their efforts merely an extension of charity? How extensively were these reforms actually applied institutionally? How many settlement houses and institutional churches existed in Alabama? How many laws by the Alabama legislature were enacted as a consequence of their lobbying? How did their reforms affect women? What were the limitations of their social involvements?

Questions regarding the scope and definition of social Christianity are the easiest to answer. Commitment to Christianizing the social order became widespread among pastors of urban churches but had less impact on rural congregations. As for definition of this phenomenon, Alabama Baptist advocates of social change described their undertaking almost exactly like northern advocates of the social gospel defined their task.

Alabama advocates of social Christianity never envisioned a world in which the social gospel would replace personal evangelism. Like Walter

Rauschenbusch and Shailer Mathews, they espoused a "new evangelism" where social service would be an alternative way in which the church presented the invitation of Christ for new birth.

This fact resolves much of the apparent contradiction between Frank Barnett's editorials in the *Alabama Baptist* that seem to condemn the social gospel in one issue and endorse it in the next. Barnett never allowed social service to become a substitute for evangelism; both were forms of evangelism and must work in harmony, not in conflict. Throughout his career, Barnett warned against excessive emphasis on social salvation. His education in Europe certainly explained much of his enthusiasm for social change. While studying in Paris in 1882, he had observed food riots and inflation that threatened to starve the urban poor. It was while studying in Paris, Vienna, and Berlin later that he became interested in socialism.[60]

Believing that social reform alone could improve society only superficially, Barnett constantly warned against the excesses of "the new social gospel" and "the new reform movement." The church must not be converted into "a mere place of amusement," with swimming pools, gymnasiums, and other athletic and educational programs. Such "institutional churches," he warned, emphasized the material world over the spiritual and devoted more time to "filling a man's dinner-pail than to filling his soul." Although he called for government regulation of impure milk on the same page with warnings against the social gospel, he warned that reforms must proceed cautiously. The church must not be turned into a "socialistic democracy of economic equality." Only Christ could redeem society one regenerated soul at a time. To virtually every editorial advocating a social gospel reform, Barnett attached a warning label that social service could not replace personal salvation. In this way, Barnett was not so unusual. Rauschenbusch and Mathews issued similar warnings. They understood the social gospel to be the finest expression of a "new evangelism" that sought to save the souls of the working class by a deeper commitment to their physical welfare.[61]

Barnett's qualifications about the social gospel must be balanced by dozens of articles calling attention to it, opening the pages of the *Alabama Baptist* to its northern practitioners, enthusiastically endorsing its major tenets, and addressing virtually every contemporary social problem in Alabama from its perspective. He also appointed "contributing editors" who vigorously championed the social applications of Christianity, including A. J. Dickinson, Charles A. Stakely, A. C. Davidson, and W. F. Yarborough.

During 1912–1913, Barnett devoted considerable editorial space to reprinting essays by the most prominent northern advocates of the social gospel. Charles Stelzle, an advocate of labor reform for workingmen, wrote a series of essays on the church and social change. Evangelistic preaching, Stelzle argued, must proceed arm in arm with the social gospel. In 1913 Barnett published essays by Mathews and Rauschenbusch challenging churches to endorse reform for child and female workers, antipoverty programs, environmental protection of workers, social security for aging and injured workers, a maximum six-day work week, and a minimum wage law.[62]

Barnett used his paper to publicize the ideas of many other reformers as well. He opened his pages to the reform ideas of Jane Addams, the leader of the settlement house movement. He reported the annual convention of the Southern Sociological Congress, the leading advocate of social change in the region (and an organization that enrolled many Baptist social workers, ministers, educators, and lay persons). Barnett particularly broadcast the opinions of William L. Poteat and Charles S. Gardner. Poteat (North Carolina Baptist preacher who had studied at the University of Berlin, held a Ph.D. in biology, and served as president of Wake Forest College) became president of the North Carolina Anti-Saloon League and the state's Conference for Social Service. Charles Gardner was professor of homiletics and sociology at Southern Baptist Theological Seminary, where he endorsed many elements of the social gospel.[63]

In addition to Poteat, Barnett also praised prominent progressive political leaders. Through his brother, Barnett came to know Tom L. Johnson, reform mayor of Cleveland, Ohio. He admired Johnson's "practical, militant sympathy with the poor and oppressed" and identified such political causes with following Christ. Barnett also admired Baptist layman and Missouri reform governor Joseph W. Folk.[64]

As for Barnett's personal view of the social gospel, his caveats about its excesses should not obscure his basic commitment to it. He vowed to make the *Alabama Baptist* a thoroughly progressive paper that would implement Baptist ideals in family, social, and political life. Broadly viewed through history, he wrote in 1907, all important movements for change had been led by progressives and opposed by "ultra conservatives." That same year he denounced Congress for defeating a dozen important reforms (including prohibition and anti–child labor legislation). Five years later he called on the church to become involved in stopping child labor, exploitation of workers, and abuses of female labor. It should work for decent housing for the poor and programs to prevent diseases and industrial injuries. In 1917 he declared war on poverty. The times might not yet be ripe for implementation of the New Testament idea of Christians sharing their wealth in common, but "the passionate cry for social righteousness" was moving toward that ideal. Christian socialism was spreading across the nation and would soon eclipse industrial materialism. In the twentieth century, economic thought would be redirected from the production of wealth to its equitable distribution. Socialism was one expression of social democracy, was inevitable, and had profoundly influenced conceptions of the Christian gospel. Earth was to be the scene for the unfolding drama of the kingdom of God. So long as socialism and the social gospel were subsidiary to the gospel and not primary in it, then the church must be involved actively in assuring that all people were adequately fed and housed and received a fair wage.[65] By 1918 Barnett had endorsed virtually every social gospel reform that Rauschenbusch and Mathews had proposed in their 1913 essays.

Such ideas, radical though they seem from the distance of nearly a century, apparently offended few of Barnett's contemporaries. Letters poured into the editor's office congratulating the paper for publishing "honorable controversy." Apparently most readers agreed because circulation doubled and Barnett became a popular and influential leader not only within his denomination but of Birmingham civic life as well.[66]

Advocacy of the social gospel was not a one-man show. Many shared Barnett's concerns. L. L. Gwaltney came to the social gospel through his own pastoral experiences. His first pastorate in Alabama was at Prattville Baptist Church, a congregation consisting of businessmen, farmers, and workingmen from Continental Gin Company and the city's cotton mills. The church also included many indigent widows who depended on the church's widows' fund. According to his biographer, Gwaltney's service as pastor at Prattville crystallized his philosophy of social service.[67]

By the time Gwaltney moved to Greenville as pastor in 1910, his understanding of the social dimensions of Christianity had taken firm shape. Extolling the new mountain school movement that had been launched by the Home Mission Board, Gwaltney praised denominational progressives who were winning the battle against "standpatters." Much of the Old Testament, he explained in another sermon, was devoted to the physical welfare of humanity. Not a word about regeneration, conversion, heaven, or hell was found in the book of Exodus, he declared in a series of sermons on that book. Instead, the writer communicated how God had delivered his people from physical slavery and distress. He told his congregation that "the man who is weighted down with the cares and sorrows and the burdens . . . of a large family, and has nothing to depend upon but his own labour wants to know if the church can bring any relief in his life; if it can you may rest assured he will more readily accept its creed." Because of the church's lack of concern, the working class was often alienated and believed the church existed for the classes, not the masses. In Greenville, he told his parishioners, they could not appreciate the problem because they all belonged to a single class. But let a half dozen cotton mills or railroad shops and a few iron foundries locate there and they would understand his point. These working parents and children would want to know what help Greenville Baptists could offer them "in this life." His application of Scripture left no doubt as to his meaning. In Exodus, forced labor had degenerated into slavery just as peonage was its consequence in south Alabama. Jews had been oppressed because of their race, just as yellow and black Americans "not so white and immaculate [like] ourselves" had been neglected. Such attitudes estranged classes and races and violated the principle that Christ was no respecter of persons. In a series of sermons entitled "Communism in the Early Church," Gwaltney noted that in the first-century church the community, not individuals, owned property. Although socialism was an impractical idea in the modern world, God did not intend for monopolies and trusts to transfer the world's goods to a few persons. God did not intend that less than 1 percent of Americans would own 70 percent of the nation's wealth. This inequity explained the growth of socialism. One beneficial result of World War I, he wrote later, would be the redistribution of the world's wealth. He applauded the graduated income tax, which sought to accomplish redistribution. As for poverty, social environment explained most of the differences between boys who grew up in slums and their mates who came of age amid affluence.[68]

A. J. Dickinson was as forthright on the social gospel as he was on modernism. "I am socialist enough to believe," he wrote in 1904, that wealth was the creation of society in earlier ages, not a private possession obtained entirely by one's own efforts. Therefore, government had the right to tax wealth to provide for the maintenance and growth of society. As an avid reader of the *American Journal of Sociology*, Dickinson traced the origins of poverty to environment. In 1908 he was elected president of the Birmingham Municipal Ownership League, which advocated municipal ownership of public transportation and utilities. At his prodding, the 1907 state Baptist convention was devoted to the study of the social applications of Christianity. He preached at the convention on the church and politics. After he resigned as pastor of Birmingham First Baptist Church in 1918, he ran for Congress advocating economic and labor reforms.[69]

Dickinson's friend, A. C. Davidson (who pastored Southside Baptist Church in Birmingham) shared his social philosophy. As one of twelve children of a pious but poor Missouri farmer-blacksmith, Davidson had a hard upbringing. His education at Georgetown College in Kentucky created an insatiable intellectual curiosity. He wrote manuscript prayers and sermons, read widely, and used elaborate clipping files to make his sermons relevant. In 1905 he wrote a four-part series for the *Alabama Baptist* on "The Attitude of the Church toward Civic Problems." He identified the most serious issues facing Christianity as poverty, politics, labor-management conflict, alcohol use, and child labor. He proposed to help the poor by direct aid given in a way that maintained their self-respect, though limited to a specified time in order to prevent idleness. He proposed compulsory school attendance laws, night schools, and institutional churches to assist child laborers. Both labor and capital had rights, labor to organize and capital to hire whomever it pleased. Citing social reformers Richard Ely and Jacob Riis, Davidson demanded that the law treat the poor man who stole a coat the same as the rich man who stole a bank or corporation. He remade Southside into an "institutional church," open every day and night of the year and containing industrial schools for working children, a free library, kindergarten, and gymnasium. During Davidson's pastorate (1898–1906), Southside's two industrial mission stations and its ministries to workers helped the church grow from 571 members to 794.[70]

At Anniston's Parker Memorial Baptist Church, a succession of pastors invoked the social gospel. Joshua Hill Foster raised money for a park to provide wholesome entertainment for the city's youth, began a Chautauqua program, and led a crusade to defeat the "whiskey slate" on the city council. In a 1909 address to the state convention, Foster urged Baptists to become politically active, to make government the guardian of citizens' welfare, and to close saloons. Foster's successor, W. F. Yarborough (1910–1916), tried to end class conflict in the church by insisting that God recognized no social and economic differences between his children. He led the church to employ a social worker (Linda Martin of Missouri) who conducted a successful ministry at the Blue Mountain mill. Church social ministries included an industrial school for children, a reading room, and free hospital beds. Leon M. Latimer replaced Yarborough in 1916 and continued the church's tradition of social ministries, working with various YMCA programs and with soldiers at Fort McClellan. Nor did this social activism deter evangelism or mission emphasis. Parker Memorial's membership grew rapidly; it regularly contributed more to missions than any other church in Alabama; and it appeared throughout the decade in top-ten categories among state Baptist congregations (fifth largest membership and second in Sunday school enrollment in 1907, ninth and eighth in these categories in 1917). Foster and Latimer left Parker Memorial for significant pastorates in other states, and Yarborough succeeded W. B. Crumpton in 1916 as head of the state mission board.[71]

Scattered around the state were many other pastors and denominational leaders who endorsed social Christianity with varying levels of enthusiasm. James H. Chapman left the pastorate of Florence First Baptist Church in 1918 to establish the department of religious education at Howard College, reportedly the first such department at any Baptist college in the South. His interest in the sociology of religion produced many pastors and denominational leaders who shared his commitment to Christianizing the social order. W. P. Wilks addressed Howard College students in 1917, rejoicing at better funding for education and the victories of progressives over "stand-patter orthodoxies" within the SBC. John N. Prestridge, who grew up in the Selma Baptist Church, left his home state for Kentucky, where he established the *Baptist Argus* (later renamed the *Baptist World*), which became the major voice of SBC progressive thought.[72]

Such opinions were not exclusive to academic audiences or to the pages of denominational papers. They appeared frequently in sermons. Around 1900, A. G. Moseley preached that environment and genetics contributed as much as food and choice to a person's character. In a 1913 sermon preached in Lawrence County, Alexander T. Sims reminded his congregation that Jesus ministered to the bodies of persons as well as to their souls. Sims recounted some thirty-five biblical cases of healing and six incidents of demon possession or mental affliction. In Alabama, Bryce and Searcy Hospitals healed three hundred mentally ill whites and blacks per year, far more than Jesus healed in all his ministry. Jesus had healed the blind, and Alabama had given the world Helen Keller, whose courage offered hope to millions.[73]

Jesse A. Cook of Andalusia Baptist Church believed that most Baptists had confined social evil to the abuse of alcohol and were unnecessarily fearful that the social gospel would substitute politics and economics for personal salvation. They considered the works of Mathews, Rauschenbusch, and Samuel Z. Batten (head of the Northern Baptist Social Service Commission) to be heretical. But while a senior at Howard College in 1907, Cook had taken a course with Dr. J. A. Hendricks in which he used Shailer Mathews's book, *The Social Teachings of Jesus,* as a text. On a trip to Birmingham from Chicago, Mathews had lectured to his class, so students could see for themselves if he were really a Christian. They also had a chance to hear Samuel Batten preach at West End Baptist Church. And they read works by Rauschenbusch. This intellectual exposure, reinforced later by the cataclysm of the Great Depression, converted Cook into a cautious advocate of social Christianity.[74]

Such journeys of revelation occurred across Alabama. The 1917 meeting of the Elmore County Association featured discussions of public schools, home economics, progressive agriculture, food conservation, health, and sanitation. New mission board secretary W. F. Yarborough cited this wide discussion of public issues as a model for other associations. "Why should not every phase of life be sanctified by relating it to religion?" he asked. The 1912 state Baptist ministers' conference in Jasper featured sermons on "The Minister and the Labor Problem," "The Minister and Politics," and "The Problem of the City." The 1919 state convention broadened the temperance committee into a social service commission.[75]

Obviously there were detractors to all these social gospel initiatives. A reader of the *Alabama Baptist* wrote in 1913 that the church made a "stupendous blunder" by emphasizing social reform instead of personal conversion. Every social problem was resolved, he wrote, "when Jesus is exhalted." In 1919 a pastor wrote that only Christian orthodoxy could stem the tide of war, injustice, anarchy, and bolshevism.[76] But these voices were remarkably mild warnings amid the din for reform. For most state Baptist leaders, the issue was keeping social Christianity subordinated to evangelism, not whether the gospel required the reconstruction of society.

The specific issues addressed in Alabama by Baptist advocates of the social gospel were similar to the ones discussed nationally. They directed the greatest moral outrage at child labor. At the head of this crusade stood Frank Barnett. Allied with Charles Stakely (pastor of Montgomery First Baptist Church) and Montgomery Episcopal priest Edgar Gardner Murphy, Barnett launched a crusade against the industrial exploitation of children by their parents and by corporations. In a revealing issue of the *Alabama Baptist*, the editor followed a scathing denunciation of the new theology with an equally vituperative attack on child labor.[77]

Barnett's campaign began almost at the moment he purchased the denominational paper. Before an important progressive victory in the 1903 legislature, Barnett dismissed conservative arguments that strong child labor legislation would close businesses and cost the jobs of mill workers. Every legislator who voted against the 1903 child labor reform bill or tried to obstruct it, he warned, "will have to give account of himself before the bar of public opinion."[78]

The 1907 legislature considered bills strengthening earlier child labor laws, and again Barnett led the charge. Calling child labor a "system of slavery" and a form of murder, he wrote emotional editorials based on his own observations of industrial injuries to young children. "I have heard the weeping of the mother who could not be comforted because her little boy had been engulfed in the great, grinding stream of coal and smothered to death. I have seen little bodies torn by machinery in the textile industries, and the scarred hands and faces of the glass-house boys. A thousand times I have cried . . . 'Oh God! that bread should be so dear, and flesh and blood so cheap.' " Such outrages continued because lobbyists for corporations controlled the state legislature, Barnett claimed, and he urged Baptists to contact their legislators on behalf of just treatment for children.[79] Once again legislators responded, making Alabama a leader among southern states in regulating child labor.

Barnett was not satisfied. Throughout the remainder of his editorial tenure, he lobbied for a variety of additional reforms. He called for creation of a federal children's bureau to monitor child labor, argued for the prohibition of night shifts by children, and favored an amendment to federal tariff legislation prohibiting imports that were manufactured using child labor. He congratulated the 1910 Southern Baptist Convention for passing a resolution opposing child labor. "Our pulpits," he admonished, "should not be silent on this great stigma on our civic life."[80] Judged by reforms promptly enacted by the Alabama legislature, the state's pulpits were effective.

The *Alabama Baptist* publicized the labor views of most northern advocates of the social gospel, including Rauschenbusch, Samuel Batten, and Charles Stelzle. Barnett, Gwaltney, Dickinson, and other Alabama Baptists generally endorsed the substance of the northern agenda: recognition of Labor Day and a special Sunday to honor working people; the right of workers to organize and bargain collectively; equitable distribution of the profits of industrial activity; a stance for social justice by the church; creation of a federal bureau of labor.[81]

Barnett's most extensive exposition on the subject appeared in a 1913 editorial entitled "Christ and Labor." He understood why laborers were disenchanted with the church. Although personal regeneration was essential to the ultimate resolution of class conflict, churches must open their eyes to the struggle for labor to earn a minimum wage, must hear the cry of children being sacrificed in mills, must help labor obtain a shorter work week and better working conditions. It was of the "utmost importance that the labor movement . . . not be alienated from organized Christianity."[82]

Barnett's most forceful contribution to this cause came in the field of health and safety. Living as he did in the Birmingham district, where he saw daily the consequences of industrial accidents and health problems, the editor developed special interest in them. At the core of the problem was a simple fact: it was more profitable to "work a man to get as much out of him as possible—'exploit him up to the last ounce of exploitability' and when he drops out to fill his place with a new man—than it has been to restrict his work to his health limit." Alabama Baptists must insist on inspections by state health officers, not a popular position among industrialists. Taxpayers had to provide the poorhouses, insane asylums, orphanages, prisons, and jails to care for the flotsam and casualties of the industrial process. Therefore, they might as well penalize industry in advance for its infractions of sanitary, health, and safety standards. Commerce and property owners, he concluded, had "too little respect for the public health" and would "rob the workman and tenant [farmer] of life and health because it happens to be more profitable at the time." Unfortunately, solutions to these problems were difficult in Alabama, where "selfish interests" had too much power and controlled politics and health policy.[83]

Barnett not only denounced threats to the health and safety of workers but also campaigned for public health reforms. He praised the landmark 1907 pure food and drug law and later urged that it be strengthened. He publicized tuberculosis and urged public schools to educate children about how the disease could be prevented. Barnett deplored the total lack of treatment facilities in Alabama for indigent TB patients, pointing out that it was mainly a disease of the poor. He prefaced a call for construction of two schools for African American children who were anemic or tubercular by acknowledging that "the reactionary will protest against this act of wisdom, as usual; but if we are ever to get the best of tuberculosis in Birmingham and the South we must care for the negro also." He urged ministers to observe National TB Sunday and endorsed a bill before Congress establishing a federal public health department. When correspondents wrote Barnett that he spent too much space in a Baptist paper discussing tuberculosis and other diseases, he replied that he believed it to be his duty as a Christian to obtain closer cooperation between city, county, and state health departments, to help foster support for a federal health department, and to counter selfish financial interests that had more power over the health of Alabamians than did civic authority.[84]

Barnett was not alone in his concern about public health. After his resignation as pastor of Birmingham First Baptist Church, A. J. Dickinson became a lecturer on social health for federal and state health services. Working out of Hillman Hospital in Birmingham and the state board of health offices in Montgomery, Dickinson spoke to various Baptist gatherings.

Speaking to the 1919 state convention on the unlikely topic "Social Sanitation and Christianity," Dickinson noted that Christ spent much of his ministry healing the sick and commanded his disciples to do likewise. No modern Christian, Dickinson added, "had met His messianic obligation" until he had become involved in social service. The kingdom of God that Jesus fostered was on this earth, and he had entrusted his disciples to improve the sanitation and hygiene of their communities. The convention was sufficiently impressed with the sermon to endorse state and federal health programs and called on churches to improve public health. In 1920 Dickinson became chairman of the state convention's new committee on sanitation and hygiene, and the following year he was elected chair of the state social service commission.[85]

L. L. Gwaltney was equally forthright. In 1919 he blasted critics of the state board of health. Having observed the board's work firsthand in its efforts to contain typhoid, malaria, and influenza in the Tennessee Valley, Gwaltney pronounced the work a positive benefit to citizens. Gwaltney welcomed into his pulpit at Florence First Baptist Church the state health officer, who used the opportunity to plead for health improvements. Gwaltney did not consider such a worship service inappropriate to gospel proclamation: "Any effort to maintain physical health and the happiness which comes therefrom is an extenuation of the spirit of the many sided Christ" who himself healed bodies as well as souls.[86]

When the annual state medical association met in Montgomery in 1908, Charles Stakely made First Baptist Church available for a traveling tuberculosis exhibit. In May of that year, the church hosted the organizational meeting of the Alabama Tuberculosis Association. Most of the early activists in the association were ministers and lay people.[87]

Constant attacks on the power of corporations and special interests and exposés about their abuse of workers and child labor or about their neglect of safety and sanitation reflected the ambivalence of Alabama Baptists regarding newly consolidated corporate America. On one hand, most Baptists saw nothing inherently wrong with capitalism or the accumulation of wealth. Rich men had a duty to use their wealth for good causes, but there was no justification for society appropriating the wealth even of selfish men. Modern socialism that sought confiscatory legislation against wealth found no support in the New Testament. Frank Barnett even urged more businessmen to run for office in order to protect society from political panaceas and demagogues. But the acquisition of wealth did not afford a person special rights or exemptions either.[88]

Certain business practices came under relentless fire as unchristian and harmful to society. Central to the corporate threat to Christianity was monopoly. Barnett wrote with alarm at J. P. Morgan's centralization of the steel industry. Such trusts as U.S. Steel had "no conscience or moral honesty," exercised undue political power, and put government under the control of a "monied aristocracy." A few years later Barnett reprinted an exposé on the "beef trust" that called meat companies "traitors to the principles of democracy." Revelations about impure milk sold to children would cause a revolution, he wrote in another editorial, were Americans a radical people. Combinations of capital with their "predatory processes of exploitation" must be held accountable to a higher law than greed. Barnett urged Alabama voters to repeal a section of the state constitution that required insolvent banks to pay business accounts before individual depositors.[89]

At Howard College, students debated the relative merits and demerits of corporate America. A prominent Birmingham attorney spoke on the trust problem at the 1902 commencement. Barnett praised the speech as precisely the sort of college commencement intelligent students should have before they assumed positions of responsibility. Seminary professor John R. Sampey spoke at the 1906 Howard commencement, calling for government control of corporations. Although he rejected "radical and impulsive" solutions, he told graduates that corporate greed often clashed with public interests. Only courageous public officials could prevent corporate power from infringing on the people's rights. At 1919 commencement exercises, the freshman-sophomore debate concerned government ownership of the nation's railroads.[90]

Alabama Baptists were equally ambivalent about the new immigrants pouring into the United States. Although the South was a secondary destination for most of them, enough southern and eastern Europeans came to the Birmingham district to cause widespread concern. Some of the natural American animosity to foreigners was limited by Baptist commitment to missions. Missionaries constantly reminded home folk how much harder American nativism made their work in foreign lands. But to many Alabamians, "heathens" looked a good deal more picturesque when they stayed in their own countries.[91]

Despite reassurances that the new immigrants were no threat to American democracy or institutions, Alabama Baptists worried about the effect of so many new immigrants with so many strange customs. The 1901 assassination of President William McKinley by an immigrant heightened their fears. Although the United States was a melting pot of peoples, the *Alabama Baptist* believed that immigrants should emerge from the pot as Americans, not as hyphenated Americans (Irish-American, Italian-American). Foreign sentiments and prejudices should be consumed by American values.[92]

Sermons of the times used nativist fears as an incentive for home missions. Clay I. Hudson told his congregation at the Athens First Baptist Church that the tide of immigration washing over the United States threatened to make it a "heathen country." Alexander Sims expressed the same opinion to his congregation in Geneva in 1909. He pointed to communities of ethnic Christians like the new Swedish Baptist church in Baldwin County as a hopeful sign. Baptists must either evangelize the cities and immigrant industrial workers or allow these "semi-heathen[s]" to "ruin our children and finally our country." The wife of R. M. Hunter (pastor of the Flomaton Baptist Church) agreed with Sims. Speaking to the women of the Century Baptist Church, she warned that unless they converted Catholics, socialists, and other threatening immigrants, foreigners would disrupt the nation.[93]

Alabama Baptists took such warnings seriously. They began settlement houses and missions in industrial communities and mining camps. They employed social workers and urban missionaries. Southside Baptist Church in Birmingham organized two missions near the Birmingham Rolling Mill. In 1909 the associational WMU established a Good Will Center for the city's Italian workers, first in the private home of Pratt City's Baptist pastor, then in a separate building. The center hired a kindergarten teacher and later a trained city missionary (Mae Campbell). She ministered both to working-class American children and to Italians, teaching literacy, cooking, sewing, and hygiene classes as well as conducting Bible study. Similar settlement houses and industrial ministries were begun in Anniston, Mobile, and Montgomery. Baptists established at least half a dozen settlement houses in Alabama cities.[94]

Such efforts were obviously helpful in promoting the growth of Alabama Baptist churches. Whereas only about 35 percent of Americans were church members in 1900, nearly 50 percent belonged by 1920. By 1910 Birmingham contained twenty-five white Baptist churches, and nine years later the Birmingham Association (with 14,500 members) was the largest in Alabama.[95]

Although Baptists had less to say about the environment, even that cause attracted attention as industrial development threatened fresh water supplies and altered landscapes. Barnett wrote in 1906 that "thinking men and women" endorsed the conservation movement. In another editorial he condemned the "intemperate use" of God's gifts to humanity, whether those gifts be pure food, clean water, forests, minerals, or other natural resources. In 1913 he opposed a bill before Congress that would have turned national forests in the West over to state governments. Such state control would ultimately result, he warned, in control by "men who have grown rich . . . by looting the public domain."[96]

Another by-product of industrial Alabama was the convict lease system. Although Baptists before 1900 had generally praised convict leasing, the revelation of horrible abuses of convicts caused them to rethink support. In 1903 an article in the denominational paper demanded swift punishment of any planter or company guilty of peonage or abuse of convicts. Four years later the president of the state board of convict inspectors wrote a scathing denunciation of prison conditions. Better to kill convicts, he wrote, than to leave them in conditions of filth and abuse. Reacting to this exposé, Frank Barnett demanded that prisoners be treated humanely. So long as the convict lease system generated income for the state, he feared that starvation and abuse of prisoners would continue. By 1913 Barnett had decided that the system must be abolished. The only appropriate purposes for penology were prevention of crime and reformation of criminals; the goal of convict leasing was to produce revenue for the state and was a "blot upon Christianity." To attempt to ameliorate conditions, Baptists supported a state chaplain to convicts and helped provide a library, literacy programs, and other assistance. But even the chaplains were under no illusions about the abuse of prisoners.[97]

Baptists maintained their strong support of public education. Former publisher of the *Alabama Baptist* John G. Harris served as state superintendent of education until his death in 1908 and was warmly supported by fellow Baptists. Believing that Christianity and education went hand in hand, Frank Barnett waged a twenty-year campaign to strengthen Alabama public schools. The state's ranking next to last in white intelligence scores demanded longer school terms. It also demanded changing the Alabama Constitution to allow counties the authority to raise taxes for their schools if local citizens wished to do so. The state superintendent of education wrote the *Alabama Baptist* in 1916, begging preachers to declare a Sunday in September "Better Schools Day." He urged them to endorse an amendment to the constitution allowing local tax referenda. Barnett endorsed the amendment, but powerful conservative interests defeated it. In 1912 the editor praised progressives within the National Education Association for wresting control away from conservatives. The progressive agenda that Barnett praised included more attention to agricultural and industrial education, sex education, increases in teacher salaries, support for woman suffrage, and instruction in international peace.[98]

Many Baptists shared Barnett's enthusiasm for public schools. John Creighton Williams (newspaper publisher, member of Talladega First Baptist Church, and moderator of the Coosa River Association) served as superintendent of schools for Talladega County, chairman of the county board of education, chair of the Talladega County Democratic executive committee, and as the county's most articulate spokesman for public schools. R. E. Pettus (Huntsville Baptist layman, secretary of the Liberty Baptist Association, and president of the city's chamber of commerce) led the 1907 effort to increase local tax support for education.[99]

Denominational leaders also paid more attention to elementary grades and underserved populations. In 1905 the Home Mission Board began a system of mountain schools in Appalachia. In Alabama the HMB helped establish four mountain schools: Gaylesville, Bridgeport, Eldridge, and Beeson Academies. Local Baptists began others, including Scottsboro Baptist Institute, North Alabama Baptist Collegiate Institute, and Healing Springs School. Frank Barnett praised such schools as the best hope for keeping poor Appalachian children in their communities and out of cotton mills and factories.[100]

In south Alabama, local Baptists began Newton Baptist Institute in Dale County in 1898 to serve the rural wiregrass area. Alabama had no state system of high schools until 1907, so private and denominational academies served a vital function. Four Baptist associations initially assisted Newton institute, with others joining later. In 1908 ownership was transferred to the state convention. Most students boarded at the school and many were too poor to attend without scholarships. The catalog emphasized the school's purpose to educate poor children by assuring them that it prized students with patched clothes more than children of wealth. The institute allowed its girls no silk or satin dresses and no dress that cost more than four dollars. The catalog sternly warned that "girls coming with four or five dollar hats will keep them about four or five minutes. The girl may get mad and go home but the hat will stay to the close of school." School discipline was severe. Students wore uniforms and were forbidden to congregate at night, smoke, dance, or perform "coon songs and jigs." The curriculum focused on mathematics, sciences, English, history, Bible, Latin, and after 1913, business. By 1909, 313 of the school's 442 students came from outside Newton and boarded with townspeople or lived in dormitories. Many of south Alabama's Baptist ministers received their high school education at the school.[101] Newton institute and most of the mountain schools closed in the 1930s when public high schools finally reached remote sections of the state.

Support for Howard and Judson Colleges continued strong despite funding problems, although iconoclast A. J. Dickinson sought to divorce the colleges from denominational control. He urged the two colleges to enlarge their endowment in order to lessen dependence on the state convention. He proposed longer terms for trustees as another way to insulate Howard and Judson from "spasmodic and occasional" storms in Baptist life. Such conditions, he believed, plagued the state's public colleges and universities. Threats to them came not from the whims of Baptists but from state politics. Trustee positions at Alabama universities, he wrote perceptively, were political spoils of the patronage system and kept state colleges from promoting quality education just as denominational control prevented Judson and Howard from doing so.[102]

The establishment of Newton institute and of mountain schools demonstrates another way in which social Christianity permeated the thinking of Alabama Baptists. They participated actively in various efforts to maintain and enhance the quality of rural life. Despite considerable attention lavished on city problems and urban ministries, Alabama Baptists were overwhelmingly part of a rural denomination. In 1915 half the rural churches in the United States were in the South. Of 24,500 SBC congregations, 20,000 were in open country or small towns. Among rural churches, 18,000 had preaching once a month and were served by "absentee" pastors who did not live on the field where they preached. Of 9,000 ministers who served SBC churches, 4,000 lived in urban areas and pastored 4,500 urban congregations. The remaining 5,000 rural pastors served 20,000 rural congregations. A 1913 survey of 716 country Baptist churches in Alabama revealed that only 29 met every Sunday and only 168 had resident pastors. Only 10 had parsonages. In the past five years 14 had been disbanded, and 194 had either level or declining membership. They paid pastors an average of only $81 a year. Between 1896 and 1916, SBC churches reported 2.3 million baptisms and .3 million deaths; but the denomination increased membership by only slightly more than 1 million. Some 865,000 members simply disappeared, most to cities where they either joined other denominations or dropped out of church entirely. Rural ministers (like their parishioners) moved frequently. They typically were called as pastor for only one year at a time, and their pastorates averaged only two years.[103] Many of these churches were simply not viable and soon passed out of existence.

The most alarming fact discovered by rural sociologists was the rapid increase in farm tenant families as a percentage of rural church membership. By 1922, 35 percent of farmer members of SBC churches were tenants. That same year, 5,600 SBC churches had fewer than fifty members, and 36 percent of country churches reported no baptisms for the previous year. Nearly one in five country SBC churches had no pastor that year. Victor I. Masters believed that the increasing dominance of tenancy in country churches would cripple if not destroy them. He predicted that this development of a white American "peasantry" would shackle the South in the twentieth century as slavery had crippled it in the nineteenth.[104]

The response of main-line Protestantism to this crisis was called the rural church movement, which grew out of the 1908 Rural Life Conference summoned by President Theodore Roosevelt. Operating as the rural wing of the social gospel, the rural church movement attracted progressives who believed in progress through rational research and surveys, efficiency, and the new science of sociology. Many rural church specialists also believed in liberal theology and ecumenism, although this position was less true of Southern Baptist rural church reformers. These reformers generally did not believe in some agrarian myth about the past (although many worried about the corrupting influence of cities). Nationally, most rural church experts blamed problems primarily on overchurching rural areas. There were too many congregations both within and among denominations. Secondary problems included roads, schools, health care, housing, low income, one-crop agriculture, and tenancy.[105]

Among Southern Baptists, two men emerged as leaders of the rural church movement: John W. Jent and Victor I. Masters. Jent (an Oklahoman and longtime professor of rural sociology at various Baptist universities) published widely on the subject. Heavily influenced by the social gospel ideas of Warren H. Wilson, his teacher at Columbia University and the leading exponent of rural church reform, Jent relied heavily on social gospel strategies. He believed that country churches must be concerned about the total life of rural communities if they hoped to survive.[106]

Victor Masters (head of the publicity department of the Home Mission Board) was less enthusiastic about the social gospel but nonetheless incorporated many of its ideas in his recommendations to improve rural churches. While emphasizing the harmful influences of cities and rejecting the idea that country churches could be saved by social service, he nonetheless chided them for failing to address the problems of rural communities and for their overreliance on individual salvation. He advised country preachers to take courses in rural sociology at land-grant universities, create ladies' aid societies, improve rural public schools and teachers' salaries, and overcome "the ultra-conservatism of rural habit."[107]

Alabama Baptists, heavily influenced by both Jent and Masters, well understood the dimensions of the crisis. They were less certain about the solutions. W. B. Crumpton expressed deep concerns about the erosion of rural church life. In his "trip reports" in the *Alabama Baptist,* he recounted experiments in crop diversification, new agricultural technology, the disturbing growth of white farm tenancy, and soil erosion.[108]

Frank Barnett published editorials under the distinctive social gospel titles, "Salvation Through Agronomy" and "Gospel Preaching and Scientific Farming." Praising agricultural reforms, he urged country preachers to help create an attitude among Alabama farmers that would be receptive to the advice of state and national agricultural experts. Barnett also endorsed the movements for better roads and rural public schools.[109]

A. J. Dickinson also wrote an essay about the crisis in Alabama's rural churches. He blamed problems on poverty, low social standing, and lack of education of rural preachers. Country churches were too small to be efficient or to afford a full-time program or pastor. Members were too individualistic to consolidate several weak congregations into a single strong one.[110]

Much of this advice was delivered as the patronizing wisdom of well-educated urban professionals who believed their ideas superior to the folk wisdom and traditional ways of country people. Not surprisingly, rural folk were not impressed. When delivered by people they loved and respected (like W. B. Crumpton), they simply ignored such advice. When delivered by theological modernists like A. J. Dickinson (whom they neither knew nor loved), they deeply resented it. Because rural pastors and laymen seldom attended state conventions, men like Dickinson often rose to prominence in the denominational hierarchy. But such leadership should not be mistaken for influence over ordinary country Baptists out in the hinterland.

The rural church movement failed primarily because rural church members rejected both the diagnosis and the remedy. They considered rural reformers outsiders who understood little about country life. They did not share reformers' beliefs about consolidation of churches, union between churches of different denominations, or the social gospel. They often feared outsiders and were not anxious for new people to join their churches and perhaps interject new ways. Reformers compounded their problems by often being as haughty, patronizing, and insensitive as country people were conservative, orthodox, and suspicious.

Neither were many Alabama Baptists prepared to have their minds changed on matters of gender despite the efforts of denominational reformers to do so. The two-thirds of Alabama Baptists who were female had usually occupied the shadows of the denomination, at first segregated in

Messengers to Central Baptist Association at Weogufka Baptist Church in 1903 reflected the all-male pattern typical of rural Baptist life. (Courtesy of Samford University Archives)

church by separate entrances and pews, then by separate rules and rituals. They could not preach. They could not serve as deacons. They could not teach Sunday school. They could not attend associational meetings or state conventions. They could not decide how the money they collected would be used. They could not even decide what kind of fund raisers they would conduct. But after 1900 conditions changed rapidly. Aimee Semple McPherson was emerging as one of the premier evangelists of the era, and even in Alabama, sexual roles became chaotic.

Key to the change was the Woman's Missionary Union. Barely a decade old in 1900, the organization over the next two decades led alterations in Baptist life that would have been unthinkable even a decade earlier. Symbolic of the new age was a new name: ladies' aid societies became women's missionary societies. "Ladies" (a name associated with Old South mythology) became "women" (a name symbolic of an emerging feminist age). "Aid societies" (associated with women banded together to perform traditional charity and aid the church in paying the pastor and furnishing the pastorium) became "mission societies" (representative of women moving beyond their own communities and entering a much larger and more complex world).[111]

Within churches, change occurred with startling suddenness. Congregations in which women had not previously served on church committees now had all-female committees. At Wetumpka First Baptist Church, nearly half of all committee members between 1900 and 1920 were women. Two single women were appointed church clerk and church treasurer during World War I. The ladies' aid society, with thirty-eight members, was the most effective fund-raising organization in the church through its rummage and bake sales. In 1911, when the church confronted a financial crisis, church leaders asked three "young ladies" to visit church members who had failed to pay pledges for the pastor's salary.[112]

In Huntsville First Baptist Church, the local missionary society took an annual offering for China missions at Christmastime. It collected clothes for the state Baptist orphanage, purchased a sweeper to clean the church, and contributed money for Howard College, China missionary Willie Kelly, China Bible women, mountain schools, the WMU Training School, as well as paying insurance on the church and covering the floors with carpet. Members petitioned the Alabama WCTU to retain Alabama's stiff prohibition laws in 1911 and that same year raised money for the destitute widow of the former pastor of Merrimack Baptist Church (a congregation located in Huntsville's cotton mill village). In 1908 a male leader asked the Huntsville WMU to help procure a new pastorium. After vigorous discussion "as to the wisest and best . . . course to pursue," the WMU turned the request over to a woman whose husband was a deacon. Designated a committee of one, she told the men how women felt about the project and asked the deacons to formulate plans. The WMU gave two gifts of $500 each to build the new home. Their money-raising projects included bazaars, the proceeds from which also purchased songbooks.[113] The formal requests made by men to the WMU, the extensive discussion, the appointment of a woman to speak further with the deacons in order to clarify details and answer questions—all reflect an immense change in gender roles at Huntsville First Baptist Church.

Other women began to modify their churches and associations as well. Alma Worrill Wright (whose husband was a prominent businessman in Roanoke) presented the WMU report to Roanoke First Baptist Church in 1904. A fine public speaker who was also active in women's clubs and was a close friend of state WMU director Kathleen Mallory, Wright became president of the state organization. The Tuskegee-Lee Associational WMU assumed financial support for A. Y. Napier (the former pastor of Auburn First Baptist Church), who resigned to go to China as a missionary. The Mobile Associational WMU raised money for Willie Kelly and sent one of its own members, Daisy Pettus, to Japan as a missionary. Dr. and Mrs. Adrian Taylor left the association for northern China and Mary Anderson represented Mobile Baptists in Canton, China. By 1914 nearly one hundred women attended the associational WMU meeting, and the eighteen mission societies were contributing nearly $5,000 a year to missions. They operated a settlement house where they taught sewing, embroidery, Sunday school, and literacy, and they employed a general missionary to the city. In 1912 the Mobile Baptist Association allowed women for the first time as delegates, a concession perhaps to the fact that WMU women had never refused a request to raise money for associational causes. The following year WMU raised more than $20,000 statewide for missions plus another $1,600 during its special Christmas offering.[114]

The ministries of these churches and associations reflected WMU work. Social service became a major component of the organization across the South as reflected in speakers at the annual convention such as Walter Rauschenbusch. Although WMU avoided using the term "social service" until 1935 for fear of antagonizing opponents of the social gospel, its personal service division focused on immigrants, industrial workers, surveys, schools, and Good Will Centers (called by that name rather than settlement houses as another concession to their critics). By 1925 the South-wide WMU conducted thirty-two Good Will Centers, including several in Alabama. Female social workers, usually graduates of the WMU Training School in Louisville, supplemented local volunteers who operated settlement houses.[115]

Alabama's state WMU publicized social service. In 1912 the state organization urged urban women to rent a house, staff it with volunteers, and begin ministries such as mothers' clubs, boys' and girls' clubs, day nurseries for children of working women, and literacy classes. In small towns, it urged construction of rest rooms for farmers' wives who came to town to shop. It recommended that rural WMU women meet once a month to sew clothes for the poor. Women must find the causes of "sin, destitution, ignorance, and indifference to religion" and remove them.[116]

Although many women ignored social ministries, others implemented them. In Montgomery they established a playground for children in a tough industrial neighborhood. State WMU women helped build dormitories at mountain schools and Newton institute. They conducted statistical surveys to determine conditions among immigrants, African Americans, and native white industrial workers. After the surveys, they established settlement houses, hired female city missionaries, and worked as volunteers staffing the facilities.[117]

Among the women brought into such work was Loraine Bedsole Tunstall, a longtime Baptist laywoman. A native of Clarke County, Tunstall became the first state child labor inspector and later served on the staff of the federal Children's Bureau and on the National Child Labor Committee. For sixteen years she headed the Alabama State Welfare Department and wrote most of Alabama's legislation affecting children. She also drafted legislation that created the Alabama Department of Public Welfare.[118]

Other women made similar contributions. Kathleen Mallory and Julia Ward grew up in Selma two blocks from each other, and both attended Selma First Baptist Church. Mallory's father, Hugh Mallory, was a prominent lawyer, progressive gubernatorial candidate in 1910, state Baptist convention president, and advocate of woman suffrage. Kathleen was chosen corresponding secretary of the state WMU,

Kathleen Mallory, longtime head of the Alabama and Southern Baptist WMUs, grew up in Selma First Baptist Church, where her father was a prominent member, president of the state convention, and candidate for governor as a prohibition-reform advocate. (Courtesy of the Samford University Archives)

then in 1912 assumed the same office in the South-wide organization. A graduate of Goucher College (where she was a Latin and history major), Mallory was a masterful tactician and fund raiser who served as head of WMU longer than any other woman (thirty-six years, from 1912 to 1948). No other person matched her influence either. When Mallory left Alabama for WMU headquarters in Baltimore in 1912, her Selma friend Julia Ward took her place in the state office.[119]

Sarah Jessie Davis Stakely recruited Mallory for both state and national WMU offices. Born in Georgia in 1861, Jessie Stakely married her preacher-husband, Charles, and almost immediately began an active life of her own.

In 1899 she was elected president of the South-wide WMU, then reelected three consecutive years (during which time, at the age of forty-one, she had her fifth child, the only WMU president to give birth while in office). In 1908 she was elected president of Alabama WMU and served continuously until 1921. In 1909 she recruited Mallory to head the state organization and as national vice-president headed the search that selected Mallory national director. Stakely was by far the dominant figure in the Alabama WMU for a generation and one of a half dozen dominant figures in the national organization. When Stakely surrendered leadership of the Alabama WMU, Kate Park Samford (wife of a distinguished judge of the state court of appeals and a member of Stakely's church in Montgomery) took her place.[120]

Stakely was a master organizer and visionary. She divided Alabama into five districts, each with a vice-president who served on the WMU executive board. Her influential advisory board included the wives of W. B. Crumpton and A. J. Dickinson.[121] Kathleen Mallory first served as corresponding secretary, and Amanda Hamilton served as state organizer. By 1911 Stakely had organized WMU in fifty of seventy-seven Baptist associations. Hamilton cautiously refused to speak to "mixed assemblies" that included men and women, a concession to lingering prejudices about the proper biblical role for women.[122]

Jessie Stakely not only was the chief architect of Alabama's WMU, she also filled a host of other roles. She established and taught a large women's Sunday school class at Montgomery First Baptist Church. She was an active member of the city's oldest literary club and the chief instigator of Montgomery's federated women's clubs. Nor did she neglect her husband or five children. When Charles Stakely became deaf, he became totally dependent upon her in all social and professional settings. When she died in 1929, he was forced to resign as pastor. She was also remarkably ecumenical for her age and denomination, perhaps a result of her club work with women of many denominations. In her 1911 presidential address to Alabama WMU, Stakely praised interdenominational women's gatherings "freed from all rivalry" that were meeting across the nation on behalf of world missions.[123]

Such cautious and careful organization paid rich dividends. In 1914 women organized ninety-nine new societies, and the following year Alabama led all states in new growth. More important, men began to grudgingly lower the barriers to full participation in denominational life. Barred from participation in the state convention since 1895 (when men hastily had amended the constitution to allow "brethren" rather than "members" to participate), women received a slight concession at the 1909 convention when, by unanimous vote, Grace Hiden Wilkerson of Birmingham was allowed to speak on WMU work for aged ministers. She completely disarmed wary males by beginning her address: "I am a daughter of a minister; you are my brothers; and so I come without fear and with much assurance that you will aid us women in this worthy and beautiful service." Male delegates praised her speech as intellectually challenging and well delivered.[124]

In 1912 a more significant breakthrough occurred. A. J. Dickinson presented a committee report recommending that women be allowed to serve as delegates to the state convention. Hugh Mallory and Charles Stakely (whose daughter and wife, respectively, played key roles in WMU) strongly supported the motion. The convention appointed a committee to change the constitution in order for women to attend in 1913. Six years later the Southern Baptist Convention also adopted such an amendment. By then, women regularly spoke to a "mixed assembly" of Alabama Baptists, and that year (1919) 109 of Alabama's 475 registered messengers were women.[125]

In addition to these dramatic breakthroughs, there were more subtle changes. The number of single women leaving Alabama for mission work increased dramatically as did students attending the WMU Training School in preparation for careers in ministry. During the first quarter century of the training school (1904–1929), seventy-four Alabama women attended. Ella Jeter and Addie Cox went from the school to China. Eva McCullough, Kathryn Rutledge Germany, Lottie Wallace, and Clara De Shazo became social workers in settlement houses. Other Alabamians became nurses, teachers in mountain schools, or state WMU workers.[126]

The lives of many Baptist women were changed less profoundly but changed nonetheless. Mrs. J. E. Weeks grew up in a small community in north Alabama where her church had no WMU. She married and moved to Florence where she joined the WMU at Florence First Baptist Church. She held every office there and in the Colbert-Lauderdale Associational WMU. "All of these years," she wrote a friend, "were years of fulfillment in my life. I seemed to have 'found myself' in the Lord's work as I worked with women and churches in my association."[127]

Not all Baptist women were so impressed with WMU. Whether because their lives were too busy, their theology too conservative, or their husbands or pastors too opposed, many Alabama women refused to join the organization. Mrs. J. A. Cheney wrote the state office in 1916 asking that her church in Allgood be dropped from the WMU roll. "We are sadly in need of enlightenment," she wrote. "We call ourselves Missionary Baptist. . . . To me it seems a misnomer. We hear, see and know so little of missions.

It is impossible to create any interest in missions." Most of the members of her church were tenant farmers who had little education. The women had too many children and were "way over worked." "What to do," she added, "is a puzzle to me." She was planning to reorganize the WMU and place a tenant wife as president ("one of their class").[128]

Similar problems arose around the state. When Addie Cox tried to organize WMU work in Blount County, a local woman explained that women in their churches wanted to keep their money at home, not send it to overseas missions. In the mill town of Cordova, a state WMU official had difficulty changing women from a ladies' aid society to WMU. Only four women agreed to contribute to missions, and the indifference "was appalling." The associational WMU superintendent resigned because of lack of support from her own churchwomen.[129]

Within churches, WMU women often opposed woman suffrage or maintained a judicious silence about the volatile subject. It seemed enough that Baptist women could now vote in church conferences, associational meetings, and state conventions. To push for women voting in state and national elections was a dangerous and divisive cause. The *Alabama Baptist* generally maintained a discreet silence on the issue, though it did endorse the 1916 Democratic platform calling for state action to enfranchise women. Even liberal, ecumenical, social gospel advocate A. J. Dickinson thought woman suffrage too radical a reform. WMU leaders refused to answer reporters' questions about their views on suffrage for women, explaining that their organization was solely concerned with missions. Generally, the same Baptists who opposed women as delegates to state conventions also opposed allowing them to vote (citing passages from I Corinthians 14:34–35 as proof that God had not intended women to vote).[130]

As with other reforms, some Alabama Baptists charted a different course through the stormy suffrage sea. W. B. Crumpton, conservative on so many theological issues, forcefully endorsed allowing women to vote. Citing the service of women during the world war and 1918 influenza epidemic, Crumpton said that women had earned the right to elect their own governing officials. As property owners, women had every right to determine how their taxes were spent. He added that male resistance to woman suffrage mainly resulted from fear of their support for prohibition. L. L. Gwaltney urged the U.S. Senate to ratify woman suffrage for the same reasons.[131]

Howard College president Andrew P. Montague was an even more forceful advocate of broader roles for women. In a series of lectures he summarized the accomplishments of university women. "The feminine intellect," he wrote, "formerly deemed by some broad enough for the piano, colloquial French, the ball-room, and the sewing machine," seemed to be able to cope just as well with higher mathematics. In the past, women had received exaggerated compliments and flattery in exchange for secondary status. But Christ had recognized the ability of women, who should be allowed to study law, medicine, theology, or any other discipline to which they felt led. If women could teach Sunday school classes, why could they not teach theology? Opponents quoted Scripture shaming women who spoke in public; but other Scripture described the speeches of women and "their words were blessed of God." Woman's proper sphere was wherever God called her.[132]

Of the leading Alabama women suffragists, one was actively Baptist. Maud McLure Kelly grew up in Anniston and Birmingham. Her father (an Anniston attorney and state legislator) allowed her to study law with him until she was admitted to the senior class of the University of Alabama law school in 1907 based on her entrance exam scores. She graduated third in her class and became the first woman to practice law in Alabama (and in 1914 the first southern woman admitted to the bar of the United States Supreme Court). Kelly, who never married, helped organize the Birmingham and Alabama Equal Suffrage Associations and served as chairman of their committees on legislation. In 1928 she became active in the presidential campaign in Alabama of Catholic Al Smith. Despite her consuming interest in law, woman suffrage, and the Democratic Party, she found time to teach Sunday school, direct Sunbeams, and serve as president of the business and professional women's Sunday school class at Birmingham's Southside Baptist Church.[133]

Internationalism and Anti-Catholicism

Progressivism affected world affairs as it did domestic life. Some Alabama Baptist leaders had studied abroad (notably Frank Barnett) and at least one was foreign born (John W. Phillips of Mobile First Baptist Church). Attention to international affairs is therefore no surprise. In the early years of the new century, sentiment favored international arbitration of disputes, pacificism, and anti-imperialism. As war clouds gathered over Europe, Baptist leaders spread the blame among all nations and urged the United States to follow the course of neutrality advised by President Woodrow Wilson. As German submarine attacks on neutral shipping increased, sentiment shifted toward the Allies. Once involved in war, ministers sought to derive theological meaning from it. After the war, they enthusiastically endorsed Wilson's League of Nations. As with so many other phases of Alabama Baptist history, the opinions expressed represent the leadership of the denomination, not its rank and file.

Frank Barnett's long study at universities in Austria, Germany, and France bequeathed him a strong legacy of internationalism. The impact of missionaries, whose letters home often applauded nationalistic movements aimed at overthrowing imperial governments in China and elsewhere, augmented Barnett's editorials.[134]

Before war began in 1914, Barnett endorsed international arbitration as the way to make war obsolete. He condemned arms and naval buildups both in the United States and in Europe and warned prophetically in 1910 that the naval race between Germany and Britain would lead to war. He praised interdenominational Christian efforts to begin an international peace movement and urged a change in Western literature away from warrior heroes and toward attention to "the heroics of peace."[135]

Barnett also criticized Western imperialism. He condemned Belgian atrocities in the Congo and demanded an international investigation. Nor was the United States immune. In an issue of the paper that featured a cartoon of Uncle Sam carrying battleships, cannons, soldiers, swords, and flags on his back, the editor charged that the nation had swapped moral leadership for physical force in the Philippines and elsewhere. For a century, the United States had protested European imperialism. Now the country followed "the reactionary and imperialistic ideas that dominate monarchies."[136]

In Asia, Barnett praised China's attempt to control the opium traffic (which Western powers had imposed in the nineteenth century), and L. L. Gwaltney praised the "open door" policy of the United States (which sought to keep any single imperial power from closing part of China to trade). Barnett also blistered imperial Russia for persecution of its Jewish population.[137]

When war began in 1914, Barnett placed primary blame on Germany but urged the United States not to intervene. Gwaltney warned against overreacting to the German sinking of the British passenger ship *Lusitania* in 1915, despite the loss of American lives. He also emphasized that the greatest suffering of the war fell on wage earners, not the upper classes who experienced only "a temporary check upon their ambitions to accumulate more wealth." Gwaltney and Barnett blamed the war on territorial aggrandizement and "fool-hearted ambitions" by both sides. European rhetoric about the need to maintain the balance of power was "buncombe pure and simple." Each nation was maneuvering to its own advantage, and "pompous sentiments from whichever side are mere banalities and pose. They fool no one."[138]

Pacificism spread rapidly during the years before United States declaration of war. An article in the *Alabama Baptist* praised a Swedish Baptist pastor who went to jail rather than serve in the army "backed by the capitalists of the state." Barnett warned against the rampant spirit of militarism that relied on "brute force." Joseph Judson Taylor, formerly pastor of Mobile First Baptist Church and vice-president of the SBC, was forced to resign his new pastorate in Savannah, Georgia, after offering a series of pacifist resolutions at the 1917 Southern Baptist Convention. Perhaps the most remarkable pacifist statement came from the congregation of the Rural Grove Baptist Church in 1915. That church passed a resolution denouncing war as "unnecessary, immoral and unchristian." The congregation asked President Wilson to submit all issues to international arbitration and to place an embargo on food and war materials shipped to Europe. "If single-handed murder be a sin against God," the congregation resolved, "we believe wholesale murder to be doubly so," especially because most casualties were innocent and helpless civilians.[139]

Once the United States declared war in 1917 and the nation's propaganda machinery began to take effect, sentiment changed. Most Alabama Baptists had long favored Britain despite reservations by their leaders. By 1917 even Frank Barnett manifested a different attitude; he began writing editorials about how to wage a moral war. Such a war must be fought for ethical precepts, not on the basis of hatred of the enemy or revenge. Combatants should avoid libeling and distorting the enemy or spreading false rumors about atrocities. The United States proved as incapable of doing so as the British had, and in fact much of the American war effort was based on demonizing the enemy. Articles began to appear under such titles as "Jesus the Fighter," which depicted Christ as justifying the use of violence when a person was threatened. Pacifism, one minister wrote, was merely an excuse for cowardice. In a sermon at the Cuba Baptist Church in western Alabama, H. D. Wilson justified Christian war in defense of property, life, and honor. He established three conditions for a holy war. Diplomacy must be exhausted. The nation must act only in self-defense. The nation must wage a "Christlike" war, not vindictively or out of hatred, but to punish sin. J. B. Laseter Jr., pastor of the Demopolis First Baptist Church, preached to the local Masons in October 1918, contrasting German materialism and nihilism with American idealism. "You have lined up with America," he lectured as he urged them to purchase war bonds, "because she is your country; she is right, she seeks to free the peoples of the earth."[140]

As soon as the war ended, Alabama Baptists supported Wilson's idealistic vision of internationalism incarnated in the League of Nations. John
W. Inzer (who as pastor of Avondale Baptist Church in Birmingham, Dauphin Way Baptist Church in Mobile, and Montgomery First Baptist Church
and as chairman of the executive board of the state convention would become one of the most influential denominational leaders of the following
generation) was an army chaplain during the war and preached an eloquent sermon on the meaning of peace. The three paramount issues facing
humanity were world citizenship, spiritual humanity, and common brotherhood. Humanity must move beyond selfish individualism of the clan,
tribe, and nation to the world citizenship embodied in Wilson's league.
M. L. Harris, in a paper presented to the Montgomery ministers' conference, described two conflicting roles for preachers in the new age. One role
assumed they were separated from the world, without concern for the conditions of present life or the welfare of humanity; their aim was to convert
as many souls as possible. The other ideal was for ministers to live as citizens of the world, demanding justice without which world peace was impossible. The League of Nations was clearly the expression of the moral
forces of the time, Frank Barnett agreed. Internationalism might not be the
intent of the nation's founding fathers, but conditions had changed since
then: "Irresistible forces are at work in the world which make us our
brother's keeper." American support of the league was a moral as well as a
political duty. L. L. Gwaltney roasted U.S. Senator Henry Cabot Lodge for
his obstruction of the league. [141]

A former Baptist chaplain, E. P. Smith, wrote forcefully on the other side
of the issue. He called the avalanche of *Alabama Baptist* editorials favoring
the League of Nations "nothing more or less than a tirade of rhetoric" that
deified Wilson. He praised Lodge's position as true Americanism. Internationalism proposed to cluster nations around a super-government in Swit-
zerland, creating yet another world empire, though this one was to be
cloaked in the fancy drapings of democracy. [142]

One consideration about the new world order was how it would affect
Catholicism. Long a concern of Alabama Baptists, Catholicism became an
obsession after the war. Many members of the denomination joined a new
organization, the anti-Catholic Guardians of Liberty. So outrageous was
its newspaper, the *Menace*, that the Catholic bishop of Mobile asked that
it be banned in Alabama. The *Alabama Baptist* energetically defended the
Guardians of Liberty as a force for maintaining separation of church and
state and public schools. When the U.S. Public Health Service sent a Catholic physician to coordinate Birmingham's disease prevention program,

Baptists led a successful effort to drive out "medical hierarchies . . . in Alabama." Even support from the chief executive officer of the powerful TCI Steel Company and organized labor could not save his job.[143]

None other than A. J. Dickinson (the theologically liberal, social gospel pastor of Birmingham's First Baptist Church) organized the semisecret, anti-Catholic True American Society in the industrial city. In 1917 Dickinson led evangelical forces aligned against George B. Ward, who ran for reelection as president of the city commission with the backing of organized labor. The True American Society opposed his reelection because Ward refused to fire Birmingham's chief of police, who was Catholic. Dickinson's forces backed East Lake physician Dr. Nathaniel A. Barrett, a member of Ruhama Baptist Church. Ward accused Dickinson of being a member of the True American Society. Dickinson disingenuously denied that he was a member of any society "that affects my religious, personal or political liberty" or that he opposed a Catholic holding public office. The issue was separation of church and state, not religious affiliation. The *Birmingham News* acknowledged that Dickinson was one of Alabama's most scholarly men but also accused him of evading "the whole truth" and endeavoring "to hide between abstractions and technicalities." Caught in a lie, Dickinson tried to extricate himself by claiming that the Guardians of Liberty subscribed to the same principles as Baptists. Despite a roasting from the press, Dickinson led his forces to a 1,000-vote victory over Ward, breaking the back of the city's traditional political elites and establishing the supremacy of anti-Catholic suburban Protestants over inner-city Catholic workers.[144]

In 1919 the *Alabama Baptist* cast the postwar world in terms of Baptist democracy versus Catholic tyranny. Every denomination would have to choose one or the other because neutrality was no longer possible.[145] The choice of Alabama Baptists would be the revived, anti-Catholic, Ku Klux Klan.

Race

Another limitation to "progressive" Baptist thought can be found in racial attitudes. Just as theologically liberal Baptists were often intolerant of Catholics, they shared the dominant racial views of their culture.

The racial upheaval unleashed by populism was arrested by the 1901 Alabama Constitution. That document used a variety of measures (poll taxes, literacy tests, residency requirements) to disfranchise black voters. The editor of the *Alabama Baptist* praised the new constitution for improving funding of public schools, restricting railroad abuses, and other reforms. But the most important feature of the document, which should "cause every white man to vote for [its] ratification," was the fact that it secured once and for all "WHITE SUPREMACY."[146]

The editor expressed racial views typical of the nation's most repressive era. He opposed a race relations conference in Montgomery because undue prominence given the African American "puffs up his vanity, magnifies his importance in his own estimation, and encourages his encroachments upon our social structure." Whites and blacks differed in every relationship of life, and no improvement in the culture, education, or experience of a black "can raise him to the dignity of the white man." The task of whites was to maintain their supremacy over blacks. The task of blacks was to remain in their separate segregated spheres. Select African Americans might be profitably educated, though providing college for the black masses "ruined [them] so far as manual labor is concerned." God had ordained the black to be "a hewer of wood and a drawer of water." Above all else, blacks should be removed from Alabama's political process.[147]

One reason white Baptists so enthusiastically supported disfranchising blacks involved the belief that they generally voted against prohibition. W. B. Crumpton wrote that black disfranchisement removed the single most powerful political weapon of the saloon interests. Other Baptists (including Frank Barnett) agreed, even attributing blame for most rapes to drunken Negroes. B. F. Riley attacked the problem in a different way, returning to Birmingham to become superintendent of the Southern Negro Anti-Saloon Federation.[148]

A. J. Dickinson's modernist theology did not reduce his racial prejudice and perhaps even enhanced it. Darwinian science and its sociological application, expressed in such theories as the survival of the fittest, tended to view society as a fierce competitive arena where superior races and classes flourished at the expense of inferior ones. This "natural law" of society favored whites over blacks. Dickinson strongly rejected allowing blacks to attend the Southern Baptist Convention, a position favored by border-state Baptists. He hoped all Negroes would move to the North, and he criticized Booker T. Washington for instilling "notions of social equality" in the minds of Tuskegee Institute students. Washington should be given "passage out of the country" where whites had determined that their Anglo-Saxon blood would pass "unpoluted [sic] and uncontaminated" to their children.[149]

Alabama Baptists deplored President Theodore Roosevelt's invitation to Booker T. Washington to dine at the White House, denounced black preachers for their political activity, and accused them of being backward and superstitious. Some even denied that Negroes had souls. To admit otherwise, one writer explained, would force a biblical literalist to admit that Adam and Eve had Negro blood inasmuch as they were the father and mother of all human beings. Only centuries of education could improve Negro character, another wrote. Sidney Catts, pastor at Tuskegee Baptist Church, urged white parents to keep their children away from too much contact with blacks lest they come to believe African superstitions.[150]

The Home Mission Board cooperated with Alabama Baptists to try to educate African Americans. When some readers objected to educating blacks, the *Alabama Baptist* defended such efforts as a religious duty. Such assistance was almost always patronizing. Whites sought to teach black ministers theology and how to preach. They provided a few hundred dollars to Selma University, the black Baptist college in the state. Charles W. Hare of Tuskegee warned ominously that if white Alabama Baptists did not do more to help their black brethren, "strangers must be looked to for help; then we must expect to see the chasm between the races . . . grow wider and more dangerous."[151]

The WMU, enlightened on many issues, was not so progressive on this one. WMU congratulated white politicians for establishing schools for blacks (not quite accurate inasmuch as most black education was begun during Reconstruction by Radical Republicans, including black officeholders). Although national WMU literature emphasized the duty of whites to help impoverished blacks, local missionary societies did not always take such literature seriously. At a 1904 WMS meeting at the Huntsville First Baptist Church to study the problems of African Americans, women presented their parts, then engaged in "a hearty and even ludicrous discussion . . . as to the best way of governing the negro in a domestic way." After the discussion, members decided "that evangelization was the only hope for the race, and not education."[152]

On the subject of violence against African Americans (especially lynching), Baptists continued to reflect middle-class white opinion against such outrages. Editorials criticized state and local elected officials for doing too little to prevent violence and praised rare acts of courage that prevented lynchings. Though admitting that lynching was not just a southern phenomenon, the editor of the denominational paper wrote that "a right thinking man" could take little comfort in the knowledge "that a pox afflicts a whole nation and not merely a single section."[153]

B. F. Riley was one of only a handful of Alabama Baptists who moved somewhat beyond racial paternalism. As superintendent of the Negro Anti-

Saloon Federation, he worked closely with black Baptists and tried to refute white racial stereotypes. He insisted on a single standard of justice
in courts, business, and education. In his book, *The White Man's Burden*,
he described Negroes as victims of "a dominant race, many of whom were
... silent friends, while many others were ... pronounced foes." Blacks
had no power themselves to appeal or redress wrongs done to them. He
denounced lynching and explained that only a southern white man could
work as he did, mediating black opinion and concerns to whites.[154]

During the two decades between 1900 and 1920, Alabama Baptists
wrestled with modernity and with one another. By no means did the dominant theological trends of the times pass them by. Modernism, ecumenism,
and the social gospel all found adherents, small though their numbers
might be. Only the social gospel seems to have gained institutional expression, although Howard College became a noisy battleground for all ideologies. What is surprising is both the number of ministers who were open to
new ideas and the prominence and influence they had within the denomination. Despite widespread disagreement over their theological ideas and
the social expressions of them, L. L. Gwaltney, A. J. Dickinson, A. C. Davidson, John W. Phillips, and Frank Barnett were widely regarded as the most
influential leaders the denomination produced. Women charted an even
more daring and independent course.

The point is not that Alabama Baptists during the first decades of the
century capitulated to theological and social liberalism. They did not. The
point is that they tolerated a variety of opinions among white, native-born
Baptists. That Alabama Baptists elected so many of these persons to positions of leadership (as convention presidents, vice-presidents, and keynote
preachers; as editors of the *Alabama Baptist*; as pastors of the largest and
most affluent churches), and remembered them with such affection decades
later, is testimony to their respect.

The fact that a Baptist was progressive did not confer upon him or
her moral superiority. Though history would prove them right on some issues, it would judge them harshly on others. The pseudoscientific ideas of
Social Darwinism tended to buttress racism and anti-Catholicism. Progressives stood at the leadership of the new eugenics movement that sought to
sterilize mentally defective people against their wills. Many progressive reforms were later criticized as attempts to impose the social, educational,
and medical beliefs of an urban, educated, elite on immigrants, working-
class people, and rural folk. In retrospect, some of their ideas seem as
flawed as the ones progressives sought to overcome.

That progressivism and modernism passed by Alabama with little influence is untrue. More accurate is a biblical metaphor. These new seeds fell on shallow soil. When the rains of reform watered the earth, a surprisingly bountiful crop sprang to life. When the harsh winds of criticism and conflict began to blow during the 1920s, the crop wilted and slowly faded.

8

The Ballyhoo Years Alabama-Style, the 1920s

"Honest seekers after the truth."

The decade of the 1920s earned its appellation as the "ballyhoo" years. Life was noisy and exaggerated. People chose sensational and showy methods of calling attention to whatever they wanted to sell, whether underwear or Christianity. Beneath the surface of brash and self-confident people, though, anxiety and conflict seethed. It was an era of cheap automobiles, easy credit, crazy fads, scandalous movies and dances, organized sports, materialism, and youthful rebellion. It was also a time of worsening agricultural conditions, growing farm tenancy, theological conflict, and rapid social change, especially for women. Although the pervasive ruralism and conservatism of Alabama muted many of these conflicts, change continued even in the heart of Dixie.

Ernest Davis (pastor of Fort Payne First Baptist Church) announced the arrival of the new age, replete with its excesses and peculiarities, in a series of sermons. Operating on the premise that it pays to advertise, he announced his catchy sermon titles in the local paper: "Full House," "Bad Stuff," "Hot Stuff," "1-2-3 and Away We Go," "A Frank Discussion of Some Prominent Folks in Fort Payne," "Tea with a Kick," "An Old Fashioned Beauty Treatment." The titles bore a striking resemblance to the titles of racy new motion pictures that ministers regularly denounced. And the titles attracted similarly large audiences. The local paper warned that if visitors expected to find seats in Fort Payne First Baptist Church, they had better arrive early. When Davis resigned in 1925 after only thirteen months as pastor, he had baptized forty and increased total church membership by one-fourth.[1]

The decade has been explained in a variety of ways. Clashes occurred between advocates of disappearing rural values and forces of modernity increasingly ascendant in cities. The localism, democracy, individualism, and traditionalism of rural people resisted the centralizing, reforming, and patronizing of well-educated urbanites. The world war had unleashed forces of moral decline that threatened traditional family and religious values. New scientific theories, especially evolution, threatened ancient Christian cosmology. Fundamentalism had become well organized, well funded, and competently led. American Protestantism had become deeply polarized between fundamentalists and modernists. The two forces battled for control of denominations in the North; where liberals managed to maintain control of denominational institutions and agencies, fundamentalists established new, parallel organizations or even new denominations. National conflicts reinforced the conservatism of southern denominations and triggered a reaction against the liberal drift of the previous two decades. Concern for poor and working-class people drifted to the background, and middle-class values prevailed. Just as two predominant ideologies separated Protestants, so did two unofficial parties. The "public" or liberal party dominated most church bureaucracies and won the allegiance of leading clergymen and seminarians; the "private" or conservative party predominated among laity and significant numbers of small-town and rural pastors.[2]

Denominationalism during the 1920s

Within the South, there was less conflict because there was less diversity of opinion. Historian Samuel S. Hill has divided southern evangelicals into four groups: the truth party, concerned mainly with establishing correct beliefs and exposing error; the conversion party, devoted primarily to missions and evangelism; a spirituality party, involved mainly with experiencing God's intimate presence; and a service party, stressing the church's work of reconciliation and ministry. Most denominations contained several of these elements often engaged in some level of conflict. During the 1920s, Southern Baptists tended to be a conversionist denomination, though with strong influence by the truth element and lesser impact from the service party. Always living on the edge of fratricidal warfare and disunion, the denomination unified less around a doctrinal synthesis than evangelism and its regional identity. It also spawned populistic resentment to the growing bureaucratization of the denomination. Preference for a small church (democratically controlled, completely autonomous, consisting mainly of plain folks, and pastored by a bivocational minister) deepened suspicion about college- and seminary-trained leaders. The folk church believed that such institutions existed to pass along unchanged the beliefs of the Baptist masses and to prepare preachers to defend the faith once delivered to the saints, not to debate competing versions of truth. The rapid growth of the denomination during these years transformed it from a bastion for dissenters who insisted on religious freedom and separation of church and state into what historian Martin Marty has called the "Catholic Church of the South." In its new role, the SBC sometimes denied freedom to others, persecuted Catholics, and blurred distinctions between church and state.[3]

Between 1917 and 1931, the Southern Baptist Convention assumed its modern organizational structure. In 1917 the SBC appointed its initial secretary-treasurer to head the Sunday School Board. The following year the Annuity Board was established to provide pensions for ministers. A year later Southern Baptists launched the Seventy-Five Million Dollar Campaign. Although successful in many ways, this gigantic fund-raising drive required a coordinated and centralized effort and left the SBC and state conventions in debt. This financial crisis led to budget, stewardship, and enlistment campaigns unprecedented in denominational history, culminating in establishment of the Cooperative Program (CP) in 1925. The CP required closer coordination between national and state conventions, with each state establishing its own ratio of funding for state and national causes. Adoption of the CP also was intended to end local church financial drives for individual missionaries, causes, and institutions. Other bureaucracies followed: in 1923, the Southern Baptist Hospital in New Orleans; in 1926, Baptist Brotherhood; in 1928, Baptist Student Union and the Education Commission. In 1927 the executive committee of the convention appointed its first executive secretary-treasurer, who became essentially the denomination's CEO. By the end of the decade, the management strategies of the 1920s had redesigned and institutionalized the denomination. Reliance on voluntary contributions to fund a growing bureaucracy put a premium on consensus and made controversy anathema. The annual convention could not easily deal with dissent or controversy because it was not designed as a political forum for competing interests. Extremes at either end of the denomination were kept under control by shrewd and powerful consensus builders, who tolerated passage of meaningless resolutions about a variety of controversial matters but seldom attempted to make resolutions binding on employees of Baptist institutions or normative for the denomination. Constantly reminding delegates (increasingly called "messengers" because in Baptist polity an autonomous church could not delegate its authority to any individual) that every church was autonomous and no convention action was binding on any of them, the annual convention increasingly became a loud, clamorous, often angry sounding board for opinion but without any coercive function. Convention leadership was determined largely by the absence of most uneducated, bivocational pastors of small churches who could not attend for financial and schedule reasons. Small church pastors and fundamentalists who did attend were generally bypassed for denominational office, whether elective or appointive, as uneducated, incompetent, eccentric, extreme, or a combination of all these disabling characteristics. Denominational leaders at both national and state levels tended to be consensus-building moderate conservatives. They harmonized Christianity and modern science, endorsed fundamental beliefs such as the virgin birth, biblical miracles, substitutionary atonement, and bodily resurrection, but refused to codify such beliefs into a creed that all Baptists had to affirm.[4]

Rejection of both extremes (fundamentalism and modernism) did not mean that Southern Baptists renounced either politics or society. Indeed, they remained fiercely prohibitionist and increasingly nativist. As more and more of their number ran for public office, Baptists often became frankly partisan. Nor did rejection of liberal theology carry with it repudiation of the social gospel. Many conservatives as well as liberals continued to believe that Christian ethics must be applied to matters other than private morality. Although the denomination's social service commission came under conservative control that narrowed its focus to prohibition and blue laws, a minority of social activists continued to challenge the denomination on matters of economic, social, and racial justice.[5]

Advocates of the social gospel and a noncreedal approach to theology were centered in denominational agencies, colleges, and seminaries: college presidents William L. Poteat at Wake Forest, Rufus Weaver at Mercer, and Rolvix Harlan at the University of Richmond; Southern seminary professors William Owen (W. O.) Carver, Charles S. Gardner, E. Y. Mullins, and Southwestern seminary professors John Price and Walter Conner; Baptist editors L. L. Gwaltney (*Alabama Baptist*), Livingston Johnson (North Carolina's *Biblical Recorder*), Z. T. Cody (South Carolina's *Baptist Courier*), and

Louie Newton (Georgia's *Christian Index*). Social application of Christianity created surprisingly little conflict within the denomination.[6]

Modernist-fundamentalist strife was another matter. Strong regional and denominational loyalty reduced the influence of fundamentalists, who tended toward interdenominationalism, which made them vulnerable to counterattack. They did wage an effective guerrilla action against seminary and college professors, particularly W. O. Carver of Southern seminary. Conservatives tried to resist both fundamentalist and modernist labels. Virtually all SBC leaders rejected higher criticism and extreme views on the social gospel, but many moderate conservatives accepted theistic evolution and rejected biblical literalism. They denied that biblical writers acted as mere stenographers, recording God's words as they were dictated. Here and there a maverick such as L. L. Gwaltney spoke against literalism and verbal inspiration, though such cases were infrequent. In fact, a Baptist teacher in western Texas was fired for suggesting that the "days" referred to in the Genesis creation story might be longer periods of time than twenty-four hours, an idea that had attracted wide support among Alabama Baptists. Led by Alabama native J. Frank Norris, Baptist fundamentalists sought to purge the denomination, but their intolerance and mean-spiritedness undermined their credibility, as did their inability to take control of state conventions or the annual SBC. Although their populism and opposition to centralized bureaucracy appealed to many Baptists, their tactics and ineffective organization undermined their cause.[7] So did unifying aspects of southern politics and culture. Moderates were not so separated from rank-and-file Baptists that they could find no common ground. On issues such as prohibition, race, anti-Catholicism, and the 1928 Al Smith presidential campaign, moderates were indistinguishable from conservative southern culture, which made them elusive targets for fundamentalists who insisted they had forsaken orthodoxy.

All these forces in the SBC helped reshape Alabama Baptists. Following patterns well established in business, the denomination reorganized. Some seventy-five local associations met each year between late August and the November state convention. In a typical meeting, the 1926 Baldwin Association voted to buy a tent that could be used for revivals near the county's eleven consolidated rural schools. Messengers especially worried about the population of Fairhope, a community that traced its roots to nineteenth-century utopian reformers who rejected individually owned property. Baptists believed that Fairhope's population was rife with atheism and infidelity.[8]

Attending associational meetings was much easier for most pastors and lay people than participating in a state or national convention. For lay people who had to take off from work and pay their own way, costs were prohibitive. Although larger churches often appropriated money to send their pastors to both state and national conventions, most Alabama Baptist churches barely covered the ordinary Sunday expenses of their bivocational pastors. The result was a state convention dominated by pastors and lay people from larger urban congregations. The officers elected reflected this pattern. From 1921 until 1924, L. O. Dawson (pastor of Tuscaloosa First Baptist Church) served as president. In 1924 the convention elected a layman from the host church, Parker Memorial in Anniston. He was reelected the next year. James R. Hobbs (pastor of Birmingham First Baptist Church) was elected in 1926, Oxford banker D. C. Cooper in 1927, John W. Phillips of Mobile First Baptist Church in 1928, and Dent F. Green (a banker and member of Central Baptist Church in Decatur and former secretary-treasurer of the state mission board) in 1929 and 1930. During the decade messengers thus elected four influential ministers and three wealthy laymen. Despite the steady growth in attendance (515 in Anniston in 1924; 1,025 in Birmingham in 1927), pastors of large urban churches dominated conventions.[9]

State conventions during the decade consolidated, reorganized, and expanded Baptist work. The 1923 meeting celebrated the convention's centennial by updating B. F. Riley's 1895 history of Alabama Baptists. The 1926 convention enlarged the convention's executive board from thirty-nine to ninety members so that each association could be represented. This concession to rural associations necessitated reducing the semiannual meetings to a single session. Because associations only nominated their representatives (who had to be elected by the state convention), power continued in the hands of messengers to that meeting. In 1929 the committee on organization and efficiency consolidated three agencies into a new department of education and training. Following the lead of the 1926 SBC, the 1930 state convention requested all denominational employees to sign a pledge assuring their full cooperation and sympathy with denominational interests.[10]

Other institutional work was begun or expanded. The centennial convention assumed as a major new ministry the location of Baptist student work on every major campus in the state. Working through local churches, the state mission board appropriated funds to provide facilities especially for students. A new Baptist hospital began in Selma supported by a statewide Mother's Day offering (nearly one-eighth of its cases consisted of charity care for the poor). Mountain schools, Newton institute, Howard and Judson Colleges, and the Baptist orphanage absorbed large quantities of money. The 1920 acquisition of Mentone Springs in northeastern Alabama as a Baptist assembly grounds provided an excellent training and recreational facility.[11]

One of the most important changes in denominational life was return of the *Alabama Baptist* to convention control. After purchasing the paper from Frank Barnett, the convention appointed L. L. Gwaltney editor in March 1919. He initially returned the paper to Montgomery but soon relocated back in Birmingham because of better train connections, cheaper printing costs, and his desire to have editorial freedom from constant scrutiny by the ever expanding Baptist state headquarters staff. Gwaltney proved a masterful businessman-editor. By cutting subscription rates in half for churches that provided the paper to every household, he added 10,000 new subscribers in the summer of 1919 alone and increased circulation from 3,500 to more than 16,000 during his first decade as editor. The paper soon turned a profit and by 1926 was included in the budgets of 125 churches.[12]

Denominational finances paralleled improvement in the state's industrial economy and the fortunes of the Seventy-Five Million Dollar Campaign. Launched in 1919, the campaign was designed to eliminate constant and competing special appeals for money. These wasteful fund raisers required that a representative of the cause physically appear in a church to ask for gifts. Such efforts favored the best organized and most articulate spokesmen, not necessarily the most worthy and needful cause. And they drained funds from the local church. The new campaign set out to raise $75 million in five years by assigning quotas to states and churches. The drive resulted in $92 million pledged (although only $58 million was actually paid during the five years). Some state conventions were hesitant about the new Cooperative Program, but Dent Green (state mission board secretary) and L. L. Gwaltney tirelessly promoted the program. At first, the convention voted to distribute 65 percent of CP funds within the state and 35 percent to SBC causes. But by 1927 the convention had settled on a 55 percent state and 45 percent SBC distribution. Although messengers recognized the right of churches to designate gifts however they wished, they urged undesignated gifts that could be apportioned according to the formula. They also permitted special Sunday school offerings for various state charities such as the Baptist hospital in Selma and the state orphanage. To better focus attention, the 1927 executive board recommended four special weeks for CP contributions: March was for home missions; June focused on a statewide evangelistic campaign, schools, colleges, and seminaries; September emphasized state and associational missions; December was the month for foreign missions.[13]

Although Alabama Baptists ranked next to last in both total and per capita contributions among eighteen states in 1920, total mission gifts more than tripled that year. Total gifts went from $750,000 in 1919 to nearly $2.5 million in 1929.[14] Unfortunately, this financial progress was uneven and narrow. Of 2,017 ABSC churches in July 1924, 301 had contributed nothing in five years to the Seventy-Five Million Dollar Campaign; 585 had given less than $50 over the same time; and 726 had paid less than $500. That left barely 400 churches of the 2,000 to contribute virtually the entire Alabama quota. Of those 400, just 4 churches paid the lion's share: Southside in Birmingham pledged $225,000; Birmingham First Baptist, $100,000; Montgomery First Baptist, $100,000; and Parker Memorial Baptist in Anniston, $104,000. In 1920, 53 of Alabama's 2,057 Baptist churches gave nearly $400,000 to missions, education, and benevolence, slightly more than half the total. Those 53 churches enrolled only 30,000 of the state's 228,000 white Baptists. At least the percentage of churches contributing something to Baptist causes rose, from 40 percent in 1910 to 75 percent in 1920. The top 6 churches in contributions that year were Southside and First Baptist in Birmingham, Parker Memorial in Anniston, and First Baptist churches in Roanoke, Tuscaloosa, and Montgomery. This disproportionate giving was consistent with other indices. In 1924, 573 churches paid their pastors salaries of less than $50 a year, and nearly 1,700 paid less than $300 annually.[15]

As Cooperative Program contributions declined sharply in 1928–1929 (the result of a declining economy and natural calamities), acrimony about the CP began to spread. Financially strapped churches, flood victims, Baptist schools, and missionaries believed either that the state kept too much of CP offerings or spent too much on South-wide causes. The executive committee urged churches to eliminate special fund raising and designated gifts, canvass every member for donations, and organize budget drives to last at least two months. When SBTS missions professor W. O. Carver criticized the state convention for keeping too high a percentage of mission gifts in Alabama, the obviously embarrassed secretary-treasurer wrote Carver that he had long favored a fifty-fifty division of the gifts but could not persuade the executive board or convention to agree. The only special fund drive he had authorized was for relief after disastrous spring floods in 1929.[16]

L. L. Gwaltney attributed declining mission offerings to a variety of causes. Of some 2,000 Baptist churches in the state, only about 150 had full-time pastors; another 250 had half-time ministers. Not more than 100 churches contributed systematically to the Cooperative Program. Much of the money from other churches came almost exclusively from women's missionary societies. Two-thirds of white Baptists thus belonged to churches that gave virtually nothing to missions. He believed that the mission spirit was dying and that Alabama Baptist institutions would either have to return to special appeals or close.[17]

Dent F. Green, secretary-treasurer of the state mission board, was the ideal representative of the new Baptist management style. As the only lay-man ever to serve in that office, he instilled the decade's preeminent values of efficiency and sound management. Like the "businessmen Progressives" who provided a new style of political leadership, Green provided a new style of efficient financial management. A graduate of Howard College, Green married a Baptist preacher's daughter, practiced law, served in both houses of the legislature, and became attorney for a group of banks in the Tennessee Valley. After becoming vice-president of a Montgomery bank, he left Decatur and served under three governors as state examiner of banks. While serving in that capacity, he was elected secretary-treasurer of the executive board in 1920, a job he continued for nearly the entire decade. Before returning to Decatur and his beloved Central Baptist Church, Green was twice elected president of the state convention.[18]

Financial trends within the state convention reflected ministerial patterns as well. As in previous decades, Baptists developed a clearly defined double tier of leadership. At the top of convention life was a small cadre of some fifty well-educated pastors of large, wealthy churches. Augmenting their numbers were convention officials and employees, who were usually selected from inside the loop of influential churches. Certain congregations furnished a phenomenal percentage of denominational leaders: Florence First Baptist; Southside, Ruhama, and First Baptist in Birmingham; Parker Memorial in Anniston; Tuscaloosa First Baptist; Siloam in Marion; Selma First Baptist; Prattville First Baptist; Montgomery First Baptist; Tuskegee First Baptist; Mobile First Baptist.

At the bottom of the ABSC was a large number of ordained bivocational ministers. Most had only rudimentary education. Their names never appeared on the executive board, as officers of the convention, or as members of its numerous committees. By 1928 the denomination had nearly 2,000 ordained ministers and about the same number of churches, but more than half the preachers pastored no church. L. L. Gwaltney believed the problem resulted from casual ordination. Men arranged their own ordaining councils, making the examination a "travesty" and resulting in self-appointed preachers.[19]

The situation seems more complicated than Gwaltney's analysis. Bivocational ministers were tied to their jobs or the land they farmed. Pastorless churches might not be located where there were surplus preachers. And many churches paid no salary or at best a pittance too small to cover even a minister's expenses. Most ordained Baptist preachers were as poor as the average white Alabamian, and that fact made them among the poorest of all Americans. More than half of Alabama's farmers during the 1920s were landless tenants, and most workers labored for the lowest industrial salaries in the nation. Bivocational ministers drawn from such ordinary folk could not subsidize a church by donating time and expenses.

Among the top tier, a remarkable array of gifted leaders served state Baptists. When volume fifteen of *Who's Who in America* appeared covering the years 1928–1929, more Alabama Baptist ministers (fourteen) were listed than from any other denomination. In fact, Baptists represented nearly half of all ministers from the state, the highest SBC percentage of any southern state. Many of the names were familiar. They were men in the final stages of illustrious careers: Charles Stakely (pastor of Montgomery First Baptist); W. F. Yarborough (retired pastor of Parker Memorial and secretary-treasurer of the state mission board); L. O. Dawson (former pastor of Tuscaloosa First Baptist and head of the Bible department at Howard College); Paul Bomar (former pastor at Siloam church in Marion and president of Judson College); Frank Barnett (former owner of the *Alabama Baptist* and then editor of a Birmingham newspaper); A. C. Davidson (then in semiretirement but still pastoring part-time in Livingston); Joshua Hill Foster (former pastor at Ruhama and Parker Memorial, retired in Tuscaloosa); William H. Smith (twice president of the state convention and pastor at Ensley Baptist Church). Other honorees represented a new generation: L. L. Gwaltney; James R. Hobbs (pastor of Birmingham First Baptist); James E. Dillard (pastor at Southside); Edward V. Baldy (president of Judson College from 1923 to 1929).[20]

Such urban ministers fit in well with their upwardly mobile congregations. They joined fraternal organizations and cultivated fashionable hobbies to occupy leisure time. Of fifty-six ministers studied from the era 1880–1940, twenty-two were Masons. Arnold S. Smith, pastor of Alexander City First Baptist for three decades, was grand master (the highest state official). Rev. William C. Bledsoe was grand chaplain for forty-seven consecutive years, allegedly the longest such term in the history of American Masonry.

So popular were Masons among Alabama Baptists that the denominational newspaper published the agenda of the supreme council as well as reprinting articles from Masonic publications. Behind Masons came Rotary clubs, with twelve members, Kiwanis with ten, and Lions with seven. Two of the fifty-six ministers belonged to labor unions and eight to parent-teacher associations. Their hobbies included fishing (twenty), gardening (fifteen), hunting (twelve), travel, golf, and photography (eight each), and reading (six).[21]

It is not surprising that pastors who made *Who's Who* also dominated denominational offices and committees. Three of them (Bomar, Stakely, and Dawson) constituted more than one-third of the 1928 state convention executive board. Many of them also served unusually long pastorates (Stakely completed twenty-nine years as pastor of Montgomery First Baptist, Dawson and Arnold Smith more than thirty years each at First Baptist churches in Tuscaloosa and Alexander City).[22]

Among the new generation, five men were destined to have particularly long and distinguished careers. Brady R. Justice was born in Geneva County, attended rural schools near Hartford, then graduated from Newton institute in 1919. He paid his way through Howard College by preaching on weekends and waiting tables in a men's dormitory. A religion professor helped him obtain his first pastorate in Calhoun County while he was a freshman, a congregation that paid him two and a half dollars per trip. Unfortunately, the church had an annual call and the next year found a Howard student willing to preach for even less. Justice moved to Weaver, where he preached twice a month for two years. After graduation from Southern seminary, he pastored at Albertville, Fort Payne, and Enterprise, where he became one of the convention's most respected and beloved leaders.[23]

The other four denominational leaders were clustered in Birmingham. James E. Dillard, a native of Missouri and graduate of William Jewell College, came to pastor Southside Baptist Church in 1918. During his service there (1918–1936), the church added some 5,500 members, a new education building, and a mission church and donated nearly $800,000 to missions. He chaired the SBC commission on Cooperative Program (1925–1927), served on the SBC executive committee (1927–1936), and was elected president of the state convention (1933–1934). As book editor for the *Alabama Baptist*, Dillard reviewed several books weekly for eighteen years, showing a preference for the most recent theological and sociological literature, much of it controversial.[24]

James C. Stivender was born in Hale County in 1888 and raised on a

Leslie Lee Gwaltney dominated the state convention from 1919 to 1950 much as W. B. Crumpton had during the previous third of a century. As a prominent pastor and editor of the *Alabama Baptist*, Gwaltney emerged as one of the denomination's most liberal thinkers on issues other than race. (Courtesy of Samford University Archives)

farm, one of eight children. He attended Howard College and received a bachelor of divinity degree from the University of Chicago and a doctor of theology degree from Southern seminary in 1919. He came to Ruhama Baptist Church as pastor in 1919 and served a quarter century before leaving for Tuskegee First Baptist Church. In Birmingham, Stivender served as president of the Protestant pastors' union and the Baptist pastors' conference and as a member of the city planning board. Twice he was elected president of the state convention. In 1929 he organized an interdenominational theological discussion group that tackled virtually every controversial topic.[25]

James R. Hobbs, a native Mississippian and graduate of Mississippi College and Southern seminary, anticipated a career in law and politics before his call to the ministry. Like Justice, he worked his way through school. As the eldest of fifteen children, his father could spare the boy only fifty cents when he began college. Although Hobbs excelled at oratory, he did not distinguish himself in the classroom. In 1918 he began a nineteen-year pastorate at Birmingham First Baptist, replacing the controversial A. J. Dickinson. Like Southside church under Dillard's leadership, First Baptist experienced significant growth, from 500 members to nearly 3,000 by 1927. Hobbs's prestigious congregation included a former governor, a former U.S. senator, a future U.S. senator, and future associate justice of the U.S. Supreme Court Hugo L. Black, who served the church as both Sunday school teacher and deacon. During his long pastorate, Hobbs served on the SBC executive committee that planned the Seventy-Five Million Dollar Campaign, headed the committee that established Baptist hospitals in

Selma and Birmingham, twice preached convention sermons at the SBC, and headed both Alabama and national antisaloon leagues (becoming both the first pastor and the first Baptist to head the national organization). A local newspaper selected Hobbs as one of Birmingham's hundred most prominent citizens.[26]

The premier denominational leader during the three decades after 1920 was L. L. Gwaltney, who took W. B. Crumpton's place as Mr. Alabama Baptist. After his graduation from the University of Richmond and Southern seminary, Gwaltney came to Prattville First Baptist Church, where he manifested considerable interest in poor textile workers and prohibition. The latter interest was a primary factor in his decision to leave Prattville. He prayed so hard in his pulpit for a dry victory in a local option referendum that some interpreted his prayer to be for some kind of misfortune to befall wets so they would be unable to vote. Some members considered him "cranky on the prohibition question." The ensuing controversy led him to accept a call to the Greenville Baptist Church. While a pastor there, Gwaltney read all fifty-two volumes of the Harvard Classics. Though he had always been well read (especially in his hobby of geology and astronomy), he frequently mentioned reading the Harvard Classics as a pivotal event in his life and recommended that all young pastors read them.[27]

After his eight-year pastorate in Butler County, Gwaltney left to pastor Florence's First Baptist Church. The sleepy Tennessee River town experienced tremendous growth during and shortly after the world war as the government built Wilson Dam on the river. The population exploded from ten thousand to nearly three times that figure in a matter of months. When the demands of the church became too great for one person, he hired Cora Goodwin as his assistant and community missionary. Their working relationship was exceptional.[28]

Gwaltney had served the Florence church only a year when a series of events shifted his career in a new direction. Cora Goodwin married, leaving him without an assistant. The state convention had decided to purchase the *Alabama Baptist* from Barnett, and Southside pastor James E. Dillard lobbied for selection of Gwaltney as the paper's new editor. Gwaltney hesitated, partly because his wife objected, but also because church leaders were angry that he had pastored their congregation so short a time. Other members were not sad to see him go. Although some considered him a wonderful preacher, others regarded his manuscript sermons as hard to follow without careful and constant attention.[29]

As editor of the denominational paper from 1919 to 1950, Gwaltney put his stamp on an entire generation of Alabama Baptists. He was innovative, an excellent manager, and opened the paper to a variety of opinions. He sought to reach and educate all Baptists, the poorest and most unlearned no less than the wealthiest and best educated. "The sweet little canaries and doves," he once wrote, "do not need the same sauce as the dear old crows and whooping cranes and eagles." Although he was willing to tackle almost any subject in his editorials, Gwaltney squelched controversies involving personalities. His editorials often ran counter to denominational opinion on theology, social concerns, and women but reflected Alabama Baptist culture on race, prohibition, Catholics, the Ku Klux Klan, and separation of church and state. His orthodoxy on these issues provided him a high tolerance level on more divisive subjects.[30]

Several aspects of Gwaltney's life seem strangely contradictory of the well-read, scientifically inclined social reformer. He was a self-described religious mystic who often speculated on humanity's connection to the divine.[31] His mysticism probably resulted from his wife's nervous breakdown and long illness, but it may have been influenced also by his contact with pentecostalism.

On a visit to Florala to solicit a contribution for Judson College, Gwaltney's host took him to a pentecostal meeting. The editor was mesmerized. The tent meeting featured a preacher in his early twenties and a mixed race audience of a hundred and fifty. Though uneducated, the evangelist was earnest and interesting. Gwaltney listened attentively. During the altar call people began to pray and cry loudly, to twitch and jerk. Some rolled in the sawdust. Having recently read a book about the second Great Awakening in Kentucky, it seemed to Gwaltney that similar events were unfolding before his very eyes. As emotions cooled, the preacher asked if any sought healing from disease, and three preachers shouted for healing of a woman who knelt with them. After their prayers, she claimed to be healed. As the service ended, a large mulatto woman accosted him and announced in an agitated voice that she was going to establish a tabernacle of Moses in Florala and become a prophetess. Gwaltney did not fully understand the unusual power that seemed to possess the people that night. Later in Springville, during a period of personal depression, he visited an uneducated cobbler whom he referred to as a Holiness preacher ("I wanted somebody with me who knew the Lord and it mattered not to me what faith he held"). Gwaltney explained his anxiety to the cobbler, and the man seemed possessed by some inexplicable presence. He began to speak in tongues exactly as the patrons of the Florala tent meeting had years earlier. Al-

though Gwaltney could not understand the phenomenon that he witnessed, he believed that New Testament references to speaking in tongues
were related to what he had twice observed in Alabama. Critics would dismiss his observances as religious emotionalism; "but it seems to me that
the emotion itself cannot be explained other than by some influence unknown to most people."[32]

Years later these experiences intruded upon his family. Gwaltney's
wife, Richie, became ill in 1929. The couple had lost two children to death
earlier, which made Richie's long illness even more devastating. After three
months of declining physical and emotional health, she was placed in a
private infirmary where she lived for four years. Physicians told Gwaltney
that she would never recover. He asked both state and national conventions
to pray for her without apparent improvement. One day as he walked down
a Birmingham street, he saw a mission operated by a woman who claimed
to be a faith healer. She had assembled a congregation of twelve or fifteen
women who shared her beliefs. Though skeptical about faith healing, perhaps Gwaltney recalled the Florala tent meeting. After initial hesitation, he
went inside. "I was like a drowning man catching at a straw," he confessed
later. He returned again and again to the storefront mission and knelt with
the women to pray for his wife's recovery. While attending those meetings,
his wife's health began to improve.

His wife's long ordeal wrecked Gwaltney's health. His neurosis prevented him from sleeping and drove him to the edge of nervous breakdown. His physician advised him to give up his work. Gwaltney discussed
his condition with his pastor, James R. Hobbs, who agreed to write editorials while the editor spent three months recuperating with relatives in Virginia. An emergency call informing him of his wife's worsening condition
brought Gwaltney back to Birmingham no better than when he had left. His
doctor refused to prescribe sedatives for fear he would become addicted.
Desperate, Gwaltney obtained help from a druggist friend who recommended a patent nerve medicine that he took for months. Gradually he was
able to sleep again and slowly to recover his health.[33] These private ordeals
were known only to his closest circle of friends, and one hardly detects any
hint of mysticism in decades of editorials or in his seven published books.
Yet, the denomination's premier leader was a complex man.

Less highly celebrated were the steady stream of missionaries who con-
nected a parochial denomination to a larger world of service and ministry.
During the 1920s, seventeen Alabamians were appointed by the Foreign
Mission Board, more than in any decade between Eliza Shuck's initial jour-

ney in 1847 and the 1950s. They sailed for China, Japan, Africa, Mexico, Brazil, and Argentina. Of the twenty-two Alabama missionaries serving on foreign fields in 1930, more than half labored in China.[34]

Missionaries came from a variety of backgrounds, although most were teachers, nurses, and physicians, not preachers. Two-thirds were single or married women. Single women often fared better than men, perhaps because men were married and usually had children. With fewer family distractions and less dependents' health to worry about, single women tended to adapt more quickly to a host country.[35]

In addition to missions, evangelism also united Baptists. L. L. Gwaltney filled the pages of the *Alabama Baptist* with calls for and reports about revivals. City-wide revivals became popular, as did tent or tabernacle meetings conducted by professional evangelists. In April 1920, thirty-four white and twenty-seven black Baptist churches in Birmingham held simultaneous meetings that netted over 1,000 baptisms. In March and April 1926, Tuscaloosa Baptist churches conducted city-wide meetings. Smaller com-

This revival at Fairmount Baptist Church in Red Level during the 1920s combined the new technology of tent meetings and old-time revivalism. (Courtesy of Samford University Archives)

munities favored traditional fall revivals. Total baptisms in 1920 reached
20,000, a figure comparable to some years during the 1980s and 1990s.[36]

The following two years (1921 and 1922) brought a marked decline that
disturbed denominational leaders. Of some 2,000 white Baptist churches,
nearly one-fourth reported not a single addition and another fourth added
less than five. In 1922 total baptisms numbered only 12,500. Gwaltney
blamed the decline on artificial figures for 1920 that had been augmented
by successful Bob Jones revivals in Montgomery and Birmingham. J. C.
Stivender probed deeper to find causes in the shifting sociology of the decade. Sunday work and amusements, automobiles and movies, the popularity of football and professional baseball—all reduced the importance of
church to a community's social life. Businessmen, sports figures, and
movie stars competed with preachers for attention. The fundamentalist-
modernist controversy divided clergy and laity and lessened confidence
in preachers. The growing importance of science, psychology, and history
in public education eroded religious confidence. Preachers were distracted
and spent too little time in prayer and study. Radio and modern advertising compensated for some of these problems by offering unprecedented access to a new audience for religion. Gwaltney, assaying the religious lan-
guor of 1921 and 1922, warned Southern Baptists not to boast of their fervor
to northern Baptists, who despite their alleged modernism were baptizing one person per eleven members while their southern brethren managed
only one baptism for every twelve. Perhaps, he concluded, Southern Baptists would do well to mind their own business and stop meddling in the
theological struggles of their northern compatriots.[37]

The following year, 1924, baptisms jumped to more than 15,000, and
subsequent years brought similarly impressive results. In a June 1927 revival, Cullman First Baptist Church recorded 68 baptisms. Two years later
Mobile First Baptist Church proved that even modernists could be evangelicals when John W. Phillips baptized 43 on an Easter Sunday evening.[38]

Styles of worship and revival changed with the decade. In rapidly
growing urban churches, worship became better organized. At Ruhama,
J. C. Stivender considered music, hymn singing, Scripture reading, prayer,
meditation, and the offering not as "mere preliminaries" to the main event
(the sermon) but as integral to worship. Reverence required a comfortable
physical environment, he believed. Music produced tranquillity and harmony of soul, articulated humanity's deepest aspirations, and reminded
worshipers to seek God beyond themselves. N. O. Patterson penned an essay on the way evangelistic music stirred listeners. A successful revival
song leader should avoid gymnastic stunts and levity, he wrote, and should

coordinate his part of the service with the evangelist. Effective song leaders needed to be psychologists who understood how different songs moved a congregation.[39]

Such careful attention to the psychology of revivals was unusual. Most evangelists took their cues from the secular ballyhoo society all around them. Folksy humor and colloquial language were the order of the day, especially in an era dominated by theatrical evangelists like Billy Sunday and Aimee Semple McPherson.

Baptist evangelist T. O. Reese preached a series of revivals in Mobile early in his career. One of his sermons, "Profit and Loss," contrasted spiritual and material values. He enjoyed recounting how he had once relied on flowery language to convey his message. Pointing to a vase of flowers on the table in front of the pulpit, Reese had declared: "The flowers are God's thought in bloom. . . . Nobody but God could have made and stretched the carpet of green! Nobody but God could have put the color in the petal of these flowers." After the sermon, an elderly lady had approached Reese and informed him: "Brother, I made these flowers. They are artificial." Afterward, Reese went lighter on the flowery imagery, though he continued to adapt to his audiences.[40]

L. L. Gwaltney made few concessions to the times. He explained that when he preached a revival he kept his sermons "free from any clap-trap or sensationalism." Then again, when he preached a revival at Springville in 1920, he had only six conversions.[41]

Whether because of sensational revivals, patient nurturing, rapid urbanization, or demographic changes, born-again people packed into churches. Old buildings bulged with the harvest, forcing congregations to build larger houses of worship. Churches forced to build new sanctuaries included Ruhama, Southside, Hunter Street, Sixty-sixth Street, Central Park, and Ensley in Birmingham; Calvary in Tuscaloosa; and First Baptist churches in Gadsden, Auburn, Dothan, and Opp. Frantic building to keep up with growth saddled churches with heavy debts, dried up Cooperative Program contributions, and often left churches strapped for funds through the Great Depression. Many churches failed to pay off their notes until the postwar prosperity of the 1940s when renewed growth forced them into new building programs and debt.

A profile of the denomination midway through the 1920s reveals both change and continuity. Between 1916 and 1926, the number of Alabama Baptists increased dramatically from 208,000 to 272,000. But the denomination remained overwhelmingly rural, with 1,974 country churches compared to only 109 urban congregations. Although membership was less one-sided (urban congregations enrolled 61,300, rural churches 210,700), Alabama Baptist congregations were a mirror image of their ministers.[42] City churches thrived. Country churches languished.

Industrial churches adjacent to textile mills, coal mines, and iron furnaces grew. At Ensley, a small congregation listened attentively to Jerome F. D'Arpa preach in Italian. "Little Italy," with a thousand Italian families, furnished the new congregation thirty-three professions of faith in the early 1920s. In Sylacauga, Methodist industrialist and former governor B. B. Comer subsidized the pastor's salary at Mignon Baptist Church and paid off the church debt in the 1920s when contributions lagged. His only condition was a troubling one. If the church was ever used for any function other than religion (perhaps as a meeting place for union organizers?), the property would revert to Comer's ownership.[43]

To avoid potential conflicts, the state mission board cooperated with the Home Mission Board to put such congregations on sound financial footing. In 1927 the executive committee of the state mission board supplemented pastors' salaries of cotton mill churches in Opelika and Opp and mining churches in Docena and Dolomite. The following year the executive committee asked the HMB for $5,000 to begin Baptist work in 200 industrial centers that had inadequate church buildings.[44]

Seeking to reach industrial workers stretched middle-class Baptist culture. R. M. Hunter of Mobile approached the problem with an updated and feminized allegory of the rich man and Lazarus. A woman already adorned with diamonds shopped at a jewelry store, carrying a poodle she occasionally kissed. She was glib but frivolous, talking mainly of men and dances. Another woman, plainly dressed and poor, fumbled for money in order to buy groceries. In her arms she carried a thin child. In time, the two women appeared again, the first wearing diamonds while she danced and chased men. The other was leading her little flock to the house of God for prayer, dispensing what food she had to the hungry. Then both died, one alone and unaided by her wealth, the other confident of eternity and beloved by her six children.[45] The moral of the allegory was clear to all who heard it.

A 1922 editorial by Gwaltney in the *Alabama Baptist* explained issues differently. Although Christ came to break down barriers between people, modern society was characterized by walls between classes. A pastor who could combine dissimilar men into a true brotherhood did the "noblest work on . . . earth." But even spiritual rebirth could not obliterate "consciousness of kind." Chinese and Americans might be "brothers in the Lord," but neither desired their children to intermarry, creating "one large mongrel family." "It has been said," Gwaltney concluded, that "the ground

is level at the foot of the cross. Well, perhaps so, but there were slants, in-
clines and declines all around Golgotha, and they might typify the classes
of men that still exist."[46]

A seemingly endless supply of rural people fed the stream of humanity
that crowded into coal camps and mill villages. Farm conditions and crop
prices declined precipitously in 1920, beginning an agricultural depression
that lasted for two decades.

Alabama Baptists had a curious double vision of farm life during the
1920s. They continued to extol life in the country as theoretically superior
to life in cities, but few of them seemed eager to return there. L. L. Gwaltney nostalgically recalled growing up on a Virginia farm; he pronounced
rural churches "the greatest single factor in American civilization." In another editorial he speculated that a majority of Baptist preachers had been
converted in churches pastored by uneducated preachers. Although such
pastors knew no Hebrew or Greek and had no "D" behind their names,
they acquired education in the school of hard knocks and served faithfully
for virtually no pay.[47] But he wrote such editorials in the bustling industrial
city of Birmingham.

From a different vantage point, the rural Eden was blighted by a multitude of modern serpents. Antimission Baptists continued to influence certain "secluded and backwoods rural districts." Remnants of Lardmarkism
survived that periodically loosed attacks on Alabama Baptist boards and
agencies. In remote rural areas, aberrations such as snake handling occurred. Expressions of "the puerile faith of some enthusiast before a morbid
crowd of people who think they have a New Testament faith" were more
evidence of "unbalanced religious enthusiasm" than of fidelity to Scripture.[48]

How to save the country church was a matter of constant discussion.
Rural church specialists insisted that congregations must be consolidated
like rural schools; then they could afford a full-time pastor and provide a
complete program of activities. Unless rural churches provided social centers for youth, young people would continue their exodus from the land.
Gwaltney criticized the sentimentality of rural people who allowed ties
to church cemeteries and tradition to keep them from disbanding dying
churches. Nonresident pastors were another problem. As better roads and
automobiles came to rural Alabama, they not only carried young people to
cities but also allowed bivocational pastors to travel longer distances. By
the 1920s some pastors lived fifty to a hundred miles from their charges.
They seldom attended associational meetings and could not minister to
members of congregations in moments of crisis. At the Unity Association

meeting near Plantersville in 1926, only three or four pastors were present to represent twenty-eight churches. Two-thirds of the pastors were nonresidents, some living a hundred miles from their fields. In the Escambia Association, two country churches closed that same year for lack of a pastor, and two others struggled to stay open despite their inability to find one. Two pastors in the county had to enter secular occupations because they could not support their families by preaching. During 1926, fifty Baptist churches disbanded as rural people left for industrial jobs.[49] Rural church experts wrote articles and books suggesting a variety of solutions that were compatible with Baptist theology and folkways.[50] Most suggestions were ignored, as was the advice of agronomists at land-grant universities who urged crop diversification, cattle dipping to eradicate ticks, fencing to improve livestock quality, and a multitude of other reforms.

Within Alabama, the state mission board strove mightily to resolve rural church problems. The 1922 executive committee investigated how to improve churches near newly consolidated schools. The committee recommended church consolidation and the employment of twelve or more seminarians each summer to evangelize rural communities. In 1927 the board hired a full-time rural field worker to train a new generation of rural church leaders to replace those moving to cities. The newly consolidated department of education and training emphasized rural work. Secretary-treasurer Dent Green organized preachers' schools during January and February, which were slack times in the country. These schools were designed for bivocational ministers. Green furnished participants free books, and WMU leaders conducted schools of missions in conjunction with them.[51] All such efforts were in vain. Despite the organization of many new churches in urban areas, the closing of rural congregations meant that the decade ended with about the same number of churches as when it began (2,085 in 1924; 2,041 in 1930).

However much rural churches might decline, the religious perspectives they bequeathed profoundly affected the denomination. Not only did virtually every preacher of the era extol rural values, but those values shaped the way Alabama Baptists perceived modernity.

Alabama Baptists and Culture

Alabama Baptists generally pronounced the 1920s a wicked decade. They believed that societal trends desecrated the Sabbath, undermined the family, and polluted the morals of youth. "Culture wars," a term widely applied to the 1980s and 1990s, began a good deal earlier.

Youthful rebellion against authority accelerated during the 1920s. Adding to the chaos was a generation of soldiers who had traveled widely and sowed a large crop of wild oats. Augmenting their numbers were rural people moving into town who often severed their relationship with rural churches and sampled urban sins against which they had been warned.

Trying to regulate urban society proved a more formidable challenge than control of rural or small-town community life. In a 1921 sermon, James R. Hobbs endorsed a law requiring businesses to close on Sunday. When Hobbs's sermon was published in the *Alabama Baptist,* it drew a negative response from one reader who insisted that "blue laws" were a violation of the principle of separation of church and state. Morality could be taught but it could not be compelled by law, he wrote. J. J. Taylor (who had returned to Alabama as pastor of Jasper First Baptist Church after being fired for his pacifism by Savannah First Baptist Church) agreed that blue laws sought to do by legislation what Christians should do out of obedience. J. V. Dickinson (one of the trio of iconoclastic Dickinson brothers) backed Taylor. But W. B. Crumpton and L. L. Gwaltney lined up behind Hobbs. Baptist patriarch Crumpton endorsed a 1923 bill in the state legislature to prohibit baseball and movies on Sunday. Gwaltney supported a 1928 Birmingham referendum that banned movies on the holy day.[52]

Gwaltney also began a section in the *Alabama Baptist* entitled "For All in the Family." He recruited Mrs. W. L. Rosamond to edit the section, and she commissioned women to write most of the articles, which focused on family issues. As with Sunday closing laws, Baptists were not of one mind about family conduct. When one essay condemned divorce as immoral, a male reader defended a man's right to divorce a wife who had been sexually unfaithful.[53]

When Dr. C. C. Davison (pastor of Decatur First Baptist Church) spoke to Howard College students in 1924 on "The Home, the Family, and Social Life," he pulled no punches. Parents spent too little time with their children and valued babies less than lap dogs. Women were as bound to fashion as "ignorant Chinese [women] with their bound feet." Sex dominated movies, plays, and literature, all of which were responsible for the skyrocketing divorce rate. The auto was a "menace to morals." Prostitution thrived in Alabama cities, and returning soldiers spread venereal disease among civilians. Another cause of the nation's moral collapse, he proclaimed, was "cigarette smoking, cock-tail drinking, pug dog nursing, half-dressed, painted woman with her 'C' collar and her 'V' back." One man, viewing such a "flapper," asked a friend, "doesn't the Bible say that when Adam and

Eve ate the apple they knew they were naked?" "Yes," his acquaintance replied. "Then," said the questioner, "it's time to pass the apples again."[54]

Although Davison's sermon must have elicited guffaws of laughter from Howard students, prostitution and sexual assault were no laughing matter. After an attempt to eliminate prostitution in Birmingham failed in 1921, a new effort began two years later when an anonymous man spoke to the Cosmopolitan Bible Class at First Baptist Church. He claimed that prostitution was worse in the steel city than in any of the 116 American cities he had studied. His charges that city officials were afraid to clean up the city drew furious denials but also provoked reform efforts.[55]

James E. Dillard explored a similar subject in a 1921 sermon before his Southside congregation. He called the rape/murder charges against movie star Fatty Arbuckle the "nastiest page in American social history." He believed the case typified Hollywood values and public taste in heroes. The United States was following the path of ancient civilizations to ruin. No woman who "smokes, drinks, swears, goes half naked, goes mid-night joy riding . . . is decent, much less moral," he stormed. Women did have as much right to engage in such conduct as men, he acknowledged, but men should be held to the same moral standards.[56]

Modern music and dance were other sources of temptation. In 1921 Gwaltney devoted an entire page of the denominational paper to the evils of modern dance. The president of Howard College reassured anxious Baptists that there would be no dancing on his campus. As for the new jazz music that was all the rage, Gwaltney dismissed it as an example of barbarism in American culture.[57]

Nor was sport exempt from criticism. Gwaltney denounced the legalization of boxing in Alabama and criticized the state's overemphasis on collegiate sports. He defended his friend Spright Dowell, president of Auburn University, whose football team did poorly when the president demanded that it conform to high ethical standards and obey the rules. Dowell was an active member of Auburn First Baptist Church and a member of the budget committee of the state convention. When Auburn alumni tried to fire the president in 1924, the convention's executive committee passed a resolution of confidence in Dowell's administration and urged the "real friends of education in Alabama" to come to his aid. They sent copies of the resolution to the Auburn board of trustees. But the school's won-loss record in football counted for more than Baptist sentiment, and the board sent Dowell packing. Years later Gwaltney contrasted Christian higher education, which valued academic standards more than the record of athletic teams, to state universities, which fired presidents in order to improve the records of their football teams.[58]

Christianity for a New Age

Despite rigid adherence to traditional standards of personal morality, Alabama Baptists could not resist some allurements of the new age. Nor did they consider all such changes bad.

The spirit of boosterism that characterized secular southern culture permeated religious life as well. Although urban ministers and business elites sometimes clashed over blue laws, their objectives usually coincided. Both groups sought economic growth, civic pride, and political tranquillity. Both endorsed conservative values. In 1923 Notasulga First Baptist Church hosted the town's preachers, teachers, and public officials for the purpose of beginning a cooperative effort to improve the town. The church modernized its procedures by appointing a committee to confer when a pastor was called or dismissed. The church also participated in a Christmas union service at the Methodist church, where the Disciples of Christ pastor preached. As University of Alabama's journalism professor Clarence Cason observed, any slackening of religious ardor in Alabama during the 1920s was "compensated by a concourse of ministers around the festive noon-tide board of Kiwanis. Mohammed has gone to the mountain."[59]

If going to the mountain meant endorsing the South's new economic patterns, then Baptists made many trips. Though all the while denying that his paper was political, L. L. Gwaltney regularly promoted modernizing Alabama's economy. He endorsed bond issues for the improved roads essential to a modern economy. He urged state officials to seek federal funds ("If Alabama does not go in favor of the issue, the federal pie will go elsewhere"). He urged tax increases for public schools. He advised farmers to join the American Cotton Association and the Alabama Farm Bureau. Gwaltney praised public health reforms and cooperated with the state health officer. He urged Baptist associations to allow state health officials to speak at their meetings because "good health and practical religion are closely related." In 1922 Dr. Carey P. McCord spoke to the Howard College commencement about public health, deploring the state's infant mortality rate and crippling childhood diseases. God had placed solutions in the hands of scientists, but a passive, traditional, ignorant public ignored health problems. Gwaltney published McCord's address and urged Baptists to support a statewide system of preventive medicine.[60]

At the same time that many Baptists endorsed the modernization of education, health, and the economy, they were ambivalent about technology. R. M. Hunter of Mobile feared that the same machines that were the key to the nation's industrial and financial vitality undermined its culture and religion. On the positive side, machines created leisure and made education, banking, and corporate life more efficient. On the negative side, they displaced millions of workers, brought people into anonymous cities, broke up homes, created strife between labor and management, and sowed seeds of bolshevism. Christianity could adapt to the new technology but not without disruption.[61]

No aspect of modernity seemed to threaten Alabama Baptists more than liberated women. Hence the frequent polemics against "painted" women who smoked, drank, danced, caroused, and were slaves to fashion. Woman suffrage, though bitterly contested by Baptists for a generation as a violation of Scripture, passed from the scene of controversy with barely a whimper. T. M. Fleming (pastor of Sylacauga First Baptist Church) preached a sermon just before the November 1920 general election, reminding women of their civic duty. He believed that much good would result from woman suffrage if women did not become so obsessed with politics that they neglected home and church. Gwaltney, long a supporter of women's right to vote, agreed. He recalled that militant suffragists in the United Kingdom and the United States had been ridiculed; yet their militancy, determination, and earnestness had kept the issue before the public until women won. The question before society was how women would use the ballot. He predicted that a decade or two of women's political power would improve the quality of national life.[62]

Gwaltney's confidence in women's capacity to utilize political power for their good depended on their willingness to impose what he believed to be salutary feminine values on rebellious men. He believed women would vote to end prostitution and Sunday desecration and in favor of prohibition, public health, and education. W. B. Crumpton urged women to organize into leagues that would vote only for men who promised to enforce prohibition laws. He also urged them to vote the national Democratic ticket, which favored the League of Nations. R. M. Hunter urged Protestant women to register in order to counter Catholic women. Although he believed that many "refined Southern women revolt at the thought of going to the polls and mingling with coarse men," new political conditions required such action. Many women worked for salaries, no longer depending on fathers or husbands. They must therefore vote to save the home and balance the "tide of ignorant emigration."[63]

Gwaltney was the most outspoken Baptist male on women's rights. Although he later concluded that woman suffrage had failed to improve the nation's moral climate, he remained convinced that women deserved fair treatment. He denied that flapper fads and fashion meant "an utter loss of morals," as many commentators wrote. To admonitions that women be silent in church and ask their husbands privately when they had questions, he responded that such advice ignored the fact that women generally knew more about the work of the kingdom of God than their husbands did. Perhaps men should remain silent and when they returned home from church ask their wives questions. There would be no "free and redeemed race of men," he wrote, "without a free and redeemed race of women." In 1927 Gwaltney told a receptive audience of two hundred female students at Judson College that neither ecclesiastical nor political rights for women had come easily. Susan B. Anthony and other "militant suffragists" had been ridiculed as "suffragettes" by contemptuous males. But thanks to their efforts, 122 women then served in state legislatures, several had been governors, and many had become lawyers, physicians, and bankers.[64]

In a 1929 editorial Gwaltney noted that Montana Baptists had ordained a woman to preach. Whether or not this was a proper decision, he declined to say. But he did point out that at one time Baptists refused to allow women to speak to mixed assemblies, sing solos in church, or serve as messengers to associational, state, and national conventions. By 1929 women did all these things with hardly a whimper of opposition. Except for women, little mission work would occur. Perhaps in time, he predicted, women would preach as well.[65]

In his lecture notes on pastoral theology (a course Gwaltney sometimes taught at Howard College), he was even more specific. Arguing for an active role for women in the church, he dealt with Paul's admonition to Corinthian women that they be subordinate to men, cover their heads, and keep silent in church. Such advice, he told ministerial students, was "no doubt due to the customs of [Paul's] day." The practical question was how Paul's advice pertained to modern society. Christians disagreed on the answer. More Baptists in the South adhered to his literal prohibition than they did in other regions. Other portions of Paul's teachings depicted women in active ways. "Besides," Gwaltney concluded, "it can be shown without a shadow of a doubt that there were deaconesses in the early church. Whatever her position was in the early church, her value to the cause now cannot be overstated."[66]

Elsewhere within the denomination, male opinions were changing. While preaching a revival at Auburn First Baptist Church, J. E. Dillard was given a book to read by the host pastor, J. R. Edwards. The new book by Madeline Southard, entitled *The Attitude of Jesus Toward Women*, emphasized the liberating nature of Jesus' ministry to women compared to prevailing customs. Dillard praised the book in his weekly *Alabama Baptist* column as a thoroughly satisfying discussion of the subject.[67]

Although it was helpful to have male allies who were being won over, the major responsibility for changing the way Baptists viewed women remained with WMU. Though WMU members represented a small percentage of all Alabama Baptist women (30,000 of 145,800 total female church members in 1926), in many ways they shaped the entire denomination.[68]

In 1921 WMU relocated its national headquarters from Baltimore to Birmingham. The move (partly initiated by Jessie Stakely of Montgomery) brought one of the state's most remarkable women, Kathleen Mallory, back home. Pleasant and accommodating in her formal relations with men, Mallory was privately a tenacious advocate of women's work within the denomination. In 1924 she wrote the director of Alabama WMU that the new Cooperative Program pledge cards made no provision for identifying gifts from members of the organization. Consequently, the money would not flow through WMU channels where it would help fund the organization's causes and expenses. "You know that people will promise to do a lot of things with our money before they get it," she wrote skeptically, "and I am ever so anxious for us to train our church treasurers to see the justice of keeping careful records of W.M.U. gifts." Mallory also lobbied the SBC to appoint women to the executive committee and all convention boards. Gwaltney endorsed this request and voted for it at the 1922 Southern Baptist Convention, although the motion failed.[69]

Once WMU headquarters moved to Birmingham, there was close cooperation between staffs of state and national agencies. Juliette Mather, the young people's secretary for WMU/SBC, became a friend and advocate of Hannah E. Reynolds, Alabama WMU college correspondent. Mather urged the state organization to send Reynolds to the interdenominational Student Volunteer Movement national convention where she could meet students from throughout the world and learn more about foreign missions. That same year, Mather joked that she heard the head of the Home Mission Board preach in Birmingham and tell one of Reynolds's stories. "I almost wanted to sue him for plagiarism," Mather wrote her friend, "but he did it so poorly compared to your finished way that I let it pass."[70]

Ida M. Stallworth, secretary of Alabama WMU, proposed that Mallory teach Howard College ministerial students a course in WMU methods. One of the serious hindrances to state work, she wrote Mallory, was uncooperative pastors. She had persuaded Howard's president to endorse the idea, and Mallory enthusiastically accepted.[71]

The function of Alabama WMU belies the controversy it caused. As an auxiliary of the convention, its tasks were to educate children about missions, enlist women in active soul winning, and cooperate in missionary, benevolent, and educational work. To accomplish these tasks, the organization had a staff during the 1920s that consisted of a secretary-treasurer, young people's secretary/college correspondent, and recording secretary. WMU divided Alabama into five geographical districts, each with a counselor. The annual WMU convention elected a president, vice-president, and fifteen-member executive board. Presidents tended to be wives of influential men (Jessie Stakely, 1912–1920, was married to the pastor of Montgomery First Baptist Church; Kate Samford, 1920–1926, to a judge of the state court of appeals; Alma Worrill Wright, 1926–1931, to a wealthy Roanoke banker). Some were also distinguished clubwomen and popular speakers. Alma Wright spoke at six annual WMU conventions in as many states, headed the national "ruby anniversary" celebration, and was regarded as one of the organization's best state presidents.[72]

The organization was blessed with a succession of gifted secretaries following Mallory's ascension to higher office. When Mary Northington resigned in 1923, Ida M. Stallworth replaced her. Born in Missouri and the daughter of a minister, Stallworth attended the WMU Training School in Louisville and afterward taught school and served as principal in Cuba, Alabama. After her husband and only child died, she accepted the job of state secretary, where she served for many years.[73]

State leaders were not timid in asking for full participation in denominational life. In 1929 they asked the executive committee to allow six members elected by WMU to serve as members of the governing board. After much debate, the matter was referred to a three-man committee. It turned down the proposal, arguing that members of the executive committee could only be elected by the state convention. It did welcome a WMU committee to discuss policies with the mission board.[74]

Women drove a hard bargain because they controlled the denomination's purse strings. When a WMU member reported how much WMU women had pledged to the Seventy-Five Million Dollar Campaign at the 1920 state convention, a startled minister responded that women were far more faithful to the church than men, who were too preoccupied with materialism. In 1925, WMU women raised $128,000 for missions; in 1927, $173,000; and in the ruby anniversary year of 1928, a phenomenal $253,000. In 1926, 30,000 WMU women contributed nearly as much as the other 240,000 Alabama Baptists combined. In 1929 they contributed $3,000 more than all their fellow Baptists.[75]

WMU used the money for a variety of causes. It furnished Alabama

Irene Jeffers (third adult from left) was one of several Alabama Baptist women missionaries who described her ministry in China as "preaching." Here she is preaching in the streets of the Chinese village of Tien Tsang. (Courtesy of Wayne Flynt and Gerald W. Berkley)

women scholarships to Judson and Howard Colleges, Newton institute, the mountain academies, and the WMU Training School. By 1921 forty women studied at the training school alone. Many of the scholarships went to orphans, girls living with widowed mothers, or women from poor families. Often scholarship holders became missionaries, as in the case of Clarabell Isdell from Sand Mountain, who went to China. Nor were Alabama women forgotten when they arrived at such remote stations. In 1928 the Alabama WMU raised $600 to buy a car for Addie Cox in China.[76]

Missionaries spoke at every state WMU convention, renewing contacts and generating interest in Baptist work abroad. Dr. T. W. Ayers, Addie Cox, and Willie Kelly were favorites. Sometimes such speakers opened new vistas. On foreign fields, cultural barriers for women were flexible, and many single women preached without apology. In 1924 Alice Huey (a native Alabamian and single missionary to China) described a ten-day itinerary

through her province during which she "taught and preached to crowds."
Three women accepted her invitation to learn of Christ. Speaking after
Huey, Kathleen Mallory noted that Jesus had commended the work of
women because they were "crazy enough to enlist ahead of men."[77]

Missions included more than service in foreign lands. WMU women
also pioneered social ministries in Alabama. They continued to serve as
directors of settlement houses at Ensley and Pratt City. Workers at such
facilities frequently reported on their work at state WMU conventions. Although organized under the personal service committee of WMU, social work assumed a basic tenet of the social gospel: salvation was designed
to be both personal and societal. Alma Wright provided a rationale for
such work in her 1927 presidential address. The kingdom of God was not
in heaven, she explained, but on earth. God's will must be performed in
Africa, China, Japan, India, and America. The United States contained 5.5
million illiterates and millions of immigrants who needed to hear the gospel. Jesus had not only saved men's souls, he had saved their lives as well.
The report of the personal service committee that year announced that sixteen WMUs had interracial committees; 139 WMU members had volunteered to work at settlement houses; 165 had worked with immigrants and
122 with African Americans. Such social ministries paled in comparison to
traditional ministries (16,314 gave clothes to the poor, 40,593 visited shut-
ins, and 488 visited prisoners). Some 1,700 women reported that they attended cottage prayer meetings while only 83 volunteered to work at industrial schools and 10 in free kindergartens.[78] Nonetheless, WMU women
persistently held a vision of social service before a denomination not renowned for such concerns.

Not all women chose to serve through WMU. One of the most important personnel decisions during the decade came in 1925 when the executive board hired Lucille Loyd to head work with Baptist college students.
She became the only woman student secretary in the South. Loyd descended from a prominent Texas family and had attended Southern Methodist
University, Rice, and Southwestern seminary. She had worked as a Baptist
Student Union assistant secretary in Texas and took over the job of secretary when her boss, J. P. Boone, left to become pastor of Tuscaloosa First
Baptist Church. It was Boone who recommended her in 1925, calling her
the best-qualified student secretary he knew. He convinced the Alabama
committee, which after her interview unanimously selected Loyd for the
job. Her letters of recommendation said she was a woman who had "sound
judgment, great prudence, and unusual gifts" and who was wonderful at
meeting, mixing with, and winning students. One deacon from a church

Even Baptist Student Union members could
be "flappers." This photograph shows coed
Sue Marsh in a fashionable 1920s dress made
of Baptist Student Union magazines. Marsh
was typical of enthusiasm generated by Alabama's BSU director, Lucille Loyd, the only
woman BSU director in the South. (Courtesy
of Samford University Archives)

in Louisiana wrote that as a platform speaker she was "a positive inspiration."[79]

Loyd's performance matched her recommendations. She organized a statewide Baptist student organization and recruited students from every white campus in the state. She taught a course on BSU work at Howard and spoke untiringly on college campuses, to women's missionary societies, and to women's clubs. Even revivalists in college towns invited her to speak. She endeared herself to students by defending flappers against negative stereotypes, and she argued that students in the 1920s were both academically serious and spiritually sensitive. She also believed that women's roles in world affairs would continue to expand. When the executive board consolidated BSU, Sunday school, and BYPU (Baptist Young People's Union) work in 1930 to save money, Loyd resigned to marry a Standard Oil official and returned to Texas.[80]

Other women carved out their own spheres of service. When W. P. Wilks compiled a biographical dictionary of Alabama Baptists in 1948, he profiled 768 males and 172 females (twenty-six of them missionaries). Thirty of the women were single, thirty-four were involved in community missions, twelve belonged to federated women's clubs, and fifty-four belonged to literary clubs. Thirteen worked for a salary. Twenty-eight attended Judson, fourteen attended Howard, and eighty-three attended other colleges. Thirty-three had attended the WMU Training School in Louisville. Twelve belonged to the United Daughters of the Confederacy, nine to the Daughters of the American Revolution and the WCTU, and seven to the YWCA.[81]

Women's lives shattered many stereotypes about Alabama Baptist females. Mollie E. Sanders served as superintendent of Pike County schools and vice-president of the county superintendents' organization and Alabama Education Association. She was also president of the Salem-Troy Baptist Association WMU. Mrs. Elmer M. Clanahan, who held a master's degree from Columbia University, directed a university nursery school and served as professor of home economics and president of the state Business and Professional Women's Club. Will Ella Hendon was a popular speaker at school commencements and civic clubs and also taught a men's Sunday school class with 120 members. She was president of the Eufaula Federated Women's Club and the Coffee County Board of Welfare. Irene Alice Ward, who held degrees from Rice University and Andover Newton Theological Seminary, chaired community missions for the state WMU, taught in a nursery school, and conducted surveys for PTA.[82] With or without the support of men, Alabama Baptist women charted a new course during the 1920s, one with far-reaching consequences.

Social Christianity

The social activism of women was part of a larger movement of social Christianity. Though less pronounced than in the two previous decades, this tradition lived on in Alabama Baptist life. There were fewer debates about the proper balance between Christianity and society during the decade, reflecting a consensus that suited Alabama Baptists. Virtually everyone seemed to agree that individual conversion was the primary task of the church. If Baptists perceived the social gospel to emphasize social change over evangelism, they nearly always opposed it. But there was also a broad consensus that Christianity must be applied to society. Historically, such belief found expression through private charity and some institutional work (orphanages, hospitals, prison ministries). But Alabama Baptists expanded their vision beyond traditional boundaries, consolidating and advancing work begun after 1900.

During the 1920s, L. L. Gwaltney assumed the mantle of A. J. Dickinson and other partisans of the social gospel, but he more clearly delineated the issues. Gwaltney believed that only spiritual rebirth permanently changed people or cured the ills of society. But he also denied that social and conversionist Christianity were in conflict with one another. Spiritually reborn people would always be essential to social progress: "It is worse than stupid to indicate that these men, both with their own denominational group and in spiritual cooperation with men of other faiths, should not bring their Christian influence to bear on all social ills of this age." He respected "flaming evangels" who preached repentance, but he valued just as highly those who trained converts to oppose fraud, oppression of the weak, unjust laws, and spiritual wickedness in political life. The task of training disciples to high ethical standards was a harder job than conversion. Nor was this radical theology: Christ himself taught humanity to apply biblical teachings to society's problems.[83]

In his course on pastoral theology at Howard College, Gwaltney told ministerial students to study anthropology and sociology because the Bible "must be transfused into the man." Ministers had two important messages—conversion and service to humanity. Some objected to a social message from the pulpit, but such critics either believed that religion concerned another world or selfishly feared that application of Christ's teachings to society would interfere with "their [material] gains or sinful pleasures." Ministers should mingle with ordinary people as well as the wealthy and fashionable. They needed to study labor-management conflicts and become acquainted with laboring people. The church had largely abrogated its responsibility for the poor to the state and must ensure that government fed and housed them adequately. He particularly endorsed institutional churches that stayed open every day of the year and provided communities with gymnasiums, reading rooms, and schools of science and fine arts.[84]

In a memoir written much later in life, Gwaltney still believed that the alleged conflict between social and personal Christianity was contrived. If a preacher followed the teachings of John the Baptist, he would tell sinners to repent, and he would preach against the social sins of his times. He would tell armies to stop fighting, reform taxes, and enter politics on behalf of justice.[85]

The institutional expression of these issues through the convention's committee on social service generally followed the conservative agenda of the SBC social service commission. Following the liberal chairmanship of North Carolinian William L. Poteat, the SBC agency came under the direction of Arthur J. Barton. Barton defined social Christianity narrowly to include personal moral questions such as divorce, alcohol use, Boy Scouts, and dancing. Taking its cue from the South-wide effort, the annual Alabama committee report also emphasized divorce, lewd literature, lynching, and prohibition. But it added other components as well. The 1928 report, for example, included a section on labor-capital relations that stressed the need for mutual justice across barriers of class, race, and religion. It also contained a strong statement on world peace that affirmed the right of citizens to know which commercial interests profited from armaments manufacture and war. Peace would become a reality only when small nations controlled their own affairs and when these affairs were controlled by Christians "thinking peace and contemplating justice, and abhorring oppression and greed and nationalistic aspirations and militarism and bloodshed under whatever pretext." The three-man Alabama committee, headed by Howard College English professor Percy P. Burns and including H. J. Willingham and H. Ross Arnold, defined social Christianity much more broadly than its SBC equivalent.[86]

Implementation of social Christianity took two forms, one consisting of traditional organized charity, the other more daring. James R. Hobbs, Charles Stakely, and H. J. Willingham served on committees that recommended establishment of a Baptist hospital. After much debate over its location, the facility was opened in Selma in 1922. The institution actually consisted of two facilities, the Good Samaritan Hospital for blacks and the Alabama Baptist Hospital for whites. That same year, Birmingham Baptist Association bought an infirmary, the beginning of Birmingham Baptist Health System. Much of the medical work at Selma, especially for poor whites and African Americans, was done for free. Unfortunately, declining contributions soon curtailed charity work.[87]

The Baptist orphanage at Troy obtained a new superintendent in 1923, James O. Colley, a native of Coosa County. An experienced pastor with degrees from Howard College and Southern seminary, Colley brought an enlightened view of child welfare to the position. The previous superintendent had refused to send students to public schools or cooperate with the new state child welfare department. Colley became an active member of the newly created State Conference on Social Work (the new name for the older Alabama Sociological Conference, which had been the spearhead of social reform between 1900 and 1920). He served on its executive committee and developed a close professional relationship with the new state child welfare department, not a difficult task because many of the agency's female administrators were Baptists.[88]

Concern about immigration and urbanization also prodded Alabama Baptists to move beyond traditional social concerns. The tidal wave of immigration that had briefly abated during the war swept across American shores again in 1919. So did a wave of labor unrest and political radicalism. These events created particular concerns in Alabama, which was affected by industrialization and immigration more than other southern states.

Birmingham was the focus of ethnic ministries. Centered in the WMU-operated Good Will Centers at Ensley and Pratt City, the work involved mainly Italians. During 1927 the centers were open for 238 days with an average daily attendance of 33. WMU volunteers from seventeen churches conducted sewing and English classes, taught handicrafts and shop, distributed clothes, and aided families with medical problems. In 1925 Mary Strange, a graduate of the WMU Training School, came to supervise the work at Pratt City. Working with two Italian pastors, J. F. D'Arpa and Arcangelo Pucciarelli, she enrolled more than 100 Italian children in her various social programs by 1928. She helped Pucciarelli with 1929 revivals in Cardiff that resulted in fourteen conversions and creation of a new mission. By 1930 Pucciarelli preached to an average of 160 each week at the Good Will Center, most of them Italians.[89]

Association with working people modified middle-class Baptist assumptions. The views of L. L. Gwaltney represented quite a departure from traditional union bashing. Gwaltney believed that the battle for industrial democracy and collective bargaining was merely an aspect of the struggle for religious freedom transferred into the economic arena. Building upon his long advocacy of child labor reform, Gwaltney broadened his commentary during the strike-prone years 1920–1921. Writing about efforts of 300 Birmingham teachers to join the American Federation of Teachers, he sympathized that they earned less than chauffeurs who sometimes delivered children to their schools. As regrettable as such unions might be, all classes had the right to earn a living wage, none more than teachers in public schools. He defended AFL (American Federation of Labor) efforts to run men for office as similar to the strategy of the Prohibition Party.[90]

Summarizing a wave of bloody strikes in 1920, Gwaltney traced the central issue to the right of collective bargaining. Sooner or later, he predicted, even Birmingham industries would recognize the right of workers to unionize. But he believed that nothing justified the "Bolshevik" violence of the area's striking coal miners. In a century, he predicted, there would be no millionaires because of the labor movement, the success of socialism, and growing belief in the desirability of equal distribution of wealth. When an angry reader chided Gwaltney for sanctioning labor radicalism and the destruction of private property, the editor responded that though labor could be as despotic as capital, he believed workers would ultimately win "the irrepressible struggle." The kingdom of God, he wrote during the 1921 steel strike, had implications for the church as well as for the entire social order. Corporations had the right to hire whom they chose, but laborers should have the right to elect representatives to bargain for them. If the church took either side in a strike, he wrote with resignation in 1926, the other side would condemn it. And if it took neither side, both would attack it.[91]

Convict labor presented a simpler issue. Abuses of convicts had become so widespread and well publicized by the 1920s that Baptists throughout the state demanded that the convict lease system be ended. During a fierce legislative debate over retaining leasing in 1923, Baptists lined up with reformers. Rev. W. E. Lockler denounced the system as similar to slavery. N. K. Murdock, a member of the Alabama Committee to Abolish Convict Leasing, wrote in the *Alabama Baptist* that the central principle of the system was to make money for the state, not to reform convicts. Theologically conservative pastor R. M. Hunter of Mobile recounted various atrocities in Alabama coal mines and west Florida lumber camps as well as one he personally witnessed while pastor at Enterprise. He had concluded that "slavery was heaven compared to the seething hells maintained by the state under the contract leasing system." Gwaltney condemned convict leasing as iniquitous, describing the leather straps used to beat convicts and the graves of convicts killed in coal mine accidents. Alabama must not be content to be the only remaining state to perpetuate such an inhuman system: "The thing is wrong and it ought to go."[92]

Despite such agitation, the Alabama legislature continued leasing convicts until 1926, when Bibb Graves ran for governor partly on a promise to abolish it. Gwaltney applauded Graves's stand and urged the new governor to act quickly. This sense of urgency resulted from yet another scandal, this one involving the killing of James Knox, a white convict who had been convicted for forging a thirty-dollar check. His death in 1924 at Flat Top Mines in Jefferson County at first was reported as a suicide. Further investigation by Attorney General Harwell G. Davis revealed that Knox had been killed by guards who beat him, then dunked him in a pot of scalding water. Davis was an active Baptist layman and a member of the convention's executive committee. His report polarized the state and created impetus for the final abolition of the convict lease system in 1928. L. L. Gwaltney wrote that Davis's revelations about "unspeakable, inhuman, and damnable treatment" of James Knox provided the final evidence that the "whole convict lease system was eternally wrong."[93]

Gwaltney became equally exercised about the injustice of capital punishment. Throughout his career, Gwaltney maintained that the New Testament clearly taught that taking life was wrong. Capital punishment, Gwaltney believed, was a Mosaic law but not a Christian concept. It belonged to "a tribal and crude stage of civilization" now outgrown. Rates of murder and lynching were higher in states such as Alabama that retained capital punishment than in states that abolished it.[94] Unlike abolishing the convict lease system, Baptists were deeply divided on this issue. Gwaltney's editorials against capital punishment nearly always drew immediate responses from Baptists (especially laymen) who cited Scripture in its defense. Gwaltney published an article in 1925 by state evangelist A. V. Reese in favor of the death sentence. Other ministers, notably Jasper's J. J. Taylor, came to Gwaltney's defense.[95]

War was closely related to capital punishment and depended upon the same scriptural arguments. If capital punishment snuffed out lives one at a time, war did so by the millions. The killing fields of France and postwar revelations of Allied cynicism and avarice fueled the debate. Although occasionally a layman denounced the League of Nations as a violation of American sovereignty, most public comment praised Woodrow Wilson and his dream of international arbitration of disputes. J. J. Taylor of Jasper First Baptist Church even denounced Baptist colleges that allowed ROTC (Reserve Officers' Training Corps) units to train students for war. L. L. Gwaltney, consistent with his views on capital punishment, endorsed the League of Nations, praised disarmament, and called war "eternally wrong." "Dogs fight," he mused, but "men ought to know better." It was useless to talk about the brotherhood of man, he wrote in 1921, until disarmament ended the prospect of war. That year's state convention at Troy expressed its concern at the failure of the Washington naval conference to abolish major armaments. In 1929 Gwaltney praised Mohandas K. Gandhi's campaign of passive disobedience against British imperialism. Gandhi, he wrote, was to Hinduism what Francis of Assisi and Leo Tolstoy were to Christianity.[96]

The Battle for the Bible: Round Two

Even more reflective of changing times was the debate raging over the Bible. After nearly half a century of festering, the boil of theological conflict finally burst, infecting all it touched.

Historians have only recently arrived at a balanced account of the fundamentalist-modernist confrontation.[97] Although some trace it to dispensational premillennialism, others find its origins more in societal tension and conflict. All agree that the decade of the 1920s was critical both theologically and politically in politicizing conservative religion. During the years from 1900 to 1920, conservative churches mobilized politically to achieve prohibition. They enlarged their agenda during the 1920s to include Bible reading and antievolution science in public schools. In 1900 virtually all American Protestants were evangelicals. By the 1920s, they were split between liberals and fundamentalists, with the term "fundamentalist" generally equivalent to the later term "conservative evangelical." Fundamentalists used attacks on evolution to gain attention and drive liberals out of their denominations. But their strident tactics alienated more inclusive evangelicals who were willing to live inside a larger Christian tent without strict creeds and with some freedom of thought. Fundamentalists were perceived, even by many tolerant conservatives, as unscientific, anti-intellectual, mean spirited, and socially callous. Retreating from center stage after the 1925 Scopes trial in Dayton, Tennessee, extreme fundamentalists tended to be the ones leaving denominations to form their own subculture. By the 1930s most American evangelicals were suspended between fundamentalism and modernism, dissatisfied with some elements of both.[98]

The evolution controversy and the broader battle over science and the Bible were equally complex. Some historians interpret the conflict as a crusade by fundamentalists to establish their religious views in public schools and subvert the First Amendment. Others emphasize the episode as a struggle between antielitist folk science (charismatic, combative, robust, and rooted in popular culture) and scientific professionals (sophisticated, rational, tolerant, and rooted in universities). Scientific creationists and evolutionists could be equally contentious, exclusive, and patronizing. Both groups understood that science could threaten religion, but Christian scientists and their allies accepted, adapted, and reconciled science to the Bible, while scientific creationists rejected evolution. Professional scientists, even Christian ones, belonged to a professional elite that used scientific language and truth in such a way as to convey "status only to the initiated," which prompted a vigorous, anti-intellectual response from those outside the academic circle.[99]

As in so many other 1920s Baptist hurricanes, Gwaltney was the eye of the storm. Tranquilly confident of his own scientific and biblical understanding, he wrote furiously while storms raged all round him. Although Gwaltney never attempted a systematic theology, he believed that change was inevitable and that Christian leaders must adapt God's revelation to new circumstances. Amid the 1925 Scopes trial, he ridiculed "old-time religion" for opposing missions in the 1830s, organization of the WMU in the 1870s and 1880s, and prohibitionists for entering politics. Throughout the fundamentalist-modernist controversy, he tried to steer a middle course, affirming traditional Baptist beliefs about the virgin birth, miracles, resurrection, second coming, and authority of Scripture without subscribing to creeds or condemning those who disagreed with him. His knowledge of church history convinced him that if Baptists could maintain denominational unity through the 1920s, the storm would subside and the polarization end. His appreciation of science, evolution, and freedom of inquiry largely protected the state convention from the divisions that occurred elsewhere and allowed a spirit of free inquiry to continue generally untrampled throughout the decade. James E. Dillard, Gwaltney's good friend who pastored Southside Baptist Church and reviewed books for the *Alabama Baptist,* lent his influence to the cause as well.[100]

Threats to Baptist beliefs seemed to come from every direction. Laity and clergy were divided both on Bible reading in public schools and on evolution. The 1924 Alabama legislature considered a bill requiring Bible reading in public school classrooms. Both R. H. Hunter of Mobile and Roy Naigler of Samson endorsed the bill. L. E. Barton (pastor in Andalusia),

Gwaltney, and J. J. Taylor vigorously opposed it as a violation of church-state separation. If the legislature compelled Bible reading, Taylor wondered, what version would it mandate, which passages would be read, and could teachers comment on what they read?[101]

Alabama Baptists divided even more deeply over evolution. An impressive galaxy of preachers enlisted in the antievolution army, including such influential conservatives as J. J. Taylor and R. M. Hunter. Gwaltney opened the pages of the *Alabama Baptist* to all of them. M. K. Thornton explained simply in 1922 that the Genesis account of creation resolved the dispute. G. B. F. Stovall agreed. Evolution could not be reconciled to the six-day creation account. Stovall found ministerial attacks on scientists and scientific criticism of preachers mutually unsavory and urged both sides to compromise. W. B. Crumpton joined the fray, denouncing the teaching of evolution in public schools. J. B. Hamic was most emphatic of all critics, decrying textbook references to evolution and evolutionist teachers both in rural schools and in denominational colleges. As a pastor, he could not ask rural Baptists to contribute their money for Christian colleges that taught "soul-destroying hypotheses [and] theories" that "nullify the Holy Word of God." Part of his animosity resulted from the harm done his own son by evolutionary biological theories.[102]

R. M. Hunter (pastor of Northside Baptist Church in Mobile) blamed evolution for everything from falling church attendance to the indifference of church members, declining contributions, the irreverence of youth, divorce, and free love. To him, youth seemed to think that if they descended from monkeys they might as well act like it. His witty pamphlet on evolution contended that Darwinism denied the Bible, infected students and faculty with infidelity, and filled pulpits with skeptics. No evolutionist could be a soul winner, he wrote. His satire perfectly captured the folk science of ordinary Alabama Baptists:

> I have heard the frogs sing, but not having the spirit of the frog, I could not interpret their songs. However, my great ancestors, who once were frogs, no doubt sang in spiritual concert with them; and the tree frog sang tenor, the toad soprano, and the big bullfrog bass profundo; and later developments made the monkey, who was the preacher of the dismal swamp settlement. . . .
>
> I had rather be a humble Christian sitting at the foot of the cross than a learned philosopher sitting on a frog stool in a dismal swamp and conversing with some imaginary God. I had rather commune with the Holy Spirit than with a Darwin, or a Huxly [*sic*], or an Ingersol.[103]

J. J. Taylor was less humorous but no less earnest. Taylor almost perfectly fits historian George Marsden's profile of the fundamentalist pilgrimage. During the war, Taylor had been a pacifist. Afterward, he denounced the SBC for becoming too political about prohibition, divorce, and the League of Nations instead of focusing entirely on spiritual matters. But by 1923 he was fully engaged in a political crusade of his own to rid public schools and denominational colleges of evolutionary science and modernistic theology. He traced the three shoots of heretical theological modernism, evolutionary science, and militarism to the same German root. When W. O. Carver (professor of missions at Southern seminary) wrote a critical review of Taylor's widely distributed book attacking evolution, the two men began a bitter and protracted public confrontation that focused popular criticism even more sharply on Baptist seminary faculty.[104]

L. L. Gwaltney led the opposing army. While dismissing rationalism and atheistic evolution, Gwaltney believed that any observant farmer understood that species evolved. He reminded antievolutionists that earlier generations of Christians had been equally contemptuous of the theories of Galileo and Copernicus. Everywhere he looked he saw evidence for the survival of the fittest. Theistic evolution rationalized science and the Bible and depended upon only one scriptural interpretation. He believed that the six days mentioned in Genesis were undetermined periods of time rather than twenty-four-hour days. Baptists needed to let their concept of God mature and preachers needed to read more astronomy and science, which had provided him "a more glorious and overwhelming concept of God." He published a multiarticle series by Southern seminary professor E. Y. Mullins during the Scopes trial to try to reconcile Baptists, and he denounced the trial proceedings as unworthy of both science and religion. Because Baptists disagreed about whether the earth was square or round, whether the sun revolved around the earth, the length of days in Genesis, and evolution, they would do well to focus on Christ as personal savior, on the inspiration of Scriptures, and on other matters about which they agreed. A steady stream of critical letters left no doubt that most Alabama Baptists disagreed with him.[105]

Indication that such criticism hurt Gwaltney can be found in two later pieces of evidence. In 1951, after his retirement, Gwaltney completed his eighth book, a manuscript entitled "This I Leave with You." In it he expressed belief in the nebula hypothesis of the formation of the universe and in evolution. Friends convinced him that publication would undermine the faith of some and reopen old wounds, so Gwaltney left the manuscript unpublished. Years later he warned a friend to "toughen up your skin a little" because many would criticize him. "Remember nothing hurts until it gets under our own skin. Keep it on the outside."[106]

Gwaltney had important allies in his battle for tolerance within the Baptist family. In January 1927 Charles Stakely delivered the prestigious Founders' Day address at Southern seminary. The occasion was important. Many Alabama pastors such as J. J. Taylor were denouncing seminary professors for defending theistic evolution. Some pastors insisted that all professors at Howard and Judson Colleges and at the seminaries should sign the recently enacted Baptist Faith and Message statement. In fact, Gwaltney interceded to persuade the president of Howard College not to force his faculty to sign the creedal declaration. It may have been Gwaltney who solicited the invitation for Stakely to speak at the seminary in 1927 because the editor was serving on the school's board of trustees at the time.[107]

Stakely's address, entitled "The Seminary and Scientific Scholarship," was widely publicized and reprinted. If Christ and science were both true, Stakely began, there could be no conflict between them. The best theologians and scientists were modest in their claims, and seminary founders had used the scientific method of inquiry. Interpretations of Scripture must be derived through research and investigation. Blind devotion to Scripture was based on ignorance, and no one understood the Bible who knew nothing but the Bible. Every seminary should employ a professor of physical sciences, and seminarians should study astronomy, geology, history, biology, anthropology, and physics as well as theology. After all, preachers must win scientists to Christian faith as well as others. In the final analysis, Stakely concluded, science was "an organic part of the revelation of . . . God."[108]

J. C. Stivender (pastor at Ruhama) also delivered a Founders' Day address at SBTS during the decade. He described the nation's scientific elite of some 12,000 members of the American Association for the Advancement of Science and pleaded for mutual forbearance. Science was neither inherently good nor evil. It reduced superstition, increased the food supply, and revolutionized technology. But science also resulted in poison gas and made war more destructive. Quoting such modernists as Harry Emerson Fosdick and Shailer Mathews, Stivender argued that intellectual acumen could not save humanity unless it was harnessed to Christian altruism and moral development. Christian education must foster social and international righteousness, must reduce racial and class conflict. Theological and scientific literature should move on different levels, without collision or conflict.[109]

Seminary professors reciprocated these visits. As Southern seminary's professor of Old Testament and Hebrew, John R. Sampey was often at the center of the theological storm. A native of Fort Deposit and a graduate of Howard College, his alma mater twice invited him back to speak. In 1925 just after the Scopes trial and a divisive Southern Baptist Convention, Howard's president invited Sampey to preach a revival and to lecture. Perhaps to reduce tension surrounding his appearance on campus, the public was not invited to his lectures or sermons. In a second appearance during 1929, Sampey deplored the lack of scientific curiosity in the South. Summarizing major accomplishments in a variety of scientific disciplines, Sampey praised Charles Darwin and others for accurately calculating the age of the earth at millions of years.[110]

Many Alabama Baptists fiercely opposed such views. H. Ross Arnold (pastor at Greenville) warned rural pastors against attending free short courses for country preachers at Vanderbilt University. He believed the courses were designed to convert rural pastors from evangelical faith to a "mess of modernist pottage 'made in Germany' and warmed over in Vanderbilt." Alabama Baptist evangelist Bob Jones, just embarking on a career that would carry him out of the denomination, promoted Bob Jones University (founded in 1927) as a college that believed the Bible and rejected evolution as well as drinking, smoking, and carousing.[111]

Gwaltney strove mightily to be fair to all sides. Like virtually all denominational leaders, he denounced "radical modernism." If by fundamentalism one meant belief in the inspiration of Scripture, virgin birth, bodily resurrection, vicarious atonement, and second coming, he claimed to know no Alabama Baptist pastor who was not fundamentalist. In 1922 he printed an essay by a New Yorker entitled "Why I Am a Fundamentalist," espousing the infallibility of Scripture and attacking evolution, rationalism, liberalism, humanitarianism, and social uplift.[112]

Gwaltney urged his denomination to be "middle-of-the-road Baptists," avoiding extremes. He contrasted Alabama with his native Virginia (whose liberal Baptists produced wonderful scholarship and pioneered religious freedom but were not evangelistic) and Kentucky (whose conservative Baptists were evangelistic but were also argumentative and doctrinaire). Alabama Baptists were a hybrid of both traditions, with a strong element of individualism mixed in. In 1926 Gwaltney wrote that religion was in "one of those many foolish periods in which argument and disputation have triumphed over common sense." Time would resolve the conflicts if Baptists would just ignore extremists on both sides.[113]

No doubt Gwaltney was sincere in his proclamation of neutrality, and according to his own interpretation, he was consistent in what he believed.

But to Alabama fundamentalists who carefully read his editorials, his middle course seemed to veer constantly left of center. In 1920 he urged pre- and postmillennialists to stop bickering and turn their attention to correcting the nation's social problems. Two years later he warned fundamentalists who constantly attacked liberals that they were in danger of creating "a coercive ecclesiasticism that freedom loving souls resent." He also denied charges by certain evangelists, preachers, seminarians, and editors that secular American colleges and universities had declared war on the Bible. He defended the University of Chicago based upon his personal acquaintance with many of its graduates who were respected Alabama Baptist pastors. During a 1923 dispute with a fellow Baptist editor over biblical literalism, Gwaltney cited Mark 16. Should Christians literally handle snakes, a practice that had resulted in two recent deaths? When Jesus called Herod a fox, did he mean the king was a "four legged chicken fox"? In 1925 the editor wrote that there might be a handful of modernists teaching in Baptist schools who denied the virgin birth, atonement, and second coming. If so, they should be fired. But the presence of three or four heretics among four thousand faithful teachers in 117 Southern Baptist schools posed less threat to the SBC than the takeover efforts of "big F fundamentalists."[114]

Perhaps Gwaltney's greatest service to moderation came in 1921 when he sought to head off fundamentalist control of the SBC by proposing the election of Southern seminary president E. Y. Mullins as president of the convention. After endorsing Mullins in the *Alabama Baptist*, Gwaltney persuaded highly respected conservative W. B. Crumpton to write an editorial seconding the nomination. Then Gwaltney wrote fellow editors in North and South Carolina, urging them to endorse Mullins. With the wheels thus greased, Mullins was easily elected. Twice reelected, he presided over a series of potentially explosive conventions and in 1925 presented the compromise Faith and Message statement that many credited with preventing denominational division. Mullins later told the editor that he had played a critical role in the election. In his autobiography Gwaltney claimed that this episode was the only time in his career when he used his paper to influence denominational politics.[115]

Although Gwaltney was the point man for Alabama Baptist moderates, he received critical support from James E. Dillard, pastor of the state's largest and wealthiest Baptist congregation and book review editor of the *Alabama Baptist*. Like Gwaltney, Dillard subscribed to biblical authority and other Baptist "fundamentals" but insisted that the Bible had to be interpreted in terms of contemporary times and circumstances. He believed that when Jesus was silent on an issue, "we are at liberty to use our own judgment so long as we do not violate the Spirit of Jesus in His teachings." Better that Baptists refrain from labeling each other fundamentalist or modernist, he believed, because such labels were inaccurate and untruthful. Better a preacher be an "honest seeker after the truth and . . . preach the message as he understands it without raising any question as to whether it is Fundamentalist or Modernist." If by fundamentalist, he wrote in 1924, one meant a person who believed "the literal, verbal inspiration of the whole Bible and therefore . . . its inerrancy and infallibility in all matters grammatical, historical, ethical, scientific, political, etc., as well as all matters religious, and who desire to discover all who do not believe as they do and would disfellowship them and drive them from the denomination . . . , then I am not a Fundamentalist."[116]

Two years after this frank declaration of opinion, the state convention chose Dillard as chairman of a twenty-five-man committee to investigate allegations of heresy against certain Howard College faculty. The committee questioned all faculty who had been accused, as well as students who secretly had lodged the charges. In each case, the committee concluded that remarks attributed to professors had been misunderstood or taken out of context. One biology professor explained that he believed his discipline strengthened rather than weakened confidence in the Bible. An accused religion professor affirmed his faith in God and biblical authority. Both professors were active members of Baptist churches. Howard's president explained that the college investigated the religious views and morals of prospective faculty and stood ready to fire any who were "out of harmony with common views of Southern Baptists." L. O. Dawson (three times convention president, beloved former pastor of Tuscaloosa First Baptist Church, and head of Howard's Bible department) affirmed his fidelity to biblical authority as well.[117]

In December 1929 Alabama Baptists finally located a real, live, self-confessed modernist, Dr. H. Calvin Day, a professor of biology with a doctorate from Stanford University. Each Howard College faculty member was assigned to lecture in chapel, and Day had intended to speak on the innocuous topic of "Friendship" until a colleague used that subject. Day should have stuck with his original topic despite the risk of redundancy. As it was, he spoke extemporaneously about various biblical stories. He told students that he had studied whales with one of the world's leading authorities, and a man could not live in the stomach of a mammal. Nor could Noah's ark accommodate 600,000 classified species of animals. Jonah got away with a "whale of a story for having been absent from home for such a long time," and Noah must not have taken every kind of animal aboard his boat. Nor did Day believe the story of Adam, Eve, and the serpent or the parting of the Red Sea. Though he proclaimed himself to be as firm a Christian as any who attended Howard College, he pronounced Genesis to contain more mythology than fact. Howard's president promptly fired Day, though expressing the highest regard for him personally.[118]

Theological divisions emerged most clearly in the battle over the Faith and Message statement adopted at the 1925 SBC and a resolution against evolution passed the following year that required the signature of all denominational employees. Moderates vociferously denounced such creeds as violations of Baptist traditions of soul liberty, the priesthood of the believer, and free thought. Although Gwaltney opposed "liberty turned to license," he considered soul liberty the heart of Baptist tradition. Coercive religious creeds had filled Christian history with "blood and gore," he wrote in 1923, and threatened to take Baptists on a journey toward authoritarian Catholicism. He bitterly opposed the 1925 Faith and Message, not because he disagreed with its doctrine, but because it led Baptists toward creedalism. At the end of the decade, he warned against trying to boss Baptists: "They have a way of not obeying commands and what is more they do not consider it worthwhile to stop long enough to tell anyone why they do not need his dictation."[119]

Even on matters of church unity moderates urged a middle course. Gwaltney praised the Federal Council of Churches for its advocacy of disarmament. His ally, J. E. Dillard, wrote in 1922 that no two Baptists agreed on what church unity meant: "One with great vehemence declared he was opposed to any kind of cooperation that in any way compromised our Baptist principles. . . . The other man with equal vehemence declared he was in favor of cooperating with all denominations . . . as long as we were not called upon to surrender . . . our convictions. . . . Surely it was a time to smile and shake hands." Gwaltney criticized denominational leaders who refused to participate in the Baptist World Alliance because of alleged heretical doctrines held by some who spoke at its meetings.[120]

Alabama Baptists clearly tolerated and even promoted a luxurious climate of opinion during the 1920s, excepting the single case of modernism at Howard College. Fundamentalists believed the climate too luxurious and accused a fraternity of seminary graduates of running the denomination through their machine. Gwaltney branded this charge "absurdly false."[121] Yet, it does appear that some fifty or so large, wealthy churches, with pastors who graduated from seminary, continued to furnish most denominational leaders. Although attendance at the state convention increased steadily to more than a thousand messengers by the decade's end, such churches were like the proverbial thousand-pound elephant moving about the barnyard. Smaller creatures had best beware.

For those smaller creatures who feared for their safety, there were alternatives. Some followed evangelist Bob Jones down the path of independence. Others remained in Southern Baptist churches but increasingly supported alternative and more orthodox institutions like the Birmingham School of the Bible (later Southeastern Bible College).[122] In such ways, they contributed in their own ways to the newly forming fundamentalist American subculture.

The Dark Side of Modernity: Race, Religion, and Bigotry

Paradoxically, many Baptists who were tolerant of theological diversity were less inclined to live in a racially and religiously pluralistic Alabama. This status was especially true of Gwaltney, whose study of sociology eventuated in a strong belief in Social Darwinism and the survival of the fittest. He derived from his sociological studies that "consciousness of kind" was a fundamental biological principle governing human societies. Commenting on miscegenation in 1921, Gwaltney wrote that the race problem was "at its deepest . . . more than half a sex problem and that the desire of African Americans for social equality was therefore unacceptable." He feared a racial Armageddon if blacks pushed for social equality. He explained that the Baptist hospitals in Selma had to segregate black and white patients because otherwise nurses and orderlies of one race would be forced to care for patients of the opposite race. His views were widely shared in the denomination.[123]

Within the constraints of the times, Baptists were not more intolerant than other white Alabamians. Paternalism was the rule in race relations. The state convention helped finance Selma University and provided charity access to the racially segregated Good Samaritan Hospital. Gwaltney not only believed in the racial superiority of whites but also believed that superiority compelled whites to prevent lynching and to educate black children and ministers. He supported the newly formed conference on interracial cooperation and praised the orthodoxy and progress of black Baptists. No man justified his own superiority, Gwaltney wrote in 1922, by giving "Negroes hell when they should have only justice."[124]

Other Baptist leaders expressed similar sentiments. A. J. Dickinson praised interracial committees that had been organized by 1920 in all but three Alabama counties. J. E. Dillard served on the state interracial commission and read widely on the subject of race relations. And one furious correspondent to the *Alabama Baptist* proposed a simple remedy to lynchings. Either sheriffs should use machine guns to "mow down the mob" or sheriffs should be fired.[125]

Noble Y. Beall took the most unorthodox stance on race. A graduate of Howard College and Southern seminary, Beall pastored in Montgomery, Ozark, and Gadsden before joining the Home Mission Board as director of its Negro missions department. In a series of perceptive publications, Beall favorably discussed African American history and contributions to civilization. He also discussed the obligations of white Baptists to racial justice, which they had not practiced. They must insist that blacks be treated fairly in the courts and economically. The economic plight of black tenant farmers, he believed, resulted from white injustice, not from Noah's curse of Ham. Baptist churches must become more involved in clearing slums, saving black youth from crime, improving living conditions, gathering accurate data about racial conditions, organizing interracial meetings, and taking a firm stand against public discrimination. Although Beall warned black churches not to become mere social agencies to improve the race, he urged that "nothing is more un-Christian than denying people certain inalienable rights . . . simply because of race; the preacher should be the first man to raise his voice in protest against such [injustice]."[126]

Alabama Baptists were more charitable in their attitude toward African Americans than they were toward Jews and Catholics. In 1923 the state convention requested the HMB to send Jacob Gartenhaus, a specialist on Jewish evangelism, to Alabama. But a variety of incidents denied him a warm welcome from the Jewish community. At the 1920 state convention, the foreign missions speaker warned that Zionism made it harder to evangelize Jews. "Were it not for the strong arm of England," he told messengers to loud applause, "civilization in the Near East would sink." The following year Gwaltney traced the failure of blue laws in the Alabama legislature to "the moving picture film trust, in the hands of Jewish financiers." Two years later the *Alabama Baptist* featured an article entitled "Jew Movies Urging Sex Vice." The article contended that "Jew-Jesuit motion picture producers persist in making the screen a school for teaching seduction" because they "always like to hear of profits." Gwaltney agreed that a trust "consisting largely of Jews" controlled the film industry, which was corrupting the morals of American youth.[127]

Anti-Semitism was mild compared to the anti-Catholicism that permeated Alabama Baptist thought during the decade. Such attitudes resulted partly from historic grievances against Catholic persecution and partly from fear of Catholic immigrants. In 1910 Birmingham had one of the highest percentages of immigrants of any southern city. Ten years later the city contained 6,000 immigrants and 10,000 citizens who had at least one foreign-born parent (most of them from Italy or Russia).[128] Although the state contained 2,083 white Baptist churches and only 119 Catholic ones in 1926 (with 272,000 Baptists compared to 36,000 Catholics), conditions proved fertile soil for the growth of religious bigotry.

In 1920 the state Baptist convention warned that European and Oriental immigrants were swarming to Alabama, threatening the very existence of the Old South. Later messengers described the South's cities as containing "cesspools of iniquity and sin."[129]

Gwaltney was partly to blame for such attitudes. He blamed Catholics for defeating prohibition candidates and for a long history of religious persecution of Protestants. He defended the Ku Klux Klan revival as a natural reaction to the Catholic Knights of Columbus and Protestant fears of papal meddling in American politics. He denied that the Klan was primarily anti-Negro, anti-Jewish, or anti-immigrant. Venerated Baptist historian B. F. Riley also demonstrated an anti-Catholic attitude when he contrasted democratic England with priest-ridden, superstitious, ignorant Ireland.[130]

Unfortunately, historical liberties by respected Baptist figures gave license to less stable personalities. Birmingham became a Klan-dominated city, and Baptists played a key role in the success of the organization. Pastors such as Theo Harris at Pike Avenue Baptist Church, J. D. Myatt at Virginia Mines, William Sentell at Avondale, and E. G. Adams at Packer Memorial received financial contributions from the Klan and defended it from critics. G. C. Eubanks and two deacons from Gate City Baptist Church frequently attended Klan meetings. Irondale Baptist Church solicited $750 in 1927 from the Nathan Bedford Forrest Klan to help pay for two lots recently purchased by the church. In return for contributions of a dollar or more, the church offered to print the Klansman's name on the interior walls of the new building. The head of the Klan in Jefferson County estimated that more than half the county's Protestant ministers belonged to the invisible empire at some point during the decade.[131]

Outside Birmingham conditions were no better. In Clay County, the Klan donated money to the Baptist church in Millerville. The Andalusia Klan gave nearly $1,600 to fundamentalist evangelist Bob Jones, who was a Klan sympathizer. At the end of a 1927 revival at the Greensboro Baptist Church, twenty-two hooded Klansmen presented the evangelist $75. In Crenshaw County, a grand jury indicted L. A. Nalls, a Baptist preacher and Klansman, for leading an assault on a divorced couple who had remarried.

After the flogging, he allegedly explained his actions to the bleeding woman: "Sister, you were not punished in anger this evening; you were punished in a spirit of kindness and correction to set your feet aright and show your children how a good mother should go." When he learned of his indictment by a grand jury weeks later, Nalls fled to Texas.[132]

The most spectacular atrocity associated with anti-Catholicism was the 1921 murder of an unarmed Catholic priest, James E. Coyle, by a bivocational Methodist preacher. Coyle had married the man's daughter to a Puerto Rican Catholic. Baptist deacon Hugo Black defended the preacher, who was acquitted when the jury accepted Black's argument that the murder was justifiable homicide. The murder and acquittal subjected Birmingham and the city's Protestants to national censure. Gwaltney justified the acquittal and wrote anti-Catholic editorials during the trial. His friend J. E. Dillard of Southside disagreed. In an August 1921 sermon Dillard expressed his respect for Coyle and his contempt for the pistol-packing Methodist killer. "I look upon gun-toting as one of the most cowardly acts of which a man may be guilty," Dillard told his congregation, adding for good measure a denunciation of lawlessness in Birmingham.[133]

Subsequent violence brought a steady escalation of criticism against Alabama Baptists from both inside and outside the state. Grover C. Hall, editor of the *Montgomery Advertiser* (who won a Pulitzer Prize in journalism for his editorial attacks on the Klan), denounced the "white trash of the second rate pulpits" for tolerating Klan violence as a method of enforcing prohibition. In 1927 Hall castigated Gwaltney by name for his silence after a wave of Klan terrorism. The best Gwaltney could offer in response, Hall wrote contemptuously, was an editorial attacking the pope. Hall wagered that no Jew or Catholic had taken part in the recent wave of floggings. Victor Hansen, publisher of the *Birmingham News,* referred to the state privately as a wilderness of Protestant- "ridden ignorance to which our people now seem utterly lost." "I fear that . . . the treatment must be a sparing administration of intelligence gradually applied" so as not to excite "too many of their prejudices at once." The *Birmingham Age-Herald* added its voice to the criticism of Gwaltney's silence, finally forcing the editor to respond.[134]

Gwaltney denied that he belonged to the Klan but defended its right to exist and engage in politics. He denied that evidence linked the Klan to the wave of floggings (even though much evidence *did* link the Klan). If the Catholic Knights of Columbus ceased to exist, so probably would the Klan. Secret organizations, he wrote, were as old as Christianity and throughout history had brought "a larger liberty to the common people." R. M. Hunter endorsed Gwaltney's defense of the Klan with his own story of a Baptist deacon in Mobile who allegedly stopped Catholics from flogging a boy. He did not defend floggings but believed Catholics as guilty of them as Protestants. From outside the state, the *New York World* called Gwaltney an apologist for the Klan and condemned the silence of the state's pulpits.[135]

While Gwaltney waffled, other Baptist ministers began to speak out. As evidence of Klan violence mounted in 1927, so did Baptist criticism of the organization. Leading the way was Southside's J. E. Dillard. In his Sunday morning sermon on July 17, he demanded an end to lawlessness in the state. The next day he addressed the same call to the Birmingham Baptist pastors' conference, which unanimously adopted a resolution calling on law enforcement to apprehend floggers and end violence. Once again, Dillard minced no words: Alabama's reign of terror by masked men "under pretense of enforcing [prohibition] law and decency" was nothing more than a cover for outrages "that would put to blush the fiends of the Spanish inquisition." The only good to come from the violence was that such excesses had finally brought Alabamians to their senses. He called on the legislature to pass an antimasking law with tough penalties. Baptists must be as quick to defend the religious rights of Catholics as they were to insist on their own. Theo Harris (pastor of Pike Avenue Baptist Church and formerly a defender of the Klan) joined in Dillard's denunciation. So did Baptist minister L. T. Mays of Montgomery, who condemned Klan cross burnings as "a vicious, un-Godly and illiterate insult at . . . the very memory of Jesus Christ and everything . . . which He taught." The 1927 state convention joined the chorus condemning "organized lawlessness" and violence.[136]

Anti-Catholicism and support for the Klan merged in Alabama politics. A slate of Klan candidates swept virtually all state and local offices in 1926 (including Klansman Bibb Graves, who was elected governor, and Baptist deacon–Klansman Hugo Black, who was elected to the U.S. Senate). Baptist support for prohibition, anti-Catholicism, woman suffrage, working-class white economic interests, and the Klan all converged in the election.

In 1920 Baptists had supported L. B. Musgrove against conservative incumbent U.S. Senator Oscar W. Underwood. Underwood had infuriated Baptists by his belligerent opposition to prohibition. He was also an economic conservative who opposed labor unions. A coalition of prohibitionists, woman suffragists, Klansmen, and unionists nearly defeated Underwood in 1920 and drove him into retirement six years later.[137]

In 1921 Birmingham Protestants mobilized behind the candidacy of

Nathaniel A. Barrett, the East Lake physician who had earlier defeated George Ward. A. J. Dickinson, who had led Barrett's forces earlier, was replaced by another Baptist preacher, R. L. Durant. Durant accused the Knights of Columbus of funding the opposition to Barrett, and Catholics did in fact form the Catholic Civic League to counter attacks against them. The next year R. M. Hunter tried to organize Protestants politically to enforce prohibition in Mobile.[138]

In 1923 Lister Hill ran political advertisements in the *Alabama Baptist* to counter charges that he was a Catholic (in fact he was of Jewish and Methodist ancestry). One friend reacted to this strategy by writing Hill, "all our people sware [sic] by their church paper."[139]

Alabama Baptists also began mobilizing against New York governor Alfred E. Smith, a Catholic "wet" and the odds-on favorite to win the 1928 Democratic presidential nomination. Gwaltney disagreed with northern Democrats who predicted the solid South would vote for Smith despite his liabilities. The *Alabama Baptist* featured one article after another denouncing Smith's religion and his opposition to prohibition.[140]

After Smith won the nomination, Gwaltney virtually endorsed Republican nominee Herbert Hoover. In the ensuing campaign Alabama Baptists were deeply split. Baptists in the Black Belt, where most African Americans lived, considered fidelity to the Democratic Party to be a racial test of faith and refused to bolt the party. But in other areas of the state, Baptists deserted the party of their fathers in droves. They denied that their political support of Hoover was a violation of their historic fealty to separation of church and state. Democratic criticism of Gwaltney's overt partisanship finally reached such a crescendo in August 1928 that he announced that the paper would no longer publish articles backing either candidate. Despite this disavowal, he continued to write editorials on Romanism, defenses of preachers in politics, and attacks on pro-Smith newspapers. John W. Phillips, perhaps the most theologically liberal Baptist pastor in Alabama, publicly endorsed Herbert Hoover in a sermon aptly entitled "Why I Do Not Believe in Tolerance." Dr. James T. McGlothlin, pastor of Parker Memorial in Anniston, also openly supported Hoover, support that divided his church when leading deacon Harry M. Ayers backed Smith.[141]

One historian of the 1928 presidential race in Alabama concludes that prohibition was a more important reason for Baptist opposition to Smith than Catholicism.[142] But Baptist attitudes toward prohibition, Catholicism, and the Klan were so inextricably mixed that it is impossible to separate the motives of those Baptists who voted for Hoover.

After the election, in which Smith carried Alabama by a few thousand votes while losing most of the South and the presidency, Gwaltney wrote that the spirit of the age was political independence. Mass movements had swept aside party traditions, and citizens would henceforth worship, work, and vote according to their convictions and not because of historic loyalty to a political party.[143]

The Baptist preacher in Camden (Wilcox County) put a different spin on the chaotic decade. These years had not been pleasant ones for John G. Dobbins. After pastorates in Orrville and Hurtsboro, Dobbins had moved to Luverne in 1923. The town was a hotbed of Klan activity, and Dobbins's son Charles visited a Klan rally at the local baseball park. The next morning Charles told his father what had transpired. His father listened attentively but said nothing. When the conversation ended, Dobbins went to the study and wrote his sermon for the next Sunday. Young Charles remembered that sermon all his life. As his father denounced the Klan, two deacons got up and walked out of the service. Other deacons joined them in refusing to pay the pastor's salary and forcing him to resign for the more tolerant Baptist church at Camden.

In 1928 Dobbins felt compelled to speak out again, this time preaching an hour-and-a-quarter sermon on why his parishioners should not vote for Al Smith. Church members in the heavily black county who knew Dobbins's intentions tried to persuade him not to preach the sermon in this Democratic hotbed. But Dobbins was no more persuaded by them than he had been by Klan members of his Luverne church. When he finished preaching, his organist (Mrs. Edgar Pritchell), a fiercely partisan Democrat, played her own benediction, a rousing rendition of "Dixie." Dobbins was not converted. Years later he told his liberal, socially activist son Charles: "We don't have politics in Alabama based on issues. All our politics is race." Perhaps he oversimplified, for in the 1920s Alabama Baptist politics had much to do with class, liquor, Catholics, and immigrants as well. But it was from his courageous Baptist preacher-father that Charles Dobbins derived his sense of fairness toward blacks and his commitment to social justice.[144] He remembered that during the troubled decade of the 1920s Alabama Baptists came in all sizes, in both sexes, and with a variety of opinions.

9

The Great Depression, 1930–1939

"We love Alabama . . . well enough to see her faults as well as her virtues."

The decade of the 1930s was neither the worst of times nor the best. But it would have taken some convincing to persuade those caught in the maelstrom of that time that life had ever been worse or would get much better. Some gave up hope entirely. The controversies of the previous third of a century were largely forgotten because Baptists had more serious problems about which to worry. Alabama led all southern states in the decline of white employment between 1930 and 1940. As unemployed families deserted cities for farms where they could at least plant a food crop, the rate of urban growth fell from 46 percent in the previous decade to 15 percent in the 1930s. Among all Alabama farmers in 1935, 65 percent were landless tenants. Most of the 600,000 industrial laborers worked in low-wage, low-skill or unskilled, nonunion jobs. Birmingham was one of the hardest hit cities in the United States; its normal work force of 100,000 was down to 15,000 full-time employees by June 1932.[1]

Because most churchgoing Alabamians were Baptists, the cataclysm of the Great Depression obviously affected the denomination severely. Fortunately, there is a more precise way to measure the effect. In September 1935, **360** President Franklin D. Roosevelt sent a form letter to half the nation's

200,000 clergymen, asking them to describe conditions in their communities. Nearly a third responded. Letters from fifty-one Alabama Baptist ministers allow the reader to peer into their anguish.

Responses came from all classes and levels of ministers: barely literate and highly educated; pastors of tiny rural churches and pastors of the largest urban congregations. In a day before junk mail and standardized letters, before political cynicism and jaded expectations about government, ministers who received these letters treated them as a sacred trust and viewed Roosevelt as genuinely interested in their replies. Most had never received a letter from a prominent politician, much less one from a president of the United States. They took out pen and paper and carefully, thoughtfully described their own circumstances as well as the conditions of their parishioners.

Rural, bivocational ministers wrote the most moving letters. Jonathan H. Darden, nearly sixty years old and a preacher for a quarter century, owned his own farm when the depression began and had always paid his debts. But five-cent cotton had cost him the family farm to mortgage foreclosure. Bryant Sanders was a tenant farmer/Baptist preacher near Dothan who interpreted the Great Depression as a sign that the world would soon end. W. L. Sprayberry pastored five churches in Clay and Randolph Counties and moderated the Clay County Association. A faithful Democrat who boasted of voting even for Catholic Al Smith in 1928, he had suffered the criticism of fellow Baptist preachers but rejoiced to be a part of God's remnant who had "rescued the people." W. J. H. Sasser lived in the country outside Andalusia. Orphaned when four days old, he had been raised by his grandparents, who were both dead. Barely literate, he begged for help for himself and his congregations: "i serve churches ever Sunday and I no about the churches in the country they need help to from some source they lots of churches going dead because they cant pay there pastors exspences i wold be glad you would help me work out some plan to help them i do not git but very little fore my exspence but i been going fore 9 years but some times it looks like i will haft to stop."[2]

Urban pastors fared only marginally better. The pastor of Mount Calvary Baptist Church in Tarrant City had to work a secular job to supplement his income. Even then he could not pay back taxes on his house, which he was about to lose. The wife of a pastor at a textile mill church in Florence wrote that she and her husband worked in a knitting mill. Like most churches in their vicinity, their congregation was in debt and needed repairs. It contributed nothing to missions. The pastor owed debts of thousands of dollars despite the fact that his wife made all their clothes. They had given up their dream of sending their children to college. Despite their troubles, others who lived in their mill town had worse problems.[3]

Pastors who chose not to share their personal anguish with the president did provide a glimpse into the lives of parishioners. A pastor from Samson pleaded for assistance to tenant farmers. Many farmers he knew cleared less than five dollars a month. Another preacher from outside Andalusia depicted his rural community as consisting of hungry, poor, hopeless people who lived in unscreened, unsanitary shacks "not fit for a horse." They kept their children out of school and worked them ten to twelve hours a day in the fields. He provided charity to keep them from starving or freezing during the winter, but prospects were not encouraging: "The poor or landless man, wage earners and sharecropper in the rural districts are nothing but slaves for the big land holders. The big landlords like the 'New Deal' because they collect big cash rentals from the government and refuse to divide it with their tenants. They also work poor men on their farms for wages that are ridiculously low. The big landlords force their tenants with threats of foreclosure or moving."[4] A pastor from Limestone County expressed similar concerns. Tenant farmers would soon have nothing to eat and no coal with which to cook or heat their houses. Tenant problems stemmed from large plantations handed down through generations, leaving most white and black people to work for others as sharecroppers.[5]

Similar letters came from small industrial towns. Jeff Ellis wrote from Cordova, where he had pastored four churches for twenty years. His travels to revival meetings revealed a confused and demoralized population; people were suspicious of their neighbors and had lost hope in God and government. From Haleyville, Joseph W. Rucker wrote the president on behalf of a women's sewing project scheduled to end in September 1935. The government project employed fifty-nine women who were sole providers for their families. They had inadequate clothing for winter, had no food stored, and were already undernourished. They begged for work and walked miles to the sewing project.[6]

Similar complaints came from city pastors. Charles R. Bell Jr. (the new pastor at Anniston's Parker Memorial Church) urged a government housing program for poor whites and blacks. They lived in the most degrading circumstances, "hounded by loan sharks and getting nothing for a crop." J. L. Aders, pastor of East Birmingham Baptist Church, described conditions in the city as intolerable, with many poor people literally starving to death. "I call daily on people," he wrote, "who will not survive the winter unless some way can be found to better care for them." Thousands on relief were trying to feed families of five to seven on incomes of three or four dollars a week. Social workers treated the poor "not as humans, but as dogs." "The United States Government," he concluded, "must be the Good Samaritan to the unfortunates in our land." "Like Lazarus at the rich man's gate this Depression has laid the poor at Uncle Sam's gate." Failure to act, he predicted, would bring revolution.[7]

A. Hamilton Reid, a future secretary-treasurer of the state convention, served as pastor of South Avondale Baptist Church during 1929. He remembered a deacon calling him on a Tuesday morning in the fall and telling him that the neighborhood bank where Reid kept his savings and the church's contributions had closed. Reid had only two dollars and the church had no money at all. His deacon (who used another bank) brought money for Reid's family. The following Sunday, offerings declined by more than 50 percent.[8]

Coping with Hard Times

Churches coped with such conditions as best they could. Montgomery First Baptist cut staff salaries. Although its 1935 contributions to the Cooperative Program remained second only to Southside's, the church changed a budget that began the decade contributing 50 percent of all funds to local needs, 40 percent to the CP, and 10 percent to the building fund to a 70/25/5 percent distribution by 1932. The congregation also established a food pantry for the needy and an unemployment registry. To earn money for foreign missions in 1933, the church sponsored an "old gold" drive that obtained 129 rings, 77 cuff links, 10 thimbles, 8 pieces of dental gold (not extracted for that purpose, one hopes!), and one gold head from a walking cane.[9]

Brady Justice became pastor of Fort Payne First Baptist Church in 1931 and promptly received a salary cut of 17 percent. Even then the church could not pay its bills; a wealthy member often paid them to keep the church out of debt. The resourceful Justice, like the denomination he served, found ingenious ways to reach people. In April 1938 he began a series of sermons with one entitled "The Meanest Man in Fort Payne." He offered five dollars to anyone who could name the person before the sermon but did not reveal how many names he received or who they were, no doubt a relief to many candidates for the "honor." Such innovative advertising kept the church growing despite its financial problems. The congregation added 460 new members during his nine-year pastorate, including 180 by baptism.[10]

Sam Jones Ezell, pastor of Clanton First Baptist Church, distributed

money and food to the poor and helped persuade Chilton County farmers
to switch from cotton farming to peach orchards. Evangelistic despite liberal views on many issues (he did not believe regenerate Christians who
had been sprinkled in other denominations needed to be immersed when
joining Baptist churches; he favored women deacons; he believed blacks
should be allowed to vote), Ezell doubled church membership during his
seventeen-year pastorate. He resigned in 1938 to become state superintendent of evangelism.[11]

The denomination experienced shocks similar to the churches. Departments of the state mission board were combined and staff positions abolished. Cooperative Program gifts declined from $180,000 in 1930 to half
that amount in 1933. They increased only to $134,000 in 1938. Total contri-
butions, which had reached nearly $2.5 million in 1929, dropped to barely
$1 million in 1934. Gifts did not return to the 1929 level until the 1940s. The
executive committee voted in 1930 to divert CP contributions temporarily
to pay interest on Selma Baptist hospitals' bonds and to eliminate all state
evangelists. In 1932 the committee heard three members of Auburn First
Baptist Church appeal for funds to pay their pastor's salary because the
church was dependent on Auburn University faculty salaries that had not
been paid.[12]

Such crises caused strains in the convention. Selma Baptist hospitals
and the state assembly grounds at Mentone had to be sold. Newton institute was liquidated, as were all the mountain schools. When the denomination persuaded Harwell G. Davis to accept the presidency of Howard
College in 1939, the school had been placed on probation by its accrediting
agency, electricity had been turned off for nonpayment of bills, pianos had
been repossessed, and debts amounted to more than $400,000.[13]

Despite these problems, the denomination not only survived but actually grew. During the 1930s the number of churches increased by 191 (to
over 2,200) and members by 82,000 (to more than 375,000). The denomination reestablished the Alabama Baptist Historical Society in 1936. Under
the energetic direction of Howard College professor James H. Chapman,
the society began systematically collecting state Baptist history.[14]

Denominational leadership remained under the control of men such as
J. E. Dillard of Southside and L. L. Gwaltney (both elected president of the
convention twice during the 1930s) and J. C. Stivender (who was elected
from 1939 to 1941). All three were Birmingham residents who represented
views considerably more liberal than the rank and file. But rural pastors
were not without a voice. The same 1939 convention that elected Stivender

president listened spellbound to R. L. Isdell, a country preacher from Sand Mountain. Gwaltney, who had known and liked Isdell for years, wrote him not to be afraid of the large crowd and to preach just as he did "in the hollows and coves of Sand Mountain." Gwaltney did not bother to request a copy of his sermon to print because he knew Isdell would not "fool away his time by writing a sermon." Isdell (whose daughter was a missionary in China and had been supported financially by the WMU while she attended college and seminary) talked about his life experiences and had his audience of city dwellers alternately laughing and crying.[15]

Though much changed among Baptists during the 1930s, more remained the same. Preachers still railed against alcohol, tobacco, and scandalous movies. They mobilized against repeal of the Volstead Act (establishing nationwide prohibition) in a losing cause but continued to resist the wet forces in local option elections. Most such confrontations were peaceful if passionate, but one in Lawrence County ended in a bloody gunfight. In 1938 W. H. Falkner was preaching on the prophetic text "The wages of sin is death; but the gift of God is eternal life" at Owens Chapel Baptist Church some miles out in the country from Moulton. One of his parishioners that day was Andrew Dutton, a converted moonshiner turned deputy sheriff who had declared war on his former associates. When Falkner's sermon was interrupted by boisterous language outside the frame building, Dutton went outside to quiet the ruckus. He was soon engaged in a shouting match with Bert Rutherford. As the argument became more heated, Rutherford's wife grabbed Dutton while her husband shot him twelve times. Ricocheting bullets killed an eighteen-year-old girl inside the church and left six others wounded. Blood splattered church benches and floors as terror-stricken worshipers scrambled for exits.[16]

In addition to alcohol, tobacco, and movies, Gwaltney believed that sports also should be regulated. In his opinion they received too much attention in Alabama. He took no national pride in Joe Louis's world boxing championship in 1937 despite the victory of the Chambers County native over the reigning German champion. Prizefighting and football, the editor warned, vented "pent up savage instincts" and demonstrated that "man at bottom is an animal." A mule could kick harder than Louis could punch, he reminded sports-crazed Alabamians, "and a mule is a half-breed ass." Although Gwaltney admitted that he personally enjoyed watching college football, he went straight home to bed when games ended, not partying and drinking as so many did. Let "the fools, if they must, have all their highballs and cocktails and headaches and chagrin which follow their folly."[17]

Rev. Elmer Merrell conducts a baptism at Mignon Baptist Church, 1939. Mignon served the Comer mill textile community in Sylacauga. (Courtesy of Wayne Flynt)

His campaign against the excesses of football and prizefighting failed. Alabama Baptists might surrender their affection for the product of vine or corn—but give up football? Never!

Evangelism remained the denomination's highest priority despite continuing debate over its form. If the fires of evangelism cooled, Gwaltney warned, the church was dead. But not just any kind of evangelism was acceptable. He deplored the "clap-trap and disgusting methods of . . . professional evangelists plus their avaricious spirit." He advised pastors to preach revivals in their own churches and rely more on Sunday school to gradually win the lost. J. E. Berkstresser agreed with Gwaltney about overemphasis on emotion. Although overly intellectual religion could not satisfy humanity's deepest religious yearning, the pendulum had swung too far toward "mob psychology" (loud speaking, "sensuous singing," too much noise). A pastor in Decatur disagreed, recalling from his own childhood how frequently revivalists wept when they preached. "Preaching from the heart," not "cold intellectualism," brought decisions for Christ, he believed.[18]

Whatever revivalistic style preachers used seemed to work. In 1929

Alabama Baptist churches baptized nearly 15,000, more than Baptists in any states except Texas, Georgia, and North Carolina.[19] As the depression deepened, baptisms declined. Gwaltney grew alarmed and urged extra evangelistic effort when only 14,000 were baptized in 1936, 2,500 less than in the previous year. In 1936, 28 percent of Alabama Baptist churches reported no baptisms (compared to rates of 25 percent in 1934 and 20 percent in 1932). But even during years when the flames of revival burned low, W. Albert Smith baptized fifty in a revival at Fairfax Baptist Church during August 1938, and Colbert Heights Baptist Church had thirty-seven conversions that same month.[20]

Such evangelistic efforts paid dividends. By 1933, Birmingham Association was proclaimed the largest Baptist association in the world, with 40,000 members in ninety-seven churches. In a city that claimed to have the highest proportion of Sunday school members in the world, Baptists had taken over as the largest denomination.[21]

One reason for Baptist success in Birmingham was the growth of its Italian missions. Begun by Birmingham WMU women about 1910, work with Italians was well organized by the 1920s into two Good Will Centers, staffed by Italian Baptist preachers and a number of social work graduates of the WMU Training School. The depression forced consolidation and cutbacks. By 1930 only Arcangelo Pucciarelli remained. The HMB paid him only $100 a month on which to support a large family, so Alabama WMU supplemented his salary with $500 annually. The WMU also provided volunteers to replace professional social workers. Pucciarelli operated the Good Will Center at Ensley and came to know Jefferson County's Italian-speaking population (of Birmingham's 5,900 foreign-born immigrants in 1930, 1,418 were Italians, though more than 22,500 Italian-Americans lived in the Birmingham district; Pucciarelli estimated that 15,000 of them still spoke Italian). Between 1921 and 1933 he baptized seventy-five of them and organized several Italian Baptist churches. Mary Headen, another trained social worker, was employed in 1933 to organize an Italian mothers' club and work with children. Four of the mothers were converted during the year.[22]

By 1939 the Italian congregation of forty worshiped in their own chapel in Ensley. Pucciarrelli preached there two Sundays a month and at other mission stations the remaining Sundays. He was assisted by Bertha Wallis, a native Alabamian and WMU Training School graduate, who supervised the seven-room Good Will Center in Ensley. According to local accounts, Birmingham Baptists experienced more success converting Italians than any other Southern Baptist effort.[23] If so, the credit goes largely to Arcan-

Arcangelo Pucciarelli, a native of Salerno, was converted in Alabama and became a missionary to north Alabama's Italian population. He established several Italian mission churches during the 1930s and 1940s. (Courtesy of Samford University Archives)

gelo Pucciarelli. A native of Salerno, Pucciarelli came to the United States with his parents in 1909. He first heard the Bible being read in his public grammar school but was not converted until he moved with his American-born Baptist wife to Alabama. After his conversion at a Baptist church in Cordova, he attended Baptist Bible Institute in New Orleans, thanks to financial help from Jasper First Baptist Church. While in seminary, he preached to Italians at Bogalusa, Louisiana, and in New Orleans. After his graduation in 1925, he returned to Birmingham to work among Italians. He also enrolled at Howard College, graduating in 1932 with a degree in languages (he was fluent in Italian, English, Spanish, and French and often interpreted for immigrants).[24]

One of Pucciarelli's converts, Rose Tombrello, continued the mission tradition. Daughter of a Baptist mother and Catholic immigrant father, she was converted at one of Pucciarelli's revivals in Cardiff. When Pucciarelli learned of her desire to be a missionary, he told the Birmingham WMU, which supplied her a scholarship to Howard College. During her high school and college years, Tombrello served her small Italian church as Sunday school teacher and superintendent, director of Baptist Training Union, and church clerk.[25]

Men and women like Tombrello continued to leave Birmingham for far-flung fields of service despite hard times. Clarabell Isdell (daughter of the charismatic preacher from Sand Mountain) left for China. Mary Ellis departed for Argentina, Walter Craighead for Rumania, Ruth Mahan for Hungary, William and Sarah Bryant for Chile. Willie Kelly continued to entertain Alabamians who visited Shanghai and inform Alabama WMU about China by letter and speech when home on furlough.[26]

To the degree that Alabama Baptists sustained mission work during the 1930s, they largely had WMU to thank. Throughout the decade, the 30,000 members of Alabama WMU continued to contribute more than half of all money for missions and benevolence (more than the 350,000 other Alabama Baptists combined).[27]

The distribution of these funds might seem impersonal to the denomination, but to recipients, each dollar given was an answer to prayer. In 1930 Alabama WMU provided eleven scholarships for women to attend Judson College and one to the WMU Training School in Louisville. Contributions of $30,000 to foreign missions, $15,000 to home missions, $31,000 to scholarships and Christian education, $3,700 to elderly and infirm ministers and to ministers' widows, $4,300 to the orphan's home, $5,700 to Baptist hospitals, among other causes, literally saved institutions and changed lives. In 1931 WMU paid the salary of a Judson professor in order for the college to retain accreditation. It also launched a five-year drive to eliminate debt on the Baptist orphanage by urging members to save coupons from Octagon soap products. The Colgate Company redeemed each coupon for a half cent. The company also donated General Electric refrigerators to the orphanage. The campaign fell short of its goal but did reduce the debt by $31,000 and earned the orphanage a number of new refrigerators. WMU funded its scholarships through the sale of cookbooks written by members.[28]

Of the many lives touched by such contributions, one was particularly poignant. Irene Long Curtis was a married woman with several children living in Haleyville when the depression began. For seven years she was employed as a WMU summer field worker. One of her daughters received a WMU scholarship to Judson, whetting her mother's appetite for learning. They enrolled together as freshmen. Mrs. Curtis was able to make her way with a $100 Judson scholarship, one free meal a day provided by the college, $20 it provided for expenses, and $135 she received from the National Youth Administration (a New Deal agency). She became too old to qualify for the NYA grant in 1936, and Judson had no funds to make up the difference. Curtis's pastor beseeched WMU for help. The Curtis family had no other income, and he feared that she would never be able to finish if she were forced to drop out. "I want to make my own way and would do so if an opportunity were give [sic] me," she wrote Ida M. Stallworth at the WMU. Yet she did not want to take a scholarship that rightfully belonged to young single students like her daughter. She wanted no special pleas to the college on her behalf and was embarrassed to learn of her pastor's request for aid. Nonetheless, the Limestone Association WMU provided some money,

and Judson officials helped her obtain a relief job at the Perry County library. The state WMU supplemented these funds, and the two Curtis
women (mother and daughter) continued as students at Judson College.[29]

Despite such uplifting stories, there was nothing sentimental about
WMU assistance. The organization carefully screened applicants for scholarships to determine both Christian commitment and financial need.
WMU officials often scolded school administrators who solicited money
from individual church missionary societies rather than funnel their requests to the state convention executive board. WMU was determined to
discipline its constituency to the Cooperative Program's coordinated funding strategy.[30]

Although Alabama Baptist churches had nearly 2,400 missionary societies and children's auxiliaries by 1930, and WMU had organized work
in sixty-eight of the state's seventy-three associations, only a handful of
congregations provided most contributions. WMU gifts from eleven
churches in 1937 constituted half the organization's funding.[31]

In light of such generosity, it is hard to understand continuing male
opposition. Most complaints seem to have stemmed from two sources: the
long antimissionary tradition of some churches, especially in north Alabama, and male determination to exercise power over church finances and
retain money in local congregations. In 1931 only 104 convention churches
had missionary unions serving all ages. Part of the problem was resistance
from pastors. The WMU secretary spoke to preachers at the 1931 Shelby,
Fayette, and Sipsey Associations. Some pastors knew nothing about WMU
and opposed it. Many changed their minds after her nonthreatening
speech and agreed to help organize their churchwomen. No amount of
talking and logic could convince others. Florence Thomasson wrote about
encountering Alabama Baptists whose "prejudice was as boundless as their
near illiteracy." Opponents included one preacher who attacked missions
as the work of the devil because he misunderstood her meaning when she
spoke of a medical dispensary organized in Nigeria. He thought missionaries were trying to centralize the sale of alcoholic beverages through a central "dispensary," a common practice for selling liquor in Alabama.[32]

The role of women within Alabama Baptist life continued to change
during good times and bad. At Salem Baptist Church in the Tuskegee-Lee
Association, women messengers represented the church at associational
meetings in 1931, 1936, and 1939. In the same association Tuskegee Baptist
Church had a female choir director who built one of the strongest adult
choirs in years. Wetumpka First Baptist Church elected a woman church
treasurer who steered the congregation through remodeling the sanctuary,

construction of a three-story education building, and support for the Co-operative Program despite depressed economic conditions. The church's Business Women's WMU Circle began ministry to women inmates of Julia Tutwiler Prison. Other church WMUs created social service committees that distributed clothes, food, medicine, books, and flood relief to the poor.[33]

Such women received strong reinforcement from many males. J. M. Cook, pastor of Phenix City First Baptist Church, spoke to the WMU at Myrtlewood First Baptist Church in 1930. His text (1 Corinthians 14:33–35) instructed women to be obedient and keep silent in church. But his treatment of the text delighted the women so much that they asked Gwaltney to publish his sermon in the *Alabama Baptist*. Cook preached that the passage had caused much confusion and misunderstanding. The specific Corinthian context was one of doctrinal confusion, speaking in tongues, and licentious women appearing in public. This context explained the verses. To use the passage to force women in the 1930s to sit quietly in church was a "faulty interpretation." Detractors of women in ministry ignored Paul's other admonitions against hairdressing, golden jewelry, strands of pearls, and costly array whenever it suited them, while focusing on keeping women silent in church. Paul also said women were to be saved by bearing children. But if that were literally so, how were women to be saved who could have no children because of their sterility or the sterility of their husbands? Such denigrating arguments about women ignored other parts of Scripture that urged women to assume roles of service. Phoebe had been a servant or deaconess in the church at Cenchrea. Women had been first at the cross and at the sepulchre and first to proclaim the resurrection. This wealth of scriptural support for women had been superseded by one passage in Corinthians taken out of context by what Cook called "Bible-twisters."[34]

Dr. James E. Dean added a defense of women deacons. Whatever the scriptural intent of the diaconate, he wrote in 1939, practically speaking it had become an executive committee for the conduct of church business. By functioning this way, it denied representation to 65 percent of the membership of most Baptist churches. No wonder women often complained that women's work, missions, and benevolence received so little attention and resources. Where women participated in decision making, missions flourished. Where they did not, the church spent its resources on itself. Rejection of women deacons was based on church tradition, Dean wrote, not on Scripture. The Greek word used to describe Phoebe's service was the word translated elsewhere as deacon. No Scripture in the New Testament barred women from such service. Nor did the writings of the early Christian fathers, who referred to female officers of the church.[35]

Just as women sustained the denomination's mission effort, they were responsible for most of its social ministries. They were the ones who visited the sick and helpless, conducted prison ministries, taught illiterates in opportunity schools, joined interracial committees, and staffed mothers' clubs, kindergartens, day nurseries, hospitals, and Good Will Centers. WMU's personal service chairman, who oversaw such work, wrote in 1937: "If Jesus walked your city or village streets, down your country roads, what needs would He see as He passed homes and people? We are His hands and feet. . . . Know your community."[36]

As in the 1920s, most women ministered more effectively to the poor and sick within their congregations than to those outside. And there was little theological depth to this commitment of the sort then being articulated by so-called Christian realists such as Reinhold Niebuhr or Paul Tillich. Christian ethics for Baptists usually originated in a format as simple as the one in Charles Sheldon's classic book, *In His Steps*. In the book, social justice began with a simple question: What would Christ do if He were in my place? Taking that question quite literally, Mrs. T. G. Bush of Southside Baptist Church became treasurer of the Alabama Boys Industrial School, a member of the board of the Birmingham YWCA, a director of the WMU Training School in Louisville, a member of the Alabama Board of Education, chair of the WMU personal service committee of her home congregation, a member of both state and national WMU executive boards, a member of Southside's executive committee, and the primary benefactor in her church's construction of a new education building.[37]

As recent Alabama Baptist history had repeatedly demonstrated, social Christianity did not have to originate in liberal theology. Lida Bestor Robertson of Mobile furnishes the best evidence of this fact. Descended from a long line of social activists (her Baptist preacher grandfather, Daniel P. Bestor, had introduced the first bill to create public schools while serving in the antebellum legislature; her cousin, Ruth Sarah Bush, also of Mobile, was a talented artist and benefactor of Baptist causes, including China missions and the Baptist orphanage), she came to social ministries from a decidedly conservative point of view. She taught Bible at Russell Creek Baptist Academy in Kentucky, taught a mothers' club and male delinquents at the Mobile Baptist Settlement House, worked with women factory workers at the Mobile YWCA, and served as a "co-city mission worker" for the port city. She also wrote articles for a number of papers, including the *Alabama Baptist* and *Sunday School Times*. In all these ways, she seems liberal for her times. When the pastor of the Campbellsville (Kentucky) Baptist Church recommended her for a job with the Alabama Baptist convention, he emphasized her role in establishing a chair of Bible at Russell Creek Academy and praised her as "one of the most gifted Bible teachers in our denomination." Apparently Alabama's mission board was not seeking a woman Bible teacher in its Baptist academies, and Robertson did not get a job.[38]

Despite such misleading appearances, Robertson's theology was not liberal. She deplored a newly published book about Christian education that "decried the divinity of Christ, the miracles, the blood atonement, sin, and the resurrection." She warned against social reforms being substituted for conversion. She denounced Al Smith in 1928 and proudly attributed his defeat to Protestant churches, women, the WCTU, Masons, and the Salvation Army. She praised Arkansas legislators for banning school texts that taught evolution. She agreed with those who taught that the Bible was dictated by God without human interference. She was kind to African Americans because "they are the lowest of races . . . , having no history, no literature, no government." She told blacks on occasion that God had created them black, and their rebellion against their status was their rebellion against God. If blacks resented living in a white man's land ruled by whites, they should emigrate to Haiti or Liberia.[39]

Such attitudes seem strange for a social reformer. On one occasion, Robertson criticized a female domestic court judge who allowed a male lawyer to cross-examine a pregnant fifteen-year-old girl, asking questions that Robertson thought only a physician or nurse should ask. The grilling had stripped the girl of "every vestige of decency." She described a visit to the Pritchard jail by a woman friend from Dauphin Way Baptist Church who ministered to women prisoners. One nineteen-year-old convict had been jailed by a woman who charged her with stealing forty-five cents, "which shocked me and disturbed me beyond measure." She asked a pastor friend to help her find the girl's name and the facts in the case so she could help the teenager. Never a shrinking violet, Robertson led a fight in the late 1930s to fire T. V. Neal, president of Howard College, because of his tyrannical conduct toward faculty and students and what she believed to be his personal dishonesty.[40]

A Baptist Critique of the Times

Baptists from all walks of life had strong opinions about what caused the problems of the 1930s. L. L. Gwaltney was the most persistent and perceptive critic of American economic injustice. Realizing that traditional economic patterns were collapsing, he deplored an economic system that imposed the family wage, requiring that women and children work in order to sustain the family. He believed that capitalism had failed completely in Europe and partially in the United States. "Men sing of liberty," he wrote, "but a liberty to starve to death is not greatly to be desired by anybody, hence many people, when put to the test, will swap liberty for security." Fascism, Nazism, and communism thrived where capitalism failed.[41]

Throughout the decade, Gwaltney provided Alabama Baptists his appraisal of the nation's economic collapse. He deplored the gap between those who lived in opulence and those who barely survived, between food surpluses in the United States and mass starvation in China. Quoting the book of James on Christian obligations to the poor, he wrote that something was radically wrong in the world's system of distributing food and other necessities.[42]

Early in the depression, Gwaltney focused his attention on what churches could do to stem a national tide of rebellion. When desperate Arkansas farmers took over a town in 1931 and forcibly confiscated food from a relief agency for their wives and children, Gwaltney warned of revolution. When 30 percent of the population owned 93 percent of the nation's wealth, rebellion was inevitable. He wrote in 1931 that only two churches in Birmingham were feeding the hungry as the Bible commanded, and both of those were Presbyterian. If Baptists did not intend to practice "practical Christianity," at least they ought to contribute to Presbyterians who did. He also praised states that were replacing poorhouses with state-operated welfare departments. This reform removed some of the stigma from the poor and allowed them to live with greater self-respect. It also kept homes intact.[43]

Social gospel ideas dominated his editorials during the 1930s. On the twenty-fifth anniversary of the publication of Walter Rauschenbusch's classic work, *Christianity and the Social Crisis,* Gwaltney praised the New York Baptist leader for awakening Christians to social oppression and injustice. Modern preachers, Gwaltney explained, must not only proclaim salvation but must also preach against armament races and unjust taxation. They must preach "both the gospel and the social gospel." Churches had a key responsibility to the "marginal population" of Alabama that earned less than $400 annually, most of whom had less than a fifth-grade education. They should support state and national policies designed to alleviate poverty. They must help direct public welfare so that it did more good than harm. "In a word," he wrote, "church people must face the question of whether we want these groups in our society to have a chance."[44]

Gwaltney recognized a form of religious communism in the early church in which all members held material possessions in common. The "partial failure" of capitalism in the United States had strengthened radical communism of the sort found in the Soviet Union. Such totalitarian communism had no sanction in the Bible or in reason. Forced to choose between two flawed systems, he preferred capitalism with all its problems to communism. Christianity could adapt to all systems of political philosophy, including socialism, and make them better, but he feared totalitarianism because the church would no longer be free.[45]

Fred E. Maxey (pastor of Mount Hebron Baptist Church near Leeds) was not so sure flawed capitalism was the best solution to the problems of an unjust society. Although the evangelist described himself as an independent, dispensational, premillennial fundamentalist, Maxey lacked formal theological education. He had been a labor negotiator in the Appalachian coal fields, and he felt deep sympathy for coal miners and tenant farmers. In his Leeds congregation he used his connections to former associates in the U.S. Department of Labor to help unemployed blacks and whites obtain work. On one occasion his intercession on behalf of African Americans earned him a warning from the Ku Klux Klan. Maxey began to write a "Pulpit in Print" column for a local radical newspaper, charging the church with neglecting its biblical mandate to care for the poor. He proclaimed Jesus a radical and tried to fuse Christianity with Marxism. He spoke at communist-sponsored rallies, opposing the poll tax and advocating that African Americans be allowed to vote. Although it is unlikely that his congregation was aware of the extent of his radicalism, it is interesting that Maxey was one of the church's most beloved pastors.[46] Perhaps even more intriguing is the fact that one of Alabama's most liberal theologians, L. L. Gwaltney, weighed Marxism and capitalism in the balance and chose capitalism, while one of the denomination's most fundamentalist preachers made the opposite choice.

Both Gwaltney and Maxey took extreme positions by the reckoning of most Alabama Baptists. J. O. Williams argued in 1931 that refusal to work or trust in God caused poverty. He claimed never to have met a poor man begging food who put the kingdom of God first in his life. The 1931 report of the state social service commission dealt almost exclusively with prohibition, neglecting poverty, tax policy, the collapse of public education, tenancy, and other social problems. It urged people to learn lessons from hard times as well as good ones and not to succumb to demagoguery.[47]

Glib dismissal of historical realities could not obscure what was clear to both Gwaltney and Maxey. The Christian church was as beset by class divisions as were other sectors of American life. An Alabama WMU report on conditions in south Alabama deplored the existence of five churches and one mission in a single community, each appealing to "a different class of people from a social point of view" who would not associate with one another. A careful study of a north Alabama community found similar conditions even when multiple classes belonged to the same congregation. The pastor of the oldest Baptist church in the community was the son of a large landowner, a fact that did not make the church particularly attractive to tenant farmers who worked the family's land. Nor were tenants or sharecroppers likely to hold positions of leadership in the church.[48]

More poignant was the testimony of a pastor's wife in Brundidge. When her husband was called as pastor of the Salem Baptist Church in 1928, they found the congregation too aristocratic for their tastes. The previous pastor would sometimes share wine at meals with younger church members. When the new pastor invited a tenant farmer to attend church services, some of the "hoity-toity type people didn't want them in the church." The wealthier clique never directly mentioned their distaste for tenants, but the visiting family realized they were not welcome. On another occasion, the preacher's wife brought a woman to a WMU meeting and members "let us know they didn't care to have her in the church, so we just had to let things pass on off." The pastor kept his peace and did not confront them with their elitism.[49]

Most Baptist churches avoided such awkwardness by catering to one class or another, an easier task in the country, where virtually all whites were either tenants or landowners, than in towns and cities, which had more complicated class arrangements. In country churches, class grievances often were expressed as feelings of spiritual superiority over more worldly urban Christians.

Rural churches confronted an anomaly. Alabama had an excess of ministers, but many rural churches could not find a pastor. The problem was both geographical and financial. Available bivocational ministers often lived in towns, not in the country. During the depression, few of them could afford to pastor a country church that could not even cover their automobile expenses, much less pay a modest salary. Nor were better educated ministers willing to pastor unprogressive rural churches that contained virtually no high school graduates. In Walker County, more than twenty of seventy-five country churches were without pastors, and many rural preachers did not have a high school education. Another county reported similar conditions.[50]

Because only about 200 of the convention's 2,300 churches were full-time during the 1930s, bivocational ministers played a critical role in denominational life. L. M. West of Opp in extreme south Alabama served as clerk of his association for more than a quarter century. The association was filled with what he called "jack leg" preachers who worked all week and preached on Sunday. During the 1930s he recalled some of them walking three to seven miles to preach for pay that often amounted to a few dozen eggs, sweet potatoes, syrup, chicken, or ham. He estimated that their cash income from preaching seldom exceeded $25 to $40 a year. He remembered them as poor, sincere men who were "mindful of the superior attitude on the part of the supposedly educated ministry."[51] The result of such itinerancy was instability in rural congregations. During the first half century of its existence (1887-1937), the Lincoln Baptist Church had twenty-seven pastors.[52]

Individual experiences of bivocational and small church pastors reveal their dedication as well as the difficulties of their profession. Edward B. Warren pastored as many as eight Black Belt churches at the same time during the 1930s, often preaching on Sundays at 11:00 A.M., in the afternoon, and at night, each time to a different congregation. Some of his services were once a month, others bimonthly. Many Dallas County rural churches, he remembered, still resisted Sunday school and WMU. They also had trouble finding a male who would serve as Sunday school superintendent. But when he suggested that his congregations ask a woman to be a superintendent, the reaction was often, "No, no, we don't want any woman."[53]

W. Albert Smith came from a background of rural poverty. At the age of fifteen, he received a call to preach but had only a grammar school education. He had been raised on a Clay County farm "with no money, no clothes, no opportunity to go to school, and no prospects of improving my situation." He prayed earnestly that his family would move to a town with a high school. His prayers were answered when his father obtained work in Sylacauga. At age sixteen Smith went to work at Mignon cotton mill, making six cents an hour. He worked one year at the mill in order to attend one year of high school and in this fashion completed three years of school in six years, graduating at age twenty-two. He began Howard College in 1928 with $45 and a scholarship provided by textile magnate Donald Comer. He pastored Mount Hebron Baptist Church near Leeds while a student, married his high school sweetheart, and attended Southwestern seminary after graduation. In Fort Worth he read water meters, fired the seminary's boilers beginning at 4:00 every morning, and pastored a church in order to pay expenses. Three years of seminary amid the financial pressures of the Great Depression on only four hours of sleep a night took its toll. Newly graduated in 1935, he had a nervous breakdown and spent two months in bed. He came home to Alabama to recover and accept a call as pastor of Bon Air Baptist Church near Sylacauga in June 1935.[54]

Andrew W. Oden was born in Blount County in 1902. His mother died while he was an infant, and his father did not make him attend school, so the boy grew up without education. After his conversion, he attended an associational meeting at which he was asked if he wanted to speak. He agreed and began to preach. That evening he felt called to the ministry. B. F. Dykes, pastor of the Oneonta First Baptist Church, befriended him and urged the young man to attend Eldridge Mountain Academy, one of the Baptist mountain schools. Though he was married and had four children at the time, Oden moved his family into a house owned by the academy, where he learned to read the Bible for the first time. He used his 1931 Model A Ford to pastor the Taits Gap and Pine Bluff churches, where members would give him quarters or half dollars to buy gas. He once complicated family finances by giving his last dollar to an unemployed family without food. Thanks to financial help from Oneonta First Baptist, he was able to graduate from Eldridge Academy. He then pastored a number of quarter-time churches in Blount, Marshall, Saint Clair, and Cullman Counties. "I still didn't never know much," he explained at the end of his ministry, "but the Lord blessed me mighty well in my ministry." Evidence of that blessing was abundant. Once he baptized forty-four converts in a single baptismal service. One year later he baptized more than all other churches in the Blount County Association combined. Though serving in an association renowned for its independence and noncooperation, Oden also preferred denominational organizations, including WMU and the Baptist Training Union.[55]

J. W. Lester grew up in rural Tallapoosa County, where he attended a Primitive Baptist church. So starved was he for worship more than once a month that he walked twelve miles into Dadeville to attend a Presbyterian church, whose pastor befriended him and gave him literature about the rural church movement. Lester left Alabama in 1928 for Detroit, where he went to work in an auto factory. Laid off during the depression, he enrolled in Chicago's Moody Bible Institute, waiting tables to pay expenses. He also joined a Baptist church and devoted his life to the ministry. After graduation from Moody, he returned to Alabama to pastor five small rural churches, but all five combined could pay him only $93 his first year in the ministry. As one of the most progressive rural pastors in Alabama, he introduced the Lord's Acre Plan, urging each farm family to set aside one acre or animal whose proceeds would go to the church. He helped each of his churches draft a budget, usually the first time they had done so. He also invited Auburn University extension specialists to conduct seminars in his churches on new agricultural techniques, diversified agriculture, poultry, and dairying. As a result of these seminars, many members began experimenting with new crops. By 1933 each of Lester's churches budgeted over $100 for the pastor's salary. His success with these five rural churches convinced him that the strategies of the rural church movement could work if energetically implemented. But his desire for further education postponed his rural ministerial career. With six dollars in his pocket, Lester caught a train for Birmingham and enrolled in Howard College. He took as many courses as possible dealing with rural life and read every library book he could find on the subject. His religion professors stressed the importance of the rural church and emphasized the need for some preachers to feel called to that particular ministry. After graduation from Southwestern seminary, he pastored rural congregations most of his career except for brief periods as associate director of Howard College's extension centers (which were designed to help educate rural and bivocational ministers), as director of pastoral institutes for African American rural ministers, and as head of the Department of Rural Church at Clear Creek School for Mountain Preachers in Pineville, Kentucky. He was chosen in 1949 as one of the South's thirteen rural ministers of the year by *Progressive Farmer* magazine.[56]

The denomination did what it could to help men such as Lester who sought to reshape and modernize rural churches. The *Alabama Baptist* explained the merits of the Lord's Acre program and urged that it be used by all rural congregations. State mission board personnel participated in rural church conferences at Auburn University. The board also employed staff who were given the responsibility of training a new generation of rural leadership, especially in Sunday school and the Baptist Training Union.[57]

Despite such efforts, the decline of rural churches continued, paralleling the decline of country life in general. An unintended consequence of New Deal agricultural policy was the displacement of millions of tenant farmers. The consolidation of land (enhanced by the acquisition of new technologies such as mechanical cotton pickers, by the decline of cotton, and by the rising importance of poultry, dairy, cattle, and timber industries) drove small landowning farmers into urban jobs, further denuding rural churches of leadership. World War II and the drafting of millions of farm youth pretty well finished the process of transforming Alabama from a rural to an urban state.

Despite efforts to preserve rural churches, the denomination subtly switched emphasis as well. Ministerial respectability came to mean a college and seminary degree and an urban pastorate. Articles in the *Alabama Baptist* extolled the merits of air conditioning in order to make worship more comfortable during summertime. One 1939 correspondent to the paper, noting how uncomfortable downtown Baptist churches were on muggy summer Sunday evenings, commented that a lightning strike would have to be fairly accurate to hit anyone worshiping in such a church.[58]

Howard College might offer J. W. Lester courses in how to save the rural church during the 1930s, but the future seemed to belong to Augustus Evans Lanier, a senior ministerial student from Birmingham who took a course in fine arts and religion during 1936. In Dr. James H. Chapman's course, Lanier learned to use art, architecture, drama, music, and literature to enhance worship. Worship should consist of sound and sight, even including symbols of the cross to substitute for the reality of the crucifixion. The new spiritual age, Lanier believed, required new forms of religious communication that could overcome differences between races and classes, diminish prejudice and ignorance, and enhance economic justice.[59] Although Lester and Lanier were classmates, the worlds of rural Tallapoosa County and urban Birmingham provided them radically different perspectives on the future of Alabama Baptists.

Despite church growth during the 1930s, some denominational leaders worried about trends they perceived. Gwaltney estimated that one-third of Alabama Baptists attended church regularly, another third attended only for marriages, funerals, and occasional revivals, and the rest never attended at all. William F. Price of Selma grieved over the growing number of pastors who were being fired or forced to resign. Although Baptists boasted of their congregational democracy, an aggressive minority often ruled congregations and forced its will on a cowed majority. Once fired, a pastor usually had a terrible time finding another church despite the fact that such dismissals were more often the fault of the congregation than of the pastor. Gwaltney denied that God always supplied a new church if a man was truly called to preach. He urged pastors who were fired to seek help actively because both human and divine elements were part of every call.[60]

The Battle for the Bible: Round Three

The reason for pastoral firings was sometimes the continuing theological battle within the denomination. Whatever liberal religion survived World War I took a drubbing from the twin forces of worldwide depression and renewed international hostility. The new theological influences arising out of Europe were those of Christian realism and neo-orthodoxy (especially influenced by Swiss theologians Karl Barth and Emil Brunner).

Christian realism provided the perspective from which Reinhold Niebuhr surveyed the wreckage of humanism and the collapse of liberal values. The new theology considered pacifism in the face of Nazism, fascism, and communism a naive position. Its reemphasis on humanity's flawed nature and the contingency of human solutions removed much of the optimism and idealism that had characterized liberal theology. Niebuhr also developed a syncretistic social theory that combined Marxist and Christian principles to address the decade's economic collapse. Classic liberalism did survive in the form of a more optimistic and pacifist spirit embodied in such groups as the Fellowship of Reconciliation, the confessional Oxford Movement, and the socially activist Fellowship of Southern Churchmen.[61]

L. L. Gwaltney's lack of systematic theology allowed him to move easily back and forth between conservatism, liberalism, and neo-orthodoxy, driven more by events than consistent philosophy. Compounding the problem of pinning down the elusive editor was his propensity to allow every viewpoint to be represented in his newspaper. Believing as he did that the greatest threat to democracy was not radical ideas but the suppression of free thought, Gwaltney published opinions with which he wholly disagreed. His popularity with ordinary Baptists owed more to his anti-Catholicism, devotion to prohibition, and populist identification with country folk than to his formal theology anyway. Though he shaped the Alabama Baptist State Convention more than any other person of his generation, he made no effort to force it into his own mold. He was generous to young preachers of all ideologies, often sending them ten-dollar Christmas gifts while they were in seminary. He could talk the language of Zion without taking it too seriously, as Sam Jones Ezell remembered from his initial meeting with the editor. Ezell had just arrived from Georgia to pastor Clanton First Baptist Church when he met Gwaltney on a train. Gwaltney greeted him warmly: "We're mighty glad the Lord sent you to help us out in the great work in Alabama," he said effusively. Ezell replied: "I am very glad to be in Alabama, but I am not sure that the Lord sent me, because the boll weevil in Eatonton, Georgia, had eaten up the crops for two years and I think [that] had a great deal to do with my coming to Alabama." The remark so amused and impressed Gwaltney that he never forgot it, and they became lifelong friends.[62]

Gwaltney considered modernism largely passé by 1935, a source of doubts and questions rather than firm faith. He continued to defend science

John W. Phillips, much beloved pastor of Mobile First Baptist Church, was perhaps the state's premier modernist Baptist. Born in England, Phillips held a Ph.D. in Egyptology from the University of London and infuriated fundamentalists with his modernist theology. He was elected president of the state convention and keynote speaker at the 1931 SBC. (Courtesy of Samford University Archives)

vigorously and deplored narrow-minded Christians who regarded Darwin as earlier generations of the faithful had regarded Galileo. Nor did their citation of proof texts from the Bible impress him. He remembered that southern Christians in the 1850s had cited Scripture to justify slavery and in the 1930s to defend war and capital punishment. Mormons even cited the Bible in defense of polygamy. He found neo-orthodoxy a convenient substitute for liberalism, writing that truth was narrow and Christians could not allow open-mindedness to turn into license to believe anything a person desired. He emphasized the sovereignty of God and deplored humanism. In a 1938 editorial praising Karl Barth, he warned that the world would plunge back into war within five years, dashing hopes of those who sought a peaceful world.[63]

Both J. E. Dillard (pastor of Southside) and L. O. Dawson (head of Howard's Bible department) agreed with Gwaltney that science and religion were compatible and that theistic evolution was no threat to Christian orthodoxy. Dawson observed that much science accepted as truth would someday be supplanted and much "truth" believed to be scriptural would be found false. Dillard boasted that he had enrolled in summer theology courses for fifteen years at the University of Chicago "and returned without as much as a smell of heresy" (though reading his book reviews in the *Alabama Baptist* did cause some Alabama Baptists to sniff a strange odor).[64]

If Dillard escaped odoriferous charges of heresy, his colleague at Mobile First Baptist Church, John W. Phillips, was not so lucky. The venerable Englishman was invited to preach the keynote sermon at the 1931 Southern

Baptist Convention, which met in Birmingham. In his sermon Phillips contrasted churches to the kingdom of God. He considered many churches to be like social clubs or businesses, operated for the benefit of the powerful. Churches were constantly tempted to rely on external power and material glory instead of simple devotion to the kingdom of God. The South's racism and injustice toward blacks was just one example of conflict between devotion to church and devotion to kingdom.[65]

Gwaltney called the sermon prophetic and urged ministers to ponder it carefully. Others disagreed. Fundamentalist evangelist T. T. Martin (who had established an educational center at Cook Springs near Birmingham) accused Phillips of modernist heresy. Phillips (who had probably preached more revivals than any minister in the state) could "sugar-coat" his deadly teachings, Martin warned, but still he denied the inspiration of the Bible, claimed Old Testament sacrifice to be relics of paganism, and believed salvation could be obtained by improving character rather than saving souls. A. D. Zbinden of Hartford penned a more temperate criticism but also accused Phillips of denying the inerrancy of the Scriptures.[66]

Gwaltney defended his friend from mounting criticism by attempting to reconcile arguments and clarify context. Phillips had come to the United States from England at age nineteen, Gwaltney reminded critics, old enough to detest the established church of his homeland. If by "church" Phillips meant "a centralized ecclesiastical institution" controlled by creeds such as Baptists seemed increasingly inclined to adopt, then Gwaltney agreed with Phillips's characterization. Such creedal churches were more dangerous to society than "anarchists or bolshevists," as Baptists should know from their own bloody history of persecution.[67]

Rather than mollifying T. T. Martin, Gwaltney's defense poured fuel on the fire. Calling Phillips's sermon "the most unscriptural, the most anti-scriptural, the most dangerous sermon ever preached before the Southern Baptist Convention," Martin attacked Gwaltney as well. He added that Phillips would never have been called to his Mobile church or elected president of the state convention if Baptists had understood his views. Such heretics, he proclaimed, often camouflaged their beliefs in order to infiltrate and corrupt orthodox churches.[68]

From England, where he was vacationing, Phillips thanked some two hundred brethren "who did not misunderstand or misinterpret" his sermon and who had written him congratulations. Rather than respond to Martin's charges, he had decided to attend noontime lectures at the British Museum on "How We Got Our Bible." There he would also read the oldest manuscript of the Bible. He wished all Baptist pastors could be with him that day, he wrote, no doubt aware of how that prospect would likely be received by T. T. Martin.[69]

J. C. Stivender explored theological issues more quietly. The ecumenical discussion group he helped establish featured formal papers by each participant after which members engaged in spirited debate. They drafted letters to the *Christian Century* defending the "Scottsboro boys" from rape charges and discussed the persecution of Jews in Germany (in 1933, years before U.S. government recognition of such problems). Dillard presented papers during the 1930s on the church and industry, the church in politics, the Oxford Movement, and the implications of psychology for religion. Other topics ranged from race relations and rural cooperatives to reforms in public education and how to make modern views of the Bible acceptable to orthodox Christians. Baptist participants included not only Stivender, who served on the steering committee, but also James H. Chapman, Lee McBride White (pastor of West End Baptist Church), J. E. Dillard, and John H. Buchanan (after he replaced Dillard as pastor of Southside). Three of the seven charter members (J. C. Stivender, James H. Chapman, and W. R. Hendrix, who like Chapman was a professor at Howard College) were Baptists. They were joined by some of the city's most liberal Presbyterian, Methodist, and Episcopal ministers.[70]

One Baptist preacher who would have enjoyed such discussions had he known about them was Charles R. Bell Jr., pastor of Parker Memorial in Anniston. The son of a deacon in the church who was president of the town's largest bank, Bell grew up in affluence. He attended Howard College and Brown University, then graduated from Southern seminary, where he was greatly influenced by W. O. Carver. At age twenty-five in 1932, he returned in triumph to his home church, determined to move it toward the mainstream of theological and social thought. Though charming and earnest, he was also innocent, idealistic, and naive. His visits to Tuskegee Institute to talk with George Washington Carver, his association with rural cooperatives, and his hosting of biracial dinners did not endear him to Anniston's social conservatives. His support of socialist Norman Thomas for president and attendance at the initial meeting of the Southern Conference for Human Welfare alienated political conservatives. His organization of a small fellowship of the Oxford Movement in his church to foster mutual confession and reconciliation made him appear elitist.[71]

Bell took a trip around the world in 1936, visiting Japan, China, and India. Long under the spell of his seminary missions professor, W. O. Carver (who had opened "a world in the New Testament which I had never heard"), Bell arranged conferences with notable Christians wherever he stopped. In Japan he was fascinated by Christian socialist Yoyohiko Kagawa. In India he talked with Mohandas Gandhi. Upon his return he wrote accounts of his travels and of missions in East Asia for the *Alabama Baptist.* He depicted Orientals as proud, sensitive people who resented imperialism and the nativism that dominated American immigration policy. How could American warships in Chinese harbors or British colonial rule of India be reconciled to Christian principles? he wondered. In Bombay he talked with Gandhi and other "heathen" who were as intense and sincere in their religion as westerners were in Christianity. Such ideas bordered on universalism and further disturbed the orthodox.[72]

Bell made his greatest impact on the denomination in May 1937 at the Southern Baptist Convention in New Orleans. Incensed by the report of the social service commission that condemned the use of tobacco while "all around us was a nation weakened by poverty, ridden by segregation," and drifting toward world war, Bell offered a four-part substitute. The first part dealt with international relations and urged Christians to work for peace and disarmament. The second part dealt with economics and held up a cooperative rather than a competitive ideal. Under the topic of labor and agriculture, he deplored "economic injustice or industrial inhumanity" that resulted in poverty, low living standards, and inequality. He also recognized the goal of organized labor for better wages and living conditions and endorsed regulation of child labor. His statement on race deplored unchristian practices aimed at African Americans. Although most of his resolutions were tabled, some were passed with modifications, and the ensuing debate attracted national attention.[73]

Although his congregation remained remarkably tranquil amid charges hurled at their pastor, attendance began to decline and some accused him of heresy. When he brought his seminary teacher, W. O. Carver, to preach at Parker Memorial, criticism escalated. Carver advised Bell to be cautious in what he said or in identifying the prophetic function of Christianity with a specific social theory or program. He admired Bell's courage but worried about his fate in Alabama. "You can easily become a thwarted martyr to an ideal," Carver wrote his young friend, "instead of a compelling witness to and exponent of an idea—even of the Christ who incarnates the ideal and the idea."[74]

James E. Dean experienced some of the same opposition as Bell. One of eleven children born to a farmer some thirty miles north of Birmingham, he worked his way through Howard College by teaching school and

preaching. For thirteen years he was at Baptist Bible Institute in New Orleans, first as a student and then as a professor. In 1931 he was dismissed
by trustees for opinions "at variance with the views of Southern Baptists."
His heresy may have developed while taking a Ph.D. in Old Testament at
the University of Chicago. For two years after his dismissal from BBI, he
was a research assistant at Chicago in Syriac languages, but he returned
home to Birmingham in 1933 unable to find a teaching job. Finally in 1936
he became pastor of Mount Calvary Baptist Church in Tarrant City, and the
next year he began a long and successful pastorate at Greensboro Baptist
Church. When he wrote FDR in 1935, he was distressed by the absence of
any vision of social righteousness. Although he regretted Roosevelt's repeal
of prohibition, he enthusiastically endorsed the New Deal.[75]

Dean began writing articles regularly for the *Alabama Baptist*, always
taking a liberal position. While pastor in Greensboro in April 1939 he endorsed women serving as deacons. A month later he warned that unless the
church showed greater interest in the poor, that class would become hope-
lessly alienated as it had in Mexico, Spain, and Russia. Usually an article
by Dean drew a quick rejoinder from William F. Price, who pastored at
Selma. When Dean extolled Kagawa's ideas, Price denounced the Japanese
Christian as an evolutionist. "If this isn't rank unbelieving blasphemy,"
Price wrote, "then pray tell me what it is?" Apparently unaware that editor
L. L. Gwaltney held the same belief, Price cited other "atheistic and modernistic statements" by Kagawa before concluding that it was time for Alabama Baptists "to come back to earth from this Oriental paradise, and leave
this Japanese teacher at home!" He warned in 1935 that modernism ("this
scourge of faith-killing and soul-destroying heresies") was on the way
South.[76]

A.D. Zbinden (pastor of Headland Avenue Baptist Church in Dothan)
took exception to the theological liberalism expressed in an article published in *Review and Expositor*, the theological journal edited by W. O.
Carver at SBTS. He protested to Carver and to John C. Slemp, a liberal
young editor at the Sunday School Board who was already under fire for
his heterodoxy. In his 1938 letter to Slemp, Zbinden chided the essay for
its view of progressive revelation (the New Testament revelation of Christ
overruled the Old Testament depiction of God) and its attribution of certain
wrathful acts to God (which seemed to Slemp better examples of man's
savagery than of God's providence). If Slemp was truly a brother in Christ,
Zbinden wrote, then the Holy Spirit would teach him the same theology
that the Spirit taught Zbinden. It was unfair that pastors had to contend

with Baptist literature that did not accept "all the Bible as the word of God." He urged Slemp to admit his mistakes and relieve "a situation that is sure to become intolerable and ultimately cause a division." Otherwise he threatened to circulate the offending passages to a circle of pastors and demand further action.[77] The incident made clear how deep theological divisions remained both within the denomination and in Alabama. But most pastors refused to identify with either camp, preferring a noncombative evangelicalism to ideological purity.

Alabama Baptists were less divided about ecumenism. Church union received no more support in the 1930s than it had in previous decades. If anything, Gwaltney was even more dubious about ecumenism, fearing that federations of both left and right might raise issues that would divide Baptists. He attacked the watering down of Christian doctrine by groups such as the International Council of Religious Education, the Federal Council of Churches, and *Christian Century.* Nor was he any more sympathetic to transdenominational organizations of evangelicals or fundamentalists. John Buchanan was more sympathetic to ecumenism while serving on a twelve-person committee to study Baptist participation in the World Council of Churches. He was part of the committee's minority that believed Baptists should join the world council and "bear our Baptist witness."[78]

Refusal to join national and international Christian federations did not necessarily translate into exclusivism at home. Many antiecumenical pastors still held Landmark beliefs that only Baptists could trace true Christian faith back to Christ. But other pastors cooperated enthusiastically in local interdenominational efforts.

Economic Depression demanded greater coordination of precious community resources. Claude M. Haygood (pastor of Tuskegee First Baptist Church) fostered cooperation between the community's Baptists, Methodists, and Presbyterians. The three churches began to hold regular union services in 1936, a tradition of ecumenism that Haygood continued while serving as a chaplain during the Second World War. In Wetumpka, Robert Edge engaged in similar interdenominational ministries while pastor of First Baptist Church. He organized a minister's council that included all pastors in the county. He allowed Methodists to use his church baptistry for immersing those requesting that form of baptism. He joined Methodist and Presbyterian churches in a community-wide, open-air union revival. He also worked with these denominations to conduct an interdenominational chapel at a local textile mill where the three ministers took turns preaching. This ministry worked so well that they cooperated in another mission in Holtville, where they built a community center to serve tenant families. Such ecumenical activities soon became a feature of Wetumpka First Baptist, extending through several decades and three pastorates.[79]

Such cooperation did not extend to pentecostals. J. E. Berkstresser denounced "the modern tongues movement" as unscriptural but warned that it was not "a fading fad." Gwaltney wrote a more perceptive sociological explanation of the movement's origins. Lumping together the Church of God, Nazarenes, and other Holiness and pentecostal groups, he wrote that the name "holy roller" had been used against them as a term of opprobrium. Such denominations appealed largely to the underprivileged, many of whom lived in "direst poverty" in backwoods or urban slums. Had Baptists been faithful in preaching to the poor, there would have been no pentecostals because the "cult is the response of the religious instinct of a neglected people." Pentecostals lacked economic and educational opportunity and expressed their deficiencies through extremely literalistic interpretations of Scripture and emotional excesses. Gwaltney believed that improving economic and educational opportunities would modify their worship. He predicted continued growth for pentecostalism and considered its excesses less disturbing than the paganism of many educated people.[80]

In sermons and editorials Gwaltney tried to redirect Christianity toward social justice. He dismissed the popular slogan of an earlier age ("Every one win one") as containing only half the gospel. Valid as evangelism was, the social impact of converted people on society was equally important. No person whose citizenship was in the kingdom of heaven could "rest quite satisfied in a world of social injustice, oppression and the exploitation of the underprivileged classes." "Every man's religion becomes a solemn mockery who does not go to his limit to right all wrongs in the society in which he lives so far as it is possible for him to do so." He believed the Sermon on the Mount to be essentially socialist in its implications, although there were many kinds of socialism. The sermon's essential assumption that people should govern themselves and not be ruled by autocracy, oligarchy, and plutocracy was also a Christian assumption. Either capitalism must adopt cooperation and profit sharing and renounce the profit motive "as the chief end and aim of business enterprise" or millions of workers would impose some form of socialism on the United States. Such obligations, he warned, were the task of biblical prophets who applied the word of God to society, not the task of the average minister who preached individual salvation.[81]

Assuming such prophetic function himself, Gwaltney wrote one of his most powerful expositions of the social gospel in 1937. Applying its themes to his home state, Gwaltney wrote:

> We want to see a state where there will be no slums . . . ; a state where no one will have to live in the miserable shacks and hovels that some of our people now call their homes; a state that sees and has compassion for its humblest citizen; a state that has an understanding heart, even when such understanding brings serious unrest.
>
> We want to see a state in which unemployment is no longer the ghost at our banquet table; a state in which underemployment and semi-employment are no longer major problems. The unemployed do not want charity any more than the rest of us. They want work that they can provide for their loved ones, just as the rest of us do. There is tragedy when men have no employment and do not know which way to turn for a job.
>
> We love Alabama . . . well enough to see her faults as well as her virtues. Such a state as we dream about will come only when one takes seriously this business of building the kingdom of God on earth, because then only will come a real brotherhood of man, whose foundation will be laid in the Fatherhood of God.[82]

Gwaltney went beyond theoretical discussions to endorse specific reforms. He endorsed the 1937 Alabama legislature's appropriation of $500,000 for state mental hospitals and public health. Praising Baptist preacher Hopson Owen Murfee, who had led the campaign to improve conditions in the state's mental hospitals, Gwaltney called care for the mentally ill "the supreme duty of a Christian commonwealth." That same year he published a frank discussion of venereal disease in order to educate the public and eradicate the problem.[83]

Many local churches also tried to implement strategies to reach the poor and helpless. Wetumpka First Baptist was notable for its ecumenical ministry to textile workers and tenant farmers. Apparently such ministries so impressed Leon Robinson, who grew up in the church, that he began mission work among Italians in New York City after completing his doctorate at Union Theological Seminary. After a long career of social ministries in the North, he returned to Saint Louis, where he managed to get his Southern Baptist Church tossed out of the local association for accepting transfer members who had not been baptized by immersion. Northport Baptist Church established a social service department in 1936. Its tasks included contacting poor families within the community who could not provide financial necessities; directing such people to appropriate welfare agencies; informing the congregation of such needs; and making recommendations to the church budget committee. The new department had a director and four associate directors and consisted of five male and five female members.[84]

Although the Alabama Baptist consensus was much more favorable to social Christianity than to liberalism or ecumenism, substantial opposition remained. William F. Price of Selma (a fierce opponent of modernism) disliked the social gospel as well. Clerical attempts to inaugurate a reign of social righteousness through "Communistic agencies and enterprises" were merely additional evidences of apostasy to Price. Baptists who sought to eliminate doctrinal differences and church creeds, who emphasized the kingdom of God as an earthly manifestation of social justice, indicated the "falling away" from the inspiration of Scripture. Such criticism was potent enough by the late 1930s to transform Alabama's social service commission into a mirror image of the SBC commission, launching annual attacks on demon rum while largely ignoring lynching, racial and economic injustice, soaring infant mortality rates, poor public schools, warfare between labor and management, and pervasive poverty.[85]

Resistance to social reform was not always a bad idea, depending on what idea happened to be fashionable at the time. In the 1920s and 1930s one popular reform involved eugenics. Growing out of Darwinian science and Social Darwinism, this new pseudoscience sought to control social progress by determining who married and produced offspring. At one level, eugenics propelled the birth control movement that flourished in the South as a way to control reproduction of poor whites and blacks. At a more sinister level, proponents of eugenics recommended that certain inferior people should be forcibly sterilized. Beginning in "progressive" states such as California, the eugenics movement spread to the South where it won support from physicians and mental health officials. In Alabama, James T. Searcy (superintendent of the Alabama Hospital for the Insane) and his chief assistant, William Partlow, authorized the sterilization of every patient released from the state's mental hospital for fifteen years. The eugenics movement reached its peak during the 1930s when Partlow and state health officer J. N. Baker praised Germany's "bold experiment in mass sterilization" and proposed that Alabama enact a similar program. Various reformist organizations (including the American Association of University Women and the Alabama Society for Mental Hygiene) endorsed a proposal to give the superintendent of any state institution for the mentally ill or retarded unlimited discretion to sterilize sexual perverts, homosexuals, rapists, mental defectives, or those who were "habitually and constantly de-

pendent upon public relief or support of charity." The proposed law even
denied patients the right of judicial review. The *Birmingham News,
Montgomery Advertiser,* and some professors at the University of Alabama
endorsed the bill. Opposition to the legislation came from an incongruous
coalition of organized labor, the American Civil Liberties Union, Roman
Catholics, the *Alabama Baptist,* and a leading Baptist legislator. Although
the bill passed the legislature, strong opposition from so many groups that
had supported his election caused Governor Bibb Graves to veto the bill.
Partlow attributed the governor's veto to "religious and political scruples,"
primarily in conservative churches.[86]

J. E. Dillard, one of the state's most liberal theologians, flirted with the
eugenics movement. He wrote that half the children born in Birmingham
were either mentally or physically "defective." Children had a right to be
"well born," he argued, and some couples therefore were not fit to be parents. He recommended that couples applying for marriage licenses present
certification from physicians that they were capable of bearing healthy babies.[87]

Gwaltney disagreed. He criticized a report by the Federal Council of
Churches favoring birth control. Although he recognized that difficult economic conditions made it hard for parents to rear and educate children, he
believed the practice of birth control would lead to promiscuity. He also
feared that whites in Europe and the United States would use contracep-
tives but colored races in Africa and Asia would not. This disparity would
give a clear advantage to colored populations in the "inevitable conflict"
between the races that he believed to be near. Yet, such unseemly views also
made Gwaltney a firm opponent of forced sterilization. Writing against passage of the 1935 "reform" backed by Partlow, he argued passionately that
"no mortal on earth, sane or insane, white or black, ought to be forced
against his or her will to [be sterilized] without any means of redress."
When discussing the resistance to eugenics in the South, one historian attributed such opposition to "values founded on traditional religion and
concern for individual rights" that served as a more effective check on the
excesses of the movement than did medicine or science.[88] Paradoxically, conservative religion helped prevent in Alabama what happened to gypsies,
Jews, and other "under people" in Nazi Germany during the same decade.

Race

That opposition to birth control should be rooted in fear of predominance by colored races was unfortunately another way in which south-

ern culture shaped Southern Baptists. Though by no means confined to the South, racism strongly influenced Alabama Baptist thought. It took root especially in Gwaltney, who prided himself on his scientific enlightenment.

Gwaltney believed that race and class consciousness—what he called "consciousness of kind"—were both inevitable and useful. Without such distinctions races would mix, and "history teaches that no hybrid or mongrel race has amounted to much." But race and class consciousness also led to war, oppression, and plunder. Although the cross of Christ guaranteed Jew and Gentile equal access to God, it did not destroy the laudable race differences between blacks and whites, without which racial amalgamation would result. If the only issues dividing the races were equal opportunity, social justice, and political rights, he wrote in 1931, the South's racial problems could be solved. But true Christian fellowship involved the thornier questions of social equality, intermarriage, and racial amalgamation, which "would defeat the highest and noblest humanity as well as Christianity."[89]

Even on this point so widely held by white Baptists, there was some disagreement. G. B. F. Stovall wrote a rebuttal to Gwaltney's "consciousness of kind" editorials. Stovall considered such a view reflective of primitive clan organization, in which every family conceived of all other families as foreign. As one came in contact with civilized peoples from all parts of the earth, such racial antipathies declined. Differences in race became signs of strength in each, not weakness. Racial amalgamation would in time perfect human society, not corrupt it, by eliminating social prejudice as well as "narrow patriotism and snobbery." Races that were most pure (Jews and Chinese), Stovall wrote, were less successful than mixed races such as the Teutonic and Anglo-Saxon. Jesus' sentiments about "consciousness of kind" certainly differed from Gwaltney's, he concluded.[90]

Most Baptists accepted Gwaltney's original premise about the divine sanctity of racial purity, as did most Americans. Assuming that limitation in their racial thought, Baptists often took positions that were enlightened by the standards of the 1930s. They continued their long opposition to lynching and other forms of racial violence. Reviewing a racial confrontation in Emelle over a debt for a secondhand automobile battery that left two whites and four blacks dead, Gwaltney attributed such violence to lax law enforcement that brought shame on Alabama and dishonored God. Gwaltney doubted the guilt of the nine black "Scottsboro boys," who were accused of raping two white textile workers on a train near Scottsboro in the spring of 1931. Charles F. Leek used his column in the *Alabama Baptist* in

January 1938 to condemn a southern congressional filibuster against federal antilynching legislation.[91]

Leek and Gwaltney believed that respectable African Americans only desired opportunity and applause for their achievements. They did not seek social equality. In that sense, Booker T. Washington and Tuskegee Institute became the embodiment of racial concord: two racially separate worlds but without restriction on individual opportunity or accomplishment. In fact Tuskegee Institute was the site of a 1938 missions conference organized by Alabama native Noble Y. Beall, who was at the time director of Negro missions for the Home Mission Board. Beall believed that bringing white and black ministers together to discuss mutual problems would help solve the region's racial conflicts. In the South, he wrote, few white ministers even knew the names of black preachers in their communities.[92]

Assumptions of black inferiority and of paternalism also underlay interracial work within the state denomination. As it had since the Civil War, the state mission board parceled out small amounts of money for Negro work. The board provided $5 to $10 a month in 1934 to pay a black female missionary and social worker. By 1936 the board also paid S. D. Monroe $240 a year to conduct social ministries and evangelism among his race in Mobile. He also received assistance from the HMB, Mobile First Baptist, Dauphin Way Baptist, and from local missionary societies in three white Mobile churches.[93]

Politics

Given the countervailing pressures of complex racial and economic forces in Alabama, it is not surprising to discover deep political divisions. Partly because of the state's poverty and the extent of its industrial work force, Alabama became a major battleground between conservative and liberal wings of the Democratic Party. Buoyed by successful organizing efforts by the United Mine Workers and other national unions, liberal Democrats, including Senator Hugo Black and his successor, Lister Hill, won a majority of the state's congressional seats.[94]

Alabama Baptists divided politically along class lines. Middle-class denominational leaders, like most middle-class Alabamians, supported FDR and the New Deal enthusiastically through the 1936 presidential election. But when the president proposed adding new liberal judges to the Supreme Court and tried to purge conservative southern Democrats in the 1938 congressional elections, they turned against him. In the backcountry where bivocational ministers held sway, enthusiasm for FDR remained high throughout the decade.

Gwaltney began the 1930s down on capitalism and Republican Herbert Hoover. He warmed to Roosevelt's ebullient optimism and praised FDR's public works and relief programs. Gwaltney agreed with Roosevelt that human rights transcended property rights and that no American should starve merely to keep taxes low. He believed that capitalism was probably doomed in the long run and would likely be replaced with some form of socialism. Gwaltney feared both Republican plutocrats who sought privileges for themselves and Democratic radicals who threatened higher taxes and welfare expenditures. At such times, he wrote, "truth and right are usually found on middle grounds."[95]

Although Gwaltney did not question Roosevelt's motives in the 1937 "court packing" dispute, he feared that enlarging the size of the court would give FDR too much power and infringe on the rights of minorities (by which he meant white southerners). Gwaltney saw enlarging the court as another step toward the loss of individual liberties.[96]

When unemployment soared again in 1938, Gwaltney renewed his support for the president, praising him for placing human rights above conservative concerns about property and higher taxes. To do otherwise simply strengthened totalitarian and antidemocratic movements such as those that had recently swept through Germany and Italy. He also praised the newly enacted Wagner Act, which gave workers the legal right to organize and bargain collectively. The law, he believed, ended the era of amassing vast fortunes. No person should "be permitted to amass . . . many million dollars . . . and not turn back to society a reasonable portion." Although he believed the 1938 congressional elections were a repudiation of the New Deal, he argued that Roosevelt had accomplished much good through the Civilian Conservation Corps, Tennessee Valley Authority, Social Security Act, banking reforms, and federal aid to public health and education. For economists who increasingly had grown critical of the New Deal, Gwaltney expressed disgust. "Of all the false prophets the world has ever heard of since 1929," he wrote, "the economists have been the falsest." "Somebody may know what is the matter with this country," he wrote contemptuously in 1939, "but it is certain the economists do not."[97]

Other Baptists were less enthusiastic about Roosevelt. R. M. Hunter (pastor of Northside Baptist Church in Mobile) scorched Roosevelt for a variety of policies. In the *Alabama Baptist* he disagreed with New Deal agricultural policies that destroyed crops and livestock in order to reduce surpluses. In private correspondence he blamed Roosevelt for helping his "African jungle friends" more than whites. As a "red bone Democrat" who favored white supremacy, Hunter believed African Americans should be shipped back to Africa.[98]

H. D. Wilson wrote in 1937 that for the sake of social security Americans were submitting to regimentation and losing their individualism, thrift, self-reliance, and sense of personal responsibility. Charles F. Leek agreed, turning against Roosevelt in 1938 because of his intervention in southern state elections to defeat anti–New Deal Democrats and because of his growing opposition to states' rights.[99]

When results from the 1935 poll of clergymen are tabulated, a clear pattern emerges, at least at that point in the New Deal. Nationally, some 83 percent of clergymen who responded to Roosevelt's letter were generally favorable toward FDR and his programs. In Alabama the favorable rating among all clergymen who responded was nearly the same (79 percent). Among fifty-one identifiable white Alabama Baptist ministers, support dropped to 77 percent. This percentage is somewhat misleading because several Baptist ministers who criticized Roosevelt did so because the president was doing too little to end the depression. They overwhelmingly scolded him for repealing prohibition even when they otherwise supported his policies. As A. C. Davidson confided to his diary: "I have stood with him in his banking matter, but we part company here. And I am against him with all I have and am. Lord paralyze the arm that would fasten on us the awful liquor saloon and evil again. I can't go any further with the party that snaps its fingers at God and puts a little income that the rich ought to pay above the well being of our people."[100] Thirteen of the fifty-one replies to Roosevelt's 1935 letter expressed the same sentiment about prohibition, though usually more tactfully.[101]

The letters communicated overwhelming support for the New Deal by every level of Baptist leadership. Enthusiastic Roosevelt supporters included predictable liberals such as Charles Bell Jr. and Charles Stakely, but other supporters included fundamentalist pastors like A. D. Zbinden. Pastors of First Baptist churches in Cullman, Uniontown, Evergreen, Huntsville, Florence, Tuscumbia, Jasper, Gadsden, and Talladega praised the New Deal, as did pastors of Boyles Baptist in Tarrant City and Central Baptist in Decatur. Some of these pastors urged Roosevelt to go further. Zbinden, for instance, believed the government should help tenant farmers locate on their own land, where they could be independent of "the selfish landlord who seeks to keep them in debt" (a liberal proposal that Roosevelt resisted in 1935 but endorsed two years later). The pastor at Central Baptist in Decatur proclaimed the Social Security Act "a gift from God." The pastor of Huntsville First Baptist urged rapid implementation of TVA despite selfish opposition from Alabama Power Company and other private utility companies.[102]

At the other end of the economic spectrum, Baptist ministers were even more uniformly enthusiastic. A sixty-six-year-old pastor in Double Springs called FDR the most sympathetic president poor people ever had. He identified himself as a mountain Republican, and Roosevelt was the only Democrat for whom he had ever voted. The pastor of Dixon's Mill church described the Social Security Act as one of the "most progressive laws this country has ever had." The pastor at Hollytree proclaimed himself "one hundred percent" for the New Deal. An eighty-year-old minister at Evergreen warned only that Roosevelt had not gone far enough to help the poor. A pastor in the textile mill town of Phenix City blamed mill owners for sabotaging the National Industrial Recovery Act. The old idea of government was that its function was to maintain order. The modern idea was that government should serve the people and strengthen the weak. If Roosevelt did not act forcefully, "the little reign of terror that has happened in other lands will be as a little pink-tea party by what will happen here." Exploitation of textile workers made the poll's question about the need for reform ludicrous: "Is there NEED for the Social Security legislation and the Works Program? Does the sun shine? Do the old and the sick get hungry? Do strong men feel the pinch of hunger, and shiver when they see their wives and children hungry for bread and shake of cold? In the name of ALMIGHTY God, Mr. President, what COULD a humane, civilized government do but feed the hungry in a time like this?"[103]

Clergy criticism of the New Deal focused on welfare dependency and loss of personal freedoms. A sixty-one-year-old bivocational preacher/cotton farmer wrote that relief programs made it difficult for him to hire cheap farm labor. The New Deal was taking away personal liberties and turning the president into a dictator. The pastor at South Highlands Baptist Church in Bessemer criticized the assumption that the Social Security Act and other reforms could permanently improve the welfare of people when only the "power inherent in righteousness" could do so. The pastor at Siloam Baptist Church in Marion condemned the political patronage that dominated work relief. The pastor of Dothan First Baptist and Vernon Baptist Churches believed the New Deal was creating welfare dependency.[104]

As compelling as domestic concerns were during the 1930s, international issues increasingly troubled Alabama Baptists. For those who traveled widely or were interested in international affairs (men such as Charles Bell Jr., Charles F. Leek, L. L. Gwaltney, J. C. Stivender, and J. E. Dillard), the storm clouds gathering over Europe and Asia were the portent of an awful Armageddon.

Just as middle-class Baptist opinion changed about the New Deal in 1936, it also changed about events in Europe. Both Gwaltney and Charles Leek initially wrote sympathetically about Adolf Hitler and Germany's new order. After attending the Baptist World Alliance in Berlin in 1934, they praised German efficiency and denied that the Nazi Party was persecuting evangelical Christians. Leek called Hitler the "prophet of a new Germany" and declared Nazism to be a step in the right direction of blocking bolshevism. Gwaltney was deeply pacifist and also believed that many European Jews had become communists.[105]

Both Gwaltney and Leek became critical of Hitler by 1936, calling communism, Nazism, and fascism merely alternative forms of totalitarianism. They praised German Christians who resisted Nazism. Alabama missionaries serving in China lodged increasingly blunt criticism at Japanese militarism as well. By the fall of 1937 Gwaltney was calling Japan "an oriental highwayman out for booty and plunder." The next year, A. Hamilton Reid brought the issue of U.S. trade with Japan before the convention's executive board. A group of Birmingham Baptist pastors organized the American Committee for Non-Participation in Japanese Aggression, which lobbied Birmingham's U.S. congressman to support an economic boycott of Japan. Gwaltney supported the Munich Agreements of 1938 as preferable to war but believed decisions at Munich only postponed the conflict. Virtually every issue of the *Alabama Baptist* during 1939 contained lengthy essays by Gwaltney analyzing world events and what he believed to be the inevitable slide into war.[106]

Although Gwaltney continued to portray Jews as greedy radicals who monopolized the professions in Germany and controlled the immoral movie industry in the United States, the editor became more sympathetic to their plight. In 1938 the *Alabama Baptist* publicized the need to help resettle 600,000 people from Germany and Austria, half of them Jews, who had suffered Nazi persecution. The article reminded readers that Christians were obliged by their religion to help suffering neighbors.[107]

A. J. Dickinson Jr., then pastor of Mobile First Baptist Church, followed in his father's prophetic footsteps in his 1938 state convention sermon. Entitled "A Militant Christianity and a Terrorized World," Dickinson traced the origins of war in Europe to hatred of the Jews. Germany had denied them equality, exiled them, confiscated their property, looted their homes, and physically attacked them. "This is the story of the treatment of Jews by Anti-Semitic hatred," he thundered, and "we should expose the skeleton in the closet and unmask the hypocrisy of this vicious prejudice." Christians must purge their own religion of hatred and anti-Semitism.[108]

When Gwaltney reluctantly announced his support of Roosevelt's military preparedness campaign in December 1938, he did so because of revelations about German persecution of Jews. Endorsing armaments was hard "for a Christian and a pacifist," he admitted, but not to face reality would be disastrous to German Jews, Rumanian Baptists, and other victims of Nazi pogroms. A year later Gwaltney published an essay on anti-Semitism by a Selma rabbi.[109]

On a personal level Baptist-Jewish relations within local communities were usually amiable. Jews and Baptists generally agreed on separation of church and state. Premillennialists also interpreted the creation of a Jewish state as a harbinger of Christ's return. Leroy R. Priest (who pastored Dothan First Baptist Church) befriended Jewish families who had no synagogue. After he left Dothan to become president of Judson College, the Jewish community built a synagogue and invited him back to speak.[110]

On a similarly positive note, the anti-Catholicism that had figured so prominently in the previous decade declined to barely a whisper during the 1930s. Whether because Catholic immigration virtually ceased, no Catholic was a prominent candidate for president, or the depression and international conflict simply overwhelmed religious prejudice, the issue virtually disappeared from Baptist discourse.

Baptists often argued that suffering eventuated in good, that God turned even evil to his own purposes. Perhaps this theology was fulfilled in the 1930s. After a decade of escalating tensions over theology, most Alabama Baptists decided to disagree without rancor or division. After a decade of declining concern for the poor, they rediscovered a prophetic voice concerning justice in this world. After being largely co-opted by their culture during the prosperous 1920s, they regained the capacity to critique society by the biblical standards of their founder. After spending much of the 1920s criticizing and even persecuting other Christians, they discovered that the world was a cold, dangerous place. Christians needed one another.

10

War and Remembrance, 1940–1954

"Right ideas possess a kind of immortality."

Junius Kendrick could not believe what he was seeing. Before him were emaciated and traumatized survivors of the Buchenwald concentration camp. Behind them were bodies stacked up like cords of firewood, five and six deep on four-wheel carts. The stench of death and unspeakable filth made him sick. Walking through the living quarters of German Schutzstaffel (SS) officers, where female prisoners had been kept as concubines, he saw lampshades made of human flesh. The experience left him shaken. "I did not think . . . that society could do such a thing." But he saw the holocaust for himself and was never the same again.

As a medic with the 456th Anti-Aircraft Battalion in General George Patton's Third Army, Kendrick was one of many Alabamians exposed to a harsh world. That experience on April 21, 1945, in Buchenwald left him despising the German people, a loathing he abandoned only after he was back home at Auburn University, where friends in the Baptist Student Union helped him overcome his hatred. In a sense he never completely overcame the sights at Buchenwald, resenting the claims of revisionist historians in the 1990s that the holocaust was a myth.[1]

Alabama Baptists and World War II

Kendrick was by no means the only Southern Baptist to have his world violently shaken by events in the 1940s. The times were out of sorts. The war and its domestic consequences literally transformed the South. For the first time its economy was fully integrated into national markets. In the 1940s six of ten southern textile workers still lived in company-owned houses. By the 1960s company towns had virtually disappeared. In 1940, 42 percent of southerners lived on farms; by 1960 only 15 percent did so. Cotton was still king of southern agriculture in 1940, even if the kingdom had declined and the crown was badly tarnished. By 1959 cotton was the principal crop in only eleven counties of the old cotton South. Only 20 percent of the region's population was urban in 1940; by 1960, 44 percent lived in towns and cities. The per capita income of the South was 60 percent of the national average in 1940; by 1960 it was 76 percent. A majority of Alabama legislators during the 1940s and 1950s could be elected by a quarter of the population because of a malapportioned legislature, and blacks held no elective offices. By the end of the 1960s, political power had shifted from sparsely populated rural counties to burgeoning urban ones, and African Americans had become a major political force.[2]

Southern Baptists were forced to change as well. The denomination continued a process of bureaucratization begun in the 1920s. Centralization made the SBC efficient, prosperous, and enormously successful. But it also marginalized rural and working-class people, effectively squashed dissent from both left and right ends of the theological spectrum, and triggered growing opposition from both liberals and fundamentalists. By the 1950s the Cooperative Program, executive committee, and Sunday School Board unofficially defined what it meant to be a loyal Southern Baptist: set aside at least 10 percent of church contributions to the CP (and nothing to non-SBC causes); obtain pastors who had graduated from SBC seminaries; purchase all support materials and literature from the Sunday School Board. Despite much rhetoric about the autonomy and supremacy of the local congregation, centralized bureaucracies conducted the daily affairs of the denomination, decided on the distribution of funds, and maintained a shaky peace by heading off controversy and electing or appointing consensus builders to key positions. Most pew-sitting Baptists focused on their local congregations and foreign missions, believing that national events had little impact on them. They supported whoever was in charge of the denomination, be they moderates or fundamentalists. For the minority who became incensed over literature, theology, race, and other matters,

Baptist polity allowed the perfect solution. They could take their church property and local budget and do precisely as they pleased.[3]

Although denominational ties began to loosen a bit in the United States, loyalty to the SBC (especially in the sectionally conscious South) still mattered a great deal.[4] Elsewhere evangelicals and fundamentalists unhappy with liberal control of their denominations began to organize against their leadership. But they had little impact in the South, where Southern Baptist consensus builders denied that the denomination strictly speaking was evangelical or that liberals influenced the SBC.

The popularity of one of their own, evangelist Billy Graham, together with the wide dispersion of Southern Baptists during the emigration of the 1940s and 1950s, made the denomination a national religious force and the largest Protestant church in the United States. As a charter member of the first SBC church in California explained in 1936: "When we came to California, I said, 'Well, I'm going to church somewhere.' So we went, but we weren't satisfied. We were longing for what we had back home." Some black congregations outside the South affiliated with the SBC, changing the denomination's racial composition and creating internal tension.[5]

Success was reflected in every statistic of SBC life. From 5.9 million members in 1945, Southern Baptists increased to 9.7 million in 1960. From slightly more than 26,000 churches in 1945, the number grew to nearly 35,000 in 1975. Total gifts increased from $98 million in 1945 to $1.4 billion three decades later. Mission and benevolence contributions went up from $2.5 million to $238 million over the same thirty years. The number of foreign missionaries increased from 520 to 2,700, with another 2,100 home missionaries.[6]

The linchpin for all these changes was World War II. Many denominational leaders were pacifists during the 1930s, as was L. L. Gwaltney. Their well-founded cynicism about Allied motives during World War I and their literal reading of the Sermon on the Mount convinced them that taking life advanced neither the cause of democracy nor Christianity. But German and Japanese aggression, sympathy for Britain, and reports of atrocities in China and Europe began to soften their resolve. By 1940 pacifism was in full retreat.

Suspended between peace and war, the social service commission urged the 1940 state convention to assist England with war materials but stay out of the conflict. The committee took the same position the following year, only a month before Japanese planes attacked Pearl Harbor. L. E. Barton (who pastored in Andalusia and Jasper) rejected both pacifism and militarism in March 1941. The Sermon on the Mount required one to sacrifice his own life but not that of the weak and helpless, he reasoned. The model of Jesus had "no bearing . . . on the right and duty of constituted civil government to maintain order and punish offenders." When Rev. Montague Cook of Montgomery responded by calling war "gangsterism practiced on a large scale" and scolded Barton for misstating the clear intent of Christ's teachings, several writers proposed even more tortured commentaries about the Sermon on the Mount. One wrote that Matthew 5:21–26, 38–39 taught Christ's disciples not to resist evil when they had no chance to win. Nor should Christians fight useless wars. But they should use all means, including war, to oppose aggression.[7] Christian realism had arrived in Alabama.

As on so many other occasions, Gwaltney set the pattern for the denomination on foreign policy. He underwent a rapid conversion from pacifist to interventionist in 1940. In January of that year he was still suspended between the two worlds. War was "godless, anti-social and wicked above anything in the world" and in time would be abolished. But such a blissful state was not yet in sight because the world had too little of the spirit of Christ. In numerous editorials and speeches and in a book published in 1941, Gwaltney connected democracy, capitalism, and religious liberty. A threat to one value was a threat to all three. Although "all right thinking men are pacifists," he believed, peace could not be obtained by appeasement of tyrants. They could be deterred only by force. Prayer might affect the outcome of the war, but Christianity would have no effect on Hitler, nor would it prevent him from enslaving the world. Extolling Britain as the source of democracy, the editor praised Roosevelt's decision to provide military assistance to the United Kingdom. He thought no nation had as wise leadership in foreign affairs as FDR was providing the United States.[8]

Summarizing his faith in both democracy and Christianity, Gwaltney wrote a brilliant overview of world affairs on July 4, 1940. The collective rights of humanity exceeded the rights of a single nation. Religious liberty depended upon political democracy, as did world peace. He did not doubt the ultimate vindication of democracy. "Right ideas possess a kind of immortality," he wrote poetically. "If truth doesn't rise from the tomb the third day, it will rise the third decade, or maybe the third century."[9]

Once war was declared in December 1941, Gwaltney quickly became a full-fledged convert to force. Four days after the Japanese attack on Pearl Harbor, he wrote that Christianity was ineffective and powerless to influence non-Christian nations. International law amounted to nothing without willingness to use force. Japan had convinced even the "peace-at-any-price pacifists" (for whom he had been a prominent spokesman only years earlier) that the time had come to fight or be enslaved. Axis aggression had united American and British public opinion at last and mobilized Baptists in favor of the war effort. The editor did what he could to help such mobilization with editorials such as "The Patriotism of Christ." Though a "lover of mankind" and a "cosmopolitan . . . citizen of the world," Jesus had also been a "lover of His little country." Suddenly in 1942 Gwaltney turned on Harry Emerson Fosdick, whom he had often praised during the 1930s, as one of the culprits in producing an entire generation of "pacifist-at-any-price" seminarians. He regularly condemned pacifism and isolationism as if he had never espoused either.[10]

Gwaltney represented most Baptist opinion in the state. Charles F. Leek, Montgomery pastor and author of a long-running *Alabama Baptist* column on world affairs, questioned the religious motivation of conscientious objectors and urged Baptist churches to display American flags. Such acts of patriotism were merely part of the times and did not contradict Baptist theology or desecrate the altar.[11]

Not all Baptists were so easily convinced. Ruhama's pastor and retiring state convention president J. C. Stivender preached his final presidential address barely a week before the attack on Pearl Harbor. In a world filled with dictatorships, he warned, Baptists must stand up for democracy and freedom. They must be loyal citizens. But they must also resist pressure to become handmaidens of the state and military. They must not promote a war spirit. Preachers must serve their country even as they remained free to criticize it, condemn unrighteousness, preach against the evils of war, and declare the whole gospel. "The church," he reminded messengers, was "the Bride of Christ and not the mistress of the state."[12]

Theological conservative H. Ross Arnold went further. He believed that Christians could not in good conscience participate in war. Secular men and governments waged war, but a soldier with only love in his heart for the enemy and with prayers in his heart for his enemy's welfare could not fight. He considered the moral courage of a conscientious objector superior to the physical courage of a soldier.[13]

Juliette Mather (who served as young people's secretary at WMU headquarters in Birmingham) agreed with Arnold. She invited pacifist Baptists to address state young people's leaders and tried to organize a support group for Baptist conscientious objectors (COs). Her nephew's death in a fighter plane accident deepened her opposition to war. At the very least, she wished Southern Baptists would emulate the attitude of Alabamian Charles Martin, who was a bombardier on a B-29 flying raids over Japan with the

Twentieth Army Air Corps. He allegedly prayed on every bomb run that God would forgive him the destruction he was causing. "I wish I could see a feeling of penitence instead of glee in our country," she wrote W. O. Carver.[14]

Charles R. Bell Jr. also confronted the war in personal ways. His brother Tartt, who grew up in Parker Memorial Baptist Church, shared his older brother's idealism and liberalism but grew much more cynical about the denomination. After attending Tulane University, Tartt completed a master's degree in economics at the University of Chicago. His reading (André Malraux, Dostoyevsky, John Steinbeck, Thorstein Veblen, Friedrich Engels, John Dos Passos, Clifford Odets) jarred him with new and different visions of the world. He increasingly considered FDR a reactionary who was steering the nation into war. He became active in the pacifist Fellowship of Reconciliation and criticized his brother's compromises, urging him to more prophetic action.[15]

Tartt Bell had no inkling of the price his brother was about to pay for his moral position as a Baptist pacifist. The 1940 SBC had acknowledged that many Baptists were pacifists and had instructed the executive committee to register COs in order to certify them to the government. The 1941 convention in Birmingham took a harder line, one that Charles Bell Jr. interpreted as endorsing "the war hysteria now sweeping" the United States. He sent a furious letter attacking the convention's action to the *Alabama Baptist*. The convention had chosen the side of those who bombed civilians, starved entire populations through blockades, promoted hatred, and eclipsed civil liberties. The SBC had become one of the first denominations "of the living Christ" to urge a country to fight an offensive war against other nations. Ends now justified means. Evil could create good. The Sermon on the Mount had been turned on its head; Christians were now obliged to return evil for evil. Could any Baptist imagine Christ machinegunning a row of advancing enemy or snuffing out lives with a grenade?[16]

When Gwaltney received the emotional letter, he begged Bell to reconsider. The editor respected his friend's right of free speech too much to reject the letter but argued at length against its premises. One by one he disputed Bell's theology and interpretation of Scripture. In an ideal world, perhaps such ethical beliefs could be sustained. But in a world of Hitlerism and international lawlessness, purity of Christian belief was naive. Gwaltney's Christian realism clashed head-on with Bell's liberal pacifism, and neither man gave an inch.[17]

Gwaltney had promised Alabama Baptists a free press, and he was as good as his word. Unable to persuade Bell that his ideas were wrong or at least dangerous to his career as a Southern Baptist preacher, he published Bell's letter in June 1941. Both men must have been surprised by the response. John H. Buchanan, influential pastor of the state's wealthiest and most influential church (and a lifelong Republican), called Bell's letter a masterful presentation of the issue much more in keeping with the spirit of Christ than the SBC resolution. Montague Cook, pastor of Southside Baptist Church in Montgomery, contrasted Bell's courage and fidelity to Christ to unworthy SBC leaders who were leading Baptists "by the paths of rationalization into murder." But Buchanan also rejected Bell's request for state convention funds to help COs as a fruitless effort that would only provoke "unwise and unchristian" debate.[18] Once war began, Bell proposed postwar treaties that were just to all belligerents, that contained no reprisals (which only seeded the ground for more terrible wars in the future), and opened trade and commerce equally to all nations.[19]

While Bell theorized about the shape of the postwar world, his congregation (which contained many military men and women from nearby Fort McClellan) became restless. During the 1930s he had survived attacks on his socialism, liberalism, involvement in interracial cooperatives, the Oxford Movement, and even hosting an interracial meal at his home. He could not survive a 1944 crisis over the U.S. flag. Some church members were determined to hang a plaque honoring Parker Memorial members who served in the military and to display an American flag in honor of the righteousness of the nation's cause. Although Bell believed display of the flag identified the church too much with an attitude of national exclusiveness, the flag was not so much the primary issue as the timing. Displaying the flag during wartime made it a symbol of armed might and thus inappropriate. When the deacons commissioned a U.S. service flag with stars placed in the shape of a cross, even Bell's younger brother, Tartt, urged compromise. But Charles Bell considered the moral issue too significant. When news of the D-Day invasion reached Anniston, members of the church determined to display their flag in the sanctuary with or without the pastor's consent. He would not relent and so resigned.[20]

Kindness and forbearance were casualties of war and racism. A parishioner wrote Bell:

> I want to congratulate you on your resignation. That is the best thing you have done for your church in ten or more years. . . .
>
> The people are tired of a negro loving traitor to our flag. . . . The place for you is in a negro church in Harlem. . . .
>
> The congregation is sorry for your mother and father, but they have no

sympathy for you and your yellow to the core brothers. . . . A white person who believes in social equality is lower than the lowest negro alive. . . . A very potential danger to our South will be removed when you shake the dust of Alabama from your feet.[21]

Some within Bell's congregation defended him. One put the issue in biblical terms: "Jesus said, 'Darkness hateth the light because their deeds are evil.' In other words, when men's desires are to murder their fellow man contrary to God's law naturally they want to find fault with those who teach the truth."[22]

From across Alabama came a similar outpouring of support from pastors who agreed with Bell or at least admired his courage: the former director of evangelism for the state convention, S. J. Ezell; theological conservative H. Ross Arnold; and Dr. T. W. Ayers, Parker Memorial's former China missionary (who, along with Willie Kelly, was the most respected of all Alabama missionaries). Southside's pastor, John Buchanan, helped Bell find a pastorate in the Northern Baptist Convention. In August Bell left to become pastor of First Baptist Church in Madison, Wisconsin. The former pastor of the Madison church, L. B. Moseley (who had carefully followed Bell's controversial career in the SBC), assured him a kinder hearing in the North: "Matters which trouble you in Alabama will be taken for granted here, unless you do too much about them. You understand that the Kingdom of God will not come without opposition. . . . You can be a prophet and stay in Madison." Moseley well understood the contrasting worlds about which he wrote. A native Alabamian, he had grown up in Selma First Baptist Church, had attended Wake Forest University and Southern seminary, then switched to the Northern Baptist Convention.[23]

As Bell prepared to depart for Wisconsin, he wrote an emotional letter to his old friend, L. L. Gwaltney. It was difficult to end so many long friendships. Bell proclaimed his love for Alabama and its hard-headed Baptists and hoped he would someday return to the state. "Yet my better evaluation tells me . . . this was a final goodbye." His premonition was correct. After a successful pastorate in Madison, Bell became pastor of First Baptist Church, Pasadena, California, the largest congregation within the renamed American Baptist Convention. He did return to Parker Memorial to visit his parents on occasion, and in 1949 his old congregation received him warmly. Always a spellbinding orator, Bell's return to his old pulpit required chairs that filled the aisles, and even then latecomers had to stand. Although few had shared his pacifism, most parishioners had forgiven what they viewed as his eccentricities. By the end of the 1940s, many expressed a grudging respect for his independence, mental vitality, and moral courage. The sermon was eloquent, powerful, prophetic, and vintage Charles Bell. The world, he warned, had influenced the church more than the church had transformed the world. Followers of Christ must reassert the radical teachings of Christ "instead of parroting in vain repetition a religion that suits our conveniences in a materialistic age." One of the congregation's historians summarized Bell's stormy career by quoting the opinion of a fellow Anniston pastor: "While I disagree with Charlie, I believe that if Jesus Christ were to return to Anniston tomorrow, he would spend the night at Charlie's house."[24]

Among the legacies of war were unprecedented financial prosperity and greater tolerance of other kinds of Christians. Financial contributions from war-swollen salaries produced the largest budgets in denominational history. Service as chaplains helped break down Baptist stereotypes about other kinds of Christians and ushered in a more tolerant and ecumenical age.[25]

Claude M. Haygood, a liberal young Black Belt pastor at Fort Deposit and Tuskegee, took theology degrees from Vanderbilt and Yale into the navy, where he roomed with a Catholic priest while in chaplain's school. Each man initially resented the other, but weeks of sleeping, eating, talking, and attending class together created a bond between them. Christian tolerance, they both agreed, was the most important lesson they learned at chaplain's school. Later at a naval air station in Maryland, Haygood worked closely and harmoniously with the Catholic chaplain. "Believe it or not," he wrote later, "but a Southern Baptist and a Catholic priest discovered that we had lots in common in the deeper things of the Christian life." South Pacific hospital service in the New Hebrides Islands was a sort of postdoctorate in his journey toward tolerance. He amused wounded southern soldiers by telling them he was a "fellow Rebel from Alabama" and amended the line to Yanks by adding that he had been civilized by a wife from Connecticut. "A little risk of life itself," he wrote, "can do a lot to clarify the meaning of faith."[26] After the war, Haygood returned to Alabama to pastor Demopolis First Baptist Church.

Theology for the World Crisis

Although neo-orthodoxy gained ground at the expense of liberalism between 1938 and 1945, the big winners (at least in terms of popular religion) were evangelicalism and fundamentalism. Doctrinally, evangelicals differed little from fundamentalists, but they tended to be less argumentative, exclusivist, and separatist. Radio ministries such as Charles E. Fuller's Old-Fashioned Revival Hour, the Billy Graham Evangelistic Association, and Campus Crusade for Christ gained new beachheads for evangelicals. They organized the National Association of Evangelicals (NAE) in 1942 and founded Fuller Theological Seminary in California a half decade later. Some thirty small denominations joined the NAE, though the Southern Baptist Convention went its own independent way. The "new evangelicalism" best represented by NAE and Billy Graham contained both Democratic, social justice elements and Republican, procapitalist supporters. These conflicting elements later gave rise to two very different evangelical magazines (the politically conservative *Christianity Today* and the politically independent but progressive *Sojourners*).[27]

Fundamentalists often denounced evangelicals as vituperatively as they did liberals. Alabama native Bob Jones (who presided over a fundamentalist Bible college in South Carolina bearing his name) denounced Billy Graham for cooperating with main-line denominations that cosponsored his urban crusades. So did independent fundamentalist John R. Rice. As a result Baptists often held fundamentalists at arm's length despite basic theological agreement on most issues. Furthermore, the NAE originated in the North and tended to be transdenominational. The regional isolation of Southern Baptists, their tight programmatic organization and focus on the denomination, and their Landmark ecclesiastical heritage of believing only Baptists preserved the true faith held them aloof or at least apart from fundamentalism. They were simply too busy doing their own thing (and in the process becoming the largest Protestant denomination in the nation and the largest missionary force in the world) to quibble about words.[28]

More characteristic of the SBC was fundamentalism by osmosis. Fundamentalist ideas simply seeped into the fabric of Alabama Baptist thought without much overt choice or connection to other denominations or leaders. Many Baptists saw the handiwork of God in the events of history and interpreted those events in the same way fundamentalists did. War, horrible atrocities, horrific fatalities, atom bomb, cold war, creation of the nation of Israel—all seemed to portend the end of history and to confirm dispensational premillennialism, which was one of the pillars of fundamentalist theology. Humanity had entered the last of many dispensations or revelations of God, and that final epoch was near an end. Soon Christ would come again to judge humanity, to separate sheep from goats, and declare judgment on all (a judgment highly merited given the sin, iniquity, and secularism so apparent in the postwar United States).

Sorting out the meaning of history was never simple for Baptists because of the variety of opinions held within the denomination. Although there were plenty of premillennialists, finding a purist on doctrines of the second coming was not easy. Most Baptists were a mixture of pre-, post-, and amillennialist, or they were simply evangelicals with no strong opinions one way or the other about the timing of Christ's return. Variety among Baptists was the theological order of the day.

The strong tradition of tolerance and anticreedalism that grew rapidly after 1900 was by midcentury well established in the hundred or so churches that provided the convention's leadership, as well as within its professional headquarters. Though modernist thought was as rare as ever, tolerance for the little cadre of modernists (so long as they did not become offensive on cultural questions like race and war) was the rule. Wiser heads adopted a simple rule to govern intradenominational relations: don't ask and don't tell.

Quietly and without fanfare the ecumenical Birmingham Ministers Discussion Group continued to meet, involving four to six Baptist pastors and Howard College religion professors. Their papers between 1940 and 1955 dealt with church unity, racism, religious liberalism, neo-orthodoxy, psychological breakdowns among servicemen, Zionism, millennialism, and labor unionism.[29]

Scattered around the state were similar sorts of people. They were not necessarily orthodox liberals but certainly were men and women who relished free inquiry and spirited debate, who read widely and sought to build an inclusive synthesis in an exclusive denomination. Jesse A. Cook, pastor at Andalusia, preached a sermon to his congregation in 1947 defining modernism as a theology devoted to righting wrongs in this world. Fundamentalism, he explained to his parishioners, endorsed the verbal inspiration of the Scriptures, awaited the premillennial second coming, and focused on the world to come. He believed the two theologies had become blurred and mixed. Modernism needed some core truths for which fundamentalists were known; fundamentalists often became irrelevant because they could not relate to the social circumstances of people's lives. The rapid gains by organized labor in the 1930s and 1940s, World War II, industrialization—all had combined to create a different church. Baptist pastors now looked out over their congregations and saw representatives of both labor and management who were deacons and Sunday school teachers. Churches were torn by industrial disputes just as communities were (Andalusia had become an important textile town and had experienced a major organizing drive in 1946). Low wages contributed to poverty, disease, immorality, and crime, Cook added, and a wage "that will not furnish a decent living for a

man and his family is a social wrong." Unions had improved conditions
for working people, and workers should have the right to organize. Southern religion had endorsed that part of labor's agenda that demanded
shorter workdays, better wages, elimination of the "stretch out" system in
textile mills, and night work for women and children. Cook reminded his
congregation that many mill workers were Baptists, and most Baptist
churches consisted of working people. But every industrial dispute had
two sides, and the church must not endorse one over the other lest it divide
the congregation. At the same time, the principles of the kingdom of God
must be applied to society as well as to individuals, and ethical neutrality
on issues of injustice, greed, selfishness, persecution, hate, intolerance, and
the violation of human rights was always wrong. The sermon presented an
ethical contradiction without resolving it. How could the church maintain
unity by not taking sides in industrial disputes and at the same time reject a course of ethical neutrality? Despite this contradiction, if modernism
meant addressing contemporary social problems, Cook's sermon certainly
fit the definition.[30]

The pastor of Greensboro Baptist Church, the erudite James E. Dean
(who held a Ph.D. from the University of Chicago in Old Testament), continued to espouse biblical liberalism. Reactionaries, he wrote in 1940, preferred creeds to the moving of the Holy Spirit, attributed too much weight
to human opinions, looked to the past rather than to the future, and feared
change. He expressed a decided preference for what he called "progressive
religion," but it is clear from numerous editorials that he meant modernism.[31]

Although Gwaltney had become less theologically liberal with the
passing years, he agreed with Dean on creedalism. Gwaltney never met a
creed he liked, even when he agreed entirely with its theology. Having traveled the ministerial backroads of Alabama for a quarter century, Gwaltney
had developed genuine respect for people unlike himself whom he met
there. He was the closest thing the denomination had to a bishop. Now
nearing the end of his career, he had not mellowed with age. If anything,
he was more acerbic and opinionated than ever. And on the issue of local
church autonomy and denominational creeds he brooked no compromise.

Gwaltney frequently compared the theological climates of the 1920s
and 1940s. Conflicts between modernists and fundamentalists had produced conservative demands for a statement of faith against which everyone's orthodoxy would be tested. Although Gwaltney was no modernist,
on this issue he sided with liberals. In the 1920s such creedalism had led

to attacks on his beloved professors at Southern seminary who had been branded as modernists or evolutionists. The only creed Baptists needed was the New Testament, he argued, and the only group that a creed applied to was the one that wrote it, not to any other church, association, or convention. Baptists had only two doctrines: the lordship of Christ and the largest freedom possible consistent with that lordship. He denounced the tendency of Baptists to organize around pre- or postmillennialism instead of the "old-line Baptist position . . . : Brother, you have your choice on that matter to believe as you please. But if you are a Baptist you will grant your brother the same right to hold his own belief." Upset by Arkansas and Oklahoma state conventions that threatened to withdraw fellowship from Baptist churches that practiced open communion or "alien baptism," he urged churches not to yield their autonomy to do as they pleased to any association or convention anywhere in the world. So angry did he become over what he viewed as this fundamental breach of Baptist polity that virtually his last act as editor of the denominational paper in 1950 was to send a copy of this uncompromising editorial to editors, Baptist college and seminary presidents, and the secretaries of every state Baptist executive board.[32]

In the event that anyone still misunderstood his position, Gwaltney penned a spirited defense of Harry Emerson Fosdick. The liberal New York pastor of Riverside Church was accused by an essayist of denying belief both in the virgin birth and in atonement. When Gwaltney received the article, he considered rejecting it because he believed it would simply stir up anger and confusion among Alabama Baptists. But when some young Alabama pastors insisted he publish it, the editor appended a typically frank introduction. Any Baptist church, he reminded the ardent young fundamentalists, including Riverside, had a right to hire a pastor who believed anything the congregation desired. Many intellectual ministers agreed with Fosdick. In fact, Baptist ministers in New York City had long been polarized into "extreme Modernists or cantankerous Fundamentalists." Whereas modernists were willing to allow fundamentalists to believe what they wanted, fundamentalists tended "to hang up by the heels anyone who did not agree with them."[33]

Gwaltney also chided fundamentalists for their war on science. As a valedictory in 1950 he wrote a series of mind-stretching essays on eternal God, the nature of time, and Einstein's theory of relativity. Filled with erudite comments from the works of philosophers such as Henri Bergson of the University of Paris, the editor urged his readers to realize how small was their stage of scientific observation and experience. Both dogmatic scientists and theologians spoke as if they knew much more than they did. Each had to rely on faith because what humanity did not understand constituted a much larger library than what was known.[34]

This series provoked a considerable amount of head scratching. But if readers were confused, at least they were parties to the conception of one of the most remarkable intellectual treatises ever penned by an Alabama Baptist. After taking his leave of the denominational paper in 1950, the editor emeritus spent the seventy-fourth year of his life writing an autobiographical memoir on science entitled "This I Leave with You." Intended as his eighth book and dedicated to his only daughter, the ninety-eight-page manuscript was never published because friends were aghast when they read it and believed it would sully his reputation. When he died shortly after completing the work, some of the twelve copies were given to family members, and one was deposited in the Alabama Baptist history collection at Howard College.

Gwaltney's chapter titles hinted at the controversy his manuscript would have raised: for example, "The Errors of Dogmatic Faith" and "God and Spiritual Mutations." He began with a description of how his faith had first been shocked at the University of Richmond by professors who questioned the teaching of his rural church upbringing that the earth was only 7,000 years old. His favorite teacher (who taught Latin and history) was the faculty member who most contradicted his inherited beliefs. Thrown off balance, he became an insatiable bibliophile, "nibbling at [the world of books] like an ant nibbling at a mountain of sugar." Ministerial students had started a "whispering campaign" against his professor. Some took their grievances to trustees and the university president. The incident furnished Gwaltney the opportunity to become a little demagogue "who could have provoked the majority of Virginia Baptists to clapping their hands in his praise." Instead, he decided to wait, listen, read, and learn for himself. The result was his belief in the nebular theory of creation. Cosmic dust or a "fire mist" had created a solid nucleus or center whose gravity had pulled matter to it as it rotated. This process took perhaps 300 million years. His readings in astronomy, geology, and anthropology revealed God's intricate, complex design for creation. Citing the works of Robert A. Millikan at the California Institute of Technology and Le Comte du Nouy of France, he reconciled evolutionary theories with the Bible but not according to any orthodox Christian system. He had been forced to "give up what might be called the traditional views of how God created the earth and man, and, instead of that was forced to accept the scientific view."

Such syncretism between science and Christianity was not popular, as numerous incidents in his Alabama career had demonstrated. When Gwaltney was preaching a revival many years earlier in Lowndes County, farmers had told him of plowing up oyster shells in their fields. They asked him if this fact was evidence of the universal flood. "No," he responded to the astonished farmers; it was evidence that Lowndes County was once at the bottom of a sea.

Gwaltney recounted a more recent story from 1950 while visiting the Cropwell community near Pell City. His hosts had a daughter studying at Howard College. The mother had found a textbook on religious education (for James Chapman's course) written by a professor at the University of Chicago. It described the "days" mentioned in the Genesis account of creation as vast periods of time, not literal twenty-four-hour days. Gwaltney allayed their concerns by explaining that the Hebrew word for "day" meant an indefinite period of time. In light of the fact that the sun was not created until the fourth day, and it controlled the rotation of the earth insofar as calculating time, the first three days could not have been twenty-four hours in duration. The anxious parents were relieved to hear such a respected Baptist reconcile an apparent conflict.

In Gwaltney's chapter on the origins of man, he postulated that ancestors of man first swam, then crawled, then walked upright. Various mutations transformed a single-cell amoeba into a primate. The unfolding pages of Gwaltney's manuscript revealed one heresy after another as reckoned from a fundamentalist point of view. He believed the story of Adam and Eve was meant to be read figuratively, not literally. Ethnology did not provide for a single set of parents for the entire race. Genesis contained two creation stories, not one. He considered the serpent and apples in the Garden of Eden story symbols of right and wrong placed before Adam and Eve. Total depravity did not result from Adam's sin (which accounted only for his fall from grace) but from the original animalistic element in every person. The baby in the womb or a saline solution given a person who was bleeding to death confirmed the "primordial and natural element [of the salty sea] from which man came."

When persons had expressed such iconoclastic views in the past, dogmatic Christians had responded with inquisitions and charges of heresy. Persecutors of Galileo or the Salem witches, Gwaltney believed, were the precursors of Baptist fundamentalists who had tried to fire seminary professors in the 1920s. It was the sad fate of all religious organizations sooner or later to become dogmatic and unyielding. In time, Gwaltney predicted, most people would change their views of how the earth and man had been created and find "a better, stronger faith." Most of them "hold to this imaginary and irrational faith about how God created man" simply because it was the traditional Christian view—and they believed that anyone who held a different view was a heretic.[35] Paradoxically, the most beloved and respected Baptist of the century left an entire manuscript full of evidence (at least by fundamentalist standards) of his heretical views. His evangelistic zeal and commitment to evangelism also demand that historians rethink the alleged apathy of higher critics toward saving souls.

That Gwaltney retained widespread respect despite such views should not be misunderstood as agreement with him. Evidence suggests that the Baptist rank and file did not share his view. Dr. C. H. Rutherford wrote in 1946 that German atrocities had been worse than Japanese because higher criticism emanating from its universities had corrupted German society. Mrs. Hawthorne J. Massie, president of Birmingham's Calvary Baptist Church WMU, attended the state Baptist Student Union convention to see if evolution was being taught. Such ideas in science and history classes a decade earlier had confused her and made her skeptical about the entire Bible. Although she had been converted in 1944, she feared that even active BSU members were being taught by "atheistic professors." At the 1950 state convention in Decatur, Henry Allen Parker (pastor of Dothan First Baptist Church) said in his convention sermon that modernism—insidiously advanced from within the denomination by college and seminary professors, theologians, and editors of state papers—posed the greatest threat to Christianity.[36]

Paradoxically, the strongest defender of orthodox theology was Gwaltney's successor as editor of the *Alabama Baptist*. A native of Whatley, Alabama, Leon Macon was one of eleven children. He graduated from Howard College in 1933 and attended Southern seminary before returning to Alabama to pastor in Bay Minette, Athens, Atmore, and Bessemer. He became editor of the denominational paper in 1950.[37]

Although in early essays before his selection as editor he tried so hard to harmonize religion and science that some fundamentalists attacked him, it was soon obvious that Macon was no L. L. Gwaltney when it came to higher criticism. In his first few weeks as editor, he attacked liberals who promoted the supremacy of reason over biblical authority. He denounced science teachers who disparaged the Bible, and he blamed declining church attendance in Europe on the spread of modernism. Although he applauded the Revised Standard Version of the Bible for correcting "some errors of translation" and conceded that no original manuscript of the Bible existed, he still believed that Scripture contained the infallible words of God. He believed modern Christianity was too academic, that textual criticism had supplanted biblical faith, and that scholarship was valued more than revelation. He did defend the authority of the local church, doubted that modernism had much influence within the SBC, and warned against denying people respect when honest differences existed about what the Bible meant. In later years he became more vehement in his denunciation of theological liberalism.[38]

Macon also announced his opposition to ecumenism in one of his first editorials, and he remained true to that position throughout his career. Macon warned Baptist women not to join the United Council of Church Women or the Federated Council of Women. Such groups drained money from their own church programs and were tainted by modernism. Speaking to James Chapman's church leadership course at Howard College, Macon told ministerial students that various church federations sought to create a universal church, eliminate theological differences, intrude in political or social arenas, endorse the United Nations, and promote the social gospel.[39]

On ecumenism (as upon virtually all issues) a variety of opinions existed. James Chapman, anxious to expose Howard's ministerial students to as wide a sample of Baptist thought as possible, invited Claude M. Haygood (former navy chaplain and then pastor at Demopolis) to present a different view. Rather than contradict Macon directly, Haygood ignored the national and international aspects of ecumenism, preferring to focus on community relations. He urged young ministers to join interdenominational ministerial conferences so as to broaden their understanding and enlarge opportunities for service. Especially should they work with black churches, he advised.[40]

Other pastors agreed with Haygood. Dr. Frank MacDonald (native of Edinburgh, Scotland, graduate of Bucknell College and Crozer Theological Seminary, and former university preacher at Vassar College) actually applied ecumenism in his own ministerial career. Enormously popular with congregations because of his heavy Scottish accent, MacDonald retired after fourteen years as a pastor of Woodlawn Baptist Church to become interim pastor of Sixth Avenue Presbyterian Church in Birmingham.[41]

John H. Buchanan was the denomination's boldest advocate of ecumenism. Chairman of the SBC's executive committee in 1946 and a member of the committee for a decade after 1937, Buchanan also served as chairman of a committee appointed by the SBC to consider joining the World Council of Churches. From the outset of deliberations, Buchanan became spokesman for a faction of denominational leaders who favored membership in the council. Backed by Southern seminary professor W. O. Carver, Foreign

James H. Chapman established study in religious education at Howard College and used his courses in church leadership to expose ministerial students to an array of viewpoints. He was also a cofounder of the Birmingham Ministers Discussion Group and the central figure in the Alabama Baptist Historical Society. (Courtesy of Samford University Archives)

Mission Board director Charles E. Maddry, and Ellis A. Fuller (pastor at Atlanta First Baptist Church), Buchanan fought first for full membership then for SBC participation as observers. Blocked by conservatives Arthur J. Barton, George W. Truett, and Southwestern seminary president L. R. Scarborough, he then waged a successful battle to at least decline membership with a courteous letter rather than with the insulting and argumentative draft suggested by Barton. Buchanan also took the considerable heat of the council's opponents in order to protect Maddry and the Foreign Mission Board (who were arguing that cooperative mission efforts would stretch resources and eliminate confusion in countries where denominational and doctrinal strife crippled evangelism).[42]

Debate over the social implications of Christianity continued to rage, with advocates of the social gospel holding their own. Until 1950 they profited from the powerful and prophetic leadership of Gwaltney. If the primary concern of the church was saving souls, he wrote in 1944, then it could not keep silent about slums, unemployment, or war. Otherwise the church engaged in hypocrisy. The issue was not whether salvation was primarily personal or social but whether Christians took God's will seriously and applied it to all aspects of life. What the nation needed, he wrote near the end of the war, was a prophet like Amos, who not only condemned the enemies of Israel but also denounced Israel's own sins. Christ, he reminded readers in 1947, came to preach to the poor, heal the brokenhearted, and preach deliverance to captives, recovery of sight to the blind, and liberty to the bruised. That was still the gospel that Christians should proclaim. Applying such teachings to himself, Gwaltney endorsed a bill pending before the 1947 legislature to abolish flogging of Alabama prison inmates.[43]

Before his abrupt departure from Alabama in 1944, Charles Bell Jr. was even more involved in social reform than Gwaltney. Having repeatedly voted for socialist Norman Thomas, Bell expressed his continuing concern for the poor by organizing a cooperative farm, supporting other cooperatives financially, helping the labor movement, and joining the Southern Conference for Human Welfare. Writing in the *Alabama Baptist* in 1942, Bell argued that any durable postwar peace must be based on correcting injustices in the United States. Unless Americans could end hunger, poverty, unemployment, and racial discrimination in their own country, they could not claim moral leadership of the free world.[44]

Members of the state social service commission (Stivender, S. J. Ezell, John Xan, Lee Gallman, and Montague Cook) provided Gwaltney enthusiastic allies. Although they predictably denounced divorce, gambling, and alcoholic beverages, they also urged arbitration of disputes between labor and management, endorsed collective bargaining and the right of workers to organize, deplored racial conflict, persecution, and demagoguery, and asked that minority races be given the same rights and privileges that the majority enjoyed. The 1947 commission favored a verifiable system of international disarmament with periodic U.S. inspections and the following year urged support for the United Nations. The 1948 report, presented during the initial phase of the cold war, advised that the best way to combat communism was by "giving the masses of the people social justice, more of the good things of life and more democracy." Under its plank on prison reform, the 1948 commission recommended segregating first offenders from hardened criminals even if more prisons and higher taxes were required. The purpose of the criminal justice system, the report added, was rehabilitation, not punishment. The 1949 report warned that Baptists (who as a denomination were becoming wealthy and powerful) were in danger of losing their compassion for the poor. The 1952 report endorsed U.S. policy in Korea, supported the UN, and condemned deficit spending, government extravagance, subsidies, regulation of markets, and overdependence on government. On occasion the state convention went beyond recommendations of the commission, as in 1941 when messengers rejected a section condemning the closed shop (a requirement that workers in certain industries must belong to a union in order to hold a job).[45]

Regarding prison reform, Baptists not only championed a bill to end flogging of prisoners and segregation of youthful offenders from hardened criminals, they also paid the salary of a prison chaplain. J. W. Sharp, himself a former convict who had been converted while in prison, resigned as pastor of Hopewell Baptist Church in 1944 in order to devote his full time to work with convicts and former prisoners. Pastor friends in the Bessemer Association created the "Friends of the Friendless Society" to support Sharp financially.[46]

Montgomery pastor Charles Leek used his column in the *Alabama Baptist* to praise Loula Dunn, Alabama's commissioner of public welfare, for administering free meals to 45,000 undernourished children in the public schools, although he also warned against "professional paupers" and welfare that destroyed the "pride of the poor." When various special interests vied with each other in 1945 for the surplus in the state treasury, Leek favored giving the money to the state welfare and public health departments.[47]

Baptist layman Hopson Owen Murfee led forces trying to improve conditions in Alabama mental hospitals. Son of former Howard College president James T. Murfee, he graduated from the University of Virginia and the University of Chicago with degrees in mathematics, astronomy, and physics. Murfee returned to Alabama as professor and then president of Marion Military Institute. He became mentally ill in 1918 and spent seven years in Bryce Hospital. After his recovery he became a crusader for mental health reform. He led a successful campaign to raise a million dollars for new construction, then mobilized Baptists and Methodists to demand that Governor Frank M. Dixon double appropriations for physicians and nurses in mental hospitals. Nearly a quarter century ahead of his time, he campaigned unsuccessfully for creation of a statewide system of mental health clinics that could provide early diagnosis of mental illness and some preventive treatment. Arguing that most mental illness could be cured, he denounced Alabama's woeful underfunding of all aspects of public health. He launched a crusade in 1942 to establish a four-year college of medicine and nursing, with services in all sixty-seven counties and free scholarships to one student from each county.[48]

Layman Charles G. Dobbins (son of the pastor of the Camden Baptist Church, Howard College graduate, and a close friend of Charlie Bell) became the liberal editor of the *Anniston Times* and later of the *Montgomery Advertiser*. As editor of the *Advertiser* (which in the 1940s was the state's most influential newspaper), Dobbins urged Baptists to vote in favor of an income tax amendment that would substantially increase funding for public schools by earmarking taxes for that purpose.[49]

Leon Macon was not as supportive of social Christianity as Gwaltney, Bell, Stivender, Murfee, Dobbins, and other reform-minded Baptists. Shortly after assuming editorship of the *Alabama Baptist*, he announced that he favored the old ways in preference to the social gospel, which was a radical change from "God's way of salvation through a new birth." Defining the social gospel as the search for a better society through the application of Christ's teachings, he cautioned that society could be saved only as individuals were converted. Jesus intended the gospel to produce "good social results" but had not divided goods among his followers. His purpose was individual salvation, and that should be the chief task of the church.[50]

Nonetheless, Macon was generally consistent with his belief that regenerate people should act justly toward others. He believed that most of the world's problems resulted from unjust division of wealth. Communism offered one solution to this problem, socialism another, but the U.S. solution (progressive taxation and organized labor) was preferable to both. Like Murfee and Jones, he considered Alabama's treatment of the mentally ill disgraceful. In an emotional 1950 editorial, he described how a sick, terrified, insane woman was strapped to a floor mattress in the Anniston jail while giving birth to her baby. Bryce Hospital was so crowded it could not admit her. Despite majority support for a vote on higher taxes for state mental hospitals, four consecutive legislatures had refused to allow such a referendum. He condemned especially a small clique of men "no larger than the politburo in the Kremlin" that determined what bills Alabamians were allowed to vote for or against. He believed that ordinary citizens were willing to pay more taxes to alleviate such terrible suffering. But some "who are well positioned themselves" "kick and growl and grumble at taxes for any such things. They are simply not good Americans, to say nothing of being Christians."[51]

Macon's philosophy of penology was similar to Gwaltney's. Primitive concepts were neither correct nor effective. Some convicts had acted out of "criminal intent," but others were in prison because of "circumstances which drove them to criminal conduct." They would be better served if forced to make restitution.[52]

Also like his predecessor, Macon enthusiastically supported public schools, both as a vehicle for promoting Protestant and democratic values and as a check on Catholic parochial education. He consistently favored tax increases for public schools and publicized underfunding and dilapidated facilities. He also defended public education from those who charged it with promoting collectivism and communism or as being wastefully and corruptly administered.[53]

Many Baptist leaders lined up behind Macon. Dr. W. R. White wrote that Christianity was not a social gospel but a redemptive and regenerative message with social implications. He praised the antislavery movement as essentially a crusade by "evangelistic evangelicals." The tragedy of modern conservative evangelicalism was that it was harnessed against no such great evil. The tragedy of modern liberalism was that it had emasculated the gospel with a materialistic concept of social redemption. One ideology minimized social sins, the other underestimated personal evil.[54]

Although the state's Baptists perceived separation of church and state as a doctrinal issue, it became inextricably linked to anti-Catholicism during the 1940s. The resurgence of antipathy toward Catholics resulted from a variety of developments and involved a wide swath of American Protestants. FDR provoked the initial reaction by appointing an ambassador to the Vatican. By May 1940 twenty-five Protestant groups had protested his action, opening a period of tension and conflict. Unlike the 1920s, when opposition to Catholicism had come from the most nativist and conservative wings of Protestantism, the post-1940 crusade involved liberal and moderate Protestants as well. This fact may also explain the altered form of anti-Catholicism during the later era. Instead of emotionalism and Klan-type violence, Protestant opposition took the form mainly of resolutions and manifestos. Catholics also responded differently. No longer primarily a religion of first-generation immigrants, many Catholics were well educated, successful, and confident. Protestants were well organized primarily through Protestants and Other Americans United for Separation of Church and State. POAU mobilized primarily around opposition to federal aid for parochial schools and hospitals.

Federal aid to education involved ecclesiastical issues for both parties to the dispute. Although theoretically neutral on matters of religious exercise in public schools, many Protestants insisted that these institutions allow Bible reading and prayer. Because virtually all teachers in public schools in the South were Protestants, religious exercises in schools were also Protestant. Catholics reacted negatively to Protestant domination of public schools and also provided parochial schools that educated many immigrant children whose first language was not English.[55]

Baptists did not always agree with other Protestants or even with each other on the manifold issues raised by church-state questions. They consistently rejected federal aid, even to the financial detriment of their own institutions. Generally, they also supported a series of Supreme Court decisions (most written by one of their own, Hugo Black) restricting prescribed Bible reading and prayer in public schools. The latter is noteworthy in light of the fact that southern congressmen by and large were the most vituperative critics of the high court's rulings. Even though Baptists were quickly becoming the power brokers of southern politics, the residual theological tradition of Baptists as outsiders endured into the 1940s and 1950s. Congregations might not be well informed on the reasons for such support of Supreme Court rulings or they might even defend Bible reading and prayer in public schools, but they were too divided to challenge their pastors, who were surprisingly united in support of the courts.[56]

In Alabama pastors of different ideologies were deeply suspicious about Catholic objectives. Gwaltney considered "Romanism" and communism similar in their autocracy, hierarchical organization, and demand for the total allegiance of followers. When a Catholic priest in Mobile criticized organization of a POAU chapter in Alabama during 1949, Gwaltney accused him of creating religious acrimony. The first president elected by the new organization was Dr. Howard M. Reaves of Mobile First Baptist Church (though with a fine sense of political balance, members selected a Methodist, a Presbyterian, and Disciples of Christ as other officers). For years thereafter, nearly every issue of the *Alabama Baptist* contained some reference to Catholicism.[57]

Occasionally, denominational leaders overstepped the boundaries of fair play on issues involving Catholics. James R. Swedenburg, the Baptist director of the Alabama Temperance Alliance, wrote the president of the University of Alabama (his alma mater) in 1954, chiding him for appointing a Catholic to a top administrative position at the university's medical college in Birmingham. Swedenburg noted that the appointment made eight Catholic department heads at the college, though Catholics constituted less than 2 percent of the state's population. He believed that Catholics used control of hospitals to proselytize patients and warned of a fight by Baptist and Methodist preachers to take control of the university's board of trustees unless the president relented.[58]

The entire range of issues relating to religion and education became greatly complicated when state courts began to rule in favor of public funding of parochial schools. Beginning with a proposed 1940 amendment to the U.S. Constitution authorizing the use of tax money for sectarian schools, Gwaltney, Macon, and the social service commission regularly denounced threatened infringements on the venerable doctrine of separation of church and state. The Birmingham ministerial association opposed a 5-4 Supreme Court decision allowing buses purchased with public funds to transport parochial schoolchildren. A. Hamilton Reid and Gwaltney opposed a bill introduced by Alabama Senator Lister Hill that permitted federal aid to sectarian schools. Leon Macon warned that such legislation would break down the "wall of separation of church and state." He also adamantly opposed tax certificates to parents of parochial school students.[59]

Such positions created a dilemma for presidents and trustees of financially strapped Alabama Baptist institutions. Never well financed, Howard and Judson Colleges (together with Baptist hospitals in Gadsden, Birmingham, and Montgomery) were perpetually in debt and struggling for their lives. When federal funds became available under terms of various federal aid to education bills or the Hill-Burton hospital construction act, they often raced to get in line for their share of the money. Occasionally a Baptist such as J. S. Brindley of Warrior publicly favored federal aid to education, despite its possible misuse, as the only way to equalize educational opportunities between rich and poor states. Usually the issue was more opportunistic. Howard College president Harwell Davis reversed his earlier opposition to the use of public funds by religious schools. Disingenuously vowing that he would accept no money that violated separation of church and state, he applied for federal funds to build four dormitories for returning veterans. When vigorously criticized for doing so, he replied lamely that he was no theologian and did not fully understand such complex issues. In 1950 the state executive committee allowed Judson College to cover its employees under Social Security because the government did not provide money for the benefits, which went to individuals and not the institution.[60]

Accepting direct construction grants under terms of the new Hill-Burton Act seemed a more obvious breach of Baptist tradition. Southside's pastor, John Buchanan, together with trustees of the Birmingham Baptist hospital, unsuccessfully pressured Gwaltney in 1949 to reverse his opposition and endorse acceptance of federal funds. S. J. Ezell and L. E. Barton, both relatively liberal on most issues, led the opposition. Finally executive secretary A. Hamilton Reid visited Gwaltney and persuaded him to reverse his position (requiring that 10,000 copies of the paper carrying an editorial against accepting the funds be destroyed).[61]

Subsequently, Gwaltney defended taking federal money. He called the Hill-Burton Act a humanitarian effort similar to public housing, Social Security, free school lunches, or state welfare programs. The precedent of federal aid to parochial schools did not apply because, unlike Catholic schools that taught sectarian religion, Baptist hospitals merely received back Baptist tax money without any sectarian purpose. At best, this was tortured logic. At worst, it was patently contradictory.[62]

Baptists remained free to proselytize any way they desired in their own institutions, but they were uncertain about how far to allow religious exercises in public schools. Gwaltney engaged in a spirited 1940 editorial debate with Yale professor James R. Angell. Angell argued that children needed personal discipline and character development and that Christianity was the surest way to instill such values. Hence, all public schools should experiment with teaching Christianity. Gwaltney responded by asking Angell which version of Christianity should be taught—the teacher's version? Angell's version? Gwaltney's version? How could public schools teach Christianity and deny equal time to other religions? If 200,000 American churches had failed to inculcate Christian values in children, how could public schools succeed?[63]

Various Alabama Baptists suggested ways to accomplish this goal. Montgomery pastor Charles Leek praised a plan by a Selma Baptist pastor to raise private money for a certified Bible teacher. The teacher would offer voluntary classes for credit in the town's schools. "Debatable" or sectarian issues would be referred to the students' parents and not discussed in class. Hal D. Bennett, associate editor of the *Alabama Baptist*, urged teachers in public schools to express their own religious opinions and to allow pupils to disagree if they chose. A pastor in Pine Hill described a religious emphasis week at the local high school where Baptist, Methodist, and Presbyterian ministers applied Christianity to literature, history, and politics.[64]

Leon Macon straddled the issue of religious observance. On one hand, he deplored the increasing secularism of tax-supported schools. On the other, he opposed requiring Bible courses in public schools. To reports from a Texas town that a public school had required students to attend a Baptist-sponsored religious meeting (and assigned "F" grades to three Catholic students who refused to go), Macon scolded local Baptists, who should be ashamed of themselves. Baptists could not claim religious freedom for themselves unless they extended it to others. He also praised a federal judge who said that teaching religion in public schools unnecessarily strained community relations. The church was the proper forum for discussions of religion, Macon argued, not public schools.[65]

On other church-state issues, Macon was more consistent. He opposed congressional attempts to amend the U.S. Constitution to recognize the authority of Jesus Christ because it would discriminate against Jews and other non-Christians, who constituted more than half the nation's population. He also urged ministers not to run for political office because it blurred distinctions between church and state.[66]

Bureaucratizing the Work of the Lord

Although Gwaltney continued to refer to Alabama Baptists as a denomination of the masses, that was less true with every passing decade. More and more people at the bottom of the socioeconomic ladder became pentecostals or joined Holiness churches, whereas Baptists became increasingly middle class.

Nor were convention officers drawn from a cross section of Baptists. No bivocational ministers or small church pastors led the convention during these years. Presidents came from laymen such as Lafayette judge W. B. Bowling or from pastors such as J. C. Stivender (Ruhama), A. Hamilton Reid (vice-president at Howard College), Frank Tripp (pastor of Montgomery First Baptist), Brady R. Justice (pastor of Enterprise First Baptist), John H. Buchanan (pastor of Southside in Birmingham), and Oscar Davis (pastor of Gadsden First Baptist).

Conventions wrestled with seemingly perpetual financial woes at Howard and Judson Colleges and wrangled over whether or not to allow their schools and hospitals to accept federal grants. In a particularly rancorous 1949 convention in Mobile, messengers voted 186 against allowing hospitals to accept Hill-Burton grants to 156 in favor. The following year the executive committee of the Birmingham Association recommended taking the funds by a 20 to 6 vote, but a special associational meeting voted 380 to 337 against doing so.[67]

Throughout the decade, Howard and Judson struggled with their debts and with each other. Howard president Harwell Davis constantly intrigued to close Judson or merge it with Howard, all the while denying any preference in how to resolve financial problems at the two colleges. The convention appointed a blue ribbon committee to study Baptist higher education and employed a number of consultants. The special committee of nine appointed in 1946 recommended combining the schools on a new campus in Birmingham. Proponents of each school began to lobby for or against the recommendation to be considered at the 1947 state convention. Tempers became so short that Gwaltney refused to publish letters for or against the report. The 1947 convention, held in Montgomery's municipal auditorium because of the large anticipated attendance, turned out WMU and Judson women in droves, who forced convention leaders to abandon the merger proposal. Subsequent conventions allocated capital funds to both schools and in 1952 authorized Howard to begin construction of a new campus in the Birmingham suburb of Homewood.[68]

Despite financial problems, both Howard and Judson retained fiercely loyal supporters among Alabama Baptists. Neither had succumbed to academic elitism, and both had concentrated on service to the denomination. A phenomenal number of pastors and missionaries claimed one or the other as alma mater. A dozen or so Judson alumnae had served as missionaries in China. Of the 1,400 students enrolled at Howard College in the late 1940s, more than a third were preparing for some form of full-time Christian vocation (408 male ministerial students, 115 female mission or service volunteers). Another 2,000 were enrolled in Howard's innovative extension program. In the fall of 1951, more than 20 "Howard boys" enrolled in the freshman class at Southern seminary. After seminary, these men and women literally scattered across the world, often sending sons and daughters back to their alma maters in subsequent decades.[69]

The *Alabama Baptist* was another well-established institution within denominational life. An important era came to an end in July 1950 when Leon M. Macon (pastor at Bessemer First Baptist Church) became editor of the paper. When he left the job, Gwaltney had served longer than any previous editor (thirty-one years) and had written an estimated 8.3 million words. He left a profound impression on the denomination. Gwaltney had proven that well-educated leaders could stay in touch with ordinary Baptists. He shared their deep devotion to the denomination and their fierce independence of thought. They loved him dearly and so forgave what they sometimes considered eccentric theological views. Within the SBC, there was no editor who was more highly regarded or influential.[70]

Macon was cut from a different pattern. Not only was his world more provincial but the boundaries of his tolerance were narrower. But he did bring energy and new ideas to a paper that had run out of steam. Gwaltney had relied upon the editorial page and the respect of the editor to sustain it. He relished the role of denominational statesman and worried little about expanding the paper's circulation base. Macon brought new ideas and fresh energy. He promoted the idea of churches subscribing to the paper for all members at a bargain basement price of only cents a copy. By 1955 he had persuaded 1,400 of the denomination's 2,700 churches to participate in the plan, and he had raised circulation from 27,000 in 1945 to 75,000.[71]

Responsibility for overseeing the expanding network of Baptist institutions belonged to the executive board of the state convention, which handled denominational policy. Its CEO held extensive power that belied his unimpressive title. He and a growing staff of professional associates managed the day-to-day operations of a large and prosperous religious bureaucracy. In December 1944 the 110-member state executive board selected A. Hamilton Reid (who had served as pastor of South Avondale Baptist Church and as vice-president and chief fund raiser for Howard College) as executive secretary-treasurer.

ABSC's executive board was somewhat less powerful than similar bodies in other states that were charged with budget preparation and administrative duties. In Alabama ten separate boards and commissions, each accountable directly to the convention, administered policy. This decentralized and often ineffective system satisfied the legendary independence and democratic proclivities of Alabamians, but it often led to confusion, duplication, and conflict.[72]

Between 1945 and 1955, the work of the convention was expanded, centralized, and made more efficient. In 1952 the convention adopted the first in a series of Five Year Advance programs that set concrete goals for all areas of denominational life, then measured success against the accomplishment of them.[73] During a period of rapid growth in both population and economy, Alabama Baptists often exceeded even their own bold projections. The Cooperative Program brought in such abundant funds that the convention authorized capital fund drives for Howard, Judson, the children's home at Troy, a new state assembly grounds (Shocco Springs), and university centers on all campuses. In 1952 the convention also adjusted CP distributions to approach the target of a 50-50 split between state and worldwide SBC causes (in 1947 the distribution had been 60-40 percent; by 1952 it was 54-46).[74] Although the executive board and its smaller administrative committee were more representative of rank-and-file Baptists (the 110-member board regularly contained a sprinkling of lay people and bivocational pastors of small churches) than convention officers, even those boards were skewed in the direction of the "first church" establishment.

The distribution of CP funds within Alabama went primarily to three recipients—state missions, Howard College, and Judson College. The state missions budget (which amounted to between one-fifth and one-fourth of total state expenditures) supported an increasingly complex bureaucracy in the Montgomery convention headquarters as well as a far-flung network of state missionaries. Having begun in the early nineteenth century with a handful of state missionaries whose task was primarily preaching revivals and distributing tracts and Bibles, the denomination was moving toward a missionary in every association whose task was essentially supportive. These missionaries started new Sunday schools and missions, organized associational meetings, provided liaison with state and SBC agencies, and promoted state and national programs and campaigns. Whereas the state mission budget had once paid a salary supplement or even the entire salary of associational missionaries, associations and the executive board now worked cooperatively to support them. The years 1940–1955 constituted a transitional time in associational work, a period of centralization and bureaucratization similar to what was taking place in the state convention. This transition allowed much freedom to experiment. Associations hired part-time associational missionaries, including some women.

A committee on state missions recommended in 1942 that the board stop "dribbling out" small amounts of money on associational work and concentrate on a few strategic locations. There were only ten associational missionaries in the entire state in 1944, and several of them were part-time. The executive board adopted principles to govern the employment of full-time associational missionaries in order to promote the denominational program. The new executive secretary, A. Hamilton Reid, quickly acted on this initiative, adding four new city missionaries and five rural district missionaries (aided by the Home Mission Board). He encouraged each association to employ a missionary and pledged executive board financial assistance to do so. Associations did the hiring with the approval of the state board. Associations usually paid expenses and the board provided salaries.[75]

Associations were not the only level of denominational life undergoing stress. Rapid growth and affluence produced a different set of problems from the hard times of the 1930s, but the local crises were just as destructive to church harmony and ministerial careers. Pastors regularly requested help from A. Hamilton Reid or Leon Macon to find new parishes. C. E. Jones pastored Concord Baptist Church, which had a reputation for running off pastors. He was no exception. He wrote Leon Macon for help in finding another pastorate, having served his church and association as well as he could. Murray Hall sent a similar letter to Macon about Moundville Baptist Church. The rented parsonage was a dilapidated house without electricity because the church had not paid utility bills. After months as pastor, Hall had added only one new member to the church's roll. Under the previous two pastors, the church had had only one addition. As a successful revivalist, Hall would not accept such a situation, which he attributed to a small clique that controlled the church and did not desire new people. He was ready to move elsewhere but would not resign until he had another pastorate.[76]

There was another side to such preacher stories. Laymen sometimes criticized ministers for trying to force their views on congregations. This authoritarianism denied lay people freedom and initiative. Macon pleaded for mutual forbearance, democracy, and open discussion. He advised preachers to try to persuade their lay people to accept new programs but never to force them. He also recommended the rotation of deacons, one-third each year of a three-year term. This practice opened a church to democracy and to younger men with new ideas.[77]

Harassed by conservative church members resistant to change and pressured by others to show quick results, underpaid and overworked pastors came up with gimmicks and desperately sought help from fellow sufferers. H. O. Hester (the energetic young pastor of Eighty-fifth Street Baptist Church in Birmingham) received national attention in 1954 for his "Silver Dollar Day." On Easter Sunday of that year, which was the twenty-fifth anniversary of the church, he urged everyone to give the silver dollars they had saved for that purpose all year long. He carted 31,000 silver dollars into the new sanctuary in two wheelbarrows; it was enough to pay off nearly the entire church debt. In order to share such ideas and no doubt gripe a bit about their respective problems, a number of pastors who liked to fish formed the "Let the Fish Talk" club. The president was the biggest liar among them, longtime pastor of Hartselle Baptist Church, Frank T. Smith.[78]

During the fifteen years after 1940, most southern states took steps to develop a more professional ministry. State populations were rapidly changing from rural and agricultural to urban and nonfarm. The South's rural culture died hard, and the transition was painful, both for displaced rural people moving to town and for country folks who remained behind. A 1954 SBC survey of nearly 2,200 Baptist pastors revealed that 73 percent were reared in rural areas (including 63 percent of the denomination's urban pastors). That year 14,700 of 30,000 SBC churches were in open country and nearly 9,000 more in "villages" and "towns." Fewer than 6,300 congregations were in cities. Average church membership was less than 300 and the average annual per capita contribution of rural church members was only twenty-nine dollars. Another SBC survey in 1949 revealed that one-third of the denomination's preachers had only a high school diploma or less.[79] Denominational leaders were deeply concerned about the future of rural churches for good reason.

Only 365 of Alabama's 2,300 SBC churches were full-time in 1940. When Sam Granade left the paratroopers at the end of the war to pastor in Conecuh County, he was the only resident Baptist pastor in that large county. Low farm income and widespread rural poverty made it difficult if not impossible to maintain a broad church program or provide a salary adequate to recruit educated, full-time pastors. Thomas M. Collins earned $120 in 1949 as pastor of Carrollton Baptist Church and $360 from Hebron Baptist Church. Most rural churches struggled hard just to stay alive, had unstable, short-term pastorates, and gave little or nothing to missions.[80]

Yet denominational officials romanticized rural churches and made herculean efforts to save them. Gwaltney wrote that boys from rural backgrounds such as his own fared better in life. Leon Macon (also born on a farm) added that he never heard of a rural church producing a modernist preacher or dying of formalism (the biographies of Gwaltney and James E. Dean prove he was wrong).[81]

Rural and small town folkways certainly continued to shape Alabama Baptist life. W. Albert Smith, though pastor of a flourishing First Baptist church in Sheffield in 1950, was originally a country man from Clay County. He offered a successful motion to the state board of ministerial education to deny ministerial scholarships to students who had sufficient funds to join a social fraternity. F. M. Barnes, executive secretary of the convention in 1941, wrote a letter of recommendation for Olin Ray to become missionary for the Bibb County Association. He referred to Ray, a graduate of Howard College, as "a big, gawky, husky young man" who came from "the mill town of Langdale and can take matters tough."[82]

Most pastors of rural and small-town churches continued to be bivocational preachers by financial necessity. One minister in Perry County pastored four churches in 1942 with memberships of thirty-five, twenty-three, fifteen, and ten. All four were weak rural churches filled with poor members. Of his four churches, only three paid anything, in each case $50 a year. His people were "so fleeced and scattered" that they could not even afford heaters for their churches. The young men were away in service. Though he described members as "a fine, lovable, friendly people," they had no in-

Hubert Williams, a bivocational preacher–coal miner, grew up in poverty during the Great Depression. Although he dropped out of school in the seventh grade to help his family survive, he enrolled in Howard College extension courses throughout his ministerial career. (Courtesy of Samford University Archives)

come except as farmers, and the land "has been scraped to the bone of its natural resources." Shelton D. Bartlett graduated from Sardis High School, was converted in 1942, and began to pastor small churches while holding down a full-time job at a Goodyear tire plant in Gadsden. He was a member of the United Rubber Workers Union and, when time allowed, enrolled in Howard College extension courses. Arthur Hurston Smith of Lincoln also received a ministerial education through a Howard extension center. He managed a grocery store, worked at Anniston Army Depot, raised cattle, and was active in county politics. He also pastored a number of rural churches in Cleburne and Randolph Counties and served on the executive committee of the Cleburne Baptist Association. C. E. Arnold of Whatley pastored eight churches at the same time in 1942, a difficult job made harder by wartime gasoline rationing. He formed committees in each congregation to inform him of serious illnesses and deaths because he had to conserve gas and tires to allow him to preach Sunday services and still tend to pastoral duties.[83]

Gordon C. Chandler was born in Cherokee County, married his childhood sweetheart when both were sixteen, and dropped out of school. After farming for a few years, he felt called to preach in his twenties. He became associate pastor of one rural church and pastor of another. Neither paid a regular salary, though both gave him occasional voluntary offerings. By 1946 he was earning a living by farming while pastoring four quarter-time churches. At age thirty-one he sold his farm and finished high school, preaching his own baccalaureate service. He began night school and supported his family by doing carpentry work. From 1948 to 1956 he pastored full-time in Gadsden and served as associational missionary for Calhoun County. In 1956 he became pastor of Blue Mountain Baptist Church, a textile-mill congregation in Anniston. Although he was a faithful student of Howard College extension courses, he never earned college or seminary degrees. Despite that handicap, he became a successful and highly respected pastor.[84]

Hubert Williams lived the industrial equivalent of Chandler's life. Born at Maben in Jefferson County and one of twelve children of a coal miner father, he dropped out of school in the seventh grade because of the Great Depression. He became a coal miner and electrician, married at age nineteen, and was converted at a revival in 1939. He began preaching the following year. Though he knew little about the Bible, he could tell congregations about Jesus. He supplemented his meager education with correspondence and Howard College extension courses. He studied the Bible by the light of a kerosene lamp until his community obtained electricity, and he pastored for thirty-five years in the Mud Creek, Birmingham, Walker, Marshall, Autauga, Cahaba, and Bibb Associations. Most of his congregations contained a mixture of farmers and coal miners.

While working in the Praco mining camp, Williams pastored Liberty Baptist Church, which was located several miles away on the opposite side of the Little Warrior River. On one occasion when the river was at flood stage and the ferry unable to operate, a member of his church died. The state road department was building a new bridge across the river, so a member of the church agreed to meet him on the church side of the river if he would cross on the unfinished bridge. He drove to the river, parked his Model A Ford, and began to walk across the bridge's scaffolding. The iron beam was only three feet wide and was high above a ravine. The raging river washed trees from the banks beneath him and swiftly carried them downstream. Halfway across Williams made the mistake of looking down. Dizzy and scared, he thought about sitting down until his friend could come and get him. Finally across the river, he preached the funeral, returned to the bridge, walked back across, and returned home. He vowed that if confronted with such a situation again, he would drive two hundred miles out of the way in order not to repeat the experience. Crossing the Little Warrior River in floodstage on an iron beam established the outer limits of his confidence in the providence of God.

Most of the time Williams pastored for free-will offerings rather than a stipulated salary. Some churches paid him less than $5 a month; the most he ever received was $450 in a single month. The coal miners, sawmillers, and farmers who made up his congregations often paid in food. Foot washing remained common in his rural churches, as did public confession of sins. He stopped the first practice because he became convinced it was not biblical and the second because many of his parishioners enjoyed confessing other people's sins more than their own.

Williams attributed the various fundamentalist-modernist squabbles of his lifetime to jealousy and Baptist politics. He preferred to ignore such differences and focus on his congregations and mission causes. He did not like centralization of the convention or the state executive committee's selection of board members, who almost always were pastors in county seat towns. He regretted that laymen and pastors of small churches were seldom selected or elected to any convention office. He argued that conventions did not build churches, churches built conventions. He attributed his ministerial success to close relationship to his people. "I never lost anything working with coal miners and sawmillers and farm people," he explained. "I put on the same kind of clothes they'd wear during week days, and go where they worked, and worked with them, and be a part of them. Then we'd all of us put on the best we had to go to church on Sunday." Unlike many preachers, Williams never kept records of sermons preached, baptisms, funerals, revivals, or number of members in the thirteen congregations he served as pastor. He explained simply, "What I have done with the opportunitites that God has given me is now history . . . [and] God holds the record."[85]

If bivocational ministers like Williams shatter stereotypes, so do many of the churches they pastored. The union church at TCI's Docena mining camp served Methodists two Sundays a month and Baptists the other two. The building belonged to the company and also functioned as a community center. The frequent social interaction between members of the two congregations softened doctrinal differences. A new preacher who did not understand his congregation well once tried to create a full-time Baptist church by criticizing Methodist practices and beliefs. But as one old-time Docena resident remembered, "he didn't have no luck . . . the Baptists run him off."[86]

State Baptist leaders realized such churches and pastors desperately needed help, and they created numerous programs to assist them. The state mission committee in 1942 recommended employing two field workers to assist rural churches. The following year the state executive committee appropriated $5,000 for rural work. The committee hired five rural district missionaries in 1945. By 1950 the committee had reduced the number of rural district missionaries (most associations had their own missionaries by then) but hired fifty college and seminary students to conduct rural vacation Bible schools. The WMU sponsored a statewide rural church conference at the new Shocco Springs assembly grounds in 1954 and paid expenses so the wives of fifty rural pastors could attend.[87]

By far the most important assistance to rural and bivocational ministers came from the Howard College extension program. As early as 1930 W. P. Wilks (then pastor in Opelika and perhaps inspired by Auburn University's Cooperative Extension Service) had called on Howard College to begin ministerial extension education to help the hundreds of Baptist preachers who were not able to attend college or seminary. Baptist and Howard officials applauded the idea, but the onset of the Great Depression delayed implementation. Later in the decade, Gilbert L. Guffin (pastor of Jasper First Baptist Church) conducted a successful school for pastors in northwestern Alabama. The idea took shape as the Extension Division of Christian Training, headquartered at Howard College but conducted in centers across Alabama. A combination of Howard faculty and local pastors and lay people taught the classes. Volunteers staffed the centers, working for only their expenses. Guffin ably headed the program initially; he was followed by Hampton C. Hopkins and J. W. Lester.[88]

The structure and philosophy of the Howard extension program was ingeniously simple. Classes began in January 1947 with twenty-five centers located in churches scattered throughout every section of the state. Each center had a local director and registrar, advisory committee, and teaching staff. Some sixty to seventy courses allowed a student to take classes for six years without repeating a course. Pastors' wives and lay people constituted nearly half the original enrollment. WMU operated a nursery on the main Howard campus to allow mothers to attend. The most popular courses included English, Old and New Testaments, homiletics, church administration, Baptist history and doctrine, and evangelism. By 1952 the number of centers had grown to thirty-eight and students to 1,665, including 475 preachers. There were no entrance requirements other than "a desire to learn." To supplement courses, the college periodically conducted rural life conferences using experts from land-grant universities and national religious personalities. Graduations (the first was in 1951 for thirty-four of the initial enrollees) were every bit as inspiring as ceremonies for regular undergraduates on the main campus.[89]

So successful was Howard's extension program that it was widely copied. Eight Baptist colleges in the South (including Carson-Newman in Tennessee, Gardner-Webb in North Carolina, and Mercer University in Georgia) created extension programs based on the Howard model. A sociology professor at Southeastern Baptist Theological Seminary in North Carolina declared it to be one of the most significant initiatives to assist rural churches not only in the SBC but in the nation.[90]

In a denomination where Leon Macon condemned proposals to consolidate rural congregations or apply "social features of the gospel," Baptists had to devise their own strategies for saving country churches. But Guffin, Hopkins, and Lester did not entirely neglect social aspects of rural life even while emphasizing the need for personal salvation. J. W. Lester often preached a this-worldly sermon entitled "Soil Conservation Fighting Soil Erosion."[91]

One expression of the influence of rural religious folkways over the denomination was the continuing battle against legalized gambling and alcohol. Baptists lined up solidly against various proposals in the Alabama legislature to allow pari-mutuel gambling.[92] They were equally adamant about the sale and use of alcoholic beverages. The Alabama Temperance Alliance (ATA) was increasingly dominated by Baptist pastors. S. J. Ezell served as president of the alliance during the 1940s and James Swedenburg became its executive secretary. Other prominent ATA leaders included A. Hamilton Reid, Leon Macon, Oley C. Kidd, Oscar Davis, and Henry L. Lyon Jr.[93]

Nor had revivalism lost its grip on the state. Developed as a mechanism to convert scattered, rural people, religious crusades had long proven their efficacy in cities as well. In the era before television, revivals still constituted an important social occasion as well as a significant religious event.

The selection of S. J. Ezell in 1938 as director of evangelism brought a man of decidedly liberal theological views to that strategic office. Under Ezell's leadership, the state entered its golden age of growth, proving again that a theological moderate could also be a soul winner. Gwaltney, who also tolerated a wide range of theological viewpoints, warned against substituting an "academic spirit" in place of "a passion for the salvation of men."[94]

He need not have worried, at least not about his own denomination. Baptists constantly found new ways to promote evangelism. The Birmingham Baptist Association targeted specific communities, establishing Belcher Memorial Baptist Church as a mission in a lumber mill village, Berney Points Baptist Church on a bus route near a large housing project, Eighty-fifth Street Baptist Church in the new Roebuck neighborhood, and Glen Iris Baptist Church, which targeted Italian and Syrian ethnic populations. Mountain Brook Baptist Church was organized south of the city in 1944. At the state level, the convention office organized in 1948 the first evangelism conference, which soon attracted more attendees than the state convention.[95]

Individual revivals and coordinated urban campaigns flourished in the fertile religious climate of the war and postwar years. John Buchanan at Southside Baptist Church persuaded the venerable Baptist patriarch George W. Truett of Dallas to preach a revival in Birmingham in 1940. The church held noon services at a downtown theater, where they often had to turn away hundreds. At night, services moved to the church sanctuary on Birmingham's Southside, where a new public address system allowed Truett to preach to three thousand. Southside also pioneered television evangelism, becoming the first church in Alabama to telecast worship services in 1950.[96]

Revivals and regular services produced 20,300 baptisms in 1945, 25,700 in 1950, and 26,500 in 1951. The 1951 results included 8,000 baptisms in open country churches, 2,500 in village congregations, 3,500 in town, and 10,000 in city churches. This season of renewal resulted mainly from simultaneous revivals in March 1951. In Mobile fifty-four of the association's fifty-six churches participated. A. Hamilton Reid estimated that statewide 500,000 Alabamians attended Baptist services during the two weeks (had each person attended only once, that figure would have equaled a staggering one-sixth of the state's total population). Simultaneous revivals the following year (March 25–April 8) produced equally impressive results. In the Birmingham Association, Acipco church baptized 21, Berney Points 13, First Baptist 45, Central Park 100, Eighty-fifth Street 24, Ensley 27, Fairfield 60, Powderly 79, Lakewood 77, Norwood 77, and Woodlawn 71. In all, nearly 1,600 baptisms were recorded just by churches in the association as a result of those two-week services. An eight-day revival in Mobile during 1953 attracted 85,000 people and registered 1,400 decisions. Evangelist Eddie Martin preached a 1954 revival at Tuscaloosa First Baptist Church that attracted average attendance of 3,500 a night. One evening the service was held at the University of Alabama football stadium and attracted a phenomenal 11,000 people (the appeal of such an event must have been irresistible; it combined Alabama's largest two religions, Christianity and football). Martin conducted successful tent revivals in Dothan and Mobile the following year. By 1955 the new goal of 35,000 baptisms in a single year seemed not unreasonable.[97]

At the end of 125 years of ministry in 1947, the Alabama Baptist State Convention published some interesting comparisons with its birth year. The 1823 convention represented 3,280 Baptists in 75 churches and reported 290 baptisms. A century and a quarter later, the convention enrolled 478,000 Baptists in 2,500 churches that registered 20,280 baptisms. That year, black and white Baptists (who had belonged to the same churches in 1823) constituted 31 percent of the state's total population; white Baptists alone constituted one-half of all Alabama church members. The icing on the statistical cake came in 1955 when *Time* magazine proclaimed the SBC the most successful Protestant denomination in U.S. history.[98]

Another dimension of Baptist evangelicalism was foreign missions. The denomination did not share in the extensive Protestant soul searching about missions that virtually paralyzed many groups by midcentury. Universalist ideas made denominations question whether Christ was the only way people could be saved. Perhaps the world's other great religions contained an adequate though incomplete revelation of God, they reasoned. Social problems in the United States made some Christians feel hypocritical exporting their religion to other civilizations. Depression-era crises dried up mission funds in all denominations, even the SBC. Secular historians increasingly interpreted missions as a form of American cultural imperialism. Most Protestant denominations absorbed such multiple shocks by sharply curtailing mission forces.

Not the SBC or Alabama Baptists. In 1940, the first full year of economic recovery in the state, a record number of Alabama Baptist foreign missionaries were appointed (eight). But that was merely a prelude to the best decade in state missionary history (the 1950s) when sixty-five Alabama-born volunteers left for foreign fields.[99]

It may be true that Alabama Baptists ignored the ecumenical, socially oriented suggestions of the rural church movement in addressing the problems of country churches. It is certainly true that they did not dispense with revivalism, as did many northern churches in the postwar period. When others disengaged from foreign missions, Baptists invested even more energy and money. In retrospect it is difficult to dispute these decisions. Small, sectarian Baptist churches in Alabama seemed to fare as well as consolidated union churches in rural New England or the Midwest. Revivalism might contain emotional excesses, but it also reaped an abundant harvest of new Christians. Missionary service might seem quaint in a new, more sophisticated age. But it continued to tap into deep roots of service and idealism among Baptist young people.

Driving much of the evangelistic, missionary, and programmatic success of these years were Baptist women. Despite women's central role in denominational life, male leaders still could not agree on their appropriate biblical sphere. While men loudly debated such issues, women quietly expanded their activities into a constantly enlarging domain.

Commenting on the twentieth anniversary celebration of the Nineteenth Amendment, Montgomery pastor and *Alabama Baptist* columnist

Charles Leek saw little evidence either of the bitter opposition of 1920 or of the amendment's therapeutic effect. At one extreme were good women whose votes had improved public life. On the other were bad women whose votes had made conditions worse. In between were most women who fell easy prey to the temptation to act like men: "wearing pants, smoking cigarettes, drinking liquors, and voting as worldings." Nonetheless, Leek did congratulate voters in the tiny Lawrence County community of Hillsboro for electing a woman mayor and six female aldermen in 1940, despite the fact that they made no promises and offered no platform. Perhaps citizens voted for them, Leek mused, because they could not "do any worse than the men."[100]

Gwaltney reminisced about his support of woman suffrage in simpler terms. It had been ridiculous that women could own property, sue and be sued, rear children and manage homes but could not vote. Enfranchising them had made the United States more democratic even if it had made the country no more moral. State WMU president Mrs. Fred Kilgore urged women to pay their poll tax and vote. "We're still in the world," she wrote, "but not of the world."[101]

If Baptist men had reached a consensus on suffrage, they most definitely had not done so on women's appropriate biblical role in society. As Gwaltney observed millions of women enter the work force for the first time during World War II, he speculated on a wide range of women's issues. He attributed the debasement of women to monarchies and rigid caste systems that glorified the warrior class and valued women as breeders of soldiers. Women fared best, he wrote, in Christian democracies. But any system that impeded "the free progress of women is a rotting point" within society. In February 1944 he endorsed equal rights for women, but that term did not include women who decided to "ape men" by smoking or entering business careers. Women ought still to value the "old-fashioned home" and domestic chores. He worried about what would happen to men whose jobs had been taken by "career girls." In the same issue of his paper, he urged Baptist pastors to send names of prospective female navy recruits to his office in Birmingham. He publicized recruitment of 91,000 Waves as a way for young women to fit themselves for their "life work" and obtain new opportunities. He also filled the denominational paper with photographs of young Baptist women in military uniforms.[102]

Men still operated within both a theological and a social order that viewed woman as a temptress, as a modern-day Eve offering Adam another apple. One leading Alabama premillennialist-fundamentalist pastor disillusioned followers by conducting an adulterous affair. The incident was widely publicized by the secular press, to the embarrassment of his cause. The attempt of his ministerial admirers to make theological sense of these events is quite revealing. They did not defend his conduct or the scandal that resulted from it. God had permitted such events throughout Christian history (they cited the case of David and Bathsheba). Such incidents were a warning to all ministers that they were not immune to waywardness. Liberal Baptists, one fundamentalist wrote, had committed "grosser sins, [that] have been covered." He wrote that perhaps his hero's sins resulted from his wife's failure to satisfy him, forcing the man to seek elsewhere what he failed to find at home. Perhaps the "other woman" was at fault because she lured him into the affair. Whatever the case, he wrote, "this is a real blow to our fundamental and premillennial testimony."[103]

Premillennial fundamentalists had no monopoly on human frailty. It is likely that theologically moderate and liberal pastors succumbed to adultery at about the same rate as fundamentalist ones, probably using many of the same theological arguments to rationalize their conduct. The point is that Baptist males were like their distant ancestor Adam, still blaming their sins on Eve. And no doubt modern Baptist Eves were still looking desperately for that illusive serpent to blame.

However little had changed in the moral conduct of men and women, much was changing in Baptist churches. Women continued a long tradition of quietly but steadily enlarging their spheres of service, pushing constantly against barriers, moving forward when obstacles receded, pausing to regroup when they did not. At Birmingham First Baptist Church, legendary WMU/SBC director Kathleen Mallory served on a pulpit committee during these years. At Parker Memorial church in Anniston, two women served on the eight-person pulpit committee that selected B. Locke Davis as pastor.[104]

Women also found unprecedented opportunities for professional service. With so many males in the chaplaincy and other places of military service, churches turned to women to staff rapidly growing churches. Women increasingly filled positions as music and education directors. Ensley Baptist Church hired Jane Groesbeck Jacobi as minister of music in 1949. A graduate of Missouri's William Jewell College and of Southern seminary, she was married to a Howard College faculty member. Fannie George Hurtt, a Howard and Southwestern seminary graduate, became full-time education director of Cullman First Baptist Church in 1951. That same year Sybil Kendrick, also a Howard alumna, was employed as youth director by Dauphin Way Baptist Church in Mobile. Kendrick's college classmate, Pheroba Ann Thomas, was called as educational secretary to

Fort Payne First Baptist Church. Zelia Woody became education director at Bessemer First Baptist Church. Two years later Lyra Nabors, Howard College and Birmingham Conservatory of Music graduate, was named music director at Oxford First Baptist Church.[105]

Women's expanding service was not limited to local congregations. They pioneered associational missionary work, an entirely appropriate sphere considering that women constituted about two-thirds of the Baptist mission force and raised most of the money to fund missions. Iona Gillespie became the first part-time associational missionary in the Calhoun Association. Women formed the core of her support and the association WMU paid $100 a month on her salary. But men did not support her, and not until she was replaced by a man did the position become full-time. The Colbert-Lauderdale Association hired Clara Thornhill in 1942 as its missionary, paying expenses that supplemented her state mission board salary of $50 a month.[106]

Annie Dopson of Eclectic spent eight years (first part-time and later full-time) as missionary for the Elmore Baptist Association. A longtime Sunday school teacher with a powerful evangelistic witness, Dopson had once returned from a trip to the Ridgecrest Baptist Assembly so burdened for unsaved women in her class that she converted every one of them. Evangelistic ardor and long involvement in Baptist work made her the obvious choice as associational missionary. During her years of service, Dopson helped organize several churches, including the Tallaweeka Baptist Church near Tallassee, which considered her its founder. Not every congregation welcomed Dopson or accepted her recommendations. A timid person by nature, she did not force her ideas on others. Her tireless efforts, as one testimonial put it, literally "worked herself out of a job." Seeing her success convinced leaders they needed a full-time person, and the association hired a male when she retired. Whether Dopson or the association initiated her retirement is not apparent from the records; but she was clearly beloved in the association. When she retired, the association held a special dinner in her honor attended by a hundred people representing fourteen churches. They gave her a generous check and presented a number of warm testimonials to her labors with individual congregations.[107]

The danger in such service was the blurring of lines between ordained and nonordained. This mystical threshold defined women's religious spheres so sharply that many churches that hired women staff refused to call them "ministers" of education or music for fear of infringing on a biblical concept that belonged exclusively to men. Other congregations either perceived no such confusion or, if they did, ignored it.

Male denominational leaders (except for occasional mavericks like James E. Dean) were adamantly opposed to ordination for women. Leon Macon began his career as editor of the *Alabama Baptist* by scolding the state church of Finland for ordaining women as pastors. He believed that God willed men to fill pulpits and found no evidence that a woman had pastored a New Testament church. The problem of other denominations was a shortage of men who surrendered to preach, which was not a circumstance hindering Baptists.[108]

The official outlet for Baptist women remained WMU, but even its corporate life was changing. As women postponed marriage and entered the work force in record numbers, the organization lost members and had to adapt to new circumstances. Many traditional WMU ministries continued. The organization faithfully maintained its official function to stimulate the missionary spirit and mission contributions of women and young people. WMU continued to staff and support Good Will Centers and provide scholarships to women mission volunteers (including one black and one Native American woman in 1951). In 1947 WMU opened a nursery at Howard College to allow wives of veterans and ministers attending college or extension classes to return to school. The organization also remained active in interracial work, sponsoring a summer camp for African American children, the Mobile Negro Center, and a Negro institute for black women. It employed an African American woman (Corenne Watts) to work with black youth.[109]

Alabama WMU measured its success in a number of ways. By 1942, recipients of its scholarships had assumed influential roles in denominational life as directors of Good Will Centers in Birmingham and Louisville, as young people's secretaries in a number of state WMU organizations, as missionaries at home and abroad, as teachers in mission schools, and as executive secretary of the Louisiana WMU. By the end of 1955, the organization had more than 1,800 local Woman's Missionary Societies, most of them in smaller churches and containing less than twenty-five members (only 236 had more than fifty members). Of 23,000 WMS members in 1945, nine associations (Birmingham, Mobile, Montgomery, East Liberty, Etowah, Tuscaloosa, Calhoun, Columbia, and Colbert-Lauderdale) accounted for nearly half. State WMU meetings attracted crowds of women as large as and sometimes larger than state conventions or the increasingly popular annual evangelism conference (in 1953 the state evangelism conference attracted 1,500, the state WMU meeting 2,000 women from fifty-three associations). Fewer than 40,000 WMU women and children continued to contribute approximately half of all funds given to missions by Alabama Baptists. They raised $300,000 in 1944 for a variety of mission causes, including a Baptist hospital in China, scholarships for children of missionaries and women mission volunteers, a Negro institute, the Alabama Baptist Children's Home, home and foreign missionaries, and elderly preachers and preachers' widows.[110]

Given the large number of indigent retired ministers who could not qualify for Social Security, the WMU practice of sending a small check at Christmastime endeared the organization to many who had been skeptical of it initially. Among letters of gratitude received from some of the 141 ministers and widows on the WMU "relief roll" were two particularly poignant ones. A retired pastor with the unlikely name of Nick O. Demus received his check at "a very trying time." He was in bad health and could no longer preach. One of his children could not attend school because he had no shoes. Owen J. Perry of Pisgah wrote a touching though ungrammatical letter of gratitude that ended: "Except my thanks for nice gift an wods of encouragement for my worke the gon By years."[111]

With the available pool of women declining because of employment, WMU organized Business Women's Circles beginning in 1942. By 1945 (when membership in Alabama WMS declined by 525) twenty-five new business women's circles increased their membership to 175. WMU sponsored the first summer retreat for businesswomen at Judson College in 1947; the retreat became a successful annual event attended by 300 by the mid-1950s. Women subsequently linked their circles into twenty-seven federations and elected nine state officers, seven of whom were single women.[112]

Leadership of the organization underwent changes similar to the state convention. An older generation of leaders retired, turning leadership over to younger, more energetic women. The organization's matriarch, Kathleen Mallory, retired as director of the national organization and returned to her hometown of Selma, where she died in 1954. Most of the Samford women (Kate Park Samford, Mrs. Yetta Samford, Katherine Samford Smith, and Mrs. Nimrod Denson), who combined for more than one hundred years of service to Alabama WMU, passed from the scene as well. Mary Essie Stephens, a native of Dothan and graduate of Judson College, ended a long apprenticeship in state Baptist work (she had been educational director at Woodlawn Baptist Church, dean of women at her alma mater, and a WMU field worker) and became state WMU executive secretary in 1954. Erma Yoe Hawkins of Gadsden First Baptist Church was elected WMU state president from 1943 to 1947. As a graduate of Cumberland Law School in Tennessee, she was symbolic of the new professional generation of WMU women, though she decided to marry rather than practice law.[113]

New leaders might come from different backgrounds, but when women's issues were threatened, they proved as tough combatants as their seniors had been. Two incidents revealed their mettle.

When male denominational leaders decided to merge Judson with Howard College, WMU mobilized against the action. Judson graduates held key leadership positions both in state WMU and in local church societies, and they rejected the idea of moving their alma mater to Birmingham and surrendering its identity. WMU women flooded the 1947 Montgomery convention and easily defeated male leadership proposals to merge the colleges.

Women's influence was not lost on Gwaltney. In a humorous valedictory editorial in 1950, the venerable patriarch praised WMU for its unequaled service to Alabama Baptists. As one who still bore scars from the 1947 pummeling, he reckoned there were some sharp thorns among the WMU roses. Elijah, he reminded his biblically attuned readers, could withstand four hundred prophets of Baal, but not Jezebel. When she "broke loose he took off to the wilderness, found a juniper tree and there prayed that he might die."[114]

The other incident began in 1950. A committee of ten WMU women and an equal number of male members of the state executive committee met to discuss the way WMU handled mission contributions. The committee addressed a sore point that had been festering for some time. Convention officials believed that the two parallel mission budgets (the WMU program of mission offerings and special projects and the Cooperative Program) should be combined. They asked WMU to agree to funnel women's regular offerings through CP channels rather than directly to WMU state headquarters. But WMU women had a long memory of male church members who had diverted women's mission offerings to their own local priorities and resisted convention entreaties. After lengthy discussions Alabama WMU agreed to discontinue separate accounting of CP contributions made by WMU members. Instead, they submitted an operating budget to the executive board for approval, drawing from CP gifts. In return men agreed to appoint five women to the 110-member executive board, two of whom would also serve on the administrative committee (something they had refused to do earlier, explaining to women that all board members were elected by the convention).[115]

An unintended consequence of this compromise was a step toward equalizing salaries of state WMU officials. With Mrs. Fred Kilgore and Mrs. Albert J. Smith sitting on the administrative committee, Quenton Porch took the opportunity at the December 9, 1952, meeting to offer a motion to equalize salaries of WMU staff with those of comparable convention agencies. His motion also provided that jobs involving equal responsibilities should pay women and men equal salaries. Whether or not the presence of two women sparked the resolution or hastened its passage, the fact remains that the motion passed, putting Alabama Baptists on a course that most secular Alabama institutions would not begin for many years.[116]

Adjusting Christianity to a New World

Tensions between men and women were only one example of many problems arising within an increasingly complex denomination. As urban Baptists became increasingly affluent and well educated, they experienced many of the pressures of urban and suburban life. Social drinking and dancing became fashionable pastimes. Movies and television became standard forms of family entertainment. Children participated in increasingly pluralistic schools and clubs. Wider use of artificial birth control (which Gwaltney and many other ministers had earlier opposed) reduced the size of families, changed child-rearing practices, and decreased teenage fears of unwanted pregnancies. Clashes between urban, middle-class religious values and lingering rural, agrarian values were fought out in Baptist colleges and seminaries over theology as well as whether dances should be allowed on campus. Moderation, tolerance, and civility became virtues to some Baptists and vices to others.

Strengthening home and family became a central concern of American evangelicals. Even their political expressions began to focus on family issues. Many of them opposed changing roles for women, especially the extent to which females were entering the work force rather than staying home to tend husbands and children. Spiraling divorce rates after World War II and increasing acceptance of sex before marriage seemed body blows to Christian values. Shifting focus away from dispensational premillennialism and on families had the double benefit of reducing differences between evangelical groups and winning them broader, secular support from people concerned about family issues. At the same time, emphasis on family made evangelicals increasingly vulnerable to despair because they divorced more frequently, were unfaithful to spouses, and had problems raising children who rejected their faith and religious values—problems identical to those of unbelievers.[117]

Both Gwaltney and Macon plunged into the debate over family values. Gwaltney worried at the end of the war that women would not relinquish exciting jobs for routine and often grubby household duties, which they had not much enjoyed even before the war. How would Baptist churches react to such social changes? "Our petty provincialism will have to be enlarged by world outlooks," he warned, and become more deeply grounded in family solidarity and religious conviction. Macon frequently expressed dismay at Alabama's spiraling rates of divorce and juvenile delinquency. He attributed such problems to a variety of factors: working women, widespread use of alcohol, unemployed youth, the predominance of sex in the media, open discussion of sex in mixed school classrooms, lack of discipline and positive role models. As a solution, he urged pastors to do more counseling, to listen sensitively to troubled couples and youth rather than "reacting with hammer and tongs."[118]

The social service commission expressed similar concerns about erosion of family values. Annual reports by the commission noted a doubling in Alabama's divorce rate between 1940 and 1945 and illegitimacy rates of 2 percent for whites and ten times that for blacks, as well as rising rates of abortion, prostitution, venereal disease, and juvenile delinquency. The commission urged renewed emphasis on the sacredness of each person and of marriage and advised churches to provide wholesome entertainment and create ministries to resolve marital and family conflicts. Public schools and colleges should offer courses in marriage and family life. Lawyers and judges should seek reconciliation of troubled marriages rather than divorce.[119]

One reason for the keen interest of the commission in family issues was the dominating presence of J. C. Stivender. Few pastors thought as deeply as Stivender about the relationship of church to postwar community. He read widely on the subject and articulated his vision for the future in a number of sermons and speeches. Communities once centered on home, school, and church had become pluralistic. Old intimacies between neighbors had been replaced by impersonal relations. Transitory populations put added stress on marriages and children.

Stivender's solutions were complex. He urged ministers, teachers, and youth leaders to approach marriage and sexual matters more frankly. He believed the church must present Christianity less as dogma, forms, and ceremonies and more as a way of life. Churches must manifest their compassion for people not only by evangelizing them but also by ministering to their practical needs. Persons should be treated as having ultimate value, not as means to an end. Churches must change the way they measured success, from statistical tables to whether they generated a spirit of hope, love, and service among members.[120]

Changing family values were matched by changing politics. Although Alabama was one of only six states that had voted Democratic in every presidential race between 1900 and 1940, fierce battles raged between the conservative, states' rights wing of the party and the loyalist, New Deal element. During the three decades after 1930, Alabama sent to Congress the most politically liberal and respected delegation of any southern state. Strong support from Baptists was central to their election, just as the defection of white Baptist voters beginning in the 1960s would install Republicans in power.

Many Democratic politicians on both ends of the ideological spectrum were Baptist laymen who helped shape the state's politics. Convention president W. B. Bowling (1941–1942) was a circuit court judge and influential Chambers County Democrat. Alabama's 1945 congressional delegation contained seven Methodists, three Baptists, and one Presbyterian. New Deal Congressman Albert Rains of Gadsden (a Baptist layman) addressed the 1945 state convention on factors necessary for a peaceful postwar world. William David Stell, son of a Baptist minister and himself an active layman at Russellville First Baptist Church, represented Franklin County in the state legislature from 1943 until 1947. He also served as secretary of the county Democratic executive committee. Harry M. Ayers, a deacon at Parker Memorial, was a close friend of Harry Truman and a delegate to various Democratic national conventions. Governor Chauncey Sparks was a deacon at Eufaula First Baptist Church.[121]

The same diversity that characterized Baptist theological viewpoints also divided them politically. On one side was layman Morris B. Mitchell, a professor at Florence State Teachers College. Speaking to the Cooperative League in 1942, he denounced those who had plundered the South's natural resources and left behind a legacy of poor housing, disease, and poverty. He praised groups causing a new stirring in the region: land-grant colleges, the Farm Security Administration, the Interracial Commission, labor unions, the Southern Tenant Farmers' Union, federal resettlement communities, and TVA (which he called "the greatest regional experiment ever undertaken by a democracy"). He praised cooperatives in north Alabama as fulfilling "the promises of Jesus."[122]

On the other political side of the denomination were men like John Buchanan and W. M. Beck. Buchanan was a lifelong Republican. In a 1952 speech to a Birmingham civic club, he deplored the rising national debt and urged government to leave citizens alone. No one should plan his son's life or guarantee his economic security. Buchanan extolled virtues of self-reliance, personal responsibility, thrift, spiritual faith, and individual initiative. W. M. Beck, a Baptist layman and speaker of the Alabama house of representatives in 1950, complained when the *Alabama Baptist* printed an advertisement for the *Southern Farmer*. He considered the Montgomery-based farm journal subversive and threatened to discontinue the denominational paper and bring the matter before his church. Other letters also complained about the left-wing politics of the magazine.[123]

Such an advertisement was not unusual in the pre–Leon Macon *Alabama Baptist* because both columnist Charles Leek and editor L. L. Gwaltney promoted a progressive and usually Democratic political course. Leek vigorously defended TVA in 1940 from criticism in the *Montgomery Advertiser*. The next year he urged industrialist Donald Comer to run for governor. When Comer refused to enter the race, the Baptist establishment actively campaigned for one of its own, Chauncey Sparks. Leek denounced the "Hitlerish refusal" of conservatives in the 1943 state legislature to allow citizens to vote on whether education should be made an essential function of state government. That same year he denounced the Democratic state executive committee for trying to select at-large delegates to the national convention rather than allowing voters to elect them. He called for repeal of the poll tax in 1945 as a device that disfranchised more white voters than black. During the 1944 senatorial primary between New Dealer Lister Hill and conservative James Simpson, Leek blistered the conservative business magazine *Alabama* for its attacks on Hill (he called them "slime-slinging," filled with "pitiful partisanship," and demonstrating the "pathetic degeneration of politics in the state"). Writing in defense of price controls after the war, he blamed greedy businesses and their price gouging for government restrictions.[124]

Gwaltney's views paralleled Leek's. He also favored repeal of the poll tax, praised FDR (without always agreeing with him) and Harry Truman, endorsed government price controls, and blamed business for inflation. Gwaltney warned against the leftist tendencies of independent candidate Henry A. Wallace in 1948 and doubted that President Truman would actually try to enforce the strong Democratic civil rights platform. Surveying state politics two years later, Gwaltney detected a "bad mental atmosphere." The gubernatorial race of that year was "so contaminated that it is hardly fit to breathe."[125]

Macon ushered in a more conservative era. He usually opposed higher taxes except for education and leaned toward Republican candidates. He stopped just short of endorsing Dwight D. Eisenhower in 1952. He believed the *Alabama Baptist* should avoid partisan politics but not controversial moral issues that affected "civic righteousness." Like a host of his predecessors, Macon advised a contradictory course: "The church should inform its members how to conduct themselves at the polls as Christians" but should stay out of politics.[126]

In the realm of international politics, Alabama Baptists (at least in their official pronouncements) were strongly internationalist, supporting the UN, welcoming the end of empires, and urging a generous peace at the end of World War II.

Gwaltney used his editorials and a new column entitled "Focus Points of the Week" to inform Alabama Baptists about international affairs. During the war, he warned that even justifiable conflicts brutalized belligerents and generated hatred of a nation's enemies. Cynical realists must make way for idealists who believed in international unity and world order. He tempered rising cries for revenge against Germany and Japan by reminding his own citizens of their treatment of Native Americans and the poor. He even questioned the wisdom of the Nuremberg trials as a precedent for future wars. Gilbert L. Guffin (pastor of Jasper First Baptist Church) agreed about the motive of revenge, warning in 1946 that U.S. occupation policy was denying Germans sufficient food.[127]

Gwaltney expressed a compelling vision of a postwar world characterized by free trade, economic justice, and international cooperation. Lasting peace could not be constructed of lies, deceit, injustice, high tariffs, and an American monopoly on the world's natural resources. He urged creation of an American relief program immediately after the war and rapid implementation of the United Nations. Nationalism must give way to internationalism. Gwaltney wrote in 1945 that the UN charter represented the "highest human hope of the race" and was rooted in ancient Christian values of peace on earth, mercy, goodwill, righteousness, and justice. He urged pastors to proclaim the UN charter as a spiritual document. World government of some kind, he believed, was both inevitable and necessary for world peace. When congressional isolationists tried to lead a U.S. withdrawal from world affairs, Gwaltney blasted them, especially Wisconsin's Senator Joseph McCarthy. Between 1942 and 1950, Gwaltney wrote literally dozens of articles on foreign affairs, all of them laudatory of the UN and internationalism. Over the objection of some readers, he even printed articles favorable to the UN prepared by the Federal Council of Churches.[128]

Despite occasional criticism, Gwaltney was on firm ground when he endorsed the UN and internationalism. The 1950 Montgomery Baptist pastors' conference endorsed UN efforts in Korea. Laymen like Harry M. Ayers of Anniston fostered internationalism through his newspaper and through the International House Foundation, which he helped establish at Jacksonville State University (and to which Ayers's church, Parker Memorial, contributed).[129]

Alabama Baptists agreed that Western colonialism was a casualty of the war. Macon acknowledged that colonialism was doomed and advised Alabama Baptists to regard more carefully the national integrity of nations to which they sent missionaries.[130]

After initial sympathy for the USSR during the war, relations between the two superpowers cooled quickly. Gwaltney warned against Russian expansionism and regretted that the long anticipated "one world" was rapidly becoming bipolar. Other Baptists were even more adamant about the origins of the cold war. W. I. Pittman, a Sunday school teacher and deacon at Dawson Memorial Baptist Church, interpreted the Bible as a defense of capitalism because of its high regard for the rights of the individual and the absence of collectivism. He even pronounced Abraham and Jacob to be capitalists.[131]

State Baptist leaders overwhelmingly opposed a peacetime draft but divided over the issue of pacifism. The pastor of Florence First Baptist Church in 1945 considered universal military training a form of militarism, as did Gwaltney. Macon agreed, adding that it also subverted the moral values of young people. Although Gwaltney maintained aspects of his earlier pacifism, his associate editor, Hal D. Bennett (who had been a World War II chaplain), had no use for conscientious objectors (whom he called "conchies"). He believed that most of them were cowards or that they were trying to avoid military service. Either way, a pacifist who came to the South would regret it: "We can make him so mad he will bite himself like a wounded snake, and that's the end of a consistent conchie." Macon, though not a pacifist himself, was more charitable, considering COs to be sincere people who sought what all Christians should desire, an end to war.[132]

Such passionate attention to world affairs brought the denomination in line with developing American civil religion. Defending the nation, displaying the flag in church, extolling the virtues of capitalism, and attributing the national economy to divine origins legitimated the nation's cause and provided a standard against which to judge it. Civil religion could be used either to defend the status quo or to effect social change. It could also assume sectional identity as a defense of a certain type of national morality.[133]

Gwaltney's definition of Americanism was broadly inclusive. A "real

American," he wrote in 1945, was a good citizen who was informed about public policy; loyal to family, friends, and country; law-abiding; liked to make money but was not a materialist; hated militarism; treated all races fairly; wanted the United States to be "the big brother to the world" without trying to rule it; and was a good loser in politics. He also believed that the most accurate symbol of the United States was a mosaic, not a melting pot. The latter image smacked of conformity, the former of creative differences and diversity. Different religious faiths, economic theories, and cultural backgrounds had created the United States, and their persistence enriched the nation.[134]

Such views positioned Gwaltney squarely in the liberal tradition of American civil religion. But these were the buoyant, idealistic values of 1945. As southern blacks articulated a different version of civil religion, one much more critical of the status quo, Gwaltney and other Alabama Baptists became less certain of their future within the postwar United States. To black Alabama Baptists, proclamations of their white brothers and sisters about brotherhood, justice, and equality smacked of hypocrisy. Black Baptists used the same words but gave these concepts different meanings.[135]

Opinions among white Baptists ranged from conservatism to extreme racism. The handful of racial liberals (men like Charles Bell Jr. at Parker Memorial) were either run out of the state or silenced by indignant parishioners. Of course, that is not the way many Alabama Baptists saw themselves. Living in a state where the Ku Klux Klan was awakening from a decade-long slumber and where lynchings still occurred with disturbing frequency, they saw themselves as tolerant, even courageous people. Compared to many of their contemporaries, they were people of goodwill.

As they had for a century, Alabama Baptists denounced lynching and violence. Gwaltney continued to publish the Tuskegee Institute's gruesome annual report on lynchings. One pastor wrote of a 1946 lynching as "a Nazi pattern" of suppressing the rights of minority groups by terrorism. Gwaltney, who had often defended the Klan in the 1920s, had nothing good to say about it in the 1940s. He condemned sporadic Klan beatings and intimidation. Blacks were not impressed. During a 1950 wave of bombings of black homes in Birmingham, a black leader wrote that the "white Christian church is so suave in its pretense of the practice of Christianity when it comes to the race question that it is practically impotent. . . . It has stood in the way with a type of deception that is little short of astounding."[136]

The denomination went as far as it dared go given the racial culture of the time. WMU was boldest, employing a black woman to work with black women and youth, helping fund a summer camp for African American children, and conducting annual interracial institutes that brought black and white Baptist women together to exchange ideas and listen to biracial choirs and preachers.[137]

The state convention initiated similar projects. In 1940 it appointed a committee to investigate the "negro religious situation" and appropriated small sums to help black ministries in Mobile, Tuskegee, and Selma. Unfortunately, pledges were not always paid; when they were, the amounts were a pittance compared to the greatly enhanced wealth of the convention. In some urban areas, white associations tried to help educate black preachers and held joint meetings, sometimes organized by biracial committees. J. W. Lester successfully lobbied for creation of a department of Negro work in 1950 under the direction of a black pastor. The white Mobile Baptist Association helped blacks purchase a Baptist center to train leaders, conduct classes, and provide a library.[138]

Individual Baptists engaged in bolder action. Many of the cooperative racial efforts resulted from the plodding of Noble Y. Beall, Alabama native and director of the Home Mission Board's Negro missions department. In a 1942 address to the state convention, Beall outlined a strategy for resolving the nation's racial conflicts. Learn to appreciate the richness of the African American cultural heritage. Recognize the many commendable traits of blacks (kindness, folk wisdom, humor, joyful approach to life). Study black literature and music. Urge white courts to dispense equal justice. Help educate black leaders. Cooperate with black churches. Be thoroughly Christian in personal racial attitudes and conduct.[139]

Claude T. Ammerman spoke to James Chapman's church leadership course at Howard College in 1947 on "Baptists and the Race Problem." Frequently citing neo-orthodox theologian Reinhold Niebuhr, Ammerman praised the accomplishments of black scientists, novelists, and intellectuals (he mentioned Paul L. Dunbar, W. E. B. Du Bois, James Weldon Johnson, Marian Anderson, Margaret Walker, and Richard Wright). Whites had responded to black aspirations with "discriminations and injustices." The result was second-class citizenship, poor housing, unpaved streets in Negro neighborhoods, high maternal death rates, and half as much spent to educate black children as whites. Whites called blacks demeaning names, denied them political rights, hired them last and fired them first. He denounced Alabama's newly enacted Boswell Amendment that sought to empower boards of registrars to disfranchise even literate blacks. He praised Swedish sociologist Gunnar Myrdal's works on race and accused his own denomination of racism. Only personal conversion followed by Christian social action would bring about change.[140]

J. C. Stivender used the convention's social service commission as a vehicle for racial change. The central issue, he wrote in 1944, was how to improve race relations without alienating whites. The 1948 report criticized
white politicians who "emotionalized, confused and used" the race issue
for political advantage. Emotion more than Christianity seemed to drive
white Alabama responses to race. The report urged whites to demand justice in the courts, better schools, and economic justice for blacks. By 1952
the report tempered these proposals with warnings against "radical demands for the rapid and complete removal of age-long discriminations by
enacting laws." More laws could not solve racial problems, the report concluded; only gradual Christian education could.[141]

Alabama Baptist columnist Charles Leek praised Houston County in
1944 for registering thirty-nine Negro voters. Long a foe of the poll
tax, Leek believed that respectable black people had every right to vote.
Although he was no integrationist, he did challenge former governor
Chauncey Sparks's call for "absolute segregation" if by that term Sparks
meant racial intolerance. Unless whites took a Christian attitude toward
blacks, Leek predicted they would "sow a racial wind and reap a racial
whirlwind."[142]

Perhaps boldest of all were the sermons of Wayne Dehoney, charismatic pastor of Central Park Baptist Church in Birmingham. Something of
a showman, Dehoney mixed theatrics and prophetic Christianity in a 1953
sermon on communism, atheism, and race. Some 2,000 attended the well-
publicized worship service, and most heard more than they bargained for.
Standing beside an empty bronze casket (representing Joseph Stalin's ideology) and a cross (representing Jesus), Dehoney asked the congregation to
choose one or the other. Honest self-analysis, he warned, revealed that most
of them had chosen Stalin's gods. Communism was a protest against injustice and won followers by promising universal brotherhood. Christianity
preached what communism practiced. The United States could not defeat
communism by caricaturing it or with "rabble-rousing investigations" that
had become "the easy path to political prominence." Nor were guns and
bombs the answer. Bullets could not stop ideas. "The colored people of this
earth who outnumber the white seven to one are turning from us to them
because there is no doctrine of 'white supremacy' in Communism." Even
with Dehoney's conclusion that proclaimed a "vital, dynamic, life-chang-
ing Christian faith" the only answer to communism, he had gone much
further down the road of racial justice than most southerners of his generation would travel.[143]

The brief window of opportunity to solve racial problems through southern initiatives passed quickly. For every prophetic Wayne Dehoney, there were a host of Baptists tied closely to their culture. In 1941 H. Ross Arnold (pastor of Jacksonville First Baptist Church) criticized BSU leaders for an incident that occurred at the state Baptist Student Union Convention in Tuscaloosa. The topic was race relations and someone invited black students from nearby Stillman College to attend. One black spoke; then other black students described personal experiences of injustice. At the end of the meeting a white female invited black students to attend a reception in the First Baptist Church where punch was served to all. Although Arnold approved the discussion topic, he insisted it be conducted "under sane conditions and with common sense." Having Negroes present was not what he had in mind. Such an incident would harm Baptists, the BSU, and race relations and would lead to social equality.[144]

During the 1949 debate in Birmingham over Baptist hospitals accepting federal funds, one argument against such a policy was that Hill-Burton grants might prohibit racial discrimination. Negro women might be placed in rooms with white women. Gwaltney tried to reconcile opponents by proposing a separate Baptist hospital for blacks.[145] For all his tolerance on matters of theology and social change, Gwaltney could still not transcend barriers of race. He made a serious theological point in 1940 with a demeaning racial story. Going into a shoeshine parlor, he had encountered "a colored boy" who "Negro like, . . . had music in his soul, and . . . began to pop the shoe-rag like unto one beating a banjo." But he did not shine the shoes. In the same way, preachers often made lots of noise but accomplished little. Though Gwaltney often proclaimed his commitment to fairness for minorities, he also declined to attend meetings in Atlanta on race because they skirted the main issue of social equality, which whites would never accept. Such idealistic meetings were full of "cheap patronage, much flattery, compliments, deep expressions of desires for fraternity and withal, camouflage and insincerity and hypocrisy." "Consciousness of kind" caused whites to defend racial purity, and no power could force them to yield. Even Christianity could not abolish racial distinctions. Gwaltney opposed intermarriage, which would produce a "hybrid people." In the late 1940s, he criticized Harry Truman's civil rights initiatives.[146]

Birmingham Baptist layman and Dixiecrat organizer Horace C. Wilkinson took the most extreme position on segregation in a 1948 essay for the *Alabama Baptist*. Denying that either the Bible or the U.S. Constitution demanded social and political equality for blacks, he cited various Scriptures in defense of segregation. Black opponents of segregation were mainly "the bastard element of the Negro race," whereas white opponents were either misguided, politically motivated, or had "a Negro strain in them." God had revealed himself to humanity through whites, who were far superior to "a mongrel race whose origin is sin and which represents the worst of all races." Racial mongrelization would destroy the church as well as the white race.[147]

Such opinions were common among white Alabamians in 1948, so what is remarkable is not so much the essay as the reaction. Rev. Kelly Johnson responded that while most Baptists did oppose racial intermarriage, they did not support denial of political rights, decent jobs and education, or social justice. White southerners must honestly face their own prejudices and resolve them, or they invited solutions imposed from the outside. Two Baptist students at Auburn University responded that Wilkinson's attack on intermarriage merely clouded the issue. The entire life and ministry of Christ refuted segregation. So did the Bible. Segregation had not prevented the "intermingling of the races" but had created discrimination, injustice, and misunderstanding. The gospel "may be extremely disturbing to us as southern white Christians," the students wrote, "but let us sincerely search for Christ's way in our relationship with those of other races." Wilkinson's essay generated so much response on both sides that the *Alabama Baptist* associate editor finally decided to suspend comment of the subject.[148]

Macon was even more adamant on race than Gwaltney. Although he approved paternalistic and self-help projects for blacks as a safeguard against "those who would seek to lead these people into rash action and fanatical conduct," he believed the South was making racial progress and that sudden change would do more harm than good. At a 1954 conference in Biloxi, Mississippi, Macon told a gathering of SBC journalists and editors that the blood of blacks and whites was sufficiently different to identify the races of donors. When a participant challenged his statement, Macon checked with an authority, who told him he was mistaken. Macon apologized.[149]

Fear of rapid population growth among colored populations of the world motivated Macon to endorse the birth control movement. Although he did not cite race as a motive, he also reversed Gwaltney's opposition to eugenics. He endorsed a 1951 bill in the state legislature that allowed mental patients to be sterilized. The bill (backed by the Human Betterment League and Southside pastor John H. Buchanan, who served on the league's board of directors) won support from many religious leaders, and Macon urged Baptists to contact legislators on behalf of its passage.[150]

As usual, not all Baptists agreed. John B. Atkins was not an educated

man; his eighth-grade education hardly matched that of the bill's proponents. But he did criticize Macon, Buchanan, and what he considered
the misnamed Human Betterment League. Citing abuses of sterilization
in both California and Germany during the war, he wondered if in time
people with only an eighth-grade education like himself might be considered unfit parents. He criticized Macon for urging Baptists to support the
bill because in his opinion it reduced human beings to the same category
as animals.[151]

Such moments of enlightenment passed quickly. Over the next decade
and a half, Alabama Baptists became obsessed with race.

11

Racial Religion, 1955–1970

"jolts and tensions of daily existence . . . jots and tittles of theology"

ews of the Supreme Court's ruling in *Brown v. Board of Education* sent shock waves through Alabama. The state's governor pronounced the May 1954 ruling "unthinkable." Newspapers denounced the decision while appealing for calm. One outspoken white minister, noting the silence of the state's clergymen, accurately predicted that government, the economy, politics, sports, schools, and the military would all acknowledge the rights of blacks long before "the Country Club and the Christian Church." The president of a national black Baptist convention meeting in Birmingham the month after the decision warned African Americans not to expect "segregationists to meekly surrender." In the same city, as if to fulfill his prophecy, terrorists tried to burn the home of Dr. John W. Nixon, state leader of the National Association for the Advancement of Colored People.[1]

Stunned disbelief soon gave way to doubt that the court really meant what it said. The tremendous energy generated by Billy Graham and Eddie Martin crusades, record-breaking numbers of baptisms and new churches, the Forward Program of Church Finance, unprecedented postwar prosperity, relative tranquillity within the denomination, enthusiasm about evangelism and foreign missions—all these things won Southern Baptists success after success and initially diverted attention from racial upheaval. The work of the state convention was conducted by competent committees representing a broad cross section of leading ministers and required the sort of compromise and moderation that kept controversy to a minimum. There was no strong, charismatic individual to rally followers to a crusade against denominational bureaucracies or institutions, which by and large remained close to ordinary Baptists. When Dr. Harold W. Seever of Mobile preached his presidential sermon to the 1957 state convention, he chose a generic, noncontroversial title typical of the times: "Alabama Baptists: Step Forward for Christ."[2]

Leon Macon's editorials in the *Alabama Baptist* were remarkable only in being so ordinary. Topics such as unity, growth, evangelism, the Cooperative Program, and missions dominated his articles. When he urged pastors to take stands on the social and moral issues of the time, he specified topics such as religious freedom, separation of church and state, control of liquor, and the tendency in the world toward totalitarianism. If ministers spoke out on such topics, he warned, they might be punished by lay people for their courage; if they did not, evil would certainly prevail.[3] It is hard to imagine Alabamians persecuting a pastor for such traditional beliefs.

Within a year or two, Macon presented pastors with a bolder political agenda. The editor slowly transformed his editorial page into a weapon against shifting moral values, racial integration, political liberalism, the dangers of centralized government, modernism, and the social gospel. He virtually endorsed conservative political candidates of both parties. Tranquillity disappeared quickly after 1954.

After Macon died in November 1965, his successor, Hudson Baggett, pursued a different course. The editorial page calmed down. Operating in an atmosphere filled with so much controversy and tension, Baggett produced a more bland and noncontroversial paper, but he did introduce a letter-to-the-editor section of sulfuric letters, mostly about controversies within the state, country, or SBC. Although Baggett seldom commented editorially on these issues, the fury manifested by individual Alabama Baptists must have been unnerving to the consensus-building editor, who suddenly found himself in the midst of a storm.

Escalating controversy was equally unnerving to many readers. In 1967 the pastor of the Gallion Baptist Church in the Black Belt urged Baggett to replace stories about integration and religious controversy with prayers and poems. A year later another letter writer begged him to remove controversial topics and "go back to publishing just the good works of God."[4]

Baggett defended his policy of opening the paper to all viewpoints, contending that Baptists were wise enough to evaluate contentious issues and reach their own conclusions. Though many preferred to read more piety and less politics, other readers congratulated the new editor for his policy.[5] The result, for the first time in the paper's history, was a page of opinion from all strata of Baptist society. Opinions were frank, unguarded, and often emotional.

Alabama Baptists had strong opinions about many subjects, especially race. The modern civil rights movement was born in Alabama, as were many of the chief protagonists on both sides (Coretta Scott King, Ralph D. Abernathy, Fred Shuttlesworth, John Lewis, George C. Wallace, Eugene "Bull" Connor). Many of the movement's leaders were black Baptist ministers. Beginning with the Montgomery bus boycott in 1955–1956 and continuing through the freedom rides (1961), the Birmingham demonstrations (spring 1963), Wallace's stand in the schoolhouse door at the University of Alabama (summer 1963), the bombing of Sixteenth Street Baptist Church (September 15, 1963), and the Selma-to-Montgomery march (March 1965), Alabama became the focus not only of American media attention but of the entire world. International observers did not perceive the profound religious irony of these events. On one side were nearly half a million black Baptists for whom the gospel proclaimed freedom, liberation, social justice, full human dignity, and economic, political, and educational equality. On the other side were equal numbers of white Baptists who affirmed the moral and intellectual inferiority of blacks, imposed second-class citizenship on them, and fiercely defended separation of the races. As texts, both groups cited inerrant Scripture. As heritage, they claimed a common spiritual lineage. A century earlier their ancestors had worshiped together in the same churches.

Although much can be made of the way in which southern culture ensnared white Baptists, the truth is that its tentacles were strong enough to ensnare Methodists, Presbyterians, Episcopalians, and Catholics as well. The head of the Episcopal church in Alabama, Bishop C. C. J. Carpenter, was a moderate segregationist paralyzed by criticism from both liberal and conservative elements of his denomination. Like Baptist leaders, he accepted racial change as inevitable, but he did not welcome it and did what he could to delay or even defeat it.

Although some Presbyterians and Methodists were far in advance of Baptists in implementing racial justice, both denominations lost members and churches in Alabama to a combination of resentment over integration and theological liberalism (which were usually combined in the minds of white Alabama Protestants). Even Catholic Archbishop Thomas J. Toolen of Mobile opposed priests and nuns coming from outside the state's boundaries to participate in civil rights demonstrations.[6]

There was no exact correlation between fundamentalist theology and resistance to integration, but prominent southern fundamentalists such as W. A. Criswell, Bob Jones, and John R. Rice were particularly active in constructing a segregationist theology. In their minds, the civil rights movement became a violation of scriptural mandates about the separation of races. They argued that integration promoted miscegenation, fostered political anarchy and violence, was instigated by communists, and was promoted by theological modernists and liberals. Rice, for instance, denounced the *Brown* decision as a product of "left wing thought" and predicted it would result in "the mongrelization of the race and the breakdown of all the Southern standards of culture." Criswell told the South Carolina legislature in 1956 not only that he favored racial segregation but that religious groups preferred to "stick with their own kind." The few blacks who desired integration, he told cheering white legislators, could "sit . . . in their dirty shirts and make all their fine speeches. But they are all a bunch of infidels, dying from the neck up." By the time Criswell was elected president of the SBC in 1968, he had moderated these views, as had Rice. Both later apologized for their racial views.[7]

Unfortunately, apologies could not undo the damage. Like white Baptist defenders of slavery a century earlier, southern racism fed off biblical literalism. Segregationists rationalized that they were defending southern civilization against secular, humanistic, liberal, corrupt mongrelization. That belief made the battle harder, longer, and bloodier than it otherwise would have been.

According to their own theological scheme of things, segregationists were quite correct about the connection between liberal views on race and religious liberalism. Although many theological liberals in Alabama (notably L. L. Gwaltney) defended segregation, such cases were unusual outside the Deep South. In fact, the civil rights movement revitalized the social gospel within main-line American churches. The National Council of Churches, established in 1950, lumbered into action, especially after 1963 racial confrontations in Birmingham. The NCC helped mobilize Christians for the march on Washington and the Selma voting rights demonstrations. It also rallied support on behalf of the 1964 Civil Rights Act. Conservative and evangelical Christians who opposed the act seemed to have little influence within their denominations. They increasingly insisted that the function of the church was to save souls, not society. If the civil rights movement mobilized nonsouthern churches toward social and political change, it sent many southern churches racing in the opposite direction.[8]

Compounding the problem for white Alabama Baptists was the fact that the SBC was acting more like main-line denominations on race. Many state conventions were more liberal than Alabama. Baptist seminary and college faculties seemed to defect to the other side as well. SBC literature, in the view of conservatives, began to brainwash Baptists in favor of equal rights. The denomination's Christian Life Commission served as vanguard for what seemed to Alabamians heretical views on race. The SBC passed a number of resolutions challenging biblical support for segregation. The slow fragmentation of racial unity among white southerners paralleled growing disruption of the SBC. One historian of SBC division hypothesizes that crises tend to appear within the denomination mainly during times of strife over race, sex, or pastoral authority. Even the White Citizens Council noticed the change. Beginning as early as 1958, the council began to denounce T. B. Maston (Southwestern seminary professor and chief Baptist ethicist), the Christian Life Commission, and other "liberal" elements within the denomination.[9]

Alabama Baptists negotiated their way through three distinct racial phases. Between 1954 and 1957, many leaders urged cautious acquiescence to the *Brown* decision, law and order, and racial peace. During the decade after 1957, white Alabama Baptists basically planted their feet next to George Wallace's and refused compromise or moderation. Their rhetoric helped enflame a populace already outraged by the civil rights movement. Constituting more than half of Alabama's white Christians, they must assume responsibility for a significant portion of its racism. The third stage began in the late 1960s when the denomination finally caught up to the social changes transforming the state.[10] Throughout these years, remarkable men and women and even some congregations transcended their culture through a special mixture of revelation, grace, and leadership. Although many of them paid a frightful price for their courage, they maintained a costly prophetic witness as the storm of racial change blew away much of their familiar world.

The brief period of accommodation between 1954 and 1957 continued the earlier optimistic era. White Baptists hoped that slow progress in race relations could pacify blacks while leaving the edifice of segregation largely intact. Except for the Montgomery bus boycott, which white Baptists roundly condemned, there was only the Supreme Court's admonition to proceed with "all deliberate speed" on desegregation to upset them.

Though some border states interpreted the Court's phrase to mean "now," the Deep South envisioned some undetermined date in the distant future. Leon Macon admonished readers of the *Alabama Baptist* in 1954 to be "prayerful, sane and Christian" in their responses, to avoid clashes and bloodshed even in the face of provocation by a court decision that had "jarred to the foundation a Southern institution." Two years later he continued to urge a course of moderation and compliance with Court orders. But he also warned that prejudices died slowly, that "outside interference" complicated matters, and that some state officials believed communists were behind the push for integration. As late as 1959, Macon denounced bills in the Alabama legislature to close public schools and use tax monies for private academies, though his opposition resulted more from the plan's violation of separation of church and state than from his concern for public education.[11]

Lines began to harden after the 1956 Little Rock school integration crisis, and opposition to integration became stiffer. In Alabama, anger focused as much on the SBC as on the federal government or civil rights leaders. Macon, under increasing pressure from lay persons, sent letters to the heads of all SBC agencies and seminaries in 1958 denouncing SBC literature that seemed to favor integration and asking their position on the subject. Most leaders equivocated. Alma Hunt (WMU executive secretary) responded that her organization took no stand one way or the other. Many seminary presidents responded similarly, though some justified integration of their institutions as a way to protect Baptists from "radical ideas" that students might encounter at heretical seminaries outside the South. The president of Southwestern seminary assured Macon that he knew of no faculty member at his institution who believed "full integration throughout the South is desirable or even possible at the present time." Only the head of the Christian Life Commission frankly repudiated segregation as a legal system that could not be reconciled to Christianity.[12]

In 1957 Arkansas congressman Brooks Hays was elected president of the SBC; he was reelected the following year. Macon declined to publish Hays's presidential sermon, which called for racial integration, because the editor claimed that it dealt more with politics than religion. At the 1959 convention, Macon, Henry L. Lyon Jr. (pastor of Highland Avenue Baptist Church in Montgomery), Jack Trammel (pastor of Shiloh Baptist Church in Sardis), and Norman H. McCrummen (pastor of Selma First Baptist Church) urged that a resolution commending Hays for his stand on integration be deleted because it would enrage laymen in their churches. Warning that Alabama Baptist churches would retaliate by reducing gifts to the Cooperative Program if the resolution passed, they won the spirited hour-long debate. They also helped elect as president Ramsey Pollard, a man Macon believed would spend more time on evangelism and less on racial issues. That same year, Macon warned SBC officials against biracial meetings of Baptist groups to discuss mutual problems. Such meetings, he wrote, only exacerbated racial divisions already present within the SBC.[13]

When Martin Luther King Jr. was invited to speak at Southern seminary and freedom riders were physically attacked in Anniston, Birmingham, and Montgomery during 1961, animosity toward the SBC intensified. Some thirty to thirty-five churches voted not to continue contributions to the seminary. George Bagley and other denominational leaders warned before King's visit how lay people would react, but the stridency of the reaction surprised seminary officials and forced them to apologize. Publicly, Macon and state convention president Howard M. Reaves of Mobile urged churches not to withhold their CP contributions; privately Macon was furious. He wrote one friend that he had traveled the state trying to cool tempers and had not met even one integrationist among Alabama Baptists.[14]

Reacting to a seminary professor's criticism of racial turmoil in Alabama, Macon wrote in 1962 that the state's white Baptists opposed integration because it would result in "a mongrel race" and lower the moral conduct of whites to that of blacks. White Baptists had a long history of financial assistance to black Baptists, and the two races enjoyed a "fine relationship" that had been jeopardized by "Communism and other foreign forces."[15]

State convention leaders rejoiced in 1963 when a fundamentalist (K. Owen White of First Baptist Church in Houston, Texas) was elected president of the SBC. White pledged to rid the convention of liberal influence that had crept in during the past decade. The convention also passed a revision of the 1925 Baptist Faith and Message that was designed to set the SBC on a more conservative course. The backlash to desegregation certainly strengthened that initiative among Alabama Baptists and won Macon's endorsement.[16]

The following year, Deep South messengers to the SBC succeeded in modifying a strong antisegregation resolution proposed by the Christian Life Commission, winning a two-hour floor debate that divided the convention essentially along conservative and moderate lines. Macon concluded that the result indicated a continuing conservative drift.[17] That same year Macon and executive secretary George E. Bagley blasted material published by the SBC Sunday School Board and WMU for recommending books written by African Americans or for controversial articles about race. Once again denominational officials wrote letters of apology.[18]

When the chairman of the Christian Life Commission wired Governor Wallace in 1965 protesting attacks on Negro marchers at the Edmund Pettus Bridge in Selma, Macon responded with a public rebuke. He informed the commission's chairman, John R. Claypool of Louisville, that no Scripture instructed Baptists to join reform movements or solve social problems. Such initiatives within the SBC were examples of the social gospel, some of whose leaders had rejected the divinity of Jesus. The violence in Selma, Macon contended, resulted from outsiders (including many ministers) plus the agitation of communists. Although Christians should not respond violently to such provocations, law enforcement officers should "react firmly" to control the "zoot-suiters" and "low class" demonstrators. When the Atlanta Baptist pastors' conference passed a resolution acknowledging their guilt of silence in the face of brutality in Alabama, Macon advised Georgia Baptists to mind their own business. Claypool ended a spirited correspondence in which Macon restated his fear of racial mongrelization by asking why a fundamentalist who believed that the human race began with a single couple would be so concerned about miscegenation.[19]

The 1965 appearance of Billy Graham for a crusade in Montgomery, where he insisted on integrated seating, did little to enhance his reputation among Alabama Baptists. The local ministers' conference did not invite him, which was a routine procedure for most of Graham's rallies, and many city fathers refused to attend. Although Macon publicly praised Graham's revival (he "stuck to preaching the Gospel"), he privately complained that the Baptist evangelist reduced his influence by public statements on "political and social situations." Macon wrote a friend that despite Graham's demand that rallies be integrated, the editor believed that God wanted the races separated. He also advised his twenty-year-old son not to attend Graham's integrated services. Although George Bagley did appear on the platform at Crampton Bowl to extend the city's welcome to Graham, he did so uneasily, believing that President Lyndon Johnson had engineered the invitation.[20]

Macon's death and the selection of Hudson Baggett as new editor of the *Alabama Baptist* changed not only the editorial page but also reaction to SBC initiatives on racial justice. Though cautious in his editorial page comments, Baggett was far less conservative than Macon. When fundamentalist Dallas pastor W. A. Criswell was elected president of the SBC in 1968, Baggett chose to emphasize the new president's renunciation of earlier rac-

Billy Graham and J. R. White, pastor of Montgomery First Baptist Church, during Graham's 1965 crusade in Alabama's capital. Graham scheduled his racially integrated crusade to coincide with escalating civil rights unrest. Many Alabama Baptists resented his timing and growing support of integration. (Courtesy of Samford University Archives)

ist positions and his statement that social action could not be divorced from
religious faith. Responding to speculation about what the 1968 SBC would
do on the nation's festering racial crisis, he listed what the convention
could *not* do: ignore the race crisis; decide the issue for individual Christians or Baptist churches; collectively confess the guilt or sins of other Baptists; or present a united Baptist position for a deeply divided denomination. The fact that the SBC response to the nation's racial crisis was selected
by Baptist Press as the most important story of 1968 did not make Alabama
Baptists happy.[21]

What made denominational criticism so painful to many white Alabama Baptists was their sincere belief that their relationships with black
Baptists were excellent (an opinion not shared by blacks). They also
pointed to what they considered generous financial support of their fellow
Baptists. It is true that the state convention, WMU, and some individual
churches and associations had long donated small amounts of money to a
variety of Negro Baptist causes. But the money was minuscule in light of
the need. The rate of black poverty in Alabama was among the highest of
any state. Nearly half the state's one million blacks belonged to one of three
black Baptist groups in 1965. Among nearly 1,700 African American pastors of 2,000 black Baptist churches, the average educational attainment
was eighth grade. There was also a desperate need for adult literacy programs for 158,000 black nonreaders.[22]

Dr. H. O. Hester resigned as pastor of Birmingham's Eighty-fifth Street
Baptist Church in 1961 to head the denomination's department of special
missions, which supervised work with African Americans. Hester was a
graduate of Howard College and Southern seminary. He also possessed an
uncommon sense of social justice and commitment to black advancement.
Despite the state's racial unrest, he began conducting small meetings in an
attempt to defuse racial tensions and persuade white and black Baptists to
work cooperatively on common projects. He was careful to avoid politics,
which would have been the kiss of death for his agency in the tense racial
climate of the 1960s. He used biblical words such as *freedom* rather than
political terms such as *integration*. He admonished white Baptists to avoid
racial stereotypes (all Negroes were not "demonstrators" or "criminals").
Hester believed that interracial work must be cooperative instead of paternalistic, and he cooperated with A. W. Wilson, black pastor of Holt Street
Baptist Church in Montgomery, who was also vice-president of the Alabama Colored Baptist State Convention. Wilson was highly respected by
white Baptists and was employed jointly by the Home Mission Board and
the Alabama white state convention.[23]

During the decade from 1956 to 1965, the white convention contributed nearly $200,000 to Selma University, a considerable sum for a school with an annual budget of only $130,000. Hester also began to study ways to provide a retirement program for black Baptist pastors. The Birmingham Baptist Association, led by John Buchanan and Leon Macon, also helped Birmingham Baptist College with fund raising.[24]

Alabama WMU continued to fund Camp Fletcher and the Mobile Negro Center but not without serious disruption. Marie Patrick Rogers (an African American who headed interracial work for WMU) announced in 1959 that "due to existing circumstances in the South it was unwise for white speakers to visit Camp Fletcher." Many whites viewed interracial meetings with suspicion and blacks increasingly interpreted such white involvement as patronizing. Black women took over the work at Camp Fletcher entirely in 1970. Such bluntness was painful to white women who thought of themselves as tolerant and committed to racial fairness. WMU adjusted to the new realities by increasing emphasis on literacy programs, instituting work with migrants and immigrants, and withdrawing from interracial activities. For several years before 1968, WMU broke its long pattern of employing a black Baptist woman as liaison to Negro Baptist churches and ceased awarding scholarships to African American women. Contact between women in black and white Baptist churches was limited to several interracial associational WMU meetings and a biracial prayer group.[25]

Even Leon Macon, who was no advocate of racial equality, began to chastise white Baptists for doing so little to help fellow Christians. He urged them to do more to help black colleges and seminaries and to help develop black leadership. He warned that Catholicism was appealing directly to black Christians, and he feared success unless white Baptists provided more help.[26] But he missed the main points. Catholicism had little intrinsic religious attraction to blacks. Its appeal resulted primarily from the racial inclusiveness and sense of social justice espoused by Catholics who became involved in the civil rights movement and the nearly universal opposition of white Baptists.

Usually preachers set the tone for Baptist religious life. But during the late 1950s and 1960s lay people charted the course on race relations. Laymen shaped the Baptist response to race from the *Brown* decision forward. One layman from Tuscaloosa wrote that blacks were immoral, and association with them would corrupt whites. Integrationist Baptists simply played into the hands of communists. A layman from Springville denounced the new SBC emphasis on Christian race relations and warned that such de-

nominational attention would lessen loyalty to the denomination. A layman from Tyler criticized the state convention for a resolution pledging
support for continued school segregation "at this time." The qualifier suggested that at some point in the future integration might be acceptable.
If segregation was a sin, he challenged the convention to cite Scripture to
prove it. But if integrationists were merely using religion "to promote
something foreign to the teachings of the Bible, then they should be exposed." Baptist laymen, he warned, were losing confidence in the denomination's leadership, which he compared to a "weakling who shivers in his
boots every time the word segregation is mentioned." Another layman
wrote Macon in 1964 of his disgust at clergymen who advocated "unChristian doctrines" identical to communist "one world, mongrelized brotherhood." Integration, he added, was "un-natural, extremely obnoxious and
highly immoral." The Kennedy and Johnson administrations were trying
to "force white Americans under the same rooftops and in the same bed-
rooms with those that are scarcely touched by civilization." After the Sixteenth Street Baptist Church was bombed and four young black girls murdered, a Bessemer layman wrote, objecting to Baptist efforts to help the
church repair damage. The use of the church as a staging area for civil
rights demonstrations during 1963 made such donations "a misuse of
money." When Baptist leaders deplored the assassination of Martin Luther
King Jr. in 1968, a Birmingham layman wrote that King was responsible for
his own death by preaching civil disobedience. A similar letter from a Pinson layman termed Baptist outrage over King's assassination hypocrisy
that "only emphasizes the depth to which our leaders are sinking to take
advantage of all opportunities for self-advancement."[27]

Nor was racism less pronounced among Baptist women. From Camp
Hill, a woman urged Macon to become more political in his opposition to
the 1964 public accommodations bill before Congress. Another woman correspondent believed the state convention spent too much time urging compliance with "man-made law" of the "liberal Kennedy-Johnson trend" and
too little defending the law of God. Numerous letters from laywomen
warned that the ultimate goal of integration was miscegenation, which
would destroy the Bible. One angry woman contrasted white men dying in
Vietnam to blacks who "lie down in the streets and kick like a bunch of
cockroaches." Such demonstrators should be "lined up and shot like rats."
Another female correspondent blamed integration "for so many of our
white women and girls [being] raped." Other women criticized King as a
communist, denounced SBC leaders and literature as favoring integration

and interracial marriage, and criticized Billy Graham for conducting integrated crusades.[28]

One central figure mobilizing Baptist lay people against integration was Montgomery circuit judge and founder of Jones Law School, Walter B. Jones. Although an Episcopalian, Jones spoke frequently to Baptist laymen. He often congratulated Alabama Baptists for their support of segregation, which preserved the "true teachings of the Bible" and the "pure . . . blood of the white race." As a founder of the *Alabama Bible Society Quarterly* and the *Alabama Lawyer,* Jones turned both journals into segregationist publications. He frequently attacked the SBC Christian Life Commission and defended segregation as decreed by God in the Bible.[29]

Jones frequently published sermons of Dr. Henry L. Lyon Jr. in the *Alabama Bible Society Quarterly.* Lyon (pastor of Montgomery's Highland Avenue Baptist Church and a graduate of Howard College and Southern seminary) was a tremendously successful preacher who had built his congregation to more than three thousand members by 1961, making Highland Avenue the largest church in the capital. Lyon was elected president of the state convention in 1955 and reelected the following year. Throughout the era he, Leon Macon, and George Bagley were among the dozen most influential state Baptist leaders. Lyon and Macon were also the denomination's most influential segregationists.

One reason for Lyon's success in the Montgomery area was his popular weekly radio program. Shortly after the Montgomery bus boycott ended, Lyon used his radio broadcast to stage a spirited biblical defense of segregation. He described how two years earlier, in the first stages of the boycott, he had been sitting on the platform about to take his place in the pulpit to preach when God had called him "in a special way to proclaim the truth concerning racial integration." This call had been confirmed by his election as president of the state convention. God's message was simple: Segregation "was good and morally right for humanity in every respect" and was the "commandment and law of God." In a televised interview with WSFA television in November 1957, Lyon argued that racial segregation was "one of the principal teachings of the Holy Bible." Integration of schools would lead inevitably to racial amalgamation. He urged Christians to use "every legal means" to preserve segregation and states' rights and to elect men to Congress who would block integration. If all else failed, Alabama should close public schools rather than integrate them.[30]

Lyon faithfully proclaimed his segregationist calling from God. He also helped organize the segregationist Baptist Laymen of Alabama. In an address to the 1958 state convention, he argued that all races derived from five different blood strains present on Noah's ark. The flood had been God's judgment on "racial intermarriage"; integration invited God's renewed fury. After violence against freedom riders at a Montgomery bus station, Lyon preached a sermon to his congregation entitled "Racial Violence in Montgomery, Alabama—The By-Product of Racial Agitation." Passive disobedience advocated by King and other civil rights activists, he explained, provoked racial violence by whites.[31]

Such opinions attracted the attention of a politically ambitious young circuit judge from Barbour County, George C. Wallace, who became a friend of Lyon and who invited Lyon to offer the invocation at his 1963 inauguration as governor. The prayer was a classic expression of southern civil religion. It invoked the Confederacy, southern ancestors, states' rights, the national flag, and the U.S. Constitution:

> Almighty God . . . we thank Thee for this glorious occasion which brings us to this sacred place, the cradle of the Confederacy—where in the yesterdays, our ancestors dedicated themselves to the cause of States Rights and freedom for the souls of men.
>
> We beseech Thee for strength as sons and daughters of the sovereign state of Alabama that we may pledge anew our allegiance to the flag of the United States of America. Fill our souls with unflinching courage as we join hand and heart with all friends of democracy to preserve the Constitution of our great nation. May we rather die than surrender this God-given heritage.

Lyon prayed that the new governor would enforce law and order, then concluded: "Our Father, in our day formal public prayers in our public schools have been declared unconstitutional. Take us back to the example set by the framers of our Constitution."[32] In its own way Lyon's prayer was as much a gesture of spiritual defiance as Wallace's more famous political proclamation of "segregation today, segregation tomorrow, segregation forever."

Wallace was delighted with the prayer and with Lyon's continuing support. In October 1963 the governor congratulated Lyon for helping rescue Alabama churches "from the hands of preachers who are brainwashing the people with their messages of racial integration." Two years later Lyon led an attempt at the SBC to amend the Christian Life Commission report to recognize that the main function of the church was evangelism and mis-

sions and that only local churches in Baptist polity had the authority to
make resolutions on social matters.[33]

Although Lyon was the most outspoken segregationist, he was by no
means alone. Herschel H. Hobbs, Alabama native and an influential denominational leader, expressed his opinion privately to Leon Macon that
Martin Luther King was a "rabble rouser" and "troublemaker." The pastor
at Andalusia First Baptist Church condemned the theologically conservative journal *Christianity Today* for depicting Alabama ministers as wicked
and outsiders as "good guys." Such ministers provoked dissension in
churches with their theological liberalism and integrationist policies, then
left local ministers to "pick up the shambles of their 'Elijah complexes,'
[and] try to explain to our people why those ministers who deny the deity
of Christ claim to be Christian [and] goad our people into strife." Sam S.
Douglas (pastor of Hilldale Baptist Church in Birmingham) responded to
criticism by a Presbyterian preacher that ministers had been silent about
racial injustice. Douglas replied that God did not call ministers "to socialize the world—but . . . to preach the Gospel." Douglas (who had grown up
in poverty and spent twenty years as a labor leader and as president of the
state AFL) had always sympathized with blacks, but he considered King
and his associates "messengers of hate, violence, and lawlessness . . . , per-
verters of truth and enemies of God." He denounced the social gospel and
theological liberalism, and he urged African Americans to "rise above the
jungle type life which predominates many Negro communities where bes-
tiality and immorality abound."[34]

James R. Swedenburg (a Baptist minister/educator and longtime executive secretary of the Alabama Temperance Alliance who had struggled up
from poverty on a sharecrop farm) found himself estranged from both his
denomination and his son in 1963 because of racial differences. He urged
Macon not to print an article by his son who had "been . . . misled by our
seminary." The son's essay on the biblical story of the Good Samaritan in-
appropriately applied it to race. He worried what effect such an article
would have on the Alabama Temperance Alliance, which contained both
integrationists and segregationists. Identifying himself as a "strict segregationist," he deplored Christians who became "excited over the sin of the
race question and . . . hurt their leadership, since it is all of the Devil
through the Jews, the Communists, the Catholics and politicians." If Baptists wanted to help the poor, he argued, they should stop agitating racial
issues and end the liquor traffic.[35]

Swedenburg's close friend, Leon Macon, was more than merely the editor of the *Alabama Baptist*. He was elected president of the 1963 and 1964 state conventions. It was unusual for the head of a convention agency also to hold its highest elected position. After several years of moderation following the 1954 Supreme Court ruling, Macon became an increasingly militant segregationist, perhaps because he was more aware than any other state Baptist leader of the magnitude of opposition to integration building up within the denomination. Macon had also become convinced by 1957 that "world communism" was behind American racial unrest.[36]

Macon became increasingly defensive about segregation and the South, blaming southern problems on outside agitators and meddling do-gooders. He claimed that racial problems were as bad in the North and denounced journalists for what he considered sensationalized press coverage of civil rights violence in Alabama.[37]

The editor included the federal government in his indictment as the Eisenhower, Kennedy, and Johnson administrations seemed to side with integration. He considered President Eisenhower's use of army troops to enforce integration of Little Rock schools a dangerous centralization of federal power. By the 1960s he warned of federal court decrees that had eroded the U.S. Constitution by substituting sociology for legal precedent. When President Johnson asked 150 Baptist leaders attending a Christian Life Commission seminar in Washington, D.C., to help promote the 1964 public accommodations bill as a moral issue, Macon denounced the move as an attempt to turn Baptist pulpits into "political rostrums." The bill, he warned, represented "an all-powerful centralized Federal government or . . . outright Socialism." He urged all Alabama Baptists to oppose the bill. He joined George Bagley in a public denunciation of the proposal, saying they spoke only as individual Baptists (though both were identified in press releases by their formal titles, Macon as president of the state convention and Bagley as its executive secretary).[38]

By 1965 Macon, like Swedenburg and Lyon, had drifted into the orbit of Governor George Wallace. He admired Wallace's advocacy of states' rights, segregation, and decentralized government. Like Wallace, he believed that blacks or outsiders had bombed Sixteenth Street Baptist Church because Alabama whites did not do such things (subsequently, a white Birmingham Ku Klux Klansman was convicted of the crime). Macon wrote Wallace privately in 1965: "You are continuing to make us an excellent Governor and I hope to speak a good word for you over the state if you run for United States Senator."[39]

As racial lines hardened, so did Macon's editorials. He endorsed using Baptist church buildings for segregated schools. He denounced demonstrators who practiced civil disobedience, blamed racial disturbances on preachers who substituted the social gospel for personal salvation, attributed violence to communism, and urged Baptist parents to teach their children to segregate themselves socially and religiously from blacks even if they could no longer do so in public accommodations. He described 1965 Selma demonstrations as a racial "holocaust," believed communists controlled events there, described open promiscuity between black men and white women, endorsed white use of force against demonstrators, and believed that qualified black voters could register in the state anytime they wanted to do so. Just before his death in 1965, Macon declared in a private letter that he was a segregationist because "the half-breed child of an integrated marriage" would be the real casualty of desegregation. The only good he discerned in the civil rights movement was that many Alabama segregationists were deserting other denominations and joining Alabama Baptist churches.[40]

Most Baptist preachers adhered to a moderate segregationist position, urging their members to refrain from violence, love blacks, and continue support of the SBC despite its mistaken racial positions. In the Black Belt, a number of segregationist pastors worked to prevent angry laymen from leaving the SBC and forming a new state convention. By the late 1960s some white pastors in Selma were meeting with their black counterparts for prayer. A number of pastors and laymen criticized the segregationist Baptist Laymen of Alabama that Henry Lyon Jr. helped organize. Several Baptist preachers participated in the Montgomery Ministerial Association's 1964 call for calm during school desegregation. A special 1965 convention committee on integration of Baptist colleges took a moderate position, acknowledging that thirty of thirty-seven Baptist colleges in the South were already integrated. Although it did not advise in favor or against integration, it did support trustees in whichever course they decided to follow. Although the ABSC's Christian Life Commission endorsed segregation in 1957, it also deplored fanaticism, extremism, and violence. The 1962 commission report emphasized the complexity of race relations and urged white Baptists to be willing to make "such adjustments in our social and political structure as may be in the best interest of all concerned." The 1966 commission, chaired by moderate John Jeffers of Auburn, noted progress in Negro voter registration, participation in politics, improvements in employment, and access to better public accommodations and schools. It urged whites to view racial conditions as Christians rather than as Democrats or Republicans, liberals or conservatives. The next year the commission offered its boldest challenge. It urged churches to recognize that racial divisions did exist and proposed that each church establish a "Race Relations Day" to focus on the economic, political, historical, and spiritual sources of racial discord. The commission sent guidelines to pastors, who were urged to take the lead in establishing the special emphasis. Unfortunately, few pastors were interested enough to do so. The Madison-Liberty Association, centered in rapidly changing Huntsville, was apparently the only association to observe a race relations day. Two churches, one black and one white, sponsored services (First National Baptist Church and Weatherly Heights).[41]

George W. Riddle (pastor of Dwight Baptist Church, a mainly textile-mill congregation in Gadsden) expressed the complexity of all Christian options in a 1965 essay. He could not decide what an ordinary Christian should do about racial conflict. He rejected "publicity seeking race manipulators" such as those promoting turmoil in Selma, but he also wanted to help blacks. He did not condone white violence or radicalism. Once a week for two years Riddle had taught a Bible class for blacks. He believed that African Americans sought dignity and respect. They wanted to be called by appropriate titles such as "Mr." and "Mrs.," not by their first names. They wanted whites to respect their opinions, to sit down and talk with them as friends, allow them to vote, and accept them socially. Legal segregation was humiliating to them.[42]

In scattered locations across the state, pastors, lay people, and even some congregations followed a courageous course. Although few of them would have been considered racial liberals by the standards of other states, they nonetheless worked for racial change, often at considerable risk to themselves. Baptist members of the Birmingham ministers' discussion group reached out for the first time to bring black ministers into their membership. Gaines S. Dobbins, venerated retired Southern seminary professor living near his son in Birmingham, began writing provocative articles on race for the *Alabama Baptist*. He participated in integrated worship services at the state assembly at Shocco Springs in 1969, describing how both white and black Baptists sometimes wept at the divisions between them. Southside pastor John Buchanan was chosen Man of the Year by the Birmingham Chamber of Commerce in 1957 for his attacks on the resurgent Ku Klux Klan.[43]

Birmingham's First Baptist Church admitted blacks to worship services and raised $40,000 in 1969 to employ a social worker and expand inner-city ministries to poor whites and blacks. Birmingham's Glen Iris Baptist Church seated blacks during the city's racial demonstrations, though in the balcony. Salem church in Lawrence County had black worshipers during the 1960s, an elderly black couple who lived in the community and had nowhere else to worship. The deacons at Athens First Baptist Church decided in the early 1960s that if blacks appeared at a worship service, they would be received courteously. When two young, well-dressed black men actually appeared and were seated, a wave of anxiety swept through the church. Some whites walked out of the service. The pastor, Kermit Gore, welcomed the visitors, then nervously interrupted his sermon several more times to repeat the welcome. One deacon repeatedly shook the visitors' hands. Some members never returned; others directed their animosity at their pastor, whom they perceived as much too eager to welcome blacks. Gore seemed not to mind, proudly introducing himself as pastor of the first integrated Baptist church in Athens.[44]

The role of pastoral leadership was important during such crises but often not decisive. The nature of the congregation, its location, and its socioeconomic makeup were also important factors. Two congregations in Birmingham followed quite different courses.

Dotson M. Nelson Jr. was the popular pastor of one of the state's newest and most affluent churches, Mountain Brook Baptist, located in a wealthy white suburb south of Birmingham. Insulated from direct economic competition with blacks, the congregation was unusually well educated and affluent. Reacting to the murder of a Unitarian minister (James Reeb) in Selma, Nelson told his congregation that his spirit was heavier than at any time since a "cowardly bomber" had killed four innocent little girls at Sixteenth Street Baptist Church. However much he might disagree with Reeb, the minister had a constitutional right to be in Selma demonstrating and speaking. "Our state once again has become a battleground," he told his hushed congregation, "and the position from which we wage war is untenable." He then outlined four principles for Christian race relations: every person must be treated as a person, not an object; every person should be treated as a brother or sister; every person was entitled to life, freedom, and all other constitutional rights; everyone was entitled to all other privileges "in so far as he is responsible and can . . . become responsible." To implement these principles, Nelson and the church WMU began a joint vacation Bible school with several black Baptist churches. The staff was biracial but included twenty whites from Mountain Brook. As one white participant wrote later, she learned a great deal more from the experience than she taught black inner-city children.[45]

Members of Mountain Brook Baptist Church could conduct such ministries confident that the recipients would not appear on their streets or in their services. The members of West End Baptist Church had no such as-

surance. Like Mountain Brook Baptist, West End had a courageous, visionary pastor, Louis Wilhite (who like Nelson was a graduate of Mississippi
College and Southern seminary). Unlike Mountain Brook, the church was
a working-class white congregation located in a transitional neighborhood.
Most members in 1964, when Wilhite was called as pastor, were older females. Wilhite immediately began numerous social ministries to try to stabilize the West End neighborhood. A hundred volunteers began a program
that provided emergency services to the elderly and infirm. A food and
clothing closet offered assistance to unemployed and poor people. A tutoring program enrolled poor children. Wilhite's active participation in Bia-
fran relief, the West End Improvement Association, and the local Jefferson
County Economic Opportunity Center reached both poor black and poor
white families. The church even became involved in persuading landlords
not to evict tenants, who often refused to pay rents because owners would
not fix plumbing or leaky roofs.

Wilhite's advanced study at Union Theological Seminary in New York
City had convinced him that the social gospel could reach poor people. At
first his congregation supported him, though with varying degrees of enthusiasm. Numbers of socially conscious Howard College faculty and students (including George Bagley's son) began to attend the church. Blacks
also began to participate in the church's ministries. The rapid transition of
the neighborhood from white to black compounded fears, as did sometimes disruptive poor white and black children who participated in church
recreation programs. By 1969 at least one white member carried his pistol
to church for fear that a black might accost him. Financial resources shriv-
eled as white members left for the suburbs. Regular visitors began to include a former bookie and two white prostitutes. By the early 1970s Wilhite's wife and children were being harassed and he was being threatened.
The church finally split in 1972, with Wilhite and more than a hundred
members forming the Arlington Baptist Church. With support from the
Home Mission Board and several suburban churches (including Brookwood, Shades Mountain, and Vestavia Hills), the new congregation pioneered a number of innovative inner-city ministries that attracted national
attention. It also attracted a dozen or so black members. Wilhite became a
bivocational minister, earning most of his income working for a community college. But the emotional price his family paid was ultimately too
great. Noting the emotional scars his three children carried from years of
being taunted as "nigger lovers," Wilhite referred to churches as "the most
reactionary institution" young ministers would ever encounter.[46] Ar-

lington Baptist Church went out of existence a few years later. So did West End Baptist.

In Auburn, both minister and congregation were different. John Jeffers grew up in Tarrant City, a segregated blue-collar industrial suburb of Birmingham. His first job at American Cast Iron Pipe Company introduced him to a world different from his own. Founded by John J. Eagan, a Presbyterian layman and one of the South's premier advocates of the social gospel, ACIPCO provided Jeffers a segregated world where blacks were generally treated with respect, were well paid, and participated on employee committees that helped manage the company. Eagan became a hero, and the belief that blacks should be treated fairly took root from industrial work experience, not educational theory. Jeffers went on to Howard College, where he was a star basketball player, then to Southwestern seminary, but financial responsibilities for a wife and five children made it impossible for him to finish his degree. Later in his pastorate at Auburn, he read an essay by prophetic Mississippi journalist Hodding Carter, who speculated about the role of southern religion in resolving racial tensions. Carter's essay inspired two sermons, "Resolving Racial Problems in a Christian Community" and "The War Nobody Wins," both designed to encourage racial goodwill in a state rapidly polarizing around color.

During these years, Jeffers was no civil rights crusader. He was merely a serious Christian trying to find his way through a cultural morass to the ideals of John Eagan: that every person, regardless of race, should be treated fairly, as a brother or sister.

Events in Alabama pulled Jeffers more and more onto center stage. Auburn ministers invited him to participate in a 1961 community-wide prayer meeting after attacks on freedom riders. He attended over the objection of some of his deacons. During the "kneel-ins" at various churches in the area, Jeffers led his church to lengthy discussions of racial problems. He made his position clear: First Baptist should be open to anyone who came to worship without regard to the person's motives. He successfully avoided a congregational vote on open membership, believing that though his position would win, it would also splinter the church. In time, he believed, segregationists would change their minds if the issue were not forced to a vote. When a segregationist proposed to the race relations committee that the church adopt a policy refusing admission to blacks, the motion failed 20 to 10. Jeffers persuaded the majority to let him handle the situation without adopting any specific policy.

Jeffers's congregation was a mixture of town and gown, but Auburn

University dominated the community. One of his parishioners, Auburn University president Harry Philpot, was a Yale graduate, ordained Baptist minister, and former military chaplain. Philpot often joked that Auburn University was the largest Baptist university in the world.

The presence of so many members affiliated with Auburn did not guarantee a liberal attitude about race. One leading segregationist was also a member of the faculty. He became a confidant of Leon Macon, bitterly complaining that Jeffers, the university's BSU director, and many students were pushing for integration, which older members did not want. He also sent Macon a devotional presented to an adult Sunday school assembly on loving one's neighbor. How could he love a Negro, the devotional speaker began, and still believe that blacks and whites should be segregated? God had created the races separate and distinctive and did not want them mixed. Segregation was "moral, Christian, lawful, and Godly," and he believed that "no Negro should be admitted to this church nor any function of it."[47]

Jeffers's determination both to maintain the unity of his congregation and to retain the integrity of his beliefs paid dividends. Blacks came and were seated and eventually some joined the church. After a bruising battle, the church began a child development center for preschoolers that enrolled many black infants. These accomplishments occurred with loss of few members to other churches.

Gradually Jeffers's racial consciousness increased. When no one would chair Alabama's Christian Life and Public Affairs Committee (the new name for the social service commission), Jeffers agreed to take the job. Working with convention president J. R. White of Montgomery and with H. O. Hester, he developed new interracial initiatives: an integrated meeting of black and white Baptists at Shocco Springs; a program to help black ministers who had been unable to obtain education. He wrote an article in his church bulletin defending the right of Southern seminary to invite Martin Luther King Jr. to speak (and received considerable criticism for his efforts). As chair of the state Christian life committee, he was one of the 150 Baptists present in Washington for Lyndon Johnson's speech on behalf of the public accommodations bill. Leon Macon and George Bagley opposed the legislation and contended that the group's polite applause did not signal support for LBJ's civil rights program. Jeffers made it clear that at least one participant did support the president's contention that public accommodations was a moral issue that should win the support of ministers. When Jeffers was asked to preach the 1968 convention sermon, he chided Alabama Baptists for opposing racial justice. Choosing a text from Amos, he emphasized the corporate nature of sin. Racism hurt SBC mission efforts and made it harder to retain young Christians. The message was not popular. That year Jeffers was one of four nominees for president of the convention. When the votes were tabulated, he came in a distant fourth.[48]

Fred Lackey's theology was fundamentalist and he pastored a different kind of church, but he was no less firm in his racial convictions or courage. Lackey became pastor of Jasper's Westside Baptist Church in 1964 and began a bus ministry two years later. Buses picked up white youth from a public housing project for Sunday school and church. Some of them began inviting black friends to attend the working-class church, which included many coal miners. Despite opposition from several families, Lackey insisted that God's word was explicit on the matter; the church must be open to all people. Several black students began singing in the choir, and an African American college student joined Westside. He was received by a vote of 497 to 8 (Lackey enjoyed pointing out that there were fewer "no" votes for the first black member than when he was called as pastor). Although three or four white families left Westside for other churches, the congregation welcomed blacks as brothers and sisters in Christ. Looking back on his forty-two-year ministry after retiring in 1997, Lackey considered the reaction of his Westside congregation to voluntary integration of their church "the greatest display of a Christ-like Christianity that I ever saw."[49]

Nelson, Wilhite, Jeffers, and Lackey did not represent the majority racial view of white Alabama Baptists. But even among laymen there was a courageous minority who transcended the predominant southern culture. Following the most belligerent of Leon Macon's editorials against outside agitators and meddling federal officials, Jerry L. Jumper of Birmingham erupted against the editor's "anti-Negro campaign." He wrote Macon that he had remained silent through the years because he realized that few Baptists agreed with him. But he had read and heard enough about racism. God was color blind. In his view, heaven would be integrated and race made no difference in character. He wondered how long the South would persist in its illusion of white racial superiority or when it would remedy the wrong it had done "Brothers who live in dark skins."[50]

Macon also received a letter of rebuttal from a deacon at Sylacauga First Baptist Church. Identifying himself as a lifelong resident of Alabama, the deacon disagreed that outsiders caused the state's racial problems. All they did was reveal the centuries of inequality and injustice in the way the state's whites had treated blacks. Outsiders inspired blacks to believe they were fully human, American citizens and were entitled to full rights. Christian southerners must surmount popular opinion, tradition, and "our Southern way of life," though to do so would require great courage.[51]

Responding to Macon's attacks on the social gospel's commitment to racial justice, a Decatur couple wrote that the editor did not speak for them. Though they were from Chilton and Dallas Counties and were deacon and Sunday school teacher in a Baptist church, they also believed in racial tolerance. Macon dismissed their letter by replying correctly that for every five such letters he received disagreeing with his stance, he received a hundred endorsing it.[52]

The ratio between racial tolerance and intolerance was closer by 1968. When the SBC adopted a manifesto on racial justice that year, pro- and antimanifesto letters were only two to one opposed. A Birmingham laywoman urged the denomination to face squarely the moral implications of racism (a word Macon refused to acknowledge as a problem for Alabama Baptists; he defined a racist as one who hated blacks, a segregationist as one who only wanted the races to live separately). According to the letter writer, the issue was simple and profoundly moral: "Should we deny Negroes their basic human rights, or should we not?" That such lay people and pastors were all too slowly changing the denomination became clear when an angry Mobile layman canceled his subscription to the *Alabama Baptist*. He wrote Hudson Baggett: "You have done nothing but try to integrate and brainwash your readers . . . on every issue."[53]

Many segregationists renounced such views in future years. Unfortunately, they could not recall the hurt they caused blacks, recapture the many racially tolerant members who left for other denominations, or remove the negative image that the SBC gained as a consequence of their statements and actions. Half a century later virtually no Alabama Baptist defended what virtually all claimed in the 1950s: that God ordained segregation and the Bible endorsed it.

Churches that had the easiest time during this tumultuous epoch were the ones with the strongest conservative consensus. Virtually no congregations were uniformly liberal on issues of race. Those that integrated usually paid a high price in discord and division. Unity around segregation maintained the harmony of a congregation and allowed it to take concrete action to defend southern racial traditions. Greensboro Baptist Church adopted a resolution in 1958 requesting all Baptist agencies to refrain from publishing articles promoting integration. Four years later, Henry Lyon Jr.'s Highland Avenue church in Montgomery adopted a resolution by a vote of 308 to 9 cutting off contributions to Southern seminary because it allowed Martin Luther King Jr. to speak there. The church also instructed its messengers to the Southern Baptist Convention to affirm the infallibility of the Bible, which allegedly had been undermined by Baptist seminaries.

Dothan First Baptist Church terminated funding to Southern seminary, the Home Mission Board, and the Christian Life Commission at the insistence of a local banker who was incensed because he believed these agencies promoted integration. Earlier the lawyer/teacher of the Baraca Sunday school class in the same church had praised W. A. Criswell's endorsement of segregation. Citronelle First Baptist Church condemned the 1964 Public Accommodations Act and the social gospel. The Silverhill First Baptist Church attacked the SBC for what it called an "ultra-liberal, non-scriptural, politically inspired and deliberate trend" to brainwash Baptists. The resolution denounced not only publications of the Home Mission Board but even the *Alabama Baptist* for "degraded, objectionable and, in some cases, obscene . . . " articles. Lanett First Baptist Church passed a resolution in 1968 criticizing the SBC's manifesto on the crisis in the nation. The church blamed national violence that bloody summer on agitators and communists and professed not to care about the "Baptist image" or how they were perceived elsewhere.[54]

In April 1965 (motivated partly by the anticipated Billy Graham crusade the following month) deacons at Montgomery First Baptist Church recommended that their congregation reaffirm its open door policy. To their surprise, members rejected the recommendation, arguing that no racial demonstrator should be seated regardless of race. Two days later, after a night of weeping for his flock, pastor J. R. White (who was serving a term as president of the state convention at the time) told his congregation that the gospel was for all people. Although he did not approve of Martin Luther King Jr.'s using the pulpit as a platform for social change or condone demonstrators using the church as a way to initiate integration, white southern churches had become a bastion for the maintenance of segregation just as black congregations had become the chief vehicle for desegregation. Neither race was as interested in the gospel as in advancing its own racial agenda. He acknowledged deep divisions within his own congregation and begged the church not to polarize around race. The church must cease to be a political forum. Members must eliminate racial prejudice from their hearts. And they must reach out to blacks. Having lost in the April vote, White had his say, then fell silent. But he did manage to hold his segregated church together. Three years later White wrote the SBC Sunday school commentary on "Overcoming Prejudice," though it was a slow process in his own congregation.[55]

Many churches, especially in the Black Belt, never recovered from the traumatic events of the 1960s. Located in counties where blacks heavily outnumbered whites and where the 1965 Voting Rights Act transferred power to African Americans, many whites fled. In Tuskegee, popular pastor James C. Stivender had increased membership in First Baptist Church from 350 to 500 by 1955. But a black boycott of businesses in 1957 caused many white residents to move into nearby Montgomery or Auburn. The Sunday school lost 50 members in six months, and the church never recovered. Of the church's 435 members in 1961, only 274 resided in Tuskegee.[56]

Many associations also defended segregation. The Selma Baptist Association helped change Leon Macon's early moderation by demanding that denominational leaders take a forthright stand for segregation. The Sand Mountain Association also endorsed segregation. Many associations denounced the public accommodations legislation before Congress in 1964 and warned pastors not to promote its passage.[57]

By 1969 the number of letters about race sent to the *Alabama Baptist* had declined dramatically. Not all members of the denomination were reconciled, and their animosity helped fuel the fundamentalist resurgence within the SBC. But there was also much internal soul searching. Morris Dees, a Baptist ministerial student at the University of Alabama, became one of many college students disillusioned with the denomination and charted a more secular career that would lead to creation of the Southern Poverty Law Center. His friend, Millard Fuller, became disillusioned as well, but in time returned to the church as founder of Habitat for Humanity.[58]

The loss of such people troubled many Alabama Baptists. The 1966 Montgomery Baptist pastors' conference discussed what future generations would consider their blind spots. They listed as their chief failure the inability to provide solutions or even open meaningful lines of communication between the races at a time of unprecedented opportunity. Already they were speculating, "If only we had. . . . " They listed as their second failure an unregenerate church membership that did not take the gospel seriously. Their third failure came from their own roles as shepherds of the church. Instead of the courageous moral leadership that New Testament Christianity demanded, they had confirmed southern culture as their parishioners had demanded.[59] It was a sobering and introspective discussion.

A year later Hudson Baggett published an interview with the former editor of the Texas Baptist newspaper. He considered the chief tragedy of Baptist history to be the denomination's stance on race. Because half of all African Americans were Baptist, the denomination should have been in the forefront of the civil rights movement. Instead, white Baptists trailed other denominations that had virtually no black members. Baptist ethicist Bill Pinson told an Alabama BSU convention the same thing in 1968.[60]

Non-Baptists were no kinder. Reflecting on his own horrific experiences as president of the University of Alabama, Frank Rose told Judson College graduates in 1968 that society needed the "guiding voice" of the church on the great issues of the day. Instead, the church was often silent on issues of social justice. Aubrey Williams, like Rose a former minister who found more satisfying work in secular reform movements, criticized Southern Baptists in the 1960s as "the most powerful force upholding segregation and the brutalizing treatment of the colored race." "If Jesus should rise and walk into any of the Southern Baptist churches today," he wrote sardonically, "you could be sure that they would at least ask him to leave, and at the worst, they would hang him." But it was an African American Baptist reader of the state denominational paper who penned the frankest critique. After years of reading Leon Macon's editorials, he reassured his brothers and sisters that they need not fear being overrun by blacks seeking membership in their churches. The emotional, social, and spiritual needs of African Americans could not be met by white churches. Whites had no monopoly on God, and black churches were essential to the maintenance of African American communities. "The only thing you have to offer that we don't have," he concluded, "is a place to sit next to a white person. You may be surprised how unimportant this has become. If you want to help us, then leave us alone."[61]

The Politics of Rage

As the involvement of Alabama Baptists in racial matters makes clear, the denomination was fully immersed in politics during the 1950s and 1960s. Providing a theological foundation for such activism was easier said than done.

Leon Macon often restated the official position. Individual Christians should be politically involved but churches should not. The only exception involved moral issues. Macon's successor as editor of the denominational paper, Hudson Baggett, agreed in principle, but he pointed out the problem in defining what was a moral issue. He could have used Leon Macon as an example. Macon was incensed when LBJ urged Baptist ministers to support public accommodations legislation as a moral imperative, branding the bill political rather than moral. Nor did he consider any other civil rights legislation to embody moral issues.[62]

Macon continued Gwaltney's practice of speaking out on a wide range of controversial matters. Macon endorsed artificial birth control as a way to limit world population and denounced Catholics for trying to limit U.S.

government export of birth control devices and information as part of foreign aid. Sex, he wrote in 1960, was not only for purposes of procreation but (in the euphemistic words of the era) "to give man and woman a rich fellowship so essential to their natures." On other national and international issues (presumably all moral by his definition of appropriateness for Baptist comment), Macon endorsed abolition of capital punishment, the cessation of H-Bomb tests, and restriction of immigration (the United States was being swamped by persons "outside the Judeo-Christian tradition"). He also denounced John Birch Society founder Robert H. W. Welch for charging that 3 percent of Protestant clergy in the United States were communists. He dismissed Welch as an "extreme rightist" and his society as "an ultra-conservative group" that was not careful with the facts.[63]

On state issues, Macon was equally outspoken. He endorsed a 1956 bond issue to provide more money for overcrowded mental institutions and a 1957 increase in state funding for public schools (Alabama Baptists "believe thoroughly in our public school system"). He endorsed a 1961 bond issue to improve conditions in Alabama prisons (Howard College president Leslie S. Wright chaired the bond support committee), including the isolation of youthful offenders from hardened criminals. Such Baptist activism probably helped pass some of these proposals, given the makeup of the legislature. Of 104 legislators who listed religious affiliation in 1963, 41 were Southern Baptists, nearly twice as many as Methodists, who were their closest rival.[64]

Alabama Baptist ideas about what was a political issue with moral consequences received sharpest challenge in the 1960 presidential elections. Macon and many pastors warned Democrats not to nominate John F. Kennedy. The state convention passed a resolution in 1958 warning that election of a Catholic president would jeopardize the nation's historic separation of church and state. One north Alabama pastor wrote just after the state convention that he considered Roman Catholicism a greater threat to American democracy than communism.[65]

After Kennedy's nomination, Alabama Baptists conducted a relentless campaign against his election. Arguing that the real issue was not Kennedy's religion but the historic principle of church-state separation, Macon wrote fourteen editorials between June and November 1960 opposing his election. He also published sixteen sermons against Kennedy's election preached by the state's leading pastors. Some of these sermons were also published as pamphlets and widely circulated. Letters from three subscribers inquiring why Macon published so many articles "kicking the Catholic religion" did not lessen his assaults on the "Catholic hierarchy" despite their charge that he was being more political in his religion than were Catholics.[66]

Although Macon urged Baptists to comply with scriptural admonitions to respect lawful authority after Kennedy's election, criticism continued. The secretary of the Selma Baptist Association believed that JFK's election had "furnished a climate for the vigorous, organized, and relentless efforts of the Catholic Hierarchy to obtain tax money for their parochial schools." The pastor of Sixteenth Street Baptist Church in Decatur wrote Macon that the "Catholic Hierarchy is not relaxing their efforts to infiltrate our administration in Washington" and was trying at the same time to destroy "southern traditions." As this letter indicates, the dangers of Catholicism and racial integration merged as Kennedy tilted federal power toward the civil rights movement.[67]

One scholar of the 1960 election has pointed out that there was more religious opposition to Kennedy that year than there had been to Al Smith in 1928. The criticism was the catalyst to a major improvement in Protestant-Catholic relations. Pope John XXIII sponsored an ecumenical council and held audiences with Protestant leaders, including former Arkansas congressman and SBC president Brooks Hays. The National Council of Churches reduced its support of POAU because of its anti-Catholicism. Academic calls for greater religious tolerance in a pluralistic society took the edge off such conflicts. Although Catholics and Protestants still disagreed over various issues of church-state separation, many southern Protestant segregationists began to find value in the Catholic position that taxpayers who sent their children to private schools should receive public funds. As abortion became a concern of evangelicals in the 1970s, they also moved closer to the Catholic position on that volatile issue. Hudson Baggett was not inclined to discuss politics as much as Macon, and he particularly avoided debates over Catholicism, while acknowledging differences on a wide range of doctrinal and policy issues.[68]

By the mid-1960s, race had completely eclipsed Catholicism as a political concern of Alabama Baptists. Macon's growing uneasiness about integration, centralization of government, infringement of states' rights, and similar issues loosened his loyalty to the Democratic Party. Like many other denominational leaders, he at first drifted into the independent Democratic orbit of George Wallace. Like Henry Lyon Jr., James Swedenburg, and others, he liked Wallace personally and agreed with him philosophically. So overt was his editorial policy that some Baptists complained in 1964 that Macon virtually endorsed a pro-Wallace elector slate in the Democratic Party primaries.[69]

After Wallace withdrew from the 1964 presidential race, Macon and many other pastors and lay people enthusiastically supported conservative Barry Goldwater and a Republican congressional slate. Macon helped persuade one young Baptist pastor, John H. Buchanan Jr., to run for Congress in order to halt the "drift toward socialism" and protect "the way of life we southerners have known."[70]

In the lead-up to the 1964 elections, Macon used his paper to criticize a variety of Democratic national policies. He condemned the growing national debt, civil rights legislation, the National Service Corps, and various measures that he believed centralized government. By late 1963 virtually every issue of the paper denounced political liberalism, theological modernism, and the social gospel, especially the involvement of churches in the civil rights movement and politics. Though he did not agree entirely with the 1964 Republican platform, Macon wrote friends that he considered Barry Goldwater "the next thing to our old Democratic Party" and was not "making a secret of the fact that I am going to vote for him. Anything would be better for us in a political and religious sense than what we have."[71]

Macon's correspondence during 1964 is filled with similar letters from Alabama Baptists endorsing Goldwater. Occasionally a particularly bold pastor followed the 1960 pattern and virtually endorsed Goldwater from the pulpit. The pastor of Andalusia First Baptist Church (though worried that his sermon might be considered too political in an election year) endorsed individualism and traditional American freedoms over collectivism and Hollywood-style moral corruption. People like himself were often called extremist because they stood for "conservative and constitutional approaches to our nation's policies," whereas any "bearded beatnik and pseudo-intellectual who advocates Marxist or Socialist philosophies is looked upon as a broad-minded sophisticate." What the nation needed, he concluded, was "not easy tolerance and namby-pamby broad-mindedness" but a "burning faith which can change men's lives."[72]

The 1964 elections were a watershed in Alabama politics. For the first time since Reconstruction, the state elected a predominantly Republican delegation to the U.S. House of Representatives (including Baptist preacher John Buchanan Jr., who won in Birmingham's Sixth District). The state also went heavily for Goldwater, one of only six states that he carried. Although Wallaceism temporarily halted white desertion to the Republican Party, traditional Democrats and especially segregationists had severed ties to the national Democratic Party, just as Alabama Baptists were cutting themselves adrift from liberal policies within the SBC. They feared that forces of integration, liberalism, and modernism had taken over Baptist colleges and seminaries, the Sunday School Board, Home Mission Board, WMU, the Christian Life Commission, and the Baptist Joint Committee on Public Affairs. If unopposed, these forces would overwhelm the SBC and state conventions. Some Alabama Baptists reacted by bolting from the denomination. Others stayed but vowed unending war on the liberal forces that they believed controlled the SBC.

The peace movement, public rallies against the Vietnam War, student radicalism on college campuses, the drug culture, urban rioting and violence, sex and violence on television and in movies all deepened Baptist alienation from mainstream American religion and politics. Hudson Baggett (a World War II veteran who normally avoided politics) weighed in against antiwar protestors, student takeovers of campus buildings, a poor people's shantytown in the shadow of the U.S. capitol, and black power radicals. By the end of the era, one of their own (Wallace Henley) had joined the Nixon White House team and another, Allan Watson (pastor of Calvary Baptist Church in Tuscaloosa), had preached in the White House for President Richard M. Nixon (who praised the sermon as the kind of "Biblical preaching" that Americans needed to hear).[73]

Within the state this drift to the political right was temporarily halted by the governorship of Albert Brewer. Elevated to the highest state office by the death of Governor Lurleen Wallace in 1968, Brewer compiled an impressive reform record during his thirty-two months in office. A devout Baptist layman and deacon in Decatur First Baptist Church, Brewer spoke constantly at Baptist events during his years in office. He appointed Samford University president Leslie Wright and convention executive secretary George Bagley to the newly created ethics commission, both of whom served terms as chairman. Brewer also spoke to the 1968 state convention and urged fellow Baptists to become more involved in politics. His obvious and oft-spoken pride in being Baptist helped him considerably in the 1970 Democratic gubernatorial primary against George Wallace. Many leading Baptist pastors and lay persons quietly supported him, and he took a surprising lead over Wallace in the first primary. The Wallace forces countered with perhaps the most virulent and vituperative racist campaign in Alabama political history, complete with vicious rumors about Brewer and his family. Brewer's lead vanished in the runoff, and he narrowly lost his bid for reelection. Although Brewer ran well among urban Baptists, he lost rural white areas of the state, and ironically he drew his strongest support from counties where black Baptists predominated. The loss was a shattering blow to Brewer, who learned an important lesson that Jimmy Carter would repeat in 1980.[74] Being a white Baptist on the wrong side of the race and culture wars of the era did not assure a candidate the vote of fellow church members.

Nor were two other flirtations with Baptist politicians more satisfying, though for personal rather than ideological reasons. Mobile mayor Lambert Mims and Alabama state auditor Melba Till Allen touted their ties to the denomination and were popular speakers at Baptist events during the late 1960s. Both likened politics to a religious calling and extolled the need for Christian ethics in government. Unfortunately, both were convicted of ethical violations and sentenced to terms in jail.[75]

Just as Baptists fudged on their vow to stay out of politics, they began to waver on their historic commitment to the complete separation of church and state. A number of factors explain their vacillation. Baptist colleges and hospitals had been strapped for money for decades. With the advent of federal programs to fund both colleges and hospitals, Baptist institutions simply could not survive if competitors accepted grants or low-interest loans while they refused. Concerns about integration caused some segregationists to advocate taking state money for church-based schools. Supreme Court rulings disallowing state-prescribed prayers and mandated Bible reading infuriated many conservative evangelicals, who believed such rulings contributed to the nation's secularism and moral decline.

Macon was most consistent of all Baptist leaders on church-state issues. He adhered to the historic Baptist position that the First Amendment to the U.S. Constitution created an impenetrable barrier between church and state. Whether the breaching of that wall of separation benefited Catholic parochial schools or Baptist hospitals made no difference. It was wrong in either case. If either set of institutions could not survive without public tax monies, then they could be dispensed with.

This thinking led Macon to positions that were controversial even among conservatives of his own time and would have been unthinkable a generation later. He attacked a proposed amendment to the Constitution in 1955 recognizing the "authority and law of Jesus Christ" over the nation. Even though two Southern Baptist congressmen proposed the amendment, Macon objected that it would trample the rights of millions of non-Christians and was a step in the direction of a state church. During the next decade he opposed a similar amendment to declare the United States officially a Christian nation.[76]

The editor objected to various proposals in his home state to teach religion or Bible courses in public schools and colleges even though their proponents promised to avoid denominational disputes and doctrine. Such courses, Macon believed, merely opened the way for Catholics and other groups to indoctrinate students wherever they were in the majority.[77]

The denomination struggled with church-state issues for a decade. The convention's executive secretary, A. Hamilton Reid, wrote a lengthy essay in 1956 on why Baptist hospitals should refuse Hill-Burton funding. The convention's administration committee lobbied the state's senior U.S. senator, Lister Hill (who had written the law), to allow church groups to borrow money at low interest rates. It also established a public affairs committee to monitor the issue for the convention. In the mid-1960s the convention engaged in sharp clashes with Baptist hospitals in Gadsden and Birmingham over acceptance of federal grants disguised as "loans." In 1967 the Montgomery Baptist Association (after a two-hour debate) voted against allowing its hospital to accept federal funds for a multimillion-dollar expansion. The Birmingham Association had already taken similar action after rancorous debate.[78]

Macon was equally opposed to federal aid to education. He believed such assistance to be a vehicle for regimentation and control of schools. He also concluded that it breached the church-state barrier. He opposed state tuition grants to parents in the aftermath of school desegregation in Alabama, grants that would have allowed parents to use the money to send children to parochial schools. His position was widely supported by associations, which passed resolutions opposing Catholic attempts to include parochial schools in various laws pertaining to federal aid to education.[79]

By the 1960s philosophical concern for church-state separation had been diluted by other issues. Macon increasingly feared federal control of schools and government centralization. He believed, correctly as it turned out, that federal aid would come with strings attached, especially a requirement that recipient institutions not discriminate on the basis of race. Such a requirement, he believed, would lead to the loss of both states' and property rights. Although the 1960 ABSC allowed its colleges to accept federal loans, it carefully monitored such applications. Macon deplored the tendency of Baptist colleges in other states to accept all forms of federal assistance, which he considered one of the most dangerous trends in denominational life. Various churches and associations, especially in the Black Belt, also objected to Judson and Howard Colleges signing compliance forms in 1965 that they would not racially discriminate in admitting students. But the convention's education advisory committee praised the schools for this action and in 1968 declared there to be no conflict between accepting National Defense Education Act (NDEA) loans and church-state separation. The financial survival of Christian higher education, the com-

mittee reasoned, was a higher priority than arcane philosophical arguments.[80]

Catholic insistence that Hill-Burton and NDEA legislation allow parochial hospitals and schools to participate helps explain emotional Baptist
opposition to John Kennedy's 1960 presidential aspirations. At the time, the
national media dismissed the debate over church-state separation as a pe-
ripheral and insincere side issue. But the context of the 1960 race makes
clear that church-state issues were central. Not only had Catholics lobbied
Congress hard for appointment of a U.S. representative to the Vatican and
on behalf of federal aid to Catholic schools and hospitals, but they also had
been instrumental in drafting a New York Board of Regents school prayer
under attack in the courts by Protestants and Jews.

Many of the sermons aimed at Kennedy's 1960 presidential campaign
focused not on religion but on church-state separation. B. Locke Davis (who
served as convention president during the 1960 election) took the lead in
opposing Kennedy's election. It was no easy decision for Davis, a gentle
man who did not fit the media stereotype of a narrow-minded, anti-Catholic bigot. A graduate of Hardin-Simmons College in Texas with a degree
in history and political science, Davis had served as a navy chaplain during the war. He pastored a dually aligned Baptist church in Missouri and
after the war weighed two offers, one from Detroit's First Baptist Church,
the other from Parker Memorial. After choosing the Alabama pastorate,
he healed the divisions left from Charles Bell's tenure, always treating his
predecessor with respect. Theologically, Davis was conservative but neither
fundamentalist nor abrasive. He rejected Landmark theology, was an excellent Greek scholar, and emphasized the grace of God over themes of judgment and damnation. His sermons leaned toward the scholarly side of
religion rather than the emotional. He was active in Anniston's interdenominational ministerial association and served as chairman of the interracial Boy Scout district committee. He subscribed to *Christian Century*
(a progressive religious journal) and frequently wrote letters to the editor
about international issues. His sermons were broadcast on the area's major
radio station, giving him a wide audience.[81]

Although Davis was widely perceived as being anti-Catholic, that was
not the case. When a local Catholic woman whose son Davis had befriended wrote a poignant letter asking for his love, not condemnation of
Catholics, Davis assured her that she had misunderstood his sermons. He
wrote that his daughter-in-law and two of his grandsons were Catholics.
His sermon (entitled "Separation of Church and State") had simply contrasted Baptist and Catholic positions on that issue. In a sermon that was
printed as a pamphlet and widely distributed during the presidential cam-

paign, Davis cast the issue facing the United States as "the cherished principle of separation of church and state." He defined the proper role of
religion in politics as Christians influencing public morality without infringing on the First Amendment. Although he used the rhetoric of the time
(he referred to "the Hierarchy of the Roman Catholic Church" to distinguish ordinary local Catholics he liked from the remote leadership he
feared), he was neither intolerant nor a bigot.[82]

Even more troubling to many Alabama Baptists than Kennedy's 1960
campaign was the complex debate over school prayer and Bible reading.
Beginning with the Supreme Court's 1962 decision declaring a New York
Board of Regents prayer for public schools to be unconstitutional, state
Baptists began to divide. Leon Macon applauded the decision and denied
that it prevented prayer in public schools or was antireligious. The church
was the proper venue to teach children about religion, not American public
schools. He also saluted a group of Jews who brought the suit for "their
forthright stand on separation of church and state." James E. Davidson
(pastor of South Avondale Baptist Church) agreed with Macon. In a July
sermon entitled "Prayer in Public Schools," Davidson quoted extensively
from Hugo Black's majority opinion as well as Thomas Jefferson's famous
description of the First Amendment as erecting "a wall of separation between church and state." He rejected the opinion of those who interpreted
the ruling as a step toward secularism and materialism. Pastors from Cullman, Troy, and elsewhere wrote Macon and Davidson their agreement. Not
all Baptists consented, however, particularly not lay people. Macon received much criticism for his editorial supporting the Supreme Court, and
Henry Lyon Jr. even denounced the ruling in his prayer at George Wallace's
inauguration.[83]

Two years later the Supreme Court ruled against prescribed Bible reading in public schools. This time more Baptist pastors joined the opposition.
Macon stood his ground, proclaiming that the genius of American Christianity was its lack of compulsion. Churches had to rely entirely upon their
own resources, making them vigorous and responsible and protecting the
nation from totalitarianism. Although he described himself as a thorough
conservative, he believed that requiring Bible reading in public schools
placed students under duress and compelled them to listen to religious
opinions to which they did not subscribe. Jews should not have to recite the
Lord's Prayer. He did not object to voluntary prayer and Bible reading in
public schools, but he denounced compulsion of any kind as "unbaptistic."
Once again he received many letters both praising and opposing his
stance.[84]

Opponents rallied behind the proposed Becker Amendment to the

Constitution that would have specifically authorized prayer and Bible reading in public schools. Southern congressmen were inundated with letters and petitions supporting the amendment. Alabama Baptist congressmen who opposed it reported that their pro-Becker mail exceeded even letters opposing the public accommodations bill then pending in Congress. Baptist congressman Albert Rains from Alabama's Fifth District warned executive secretary George Bagley that Governor George Wallace's endorsement of the Becker Amendment had placed the Alabama congressional delegation under great pressure to vote for it. He urged Bagley to launch a "massive publicity program" to counter Wallace. Bagley responded immediately and effectively. He wrote all ABSC pastors explaining the amendment's threat to church-state separation, denied that court rulings banned voluntary prayer and Bible reading, and urged them to contact their representatives. Congressmen were flooded with resolutions from churches and associations opposing the Becker Amendment, a campaign that resulted in most Alabama congressmen voting against it.[85]

Bagley's campaign was not universally approved; he received furious letters from proponents of the amendment. Jimmy C. Jones, who described himself as a lifelong Baptist, resented Bagley's opposition to the Becker Amendment and the fact that his position was widely reported as representing that of Alabama Baptists. He contrasted those who favored the measure (George Wallace, Strom Thurmond, and the "host of patriots who have stood for constitutional government") with its opponents (the National Council of Churches, NAACP, Congress of Racial Equality, Student Nonviolent Coordinating Committee, Southern Christian Leadership Conference, Methodists, Jews, Unitarians, Hugo Black, Earl Warren, Gus Hall, Norman Thomas, the "God-hating American Civil Liberties Union," and "every other communist fronter and socialist in the whole cotton picking United States of America"). Another angry writer contrasted the access that evolutionists had to public schoolchildren with the banning of "the infallible Word of God."[86]

Under such a barrage of criticism, both Macon and his successor, Hudson Baggett, began to waver. Macon had second thoughts about the New York regents prayer, which he concluded had not been sectarian after all. He criticized the ACLU for suing Washington, D.C., schools to eliminate recitation of the Lord's Prayer and Bible reading. Eliminating religion from public schools simply played into the hands of communism, he wrote. Macon reversed himself again the next year, praising Supreme Court Justice William J. Brennan's explanation of the Court's position in such cases (any version of the Bible was inherently sectarian; every community contained people opposed to any particular version of the Bible; prayer was a private religious exercise to many people; the United States had no "common core" of religious beliefs acceptable to all citizens; reading the Bible without comment or explanation to children could create confusion and misunderstanding). These arguments convinced Macon that his original position was still viable. His confusion may also be attributable to his rapidly deteriorating health.[87]

As editor of the *Alabama Baptist*, Hudson Baggett backed away from Macon's opposition to a constitutional amendment allowing prayer and Bible reading in public schools. He noted that Baptists were on both sides of the Dirksen Amendment, which clarified that nothing in the U.S. Constitution should prohibit voluntary school prayer, although it specifically prohibited prescribed prayers. Baggett wrote that he had no "serious objection" to the amendment itself, but he did not think it wise to change the U.S. Constitution unless it was "absolutely necessary." Three years later he criticized the trend toward "complete secularization of society" and proclaimed voluntary Bible reading, prayer, and devotional comments in public schools as much a part of the national heritage as the pledge of allegiance to the flag.[88]

Protracted debate about prayer and Bible reading was part of a larger debate emerging in the 1960s. Secular and religious society increasingly polarized, giving rise to what would soon be called "culture wars."

Alabama Baptists disagreed over the role that banning public school prayer and Bible reading had on the nation's moral decline. But they were of one mind on the direction in which society was headed. Citing as evidence rising rates of alcohol consumption, divorce, crime, sexual promiscuity, pornography, and lewdness in music, movies, and television, many again saw Armageddon just around the corner. Macon even returned to a favorite 1920s theme, women's attire. "When a woman dresses so that men gaze at her she originates the sin and is as guilty as the man himself," the editor wrote in 1965. "If a woman does not want to be stared at and lusted after she ought to dress in a manner that would not awaken these natural desires."[89]

Both Macon and Baggett criticized popular 1960s movies and television programs for their obscenity and vulgarity. Readers chimed in with denunciations of articles in *Ladies' Home Journal* and even a Sunday School Board "hippie concept of Christ" that depicted the Savior with long, multicolored hair. Churches began to pass resolutions denouncing lewdness in the media.

Popular music posed a similar threat. Macon denounced rock'n'roll music and dances as little more than "orgies." He deplored the use of jazz in religious services or young people's meetings. "Jazz is jazz," he wrote disapprovingly in 1959, "and can never be wholesome and beneficial to a person in his moral or spiritual cravings." In 1965 he added the Beatles to his cultural enemy's list. Their dress was immodest, and their singing was a return to "savagery." Hudson Baggett agreed, commending a campaign to ban the Beatles from Alabama. He ridiculed their "moplike hairdo and the wacky, swingy music with a kind of Congo cadence." Two popular Birmingham disc jockeys and numerous businesses joined the effort. The DJs urged their listeners to burn Beatles' records and designated businesses where records could be deposited for destruction. One business attached a sign to the container: "Deposit Beatle Trash Here." Taking note of American cultural collapse, W. A. Criswell (speaking to the 1966 state convention) predicted somberly that Christianity would be "practically non-existent by the year 2,000."

John Bob Riddle, pastor of Birmingham's Central Park Baptist Church and president of the 1969 state convention, devoted his presidential sermon to the nation's cultural and moral decline.[90] Baptists who agreed society was on the wrong path could not agree on a course correction. Some thought campaigns against the Beatles' music wrong-headed and a waste of time. Others (especially youth) liked the music and denied that it undermined morals. A young Baptist from Alexander City scolded Macon for "the same old bleat of the 'holier-than-thous' " that greeted every new musical group that appealed to youth. He was weary of Macon's superstition, fear, fanaticism, paranoia about communism, allusions to sex as something dirty, and prejudice against "mop-haired singers from England." Someday perhaps Macon would come to understand rock music and change his opinion. Meantime, the reader warned, "Keep a wary eye peeled for stray Rolling Stones, Zombies, Animals, Kinks, and Beatles."[91]

Baptists could not agree on the solution to family problems. Opposition to divorce began to soften, and increasing numbers of ministers performed marriage ceremonies for divorced couples (not a common occurrence before the 1950s). Some churches ordained previously divorced persons as deacons. Many Baptists urged Sunday School Board literature to deal more directly and frankly with sexuality, but when Baptist Training Union literature actually began to do so, numerous adult leaders criticized the lessons as inappropriate for mixed groups of teenagers and threatened to switch to non-Baptist material. These protests generated a spirited defense of the literature by one Baptist marriage counselor who wrote that ignorance and misconceptions about sex were major causes of marital unhappiness and adultery. Hudson Baggett wrote that the widespread reaction of

Alabama Baptists against even church-based sex education made it difficult to counter the popularity of pornography. He regretted the fact that
many church members simply refused to deal with sex education and even
opposed mention of sex in church. His editorial provoked an avalanche of
letters in opposition to church-based sex education.[92]

Theology

Cultural wars separated Baptists on a line roughly approximating
long-standing theological divisions. Large suburban churches with well-
educated, middle- and upper-class congregations and small-town First
Baptist churches tended to be more theologically liberal and culturally tolerant and diverse than working-class, inner-city, or rural churches. During
the 1950s and 1960s, theological debates increasingly became enmeshed in
larger sociological struggles over race and cultural modernity. When that
happened, the earlier disputes (which had remained largely cerebral and
respectful) became angrier and more emotional.

There are nearly as many interpretations of the modernist-fundamentalist debate within the SBC as there are historians discussing it. Books devoted to the topic fill entire shelves of libraries. Historians do seem to agree
on some issues. The battle began long before fundamentalists took control
of the SBC in 1979. It involved more than theology. Southern Baptists
within the broad scheme of American Protestantism have always anchored
the most conservative line. But diversity thrived within their autonomous
churches because historic Baptist theology was rooted in the priesthood of
each believer to interpret Scripture for himself/herself; because their emphasis was on soul competency; and because southern culture was strongly
individualistic. Baptists historically had resisted creedalism and theological conformity. One result of the Civil War was belief that southern religion
had been purged in the refiner's fire, leaving Southern Baptists with a sacred mission to save the United States from apostasy and heresy, mainly
imported from Germany. The South's agrarianism, ruralism, and anti-intellectualism strengthened these religious assumptions. At first most
Southern Baptists assumed they were all of one mind on such matters.

By 1900 it was obvious that even Southern Baptists produced seminary
professors, preachers, and lay people who were theologically tainted by liberalism in one way or another. Although their sectionalism, geographical and intellectual isolation, and fierce denominational loyalty kept them
aloof from interdenominational fundamentalism, they certainly shared
many of its assumptions, especially about scientific evolution and inerrancy of Scripture. Fierce debates between the denomination's fundamen-

talist wing and its moderately conservative contingent (augmented by what few liberals the SBC contained) ended in a draw.

Fundamentalists got their creedal statement in 1925 (the Baptist Faith and Message). But the 1925 declaration was broad enough to cover virtually all factions who had taken refuge in the Baptist camp. It turned out to be an expandable tent that could encompass all who wanted to be Southern Baptists. And people desired to be Southern Baptists for a variety of reasons: they were born in the South and grew up in SBC churches; they endorsed historic Baptist doctrines such as the priesthood of the believer, religious freedom, soul competency, separation of church and state, and baptism by immersion; they were committed to evangelism and foreign missions; they were theologically conservative; they were fundamentalist. By the 1950s and 1960s some southerners also chose to join SBC churches because their own denominations were becoming too liberal on race.

Although theological fundamentalists might be numerous in Baptist ranks, the denomination's seminary-trained leadership was more moderate and tolerant of diversity. SBC seminaries did not suddenly succumb to liberalism after World War II. Seminary professors as far back as the late nineteenth century had studied in Germany and were conversant with European scholarship. Some of it they accepted; other parts they rejected. Students who studied with them were exposed to a wide spectrum of theological opinion, though with a preference for conservative viewpoints. The SBC seminary climate was not polemical or particularly provincial, as perusal of the private papers of W. O. Carver, Victor Masters, and a host of other professors makes clear. The leadership of state conventions by the students of such professors was a product of many forces. Their devotion to the SBC and southern culture (including its racism) was indisputable. The fundamentalist-modernist debate occurred among men who knew each other well, which kept them from demonizing one another. Well-educated pastors of "first churches" had equal opportunities to exercise denominational leadership regardless of their theological beliefs. The pastors shut out of the bureaucracy were eliminated because of lack of education or because they had insufficient financial resources to attend state conventions and the SBC, not because of theological beliefs. In Alabama at least, becoming president of the state convention had more to do with service and name recognition than it did with ideology, and laymen served half the time between 1875 and 1925. After the state bureaucracy expanded following World War II, it was dominated by moderate conservatives who pastored large churches that gave most of the money. But the convention often elected fundamentalists and conservatives as president, including Brady Justice,

Henry L. Lyon Jr., and Leon Macon (fundamentalists W. A. Criswell and K. Owen White were also elected to the SBC presidency during the 1960s).[93] Moderate conservatives were also elected president of the ABSC (John H. Buchanan, Harold W. Seever, B. Locke Davis, Howard M. Reaves, and J. R. White).

The dominant Alabama Baptist figure between 1950 and his death in 1965 was Leon Macon. As editor of the denominational paper, twice president of the state convention, and chief ABSC national spokesman, he eclipsed both executive secretaries A. Hamilton Reid and George Bagley. Macon had solid fundamentalist credentials.

Although Macon agreed with L. L. Gwaltney that theoretically science and religion were compatible, he adopted a more adversarial position. He deplored the tendency in the post-Sputnik era to glorify scientists and their emergence as a special and influential elite. He believed that public school students should be taught evolution as theory, not as fact.[94]

By the 1960s Macon had connected four negative elements into a holistic theology: antimodernism; anti–social gospel; antiecumenism; anti–political liberalism. Fused by his growing concerns about government centralization, moral decay, and racial integration, he expressed this theology largely in reaction to dangerous trends he detected: too much emphasis upon the rights of citizens, too little on responsibilities; too much emphasis on scholarship, too little on authority; too much attention on government to solve problems, too little on states and individuals; too much attention on new science, too little on traditional ways of life; too much influence by communism, modernism, liberalism, and ecumenism.[95]

Macon increasingly centered his attacks on modernism. He blamed SBC declines in baptisms on "creeping liberalism," not on the denomination's racism, as some claimed. He contrasted the decline of the American Baptist Convention (which had adopted an inclusive policy designed to accommodate a variety of views) to the growing SBC, which had tried "to freeze the liberals out in the pulpits, colleges and seminaries." Liberalism, he added, was a "parasitic movement which endeavors to take over the churches and institutions that conservatives build and pay for." He defined liberalism as a departure from Christian orthodoxy in favor of socialism and humanism, which majored on doubt and uncertainty. Its origins in Germany owed much to academics who felt obliged to do original research that had led students to write "absurd theses on the Scriptures." This academic elitism (he called such scholars "silk hats of distinction") replaced personal Christian faith with textual criticism. Fortunately, Southern Baptists continued to adhere to fundamentalist belief in a literal, infallible

Bible. He wrote in 1955 that he knew not a single Southern Baptist who did not accept the Bible as "completely infallible."[96]

None of the Christian alternatives to fundamentalism—Christian humanism, existentialism, or neo-orthodoxy—appealed to Macon. Humanism substituted faith in man for faith in God. Existentialism emphasized historical relativism and shifting perceptions of God. He did have some favorable opinions of neo-orthodoxy. Like its practitioners, he believed that textual criticism alone would not allow one to understand the Bible (reason had to be employed as well). He also applauded neo-orthodox emphasis on humanity's fallen nature and the need for redemption. But he linked neo-orthodox theologian Paul Tillich with liberalism and believed neo-orthodoxy undermined the authority of the Bible by employing the historical-critical system that reduced many biblical stories to myth.[97]

Although Macon was the most outspoken fundamentalist, he expressed the views of many other Alabama Baptists, as his personal correspondence confirms. One correspondent in 1955 wrote Macon that Baptists were beginning to compromise with modernism, to substitute rationalism for revelation, and sacrifice "Bible principle" for popularity. He even criticized Macon's newspaper, which he suggested should be renamed "The Protestant Compromiser." A 1961 correspondent criticized Southern Baptist literature for emphasizing the right of individual Baptists to interpret Scripture. It was meaningless to claim the Bible as textbook and at the same time allow every person to "put whatever interpretation he may please on it and imply . . . that any number of such interpretations are 'reasonable.' " Macon probably agreed with this thesis but not the application his friend made. The friend cited as example Baptists who said they believed the Bible but rationalized evolution by claiming the "days" in Genesis I were of indeterminate time, which was precisely Macon's position.[98]

The catalyst for much of this fundamentalism was a series of conflicts originating in SBC colleges and seminaries. Conflict erupted at Southern seminary in 1958 in an internal dispute between faculty and administration. Three years later controversy broke out over a different and more theological issue. Ralph Elliott (a professor at Midwestern Baptist Theological Seminary) wrote a book about Genesis describing parts of it in mythological language. Coming as it did among heightened tensions about race and national politics, the contoversy over Elliott's book riveted attention on the widening theological chasm between ordinary Baptists and a theologically educated elite.

In Alabama Macon used these controversies as occasion for wider commentary on Baptist orthodoxy and higher education. Having no pre-

tensions to the sort of intellectualism that had characterized L. L. Gwaltney, Macon argued that humanism and liberalism were infiltrating Baptist higher education. Having declared five years earlier that he knew no
Southern Baptist modernist, he found them behind practically every book-
case on college and seminary campuses by 1960. Modernism was the natural outgrowth of "a strong emphasis . . . on scholarship in religious institutions." Academic freedom should not extend so far as to allow a professor
to undermine the foundations of Christian faith.[99]

As early as 1960 Macon wrote five SBC seminary presidents complaining about professors who treated portions of the Bible as myth. The presidents initially mollified the editor by explaining that use of the word *myth*
did not imply rejection of miracles or the supernatural; it was only a technical word for a traditional story, ostensibly with a historical basis but more
important as an explanation of religious phenomena. Although the word
could also mean that a story was fictitious or imaginary, that was not the
intended meaning that professors gave it. Macon preferred that professors
use another word because to most Alabama Baptists the word *myth* meant
"false"; but he was temporarily satisfied that the seminaries were faithful
to Baptist doctrine.[100]

The Elliott affair convinced him otherwise. Although Macon considered Elliott sincere in his beliefs, the editor believed his writings were "not
true to Baptist interpretations." Academic freedom was not so inclusive as
to allow departure from the Baptist "Statement of Faith," and Macon called
for an investigation of the seminaries. Although he opposed a proposal to
appoint a new board of trustees for Midwestern that would pledge to fire
Elliott, he warned against people who were more interested in philosophical speculation about the Bible than in finding favor with God. When the
seminary finally fired Elliott in 1962, Macon applauded the decision. He
privately wrote the fundamentalist president of the SBC that many other
seminary professors shared Elliott's views. To other correspondents, he
confirmed his own belief in the infallibility of Scripture and the "modernistic tendencies" of seminary faculties. A pastor from Ozark shared with
Macon his own experience as a rural preacher who was shocked when his
psychology professor at a non-Baptist denominational college told the class
that Adam, Eve, Noah, Lot, and Abraham were all fictitious characters. He
feared that Baptist colleges and seminaries were on the same path toward
liberalism, agnosticism, and atheism.[101]

In reaction to the Elliott controversy the 1963 SBC adopted a revised
"Baptist Faith and Message" largely drafted by Alabama native Hershel H.
Hobbs, who served as convention president during the critical years of the

controversy. Elliott's firing stoked the fires of controversy temporarily, but the affair left deep scars in Alabama. Macon began privately praising Luther Rice Seminary as a scripturally based alternative to increasingly liberal SBC seminaries. The resignation of four professors at Southeastern Baptist Theological Seminary in 1965 in response to criticism of their historical-critical methodology typified the preference of some seminary professors for "secular scholarship" over "Biblical theology," he wrote. Letters to the *Alabama Baptist* attacked Baptist religion professors who criticized W. A. Criswell's book on the infallibility of the Bible. The "gullible bourgeois" who supported Criswell, who constituted grass-roots Baptists, and who paid for the denomination's academic institutions were contrasted by one evangelist to the sixty-eight professors who signed the document criticizing Criswell and who were corrupting the children of Baptist parents. A woman from Geneva described young preachers who had been ruined by the "historical-critical method" and affirmed that the Bible was infallible on matters of geology and anthropology no less than on theology. The East Walnut Baptist Church passed a resolution demanding that any employee of a Baptist institution or agency who did not "believe without mental reservations" that the Bible contained no error should be fired.[102]

Macon was transformed between 1956 and 1963 from an opponent of creeds to their advocate. But careful scrutiny of the kind of creedalism Macon rejected is important. He feared not so much the creeds of fundamentalists within his own denomination as he did the creeds of a growing minority of Southern Baptists who were leaving what they viewed as a liberal denomination for the status of independent Baptists. Many were fiercely premillennial in theology and demanded that all conform theologically to that view. Though a premillennialist himself, Macon refused to make that doctrine a condition of theological orthodoxy. Such people could become as fanatical and destructive as liberals, he wrote in 1963, and whatever the mistakes of the SBC, at least it was trying to correct them and had remained essentially true to the Bible.[103]

Organization of the Independent Christian Association in 1965 by former Alabama Baptist ministers formalized the split in the denomination. Citing concerns about Sunday School Board literature and false doctrine taught in Baptist colleges and seminaries, the association's leaders detailed their charges in letters to Baptist laymen and ministers. They challenged Macon and other leaders to debate them, a challenge he ignored. The charges won some converts, such as the pastor of Highland Baptist Church in Plateau. He complained about denominational sponsorship of "race relations Sunday," promotion of integration, and support for liberalism and modernism. Though formerly a loyal Southern Baptist, he now proclaimed himself "an enemy of the convention."[104]

Combating such views was an intriguing coalition of denominational loyalists who held most positions within the convention. They included tolerant theological conservatives, moderates, and even a few liberals. Denominational loyalists defended Howard College against rumors circulated about the school's faculty in the mid-1950s. Howard's dean of religion and the founder of the school's extension program, Gilbert L. Guffin, argued in 1963 that the denomination should follow a "middle of the road" approach to theology that rejected extremes. Walter G. Nunn, influential pastor of Gardendale First Baptist Church, considered the SBC the nation's most conservative denomination. But he also criticized W. A. Criswell's book, *Why I Preach That the Bible Is Literally True,* as a bombastic, nonscholarly work full of contradictions. He believed that neither the Bible nor Christ taught verbal inspiration of Scripture. He also criticized Criswell for rejecting theistic evolution as a Christian option and for his intolerance of those who did not share his beliefs.[105]

Charles T. Carter was another theological conservative who demonstrated tolerance toward dissenters. A native of Birmingham and graduate of Howard College and Southern seminary, he returned to Birmingham to pastor Hillview Baptist Church. During the 1962 Elliott controversy, one of Carter's seminary professors, Dale Moody, was accused of heresy for his challenge to the historic Baptist doctrine of the perseverance of the saints ("once saved, always saved"). Leon Macon was particularly severe in his criticism of Moody and argued for replacing the trustees if they did not remove the professor. In the midst of the controversy, Carter invited Moody to speak at his church's annual summer Bible conference.[106]

Hudson Baggett, Macon's successor, was more tolerant of diversity. He wrote a rebuttal to those who thought they could resolve all debates by saying "the Bible tells us. . . . " Baptists interpreted the Bible in so many ways that what was right and wrong was not always clear. Biblical principles constituted ethical guidelines, but even the Bible could be rationalized to serve "our own ends and purposes." The problem was not God's faulty revelation but humanity's faulty understanding. When W. A. Criswell deplored diversity in the SBC and urged Baptists who did not accept the Baptist Faith and Message to leave the denomination, Baggett replied that the problem was how Baptists interpreted the statement.[107]

Additional rebuttals came from a group of Alabama Baptists who might more properly be called moderates. Dr. William Lucas, a scientist at Marshall Space Center in Huntsville, told the 1967 state WMU meeting that scientists were neither irreligious nor anti-Christian. The apparent conflict between science and religion stemmed largely from Christians who feared they could not defend their beliefs and used the Bible in spheres outside religion. "The Bible is not a book of science," he explained in contradiction of most fundamentalists, who insisted that it was as valid on matters of science as for theology. But he did endorse orthodox Christianity and criticized scientists who thought of themselves as authorities on religion. "While the circles of science and theology may intersect," he explained, "I believe . . . that the center of each lies beyond the compass of the other." He believed that scientific and technological changes would also demand a different approach to evangelism in the future.[108]

William E. Hull tried to reconcile Alabama Baptists to new patterns in theology. A native of the state, Hull had attended the University of Alabama as a pre-med student before his call to the ministry, after which he transferred to Howard College. After completing Southern seminary, he did additional study at the University of Goettingen in Germany. As a professor of New Testament at Southern, he wrote several influential books embodying his desire that Southern Baptists make their own distinctive contribution to biblical scholarship. He urged fellow Baptists not to ape European scholars nor close themselves off from such contacts.[109] Some fundamentalists date the modern split in the SBC to a series of articles Hull wrote explaining why he thought the Bible was not inerrant.

Howard M. Reaves (pastor of Mobile First Baptist Church and twice president of the state convention) used his first presidential address in 1961 to refute attacks on seminary professors. He reminded messengers of earlier attacks on the writings of professors presently regarded as pillars of orthodoxy. Baptists must affirm their historic belief in the right of individuals to think for themselves. That belief would always create questions about someone's orthodoxy; but he remained confident in the "essential soundness" of SBC seminaries.[110]

A year later Reaves created an uproar with a sermon to an associational program in Birmingham. Although he avowed his fidelity to the authority and authenticity of the Bible, Reaves rejected the plenary verbal theory of inspiration. Some Baptists were trying to impose such views as the only orthodox position of biblical interpretation. Reaves believed that this demand for conformity would alienate the "most intelligent minds among us" and drive them into other denominations. His remarks led the Mount Olive Baptist Church in Trussville to pass a resolution accusing him of believing the Bible to be fallible. Macon also expressed his disagreement with Reaves, though in the letter ostensibly affirming verbal inspiration, he described the "days" mentioned in Genesis I as periods of time that could vary from twenty-four hours to twenty-four million years.[111]

Some liberal Alabama Baptists did precisely what Howard Reaves predicted: they left the denomination. John Bush was a bright, committed ministerial student at Howard College during the early 1960s. He decided to attend Midwestern seminary partly to work with Ralph Elliott. Bush had grown up in and had been ordained by Montgomery's Clayton Street Baptist Church, where his mother was a WMU leader and his father a deacon. At Midwestern he was appalled by "the utter cruelty and absolute absence of Christian love" expressed toward his major professor. He helped form a student group to defend Elliott and wrote in his diary in April 1963: "I'll not long bother Baptists with my presence." When he sought ordination as a Presbyterian, some Alabama Baptist officials suggested he surrender his Baptist ordination, which Bush refused to do. Bush went on to a distinguished career as director of the Interchurch Coordinating Council in Clinton, Missouri, which pioneered regional social ministries. His brother Bill, a ministerial student at Baptist Bible Institute in Graceville, Florida, when the Elliott affair broke out, considered the professor's writings heretical. He defended Elliott's right to his opinion, although he believed that a book that caused even one person to be lost was not worth publishing. As he wrote his brother shortly before dying of a spinal disease in 1965, "I hope we can always talk without getting mad at each other." They could. Unfortunately, many Alabama Baptists could not.[112]

Opposition to the social gospel remained less pervasive than resistance to modernism and ecumenism. W. A. Criswell led SBC opposition to social Christianity, which he defined as different from the social righteousness espoused by social workers and community betterment associations. Never one to mince words, Criswell called the social gospel "dry rot that is destroying Christendom" and declared that its fruits were "a dead church, a dead gospel, a dead denomination, a dead seminary, and a dead preacher." Speaking to the Mobile Baptist pastors' conference in 1968, Criswell warned that when the church became a social reform agency, it ceased to evangelize people.[113]

Leon Macon was the point man leading attacks on social Christianity. During the mid-1950s the editor's animosity was muted and ambiguous. He conceded that God was as interested in the material needs of persons as in their spiritual hunger. He praised the goals of the movement—to end war and economic and social injustice and to make the world a better place to live. He regretted that Alabama Baptists were doing so little to improve conditions in the state's prisons and mental institutions. But he also in-

sisted that the proper way for the church to change society was by changing individuals. There was neither scriptural support for the social gospel
nor precedent in the ministry of Christ. By the 1960s Macon attributed
everything from the nation's rising crime rate to urban violence, civil rights
agitation, and declining baptisms to the social gospel. He criticized the
SBC Christian Life Commission for its reform activities, denounced the social gospel in his presidential address to the state convention, and criticized
LBJ's attempt to define poverty as a moral issue.[114]

Many pastors expressed similar views. One condemned "Social
Gospellers who are so bored with life they find no excitement as a pastor,
and seek it in the street marches in someone else'[s] community." He was
tempted to tell his congregation "about these eggheads . . . from the Baptist Hindquarters . . . that we're supporting with our mission money." He
expressed no sympathy for Selma demonstrators "who got their heads
skinned while fraternizing with the Philistines."[115]

Others expressed a similar if more humane opinion. Samford's dean
of religion, Gilbert Guffin, criticized the social gospel for emphasizing social over personal salvation. Ralph D. Field, pastor of Center Point Baptist
Church in Birmingham, denied that the United States could create a "Great
Society" with civil rights and antipoverty legislation because only the gospel could accomplish that goal.[116]

Lay persons were just as critical. A layman from Scottsboro criticized
Billy Graham for endorsing LBJ's war on poverty. A woman from Prichard
who had recently left her denomination (which had "sacrificed itself on
the altar of Social Reforms") to become a Baptist warned that now Baptists
were "promoting racial integration as well." She called leaders of the social
gospel "false prophets."[117] Such opinions fit the stereotype of Alabama Baptists during the 1960s. But they do not reflect the widespread disagreement
about the social gospel.

George D. Lovett, a layman from Alexander City, disagreed with Macon's constant attacks on the social gospel. Individual salvation was the
chief responsibility of the church, but Christians lived in a social environment. He had concluded that Macon's condemnation of social Christianity
was "only a camouflage means of voicing tolerance, even approval of such
anti-Christian and anti-democratic philosophies as racial segregation."
Russell J. Drake of Gardendale felt equally strongly about Macon's criticism of LBJ's poverty program. As a bus driver and teacher at a Headstart
school, he listed the program's numerous benefits and believed Southern Baptists were "foolhardily clinging to the fundamentalist approach" in
the face of a rapidly changing world. Another advocate of the social gospel

cited the opinions of L. L. Gwaltney and Billy Graham as precedents for his views.[118]

Mention of Billy Graham was critical. In June 1967, for the first time in his ministry, the highly respected evangelist endorsed a government program, Lyndon Johnson's war on poverty. In an address to 150 congressmen and business leaders, Graham expressed his opinion that churches and individuals could no longer solve the complex problem of poverty. He had initially opposed the war on poverty, but intense study of the Bible had changed his mind. This news on the front page of the *Alabama Baptist* softened opposition in Alabama. So did the 1967 SBC. At the Miami convention, Republican U.S. senator Mark Hatfield of Oregon, a Conservative Baptist, told messengers that if churches had done their jobs, government would not have to feed the hungry, heal the sick, and minister to the needy. After failing in these tasks, Hatfield chided, evangelical Christians were the loudest in criticizing federal welfare and poverty programs. By 1968 SBC literature from a number of agencies dealt sensitively and in some depth with what Southern Baptists could do to reduce poverty.[119]

Denominational change was mirrored in Alabama. The state Christian life organization took a cautious leadership role. Under the chairmanship of George W. Riddle (pastor of Gadsden's Dwight Baptist Church) and Auburn's John Jeffers, the commission wrestled with capital punishment, militarism, economic and racial justice, and prison reform. Although Riddle concluded that Southern Baptists were less involved with social justice issues than their northern brethren, he perceptively attributed that fact largely to the conflicting influence of two secular cultures. Southern pastors became excited by alcohol "while controlling quite well their feelings on social matters generally," whereas civil rights interested northern ministers more. John Jeffers, who agreed to serve as the committee's chairman because no one else would take it, preached the 1968 state convention sermon on "The Gospel and Social Order." Although he centered his discussion on race, he dealt with other issues as well. Sin, he insisted, was as much a problem of the social order as of the individual. As in Old Testament times, the wealthy still exploited the poor. Quoting Reinhold Niebuhr, he chided Baptists for too narrow a view of sin (murder, adultery, theft, lying). Southern Baptists had extolled the New Testament emphasis on the redemption of individuals but had largely ignored Old Testament emphasis on corporate redemption. The holistic gospel spoke both to personal salvation and to social issues such as war, peace, and domestic injustice.[120]

L. Dudley Wilson, pastor of Fairfield First Baptist Church and guest editor after Leon Macon's death in 1965, wrote an editorial on "Christ and the Poor" in which he refuted critics of the poverty program for using as text "the poor you have with you always." That quotation represented Jesus' tacit acceptance of the inevitability of poverty and its resultant suffering. But to suggest that the verse reflected his insensitivity to the poor misrepresented Christ's entire ministry. Though not the central theme of the gospel, concern for the material needs of people had always been a product of Christian faith and an "integral factor in every church's ministry." Christians "agree with one voice that to exploit the poor for political or personal profit is appalling."[121]

Hudson Baggett changed the editorial policy of the *Alabama Baptist* when he replaced Macon in 1965. Citing Michael Harrington's influential book, *The Other America,* and Arthur R. Simon's *Faces of Poverty,* the new editor puzzled over why extensive poverty and unparalleled wealth existed side by side in the United States. Many middle-class values, he concluded, came not from Christ but from "the standards of the world" and "our lack of compassion for the poor." Poorly designed and ineffective welfare programs did not excuse Christians who ignored the poor. He urged a middle course between exclusive concern either for the social gospel or for personal salvation. His editorials attracted strong support and opposition.[122]

In practical terms Alabama Baptists cautiously expanded social ministries. They organized a prisoners' aid society to help convicts and their families. The Baldwin County Associational WMU provided health kits to migrant workers as did the Sand Mountain Association, though in both cases assistance lacked any organized social ministries. A number of churches began language classes for international students, including Southside in Birmingham and Auburn First Baptist. Louise Pittman, Baptist laywoman and director of the Alabama Bureau of Child Welfare, worked to improve dreadful conditions for the state's children. Her sixty years of child advocacy earned her awards from both the Children's Health System of Alabama and the National Association of Child Advocates.[123]

At best these efforts were halting. The social involvements of white Baptists as the 1960s ended did not approximate the extent of their social activism half a century earlier. The prominence of race in social reform had turned the denomination in a conservative direction despite the fact that more than half of Alabama's poor were whites, many of whom were also Baptists.

Denominational Life

Whatever tensions resulted from internal disagreements did not hinder denominational growth. With the baby boomers of the late 1940s enter-

Robinson Springs Baptist Church, created as a mission in Elmore County in 1963, was typical of the new churches forming during the 1950s and 1960s. This photograph shows the sixty-five charter members of the new church formed in April 1964 in front of their first worship center. (Courtesy of Samford University Archives)

ing adolescence, demographics favored rapid church growth. Alabama Baptists took nothing for granted. Their central focus on personal salvation might hinder social ministries but it gave them a distinct advantage over main-line denominations in evangelism. And on the primacy of evangelism there was near unanimity. As the pastor of Fort Deposit Baptist Church explained: "A church is nothing better than an ethical club if its sympathies for lost souls do not overflow." Hudson Baggett agreed. He constantly extolled the centrality of evangelism and published numerous articles on how to do it more effectively. The state evangelism conference (which always featured a bevy of popular pastors and evangelists such as W. A. Criswell and Herschel Hobbs) continued to draw large crowds. Special evangelistic emphases through simultaneous revivals across the SBC created convention-wide excitement.[124]

Evangelism paid off in record-setting rates of growth in baptisms, church membership, and contributions. Alabama Baptist churches reported 26,600 baptisms in 1954. By 1959 they listed a record 30,500. Although numbers fell during the 1960s from that peak, baptisms continued at between 25,000 and 29,000 per year. Although secular diversions such as television reduced Sunday school, Training Union, and WMU enrollment, church membership increased by more than 15 percent to 855,600 and the number of churches by 96 to 2,954 (organized into seventy-six associations). Some 61 percent of the state's white church members belonged to ABSC churches (the next highest were Methodists with only 26 percent), a total that represented one-quarter of the total population. More than two-thirds of ABSC churches (which contained one-third of the members) were still located in open country or villages under 500 population. Forty percent of these churches had fewer than 10 resident members, a source of growing alarm. Most of the nearly 3,000 churches had no frills. In 1970 only 161 had kindergartens and less than 10 percent had mission committees.[125]

Numerical growth sparked a boom in building new sanctuaries unparalleled since the 1920s. Churches in Cullman, Vinesville, Scottsboro, Tuscumbia, Trussville, Jasper, Selma, Addison, Pell City, Oxford, Dothan, Huntsville, Bemiston, Red Bay, and Birmingham built new structures. Many of the new sanctuaries departed from traditional Greek column and steeple construction, featuring such innovations as space motifs (Huntsville First Baptist) and elevated pulpits.

Finances kept pace with membership growth. A. Hamilton Reid launched the state's first five-year financial plan in 1952, and CP gifts increased by 116 percent by the end of 1956. The CP increase from 1944 to 1962 was a phenomenal 885 percent. By the 150th anniversary of organized Baptist work in Alabama (in 1958), total gifts reached nearly $25 million and CP gifts totaled $3.8 million. By 1970, CP contributions reached $7.8 million, led by four churches (Southside, Dawson Memorial, and Mountain Brook in Birmingham and Dauphin Way in Mobile). In the 1950s, ten of the seventy associations contributed nearly half of all contributions. Six of the ten were within fifty-five miles of Birmingham, and the others were in Mobile, Montgomery, and Huntsville.[126]

Every aspect of denominational life reflected similar growth. Leon Macon's determination to have the denominational paper included in all church budgets raised circulation from 45,000 in 1950 to 135,000 by 1965 (making it second in the state to the *Birmingham News* and second in the SBC to the *Texas Baptist Standard*).[127] Denominational offices in Montgomery moved into a new headquarters building in 1963.

Baptist higher education grew as well. In 1957 William K. Weaver Jr. (a former World War II chaplain and then pastor of Sylacauga First Baptist Church) chaired a convention committee to investigate establishing a Baptist junior college in Mobile. His committee recommended creating a branch of Howard College in the port city, which had no state institution

Huntsville First Baptist Church typifies the new, nontraditional church architecture of the post-1960 period. Its architecture and stained-glass windows contain space and creation motifs, though its interior worship area captures historic theological concepts. (Courtesy of Samford University Archives)

of higher learning at the time. Although Mobile citizens generally greeted the proposal with enthusiasm, the city's two leading Baptist pastors split on the proposal. Howard Reaves (pastor of First Baptist) favored it; Harold W. Seever (pastor of Dauphin Way) opposed. Both were denominational heavyweights, Seever having served as president of the state convention in 1957–1958 and Reaves in 1961–1962. Leon Macon sided with Reaves, and by 1961 plans favored a separate, convention-owned college. That same year Weaver was selected as the initial president of Mobile College. Despite the legislature's creation of state junior colleges and the University of South Alabama in Mobile during the mid-1960s, Weaver provided exceptional leadership and established a strong local base of support. The Oxford native (who held degrees from Howard College and Southern seminary) had a winsome personality and a genuine interest in people that endeared him to local Baptists as well as to the business community.[128]

Howard College also underwent dramatic change. The school acquired Cumberland Law School in 1961 and, with establishment of graduate studies in 1964, began to consider a name change. After pondering several possibilities, trustees decided on Samford University to honor a distinguished Alabama Baptist family that had played key roles in the WMU, state convention, and Howard College. Frank Samford, CEO of Liberty National Insurance Company and a prominent layman at Southside church, had served for many years as chairman of the college's board of trustees and had rescued it several times from financial disaster. Both the acquisition of the law school and the name change sparked criticism. Some pastors believed that trustees had exceeded their authority; others objected to naming the college for a living person. When the president of the 1965 state mission board ruled such arguments out of order because the school's charter required all measures dealing with the college to be initiated or approved by the trustees, members engaged in a heated exchange. They finally approved the change. Although some associations adopted resolutions opposing the name change, the convention approved the action.[129]

Howard College quickly repaired damaged feelings and maintained its close ties to local churches. By 1962 it conducted sixty-six Howard College extension centers, including many in small towns and rural areas. In the mid-1960s the college also enrolled 500 students who were preparing for church-related vocations, 67 of whom held part- or full-time pastorates and many others who served as youth and music directors. The college's H-Day program placed ministerial students in local churches every Sunday, giving the students experience and tying the school more closely to its constituency. Nearly half the state's associations participated in the program during 1965–1966.[130]

In the mid-1960s the denomination authorized a special study of Baptist higher education. An outside consultant hired by the committee made a number of recommendations: eliminate designated funding in order to provide colleges more budget flexibility; end racial discrimination in admissions; combine some of the schools; accept federal funds that did not violate the principle of church-state separation.[131] Most of these suggestions were enacted, though Judson alumnae and WMU opposition convinced wary males that they wanted no part of renewed battles over combining Judson College with another institution.

The allocation of a third of all ABSC revenue to the three colleges represented an unprecedented level of state support made necessary by almost total lack of endowment and tuition kept low so ordinary Baptist young people could attend. The result was a state convention budget that fundamentally misstated allocations of funds. For benefit of public relations, the convention advertised a 50-50 CP split between state and SBC causes. But because the figure did not include capital funds used for construction of college buildings and BSU centers on state campuses, the actual figure was 65 percent state, 35 percent SBC.[132]

As the convention grew, its organization became more complex. The 1958 convention changed representation, basing allocation of messengers on either membership or financial contributions. Some departments were combined and others were enlarged. The 1969 administration committee recommended that the convention's executive board be limited to 125 members to keep it from becoming unwieldy.[133]

Such bureaucracy troubled the populistic Leon Macon. He warned that many Baptists feared a tendency in the denomination toward centralization and urged the convention hierarchy to be more inclusive on committees and boards. He also argued against the denomination accumulating too much wealth, a factor in the rise of anticlericalism in Europe. He praised rural pastors who had little education and admonished his increasingly powerful and affluent brothers and sisters that aloofness had "no place in a great and vital Christian movement." They must not lose touch with common people or make them feel uncomfortable.[134]

To a remarkable degree the denomination followed his advice. Although it lost members at both ends of the socioeconomic spectrum, it retained remarkable appeal to middle-class Alabama whites. George Bagley instituted "listening sessions" where denominational officials traveled the state holding meetings where grass-roots Baptists could have their say. Although most were sparsely attended, they did establish a sense of participation in the life of the denomination.[135] The convention's executive board, which set policy, always contained a mixture of bivocational and rural pastors. The more influential administration committee (which seldom contained either) at least represented a range of theological viewpoints. During the 1960s such prominent fundamentalists and conservatives as Leon Macon, Edgar M. Arendall, John Bob Riddle, Charles T. Carter, and Henry Lyon Jr. served on it. So did at least two women from the WMU and a variety of moderates.

State convention presidents tended to be less representative. Between 1,100 and 1,600 messengers tended to elect as president pastors of large urban churches (presidents during the 1960s came from Highland Avenue and First Baptist in Montgomery, Dauphin Way and First Baptist in Mobile, and Parker Memorial in Anniston). No laymen were chosen, provoking a Centerville man to suggest that more be asked to serve on committees and boards in order to give them greater visibility.[136]

Presiding over official convention life was a new generation of leaders who had been educated during the depression and who had come of age during the war. George Bagley replaced A. Hamilton Reid as the convention's executive secretary in 1963. The contest for the office was spirited, with nominees such as Herschel Hobbs, Edgar Arendall, Gilbert Guffin, Henry A. Parker, Brady Justice, Leon Macon, Howard Reaves, Harold Seever, and J. R. White. B. Locke Davis was appointed chairman of a nominating committee that unanimously recommended Norman H. McCrummen for the post. McCrummen was an honors graduate of Mercer University and Southern seminary, an air corps chaplain during the war, and president of the Baptist pastors' conference. But the executive board discovered who the nominee was to be and politicking began. At the June meeting Henry Lyon Jr. and other members suggested George E. Bagley instead. He won a two-thirds majority after several ballots when Locke Davis changed his vote to break the deadlock.[137]

Bagley was the youngest man to be elected executive secretary and was the only one to that time to have worked as a staff member of the executive board. He also served a longer tenure than any of his predecessors (1963–1983). Career-long service as an employee of the convention provided Bagley with both advantages and disadvantages. He was familiar with convention activities and procedures, but he also had a proprietary concept of his role. He constantly suggested new programs, which required ever expanding staff. Like many pastors and corporate CEOs of the era who tried to control who served on their deacon or corporate boards, Bagley tried to influence who was elected to the administration committee. He had a "take charge," "top-down" approach to administration in which decisions were made by him and administered by others.[138] But he also presided over a period of remarkable growth and tension, holding a volatile convention together.

Editorship of the *Alabama Baptist* changed hands two years after Bagley's selection. Macon died in November 1965, and the paper's board tried a series of prospective editors. They chose Hudson Baggett, a witty, down-to-earth Samford University religion professor, as the new editor in June 1966. A Cullman native and graduate of Howard College and Southern seminary who had pastored Florence First Baptist Church, he followed a path to leadership common to many in the twentieth century. He pledged to be balanced in his news coverage, to neither attack the denomination nor be its parrot. He opened the paper to a wider range of opinion and controversy and added a popular letters-to-the-editor section. His simple, noncontroversial editorials were short on substance but long on common sense and folk wisdom, reflecting his belief that most people were bothered more by "the jolts and tensions of daily existence" than by the "jots and tittles of theology."[139] An avid University of Alabama athletic fan and skilled story-teller, Baggett helped hold the denomination together. Though a theological moderate and denominational loyalist, he was counted a friend by virtually all camps in the increasingly fractured convention.

Along with crises of race, theology, and growth were more mundane challenges for the new leadership team. Chief among these was the rural church. Though Alabama's population was nearly 60 percent urban by 1970, small rural churches abounded. As late as 1970, 2,257 of the convention's 3,000 congregations were in rural areas, and they declined in numbers by only 6 percent between 1950 and 1990. Their health was partly due to an aggressive ABSC rural church program and even more to the Howard College extension system and the determined leadership by rural pastors. The administration committee created a rural church department in 1955 and made available pastoral salary supplements, building funds, and other programs. Convention staff held annual rural church conferences at Shocco Springs and regional town and country conferences at Judson College. The SBC and Home Mission Board also began to take a more active role in addressing rural church problems. Due to their help and an improving rural economy, Salem Baptist Church called its first full-time pastor in 1965, selecting him because of his interest in rural life.[140]

Typical of many such rural areas was Blount County, which was filled with small, fiercely independent churches. Few of these churches supported the Cooperative Program, but they nonetheless preserved a strong sense of fellowship and community. Once a year in October the churches pitched a tent in the county seat of Oneonta and held what was usually the largest associational meeting in the state. No one from the state convention spoke unless invited to do so by a local church. Not particularly fond of college- or seminary-educated preachers, Blount County churches also focused their mission attention on their own area. A few of the larger and more cooperative churches established Friendship Association in 1956. But the Blount Association retained three times as many churches and continued its independent ways. As late as 1988 only seven of the association's sixty-two rural churches contributed to the Cooperative Program.[141]

Urban churches had a different set of problems. Racially changing neighborhoods and urban renewal weakened congregations. Poverty, crime, delinquency, and other problems caused some downtown churches either to dissolve and sell the buildings to blacks or to move to white suburbs. Calvary Baptist, West End, Arlington, First Baptist, and Hunter Street in Birmingham, Dauphin Way in Mobile, and Goode Street Baptist in

Montgomery were early casualties of urban change. Other congregations vowed to stay, even if the price they paid was long commutes from suburbs or opening doors to blacks. Fairfield First Baptist and Southside in Jefferson County, First Baptist in Mobile, Southlawn and First Baptist in Montgomery vowed to remain downtown and minister to increasingly diverse populations. These churches were augmented by six Good Will Centers that provided services to inner-city populations.[142]

As culture wars and race conflicts heated up, Baptist concern about traditional moral crusades (dancing, alcohol, Sabbath observance) slackened. Although Leon Macon expressed his opinion that dancing should not be allowed on denominational campuses, Baptists paid less attention to such issues. By 1968 "wets" had won in only twenty-eight of the state's sixty-seven counties, but each election seemed closer. Changing urban mores soon ended prohibition in virtually all of Alabama's larger towns and cities.[143]

Macon was more sympathetic to other changes. He endorsed the trend toward rotating deacons every three or four years, but he considered the use of alcoholic beverages a disqualifying sin for deacons. More and more urban churches disagreed, following a "don't ask, don't tell" philosophy of simply not raising the issue. Radio and television broadcasts also became more common among urban congregations, extending their outreach. One form of communication Macon resisted was glossolalia. Although he conceded gifts of the spirit were authorized by the New Testament, he believed that speaking in tongues referred to foreign languages, not gibberish. He denounced its spread to main-line churches as a reaction to excessive formalism and liturgical worship.[144]

Polarization of the convention over race and theology took a frightful toll on church staffs. Congregational churches often exact fierce retribution on prophetic pastors. During times when such an innocuous sermon title as the "Good Samaritan" could be misinterpreted as the ravings of an integrationist, the normal perils of ministry increased.

Normal perils were bad enough. According to the 1960 census, the average ministerial salary in Alabama was only $3,647 a year, one of the lowest in the United States. Churches often paid as little as they believed their pastor would accept. Many pastors considered it unseemly in light of their divine calling to ask for more. Sometimes parishioners unhappy with a pastor for a variety of reasons opposed pay increases as a way to force his resignation.[145] The result was often stressful for a pastor and his family. Many "preachers' kids" and spouses resented the lack of material advantages enjoyed by church friends. Pastors often found themselves struggling

not only with an escalating load of reading, sermon preparation, endless meetings, and counseling but with increasing debts as well. Often the
stress became too great, and nervous breakdowns were common. W. Albert
Smith, who had such an experience while trying to complete seminary during the depression, assumed a personal ministry of encouragement to those
with similar problems.

Though a self-described theological conservative, Smith often referred
friends and parishioners to psychiatrists and professional counselors. He
believed that mental illness was usually caused by a family crisis or prolonged stress and that it could be treated without institutionalization. He
encouraged professional counseling for people with mental problems and
was extremely encouraging to pastor friends in such crises. Once, when a
staff member had an affair with a female member of his church, Smith advised the woman's husband to seek professional help for his coldness and
lack of affection. The man's obsession with money and his job led to the
neglect of his wife and children and had caused the affair, Smith believed.
The pastor attributed the woman's "immature crush" to her "hunger for
love and affection which was denied so long." Conversely, he described another case in which a woman had a nervous breakdown because her deacon
husband had been "caught in a morals case and she felt disgraced before
her church and society." Such sensitivity and reliance on professional
counseling was not common in the 1950s and 1960s when many pastors still
considered the need for counseling an admission of inadequate spirituality.
Smith's empathy for women was even more unusual. His voluminous
correspondence to pastor friends experiencing mental or physical problems
was a largely unknown but enormously appreciated personal ministry.[146]

Women were experiencing complex pressures in a world of shifting
gender roles and expectations. Many pastors, including Leon Macon,
thought women should not work outside the home. Nor did most Baptists believe that women should preach. When a Pinson man objected to the
election of a woman as vice-president of the SBC in 1964, Macon agreed
"that we should keep men in the leadership of our work for that was certainly the practice of Jesus in selecting his apostles."[147]

Try as men did to hold back change, Baptist women continued to push
gently (and sometimes not so gently) for new opportunities. When the state
WMU celebrated its seventy-fifth anniversary in 1964, more than 2,000
women from seventy-two of the state's seventy-six associations attended.
WMU (with 125,000 members) was affected by large numbers of women
entering the job force but managed to hold its decline to minimal numbers.
Despite numerous problems, Alabama WMU began new ministries for il-

Despite the important role that women played in the early development of associational missions when missionaries worked part-time for small salaries, the professionalization of the office marginalized them, a phenomenon common also in secular society. The three females in this photograph of associational missionaries during the 1950s/1960s reflect the declining status of women and their separate religious spheres. George E. Bagley, longtime director of the state mission board, is sitting in the front row on the right. (Courtesy of Samford University Archives)

literate adults and migrant workers and attempted new ways of relating to blacks. It also continued to provide Baptist women (both black and white) large numbers of college scholarships and sponsored an anniversary history of the organization. Hermione Jackson (wife of Southside's pastor and a trained historian with a master's degree) agreed to write the history. Jackson's history not only was scholarly sound but contributed to women's history. Where possible she carefully provided women's full names rather than calling them by their husbands' names. She wrote the book not for eighth-grade women who read "between churning buttermilk and snapping beans" but for women who were leaving the denomination because they were tired of being "preached down to or written down to."[148]

Mary Essie Stephens served as WMU's executive secretary from 1954 until 1984. A native of Dothan, Stephens was a fine student and athlete at Judson College, where she developed self-discipline by beginning each day at a 7:00 prayer and devotional session. Her kindness, gentleness, and hard work made her highly effective. Unconcerned about who received credit, she inspired loyalty and devotion from her staff. She was active in the Business and Professional Women's Club and the American Association of University Women, as well as in denominational life. Although she was offered the directorship of national WMU, she turned it down for family reasons.[149]

The decision in the 1950s to centralize WMU fund raising in return for guarantees of female representation on the executive board and administration committee continued to pay dividends for women convention staffers. In 1958 Mrs. Albert J. Smith of Monroeville, a past president of the state WMU, successfully lobbied the executive board for the inclusion of all WMU employees in a 5 percent staff salary increase. Nan Hall of Parker Memorial church, who served on the administration committee in 1965, made a similar successful motion. In December 1968 another female member made a motion to increase the housing allowance of one of the few non-WMU female convention staffers (Sunday school department worker Lillie Falkenberry) to $2,000 a year, the same as a single male's allowance. The other female member seconded the motion, but it was defeated by male members. Reorganization of the executive board in 1967 provided for five women to be elected at large to the board, no two from the same association. The reform committee also proposed changes that would combine various WMU mission offerings to eliminate duplicate bookkeeping. This and other recommendations increasingly troubled WMU staff, causing them to ask for a meeting with convention officers. They were concerned because WMU's work would be under the domination of male pastors and because the state convention never elected female officers. They feared WMU's staff would be reduced, which would further erode lay influence in the convention. Forceful WMU opposition delayed these changes until the mid-1970s.[150]

Outside WMU, Lillie Falkenberry rose highest in the male-dominated Baptist bureaucracy. Raised on a farm in Monroe County where her family read chapters of the Bible each evening, Falkenberry taught school in the fall and winter so she could attend Alabama College for Women in the summer. During her fourteen-year teaching career she felt called to Christian ministry. She volunteered in the early 1940s to serve the Bethlehem and Pine Barren Associations before either could afford a full-time associational missionary. They paid her a dollar a day, about the same salary a farm laborer received. One pastor told her she was crazy to work so hard for such low pay. But work she did, traveling the backcountry, conducting Sunday school, Baptist Training Union, and vacation Bible school conferences and teaching study courses.

John A. Davison, pastor of Selma First Baptist Church, heard about the resourceful woman and hired her as education director. For twelve years Falkenberry developed missions in Dallas County, which in time produced four new churches. She also began working with blacks at Selma University, conducting Sunday school and vacation Bible school clinics. She resigned in 1957 to attend Carver School of Missions in Louisville, where she particularly enjoyed Bible courses with Ralph Elliott before his controversial book on Genesis forced him out of the denomination.[151]

Falkenberry's social work curriculum carried her to a settlement house in a poor neighborhood of Louisville where she befriended delinquent girls. She also decided on a future ministry working with blacks, but rising racial tensions in Alabama made that goal impractical. A. Hamilton Reid offered her a job with the Sunday school department in Montgomery working with two male staffers, planning and promoting vacation Bible school clinics. After six years of this work, she concentrated on preschool and children's programs after a male was assigned VBS. She worked sixteen years, then served as a VBS consultant for New York and other states for another decade. After her retirement in Monroeville, she developed a prison ministry, visiting women jail inmates each Sunday, buying them electric fans, writing them after their transfer to Julia Tutwiler Prison, and visiting their relatives in Monroe County. She also worked with Cambodian refugees who settled in the county. Edward Warren, who worked with Falkenberry in Dallas County, considered her one of the most remarkable church starters in the state.[152]

Although Falkenberry and her cohorts were not necessarily feminists (any more than her cautious male colleagues who favored expanded rights for African Americans were liberals), they nonetheless broke new ground among Alabama Baptists. During the 1960s in the "heart of Dixie," change came by inches, not by miles.

12

Race and Politics
during the 1970s

"Enter at your own risk."

racking down the accurate version of a highly controversial event is never easy. Everyone seems to have a different memory of the incident. One version of what happened at Normandale Baptist Church traced the origin of the event to a visit by a young black woman who had lived in the Midwest before settling in Montgomery. She visited the church several times, bringing her small child to the nursery. Several deacons asked the pastor to visit the woman. He did so and reported back that she preferred Normandale because it was more like the church she had attended in the Midwest than were the city's African American congregations. Some church leaders complained that they did not care why she attended, the point was she was not wanted. Despite a return visit by the pastor to explain the attitude of the members, the black woman persisted, forcing the church to take formal action. A vote on whether African Americans could attend was scheduled for a Sunday morning service. Deacons presented a simple resolution denying church access to any minority and allowed no debate. The motion won by a narrow margin. Harold E. Martin, editor of the *Montgomery Advertiser* and a Sunday school teacher at Normandale, decided to join another church as a result of the action. Members of the convention staff who attended Normandale remained, perhaps because they approved the policy, feared for their jobs, or thought by staying they might be able to change the church's racial policy.[1]

The incident at Normandale was not widely reported, perhaps because such incidents occurred with such regularity that they were not considered newsworthy. Wherever they happened, the incidents left churches in the same condition as Normandale: lifetime relationships damaged; congregations divided. Like the denominational staff that attended Normandale, some members hunkered down and kept silent, trying to ride out the storm and repair the shattered pieces of a divided church. Others could not reconcile so egregious a violation of the Christian spirit, and they left the church. Some left the denomination as well. Still others had their say, disapproved the church's racism, but for the sake of family or place in the community learned to live with moral ambiguity.

That such disputes occurred at all was profoundly important. Whereas public schools and accommodations had come under the purview of the courts and were compelled to desegregate, a church was subject only to the moral constraints of the spirit of God and to the dictates of conscience. Controlled entirely by the Christian vision and free choice of its members, the church was tragically the last southern institution integrated (along with private clubs) and at the same time the most symbolically important because its integration resulted from choice and not compulsion. At least during the 1970s Alabama Baptists struggled over the issue. During the 1960s there had been too few prophetic voices even to hold a serious debate in most churches.

This change resulted from a variety of causes. The Southern Baptist Convention, largely silent on racial injustice, finally bestirred itself and lumbered into action. Agencies that had been active in the 1960s (the Home Mission Board, Christian Life Commission, and WMU) produced literature that dealt frankly with racial prejudice. A series of Southern Baptist conventions passed increasingly bold resolutions. Fundamentalist leaders like W. A. Criswell recanted earlier segregationist opinions.[2]

Such top-down initiatives did not sit well with many segregationists, whose opinions consisted of several parts. A few were so completely identified with political, economic, and social racism that they personally disliked blacks. But such individuals seem to have been a fringe element, making more noise than exercising influence. More common was a kind of structural blindness to racist elements of society. Having never been the object of racism themselves and knowing little about how blacks were constantly subjected to it, they took for granted what was deeply offensive to African Americans. Passive racism simply accepted the inferiority of African Americans as a people whether the cause was genetic or lack of cultural and educational opportunities.[3] These tentacles of southern culture encircled church members, perhaps here and there releasing an arm or leg but constantly struggling to hold the body within southern traditions.

Cutting cultural tentacles proved a formidable challenge everywhere in the South. "Race Relations Sunday" was not the convention's most popular special event. Controversy over the way in which denominational literature dealt with race was voted by Baptist Press as the top Baptist news story of 1971. In Macon, Georgia, and Wake Forest, North Carolina, churches fired staff whom members believed to be too integrationist. And these were liberal states compared to Alabama, where George Wallace had stirred the flames of racial discord white hot during the 1970 gubernatorial primary. In fact it was during and just after that campaign that the worst racial incidents occurred in Baptist churches.

Unlike the Normandale incident, the split at Birmingham's First Baptist Church during the summer and fall of 1970 was extensively documented by both sides, although accounts differ on the meaning of nearly every event.

Both sides agreed on some facts. From 1953 to 1968 the church had a succession of six pastors. Located in the center of town with a public housing project within walking distance, the church increasingly became a commuter congregation as members drove in from all-white suburbs. As downtown changed, the church became a white enclave within a black sea. J. Herbert Gilmore Jr., called as pastor in 1968, represented a new commitment by the church to remain downtown and minister to its neighborhood. One aspect of that ministry was hiring a social worker, Betty Bock, and beginning a tutoring program at Powell School, which was located only blocks from the church. Like the new social ministries begun by Louis Wilhite at West End about the same time, these ministries attracted the interest of black children, who began to attend church activities. An African American woman, Winifred Bryant, and her daughter Twila Fortune, together with several other black children, joined Sunday school classes, causing some white members to leave. But most accepted Bryant, and the children attended church picnics, swam with white children, and attended church events in members' homes. But when Bryant and her daughter tried to join the church, members rejected them. Conflict raged in the church from July to November. On August 27 nearly 500 members argued for eight hours and cast ten ballots on firing Gilmore and Bock (the final vote to retain them, 241 to retain and 237 to fire, occurred at 2:30 in the morning). On September 10 the church defeated by a vote of 240 to 217 a resolution to consider members without regard to race. Opponents of integration also managed to elect their own slate of deacons over those proposed by the nominating committee. Finally, on November 1, 1970, some 250 members left First Baptist to form a biracial church, the Baptist Church of the Covenant.[4]

Participants disagree about the meaning and causes of these events. During the debates and in subsequent accounts, those who sought Gilmore's resignation cited as reasons the pastor's refusal to visit elderly members, his failure to promote evangelism, lavish expenditures on new staff offices, and his "liberal and humanistic preaching which de-emphasized the Bible."[5] Gilmore denied these charges and attributed the split exclusively to race. Given the fact that Gilmore later fell out with his new congregation, personality conflicts may have played a role. But even Gilmore's opponents could never explain why, if the split was not primarily about race, controversy exploded only when blacks began to attend in 1970 during the divisive gubernatorial campaign.

Theological differences complicated the situation. Although Gilmore's opponents spread various rumors privately (the pastor opposed the free enterprise system and/or was a communist; the NAACP precipitated the controversy; Mrs. Bryant had six children by six different men), public debate focused on his theology. Critics (some of whom had attended fundamentalist Southeastern Bible College and were aligned with the First Conservative Baptist Church) claimed that Gilmore did not believe the Genesis account of creation, the flood or Jonah stories, the virgin birth of Christ, or the infallibility of the Bible. Gilmore denied these charges.[6]

Because of the prominence of First Baptist, the division included influential people on both sides. The traditional church leadership strongly backed Gilmore and included such influential figures as physician Byrn Williamson, federal judge Hobart Grooms, and Grooms's daughter (and future Birmingham city councilwoman) Angie Grooms. Opponents were led by Ollie Blan, a local attorney.

Many relationships were severed by the dispute, including some between parents and children. Some WMU leaders who helped sponsor the tutoring program that attracted blacks to the church refused to support opening its membership. Betty Bock, one casualty of the split, had a hairdresser who did not attend church but whose husband was an Associated Press photographer who had been shot at by segregationists during Birmingham's 1963 racial agony. One of the woman's customers, unaware of her friendship with Bock, began to discuss the protracted church conflict while having her hair done. In the course of the conversation, she accused Bock of being a communist. Some months later both customers happened to be in the shop at the same time when the hairdresser introduced Bock: "I want you to meet Miss Bock. I have told her you are telling everybody she is a communist." The irate customer stormed out of the shop to the hairdresser's delight. "I don't care, for I never did like her anyway."[7]

Although the *Alabama Baptist* carried a factual account of the church split and a follow-up article by Gilmore's opponents, the *Washington Post* covered the conflict more thoroughly than did the denominational paper. Hudson Baggett declined to publish an article analyzing the affair. He also published little news about the new Baptist Church of the Covenant. Baggett considered church splits, whatever the cause, to be local problems and particularly avoided those involving race. He explained his refusal as a way of protecting ministers who might have problems finding pastorates if their integrationist positions were known. He also worried that such controversies portrayed the denomination in a bad light.[8]

Baggett was not the only person the First Baptist staff felt had deserted them. The wife of one staffer grieved about the silence of local Baptist pastors and the national WMU director (whose staff included many First Baptist members). One pastor who did publicly take a stand (Otis Brooks, pastor at Vestavia Hills Baptist Church) was scolded by his own deacons for identifying the church he pastored in a letter to the *Birmingham News* supporting Gilmore and Bock.[9]

Although Birmingham First Baptist experienced the most widely publicized split over race, other churches went through similar trauma. The result for staff was often the same: Either accept segregation (perhaps with some token protest), resign, or be fired. Louis Wilhite was forced out as pastor of West End in 1972. Robert G. Wilkerson was fired by Inglenook Baptist Church in 1973. George Steincross, pastor of Montevallo First Baptist Church, was fired by a 7 to 6 vote of deacons and a 147 to 136 vote of the congregation. Rodney Ellis, campus minister at the University of Montevallo, was fired as well. Both Steincross and Ellis were dismissed for bringing black students to the church. Seventy-seven families left the church and formed University Baptist Church. Once again Baggett at first ignored the story, and when he did comment, he wrote that it was better to keep such conflicts within the church.[10] In each case, congregations insisted race was not the issue even though race clearly precipitated each crisis.

Black Belt churches were particularly vociferous about race. Historic Siloam Baptist Church lost some Judson College students when members voted to bar blacks. Shiloh Baptist Church near Selma was the home church to some one hundred fifty boys from the Sheriff's Boys Ranch at Sardis.

When federal courts ordered the ranch integrated, deacons told the administrator that the church would not allow black boys to attend. As a result the supervisor stopped bringing any of the boys. The church later ran off the pastor for what it considered his softening stance on segregation.[11]

Selma was the center for a number of such controversies. The 1965 voting rights demonstrations left the city racially divided. The federal decision to close Craig Air Force Base hurt the local economy. As Hudson Baggett wrote privately in 1977, "most of us realize that there is a good bit of racism left in Selma, as well as other parts of our dear State. Furthermore, it is quite obvious that we have not solved the race problem in our churches. In a way, it is more intense there than anywhere else."[12]

In 1975 renowned Baptist lecturer Dr. Chester Swor was invited to speak at Selma First Baptist Church. The president emeritus of Selma University, Dr. William H. Dinkins, admired Swor and came in quietly after Swor had begun speaking, got a folding chair, and sat by himself in the corner. One deacon saw him and started to the back to evict him. But the man sitting next to him restrained the man, explaining who the distinguished, elderly black Baptist minister was. Swor greeted the president emeritus warmly after the service, but the church maintained its policy of racial exclusion throughout the decade. Selmont Baptist Church in Selma refused to allow one of its air force families to bring a black child to visit from Craig Air Force Base.[13]

Fairview Baptist Church in Selma split over admitting blacks. Pastor John Hollingsworth, a native Alabamian, and 125 other members left to form Good News Baptist Church (Hollingsworth later joked that they should have named their new church "Grandview"), the only biracial Baptist congregation in Selma during the 1970s. The congregation of mainly working-class whites had only three black members, but the Selma Association refused to admit the church. As with the Birmingham First Baptist incident, opponents of Good News insisted that the real issue was theology (some claimed the church allowed pentecostal practices) and polity (the church used some non-SBC literature, contributed little to the Cooperative Program, and did not have a WMU). However, the church did record more baptisms than any other church in the association and was the fastest growing Baptist congregation. A number of the new members came from Baptist churches that refused to accept blacks, even including one Judson student from Marion. Once again Baggett chose to ignore a story that received widespread coverage in secular papers, though he later regretted not paying more attention.[14]

Wendell F. Wentz (a native of Eufaula, where his father ran a meat market) was the only pastor who left a contemporary account of one of these congregations.[15] Called to pastor Benton Baptist Church near Selma in 1970, the thirty-nine-year-old Mercer graduate found himself almost immediately immersed in controversy. He alienated many local pastors when he led the attempt to win membership for Good News Baptist Church in the Selma Association. His blue-collar opposition to country clubs and private schools did not endear him to Dallas County's white power structure, which included many Baptists. His avowed integrationist views infuriated the three leading deacons at Benton Baptist Church. They met with Wentz in December 1976 and warned him about his support of Good News Baptist. They believed admitting the church to the association would erode support for segregation in other churches as well. When Wentz asked them to consider seating blacks at Benton's services, they categorically refused. If Wentz tried to integrate the church, they vowed either to force him out as pastor or to leave themselves. They also decided to stop advertising their services in the Selma newspaper lest blacks attend. They criticized films Wentz used in Baptist Training Union, young people's literature, and the way the pastor had the congregation read Scripture. One deacon also criticized him for asking people if they were saved, arguing that the question was too personal.

Wentz blamed much of his trouble on the deacons' wives (whom he called the "bridge club"). In his opinion, they really ran the church. In May 1977, deeply in debt and still under fire, Wentz left Dallas County for the more racially hospitable climate of southwestern Missouri.[16]

How many resignations, firings, retirements, and moves resulted from racial confrontations will never be known. But four in Dallas County alone suggest the number was much larger than anyone realized at the time. That such racial attitudes existed among many Alabama Baptists is well documented in their own words.

Integration crises at Birmingham First Baptist generated several revealing letters. James Swedenburg (the longtime secretary of the Alabama Temperance Alliance whom Governor Wallace had appointed head of the Alabama Educational Television Commission) criticized Baptist leaders who challenged the morality of segregated churches. During the dispute at First Baptist, Swedenburg advised denominational leaders who criticized segregation to mind their own business, and he deplored newspaper coverage that made the church a "whipping post." The man beloved among Baptists as "Brother Jim" was in many ways a product of his time and culture. Born into a poor family in Millport, Swedenburg had pastored twenty-four different churches during his long career. A graduate of Howard College and the University of Alabama, he had also served as superintendent of Pickens County schools. In a traditionalist moral world defined largely by his rural upbringing, sin still consisted mainly of dancing, drinking, gambling, and sexual excesses.[17]

It did not occur to Swedenburg that sin might also encompass attitudes such as those expressed by a member of West End Baptist Church in Tuscaloosa. The layman condemned the *Alabama Baptist* for publishing articles favoring racial integration. Billy Graham, he believed, had begun this "hog wash" by claiming that heaven had no color line. The denominational paper had abetted this "brain wash," as had various Baptist centers across the state where Negroes and whites worked side by side. He knew his demand for rigid segregation would result in criticism but did not care: "Well, I am a white racist and am proud of it and make no apologies to anyone."[18]

Other correspondents blamed the National Council of Churches or their own denomination for integration. A woman correspondent believed the NCC was procommunist. A Sheffield layman denounced the SBC for allowing "black militants" to appear at the 1970 convention. A laywoman disputed an article in the *Alabama Baptist* that contended Jesus' trip through Samaria was a biblical precedent for integration. Race mixing was a sin, she wrote, because God had made the races separate. Lafitte Baptist Church in Saraland objected to inviting civil rights leader and Baptist preacher Andrew Young to the 1977 SBC because he was a spokesman for the theological and political "far left." When Montgomery First Baptist pastor J. R. White commented on the first of four Sunday school lessons dealing with race relations, a letter writer accused the series of being communistic, like so much other SBC literature. A layman from Talladega opposed deleting the word "southern" from the denomination's name. He placed this issue within the context of a world where white students were not allowed to wave the Confederate flag or sing "Dixie" and where the NAACP and federal courts controlled hiring of Alabama state troopers. A layman from Scottsboro denounced school busing to achieve integration and criticized "a kind of intellectual church hierarchy" for assuming the authority to speak on behalf of ordinary lay people. Even the usually noncommittal Hudson Baggett publicly opposed busing of children to achieve integration.[19]

Race contributed to another significant denominational problem, the rapid demise of urban congregations. The fate of Birmingham First Baptist and West End was common to many urban churches. A committee of the Birmingham Baptist Association revealed some deeply troubling statistics. By 1971, twenty-two of thirty-eight downtown congregations belonging to the association had significant declines of resident members from their twenty-year highs (declines of more than 20 percent). In seven cases, the decline was more than half the membership. These declining congregations included some of the most influential Baptist churches in Alabama: Central Park, Fairfield, Birmingham First Baptist (which had lost 64 percent of its 1951 total), Southside (which had lost 68 percent), West End, and Woodlawn. Nine Baptist churches had closed by 1974. Conversely, suburban church membership boomed during the same two decades (Center Point from 280 to 2,219, Dawson Memorial from 1,044 to 3,719, Gardendale from 425 to 1,420, Mountain Brook from 226 to 1,345, Ridgecrest from 375 to 2,226, Shades Mountain from 206 to 2,070, Westwood from 166 to 850).[20]

Other Alabama cities experienced similar problems. Toulminville Baptist Church in Mobile moved when membership dipped from 1,100 to 300 in a racially changing neighborhood. Dauphin Way was not far behind. By 1977 only two white Baptist churches remained in the western quarter of Montgomery.[21]

The state convention as well as local associations desperately sought ways to stabilize declining inner-city churches. The 1972 administration committee debated a report about the needs of churches in changing communities. Identifying thirty-eight such churches in Birmingham alone, it established a pilot project at West End. The convention also held annual conferences on the subject at Shocco Springs. The Home Mission Board placed one of six projects in Birmingham. It matched three inner-city churches (Arlington, South Park, and Parkview) with prospering suburban congregations. The Birmingham Association also created an inner-city committee to study the problem.[22]

Remedial strategies focused on various kinds of social ministries. The Montgomery Association, state convention, area National Baptist churches, and the HMB sponsored a biracial Baptist Fellowship Center in downtown Montgomery directed by a black Baptist minister and sociology professor at Alabama State University. Arlington Baptist Church in Birmingham operated a mobile missions van that distributed hot meals and medicine. Parkview Baptist Church, located in the shadow of Legion Field, began special programs for single mothers and divorcées (90 percent of children in the church lived in broken homes) and the elderly. The church was paired with suburban Shades Mountain Baptist.[23]

Birmingham Association's committee on urban churches in transition, created in 1972, was one of the most prophetic regarding social ministries. Chaired by Louis Wilhite and including Dotson Nelson (Mountain Brook Baptist), Lamar Jackson (Southside), Gaines Dobbins (retired seminary professor and longtime advocate of social Christianity), Oley Kidd (who was equally committed to inner-city social ministries), as well as others, the committee proposed a bold strategy. Betty Bock contributed an important position paper to the deliberations. Committee recommendations came straight out of the social gospel: escort services for the elderly; food co-op warehouses; interracial ministries. Bock's report deplored the artificial divisions between evangelism and social ministries. She also urged Baptists to help form community organizations, increase cooperation with community action agencies, and become more involved in changing the political and economic structures that resulted in many of Birmingham's problems. The entire committee emphasized that suburban churches would have to become more involved in helping inner-city churches through counseling, staff, and finances.[24] None of these things happened to any considerable extent, and the three pilot churches—Arlington, South Park, and Parkview—were soon either defunct or all black.

Some urban churches found traditional ways of coping with racially changing neighborhoods. In Huntsville, Highlands Baptist Church became the most racially mixed SBC congregation in Alabama through an active bus ministry rather than social ministries. The congregation's fundamentalist white minister hired a black associate pastor to conduct Sunday school and worship at a nearby public housing project. By 1977 about one-third of the congregation's 775 members were black.

The pattern in Montgomery was quite different. A minister fired by Fairview Baptist Church in Selma because of his racial views became pastor of Trinity Baptist Church near Maxwell Air Force Base in 1978. The church had an interesting history. In 1975 Westgate Baptist Church, located two miles from Trinity in a racially mixed neighborhood, refused to integrate. The split congregation decided to dissolve and deeded its property to the Montgomery Association. Trinity began Westside Mission in the old Westgate Baptist Church building. The state convention helped Trinity hire Milton Boyd, a black retired air force officer, to head the mission. Trinity helped Westside become a full-fledged church, the first recorded effort in recent history of a white church sponsoring a black mission. During its transition to church status, the mission sponsored a black Royal Ambassador chapter for boys that became the first African American chapter in the ABSC. In 1977 Trinity voted to open its doors to black members, causing forty members to leave within three months of the decision. But eighty new members joined (only one of them black) during the same time.[25]

Eastdale Baptist Church in Montgomery followed a less democratic but equally successful course to integration. The crisis began innocently

Westside Baptist Mission began as a racially integrated church in a predominantly African American section of west Montgomery during the late 1970s. (Courtesy of Samford University Archives)

enough in a vacation Bible school promotion in a racially mixed neighborhood. Three black children responded to the invitation. The pastor and assistant pastor, Perry Neal and Steve Sullivan, decided it would be hypocritical to turn away children attracted by their own advertising. Several deacons had different ideas. They told Neal to send the black children home, a request that the pastor ignored. The deacons then demanded a church vote on open admission. Neal replied that Jesus died for all men, including blacks, that the church was the body of Christ, that the body of Christ was not just a white body, and all that was a fact not requiring a vote by Eastdale Baptist Church. The discontented deacons left for another congregation, and the black children attended VBS at Eastdale.[26]

Vestavia Hills Baptist Church (which had many national WMU staffers and Samford University faculty as members) admitted its first black member in the 1970s when a Samford University couple who belonged to the church brought a Nigerian pharmacy student with them to church. After some debate, the church decided to open its doors. The church's pastor, Otis Brooks, was also one of the few local Baptist ministers to support publicly the beleaguered staff of Birmingham First Baptist and Louis Wilhite at West End.

During the 1970s, an increasing number of Baptist ministers took similar stands. Retired Southern seminary professor Gaines S. Dobbins attacked segregation in a series of articles he wrote for the *Alabama Baptist.* Evangelist Leslie Woodham of Clayton preached to one segregated congregation and one integrated church in 1971. He wrote that white Christians must realize the contradiction in demanding that blacks accept treatment as second-class citizens while also proclaiming that God loved them. Racism and its by-products, he wrote, constituted "our most pressing spiritual, moral, and social problem."[27]

Abe G. Watson, pastor of Brewton First Baptist Church, preached sermon after sermon during the 1970s on interracial understanding and the need for tolerance and moderation. Extremism in either religion or politics, he told his congregation in 1970, resulted from irrational fears and oversimplification. Such an atmosphere led to violence, coercion, and the intimidation of dissidents. In the face of groups that branded Protestant clergy as communists without evidence, Christians should insist on tolerance, fairness, and love. He opposed violence but also the silence that allowed extremists to "run over innocent people." Many men who had prophetically proclaimed the gospel had been considered troublemakers, he reminded his congregation in another 1970 sermon. He used a Broadway play (*The Deputy,* which dealt with the silence of the German church during the rise of Hitler) and a movie (*A Man for All Seasons,* which based its story on England's Reformation martyr, Sir Thomas More) to argue that church members should be more concerned about God's opinion of them than about the status they had in private clubs, congregations, or among their friends.[28]

Convention leadership was not outspoken but cautiously began to facilitate better race relations. In March 1970 the administration committee voted to allow the state Baptist assembly at Shocco Springs to be used for joint meetings of black and white Baptists. Staffer Mac Johnson and committee member Dotson Nelson proposed that African American boys who were members of ABSC Royal Ambassador chapters be allowed to participate in all Shocco Springs activities. At its July meeting, Vernon St. John proposed that the executive board endorse public schools and discourage private schools created by churches merely to avoid integration. Although the motion was tabled, it won strong support. The department of special missions under H. O. Hester sponsored a biracial annual human relations conference in May at Shocco Springs, provided scholarships to National Baptist ministerial students, worked with churches in changing urban communities, and tried to increase SBC/National Baptist cooperation. After his retirement in 1977, Hester received an award from the SBC for his exemplary contributions to racial reconciliation (honoring men who "have been called nigger lovers"). The administration committee also approved changing the Judson College charter in 1973, declaring the school open to women of any race. The Howard College Extension Division opened to blacks in 1968 and enrolled 115 African American students by the 1973–1974 term.[29]

State convention programs also began to feature black speakers. In 1973 at the 150th anniversary celebration of the founding of the ABSC, the black pastor of Salem church in Greensboro (where the convention had begun in 1823) spoke. Three years later five thousand black and white Baptists attended the special U.S. bicentennial session of the convention. This historic meeting at the Birmingham–Jefferson County Civic Center momentarily brought together the ABSC with four black Alabama Baptist conventions that had split from the white convention after the Civil War. One of the speakers at that convention, Birmingham Baptist preacher and Republican U.S. congressman John H. Buchanan Jr., praised Democrat president-elect Jimmy Carter as a born-again Christian who had helped form an integrated church in Plains, Georgia. He urged the ABSC to be equally bold in its outreach.[30]

A joint effort in 1974 by black and white Baptists (supported financially by the Home Mission Board) resulted in creation of the Inter-Baptist Fellowship Committee and Human Relations Conference. Led by a black minister and headquartered in Birmingham, the fellowship was designed to plan such projects as the 1976 joint conventions, foster cooperation between white and black churches in transitional neighborhoods, distribute disaster relief, and produce a newsletter called "Crossing Barriers." It sponsored integrated meetings at Cook Springs, the Birmingham Baptist Association camp, and developed materials and provided resource persons for Human Relations Sunday. It also developed biracial teams for the statewide, biracial revival, "Good News, Alabama." It became the formal link between the ABSC and the state's four African American Baptist conventions.[31]

Culture Wars

No single subject demonstrates how dramatically Baptists were changing than the rapidly escalating culture wars of the 1970s. Issues that had

The biracial teams for a 1977–79 statewide Baptist revival called "Good News, Alabama" were developed by the Inter-Baptist Fellowship Committee, an integrated
leadership initiative begun in Birmingham in 1974. Many of the whites in this photograph (Camilla Lowry, Frank Wells, Earl Potts, Dotson Nelson) played key roles
in the moderate Cooperative Baptist Fellowship during the 1990s. (Courtesy of
Samford University Archives)

dominated Baptist attention for a century and a half (alcoholic beverages,
dancing, gambling, Sunday closing laws) received less and less attention.
Issues that had received little attention (movie and television program-
ming, abortion, human sexuality, homosexuality, sex education, feminism)
received dramatically increased attention.

This shift reflected profound changes in American culture. Increasing
secularization of all aspects of society made many evangelical Christians
feel like aliens in their own land. To some degree, the extent of their alienation depended on the subculture to which they belonged. Many rural and
small-town churches still considered even moderate drinking to be a grave
matter. But affluent suburban churches, even fundamentalist ones, often
dropped the moderate use of alcohol from status of a religious felony to that
of misdemeanor. Except for a few small towns, urban and suburban Bap-

tists were not willing to go to war about K-Marts opening on Sunday
or their children attending dances. Gambling was more of a concern, but
members began to split even on this issue. Although few Baptists actually
endorsed legalized gambling, some members pointed to an obvious inconsistency in the denominational position. For decades the *Alabama Baptist*
had endorsed tax increases to support adequately the state's prisons, mental hospitals, and public schools. Just as regularly, antitax groups and reluctant voters had defeated such increases. If Baptist voters resisted new
taxes for such worthy projects, then some Baptists decided that perhaps
revenue from gambling was less an issue than the suffering of people condemned to poor schools or scandalously inadequate mental hospitals and
prisons. Dr. William D. Geer, a Baptist layman and dean of Samford University's school of business, wrote an article in 1972 on the economics of
dog racing. Believing that Baptists should not only oppose gambling but
should advocate alternatives to it as well, Geer proposed a four-mill property tax increase to fund a new cancer hospital, mental health facility, and
civic center for Jefferson County.[32]

Although Baptists were criticized for negative moral positions rather
than for advocating positive alternatives, the criticism often came from citizens who merely belonged to a different and competing subculture. Sophisticated, educated urbanites who resented Baptist attitudes on drinking, movie and television censorship, Sunday closing laws, women's rights,
or abortion represented no less a discrete subculture than the people they
criticized. And Baptists were not of one opinion on any of these issues
either, reflecting the multiple subcultures that produced them. As Baptists
became increasingly well educated and affluent, they were also likely to become more tolerant. Thus strains within the state convention, like mounting tensions within society, owed much to the diversity and pluralism of
American life during this decade.

Part of the 1970s culture wars involved public schools. Integration
and the rise of church-sponsored private schools eroded white support for
public education. As made clear by Vernon St. John's resolution condemning Baptist schools created to thwart desegregation, many denominational
leaders took no pride in this development. Early in 1970 a group of ten religious leaders, including George Bagley, adopted a resolution supporting public schools. Given the number of letters written in opposition to
Bagley's role in the statement and to school integration, it is obvious that
Baptist support for public education was flagging. Supreme Court rulings
on prayer and Bible reading further undermined confidence, as did the continuing teaching of evolution and the use of objectionable textbooks. The

1973 state convention approved a resolution calling for teaching the biblical view of creation as well as evolutionary theory. Hudson Baggett opposed a prolonged battle with science teachers over the subject, noting that creationism could be taught more effectively in homes and churches by people who believed in it than in schools by teachers who did not. He also opposed a constitutional amendment allowing nondenominational prayer, arguing that the courts had not banned voluntary prayer. But many Baptists disagreed with him on both issues.[33]

Disagreements over other issues were equally fierce. A new soap opera offended many Baptists, as did a variety of 1970s movies and music. When Oklahoma evangelist Sam Cathey told the 1977 ABSC that Elvis Presley was in hell, readers of the *Alabama Baptist* responded with angry letters, and teenagers complained that attacks on mod fashions and music were a product of the denomination's narrow-mindedness. But many others agreed with Cathey's attacks on television content and popular music.[34]

Never before had Baptists exerted so much denominational energy debating intensely personal and family issues. Topics such as human sexuality, in-vitro fertilization, abortion, and homosexuality either appeared for the first time in the *Alabama Baptist* or received extensive discussion. Broader issues such as marriage, divorce, and the role of women in church and society also received unprecedented coverage.

Entire series of articles in the *Alabama Baptist* dealt with marriage and the family. Divorce (which earlier had been treated as a problem that only occasionally affected Baptists directly) became a primary concern of the church. Denomination-sponsored family life conferences and the Christian Life Commission deplored the denomination's lack of such a ministry. Vestavia Hills Baptist Church sponsored a seminar for divorced persons in 1977, with workshops on legal, financial, and personal aspects of divorce. Church members who were psychiatrists, counselors, lawyers, stockbrokers, college professors, and ministers staffed the workshops. Hudson Baggett publicized Alabama's above-average divorce rate, noting that white Protestants divorced at a higher rate in Alabama than any other group. He pleaded for Baptists to be more tolerant and not to "shoot their own wounded." A divorced woman praised his editorial, commenting that "God never lets us down, [but] churches often do." Hurtful and judgmental attitudes, she warned, were driving many divorced persons out of the denomination.[35]

Divorce ceased to be an abstraction to the denomination in 1974 when the campus minister at the University of Alabama in Birmingham and his wife ended their marriage. The convention's executive board fired the minister even though its personnel committee conceded that neither had engaged in immoral conduct. Board member Bob Curlee, a Birmingham pastor, moved that the minister be reinstated; he argued that the denomination's credibility with the university community would be damaged. Firing a convention employee because of divorce also set an unfortunate precedent. A number of ministers opposed Curlee's motion, arguing that the Bible prevented ministers from divorcing regardless of circumstances. Curlee finally withdrew his motion for lack of support.[36]

Curlee's prediction about the reaction of Birmingham's university community could not have been more accurate. Two other Birmingham-area campus ministers resigned in protest. The divorced minister's home church passed a resolution of support. Birmingham-area Baptist students protested the firing as did the state BSU president.[37]

Human sexuality was an even more sensitive issue and one long ignored by Southern Baptists. The trend toward later marriages, the introduction of the birth control pill, increased rates of premarital sex, teenage pregnancy, and illegitimacy all demanded some response. Training Union and Sunday school literature began cautiously to address these issues. But what seemed cautious to persons from an urban, middle-class Baptist subculture often seemed libertine to rural or small-town Baptists. Few issues (including racial integration of churches) stirred more furor than a 1970 series of Training Union materials on sexuality. A resolution from the Malvern Baptist Church in Slocomb began the onslaught. The church found the materials inappropriate for "mixed unions" and offensive to adults. The Pleasant Grove Baptist Church in Moulton discontinued the use of Southern Baptist literature over the issue and urged SBC action "to rid ourselves of this insidious 'enemy from within.' " The Liberty Baptist Church in Tallassee agreed, as did Robinwood Station Baptist Church, Cedar Hill church in Jasper, Mount Hebron West in the Elmore Association, and many others. Several churches and many teenagers endorsed the literature, provoking a full-fledged denominational fight.[38]

An SBC Christian Life Commission (CLC) meeting that same year exacerbated the conflict. Sponsors of the seminar invited Episcopal priest and ethicist Joseph Fletcher to speak, and he discussed such topics as *Playboy* magazine and situational ethics. The Birmingham Baptist pastors' conference denounced the seminar, as did many individual ministers. Gene Walley, pastor at Thomaston Baptist Church, proposed that funding for the commission and the Home Mission Board be terminated: "Too long I have sat smouldering inside concerning the trends and issues of our day in the convention. How long before 'grass roots' gets all it can stand and begins to rise up?" As it turned out, the answer to his question was, "not long." A torrent of criticism poured from Alabama Baptist churches and pastors.[39]

Not all Baptists agreed. The pastor at Vernon First Baptist Church, who had attended the controversial seminar, praised it. So did Otis Brooks, pastor of Vestavia Hills Baptist Church. Had the seminar's critics forgotten, Brooks questioned, that Christ was not threatened by the company of harlots, traitors, and pagan philosophers? "Our present defensiveness and spiritual insecurity," he wrote, "may mean that we are not keeping company with our Lord."[40]

A follow-up CLC seminar in 1975 focused on family issues and met at Birmingham First Baptist Church. One speaker attributed the increase in abortions partly to evangelicals who blocked sex education. Abortions also resulted from unwanted pregnancies by married women who could not afford more children. Hudson Baggett gingerly weighed into the dispute, admitting that conflicts over money and sex did create marital disharmony and often required professional counseling. Baptists, he admonished, needed to avoid attitudes that produced guilt and anxiety. Divorce might be a bad solution, he wrote, but remaining together in a loveless or abusive marriage "may be worse and the cost may be higher." Churches should help couples remain together if possible. If not, they should help divorced persons adjust as best they could. Issues such as in-vitro fertilization ("test-tube babies"), Baggett warned, were fraught with moral dangers but also offered hope to childless couples. People were increasingly tempted to play God. "What is morally and legally correct," he concluded, "becomes more difficult to decide."[41]

No better example of this moral ambiguity existed than abortion. Although the denomination later treated the issue as if Baptists had historically maintained an antiabortion position, that was not the case. Leon Macon had written in 1955 that life began with the birth of a baby, but the first specific reference to abortion in the *Alabama Baptist* occurred in the April 30, 1970, issue. The first reference was to a poll that revealed three-fourths of Baptist leaders surveyed opposed legalized abortions, a much higher percentage than for the general U.S. population. When asked if they favored permitting abortions to protect the mental and physical health of the mother, Baptist opinions shifted dramatically. Seventy percent of pastors and 78 percent of Sunday school teachers would allow abortions in such cases. In cases involving pregnancies that resulted from rape or incest, 71 percent of pastors and 77 percent of Sunday school teachers would allow abortions. Nearly the same percentages agreed to abortions in cases of fetal deformity.[42]

The 1973 Supreme Court ruling *Roe v. Wade*, which declared abortion to be legal, created surprisingly little reaction compared to the 1970 sex education flap. Other than a resolution opposing the legalization of abortion drafted by the WMU at Jacksonville First Baptist Church, there was little reaction. A 1974 *Alabama Baptist* series on sanctity of life issues included abortion among discussions of euthanasia and capital punishment. The essay on abortion contended that the Bible said nothing directly about induced abortion, although it did contain brief mention of spontaneous abortion or miscarriage. The principle of sanctity of life applied nonetheless. Fetuses had rights, and guilt and depression often accompanied abortion. But the author also noted that the biblical penalty for murder was more harsh than the one for causing the death of a fetus, suggesting that the issues were of different magnitude. Induced abortion, though never morally right, "under certain circumstances . . . might carry fewer tragic, painful consequences than other possible courses of action. All possibilities should be carefully weighed and judged in the light of the best spiritual and medical counsel available." The author believed that abortion was the toughest ethical issue facing the Christian church.[43]

The 1976 SBC agreed. Messengers defeated two antiabortion amendments before passing a compromise affirming the limit of government's role in abortion. It also affirmed a mother's right to a full range of medical services and affirmed the biblical concept of the sanctity of life. During the ensuing presidential campaign between Gerald Ford and Jimmy Carter, Hudson Baggett deplored the use of abortion as a campaign issue, writing that politicians were trying to "state a complex issue in simple terms." The Bible taught reverence for life and opposed taking life for any reason. But "who would be against abortion if it meant saving the life of a wife, sister, or daughter? Abortion for medical reasons, should be considered."[44]

Homosexuality was a less ambiguous issue. Like abortion, virtually nothing had appeared about this issue in the *Alabama Baptist,* nor had it been discussed in Baptist literature. But the same 1976 Southern Baptist Convention that waffled on abortion passed the first resolution enacted by Baptists condemning homosexuality. Messengers even deleted a phrase expressing compassion for homosexuals.[45]

The roles of traditional Baptist women (who advocated neither abortion nor homosexuality) proved just as divisive an issue in the emerging culture wars. Other states moved much more quickly than Alabama to address women's issues. A Baptist church in Durham, North Carolina, had ordained a woman to pastor an American Baptist church in 1964. A South Carolina congregation ordained a woman as chaplain at the state hospital

in 1971. The following year a Virginia woman was ordained as chaplain of
the state industrial farm for women. Other churches in North Carolina and
Virginia took similar actions in 1973. The Metropolitan Baptist Association
(SBC) in New York City accepted a black Baptist church that had a female
pastor in 1972, giving the SBC its first woman pastor. The following year
Deacon magazine carried an article acknowledging that Southern Baptist churches had ordained women as deacons since the 1920s. A professor
at Southern seminary wrote that the biblical evidence for women deacons
could be used to bolster either side of the dispute. By 1976, Virginia Baptist
churches alone had ordained more than 500 women deacons. Their numbers by the end of the decade numbered in the thousands, though they were
mostly clustered in Virginia, Kentucky, North Carolina, and Texas (these
states also accounted for nearly half of all ordained Baptist women clergy
and half the churches and institutions employing them).[46]

Many SBC agencies cautiously joined the debate. In 1974 the Christian Life Commission proposed that the SBC set aside one-fifth of all board,
agency, and committee positions for women. Instead, the 1973 SBC passed
a resolution proposed by the wife of a Texas pastor, attacking the women's
liberation movement and affirming that woman was made for man and that
they were mutually dependent on each other. The 1974 SBC even tabled a
resolution affirming "the Bible's teaching that every individual has infinite
worth and that, in Christ, there is neither male nor female." The following year the national president of WMU announced that she respected the
right of women to seek ordination as pastors and that such a call was a
personal matter between God and a woman. In 1978 the denomination
sponsored the first Consultation on Women in Church-Related Vocations,
and that same year was the peak for female representation on convention
boards and agencies. By 1991 there were more than 800 ordained Southern
Baptist women ministers but only 38 who served as local church pastors.
In fact, more women had served on SBC local church staffs during the
1940s and 1950s than did so in the 1990s.[47]

WMU became increasingly concerned about opposition to women in
ministry. Carolyn Weatherford became executive director of WMU/SBC in
the 1970s. Although a native Floridian with degrees from Florida State University and New Orleans Baptist Theological Seminary, she had worked
in Alabama as director of Young Woman's Auxiliary and been trained in
WMU work by Mary Essie Stephens. She also attended Vestavia Hills Baptist Church, one of the more supportive congregations for women in the
Birmingham area. In 1978 Weatherford denounced "the manipulation and
self-deceit of the 'Total Woman,' " a book that accepted a subordinate role

Catherine B. Allen (left) and Earl Potts attended the controversial 1978 "Consultation on Women in Church-Related Vocations" conference in Nashville. The conference helped reveal the deep split among Southern Baptists on gender issues. Allen was an influential executive with WMU/SBC based in Birmingham, and Potts was on the staff of the Alabama Baptist State Board of Missions. (Courtesy of Samford University Archives)

for Christian women but also recommended ways women could use their sexuality to manipulate men. Weatherford did not consider the book to offer a Christian approach to relations between the sexes (prompting one Alabama Baptist woman to insist that Weatherford could not understand the book because she was single). Weatherford did acknowledge that women who assumed leadership roles in churches usually received more criticism from other women than from men. She not only urged a broader role for women in the SBC (only 114 women were among 1,053 members of denominational boards and agencies) but also noted that only 14 percent of divorced women received alimony, 44 percent of divorced mothers received child support, and 58 percent of men arrested for forcible rape were not prosecuted. Many Alabama Baptists responded negatively to Weatherford's speeches and articles.[48]

Catherine B. Allen, another WMU executive from Birmingham, received similar criticism as chairperson for the 1978 Consultation on Women in Church-Related Vocations. Although SBC agency heads pledged greater sensitivity to the professional needs of women for equal pay and respect, one participant insisted that "when Eve misbehaved in the Garden she showed that women have an inherent weakness that is built into woman-hood." He accused the WMU of bringing the women's movement into the SBC by encroaching on male prerogatives within the church. Earl Potts, a member of the state convention staff, attended the consultation with his daughter Libby, who had joined the staff of Woodlawn Baptist Church after seminary. Although he disagreed with some of the more vociferous advo-cates of ordaining women, Potts supported individual women who sought ordination, as well as the churches that ordained them.[49]

In Alabama the continued leadership of WMU by articulate women such as Hermione Jackson (Southside Baptist Church) and Camilla Lowry (Auburn First Baptist), combined with the presence of national headquar-ters in Birmingham, gave the woman's mission organization a particularly prominent place in the culture wars. The 1972 state convention for the first time in ABSC history elected a woman (Miriam Jackson, dean of women at Jacksonville State University, a Howard College graduate, and the widow of a Baptist pastor) vice-president. Although Jackson hoped her election was not interpreted as a victory for "women's lib," Hudson Baggett used the occasion to speculate on why no women had been elected before. He did not agree with everything "women's lib" advocated, but neither did he agree with those who proposed to "keep women in their place" by quoting biblical passages written "in a man's world" where women were consid-ered property. Jesus never discriminated against women. Baggett endorsed more women on SBC boards but rejected the CLC's call for a quota sys-tem.[50]

Not even racial integration drew as much fire during the 1970s as the shifting roles of women. Every incident created a controversy. Opposition to ordaining women as deacons or ministers drew most opposition, much of it from women. The pastor of the Mount Hope Baptist Church in Crane Hill cited passages from Corinthians and Timothy to deny that women had a right to exercise authority over churches. This assertion would of-fend some women "who need a recognition of their professional status as a boost to their ego," he wrote, but it was biblical nonetheless. Ed P. Wallen of Hueytown rejoiced at this "grass-roots" opposition to the ordination of women because the real issue was "denial of the authority of the Bible." Most congregations reacted like the one in which Mary Anne Forehand grew up, which refused to ordain her when she was called to pastor a Washington, D.C., church.[51]

The Equal Rights Amendment created additional conflict. Although Hudson Baggett approved many goals of ERA (upgrading the status of women, greater employment opportunities, equal pay for equal work), he questioned whether the amendment would improve treatment for women. A Columbiana woman called ERA an attack on marriage and the church. She believed that passage would open rest rooms and jail cells to both sexes. Another woman, who identified herself as the chairman of the Franklin County "Stop E.R.A.," denounced Baggett for using "Ms." as a prefix for women's names in the *Alabama Baptist* because the abbreviation had been "invented by the female liberalists movement" to help pass ERA. Use "Mrs.," she berated the editor, because single girls should aspire to marry. The 1977 executive board attacked ERA, the National Organization of Women, lesbianism, federal child development programs, and the International Women's Year (which members called the "Federal Festival for Female Radicals Financed with Your Money"). The state's Christian Life and Public Affairs Commission took up ERA in May 1978, dealing with a resolution critical of the measure passed by the previous year's ABSC. The chairman distributed a statement by Olivia Byrd opposing the amendment and allowed laywoman Sue H. McInnish to speak in favor of it. Citing conservative columnist James Kilpatrick and Republican North Carolina senator Jesse Helms, Byrd argued that ERA was a moral, not a legal or political issue. The amendment was an attempt to create a unisex society, to promote lesbianism, abortion on demand, and federally funded child care centers, and to undermine the home. She criticized articles in the *Alabama Baptist,* chided Carolyn Weatherford for her attacks on "the Total Woman," and said ERA really stood for "Exceedingly Radical Amendment." McInnish denied Byrd's charges and explained ERA as an extension of Christian beliefs in fairness and justice. The commission was deeply divided and decided to take no action. A member of the convention staff wrote the CLC/SBC for some objective information on the "explosive issue." Other than a report that many anti-ERA leaders were associated with conservative Republican activist Phyllis Schlafly, he received little help.[52]

Other women endorsed ordination of females. Citing scriptural references to women who served as prophetesses and deacons, they argued that the Bible supported their cause. Some attributed opposition to male insecurity. One woman charged that opponents picked and chose their proof texts, conveniently excluding Galatians 3:28, which proclaimed that in Christ there were no distinctions against women because of their sex.[53]

Some men expressed support as well. Otis Brooks, Carolyn Weatherford's pastor at Vestavia Hills Baptist Church, believed there was scriptural authority for women deacons. A layman from a rural church near Billingsley expressed a folksy defense. He wrote that he was tired of women being "hammerbacked." "I think if a woman feels like preaching, she should preach. It's no more harm for a woman to preach than it is for her to teach a Sunday School class." He listened to a woman preacher each Sunday on a Clanton radio station, "and she's a real preacher guided by the Lord." Male preachers were unwilling to serve rural churches; so when a country church declined to twelve or fourteen members, he advised the male preacher to pack his bags, move, and give a woman a chance.[54]

Ruby Welsh Wilkins followed his advice. She entered the debate over women preachers in 1973, carefully detailing the biblical contributions of women. She received severe criticism for her efforts. One woman admonished that if "women would stay home doing for their families and neighborhoods instead of trying to get more worldly recognition and intellectual learning they could . . . do more for the spiritual Kingdom of God."[55]

Worldly recognition was hardly the object of Ruby Welsh Wilkins's preaching. She was trying to save her rural congregation, Antioch Baptist Church near Wadley. When she arrived in the community as a bride in the 1940s, the historic church was down to two resident members, a widow and her daughter. She helped Antioch conduct a vacation Bible school, assisted rebuilding the church in a new location after it burned, and felt a distinct call to preach in 1948. Neither her husband nor pastor understood, but her father, a Baptist deacon, supported her. She received more important support from God: "The Lord . . . walked the way with me. He stilled my spirit and sat me down at the feet of the Holy Spirit, who opened the wonders of the Word. I fed hungrily, searching for answers to myriad theological questions and for scriptural support of my calling." She concluded that Baptists were sound in their doctrine of the personhood of Jesus Christ but unsound in church practice.

For a dozen years, Wilkins taught Sunday school, vacation Bible school, and study courses, cooked Sunday dinner for preachers, and saw a steady stream of pastors come and go at Antioch Church. She finally left Antioch and the denomination for a more congenial church and began to publish a monthly paper as an outlet for her calling. Then in 1970 some members of Antioch asked her to return. Yet another pastor had resigned, so she returned to teach Sunday school. The church licensed her to preach, which resulted in its exclusion from the Tallapoosa Baptist Association. Nor would any pastor participate in her ordination.

For the next few years, the church prospered. Members reworked the basement, installed new lights, replaced windows and pews, and had services each Sunday morning. Wilkins preached a revival, baptized new converts (including her son), and performed funerals. As a bivocational minister, she continued to work full-time as a machine operator at a sewing mill in Wadley, and she kept house for her husband and children. One male, a follower of Baptist fundamentalist John R. Rice, "dumped women preachers into the same pot with 'bobbed-hair hussies' and 'bossy wives' " and left. His family's departure, together with the escalating fundamentalist battle in the SBC, created divisions at Antioch. Membership fell from twenty-four resident members to only four or five, and Wilkins's husband developed Alzheimer's disease. The stress of caring for him led to her resignation as pastor in 1985. An independent Baptist preacher had persuaded the fundamentalist family to return, and they briefly conducted services before giving up the effort to reconstitute Antioch as a fundamentalist congregation. As a result, Wilkins and her son began services again, completing the cycle that had started when she arrived as a bride in the 1940s. Widow and daughter had kept the church alive then; widow and son kept it alive in the 1980s. As a child of the depression, Wilkins had never been able to attend college, so she enrolled at Southern Union Community College, from which she graduated with a perfect 4.0 academic average at age seventy-two. Despite considerable ridicule, she and her son (the only remaining resident members) kept up the church and grounds into the 1990s. As Wilkins explained simply: "I can't believe that God is finished with Antioch. Nadir may yet widen to apogee; the phoenix may rise again. However that may be, we shall continue our labor of love."[56]

Grace Philpot Nelson followed a different route to the same conclusion. Nelson was a surgeon's daughter who had worked in his hospital before her marriage. After her marriage to Dotson Nelson (later pastor at Mountain Brook Baptist Church), he urged her and their children to base decisions on their understanding of Christian discipleship, not their roles in a preacher's family. When their children wanted to attend dances, the Nelsons decided that if deacons' children could dance, then the preacher's children should be allowed to do so as well. Grace Nelson staked out her own ministry as a Sunday school teacher, where she discovered her gift for teaching the Bible. She began working to become a hospital chaplain at Baptist Medical Center in 1978. At age fifty-nine, she enrolled in a program of clinical pastoral counseling, encouraged by her husband. Work with a dying coal miner and with an illiterate black man terminally ill with cancer convinced her she had heard God's call clearly. Two days before the black man died and after weeks of reading the Bible to him, he told Nelson he would greet her in heaven. Thus inspired, she completed work in clinical counseling and obtained a master's degree in pastoral care at Samford University. Believing that ordination represented a sending out by the church as well as by Christ, she requested and was granted ordination to the "full Christian ministry" by Mountain Brook Baptist Church, where she had taught Sunday school for so many years.[57]

The Battle for the Bible: Round Four

Culture wars dovetailed with fundamentalist theology during the 1970s, greatly expanding the popular base for the conservative resurgence. Baptists who through the years had paid little attention to arcane theological debates about strict Calvinism or biblical infallibility because their leaders had assured them that virtually all Southern Baptists were conservatives began to wonder if that were true. If all Baptists were so conservative, they began to wonder, why did so many oppose constitutional amendments to restore prayer and Bible reading in public schools or to ban abortion? Why did so many advocate the ordination of women and ERA? Why did they endorse the racial integration of churches and public schools? Although it was not necessarily the intent of theological fundamentalists to link biblical authority to the preservation of the South's social and racial status quo, the linkage occurred nonetheless.[58]

Dispensational millennialists found hope as much in strengthened homes and families as in Christ's imminent return. This focus reduced tensions between various conservative religious groups (including historic conflicts with Catholics).[59]

Theological disputes in Alabama were subplots in a much larger drama. The SBC swung sharply right during the 1970s, culminating at the end of the decade in the election of a fundamentalist president who pledged to cleanse the seminaries of modernists. But the entire decade was characterized by controversy. The Denver convention in 1970 featured demands for recall of the Broadman Bible Commentary because of its alleged modernist treatment of Genesis. Baptist Press chose three controversies as the top stories of the year: Baptist efforts to grapple with racial prejudice; a controversial CLC seminar featuring discussions of *Playboy*; and in first place, doctrinal polarization of the SBC. The top story for 1972 was continuing conflict over recall of the Broadman commentary volume on Genesis.[60]

These disputes were merely prelude to what many consider the most divisive and important convention in SBC history. Grievances (some of which had festered for decades and some of which were of recent vintage) had led fundamentalists to organize various splinter groups such as the

Conservative Southern Baptists and the Baptist Faith and Message Fellowship. The publication of Harold Lindsell's book, *The Battle for the Bible* (1976), which attacked liberals such as William E. Hull (former provost at Southern seminary), heightened tensions. So did regular fundamentalist attacks on liberalism and modernism at SBC pastors' conferences that preceded the general convention. Then in 1979 Paige Patterson and Paul Pressler, two Texas Baptists, held a series of meetings across SBC territory devoted to mobilizing fundamentalists, getting them to the upcoming Houston convention in large numbers, and electing a fundamentalist president. The strategy worked, as busloads of messengers arrived on the day of the vote, and Adrian Rogers, the fundamentalist candidate from Memphis, won by a majority of 51 percent. A succession of fundamentalists followed Rogers (Bailey Smith, James T. Draper, Charles Stanley, Jerry Vines). Moderates at first resisted organizing; nor could they agree on a single candidate. By the time they established unity and organization in the mid-1980s, it was too late. Fundamentalists were entrenched in power and were purging boards, agencies, and seminaries of any person who would not swear allegiance to biblical inerrancy.[61]

Alabama reaction to the 1979 convention reflected the ambivalence of moderates, who desperately desired to maintain control and allow some theological diversity but were reluctant to become enmeshed in denominational politics. Hudson Baggett criticized the frenzied political activities that led up to Rogers's victory, but he predicted that little of substance would change in the convention. Harper Shannon, pastor of Huffman Baptist Church and president of the ABSC, also criticized the excessive politics preceding the convention, disagreed with Rogers's allegations of widespread liberalism in Baptist seminaries, and pleaded for theological tolerance of the "broad spectrum" of Baptists. But he also considered Rogers a friend and predicted he would be a good president. Like Baggett, he incorrectly predicted that little would change as a consequence of Rogers's presidency.[62]

Convention conflicts revealed many subterranean currents within the SBC. To some degree, the conflict was mainly a battle among preachers and professional church staffs. A survey of the 1978 convention revealed that three-quarters of the 23,000 messengers were employed on church or denominational payrolls. That does not mean that lay people were apathetic about the outcome of theological disputes. Probably a fifth or so of urban Southern Baptists thought like tolerant, main-line Protestants. Close to half identified themselves as fundamentalists. The others identified themselves as pentecostals or conservatives without any particular political agenda.

Many were simply loyal to the denomination and would support whoever was in power. As with many other groups, intramural battles became more important than battles between denominations.[63]

The SBC had always lived on the edge of doctrinal division. The miracle was that unity had been maintained into the 1970s. Denominational unity had always rested more on regional identity (its "southernness") and denominational loyalty to missions and evangelism than on theological consensus. What historians often referred to as the "grand compromise" had kept ideologues of the left or right from controlling the denomination. Centrist conservatives who favored missions, evangelism, and the Cooperative Program controlled the centers of power and forced frustrated proponents of each extreme to leave the convention. But control by the right wing of the generally conservative denomination beginning in 1979 alienated not only the small cadre of denominational liberals but a substantial part of the loyalist conservative center as well.[64]

Polarization within the SBC quickly swept into Alabama. Letters to the editor of the *Alabama Baptist* extolled inerrancy and urged liberals to get out of the denomination. One irate pastor wrote just after the 1970 national convention that "the liberal forces are our enemies, and God's enemies." Pastors from Liberty Baptist Church in Duncanville and Hartselle First Baptist vowed their belief in inerrancy, as did the executive committee of the East Liberty Baptist Association. Some letters even criticized the popular new Bible translation, *Good News for Modern Man,* as a modernistic paraphrase of the Bible. The writer extolled the King James Version, which he said had led to three hundred years of English domination of the world through the British Empire.[65]

Within Alabama, the annual evangelism and pastors' conferences became primary forums for inerrantist speakers, although many also preached at state conventions. In 1971 and 1978, W. A. Criswell was a featured speaker at the state evangelism conference. He denounced modern trends in religion both times, saying that the Christian message should be authentic, authoritarian, absolute, and apocalyptic. Adrian Rogers and John Bisagno spoke to the 1976 conference, and Bailey Smith was the keynote preacher in 1978. The conference was the best-attended state Baptist meeting, drawing as many as 3,000 and even outstripping the annual WMU convention. Featuring "old-time preaching and singing," it was in many ways a continuation of rural southern religion. Hudson Baggett wrote that the services reminded him of the "simple and sincere" religion of his youth in a small rural church in Cullman County. Although he admitted that evangelism sometimes employed objectionable tactics to win people, Baggett frequently promoted it as the central component of Baptist life.[66] Within the state delegation, pastors Fred Wolfe, Jerry Vines, and Harper Shannon were also popular preachers. Nor was the program all white. Black California Baptist preacher Manuel Scott often stole the spotlight from his white brethren in his numerous appearances during the 1970s.

Many leaders of the evangelism conference emerged as spokesmen for the fundamentalist cause. E. P. Wallen, pastor at Hueytown, invoked a strict Calvinist view of Scripture as central to Southern Baptist theology, and he endorsed political and social views equally as conservative. Jerry Vines (a graduate of Mercer University and New Orleans Seminary with a Th.D. from Luther Rice Seminary) pastored Dauphin Way Baptist Church in Mobile to leadership both in total membership and in number of baptisms. When only thirty-eight years old in 1976, Vines was elected president of the SBC pastors' conference and would soon be elected president of the SBC (though after leaving Alabama). Speaking to the third annual meeting of the Baptist Faith and Message Fellowship at Birmingham's Center Point Baptist Church in 1975, Vines called the "wolf of liberalism" inside the SBC the greatest danger to the denomination. He berated one of his Mercer professors who imposed "intellectual intimidation" on conservative students to make them feel dumb if they believed in biblical inerrancy. "Liberalism gives you a Bible full of holes," he thundered, "it gives you social reform instead of evangelism." He also denied that all fundamentalists were racists. Fred Wolfe, graduate of the University of South Carolina and Southwestern seminary, came to pastor Mobile's Cottage Hill Baptist Church in March 1972 and emerged as another major leader of the conservative resurgence.[67]

Harper Shannon and Hudson Baggett used their considerable influence to mediate the dispute. Though both claimed to be theological conservatives who rejected the social gospel and modernism, they were not as political as Wallen, Vines, and Wolfe. Shannon was a frequent speaker at the state evangelism conference and drew a standing ovation at the packed 1978 meeting for his sermon, "Worthy Is the Lamb." Even though Shannon drifted closer to fundamentalists after their triumph in 1979, he maintained broader ties than Wallen, Wolfe, and Vines. Baggett constantly proclaimed his fealty to evangelism and the Bible but maintained an even more independent stance than Shannon.

Theologically Baggett was unpredictable. In 1971 he rejected the social gospel as misleading and divisive, but he added that one could not be Christlike and ignore injustice, oppression, and cruelty. That same year he wrote an editorial on Christian environmentalism, arguing that protection

of water, land, and air from pollution was a matter of Christian stewardship. He regularly proclaimed Southern Baptists to be "middle of the road-
ers" theologically and denied the central tenet of fundamentalists, that the
primary threat to the denomination came from internal liberalism. Proclaiming 99 percent of Southern Baptists to believe the Bible, he admitted
that they would not agree on what particular passages of Scripture meant.
But to "assume that a person is a heretic, unChristian or does not believe
the Bible just because they disagree with us is a witness in reverse for
Christianity." In another editorial, he praised the SBC for resisting efforts
by the "watch dogs of orthodoxy" to push policies too far toward creedalism. In fact, his frequent warnings against creedalism were similar to L. L.
Gwaltney's before the 1925 SBC. Although Baggett praised fundamentalists like W. A. Criswell, he also rejected demands that the Sunday School
Board recall the Broadman Bible Commentary as "ridiculous" creedalism and "un-Baptistic." In 1971 Baggett led forces opposed to changing
the constitution of the state convention to define a "cooperating" Baptist
church as one that baptized by immersion. Although Baggett agreed with
the theology, he denounced the change for imposing a creed on Baptists.
The November 1971 state convention defeated the change by a vote of 317
to 313. Baggett also avoided comment on internal church divisions over
race, culture wars, and theology, making the state denomination appear
much more united than it really was.[68] His self-censorship and the relative
conservatism of state convention leaders and staff unquestionably played a
role in keeping the state one of the most tranquil during escalating denominational strife.

Although Alabama's moderates were heavily outnumbered, they
did contest each inch of ground. John Jeffers, pastor of Auburn First Baptist
Church and one of three Alabama trustees on the Sunday School Board in
1972, refuted charges of heresy against the Broadman Commentary. James
A. Auchmuty Jr., pastor at Birmingham's Shades Crest Baptist Church, attended evangelism conferences but regretted how evangelism had been
severed from commitment or mature discipleship. He noted that 3,000 Alabama Baptists often attended annual evangelism conferences but only 60
or so showed up for seminars on conserving church members. Evangelism
focused too much emphasis on Christ as savior and too little on Christ as
Lord. Auchmuty and Baggett also took the lead in defending seminary professors against charges of liberalism by Harold Lindsell.[69]

Native-born Alabamian and Howard College graduate William E. Hull
was one of Lindsell's favorite targets. Hull published an essay in 1970 entitled "Shall We Call the Bible Infallible?" Although the essay tried to rec-

oncile some of the differences between fundamentalists and moderates, Hull wrote that the Bible did not claim to be infallible. That same year he spoke at the state Baptist convention in Mobile and affirmed the right of a Baptist to be either conservative or liberal. A number of pastors and laymen wrote rebuttals, notably the pastor of Calvary Heights Baptist Church in Alexander City. How could he ask members of his church to support the Cooperative Program when it supported seminary and college professors who did not believe the Bible was "the infallible inerrant Word of God"? He also attacked Hudson Baggett for printing Hull's convention sermon. Many others defended Hull's views and asked for tolerance of other viewpoints. The pastor at Bluff Park Baptist Church denied Lindsell's charges of liberalism in the SBC and accused fundamentalists of "bibliolatry" (worshiping the Bible).[70]

Abe Watson, pastor at Brewton, preached to his congregation on "The Rediscovery of the Bible" during the debate over Hull's 1970 convention sermon. The Bible was written by ordinary, fallible men, he explained. Nor did modern Christians have original copies. Copiers had made errors in translations. When people believed they had a monopoly on truth, they inevitably tried to force everyone to think alike. The best antidote to intolerance was for people to study the Bible constantly, alone and in families, to find new meaning in it through the leadership of the Holy Spirit.[71]

John Wiley Jr. held similar views. A native of Ensley, Wiley began Howard College in 1940 but left after the Japanese attack on Pearl Harbor to serve four years as a Marine Corps chaplain in the South Pacific. When he returned to Howard, he had found his calling as a pastoral counselor. After graduating he attended the pastoral counseling program at Andover Newton Theological Seminary, completing his internship at Boston City Hospital. He turned down an opportunity to continue his studies in counseling at Harvard in order to return to Alabama in 1951. He spent five years at Southside Baptist as assistant in charge of counseling, then became pastor of the newly formed Vestavia Hills Baptist Church. At the time, there were only three psychiatrists in Birmingham, and many evangelicals distrusted the mental health movement as an admission of God's inadequacy to heal mental problems. During nearly twelve years in the pastorate, Wiley avoided sermons on hell as an abstraction few understood, and he emphasized forgiveness (which "is what the New Testament is all about"). Jesus, he believed, came into the world to rid it of fear and guilt, "and that was my orientation in preaching." Admitting that he was not a conventional Baptist preacher, he sometimes even doubted that he was a Southern Baptist. He saw no way of reconciling his belief in the historic Baptist principle of the soul competency of every person before God with hardening creedal-ism within the denomination. Concluding that he was a liberal in the sense of tolerance for other viewpoints, he also felt increasingly alienated by his denomination's racism. At Southside, he had tried to use the church gym-nasium for community waifs and to begin a kindergarten for the children of divorcées, but he was told these were inappropriate ministries. At Vesta-via Hills, his racial liberalism caused him additional problems. So in 1969–1970, with the support of Earl Potts (pastor at McElwain Baptist), Dotson Nelson (pastor at Mountain Brook), and others, he began one of the city's first family counseling practices. Believing "with all my heart that Jesus in his teachings was grounded in the psychological principles of mankind," he believed his new ministry allowed him to maintain "the deepest rela-tionship to God."[72]

The Birmingham ministers' discussion group continued to provide moderate Baptists a theological forum. By the 1970s six of the seventeen members were white Baptists. The director of pastoral counseling at Bap-tist hospitals, Joe Boone Abbott, Samford religion professors Mabry Lunce-ford, Arthur Walker, and W. T. Edwards, and pastors Dotson Nelson and Lamar Jackson (who took John Buchanan's place as pastor at Southside) presented papers on bioethics, feminist theology, mental health, psycho-analyst Rollo May, and theologians Harvey Cox and Davie Napier (who was a Yale theologian and son of an Alabama Baptist couple in China). The group also accepted its first two African American members during the 1970s, both Baptist pastors.[73] The Baptist ministers represented a wide range of moderate theological opinion, but there were no fundamentalists among them.

Although Alabama Baptists had little to fear from liberals, they had reason to be concerned about pentecostalism. Charismatic religion was making inroads into main-line denominations and Southern Baptists were no exception. There had been periodic defenses of pentecostal practices during earlier decades, but the debate escalated during the 1970s. Moder-ates proved relatively tolerant (at least in spirit), whereas fundamentalists gave no quarter.

Periodic descriptions of pentecostal practices drew heavy fire. Al-though the moderate president of the SBC in 1975 and an Alabama Baptist pastor pleaded for tolerance and understanding, W. A. Criswell blasted pentecostalism as an "aberration and a heresy." Letters flooded the *Alabama Baptist* on both sides of the issue in response to Criswell's criticism.[74]

A 1976 Home Mission Board survey located more than one hundred charismatic Baptist churches with some 10,000 members and estimated the existence of that many more participants in charismatic prayer groups. Criswell met this report by denouncing speaking in tongues as "senseless, insane, and idiotic." Baptist pentecostalism was voted the top story in 1975 by Baptist Press, which elicited three letters from charismatic Alabama Baptists. James Auchmuty wrote a five-part series on charismatic gifts for the *Alabama Baptist* the following year. Evangelist Sam Cathey condemned the charismatic movement as heresy at the 1977 state convention. He accused charismatics of tearing up SBC churches and draining money from the Cooperative Program. But his attacks on charismatics provoked far less response than his pronouncement that Elvis Presley was in hell.[75]

One source of increased tension within the denomination was the application of Christianity to social problems. Alabama Baptists had been content to apply their faith to prohibition of alcohol and even to the problems of poor whites (child labor, mental health, public education). But the application of Christian conceptions of social justice to race and war had created a witch's brew of confusion and bitterness during the 1960s and alienated Southern Baptists. Many Baptists already had theological objections to social Christianity; now they had racial and nationalistic objections as well. The peace movement might think of itself as drawing from the Sermon on the Mount; most evangelical Christians believed it originated in Hanoi. And white Alabama evangelicals had already made clear they believed that the African American struggle for social equality owed more to communism than to Christ.

Opposition came from two directions. Reacting to the peace and civil rights movements and citing fundamentalist theological interpretations of the Bible, many critics insisted that the only task of the church was saving souls. Society would be redeemed when lives were changed by conversion. In July 1970 a friend with a talent for alliteration wrote Hudson Baggett that preachers should preach salvation, not sociology; redemption, not reform; conversion, not culture; pardon, not progress; the new birth, not the new social order; Christ, not civilization.[76]

Baggett, Walter G. Nunn (book review editor of the *Alabama Baptist*), and other denominational leaders conceded that personal salvation had to change society for the better if it was genuine. But they agreed with critics that the principle task of the church was evangelism, which was usually neglected by denominations that stressed social involvement.[77]

Despite the dominance of such views, individual pastors, lay persons, and even entire churches struggled valiantly to construct a conservative theological rationale for a liberal commitment to social justice. Gaines S. Dobbins used the intellectual freedom of retirement to have his say on the connection between personal salvation and social action. In his regular column in the *Alabama Baptist*, Dobbins praised Walter Rauschenbusch as the apostle of applied Christianity and defended social Christianity with biblical quotations. Although he conceded that Rauschenbusch may have taken the social gospel too far, he challenged Alabama Baptists to take it a great deal farther.[78]

Robert Ferguson (pastor of Oakdale Baptist Church in Mobile) denied that concern for social justice was the same as the social gospel. He did not equate social improvement to utopia (his definition of the social gospel); he did insist that Baptists must help people who suffered. Baptists had always been involved in addressing social issues (alcohol, health, hunger, prostitution). They just needed to define social problems more broadly.[79]

Alvin H. Hopson, pastor at Huntsville First Baptist, addressed the issue in a 1972 sermon. Postulating that Christians were active participants in a particular economic system, he applied biblical principles to that system. Wealth was not inherently evil, but greed and materialism were sources both of spiritual danger and of social injustice. The proliferation of middle-class values of production and consumption had resulted in social improvement as well as social stress. Christians needed to be not only participants within the economic order but also its critics. Citing a favorite source for such sermons (Reinhold Niebuhr's *Moral Man and Immoral Society*), Hopson grieved over the existence and extent of poverty amid unprecedented middle-class affluence. Using Appalachia as example, he ruminated about a country so rich where a sixth of the population was so poor. Although he conceded that the blame for some poverty fell on the poor themselves, he traced other sources to corporate and individual greed. Christians must bring more influence to bear on the national economy, participate in national planning and decision making, and confront problems of environmental pollution and inadequate health care.[80]

Of course the test of such theology is not the pen that writes it or the tongue that proclaims it. The test is in the implementation. By that standard the vision of social action survived within the denomination, through both the prophetic vision of individuals and the corporate ministries of churches. Harold E. Martin (Howard College graduate, Montgomery layman, and editor/publisher of the *Montgomery Advertiser-Journal*) left his church over the way it excluded a black woman and her child. He also won a Pulitzer Prize in journalism for a series of articles revealing medical experimentation on state prison inmates. Speaking at the 1976 dedication of a new building for the *Alabama Baptist*, Martin urged the paper's editor and staff to take stands on issues confronting society. They had the responsibility to analyze, criticize, and persuade readers toward a more just society.[81]

Many churches already engaged in ministries designed to make society more just. Ministries to migrant workers continued, though they sought more to mitigate the harmful results of exploitation than to address the economic system that caused them. Six associations (Birmingham, Etowah, Madison, Mobile, Montgomery, and Russell) created Christian social ministry programs, and several employed directors to coordinate these ministries. The Birmingham committee (directed by Robert G. Thompson) operated the Marks Village Community Center, which it leased from the city. Programs included a day kindergarten for five-year-olds, women's groups, boys' and girls' clubs, a gymnasium that was open four nights a week and enrolled more than a hundred boys, senior citizens' groups, and an emergency food pantry and clothing center. Members of Crestway Baptist Church, Samford University students, and other volunteers staffed the programs. Louis Wilhite's Arlington church and Baptist Church of the Covenant conducted extensive social ministries.[82]

Auburn and Montgomery First Baptist Churches launched similar social initiatives. The Auburn congregation institutionalized such work through its Christian Life and Ministries Fellowship, one of whose members (Mary Lynn Porter) pioneered the Auburn Day Care Center and became an important figure in preschool reform for poor children statewide. The church participated in a variety of social ministries, including the Auburn Crisis Center, Dental Care Unit/Emergency Medical Fund, Project Uplift, Shelter for Battered Women, Auburn Charity Fund, Auburn Social Concerns, Presbyterian Community Ministries (which provided no-interest house repair loans and emergency utility grants), Clothe-A-Child, Habitat for Humanity, Loaves and Fishes, AIDS Outreach, and Alabama Caring Foundation (health insurance for children of working poor families).[83]

Russell Association participated in joint Christian social ministries through a project cosponsored by the state convention and Home Mission Board. Joycelyn Kay Long, a social work graduate of Howard Payne College and Southern seminary (who had done inner-city social ministries in Corpus Christi, Texas) headed the ministry. A number of Christian social centers remained active in the state's largest cities. The state convention also helped the Brother's Brother Foundation purchase tuberculosis vaccine for a massive immunization program in Haiti, partly organized by Ira Myers, state health officer and a Baptist layman.[84]

Baptists increasingly felt uneasy that they had taken bold and public political positions on alcohol, gambling, pornography, and Sunday closing legislation but ignored nonconsensus political issues such as poverty, governmental corruption, tax policy, housing, discrimination against women, abortion, welfare reform, and the war in Vietnam. Gradually the SBC edged forward on all these issues, to the increasing dismay of both fundamentalists (when the stance involved poverty, women, welfare, and tax reform) and moderates (when the stance involved abortion or conservative views of welfare and taxes).

Hudson Baggett suggested the new political realities in 1970. He warned those who adhered to rigid separation of church and state that the federal government was no longer remote from people's lives. Which religious group was seeking favored status was less a problem, Baggett wrote, than the tendency to minimize or even eliminate religious influence altogether. The revolutionary events of the 1960s had awakened Baptists "from a deep slumber" and forced them to confront the secularization of American society. If political apathy meant silent acquiescence to moral evil, then pastors and churches must become more involved. Many letters to him agreed, though they expanded "moral evil" from liquor and gambling (Baggett's preferred subjects) to racial prejudice, hatred, and injustice.[85]

Baggett practiced what he preached, at least during his first decade as editor. In 1972 he endorsed a 5 to 4 Supreme Court ruling that struck down capital punishment. He interpreted the commandment "Thou shalt not kill" to be an absolute ethical principle, not a relativistic standard. A year later Baggett and George Bagley (who served on the Citizens' Conference on Alabama State Courts) endorsed a judicial reform package advocated by chief justice Howell Heflin that overhauled the Alabama court system. Bagley explained that morality and justice were goals of all religions, and all churchmen should endorse the judicial article that was designed to reform the court system. Baggett also opposed attempts by legislators to weaken the state ethics law. Both Bagley and Samford University's Leslie Wright chaired the state ethics commission during the decade, and they employed Baptist layman Melvin Cooper as its director.[86]

Politics had always been an important part of Alabama Baptist life either formally or informally. In February 1974 Vestavia Hills Baptist Church invited former SBC president and presidential adviser Brooks Hays to the church to speak. In his lecture at the church and again at Samford University, Hays called politics "a religious adventure."[87]

Republican congressman John H. Buchanan Jr. agreed. Buchanan's ministerial background made him an unusual Republican. Although partisan on most issues, he developed a keen sense of racial justice that often put him at odds with his party's positions. While representing the Sixth Congressional District (Birmingham), Buchanan served as interim pastor of Riverside Baptist Church, an inner-city, biracial congregation. His wife was the congregation's music director. Raised in a racially tolerant home in which his father (who was pastor of Southside Baptist Church) combined fiscal conservatism with enlightened racial views, Buchanan joined African American congressmen to try to enact a constitutional amendment giving Washington, D.C., home rule and its own congressional representative. Under heavy criticism from some whites in his home district, Buchanan conceded that his stance might cost him reelection in 1976, but he vowed that he would no "longer compromise on civil rights." Rather than cost the Baptist preacher reelection, his stance won him many black votes to add to his traditional base among middle-class Jewish and Baptist voters.[88]

Baptists on the other side of the racial divide were also well represented. Russell Yarbrough, a deacon at Woodlawn Baptist Church, served on the Birmingham city council during the 1970s. A Democratic conservative who won with heavy white support, Yarbrough was perhaps the most popular councilman during these years of transition in city politics. His friend Frank Parsons ran for mayor in 1979 against Richard Arrington Jr., the city's first black chief executive. Parsons was a member of McElwain Baptist Church, and his campaign manager was a member of his Sunday school class. Parsons's initial campaign contributions came largely from church members. He frequently mentioned his religious beliefs, and his campaign in some ways anticipated the Moral Majority efforts a year later.[89]

As theology, race, and social issues began to intersect, Baptist politics became increasingly secular. W. A. Criswell, a frequent speaker in Alabama at state conventions and evangelism conferences, stopped just short of openly endorsing Republicans. In 1975 he preached a well-publicized sermon entitled "Death in Detente, or Courting and Cultivating the Cancer of Communism." Announcing beforehand that the sermon was highly political, he invited a Republican U.S. congressman to sit on the platform with him as he preached. In the sermon he claimed that U.S. foreign policy since FDR had appeased the USSR. Hudson Baggett reported the sermon but felt compelled to include Republican presidents Richard Nixon and Gerald Ford in the indictment. During the Nixon impeachment proceedings (which seemed at least to some Baptists to involve serious ethical lapses), one partisan Alabama Baptist insisted that "Watergate should be of no concern to the church . . . because of the political nature of the accusations." Reluctance to criticize President Nixon resulted partly from strong Southern Baptist support for him in 1972. Many Baptists despised liberal Democrat George McGovern despite his early career as a Methodist minister. The SBC invited Nixon to speak at its 1972 convention. John Buchanan subsequently defended Nixon passionately throughout the Watergate hearings, jumping ship only days before the president's resignation.[90]

Jimmy Carter's campaign for president in 1976 temporarily restored some balance to a denomination leaning precariously toward partisan politics. Baptists had long played a major role in Georgia politics. Governors Lester Maddox, Jimmy Carter, Carl Sanders, and Herman Talmadge, Senator Walter George, and Republican gubernatorial candidate Bo Calloway were all Baptists, though of widely varying ideology and representing both parties. Carter was a trustee of the SBC Brotherhood Commission, and the SBC's Broadman Press first published his campaign biography, *Why Not the Best?* Carter's opponent, President Gerald Ford, became the first sitting president to speak at the convention (Nixon had declined four years earlier). Ford's speech generated a chorus of criticism in the *Alabama Baptist* from writers who believed it unwise to invite an incumbent president to speak during an election year, especially when a Southern Baptist was running against him. Baptist leaders replied that Ford was invited because he was president, not because the denomination endorsed his positions. (The argument was not convincing; in future years neither Carter in 1980 nor Bill Clinton in 1996 was invited to speak at the SBC, although both were incumbent presidents and members of Southern Baptist churches; conversely, Republicans Ronald Reagan and George Bush, neither of whom was a Southern Baptist, were both invited.) Carter did carry Alabama, thanks to the endorsement of George Wallace and strong Baptist support. But a letter during the campaign made it clear that black Baptists liked him better than whites did. A writer from Opp urged Baptist voters to cast ballots for candidates who supported scriptural positions such as capitalism, states' rights, the return of welfare to the states, outlawing abortion, and ending State Department meddling to undermine the white government in Rhodesia.[91]

Carter's election in 1976 did as much to bring Southern Baptists into the mainstream of American religious life as John Kennedy's election in 1960 had to bring in Catholics. It was a public demonstration of the diversity and sophistication that had long existed but had been largely ignored by those outside the denomination.

At first, Baptists took considerable pride in Carter's presidency. His biracial policies demonstrated that not all Southern Baptists were racists, as many Americans believed. His sincere compassion for the poor and his obvious debt to Reinhold Niebuhr and neo-orthodox theology promoted issues such as adequate housing, nutrition, education, and idealistic foreign policy to the forefront of public debate. In May 1977, only months after taking office, Carter proposed that Baptists create a Mission Service Corps to place five thousand short-term volunteers on domestic and foreign mission fields both to evangelize and to perform social ministries. The Alabama state convention responded slowly to this initiative, but a number of communities applied for volunteers (the Montgomery Christian Social Center in a black public housing project requested a director; the state convention asked for a coordinator for prison ministries). By 1979 Alabama counted twenty-six volunteers from churches large and small (volunteers came from Montgomery's Normandale and First Baptist, Mobile's Cottage Hill, Huntsville First Baptist, Lakeside and McElwain in Birmingham, as well as Addison church in Winston County, Lebanon in Morgan Association, and North Highland in the Bessemer Association). Unfortunately, funding was a problem. The ABSC allocated no funds to the program, zealously reserving gifts for the Cooperative Program.[92]

Perhaps the most remarkable Mission Service Corps volunteer was seventy-four-year-old Ella Thomas Steele of South Roebuck Baptist Church in Birmingham. A native of Birmingham and former voice and piano student at Howard College and the Chicago Conservatory of Music, Steele had taught music for forty years in Chicago and Birmingham. After her husband died in 1978, she decided to satisfy her lifelong interest in missions by volunteering for the Mission Service Corps. She was sent to Spokane, Washington, where she played organ and directed the choir for Sunset Hill Baptist Church. She also was the congregation's "one-woman visitation committee," visiting shut-ins, sick members, and new prospects. She lived with a church family, paid her own expenses, and loved her new life.[93]

Such Carter administration successes were soon buried in a sequence of domestic and foreign policy crises that increasingly soured Americans in general and Southern Baptists in particular. By 1979 letter writers were regularly blasting the president for "giving away" the Panama Canal and recognizing the People's Republic of China. Others denounced his policies on abortion and controversial social issues. Jerry Falwell had already begun to mobilize Moral Majority, a fundamentalist and conservative political lobby that would soon help defeat both moderate Democrat Jimmy Carter and moderate Republican John Buchanan Jr.[94]

Although Alabama Baptists were more deeply politicized by 1980 than in decades, there was a price to pay for political partisanship on the left or right. In 1970 Albert Brewer's candidacy for reelection as governor deeply divided the convention. Brewer's Montgomery pastor, Dr. J. R. White of First Baptist Church, wrote a letter to Alabama Baptists explaining what a fine Christian Brewer was and endorsing his reelection. Although White acted on his own and spent neither ABSC or First Baptist funds, the letter did require someone to supply addresses. Many angry backers of Governor Wallace accused Hudson Baggett of supplying the *Alabama Baptist* mailing list. Baggett vigorously denied this charge. An embarrassed J. R. White explained to his divided congregation that he had assumed the mailing would go only to pastors and church leaders, not to virtually every Baptist home in Alabama. Charges and countercharges poured onto Hudson Baggett's desk, all of which he refused to publish lest they polarize the denomination. George Wallace obviously had strong support among rank-and-file Alabama Baptists, and they did not appreciate the obvious pro-Brewer sentiment of their leaders.[95]

Another incident involved Republican partisanship. President Richard Nixon had portrayed himself as a deeply religious man by bringing ministers to the White House to preach. The impressive surroundings and aura of power overwhelmed visiting Baptist ministers as normally cautious as Billy Graham. One young Alabama Baptist flew particularly close to the alluring flame of presidential power. Wallace Henley was a Samford University graduate, minister, and religion reporter for the *Birmingham News* when he became active in the 1968 Nixon campaign. Three years later the White House invited Henley to become assistant director of the cabinet committee on education. Later he became director of public and congressional affairs in the Justice Department. Although Henley could not have known it at the time, he was also a pawn in a political strategy. Nixon believed that Alabama governor George Wallace was the chief barrier to his reelection in 1972. By splitting the antiliberal vote between himself and Wallace, Nixon feared a Democratic victory. The appointment of southerners like Henley was designed to appeal to Southern Baptists and neutralize Wallace's popularity in the South. Like John Buchanan, Henley initially defended the president during the Watergate scandals but quickly realized the ethical quagmire in which he found himself. He resigned in 1973 and wrote a book (*Enter at Your Own Risk,* 1974) to explain how he had allowed his support of Nixon's political ideology and the trappings of presidential power to suck him into a cynical world where politicians used religion to manipulate a gullible public. The autobiography was the first step on a path that led Henley back into the pulpit, to the presidency of the state convention, and ultimately into a charismatic Baptist ministry.[96]

The Alabama Baptist State Convention

As Hudson Baggett and many pastors constantly reminded an increasingly politicized convention, the primary goal of Alabama Baptists was evangelism. To refocus attention on that priority, the SBC launched "Bold Mission Thrust" in 1976, a twenty-five-year program to carry Baptists into a new millennium. Buoyed by phenomenal success in the early 1970s (more than 400,000 baptisms a year and rapidly increasing Cooperative Program revenues), the convention set ambitious goals. In Alabama baptisms averaged more than 30,000 a year during the early 1970s, and nine-year totals at middecade listed more than 266,000 baptisms, a total surpassed only by Texas among SBC states.[97]

Unfortunately, the first few years of Bold Mission Thrust saw baptisms go down, not up. Although total church memberships and contributions continued to grow, baptisms declined for four consecutive years (1976–1979). In 1975 the denomination baptized 421,000. In 1978 SBC churches baptized only 334,000 before recovering ground the next year. In Alabama total baptisms declined from 32,266 in 1972 to 21,944 in 1978 and recovered only to 28,435 in 1980. Numerous reasons were cited for these declines: demographic changes in the U.S. population, especially declining numbers of teenagers; the rise of para-church organizations; lack of emphasis on evangelism; smugness over growing denominational power and influence; theological liberalism.[98]

Numbers of baptisms became the litmus test for Alabama Baptist preachers, and the standard was unforgiving. The criteria made no allowance for considerations such as pastoring an inner-city church in a transitional neighborhood without adequate parking, or a small-town church in an area of closing factories and declining populations. Pastors of dying rural churches received no credit for ministering to small, elderly bands of faithful worshipers after all the young people moved to cities. The unremitting standard of success was, "How many did you baptize?" By that standard a handful of churches baptized a phenomenal number of new members, led regularly by Dauphin Way and Cottage Hill in Mobile, Whitesburg and West Huntsville in the space city, Center Point and Dawson Memorial in Birmingham, Flint Hill in Bessemer, and Cottondale in Tuscaloosa.[99] Although not all were pastored by theological fundamentalists, most were, lending credence to their charge that declining numbers of baptisms resulted at least to some degree from lack of evangelical zeal.

Pastoring such a church almost immediately promoted the pastor to celebrity status, especially at the state evangelism and pastors' conferences. Charles T. Carter, who pastored Whitesburg in Huntsville to 211 baptisms in 1970–1971, was called to Shades Mountain in Birmingham to accomplish similar feats. Donald H. Watterson, who baptized 98 at Cottage Hill Baptist in Mobile during 1970, was selected the following year as state Sunday school director. Jerry Vines baptized 264 at Dauphin Way in Mobile during 1975 and was soon elected president of the SBC. Bob Barker, pastor of

558   R a c e   a n d   P o l i t i c s

Chickasaw First Baptist until 1978, baptized 3,600 during his twenty years there, hosted a popular television program ("Coffee with the Pastor"), and became an influential figure in the evangelism conference.[100]

Membership and financial growth outstripped baptisms. The state convention began the decade with 838,000 members in 2,960 churches. It ended the 1970s with 974,000 members in 3,033 churches, a membership increase of 14 percent. Although Sunday school and WMU membership remained static or even declined a bit, church membership growth outpaced Alabama's population increase, rare for states during that decade. Dauphin Way edged into the top ten SBC churches in membership growth in 1979, but in Alabama three churches added more members during the previous year: Cottage Hill, Dawson Memorial, and Shades Mountain. In 1971 Southern Baptists led all other denominations in sixty-six of Alabama's sixty-seven counties, and the percentage of Southern Baptists to total church members topped all states, reaching 64 percent.[101]

Contributions grew even faster than membership, a reflection of both the increasing prosperity of the Sun Belt and the mobility of Alabama Baptists into middle and upper classes. Offerings increased by 9 percent in 1973 and 13 percent two years later. But different churches often led the increase in mission gifts. Some large fundamentalist churches, disenchanted with what they interpreted as liberal leadership in the denomination, gave small percentages to the Cooperative Program. Other conservative churches were simply growing so fast that they had to devote most of their contributions to adding space and staff. As a result, Cottage Hill, which often led the state in baptisms and membership growth, gave only 4.5 percent of its income to the CP, whereas more "liberal" churches such as Vestavia Hills (8.9 percent) and Auburn First Baptist (13.3 percent) gave twice or three times as much. Stable, traditional First Baptist churches often led the state in percentage of contributions going to missions (Mobile First Baptist gave 15.7 percent to the CP in 1975, Oxford First Baptist 14 percent). In 1978 the top four contributors to the Cooperative Program were Mountain Brook, Dawson Memorial, Montgomery First Baptist, and Dothan First Baptist, which were considered either moderate or nonaligned. Top contributors to the Lottie Moon Christmas offerings for foreign missions that same year (Montgomery First Baptist, Shades Mountain, Dauphin Way, and Dothan First) included churches pastored by both fundamentalists and moderates.[102]

The convention's structure struggled to keep up with change. A new office of church-minister relations (reflecting the tensions within the denomination) helped ministers seeking pastorates and counseled ministers and churches engaged in strife. Disaster relief programs were instituted. Listening sessions around the state continued. Catholic-Baptist dialogues, conferences on the rural church and Black Belt, interracial conferences, and many other such efforts occupied state and associational leaders. The *Alabama Baptist* moved into new offices in Homewood. The convention staff rose to a hundred persons.[103]

Baptist higher education remained a high priority of the denomination. The ABSC appropriated nearly a third of its contributions to the state's three Baptist colleges, the highest percentage of any state convention. Even with that level of support, all three continued to struggle with small endowments and increasing costs. Retired Howard College president Harwell G. Davis spoke at Mobile College's 1970 commencement. Arguing that separation of church and state had never been complete in the United States, he urged Alabama Baptists to allow their colleges to accept some forms of federal aid. This reversal by a man who had fought such blurring of church-state distinctions all his life demonstrated how serious the funding crisis had become. Denominational schools that refused to accept some forms of federal education monies were simply not going to survive competition from Alabama's low-cost, far-flung, public college empire. Although some correspondents rejected Davis's proposal, his speech precipitated a re-thinking of the issue. In July 1972 the executive board adopted a resolution allowing Alabama Baptist colleges to accept federal aid to students provided the assistance did not compromise the religious freedom of the institutions. Only six of the sixty-nine members of the executive board voted against accepting federal student loans. Edgar Arendall, pastor of Dawson Memorial Baptist Church, did question Samford University president Leslie Wright's contention that trustees could take such action unilaterally, without the approval of the state convention. Arguing that such reasoning allowed the convention to control the colleges only through election of trustees and restrictions on indebtedness, Arendall vowed to take the issue of convention control to the floor of the convention.[104] The ensuing debate left the question of trustee-convention control of the colleges unresolved.

Convention leadership continued to draw from the same mix of prominent pastors of large urban churches, with an occasional layman mixed in. Women need not apply. In 1970 the convention elected Mobile mayor Lambert Mims president, the first layman elected in twenty-eight years. The next year messengers selected Walter G. Nunn, pastor of Jasper First Baptist Church. Dotson Nelson (Mountain Brook pastor, twice a "Baptist Hour" radio network speaker, and a former SBC vice-president) was chosen president in 1973. Dan Ireland, pastor of Jackson Way Baptist Church in Huntsville, and Drew J. Gunnells Jr., pastor of Mobile's Spring Hill Baptist Church, also won terms. Gunnells defeated Dauphin Way pastor Jerry Vines in 1979 in a race that pitted an avowed moderate (Gunnells) against an outspoken fundamentalist. Walter Nunn presided over the 1973 convention in Greensboro, which celebrated the 150th anniversary of the convention.[105]

Among the many problems the convention had to resolve was the continued crisis in the countryside. Small-town and country churches continued to face a variety of crises as Alabama's rural population declined: Alabama's rural population dropped from 83 percent of the state's total in 1910 to just 40 percent in 1977. Between 1964 and 1976 alone, Alabama's rural population declined by 4 percent, about the same percentage as the decline in ABSC churches.

Problems abounded in such congregations. The annual turnover rate of pastors was 30 percent, and a tenth of Alabama's rural Baptist churches had no pastor at any given time of the year. The educational attainment level of Alabama pastors in the 1970s was the lowest of any older SBC state: only 24 percent had completed college and seminary (compared to 37 percent in the SBC as a whole). Among full-time pastors of churches with under 300 members, 71 percent earned less than $7,500 a year. As a result, their wives had to earn a salary for the family to survive. In 1978 nearly 1,200 Baptist churches in the state employed bivocational pastors, more than any other state (the next highest, Georgia, had only 995). Lack of leadership or stability resulted in many congregations that were Baptist in name only. They reported no baptisms and contributed nothing to the Cooperative Program.[106]

These problems were not unique to Alabama. In 1978 there were 9,400 bivocational ministers in the SBC, most of them only casually involved in denominational life. Many associational meetings and state conventions were held when they could not attend because of secular jobs. Nearly a third of them had never taken a course designed for pastors. A quarter had no college degree. They often felt isolated and inadequate. In churches with fewer than 300 members, more than half the SBC pastors were bivocational. One-third of their wives were employed outside the home.[107]

The state convention addressed problems in a number of ways: annual rural church conferences at Shocco Springs; observation of "Rural Life Sunday"; special recognition for outstanding rural pastors; continuing education programs; proposals for a Bible institute for bivocational ministers at Cullman. A rural pastor urged the convention to invite country preachers to speak at the annual evangelism conference and state convention. He observed that country pastors were never elected to office in either and were not much noticed by the denomination.[108]

In the listening sessions begun by George Bagley, the most frequently mentioned subjects in 1972 were the need for help by local church leaders, education for preachers, and assistance for rural and weak churches. Although the sixty Howard College extension centers addressed all these questions, some denominational leaders thought more needed to be done. One proposal stemming from this concern was a Bible institute in Cullman to train black and white bivocational and rural pastors. But the Howard extension director vigorously opposed this proposal, pointing out the obvious duplication and reminding convention officials that Howard's extension service had enrolled 25,000 persons (5,000 of them preachers) during its existence. In 1976–1977, the centers enrolled more than 600 ministers, 225 of them African Americans. The center at Cullman enrolled 325, making the Bible institute redundant. The director described the Howard extension center as "THE militant and clear voice in that section of the state against the independent, anti-board, rebel, and superstitious movements which have at times invaded some of our churches." After this spirited rebuttal, the idea of a Bible institute was dropped.[109]

Hudson Baggett warned rural churches that some of their problems were of their own making. In Shelby, Saint Clair, Walker, and Blount Counties, suburban spillover from Birmingham was bringing lots of new people into rural areas. But many country congregations refused to reach out to newcomers, fearful that traditional worship practices would be changed. Blending town and country into a single church was more of a challenge than many rural congregations wanted.[110]

Nor did other problems have easy solutions. The 1972 report of the layman's committee on pastors' salaries was sobering. The committee carefully surveyed seventy-seven churches with resident membership of 101 to 200. It discovered that the average family income for pastors of such churches was only $4,900 (compared to $12,600 statewide). The average pastor receiving such an income had four years of education beyond high school and thirteen years of experience. Fewer than half these churches paid their pastors' expenses to the state convention or automobile costs. Only six paid Social Security for them, eight medical insurance, forty retirement, and fifty-four a housing allowance. As category of church size increased, the survey revealed, so did salaries and fringe benefits, resulting in a two-tier system. Middle-size and large churches provided adequate though not opulent salaries and benefits. Small churches paid so little that only a bivocational pastor could afford to serve. Only a handful of wealthy or megachurches paid salaries comparable to executives in secular jobs. Later in the decade Hudson Baggett reminded churches that inflation had increased by 36 percent between 1973 and 1977, with a resultant loss of earning power to many church staff members who had not received regular and substantial salary increases.[111]

An anonymous wife of a rural pastor related their personal experiences. Despite college and seminary degrees, her husband had to teach school to supplement his income of seventy dollars a month as pastor. He had to pay his own utilities, retirement, and car expenses. During two years as pastor of his church, he had received no salary increase even though church contributions had increased by 80 percent and the church had installed air conditioning. Of the twenty-six pastors in her association, either all worked at secular occupations or their wives did so. To make ends meet, she was a substitute teacher.[112] It was well and good for conservative Baptists to insist that women should stay home and tend their families— but many churches made that impossible by the salaries they paid.

The most poignant correspondence about salary came from the mayor of Pensacola, Florida. His father, an Alabama Baptist preacher who had quit school in the sixth grade, had felt called to preach at age twenty-five. When his oldest son had entered the first grade, the father attended the same school. Despite many jokes and much humiliation, he persevered and finished high school, Howard College, and Southern seminary. When he graduated from seminary in 1939, he was thirty-nine years old and had a wife and seven children. His first pastorate after seminary did not pay him for three months, so he finally asked the chairman of the deacons when they were going to pay him so he could settle his debts. The chairman summoned the deacons, who debated for three and a half hours whether their pastor was too "mercenary-minded." They finally voted to pay him once a month *after* all church bills had been paid. That first pastorate was typical of a series of churches that expected him to take a vow of poverty and made it impossible for him to care adequately for his children. When he retired, his total resources amounted to three hundred dollars, requiring his children to provide for his old age.[113]

The letter reminded readers that cosmic conflicts over race and theology often took second place to more mundane matters. People became ill, old folks died, churches declined, preachers did not make enough money to pay their bills, wives had to go to work, sermons had to be preached, people had to be encouraged. It was in the faithful discharge of such duties, often under duress, that a generation of ministers earned the respect of their congregations.

13

The Fundamentalist Controversy in Alabama, 1980–1998

"See how they love one another."

n 1993 Hudson Baggett wrote a friend in Montgomery who had left the Baptist denomination and joined a Methodist church. The church, according to Baggett's acquaintance, was filled with "ex-Baptists." Baggett sympathized. He wrote his lifelong friend: "I am saddened with you regarding the increasing infighting and polarization among Southern Baptists. We cannot eliminate diversity, but the key thing is how we deal with it, and we are certainly not doing a good job of that."[1]

For people who claim to take the Bible seriously, Southern Baptists pretty well ignored the parts about loving one another. From the fundamentalist ascendancy in 1979 to 1998, Baptists battled more furiously with each other than with the forces of Satan (although both sides did a thorough job of "demonizing" the other). At least in their fighting, Southern Baptists finally joined the American religious mainstream. Few denominations escaped polarizing struggles between liberal and conservative wings.[2] Many such disputes led to schism.

The context of religious controversy is essential to its understanding. The percentage of Americans who told pollsters that religion played a "very important role" in their lives dipped to 52 percent in 1978 before climbing **563** back to 59 percent in 1993. Although the percentages were far below the 1952 high of 75 percent, religious interest clearly rebounded. According to surveys, religion was more important to women, blacks, southerners, people with annual incomes below $20,000 and non–college graduates than to men, whites, nonsoutherners, the affluent, and college graduates.[3]

Denominations profited to different degrees from this increasing interest. Main-line denominations suffered continuing declines. Between 1965 and 1990, five denominations (Disciples of Christ, Evangelical Lutheran Church, Presbyterian Church U.S.A., United Church of Christ, and the United Methodist Church) lost 5 million members (between 10 and 50 percent of total membership). Southern Baptists grew rapidly during the decade 1965 to 1975 but then leveled off to a nearly flat rate. Pentecostals experienced fastest growth.[4]

Evangelicals nestled between main-line and fundamentalist denominations, precisely the niche occupied by the SBC before 1979. They stressed personal commitment to Jesus, confidence in the Bible, and evangelism. They were sustained by robust student movements and enthusiastic lay people. They united around key doctrinal positions such as the second coming, the substitutionary atonement of Christ, the virgin birth, and the physical resurrection. Evangelicals considered liberals to have lapsed into agnosticism. They criticized fundamentalists for arguing endlessly about dispensational millennialism and biblical inerrancy, for being intolerant of other viewpoints, and for being close-minded.[5]

Although historically the beneficiary of fierce regional and denominational loyalty, the SBC could no longer count on such support. Ideological and political beliefs counted for more than institutional loyalty as the twentieth century came to an end. Members were no longer tied to denominations by long patterns of kinship. They surfed denominations like they did the Internet, pausing to join a church because of its youth programs when their children were young, because of aerobics and recreation facilities when they were middle-aged, and because of seniors' programs when they retired. Floating allegiances, blending of beliefs, variety of programs and worship, loyalty to congregation rather than denomination became the pattern of the times. In 1955 only one in twenty-four Americans left the faith of their childhood to join another denomination. By 1985 one in three did so.

Within American Protestantism the SBC remained the towering giant. Not only was it the largest Protestant denomination in the United States, but it was predominant in more counties than any other religious body (42 percent), followed by Roman Catholics, Lutherans, and Methodists. As the denomination spread, it also changed. Many congregations of ethnic Southern Baptists (African American, Hispanic, Korean, Chinese) enlarged diversity, as did white congregations outside the South. Although leadership of the SBC became increasingly fundamentalist, research indicated that only 21 percent of Southern Baptists strongly supported the fundamentalist social program. Considerable confusion also existed over its theological agenda.[6]

Some non-SBC evangelicals interpreted modern trends in religion as the final stage in a northern evangelical takeover of the SBC. As the "most adamantly self-sufficient and fiercely loyal denomination" in the United States in the twentieth century, the SBC seemed to be fragmenting into numerous pieces. Many conservative Baptists were more loyal to the national and even international fundamentalist movement than they were to the SBC and would leave it at the first moderate "course correction" or "takeover." Main-line Protestant elements within the SBC had already effectively left it by the 1990s to form the Cooperative Baptist Fellowship. What was left of the denomination, one national evangelical leader suggested, was likely to be absorbed into mainstream American evangelicalism as the final stage of pluralistic northern thought overwhelming southern parochialism. A kinder way of explaining this phenomenon would be to describe it as the continuing integration of the South into mainstream American society and culture. The fact that SBC theologians were neither widely known nor highly regarded in national evangelical circles, plus the fact that the fundamentalist wing of the SBC was out of touch with mainstream conservatives on both inerrancy and dispensationalism, made this prospect more likely. So did growing disagreement over the definition of inerrancy among fundamentalists and its declining importance in the SBC controversy. By the 1990s the cultural and political agenda of fundamentalism preempted the so-called battle for the Bible.[7]

The pronounced growth of political conservatism within the SBC demonstrated these tensions. After supporting one of their own, Jimmy Carter, in 1976, Baptists voted heavily Republican in 1980 and thereafter. Swept into political activism by the Moral Majority and the Christian Coalition in the 1980s and 1990s, Baptists had difficulty reconciling their political enthusiasms with millennialism. The real desire of conservative Southern Baptists seemed not to be the end of the world after all, but repentance and moral rearmament to prevent the end. The more millennialistic Baptists were, the more likely they were to oppose social change resulting from modernity. They also voted heavily for fundamentalist candidates to lead the SBC. Defeat of liberalism became a substitute rapture, perhaps not quite as good as the real thing, but a close runner-up.[8]

Numerous social and political positions became central elements in the fundamentalist resurgence: reestablish male hierarchy; reestablish pastoral authority over the church; end erosion of families; impose conservative Protestant values or at least demand an equal hearing in public schools and in courts; impose grass-roots control on Baptist colleges and seminaries.

More controversial was the relationship of racism to fundamentalism. Southern reactions to racial integration generated support for fundamentalist leaders during the 1960s and 1970s. Like political code words for racism that became popular ("law and order"), attacks on public education, support for private schools, and erosion of historic belief in separation of church and state owed much to continuing Southern Baptist support for segregation.[9] However, many moderates were also segregationists, and many fundamentalists were among the first Southern Baptists to integrate their churches. No Baptist controversy was ever entirely political or theological, so debate centered on whether religion or politics played the larger role.

Whatever the mix of causes for the SBC controversy, fundamentalists clearly won it. Moderates had no ideology to match the popular appeal of biblical inerrancy. They were too slow to react to successful political organizing by fundamentalists. They relied too heavily on their control of the denominational bureaucracy and the strength of the "grand compromise" that had permitted broad theological diversity within a consensus forged by commitment to missions and evangelism. Having held against extremist attacks from both left and right many times before, centrist leaders assumed it could absorb the fundamentalist challenge by drifting to the right while maintaining broad diversity of belief. Moderates tended to avoid politics and had no convincing response to the charge that they no longer had a passion or strategy for adult evangelism.[10]

As fundamentalists consolidated their control, the conflict switched to the states. Both sides of the controversy were well represented in Alabama, although denominational leaders made a valiant effort to stay nonaligned. The political and theological center of Alabama fundamentalism was Mobile. When whites from rural Alabama and Mississippi poured into the city during and after World War II, Mobile was transformed from the state's most culturally diverse and tolerant city to a center of racial and religious conflict. It was the only large city in Alabama that George Wallace regularly carried. It was also site of two Baptist megachurches that produced a succession of fundamentalist leaders.

Dauphin Way not only moved from downtown to the suburbs but also moved from theological mainstream to fundamentalist. Jerry Vines, who pastored the church in the early 1980s before leaving for a Florida pastorate, was elected president of the SBC in 1988. Darrell Robinson (who was then pastor at Dauphin Way) was elected first vice-president. Asked about the prominence of Dauphin Way in SBC politics, Robinson responded: "I don't want to sound presumptuous, but there is something of the anointing of God's hand on the church."[11]

Cottage Hill Baptist Church also played a major role in both SBC and state fundamentalism. Established in 1944 during a disruptive four-year period when Mobile's population nearly doubled, the church reached 2,000 members in 1963. Fred Wolfe came from an extremely successful tenure in Decatur, Georgia, to pastor Cottage Hill in 1972. Wolfe was a star athlete who had played football at the University of South Carolina. Like Fred Lackey in north Alabama, Wolfe had taken a courageous stand on racial integration. He was a pioneer of bus ministries and urban evangelism. When these efforts brought the first black youth to Cottage Hill in the fall of 1973, several men asked him to talk with a group of members about integration. The "group" turned out to number more than a hundred. Wolfe refused to back down, citing Scripture to support his call for a racially open church. A dozen or so left the church and others were disgruntled for nearly a year, but most members accepted the new black members (by 1997 Cottage Hill had between 100 and 150 black members and a black deacon). Wolfe attributed the phenomenal growth of his church to its fortuitous move to the western edge of Mobile, where it was suddenly swamped by whites moving to the western suburbs. During the years after 1979, Wolfe emerged as part of the inner circle of the fundamentalist resurgence in the SBC, though he played a smaller role in ABSC politics. He was elected vice-president of the powerful SBC executive committee and in 1990 emerged as the fundamentalist candidate for president. But in February he changed his mind and dropped out. Later he lost a closely contested battle for president to a less exclusivist fundamentalist. When offered the presidency in the mid-1990s, he declined.[12]

Al Jackson (pastor of Lakeview Baptist Church in Auburn) was a key leader of state fundamentalist forces. Like Wolfe he had been disillusioned by professors while attending Baptist institutions, and he led attacks on Samford University as a trustee of the school and as an activist in the national fundamentalist movement. He helped rally support for Vines, Robinson, and Fred Wolfe at the SBC and allied closely with transdenominational fundamentalists. As he explained in 1996, inerrantists found they had more in common with like-minded evangelicals of different denominations than they did with noninerrantist Southern Baptists (a discovery moderates were also making). Jackson tended to be confrontational, explaining: "Many a Christian has failed because he had a wishbone where he needed to have a backbone." Believing that the church had been ignored because of its compromises and lack of courage, he proposed an activist political agenda. Although secularists and humanists denounced his cause as part of the "religious right" and tried to isolate its influence, Jackson proclaimed the obligation of ministers to "speak the message of life into every area of life," especially on controversial public policy issues such as abortion.[13]

Perhaps the most influential political fundamentalists in Alabama were Albert Lee and Eunice ("Eunie") Smith. Albert Lee Smith cut his political teeth as head of the Jefferson County John Birch Society. In subsequent years he headed the local Republican Party and defeated fellow Southside church member John Buchanan Jr. in the 1980 Republican primary. Eunie Smith was a founder of Eagle Forum and its longtime president in Alabama. As an opponent of abortion, evolution, and women working outside the home, Smith was a perfect complement to her husband's crusade to purge moderates and liberals from the SBC. He led the fight to defund the Baptist joint committee on public affairs because of what he called its leftist agenda and became chairman of the SBC public affairs committee that replaced it. He also led efforts to purge Samford University's faculty and administration of persons he considered liberals. In 1990 he led an unsuccessful mass mailing and organizing drive to elect a fundamentalist president of the state convention.[14]

Alabama also produced a number of moderate leaders. Carolyn Weatherford (executive director of WMU/SBC and member of Vestavia Hills Baptist Church) resisted fundamentalist control and was runner-up for first vice-president of the SBC in 1989. After her retirement from WMU and marriage, she was elected president of the Cooperative Baptist Fellowship.[15]

Steve Tondera (a Huntsville layman and member of the city's First Baptist church) served two terms as president of the state convention and a term as head of the state convention presidents' organization. He played a leading role in a number of moderate efforts to regain control of the denomination, running for second vice-president in 1990 on the ticket with Carolyn Weatherford Crumpler. Crumpler won 40 percent of the convention vote for first vice-president, Tondera 22 percent for second vice-president.[16]

Dotson Nelson (pastor of Mountain Brook Church) voted against the 1963 Baptist Faith and Message because he believed fundamentalists would turn it into a creed and attempt to enforce it as a loyalty oath on ministers and teachers. He was also defeated for vice-president of the SBC, though like Crumpler and Tondera, he emerged as a leader of the new Cooperative Baptist Fellowship.[17]

Pastors Dan Ivins and John Jeffers also occupied key roles in the moderate camp. Ivins (pastor of Baptist Church of the Covenant) was elected to the board of directors of the new Southern Baptist Alliance, an organization of moderate Baptists formed in 1987. Church of the Covenant and University Baptist Church in Montevallo, both of which had resulted from racial splits during the 1970s, actively supported the alliance. John Jeffers (pastor of Auburn First Baptist) served as an organizer for moderates South-wide after they decided to try to match the political efforts of fundamentalists. In a series of articles and sermons, Jeffers became one of the few Baptists to claim the label of "liberal," though he defined the term to mean racially open, theologically tolerant, willing to ordain women, preferring structured and liturgical worship services, affirming the inspiration and authority of the Bible without rigid literalism, and committing to evangelism. Jeffers defined fundamentalism as "orthodoxy gone cultic." It was, he said, extremist, antieducation, negative in its ethics, and shallow in its evangelism.[18]

Although they did not reside in Alabama at the time, a number of moderate denominational leaders who were casualties of the controversy were natives of the state. Their ties to Alabama churches and prominent Baptist families strained emotions already frayed by years of conflict. Randall Lolley (president of Southeastern seminary) was the first seminary president forced to resign after fundamentalists took control of the convention. Jack V. Harwell, member of an influential Alabama Baptist family, was forced by fundamentalists to retire as editor of the *Christian Index*, Georgia's state Baptist paper. Both were Howard College graduates and friends of Hudson Baggett. State fundamentalist leader E. P. Wallen, pastor of Vineland Baptist Church in Hueytown, criticized Baggett for not publishing the real reason Harwell was fired, which according to Wallen was his "heresy" (Harwell rejected the plenary interpretation of inspiration and biblical infallibility). Wallen's letter provoked a spirited exchange in the *Alabama Baptist* and an anguished private letter from Baggett to Harwell. Baggett sympathized with his friend for reaching the limit of his endurance. Describing the

wrath of God as a situation in which God left man to his own devices, resulting in self-destruction, Baggett believed such a fate awaited the SBC.
Despite a brave public posture of optimism, Baggett's private mood was
one of bleak pessimism about the future of Baptists.[19]

Alabama Baptists were kept well informed throughout the national
conflict. Baggett ran articles almost weekly about one aspect or another of
the battle. One 1989 series entitled "On the Ends of the Spectrum" explored
fundamentalist J. Frank Norris as well as liberal and moderate traditions
within the SBC.[20]

Each side brought its warriors to the state. Samford University sponsored a 1987 debate between fundamentalist Paige Patterson and moderate
Kenneth Chafin (a Southern seminary professor) over attempts to control
what faculty taught at Baptist institutions. Patterson's view that "Southern
Baptist Christians . . . have every right to insist that their institutions teach
according to their common beliefs as expressed in public sessions" fulfilled Dotson Nelson's prediction that the Baptist Faith and Message as interpreted by messengers at any given state convention or SBC would become a creed against which to judge the theology of Baptist professors.
Chafin pleaded for toleration of theological diversity.[21]

Various churches hosted fundamentalist SBC presidents and moderate
seminary officials. Lakeview in Auburn hosted rallies by Paige Patterson
and Paul Pressler. Valleydale Baptist Church in Birmingham hosted 1990
SBC president Morris Chapman, who proclaimed his allegiance to inerrancy. That same year, moderate Southern seminary president Roy L. Honeycutt addressed more than a hundred pastors at Brookwood Baptist
Church in the same city.[22]

Views from both sides filled the letter-to-the-editor section of the *Alabama Baptist*. Of the hundreds of letters that appeared, two captured the
emotions of their respective sides. A pastor at Adamsville wrote in 1991 that
Southern seminary tenured professors "spew forth their own ideas and interpretations of scripture without regard to Baptist Standards adopted by
the Convention." They held the faith of young men hostage to scholarship.
Page Kelly, a native of Hartford and professor of Old Testament at Southern, denied these charges, proclaiming his orthodoxy on the virgin birth,
resurrection, biblical authority, and other issues. Baggett, though meticu-
lously neutral on his editorial page, wrote Kelly privately that he had researched one of the seminary's critics and discovered that he proudly identified himself as pastor of an independent Baptist church.[23]

The young pastor of the River Road Baptist Church in Tallassee was equally outraged over the firing of Russell Dilday, a self-described biblical inerrantist who nonetheless proved too liberal for new trustees at Southwestern seminary. The young pastor led his rural church to designate all its Cooperative Program gifts to Alabama causes rather than fund "the despicable actions of the board of trustees at Southwestern."[24]

Every action by SBC fundamentalists had an equal or opposite reaction in Alabama. When inerrantist SBC president Bailey Smith proclaimed that "God almighty does not hear the prayer of a Jew," George Bagley and Drew J. Gunnells Jr. (the executive secretary and president of the state convention, respectively) called the remark "unfortunate." Declaring that Smith spoke only for himself and fearing his remark jeopardized relations between Baptists and Jews, Gunnells and Bagley thought it presumptuous to declare whose prayers God heard.[25]

The filter for much of this controversy was the state administration committee and executive board, which usually contained a substantial number of moderates and fundamentalists; conservatives aligned to neither side held the balance of power. In 1983 fundamentalists narrowly passed a resolution calling for defunding the Baptist joint committee on public affairs. The following year a similar resolution was presented to the administration committee. Fred Lackey warned the committee that grassroots Baptists had a right to withhold their support as a last resort if the convention continued to support liberal causes. After heated debate, the motion was tabled. That same year members of the committee warned that divisions within the denomination were affecting contributions. Fundamentalists urged that a higher percentage of CP gifts be sent to SBC causes, a move all endorsed in theory but which they repeatedly delayed in practice.[26] The convention also passed resolutions recommended by fundamentalists on a number of issues pertaining to the culture wars (abortion, school prayer). In fact the inerrancy debate declined in ferocity by the 1990s because inerrancy ultimately proved as illusive a term as biblical authority, allowing many a tolerant Alabama conservative to crawl inside the fundamentalist tent. Nonetheless, former convention presidents like Howard Reaves of Mobile considered both state and national conventions to be dominated by fundamentalists.[27]

It is true that virtually all state convention presidents referred to themselves as conservatives. But such events as the firing of Russell Dilday demonstrated the variety of conservatism inside the power structure. Alabama's trustee on the seminary board (the pastor of West Mobile Baptist Church) defended the firing. But many Alabama alumni of the seminary denounced the trustees. Hudson Baggett wrote that the firing of a theologi-cal conservative further eroded the "already tarnished . . . Southern Baptist image," and he renewed his call for an end to the conflict.[28]

The denomination's patriarch, Alabama native Herschel H. Hobbs, be-came increasingly distressed by the conflict. Aware that the Baptist Faith and Message, which he largely wrote, had been turned into a creedal state-ment, he deplored Southern Baptists who acted like "animals devour-ing one another." Had fundamentalists been willing to appoint moderates to leadership positions, he wrote shortly before his death, the Cooperative Baptist Fellowship would not have been successful.[29]

The weariness of Baggett and Hobbs increasingly reflected attitudes of ordinary Alabama Baptists. A concerned, conservative pastor of a small church in central Alabama, upset by the political state of the convention, asked three times that his name be removed from the mailing list of a con-servative tabloid that used "tactics of personality and character assassina-tion." He was equally unhappy with a moderate pastor who sent his church a tape "with political overtones." A layman from Selma brought up the SBC controversy in his Sunday school class, and members agreed it was "noth-ing but college professors and preachers at the big churches fighting for control of the SBC, and the SBC doesn't solve any of our problems."[30]

Many of the issues that energized the fundamentalist movement na-tionally seemed remote to ordinary Alabama Baptists. In order to elect their candidates as president of the state convention, fundamentalists tried a variety of strategies. Because virtually all denominational leaders de-scribed themselves as conservatives who believed every word of the Bible, inerrantists followed their national leaders and turned their aim on one of the denomination's educational institutions. For a decade and a half, Sam-ford University was at the center of the theological storm.

After a brief honeymoon, Samford's new president, Thomas E. Corts (who was named president in 1983), stepped into the abyss of state Baptist politics. Fundamentalist Al Jackson strenuously objected to Corts's deci-sion to allow dancing on campus. Calling dancing "a morally unacceptable practice" that stimulated sexual activity, Jackson warned Corts that his ac-tions simply added more fire to the state's denominational conflict.[31]

Religion professor Karen E. Joines had long been a target of Jackson and other fundamentalists. Gary A. Enfinger (pastor of Thomasville Bap-tist Church) presented Corts a tape recording of a Joines class allegedly proving his heresy. Enfinger and Albert Lee Smith led criticism of the pro-fessor at the 1987 state convention after Corts refused their request to fire Joines. Some of Joines's students defended their professor's teaching and scholarship. One called him "thoroughly Biblical in his teaching and his theology, . . . a great communicator and motivator" who demonstrated "a love for his students and is most receptive to their expressing views which may be contrary to his own." He particularly blasted Smith's "altogether unconscionable manner" of attacking a man he had never met and with whom he had never discussed his grievances. The upshot of the 1987 convention squabble over Joines was that Dr. Max Croft, a Huntsville layman who had served part of a trustee term at Samford and been recommended for a full four-year term, was rejected by the convention. Messengers replaced Croft with a twenty-six-year-old Baptist preacher from Hartselle. Moderate leaders privately warned that this was the first step in a purge of Samford similar to what had happened at SBC seminaries. Croft's pastor described him as a biblical inerrantist as conservative as the preacher who replaced him, and he denounced the entire affair as petty power politics.[32]

The 1987 replacement of Croft was only partly aimed at Joines. The bigger fish to be fried was Samford's newly appointed provost, William E. Hull. An Alabama native, experienced seminary administrator, and popular pastor, Hull seemed an ideal choice for the Baptist university. But his defense of tolerance and diversity and his refusal to endorse inerrancy made him a pariah to fundamentalists. No sooner had his selection been announced than anti-Hull letters began to pour into Corts's office. Al Jackson of Auburn protested that Hull for many years had been identified with "the left-wing of the theological spectrum in Southern Baptist life." He urged trustees to block the appointment lest Hull lead Samford to forsake commitment to missions and evangelism. Albert Lee Smith urged fundamentalist pastors to contact trustees in person to oppose Hull as "a lightening [sic] rod" liberal. He also helped organize a letter opposing Hull signed by 238 people. The letter contained many undocumented personal and political assertions, and Hudson Baggett (on the basis of legal counsel he requested after receiving the letter) refused to publish it. Hull did meet with sixty-four of his detractors, but the agenda quickly switched from Hull's alleged failings to "long-held grievances" against the university. When his new duties as provost prevented his response to a list of complicated theological questions presented by two of the pastors, they accused him of an "uncooperative spirit" and criticized him at the state convention.[33]

Corts defended Hull in a memorandum to the trustees and in an interview before the convention. Hull represented the "more tolerant element in . . . the convention," he wrote. Corts explained that the university's freedom "to make responsible choices" of faculty and staff was "non-negotiable" to accrediting agencies. Hull's position was strengthened by numerous letters from supporters. Harold D. Wicks (a Howard alumnus and director of missions for Salem-Troy Association whose daughter attended Samford) praised Hull as a fair-minded theologian who would foster a climate of honest inquiry at the university.[34]

Fundamentalists also denounced the appointment of theologian John Killinger because he was a Presbyterian and a liberal and because he objected to parts of the Baptist Faith and Message. The Bessemer Association's pastors' conference contrasted Killinger's tenured position to the untenured status of the inerrantist dean of Beeson Divinity School. Corts responded that no administrators (including the president) had tenure.[35]

Even the largest gift ever received by an Alabama university (and one of the largest in the history of American higher education) brought Samford as much criticism as applause within the Baptist family. In 1990 Presbyterian businessman Ralph Waldo Beeson (who had already given the school $10 million) bequeathed Samford nearly $39 million more. After a century and a half of constant financial struggle (and a decade when the executive board consistently rejected proposals by the denomination's education commission to launch an endowment drive for its three Baptist colleges), Samford suddenly became one of the best-endowed American universities.[36]

Jonathan D. Reaves (president of the Bessemer pastors' conference, who had opposed the hiring of John Killinger) led his group in opposition to the Beeson endowment as well. He argued that the money would weaken Baptist distinctiveness because Beeson had stipulated that the primary beneficiary of his philanthropy, the Beeson Divinity School, must employ some non-Baptist theologians.[37]

Although Hudson Baggett (who privately pronounced himself "unashamedly ecumenical in my outlook," which was quite a contrast to his public opposition to ecumenism) endorsed the new divinity school, representatives from all sides of the denominational controversy attacked Corts's decision to establish Beeson. Moderate Huntsville pastor Ralph Langley observed the appointment of fundamentalists and liberals like John Killinger and called the mix "to say the least an unusual combination." He worried that Corts planned to build a "Fuller Seminary-East" (a reference to the conservative, interdenominational California school). A fundamentalist pastor from Cullman worried that Beeson was intended as "the Moderate's seminary." Corts assured him that he planned to hire inerrantist professors as well as moderates. Nonaligned conservative Drew J. Gunnells Jr. (pastor of Spring Hill Baptist in Mobile and a trustee of Southwestern seminary) privately protested that the denomination needed no more institutions to educate ministers. He believed that Corts's decision to establish a divinity school had alienated both moderates and fundamentalists.[38]

The announcement that the Beeson school would focus on a practical master of divinity degree to equip local ministers defused some opposition (the state had 3,500 pastors who had no formal ministerial education). The selection of self-described inerrantist Timothy George as dean silenced other critics. A Harvard graduate and church historian, George declared his fealty to the Chicago Statement on Biblical Inerrancy but denied that he belonged to either side of the protracted denominational controversy. As dean, he hired both inerrantists and moderate conservatives (though no liberals). His subsequent decision not to allow John Killinger to teach courses in the divinity school and the rejection of a Jewish rabbi earned the school national attention and some criticism from moderates but applause from fundamentalists. The subsequent employment of moderate church historian Bill Leonard to head Samford University's religion department created tension between the two divisions of the university but also won applause as a genuine effort by the school to promote a civilized dialogue on the central theological issues of the times. Samford was one of the few Baptist schools to provide fair representation to the full conservative spectrum of opinion (though, unless Professor Joines's critics were correct, the school seems to have been unwilling to add a liberal voice to the dialogue).[39]

E. P. Wallen became the point man for attacks on Samford for more than a decade. A retired military officer, Wallen pastored a church in Hueytown. Beginning with his denunciation of William Hull, Wallen wasted few opportunities to attack the school. In 1988 he demanded that Corts appoint at least half inerrantist professors to the Beeson Divinity School faculty. When Corts added Killinger to the faculty, however, parity was no longer Wallen's goal. Killinger was unacceptable. The selection of Timothy George as dean, which Wallen praised, did not make William Hull any more acceptable to him. Corts responded to Wallen's criticism of Killinger by writing that he felt "whip sawed" by the continuing criticism of his appointments. When he appointed former faculty from fundamentalist Criswell College in Dallas, moderates attacked him. Now Wallen and others demanded to know Killinger's views on abortion. He did not know Killinger's view on that or any single issue and assured Wallen the new professor would not be perfect (nor did Corts know any perfect pastors).[40]

Wallen soon found another issue. "We are concerned about the glaring absence of both faculty and trustees who reflect conservative views," he wrote in 1993. Arguing that Corts recruited faculty who sought "to destroy, tear down, and deny the biblical teaching that we, as pastors, are giving our young people," he broadened his criticism beyond the religion faculty. He also criticized various speakers who had been invited to campus, deplored the lack of fundamentalist trustees, and declared that academic freedom did not extend beyond the doctrinal statements contained in the Baptist Faith and Message.[41]

In 1992 Wallen and Wayne Dorsett (pastor at Central Park Baptist Church in Birmingham) became furious when they were not allowed to attend a closed Samford trustee meeting. They mailed criticisms of Corts (the school had "sunk to an all-time low in morality") to Baptists throughout the state and organized meetings at which Samford was the major target of criticism. Corts reacted with his own mailing, calling the charges "pure falsehood and an affront to the dedicated Christian students and faculty who devote themselves to a high moral tone." Wallen, Dorsett, and Rick Cagle (pastor of Gadsden First Baptist) could not rally enough convention support to take action against Samford. Samford trustee Lawrence Phipps (pastor of Enterprise First Baptist) dismissed the charges as merely an extension of fundamentalist attacks on seminary faculty. It was harder to make such charges credible in a small state like Alabama where so many Baptists personally knew many Samford faculty. Samford's critics expressed frustration at their inability to change the university's course, and Dorsett and Cagle (who were also members of the University of Mobile's governing board) threatened to let "Samford be Samford" and direct their support to the University of Mobile (Mobile College was renamed July 1, 1993), which they called "the conservative flagship university." They admitted that conservatives were divided about Samford. "Some want to go dead at them," but others proposed to switch support to the University of Mobile and leave Samford alone.[42]

Despite such frustration, fundamentalists continued their assault. They switched their campaign to limiting the number of trustees from any single church and adding more pastors. This new strategy was the last straw. Despite a vow by Corts at the 1991 state convention to maintain close ties between university and convention, Samford trustees decided in September 1994 to move toward a self-perpetuating board without approval of the state convention. Fundamentalists and even many nonaligned conservatives denounced this decision. Beeson's dean, Timothy George, issued his own demurral, noting that few denominational schools that broke ties with their founding constituency retained "a lively commitment to the Christian faith . . . [instead of] a thin veneer of religiosity." This press release provoked some internal debate between George and other deans who believed an independent board was essential to protect Samford from the fate of Baptist seminaries. Trustees (all of them Baptists) explained that the action was necessary to save the university from the seemingly endless power struggle within the denomination. But pastors and laymen (who were unaware of events well documented by more than a decade of private correspondence to Hudson Baggett and made available after his death) did not perceive any threat to the school.[43]

For the next two years, Samford and the convention worked to restore their relationship. Samford's critics could never mobilize sufficient strength at the convention either to cut off funding or to authorize a lawsuit. Finally, at the 1996 state convention, Samford and the ABSC agreed to a new "covenant of trust" that allowed the convention to retain authority to approve trustees but permitted the school to initiate trustee recommendations and to appoint replacements for any turned down by the convention. Samford essentially vested the school's final authority in its board, although the convention retained a symbolic right of approval. Some inerrantists remained opposed, but most simply switched their allegiance to the University of Mobile and conceded the compromise as the best they could hope for short of a lawsuit. In 1997 fundamentalists were embarrassed by a series of financial scandals at the University of Mobile and the forced resignation of its president.[44]

Culture Wars

In addition to the battle over Samford, Baptists divided over the escalating culture wars. Traditional concerns about dancing and drinking continued but in greatly reduced fashion. In 1988 no wet county had voted dry in more than three decades. As middle-class culture swept over the convention, many more deacons and church leaders consumed alcoholic beverages. Despite furious attacks against moral compromises in other areas of Baptist life, references to alcohol faded away. So did concern about dancing and blue laws, which had become largely nonissues by the late 1990s.

The old Alabama Temperance Alliance (renamed the Alabama Citizens Action Program or ALCAP and headed by Baptist preacher Dan Ireland) broadened its agenda to include drug and tobacco education, opposition to legalized gambling, and prohibition of pornography. Under Ireland's direction, ALCAP and the Christian Life Commission were particularly successful in lobbying against extending legalized gambling.[45] The convention hired its first full-time director of the Christian Life Commission in 1988, providing Ireland assistance in lobbying the legislature.

One of the most dramatic shifts in the ethical agenda of Alabama Baptists was their waning support for public schools. Having played a key role in the creation of public education, they had maintained an unbroken record of vigorous support, even in the face of public resistance to increased taxes for education. Racial integration had eroded that support during the 1960s, and Supreme Court rulings limiting prayer and Bible reading further dampened enthusiasm. Allegations that textbooks promoted New Age religion, evolutionary science, and alternative life-styles became part of the agenda of school voucher and private school forces. Such arguments caused many fundamentalist churches to begin their own schools. As a result, Baptist support for public schools eroded rapidly after 1980.

Debates on school prayer, Bible reading, and textbooks followed predictable lines. Fundamentalists were prominent in the debate to pass a constitutional amendment allowing voluntary school prayer and Bible reading. Al Jackson of Auburn argued that this was a traditional Baptist view. David O. Dykes, pastor of Oneonta First Baptist Church, argued that even if such an amendment reversed the historic Baptist position on church-state separation, the challenge of humanism and sensuality made such a reversal necessary. Albert Lee Smith helped with the SBC lobbying drive for the amendment in Washington.[46] Other Baptists thought such an amendment unnecessary, believing that voluntary prayer was legal under existing court rulings. Hudson Baggett and Walter G. Nunn (then pastor at University Baptist Church in Huntsville) both held that view, and many individual correspondents to the *Alabama Baptist* agreed. Several of them also mentioned the problem of who would write the prescribed prayer to be recited.[47]

Typical of the dilemma facing Baptists were the experiences of Bessemer businessman James (Jimmy) Moore, a graduate of Samford University and active layman in Bessemer First Baptist Church. Moore recalled morning devotionals in his public school when teachers read the Bible and offered prayers. His fourth-grade teacher had a contest each Monday, placing stars by the names of children who had attended Sunday school and church the previous day. He hated to miss his star and believed that the teacher's emphasis instilled morality in children. To Moore, such religious observances seemed an innocent method of building character.[48] To non-Christians, such religious rituals seemed a way of proselytizing students in a public school that they were required by law to attend and supported by taxes paid by Christians and non-Christians alike.

Public school textbooks complicated these issues. Throughout the era, Baptists directed mounting criticism at textbooks for allegedly teaching New Age and Eastern religions that they believed were harmful to students. Many conservative organizations barraged the state textbook committee with criticism of science textbooks. Baptists pushed for equal treatment of biblical creationism in science classes.[49]

When Eagle Forum led an effort in 1984 to require teaching creationism in science classes, the state superintendent of education and many science teachers fought the proposal, calling creationism a religious and not a scientific argument. Although many Baptists endorsed the recommendation (including M. G. "Dan" Daniels of Cottage Hill Baptist Church in Mobile), others opposed it. Mary Ball and Charlotte R. Ward, professors of zoology and physics, respectively, at Auburn University and both members of Auburn First Baptist Church, testified against the resolution.[50]

Despite solid opposition from Alabama's scientific community, creationism remained an attractive option to many Alabama Baptists. At the 1994 pastors' conference in Mobile, an Australian leader of Creation Science Ministries affirmed his belief that the world was created in six twenty-four-hour days, that dinosaurs were present on Noah's ark, and that evolution was wrong. The pastors enthusiastically applauded his views. One explained after the sermon that "evolution is at the root of our social problems. It deifies man." Another pastor noted that the local Christian Coalition had endorsed a candidate for the Mobile school board who supported teaching creationism, and he had won the November election.[51]

It was appropriate that this convention occurred in Mobile. Not only was the city the center of Baptist fundamentalism in the state, but it had also been the scene of a series of bitter disputes over public education. In 1983 Muslim Ishmael Jaffree had sued to overturn an Alabama law allowing silent prayer. Cottage Hill Baptist Church had assumed leadership in opposing Jaffree's suit. Dan Daniels, chairman of the church's moral actions committee, filed a countersuit three years later, challenging public school textbooks that he alleged brainwashed children in favor of secular humanism. The church began to send a moral issues survey to candidates for public office in Mobile. A typical questionnaire asked if the candidate were willing to reduce violence on TV and eliminate vulgar ads and sexually explicit movies, antifamily broadcasting, and employment of homosexuals as schoolteachers or in national defense jobs. The church distributed candidates' responses to between fifty and seventy-five congregations affiliated with the SBC, independent Baptists, Assembly of God, and Church of God. Pastor Fred Wolfe claimed a political base of 30,000 to 40,000. Jan Bolla (a member of Shades Mountain Baptist Church in Birmingham, chairman of Eagle Forum's education committee, and a teacher in a private high school) testified for the plaintiffs in the case. The state convention also contemplated establishing a textbook review committee to publicize the content of texts used in Alabama schools.[52]

As usual, Baptists fought fiercely over these issues. Several families who intervened on behalf of the state board of education against Bolla's argument that secular humanism was a "religion" were members of Hillcrest Baptist Church, a moderate Mobile congregation.[53]

As debate continued, many Baptist public school teachers, administrators, and college professors defended public education and assumed major roles in trying to strengthen it. Other Baptists charged the schools with promoting outcome-based education (allegedly a social agenda hostile to Christian values), secular humanism, and evolutionary theories contrary to the Bible.[54] This dispute, like the 1986 Mobile suit, closely followed fundamentalist-moderate theological lines, with fundamentalists supporting private schools and creationism in state textbooks, moderates supporting public schools and uncensored texts.

Sexuality also remained a source of tension. The convention's family ministry department provided a biblically based sex education packet that advocated total abstinence and provided information for those who "have homosexual tendencies."[55] The problem came in implementation. Few churches requested such packets. Although Baptists played prominent roles in banning from Calhoun County schools what they called "vulgar trash" by Pulitzer Prize–winning novelist John Steinbeck, they were reluctant to discuss sex in their churches. They condemned homosexuality and AIDS but generally did not engage in ministries to persons with AIDS. That moral problems seldom had easy solutions was illustrated by correspondence between Hudson Baggett and a Baptist woman who objected to listing Holiday Inn motels as lodging for messengers to the state convention. She complained that the hotel chain served liquor and showed adult movies. Baggett replied that if Baptists boycotted all hotels in convention cities that served liquor and showed adult movies, there would be no place for messengers to stay.[56]

Abortion became the central moral issue of the times. The SBC came to its antiabortion position late, not endorsing a proposed constitutional amendment prohibiting abortion until 1980. This decision began a Baptist-Catholic dialogue both in Nashville at SBC headquarters and in Alabama. Bishop Joseph Vath of Birmingham and some priests met with Alabama Baptist leaders at Shocco Springs in September 1980. They emphasized areas of agreement, and Hudson Baggett subsequently began corresponding with Archbishop Oscar Lipscomb of Mobile. Although Baggett's genuine concern about reducing Baptist-Catholic animosity and misunderstanding played a role in this dialogue, so did mounting Baptist support for federal aid to parochial and private schools and opposition to abortion.[57]

The abortion issue did not divide Baptists along fundamentalist-moderate lines. Many tolerant conservatives such as executive secretary Earl Potts and editor Hudson Baggett believed that taking life was wrong in all situations, that a fetus constituted life, and that abortion was therefore morally wrong. Potts joined fundamentalist Fred Lackey in lobbying on behalf of an amendment that guaranteed hospitals receiving federal funds would not be forced to allow abortions. Lackey also urged the convention to establish homes for unwed mothers to make the convention's antiabortion position a more positive statement of concern for women.[58]

Birmingham-area fundamentalist leaders (Doug Sager, pastor of Roebuck Park Baptist; Wayne Dorsett, pastor of Central Park; and Calvin Kelly, pastor of Valleydale) formed Alabama Baptists for Life in 1989 and mobilized for a massive march on Montgomery planned for the following year. Prolife evangelicals spent a year planning the rally and hoped to mobilize as many as 100,000. Some began to discuss civil disobedience at abortion clinics. The *Alabama Baptist* also helped mobilize the denomination for the January 23, 1990, rally in Montgomery. Fundamentalist leader Derek Gentle (pastor of Boyles Baptist Church) interpreted abortion as a simple moral issue like slavery or wife abuse: "You can't say, 'Personally, I'm opposed to it, but I don't want to get involved.'" For him, there was no middle ground.[59]

The 1990 rally drew between 15,000 and 30,000 and a follow-up march the next year attracted 14,000. Many Baptist churches sent bus loads of demonstrators. Numerous prolife letters poured into the *Alabama Baptist*, and state senator Albert Lipscomb (a member of Vernant Park Baptist Church in Baldwin County) introduced antiabortion legislation.[60]

During this extended debate, two issues became clear. A 1996 national survey revealed that nearly one in five women who had abortions described themselves as "born-again" or evangelical Christians. And Alabama Baptists could not agree even on this issue. Polls of Alabama citizens consistently revealed that about two-thirds favored stricter abortion laws and about the same percentage favored permitting abortions in cases of rape, incest, or health problems involving mother or fetus (much wider latitude than the position endorsed by the state convention). Obviously many of those dissenting citizens were Baptists, as a regular stream of letters to the *Alabama Baptist* revealed.

Ed Culpepper (pastor of Mountain View Baptist Church in Huntsville) disagreed with Derek Gentle on the absoluteness of the moral issue. "The struggle of Baptist pastors," he wrote, was that "anywhere you turn, you are dealing with tragedies: unwanted pregnancies, an inadequate system of care for mothers and newborns, an inefficient system of adoption. Most people want to deal with tragedies redemptively. To condemn women with unwanted pregnancies is not the heart of the gospel. Therefore, legislation which is absolute compounds the tragedy."[61]

Many others agreed. Birmingham pediatrician Linda Reeves, a Baptist laywoman, considered herself prolife but also favored choices that allowed abortion in sanitary, safe facilities. Admitting that abortion "is a terrible thing," she nonetheless discussed the complexities of the choices available and opposed outlawing the procedure. Dan Ivins (pastor of Baptist Church of the Covenant) helped organize Clergy for Choice and argued that many Baptists opposed legal restrictions on abortion. Moderate James Auchmuty (pastor of Shades Crest Baptist) preached a sermon on "What Does It Mean to Be Pro-Life." He took a position between what he called prolife and pro-choice "extremists." He called for more attention by prolifers to sex education and to the wretched quality of life for children in Alabama.[62] At the 1981 state convention, John Brantley (associate pastor of Auburn First Baptist) challenged messengers to pass a resolution endorsing nuclear disarmament as well as a resolution opposing abortion. The resolutions committee rejected Brantley's proposal because it "dealt with issues well beyond our competency as a committee to make a sound judgment." One correspondent to the state journal wondered how the committee could so easily sort out complex issues involving abortion and be so perplexed about nuclear war.[63]

The convention also denounced homosexuality. Timothy George laid out the historical and biblical basis for such a position. One troubled Baptist layman wrote privately that his problem with the argument was not whether homosexuality was pleasing to God. He believed it was not. Rather, he criticized the judgmental condemnation of other people and the use of the issue against Bill Clinton in the 1992 presidential race. Baptists would be better Christians, he wrote, if they spent more time forgiving and less time judging others.[64]

Even as Baptist positions on abortion and homosexuality hardened, their historic opposition to divorce softened. Many churches ordained divorced persons as deacons (ironically, including some that would not ordain married females). Special Sunday school classes and programs for divorced church members became common in Baptist churches. One bivocational, divorced pastor of two small rural churches praised his members for giving him a second chance to preach and discussed the warmth of their love for him. Other pastors preached sermons exploring the issue and reassuring members of forgiveness and hope for the future.[65]

Another dimension of the culture wars involved the proper sphere of women. Attitudes came to dominate the SBC during the 1980s that had not been prominent in Baptist thought since the nineteenth century. Fundamentalists argued that women should marry, have children, stay at home, and care for their families. They should be subordinate to males both in family and in church. Their subordination resulted from their having been first to sin in the Garden of Eden. Eternal subordination to men was the price of their sin and the prescription of the Bible. Secular American society headed in the opposite direction and carried main-line denominations and many Southern Baptists with it. They endorsed equal pay for women, passage of the Equal Rights Amendment, guilt-free careers in business and the professions, and recognition of women's service in the church (whether by ordination or election to other leadership roles). These two subcultures collided in the 1980s, with considerable noise and furor.

WMU had been the rather conservative vehicle through which most Southern Baptist women had exercised their discipleship. Despite some membership decline as women entered the labor force, WMU membership remained high. As fundamentalist leaders increasingly questioned the right of women to be ordained and discouraged WMU organizations in the churches they pastored, women counterattacked. Affirming the autonomy of Baptist women to respond to the call of God as they understood it, Carolyn Weatherford (national WMU executive director) encouraged the new Women in Ministry, SBC, a network of ordained Baptist women. When the group was established in 1983, WMU allowed it to use its meeting space at the SBC. Though WMU took no stand on ordination of women or on women's subordination, the very existence of the organization and its professional staff ran counter to most fundamentalist tenets about women's proper sphere within the church. Dellanna O'Brien, who succeeded Weatherford as executive director in 1989, continued the same basic strategies and also agreed to produce mission materials for non-SBC groups, including the moderate Cooperative Baptist Fellowship (CBF). This action outraged fundamentalists, who were already angry that the completely autonomous WMU refused to become subservient to the new male convention leadership.[66]

Carolyn Miller (a native of Boaz and member of Huntsville First Baptist Church) served as national WMU president from 1991 to 1996, the first native Alabamian in the twentieth century to do so. She not only endorsed a ministry-centered agenda for the organization (hunger, AIDS, and child advocacy), which ran counter to the fundamentalist direction of the SBC, but also defended O'Brien's decision to publish mission materials for CBF. The result was public criticism of WMU unparalleled since the nineteenth century. Alabama Baptist WMU members generally defended their organization. The North Jefferson Associational WMU (representing thirty-three churches) endorsed the new missions publication program. Hudson Baggett affirmed WMU, regretted the criticism of the organization, and defended publication of anti-WMU letters as a way of revealing that "some unholy things . . . are going on in the Southern Baptist convention that people should know about."[67]

The location of national WMU headquarters in Birmingham caused the state to play a larger role in women's issues than in most other denominational squabbles. Longtime state secretary Mary Essie Stephens retired in 1984 and was replaced by a vigorous Texan from the national WMU staff, Beverly Sutton. Two years later, Sutton reported the largest enrollment increase of any state. But the state organization also came under tighter convention control. Alabama WMU objected to combining Lottie Moon Christmas and Annie Armstrong Easter offerings. But in 1989 separate WMU and convention budgets were combined. Such control did not diminish the organization's independence. In fact, one president during the 1980s (Camilla Lowry of Auburn First Baptist) was an ordained deacon in her home church and later became state treasurer of Alabama's CBF organization.[68]

Fundamentalists (not pleased with the independence of women such as Miller, Lowry, Stephens, and Sutton) launched a countereffort in 1980. Joyce Rogers, wife of an inerrantist SBC president, sponsored a Mid-Continent Christian Women's Conference in Memphis. Attracting four thousand women, the conference denounced what it termed humanistic approaches to family, the feminist movement (which it called "a demonic attempt to make men and women alike"), and ERA. It also advocated submission of women to their husbands.[69]

Such attitudes clashed with the predominant American cultural pattern of enlarging opportunity for women as well as the autonomy of local Baptist churches. With the SBC defining women's opportunities in ever diminishing ways (fewer women served on boards and agencies, as trustees or convention officials) at the same time that churches were ordaining unprecedented numbers of women deacons and ministers, conflicts became inevitable. A number of associations refused to seat messengers from churches that ordained women deacons. The Foreign Mission Board refused to appoint a missionary couple because the wife had been ordained to preach. Many Alabama Baptists wrote their state paper opposing the ordination of women as a violation of Scripture.[70]

Equal numbers of men and women endorsed such ordination. They insisted that Paul's admonition for women to be silent and submissive in the Corinthian church was culturally based advice to that time and place and did not apply to all women for all time.[71] Scarlett C. Emfinger of Cottondale delivered what can only be called the "steel magnolia" response to calls for submissive females:

> I don't care what Paul thought women ought to do about their heads. I will not cover mine and it does not take away from my standards. The problem is that churches will not let women participate as they would like and the Bible does not say that they cannot. In most churches, women keep the babies, wash the dishes, clean up after dinner, clean bathrooms, etc. Why can't women take up collection, read the Bible, pray, serve as deacons? There are some women wanting to be deacons that would certainly be of higher caliber than men deacons we have now.
>
> I agree that someone in the family unit needs to make sure things get done by assuming authority. But in most family units it is the woman who is doing the deciding and the man gets the credit.
>
> I feel that Paul put women as low as he could put them. He had no use for them and we are paying for this today. Women are afraid to speak out in church or anywhere for fear that their husbands might get wind of it.[72]

These issues came to a head in the mid-1980s. By a narrow margin, the 1983 SBC defeated an attempt by Joyce Rogers to amend a resolution of gratitude for contributions of women to ministry to add words denying support for ordination of women. The following year, messengers to the Kansas City convention resolved that women had been first to sin and that the Bible prohibited their ordination.[73]

Not only did the 1984 action provoke non-Baptist ridicule and satire, it also divided Southern Baptists as few issues had before. Hudson Baggett wrote a lengthy editorial about ordination, calling it merely a way of affirming or approving a person for service. It was the province of the local church to decide who should be ordained, he wrote. Many pastors agreed, endorsing the ordination of women and calling the debate more a dispute about male power over women than about the Bible.[74]

Women debated the issue in separate letters to the state convention president. Beth Baldwin of Scottsboro believed women who sought ordination desired "public affirmation for doing God's work." Women's primary responsibility was the home, she declared, and their neglect of that sphere for outside jobs was responsible for divorce, teen suicide, drug abuse, child runaways, and illicit sex. Motherhood was woman's greatest career, and only women's return to full-time home duties could save the United States.[75] Fay White, president of Rocket City International Training in Communication of Huntsville, represented the other side. Infuriated by the SBC resolution on women in ministry, she noted that such males neither acknowledged nor accepted women equally in Christ. Their attitude was demeaning:

> We must have you women to continue on with your detail work so that we men can continue with boasted egos to lead and work in the ministry! But . . . no way will the Baptist Convention take a stand for equal rights! . . . just throw that crazy issue back to the individual churches, then those women who aren't happy being held down and taking a back seat, well maybe they'll find a more liberal Protestant church to attend. But if they do, just what have we lost? In our opinion they should be thankful we even allowed them ever to become members of a Baptist church in the first place![76]

The controversy descended on the state convention in 1987. A resolution affirming women's role in the church was defeated by a vote of 748 to 644 because opponents feared it might be interpreted to endorse ordination of women. The decision infuriated former executive secretary George Bagley, who exclaimed after the vote: "I'm thankful women have not waited for this convention to serve God."[77]

Two years later the Calhoun Baptist Association disfellowshipped First Baptist Church of Williams for ordaining two women deacons. The church refused to reverse its action, causing the association by a vote of 331 to 269 to refuse to seat the church's messengers, then to expel it from membership in the association. Most associations followed the pattern of Tuskegee-Lee, which had only one church (Auburn First Baptist) that ordained women. Though most messengers disagreed with the practice of Auburn First Baptist, they also considered it an issue of local church autonomy and retained the congregation in good standing. The Calhoun County dispute launched yet another wave of animosity about the service of women. Dorris Chitwood of Moulton suggested that if Baptists were serious about silencing women in church, they should remove them as organists, piano players, Sunday school teachers, and missionaries. Chitwood (who identified herself as a forty-five-year veteran of church service, not a "young whippersnapper with so-called radical ideas") wondered if men were willing to take their places.[78] Pastors who agreed with her preached sermons that emphasized women's biblical roles as prophetesses and deaconesses.[79]

As battle raged between these two camps, women's roles continued to change. From a handful of Alabama Baptist churches that ordained women in the 1970s, the numbers reached into the dozens by the 1990s, including many of the state's oldest and most influential congregations. Mountain Brook in Birmingham, Hillcrest in Mobile, Auburn First Baptist, Huntsville First Baptist, and many others ordained women as ministers. By 1996 more than 1,300 Southern Baptist women had been ordained to the ministry and 50 had served as pastors of Southern Baptist churches. In Birmingham, Marilyn A. Mayse (a chaplain and clinical pastoral supervisor at Baptist hospitals) organized a group of nine ordained Southern Baptist women who lived in the Birmingham area. Paradoxically, during these same years the number of women serving in traditional staff positions as ministers of music and education declined. By 1991 Leslie Poss of Greensboro First Baptist Church was reportedly the only full-time female minister of music in the state convention's three thousand churches. Although women such as Dorothy Frady of Seventh Street Baptist Church in Cullman and Betty Pittman of Dawson Memorial and Hunter Street Baptist in Birmingham excelled as ministers of education, their numbers were also down sharply from the 1950s.[80]

Three factors explain this decline. Many churches, confused over the difference between ordained and unordained staff, simply preferred to take no chances; they refused to employ women on the professional staff. Fundamentalist clergymen also preferred not to employ women professionals. And as ministerial pay increased, such jobs became more attractive to males, who competed for staff positions that had once gone to females by default.

Politics

Both moderates and fundamentalists continued the long tradition of Alabama Baptist involvement in politics. Melvin Cooper and his successor as director of the Alabama Ethics Commission were both active Baptist laymen. Former progressive Democratic governor Albert Brewer remained politically active in judicial reform as organizer and head of the highly regarded Public Affairs Research Council of Alabama, housed at Samford University, where Brewer taught law and government. Claude Harris, Democratic congressman from Alabama's Seventh District, belonged to a

Tuscaloosa church. Terry Everett, Republican congressman representing the Second District, was an active member of Enterprise First Baptist Church. Democratic U.S. Senate candidate and influential legislator Roger Bedford belonged to Russellville First Baptist Church. Supreme Court associate justice Hugh Maddox and state legislator Leigh Pegues both belonged to Montgomery First Baptist Church.[81]

Alabama Baptists had long been active in both political parties and espoused a variety of ideologies, but that began to change in the 1980s. Moral Majority and Christian Coalition, representing the conservative politically activist wing of evangelicalism, began to define a "Christian" political posture. Baptists had always moved cautiously in politics, avoiding partisanship unless there was a compelling moral issue involved—and even the moral issue had to result in a Baptist consensus. Generally if church members were deeply divided, pastors decided it was not a "moral" issue (segregation, women's rights, pacifism, capital punishment were all issues that many religious people considered "moral" but that Baptists defined as "political" because of denominational divisions about them).

Increasing politicization of Alabama Baptists was part of larger trends. The rise of what political observers called the "New Religious Right" owed much to two southern Baptists who were not members of the SBC, Jerry Falwell and Pat Robertson. Falwell had left the SBC for independent Baptists, and Robertson was suspect because of his pentecostalism. These differences were largely forgotten as the culture wars took center stage and denominational loyalty declined. Falwell's Moral Majority organization and Robertson's Christian Coalition became the political vehicle for evangelical Christians. They began to take control of Republican Party organizations in many southern states.[82]

Middle-class Southern Baptist ministers were attracted both to the fiscal conservativism and to the cultural agenda of this newly "Christianized" Republican Party. A 1980 poll found that only 29 percent of Southern Baptist ministers considered themselves Republicans; by 1985, 66 percent did so. The most dramatic shifts during that half decade occurred in the Deep South. Preachers also became much more political and conservative during these years. In the 1970s progressive Baptist clergymen were more likely than conservatives to be politically active. By the 1990s, the reverse was true. Three in four Southern Baptist ministers expressed more than "mild interest" in politics in 1992. After voting three to two for Jimmy Carter in 1976, Southern Baptists voted against him by about the same margin four years later. Organization of Falwell's Moral Majority in 1979 hastened this switch.[83]

Toward the end of the century, Alabama WMU expanded its community ministries programs to include comprehensive job training for women, Habitat for Humanity, literacy programs for the poor, and English as a second language for international students. (Courtesy of Samford University Archives)

Close identification with Falwell and Robertson and fundamentalist dogmatism and intolerance hurt the religious right during that decade. But by the 1990s, religious conservatives had moderated some of their more extreme positions. Moral Majority and Religious Roundtable of the early 1980s had become the Family Research Council, American Freedom Federation, and Freedom Council of the early 1990s. Prayer in public schools was redefined as student rights and equal access legislation. Leaders became more conciliatory and willing to compromise, but there were still trade-offs; nonfundamentalist voters often expressed revulsion at the dogmatism and extremism of the religious right; as more fundamentalist churches invested time, energy, and money on surveying politicians and electing conservative candidates, evangelism and missions received less attention. Whatever way Southern Baptists justified their growing political involvement, they discovered that when religion becomes involved in politics, it becomes more compromising, divisive, polarizing, and secular.[84]

Moral Majority won one of its earliest victories in Birmingham in the 1980 Republican primary when two members of Southside Baptist Church squared off. Albert Lee Smith beat incumbent Republican congressman John Buchanan Jr. Though elected in the 1964 conservative Goldwater sweep, Buchanan had followed an independent ideological course. He had developed close ties to Birmingham's Jewish community and demonstrated genuine interest in racial justice. He had also voted to extend the deadline for ratifying the Equal Rights Amendment, and that vote became Smith's primary target. Jerry Falwell singled out Buchanan for criticism at a March rally in Montgomery. Political pundits credited Moral Majority with Smith's upset victory in the Republican primary and recognized Birmingham's affluent, white suburbs south of the city as a major center of the new organization.[85]

What was more surprising than Smith's victory was the level of Baptist criticism that greeted Moral Majority involvement in the campaign. James Auchmuty (pastor of Shades Crest Baptist Church) criticized the group from his pulpit. He questioned Falwell's ethics in recounting a story about President Jimmy Carter. Falwell alleged that Carter had said he allowed homosexuals on the White House staff because the president represented all segments of society. When recordings revealed that Carter had made no such statement, Falwell admitted that he had made up the conversation. The account, Falwell explained, was "hyperbole" to communicate to his audience Carter's stand on gay rights. To Auchmuty, Falwell's "hyperbole" sounded a lot like most people's "lie." Auchmuty told his congregation: "After prefabricating the story about the president, he said that was just an anecdote. . . . Their arrogance is something that just galls me. They say, 'We have the Christian position,' and I do not think that at all." Drew Gunnells (president of the state convention at the time) also preached on the subject. He favored some of Moral Majority's positions (such as opposition to pornography) but deplored the organization's tactics and misrepresentation of opponents' positions. The pastor of Montgomery's Ridgecrest Baptist Church, Charles Stroud, worried about the organization's reliance on force and political pressure to influence political processes. Tom Roote (executive director of the Birmingham Association) said that Baptist preachers in his area were deeply divided about Moral Majority.[86]

The convention's Christian Life and Public Affairs Commission held a workshop on Christians and politics in 1982 to explore the new organization as well as other approaches to political action. The leader of the seminar argued that Christians should strive for peace and justice when they entered the political arena. With that in mind, he endorsed a Baptist public policy agenda (antipornography, separation of church and state, anti-state-prescribed prayers in public schools, anticreationism in public schools).[87] These positions coincided with those of the moderate wing of the state convention but did not convince conservatives. Defeated congressman John Buchanan left Birmingham for Washington, where he became chairman of People for the American Way, a group created to counter Moral Majority.[88]

Meanwhile, Charles Stanley, SBC president and a leader of Moral Majority, openly campaigned for Republican Ronald Reagan in 1984. Letters to state Baptist officials talked less and less of missions and evangelism and more and more about abortion and Robert Bork, Reagan's nominee for the Supreme Court. In 1987 a Baptist layman wrote Earl Potts angrily blaming the Senate's rejection of conservative Robert Bork (who was an agnostic) on those who supported abortion, homosexuality, drug abuse, and "female dominance." God intended government "to be the means of enforcing justice rather than contributing to the corruption of its people," he wrote. A female member of Pinedale Baptist Church in Montgomery wrote about the same time, endorsing a different political savior, Pat Robertson. She had heard "separation of church and state until I am sick of it," she wrote. It was time for Christians to endorse Robertson and get off "the bench of football politics."[89]

When Pat Robertson launched his 1988 presidential campaign, he had strong support in Alabama Baptist churches. The honorary chairman of Robertson's state campaign was a member of Locust Fork Baptist Church near Birmingham. Gary Fleming (pastor of Mount Signal Baptist Church near Chelsea), Richard Rhone (a deacon at Tuscaloosa's Forest Lake Baptist Church), Lenny Bolton (pastor of Montgomery's Chisholm Baptist Church), and Von McQueen (pastor at Wetumpka's Blue Ridge church) also played prominent roles in the Robertson campaign (which was also endorsed by prominent SBC fundamentalists Adrian Rogers and Charles Stanley). Bill Whitfield (pastor of Cypress Shores Baptist Church in Mobile and a former Republican Party activist in Los Angeles) spoke for many Baptists when he explained that "to stay out [of politics] would ultimately lead to one's own bondage."[90]

W. O. Mozingo (a member of Mobile's Government Street Baptist Church) agreed with Whitfield's demand for political involvement—but in another party and with a different agenda. As a Democrat activist and president of the Southwest Alabama Labor Council for twenty years, Mozingo believed his political causes were also those of the church. Obviously, either Mozingo or Whitfield must have perceived God's revelation incorrectly if one judges by their politics. If God's political will was determined by a referendum of Alabama Baptists (at least judging by the letters that appeared during these years in the *Alabama Baptist*), he had joined the GOP.[91]

The 1992 and 1996 national campaigns deepened Baptist alienation from the Democratic presidential ticket, which ironically was led for the first time in history by two Southern Baptists. Even mentioning that fact earned publisher Hudson Baggett a reprimand. Vernon Offord Sr. accused Baggett of essentially endorsing the Democratic ticket by identifying Bill Clinton and Al Gore as Southern Baptists. Accusing Baggett of favoring "Teddy Kennedy Clinton and Jesse Jackson Gore," Offord had decided that Baggett was "not a dedicated servant of Jesus Christ. You talk out of both sides of your mouth so as to confuse the issue. As far as I am concerned, you can go please your Yellow Dog and Satanic friends all that you want to. I am dedicating my life to having you fired." Gail Hoecherl wrote Baggett that the fact that Clinton and Gore were Baptists should influence no one in their favor. "God's word and the Southern Baptist Convention," she added, "have made it very clear to Baptists that homosexuality and abortion are wrong and not condoned." Because Clinton and Gore ran on such a platform, Baptists should vote Republican. Another writer expressed his opinion that "only one national political party . . . even comes close to supporting the morals that Christians try to live by based on the Bible" (the Republican Party).[92]

Such letters had always been common in the correspondence of political candidates of all parties. But their increasing prominence in the correspondence of Baptist officials demonstrates the secularization of religion once it intruded into partisan politics.

The stridency of such debate and the deepening political polarization of churches bothered many Baptists. As early as 1985 Billy Graham wrote that Christian ministers and evangelists "went too far" in their partisan support of both parties. Hudson Baggett (aware from his own correspondence of the growing animosity and bitterness of the debate) pleaded with Alabama Baptists for moderation and balance. Politics, he wrote sardonically in 1988, was "humanism writ large" because it exalted human effort to save society. Moral Majority had introduced divisive and controversial politics that had diverted Christians from their primary task of soul winning. Though he believed Baptists should be politically involved, Baggett warned about the dangers of such engagement. By 1996 some Baptists participated in organizing the Alabama Christian Faith Alliance, which denied that either political party had a claim on God or morality. Former governor Albert Brewer warned that some churches were in danger of violating Internal Revenue Service guidelines that restricted charitable agencies from endorsing political candidates. He added that "one does not find Jesus making choices between rulers or governors or other officials," whether they were left wing or right wing. "No political label can define or limit Jesus. He defies classification as a politician."[93] Such admonitions had little effect in 1996 Alabama elections, in which most black Baptists worked hard for the election of Democrats and most white Baptists labored zealously for the election of Republicans.

Race

Paradoxically, white Alabama Baptists got along worse with each other than with black Baptists during the era. Deepening divisions in their own convention obscured real progress in race relations. One factor aiding reconciliation was the fact that African American evangelicals tended to be more fundamentalist in theology than whites (even though they were also more economically and politically liberal).

Part of the improvement came from the Home Mission Board's decision to employ Emmanuel McCall as director of black church relations. An enormously popular evangelism conference speaker in Alabama, McCall and Willie McPherson (a consultant for the HMB) confronted racism head-on. McPherson criticized "superior and patronizing white ways of relating to blacks." McCall was equally outspoken, referring to racism as a continuing problem in the SBC. Use of the term "racism" to describe any aspect of SBC thought or life was a flashpoint for white Baptists. The pastor of the Friendship Baptist Church in Pine Apple responded to McCall's article by demanding he be fired.[94]

Periodic vestiges of the past continued to resurface. In 1989 a black Selma University ministerial student and two friends were turned away from worship services at Central Baptist Church in Selma. That same year, Loachapoka Baptist Church fired its pastor, John Clark, for inviting blacks to attend revival services. Clark, a twenty-one-year-old student at Auburn University, was not a confrontational liberal. He attended fundamentalist Lakeview Baptist Church and planned to attend either conservative Mid-America Seminary in Memphis or Luther Rice Seminary in Jacksonville. His pastor, fundamentalist Al Jackson, offered the young minister enthusiastic support, and Lakeview led a move to disfellowship the Loachapoka congregation from Tuskegee-Lee Association.[95]

Half a decade later, a plaintive letter from a student at Samford University revealed a dark undercurrent of racism still alive in the denomination. When assigning African American ministerial students to churches for preaching experience, he had discovered that many of the churches refused to allow them to preach. One association told him that none of its churches would accept a black student-preacher.[96]

When racial conflict descended on Selma again in August 1990, the goodwill slowly constructed by two decades of mutual forbearance and grace swiftly evaporated. Even though Selma First Baptist, along with other congregations, had opened its doors to black worshipers and its pastor Michael Brooks had his children in predominantly black public schools, polarization spread quickly.[97]

The legacy of racial turmoil lived on in two congregations that had divided in 1970. Birmingham First Baptist put a brave face on its problems but remained a deeply troubled church. In August 1980, a decade after racial problems divided the congregation, Samuel R. Jones Jr. ended his three-year pastorate. He explained that he had "grown weary of having to continually secure my ministry." He had proposed twenty-five programs to the members of his declining congregation "with little success." In his resignation he used the analogy of a physician who had done all he could to save a patient who had not responded to treatment. The church began to prosper only when it moved to the white suburb of Homewood.[98]

Meanwhile, Baptist Church of the Covenant had its own problems. Members divided over whether it should stay on Birmingham's southside or move. Pastor Herbert Gilmore felt abandoned by fellow Baptist pastors. He wrote that he had received more support from the city's Jewish community than from his own denomination. Yet, Church of the Covenant survived as well. Wounds healed, Gilmore retired, and the church celebrated its quarter-century anniversary in 1995 as a vigorous congregation with a new $1.2 million sanctuary, many social ministries, and a biracial congregation.[99]

The history of the two churches—one remaining downtown, the other moving—represented alternative ways of coping with racial and urban change. When First Baptist voted to move in 1984, only 143 of the church's 1,100 remaining members showed up for the vote. White flight to the suburbs created tremendous problems that few churches of any denomination overcame. Only a fierce commitment to biracial membership and inner-city ministries kept such a church downtown. Few white Baptist churches had either. Norwood Baptist closed in 1987. Hunter Street moved to Hoover after membership declined by half between 1980 and 1986. Even Parkview Baptist (which became biracial, conducted numerous social ministries, and participated in a model project of the Birmingham Association and Home Mission Board) succumbed, closing its doors in 1980.[100]

Other churches survived downtown. Westside Baptist (an integrated church in western Montgomery) grew to over 200 members. Fairfield First Baptist and Central Park in Birmingham bravely fought on under the leadership of vigorous, committed pastors. Central Park's Wayne Dorsett vowed to stay in the most densely populated area of the state. He insisted that inner-city churches not reconcile themselves to decline. Instead, he proposed a mixture of ministries (notably a thriving K-12 school) and focus on numerical growth. Fairfield First Baptist, pastored by Jack Still, rebounded from a low of 169 in Sunday school and no conversions in 1986 to sixty-nine baptisms in the early 1990s, which led the Birmingham Association in baptisms per resident member. In Mobile the nontraditional New Song Community Church (sponsored by Cottage Hill Baptist Church) located downtown and attracted biracial worship attendance of 250 by 1991. Beacon Light, another nontraditional church sponsored by Tuscaloosa First Baptist and the Tuscaloosa Association, was all black in membership but mainly white supported.[101]

Many churches opened their doors to blacks, including Opelika First Baptist, Normandale in Montgomery, Selma First, and Greensboro Baptist. By 1982, sixty-two SBC churches in Alabama had at least one black member. Judson College president David Potts hosted dinners for Black Belt leaders of both races to reduce racial polarization. When arsonists burned a number of African American churches in the Black Belt in 1996, the state convention responded with generous assistance.[102]

Racially mixed revivals and cooperative meetings became routine. The annual human relations conferences, begun during the 1960s, brought black and white Baptists together every year at Shocco Springs. Powell

Brewton, a Dothan businessman, wrote a friend after the 1992 conference that white Baptists must not only study the teachings of Jesus but must also apply them to life. The church, he wrote, must articulate "an inclusive ministry that recognizes the worth of a human soul, whether that soul is covered with a white outer covering or one of a darker shade." White and black Baptist churches in Montgomery held joint worship services, and Birmingham congregations continued a 1970s tradition of biracial, city-wide revivals.[103]

Evidence of measurable progress in race relations could be seen throughout Baptist life. When the director of Samford's student-preacher program revealed that many churches refused to allow African American students to preach for them, the minister of education at Maranatha Baptist Church in Rainsville praised just such a speaker, John Mokiwa of East Africa, and urged all churches to accept black Samford ministerial students. The Rainsville church and a black congregation had subsequently formed a biracial fellowship. Billy Webb, a bivocational Baptist preacher, overcame a lifetime of religious arguments against interracial marriages and married an African American woman. Biracial couples belonged to a number of congregations, including both Lakeview and First Baptist in Auburn.[104]

Convention agencies hastened changes by hiring African American staff. In 1986 the state board of missions employed a black campus minister for Alabama A&M University in Huntsville. Two years later, a coalition of HMB, Birmingham Association, and National Baptist churches hired a black director of inter-Baptist relations for the Birmingham area. Another African American was hired by the state board of missions in 1993 to work with the twenty-two predominantly black ABSC churches. That same year the state board elected one of those twenty-two pastors as the first black missions board member (Robert Mays, pastor of Rock of Ages Baptist Church in Tuskegee-Lee Association). The professional staff of the state board of missions included three African Americans by 1996. That same year twenty-five predominantly black churches belonged to the state convention.[105]

Some of those black congregations were among the most distinguished in the state. In 1990 Birmingham's largest and wealthiest black church, Sixth Avenue Baptist (with 2,800 members), applied for membership in the Birmingham Baptist Association. Although the church remained aligned with the National Baptist Convention USA as well, its ABSC membership was historic. The pastor, John T. Porter, held a master of divinity degree from Morehouse College School of Religion. He had been an assistant to Martin Luther King Jr. at Dexter Avenue Baptist Church in 1954–1955 during the first stages of the Montgomery bus boycott. He had also been arrested with King during the 1963 Birmingham demonstrations. Later he served in the state legislature, as a member of the state parole board, as a Samford University trustee, and as a member of the Birmingham ministerial discussion group. He interpreted the congregation's membership in the Birmingham Association as the end product of the civil rights movement: "We are still uncertain about each other, but we have to start somewhere. I hope white and black Baptist churches will find a counterpart . . . and try it. . . . It will help us overcome our fear of each other." When Baptist historian Bill Leonard became chairman of Samford's religion department, he and his family joined Sixth Avenue church, completing a symbolic reunion of a religious family long severed. In 1997 Michael Fox Thurman, a graduate of New Orleans seminary and a former employee of the Home Mission Board, was called as pastor of Dexter Avenue King Memorial Baptist Church in Montgomery, the church most closely associated with the civil rights movement.[106]

The 1995 SBC speeded racial reconciliation when it acknowledged its responsibility for slavery and racism, formally apologized to African Americans, and committed the SBC to eradicating racism in its corporate life. This repudiation of centuries-old methods of interpreting the Bible on matters of race drew favorable national attention.[107]

Two responses from Alabama demonstrated the distance Baptists had traveled and the miles still left to go. Rheta Grimsley Johnson grew up in a Montgomery Baptist church during the 1960s. Her church had developed a plan to deal with blacks if they came. Deacons were assigned to act as decoys to delay black visitors at the entrance to the sanctuary while whites would file out of the building. Blacks would find themselves seated in a deserted sanctuary. Some members protested this plan, including a beloved pastor who left because he would not accept such conduct. The church divided into two camps. Blacks never came to test the evacuation plan. But her church did return Sunday school literature that featured a black child as part of a rainbow of faces around a portrayal of Jesus. Like many white Baptist young people during the 1960s, Johnson dropped out of church. As a student at Auburn University and later as a local newspaper reporter, she wrote about the integration of Opelika First Baptist Church. It was not until the 1995 SBC resolution that she felt relieved of the Baptist racial burden of her youth. Calling the resolution courageous and meaningful, she wrote in her nationally syndicated column that "guilt, like injustice, is a heavy, horrible, eternal thing" that Baptists had finally begun to lay aside.[108]

A Baptist minister from Billingsley, Alabama, disagreed. Although he conceded that Christians should treat all races respectfully, he denied the authority of the SBC to repent for personal sins. "All this seems to me," he wrote, "to be an act of political correctness and an attempt to build the 'Southern Baptist kingdom' instead of the kingdom of God."[109]

Perhaps the three men most responsible for changing racial attitudes within the convention were H. O. Hester, Billy Nutt, and Earl Potts. Hester directed the state convention's special missions department, working with National Baptists. More than any single person, he kept open lines of communication during the worst days of racial tension in Alabama. Hester's successor, Billy Nutt, continued and expanded interracial work. Earl Potts not only was personally involved in interracial issues while pastor in Birmingham but helped foster such a spirit in his tenure as executive secretary of the ABSC. After his retirement Potts continued this work as director of a new interdenominational, biracial ministry called "Mission Hope," which focused on job training, health care, and family life enrichment as well as evangelism and church growth. His active participation in Voices for Alabama Children and the Alabama Poverty Project also brought him in touch with biracial ministries designed to help the poor, especially African Americans.[110]

In all social movements there are decisive turning points. Once passed, the momentum of history seems clearly in one direction. Although many white Baptists still resisted that momentum in the 1990s, people like Porter, Potts, Hester, Nutt, Fred Wolfe, Fred Lackey, and Al Jackson seemed to have moved the denomination beyond a critical juncture in the road. The biracial Baptist churches of the early twenty-first century would not be like the ones of the early nineteenth, when blacks and whites sat in the same buildings but as part of different Christian communities. Liberals, moderates, conservatives, and fundamentalists (none of whom brought unspotted records to this issue) seemed to have resolved that race would no longer be the one insurmountable barrier to Baptist fellowship in Alabama.

Social Christianity

How to accomplish this change in racial attitude and behavior was another matter. Some believed social ministries stood at the heart of the issue. Others continued to insist that the economic and political legacy of racism must be destroyed one saved soul at a time. On issues of social justice, Alabama Baptists were no nearer agreement than at any time in their history.

Officially, intramural arguments continued about social Christianity. Fundamentalists especially condemned the social gospel as a sinister force second only to secular humanism as a threat to Christianity. But much of the steam evaporated from their argument as critics pointed out the obvious. If abortions and welfare systems were to be abolished, unwed mothers and poor pregnant women had to be cared for. Medical expenses had to be paid; decent housing had to be found; jobs, education, and job training had to be provided. These were all social functions of Christianity. Some critics insisted that prolife fundamentalists seemed to care more about fetuses than children, based on the ten measurements of child welfare developed by various child advocacy groups (and measured against which Alabama rated near the bottom in most categories). Stung by such criticism, even fundamentalists became more involved in social ministries.

The leading agents of social ministry continued to be Baptists of moderate or liberal persuasion. Churches and the state convention generally feared the label of social gospel and seldom reached a broad enough consensus to allow any ministries beyond traditional charity or crisis intervention. The chief traditional charity was world hunger. Devastating droughts in Africa during the 1980s mobilized the SBC into a world hunger ministry. The ABSC designated $200,000 to famine relief in 1981. Unfortunately, Baptists could not sustain interest in world hunger, and donations from Alabama Baptist churches fell from $746,000 in 1985 to $627,000 in 1995 (in 1991 SBC gifts to world hunger averaged only 52 cents per member). In Alabama, churches identified as moderate tended to give most, though some fundamentalist churches became more involved by the 1990s.[111]

Other traditional social ministries fared better. The state convention bought and equipped an $85,000 trailer to use in disaster relief. Disaster teams were trained to operate the trailer, and it was used during numerous natural disasters throughout the United States. Literacy programs remained popular, and state convention agencies sponsored various workshops to train Baptists to work with both illiterates and foreign nationals who did not speak English.[112]

A different kind of crisis produced a short-lived jobs ministry in 1996. The closing of dozens of textile mills created severe economic crises. Monroeville First Baptist Church organized services for displaced workers and invited the convention's church-minister relations director, Dale Huff, to bring a team to Monroeville to discuss stress management, job retraining, interviewing, job search, and related issues. All five resource persons were members of Montgomery First Baptist Church, one of the premier congregations in providing social ministries. Unfortunately, response to the program was limited, and it was not systematized into a regular ministry.[113]

Churches were better able to reach consensus about social ministries than the state convention was. As a result, individual congregations sponsored bolder projects. Southside, Church of the Covenant, Vestavia Hills, and McElwain churches in Birmingham organized language instruction for internationals and Southeast Asian refugee resettlement programs. Central and Oak Park churches in Decatur operated a hospice program. Wallace Henley (pastor of McElwain at the time) headed a Birmingham Association unemployment ministry during the 1982 national recession.[114]

Churches that had been deeply committed to social ministries for decades led in such activities. The Pilgrim's Sunday School class at Auburn First Baptist provided insurance for sixteen children through the Alabama Child Caring Foundation, and the church as a whole cared for twice that number. The congregation's innovative global ministries offering (which was over and above its gifts to Cooperative Program SBC, Cooperative Baptist Fellowship, and local social ministries) funded overseas missions and seminaries (in Africa and Europe), Habitat for Humanity, the East Alabama Food Bank, Loaves and Fishes (meals for homebound people), as well as many traditional SBC programs.

Several Birmingham-area churches remained well known for their social ministries. Church of the Covenant supported a shelter for homeless women, a ministry for children in a public housing project, an unemployment–job assistance program, and AIDS care teams. Ministers Dan Ivins and Betty Bock explained the church's commitment in 1986: "Ministry is our way of sharing Christ. This is our way of witnessing. . . . Christ showed a radicalism that few people are willing to live out. What comes out strongest in the Bible is Christ's ministry to the poor, the lame and the sick. . . . We don't want to say that we minister only to those who are just like us."[115]

Montgomery First Baptist led the state in social ministries. Organized by social worker Jane Ferguson, who headed the community ministries program of the church, First Baptist allocated 4,000 square feet of its downtown church to such activities. Under the leadership of pastor Dale Huff, the church offered a variety of social ministries: English as a second language, food and clothing centers, employment counseling, teaching parenting skills, support groups for the unemployed, tutoring, prison ministries. Ferguson was also instrumental in establishing the Alabama Baptist Network of Community Ministers. Montgomery First Baptist received the 1983 Jewell Beall award from the HMB/SBC in recognition of its community ministries. Thanks partly to Ferguson's energy, the city also had five Baptist centers supported by the association and headed by a Southern seminary social work graduate.[116]

Only a handful of congregations matched these churches in social ministries. More typical was the involvement of single individuals, and un-questionably the most remarkable example was Millard Fuller. Fuller began to work with a disaffected former Baptist ministerial student, Morris Dees, on a variety of money-making schemes. The two Baptist young men re-placed a Christianity they had found wanting with capitalism, in which they were spectacularly successful. Though both became millionaires in their twenties, they experienced spiritual crises. Dees satisfied his spiritual needs through the Southern Poverty Law Center, which he founded and used to attack racism, the Ku Klux Klan, and armed militias. Fuller used his money to found Habitat for Humanity. Accepting a salary of $800 a month as director of Habitat, he left Montgomery for Koinonia Farms near Americus, Georgia, site of an interracial cooperative farm established by unorthodox Baptist minister Clarence Jordan in 1942. As the spokesman for what he called the "economics of Jesus," Fuller used Habitat volunteers to help poor people around the world build no-profit, no-interest homes. After its beginning by Fuller and Jordan in 1968, Habitat for Humanity became one of the most successful worldwide Christian social ministries in history when former president Jimmy Carter became active in the volunteer pro-gram.[117]

State health officer Earl Fox used his Baptist affiliation and leadership of the state's public health program as a bully pulpit for improved medical care for the poor. He urged Baptist ministers to act as catalysts in dealing with teenage pregnancies, the nation's highest infant mortality rate, and AIDS. He also urged the convention's executive committee to take action on these problems. He endorsed higher cigarette taxes to provide school counseling for sexually active teenagers, more money for AIDS patients, legislation to protect mothers and babies, adequate prenatal and infant health care to prevent abortions, prenatal clinics in every county, free preg-nancy testing, free care for high-risk maternity cases, outreach services and hospital care for babies to the age of two, and family planning for low-income women who did not want additional children. Unfortunately, Bap-tists listened without acting. They took no collective stand on these bills when they were before the legislature, nor did they take an institutional stand for "children first" legislation during the 1995, 1996, and 1997 legis-lative sessions that would have increased tobacco taxes to help at-risk youth.[118]

Other individuals initiated equally creative ministries. Lloyd H. Lauer-man Jr. and Paul Smith (both members of the veterinary faculty at Auburn University and of Auburn First Baptist Church) formed the Alabama Bap-tist Veterinary Fellowship. Together with vet school colleague and fellow

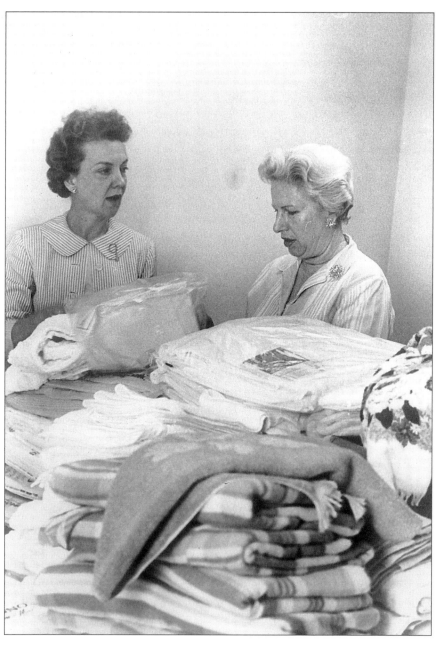

Mary Essie Stephens, director of Alabama WMU, and Byrd Ousley, treasurer of state WMU, sort towels and linens to be given to Shocco Springs. (Courtesy of Samford University Archives)

church member Dwayne Beckett, they organized a number of overseas veterinary ministries to Belize, Thailand, East Africa, Central America, and Brazil. Dan Merck, a surgeon at Baptist Medical Centers in Birmingham, organized the Baptist Medical-Dental Fellowship to supply volunteer medical services on a short-term basis at mission stations around the world. The Alabama Poverty Project, founded in the early 1990s, was led by a number of Baptist lay persons and ministers. Earl Potts was one of the founders and longtime officers. His son David, president of Judson College, was a member of the board. So were former governor Albert Brewer, Samford University president Tom Corts, and Cynthia Allen Wise, a laywoman, teacher, and historian at Dothan First Baptist Church.[119]

Resistance to such ministries continued. Despite their size, affluence, and power, Alabama Baptists had minimal influence on strategies aimed at social change. Their prophetic ministries depended on a handful of churches and individuals. Though active in their opposition to legalized gambling, they offered no alternatives for raising revenue to pay for critical social services. The denomination was nearly invisible during campaigns for tax and education reform, although individuals such as Albert Brewer and Earl Potts lent their support. As a deeply cynical Herbert Gilmore reminisced late in his life: "If you have a conscience about social justice, you are a social gospeler. The deepest problem in Southern Baptist ranks is the way our spiritual leadership has been as silent as a gravestone regarding the real issues of theology and social justice."[120]

The State Convention

Controversies over theology and social issues split the SBC and most state conventions after 1979, but Alabama Baptists remained remarkably united. A number of factors explained this relative peace. Many leading conservative pastors were politically nonaligned. No major fundamentalist or moderate leader polarized the state convention (though several took leading roles on both sides within the SBC). Consensus builders dominated the state convention and mission board. Hudson Baggett, who controlled the Baptist media, "relentlessly focused" on any promising sign and pleaded for understanding and tolerance. George Bagley became increasingly outspoken on behalf of the moderates in the early 1980s. Like many long-term denominational officials, he thought the SBC would quickly return to a centrist consensus as it had so many times before. By the time its rightist drift had gained momentum, Bagley retired. His retirement was fortunate for convention harmony because leading fundamentalists considered him unfair.[121]

Earl Potts, a workmanlike mission board employee and Bagley's assistant, was chosen as acting executive secretary in 1983. He was the perfect candidate to prevent a rift in the highly charged atmosphere of the convention. Pastors believed the sixty-two-year-old Potts was too old to be a candidate for the permanent position. As a longtime pastor and denominational bureaucrat, he was well known and experienced. Born in rural Randolph County the son of a farmer, dairyman, and service station operator, he had worked at a dairy and cotton mill as a young man. After graduating from Howard College and Southern seminary, he had pastored numerous small churches before moving to McElwain church in Birmingham, where he also taught in the Howard extension program. Soft-spoken and well-mannered, he was scrupulously fair to all sides of controversies. He never forgot his humble origins, which allowed him to identify with ordinary Baptists.

His age and disavowal of interest in the job led the search committee to name him acting head. The obvious ambition of others, deepening denominational controversy, and Potts's inclusive, team-oriented administrative style endeared him to a wide range of Baptists. Other choices threatened to polarize the state, so in April 1984 he was chosen permanent secretary.[122]

The choice was providential. As the second mission board professional selected to head the staff, Potts was a consummate compromiser. During his five years in office, he steered the denomination like an expert pilot through waters filled with snags and bars. Hudson Baggett, recalling Potts's role in quelling Birmingham racial strife and building bridges to National Baptists, described him as a man of "gumption, grit, and grace." An SBC official called his style "a ministry of the towel." When fundamentalist leader Rick Cagle, pastor of Gadsden First Baptist Church, commented in 1989 that the atmosphere in Alabama was different and more tranquil than in other states, ABSC president Charles Carter attributed the difference to Potts: "Institutions reflect the personality of their leadership, and Earl Potts is characterized by congeniality and cooperation." In 1990 when Potts retired, 2,500 Alabama Baptists attended a reception in his honor.[123]

The mission board chose Troy L. Morrison to succeed Potts. A self-described inerrantist, Morrison was the third consecutive state board employee chosen. As director of church-minister relations after 1985, he was fifty-eight when elected, close to Potts's age at his selection. A native of

Hudson Baggett, editor of the *Alabama Baptist* from 1966 until 1994, helped steer the convention in a centrist course away from theological extremes. A tolerant conservative, he privately criticized fundamentalism while publicly remaining friends with many fundamentalist leaders. (Courtesy of Samford University Archives)

Cherokee County and owner of a building supply company before he entered the ministry, Morrison had pastored Twelfth Street Baptist Church in Gadsden.[124] He was chosen for the same reasons that Potts had been; he was a team player and consensus builder. To pick a pastor from a prominent church in a time when most pastors were identified with one of the contending factions threatened to tilt the denomination in one ideological direction or the other. Better a proven administrator for executive secretary who was politically nonaligned.

Another reason for the denomination's relative harmony was Hudson Baggett. As editor of the *Alabama Baptist* (whose circulation of 120,000 in 1996 continued the paper's second-place rank among Alabama newspapers), Baggett followed a course of balance and fairness. His goal was to hold the denomination together. Moderates who knew him well criticized Baggett for tepid editorials that masked his private rage at fundamentalist tactics and creedalism. Fundamentalists who knew him well accused him of favoring moderates. Both charges were valid. He steered as straight and balanced a course as anyone could have under the circumstances.

One of Baggett's major assets was his personality. He loved to tell sto-ries from his rural Cullman County childhood. Hardly a Sunday passed that he was not in some pulpit, likely as not in a rural church or small town. Baggett learned the same lesson that L. L. Gwaltney had discovered de-cades earlier: Alabama Baptists would tolerate a variety of opinions from persons who obviously cared about them but would not long suffer con-trary viewpoints from remote or callous leaders, be they moderate or fun-damentalist.

Baggett defined the function of a denominational paper to be both an echo of popular sentiment and a prophetic voice. By prophetic, Baggett seemed to mean a paper that was open to multiple viewpoints rather than taking public stands in advance of the constituency. His editorial comment was relentlessly upbeat. Controversy was not altogether bad. Divisions were not as deep as they seemed. Almost all Baptists were conservatives. On the major issues of missions and evangelism, Baptists were united. Poli-tics had always been present in convention life. Baptists must be tolerant of one another's differences and grant each other freedom of belief. After every convention or major controversy, Baggett published brief comments by Alabama Baptists on both sides of the controversy.[125]

Baggett liked and respected many inerrantists. Politically he was quite conservative himself. In editorials he frequently praised fundamentalists such as Adrian Rogers and W. A. Criswell, although he warned against a spirit of "witch hunting and narrow views regarding the definition of a heretic." His personal correspondence with inerrantists Fred Wolfe and Junior Hill was warm and affectionate. In 1993 he took the initiative in pro-moting the candidacy of inerrantist Timothy George as president of South-ern seminary (George was "not a moderate," he wrote, but possessed "a moderate spirit and attitude").[126]

As a consequence of his personal charm, Baggett received constant praise for his evenhandedness. One friend believed he was the consum-mate Baptist editor for controversial times: a man "with the hide of a rhi-noceros as well as a keen mind and a warm heart."[127]

Privately Baggett frankly expressed his own opinions. Although he did not dwell on the SBC controversy in the paper, he read every book and ar-ticle that appeared about it. He published correspondence from all points of view while often refusing to print inflammatory letters. One correspon-dent sent the editor a copy of a letter to George Bush during the 1992 cam-paign, backing the president and calling AIDS a judgment of God on those who lived immoral lives. The letter earned the writer a rejection and an icy sermonette. Baggett explained that the *Alabama Baptist* did not publish letters to politicians and that AIDS was also transmitted through blood transfusions. In letters to friends Baggett linked fundamentalism to "thought control and brainwashing" that were more psychological than theological. He responded to a friend's request for an explanation of the SBC controversy by replying that it originated in a desire by some preachers for a rigid and inflexible litmus test. He denied categorically a central fundamentalist tenet, that many Southern Baptist leaders did not believe the Bible to be true. The controversy was, in his view, primarily political. "All of the politicking and ego exercising is done by a definite minority of people," he wrote another friend. Although he did not doubt their sincerity, he insisted that Christianity was more than a "set of rules, regulations, and legalistic pronouncements." He particularly criticized one fundamentalist pastor as "a good young preacher but . . . extremely ambitious and political." "The bottom line for a lot of these young fellows," he added, "has to do with climbing the ladder to get a better church and a more prestigious platform as an ego stage." Baggett declined to attack such preachers publicly, he wrote another friend, recalling the advice of evangelist Vance Havner, who had once said: "A bulldog can whip a skunk but it isn't worth it."[128]

Especially during the 1990s Baggett made no attempt to disguise his feelings to friends he felt he could trust. He wrote Herschel Hobbs to confirm the worst fears of the aging patriarch: the peace committee report, like his earlier Baptist Faith and Message statement, had been made into a creed "by which people in our agencies and institutions were measured." Baggett responded factually and fairly to inquirers about the new Cooperative Baptist Fellowship, assuring them that it did not reject biblical authority. He congratulated a fellow editor for pointing out the inconsistency of fundamentalists who welcomed independent Baptist Jerry Falwell (who had never supported the SBC) while demanding that members of Cooperative Baptist Fellowship (who had been some of the denomination's most faithful supporters) leave the denomination. A lawyer friend who engaged Baggett in dinner conversation about the SBC controversy was delighted they thought so much alike. "The Inerrantists are certainly intellectually dishonest," he summarized, and the moderates were "unfortunately fuzzy brained." Inerrantists had the shrewd leadership of Texas judge Paul Pressler. Moderates had "no Brain nor Strategist. So we lost."[129]

Fundamentalists who knew Baggett well had doubts about him. His public fairness won their admiration, but they could never quite forgive his private opposition. Gary A. Enfinger of Thomasville Baptist Church criticized Baggett for using articles by the independent Associated Baptist Press, which, he accused, was formed "by disgruntled individuals who have a reputation for writing with a clear bias against current SBC leadership." When Baggett continued to use the new press, Enfinger asked the newspaper's board of directors to discontinue it. Other fundamentalists accused Baggett of bias against inerrantists and asked that he allow one of their leaders to present their side in the paper. They also criticized Baggett's journalist son, Mark, for interviewing people outside Cooperative Program–supported agencies. Michael J. Bryson Sr. of Birmingham addressed a letter "To the Bible Believing People of Southern Baptist Churches in Alabama" to have the two Baggetts fired as "trouble-making liberals." Although new inerrantist Southern seminary dean David S. Dockery did not go that far, he did criticize several articles published in the *Alabama Baptist*.[130] Baggett's sudden death of a massive heart attack in November 1994 should have been a warning to all Baptists of the toll their fighting had taken. Baggett's private correspondence makes one point obvious. Beneath the surface tranquillity of Alabama Baptists, relations were churning and tumultuous.

Dominance of the state convention (like control of the *Alabama Baptist* and the executive secretary's job) was a central objective of both fundamentalists and moderates. Though polite and conciliatory in public, they privately worked like demons to elect their man president. Virtually every presidential election during these two decades pitted a conservative aligned with SBC fundamentalists against a conservative who was politically nonaligned (often referred to by both sides as a "denominational loyalist"). Moderates and women active in WMU backed nonaligned inerrantists, as did many theologically conservative pastors who resented the politicizing of the convention and who feared that the animosity of the SBC controversy might take root in Alabama.

The first three elections in the 1980s (not counting reelections for second terms, which were customary) arrayed factional candidates against each other. In 1981 moderates backed James Auchmuty of Birmingham's Shades Crest Baptist Church, and inerrantists endorsed Fred Wolfe of Cottage Hill Baptist Church in Mobile. Gadsden First Baptist pastor Harold Cushing, a less strident conservative, won a runoff against Wolfe, and state health officer Ira Myers was elected as vice-president. Cushing specifically disassociated himself from Moral Majority but also opposed abortion.[131]

Cushing's successor, Wallace Henley of McElwain Baptist Church, beat moderate layman Ira Myers of Montgomery by only eighteen votes in a 1983 runoff. Henley was a self-described theological liberal turned fundamentalist. Like Cushing, he refused to join Moral Majority or endorse Jerry Falwell or Pat Robertson for U.S. president. His participation in the

Nixon administration had left Henley cynical about political power and suspicious of demagoguery. On many social issues he took a New Right position, but he also allowed his female minister of recreation to "speak" in his absence from McElwain and refused to become involved in adversarial relationships. He also was an admirer of Earl Potts (his "heart is so pure," Henley explained, that people "can give [him] total and absolute trust").[132]

Lewis Marler (who had pastored Gardendale First Baptist before moving to Mount Philadelphia Baptist, a small church in Walker County) defeated inerrantist Jimmy Jackson of Huntsville's Whitesburg Baptist Church in 1985.[133] Marler disavowed interest in politics and was theologically nonaligned. His first vice-president, Steve Tondera of Huntsville, was elevated to president when Marler became ill late in 1986.

Tondera was a native of Waco, Texas, a graduate of Baylor University, and a computer expert and administrator at Huntsville's National Aeronautics and Space Administration. He also owned Diamond T. Ranch, where he raised Santa Gertrudis cattle. An active Mason, president of the politically powerful Alabama Cattlemen's Association, and former chairman of the deacons at Huntsville First Baptist Church, Tondera called himself a theological conservative who was tolerant of other viewpoints and who deplored the theological controversies splitting the denomination. Garrulous and a wonderful jokester, he entertained crowds with self-deprecating stories. Elected with 65 percent of the vote in November 1986 over Glenn Weekley of Jasper First Baptist Church, Tondera was the first layman elected president since 1970.[134]

Following his election, Tondera tirelessly promoted denominational causes. During three months of speaking at churches and associational meetings in 1987, he drove 22,000 miles. One story he used when speaking to such audiences concerned an incident that occurred when he was returning home late from speaking and exited at a Cullman truck stop for coffee. The waitress recognized him as president of the ABSC from his photograph in the paper. She told him that her parents had died when she was a child; she and her sister had been raised at the children's home in Troy. She asked him to express her gratitude to Baptists for the facility and what it had meant in her life.[135] Such stories left many a misty eye in Baptist churches and endeared the folksy president to Baptists who heard him.

There was another side to Tondera. From the beginning of the SBC controversy, he sided with moderates. He became active in the statewide campaign to publicize the AIDS crisis and served on the state AIDS Prevention Council. His proposal that sexually active people use condoms to prevent the spread of the disease raised a furor among Baptists. Keith Adams, who identified himself as a "fundamental, independent" Baptist preacher, condemned Tondera and SBC pastors (who "need to . . . cut the lace off their underwear and let's preach salvation and righteousness and forget those social committees"). Another independent Baptist scorched Tondera for suggesting education and condoms as a solution to AIDS instead of salvation, which was "God's AIDS Prevention Council." Tondera also said that the ordination of women was a local church issue. He strongly supported WMU when fundamentalists began to attack the organization. Even his presidency of the state SBC presidents' fellowship, which pushed for a peace committee to compromise differences within the convention, came under fire.[136]

The crowning indignity to many Alabama fundamentalists was Tondera's refusal to support their attempts to fire William Hull, Samford's provost. The controversy over Hull peaked in 1986–1987, and Tondera forcefully backed the university administration. Bob Pitman (pastor of Muscle Shoals First Baptist Church) launched a short-lived campaign to prevent Tondera's reelection in 1987. But Pitman was hurt by his opposition to a customary second term for Tondera and by the fact that his church did not have a WMU organization. Tondera had amassed considerable support by his "aw shucks," laid-back cowboy boots–wearing affability, and Pitman withdrew from the race the week before the state convention.[137] After his term of office ended, Tondera became active in the Cooperative Baptist Fellowship and was a leader of both national and Alabama moderates.

Tondera, a layman with moderate credentials, probably would never have been elected had he not inherited the office when Marler became ill. But Tondera's successor, Charles Carter, was a predictable candidate. He had pastored one of the state's premier fundamentalist churches, Whitesburg in Huntsville, was pastor of Shades Mountain Baptist Church at the time of his election (a church that was emerging as one of the SBC leaders in both baptisms and gifts to the Cooperative Program). Carter was an inerrantist and an innovative evangelist. He was also a superb administrator who planned ahead and alerted others to his ideas so he could solicit their thought and reflection. He was resolutely upbeat, a tolerant fundamentalist who refused political identification. He had also been one of the early advocates of an SBC peace committee representing all sides of the theological controversy. His election in 1988 without opposition ushered in two years of relative harmony, and his evenhanded appointments continued a tradition of giving both sides significant representation on committees and boards.[138]

Following the relative tranquillity of the Carter years, the warring factions reengaged in 1990. Moderates and nonaligned conservatives backed
Rick Lance, pastor of Tuscaloosa First Baptist Church. Albert Lee Smith described Lance as a moderate and backed Doug Sager, pastor of Roebuck
Baptist Church. But Lance had nominated Charles Carter for president two
years earlier, avowed his conservative credentials, and promised to focus
on evangelism and missions, not on the SBC controversy. Lance was elected
with 54 percent of the vote in something of a surprise because the convention was held in the fundamentalist stronghold of Mobile.[139]

After Lance's uncontested election to a second term, inerrantists waged
perhaps their most politicized campaign for the presidency in 1992. The
atmosphere in the state convention was tense. Organization of the Cooperative Baptist Fellowship, level funding of the Cooperative Program, controversy swirling around Samford University—all contributed to a particularly sour environment. Two other incidents had significant impact on the
outcome of the election. Just before the convention, inerrantists published
a newsletter, the *Alabama Baptist Observer*, which endorsed Fred Lackey for
president. It was sent to pastors and passed out to messengers as they entered the convention church, a familiar tactic to those who attended SBC
meetings. The strategy backfired, according to some messengers who worried that such tactics introduced SBC-style politics to Alabama. Inerrantists
denied that the newsletter was divisive or influenced the outcome.

The other issue had a more demonstrable but subterranean effect. For
a year the SBC had been wallowing in an unlikely squabble over the Masons. A fundamentalist physician from Texas, Larry Holly, had condemned
the organization as nonbiblical and satanic. The initial charges and a Home
Mission Board investigation generated some favorable support in Alabama.
Crystal A. Haynes of Jackson's Gap wrote a lengthy article claiming that
the Masonic order was a religious cult. Hudson Baggett refused to run the
article because it did not conform to the required length, and he considered
parts of it libelous. Haynes believed the real reason Baggett rejected her
letters was because so many Baptists were Masons. The latter charge was
probably correct. More Baptist preachers had belonged to the Masons than
to any other group during the heyday of fraternalism. In fact, the man to
whom she sent her letter, Hudson Baggett, was a Mason, although he hardly
considered it a rival to Christianity. Another critic tried to run an advertisement against Masonry. When Baggett refused the ad, he threatened to
sue the editor and accused him and half of all Baptists of being "involved
in this cult."[140]

As the controversy spread, angry Masons flooded Baggett with rebut tals. A Mason from East Gadsden accused Holly of "tap dancing" through the Bible in order to sow discord among Baptists. Margaret Bryan and her daughter were members of Eastern Star and her husband and two sons were Masons. They had been Masons, she wrote Hudson Baggett, "about as long as Baptist" (fifty-four years). Her father had been a Mason and Baptist deacon. "Who ever the man was that wrote . . . that the Masons are Satan worshippers either don't know what he is saying or he is telling a lie," she wrote in fury. "Instead of Southern Baptists (who are not like they were when I was growing up) trying to down the Masons, why don't they do like they did years ago and fight the devil." In an ominous conclusion, she warned: If Southern Baptists wanted to keep their finest members, "they had better lay off the Masons."[141]

Although Baggett refused to publish these letters as well, he was sympathetic with their content. No other part of his private correspondence matched his venom toward Holly, whom he called "a vicious man" with a "wrecking crew mentality." "Though he is a physician," Baggett wrote one friend, "he is one of the sickest persons I know. His charge that Masonry is satanic is a projection of his own demonic spirit."[142]

Coming as it did just before the 1992 convention, the Masonic controversy contributed to the backlash against fundamentalism and the introduction of such fringe controversies into Alabama. Although little attention has been directed at the Masonic debate, it obviously was a strategic fundamentalist miscalculation.

The 1992 convention pitted inerrantist Fred Lackey (pastor of Athens First Baptist Church) against Dewey Corder (pastor of Trussville First Baptist Church). Corder won with 51.6 percent of the vote. An inerrantist and a moderate were elected vice-presidents. Corder described himself as "theologically conservative and politically nonaligned." He did not favor ordaining women but believed the matter should be left to each church to decide. His church had two women in full-time professional ministerial roles, but neither was ordained.[143] Lackey accepted his defeat gracefully and pledged to work with Corder.

Lackey's cooperative attitude and patience paid dividends in 1994 when he won a close victory over Earl Potts, 1,258 to 1,113. Moderates had long favored Potts. Strong advice from his friend Charles Carter and others had kept him out of the 1992 race, but he was persuaded to enter the 1994 campaign partly because of the constant attacks on Samford University, for which he worked part-time after his retirement as executive secretary.[144]

Following Lackey's second term, the factions renewed their conflict in 1996. Politically aligned inerrantists backed Mike McLemore, pastor of

Lakeside Baptist Church in Birmingham. Nonaligned and moderate forces backed Leon Ballard, pastor of the 227-member York First Baptist Church. The resolution of the Samford University trustee controversy on the first day of the convention created a more harmonious spirit than in previous conventions and removed the central controversy. Nominating speeches for Ballard were also effective, touching a populist nerve in the convention by emphasizing that the ABSC had not elected a small-church pastor president in decades. Ballard won with 60 percent of the votes.[145]

Nonaligned inerrantists played the critical role in preserving convention harmony. The refusal of many fundamentalists to include noninerrantists in convention life divided other states and drove moderates into the new Cooperative Baptist Fellowship formed in 1990. Although many Alabama moderates played key roles in the new organization (John Jeffers, Dotson and Buddy Nelson, Philip and Cynthia Wise, Jim Auchmuty, Steve Tondera, Gary Burton, Camilla Lowry, Roger Lovette, John and Deb Loftis, Laura Hargrave), it failed to win widespread backing in Alabama because fundamentalists did not precipitate the kind of crisis that forced nonaligned conservatives to choose between CBF and SBC. The organization produced its own state newsletter (the *Baptist Light*) and met twice a year. Women and lay persons played a much larger role in the state CBF's biannual meetings than they did in the state convention. Members regularly elected women as moderator and members of the governing council. Although the number of churches financially supporting CBF was small (twenty-seven in 1993, forty-five in 1996), many of those churches were influential and wealthy. Of the leading twenty-five churches in Cooperative Program gifts to the 1993 state convention, seven also contributed significantly to CBF (Dawson Memorial, Dothan First, Mountain Brook, Huntsville First, Brookwood, Decatur First, and Southside). In 1994, 145 individuals and thirty CBF churches in Alabama contributed $556,000.[146]

Pastors were major casualties in many CBF-SBC struggles. Although most churches were united in favor of remaining in the SBC, many contained alienated members furious over attacks on Masons, favorite professors, colleges or seminaries, or for what many Baptist women considered demeaning SBC attitudes toward them. The resulting tension divided churches into warring factions. Sometimes pastors led one faction or the other; at other times, they were hapless victims caught in the middle. Many times the forced resignation of a pastor had little to do with either theology, SBC controversies, or moral turpitude. The culprit was often the pastor's poor administrative or interpersonal skills. At other times, firings resulted from the unrealistic expectations of parishioners. Congregations often gave equal weight to a dozen or more characteristics of pastoral leadership, creating impossible conflicts and demands on any preacher trying to maintain family stability and his own physical and emotional health. Domestic problems that ended in spousal separation or divorce usually ended a pastor's ministry regardless of circumstances. So did mental problems such as depression, even if it could be controlled by medication. The pervasive negativism took its toll even on noncombatants. Many churches also preferred young pastors, tiring quickly of ministers in their fifties and sixties, whose energy levels often waned.[147]

The result was a spiraling number of forced resignations. In the SBC some estimates of forced resignations reached 5 to 10 percent annually by 1991. Within Alabama one pastor claimed in 1982 that he personally knew eighty-seven pastors who had been forced out of churches in a half year. In 1988, fifty-eight terminations were reported to the church-minister relations office.[148]

Individual cases were tragic. One pastor (accused of neither moral malfeasance nor theological deviance) experienced hurt, anger, and frustration when forced to resign without severance pay. Another pastor who became a Methodist minister after being forced to resign blamed the root cause on the autonomy of local churches. In such a governance system a small number of members could vindictively drive a pastor or even successive preachers out of the pastorate.[149]

The state convention helped as best it could. The church-minister relations department provided emergency funds for terminated staff as well as counseling for staff and churches.

Many church problems (according to the state office and wizened veterans like Hudson Baggett) resulted from idealistic and unrealistic expectations by young pastors. Baggett tried to demythologize the "call" of young ministers. He warned that they were entering a highly political profession that put a premium on "a glib tongue and a willingness to bend to whatever degree necessary to . . . satisfy the expectations of people." Prophets would not last long in the pulpit ministry. One young minister wrote to Baggett to request help in finding a pastorate. The pastor urged Baggett "to let God tell me where to cut the letter" of recommendation. Such theology was part of the young man's problem, Baggett responded frankly: "We think God is doing everything and do not really understand sometimes that committees, congregations, and individuals make the decisions, and they do not come directly from heaven. If [we] think God is doing it all then we get clobbered in the process; we are really victims of our own preaching."[150]

Baggett also showcased successful pastors as models for younger colleagues. He spotlighted pastors across the theological spectrum: Buddy Nelson, Darrell Robinson, Larry Wimberly, Allen Walworth, Ralph Langley, and Edgar Arendall. He also surveyed Baptists to determine what they most valued in pastors (sincerity, authenticity, practicality) and identified pastors who best exemplified them (Drew Gunnells and Charles Carter, among others).[151]

Bureaucracies Surviving Crises

Measuring the statistical impact of two decades of fierce controversy is not easy. But Baptists have always insisted on evaluating their successes and failures numerically, so they could hardly change the rules. Bold Mission Thrust, the name given to the massive denominational mobilization at the end of the twentieth century, sputtered as the century ended. The state convention and SBC established specific numerical goals in every area of Baptist life.[152]

Bold Mission Thrust had many misadventures, and decades of controversy did not help. Fewer non-Christians attended church, and evangelical influence began to wane by the 1990s, especially among "baby busters" (adults born during the downturn in birth rates during the 1960s and 1970s). By 1995, 52 percent of Alabama Baptist churches had plateaued or were declining (the Home Mission Board defined a church as having "plateaued" when resident membership had increased by less than 10 percent during the previous five years). Even worse was news that 70 percent of Baptist Sunday schools were in the same condition. Bold Mission Thrust missed many 1995 SBC goals badly (1.885 million baptisms instead of 2.1 million; undesignated gifts of $4.5 billion instead of $12 billion; 4,139 career missionaries instead of 4,800).[153]

Sometimes urgency to stay on target led to embarrassing fiascoes. The Home Mission Board produced a study calculating the number of unsaved Alabamians. Rather than using traditional estimates based on unchurched persons, the HMB estimated what percentage of each denomination was unsaved. Although evangelicals understood the logic behind the estimate, release of the study to the *Birmingham News* created a public relations nightmare. The report became grist for a nationally syndicated column by Rheta Grimsley Johnson (who grew up Baptist in Montgomery). "Baptists today are forever whining that they are portrayed as intolerant," she ended one column. "Maybe it's because they are intolerant. You cannot commission a study to decide who is saved and who is lost without somebody, somewhere taking offense at the labels. Especially those told they're going to hell." Even her column was kinder than a BBC broadcast in the United Kingdom that centered on Shelby County. Though the program followed an earnest pastor through the county, the underlying spoof and satire did not depict Alabama Baptists favorably.[154]

Although many Baptists defended the survey and expressed disdain at how Alabama Baptists were depicted to the rest of the world, Hudson Baggett was mortified. He wrote an Episcopal friend congratulating him for a satire on the "ill-conceived" HMB study. To another friend he wrote that the SBC controversy had conditioned people "to see us intolerant, judgmental, and unkind even to our fellow members." The HMB study had compounded the damage.[155]

Statistics hurt in other ways as well. The constant growth of the 1940s through the early 1970s ended. Within the SBC, baptisms peaked in 1980 at 430,000 then fell to as few as 338,000 in 1987. Membership growth between 1994 and 1997 was less than one-third of 1 percent. By 1996 baptisms had reached 380,000, but the decade and a half had not been a good time. In Alabama, baptisms declined from 35,000 in 1972–1973 into the low 20,000s. The figure for 1995 was 24,100; in 1996 it fell to 23,400. Membership growth slowed to about 1 percent a year (974,134 in 1980 to 1,071,600 in 1995). The 1996 figure of 1,072,000 represented virtually no growth. WMU membership declined from 102,000 in 1992 to 90,000 in 1995; Sunday school enrollment fell from 607,000 in 1992 to 599,000 in 1995.[156] This slump was no small embarrassment to fundamentalists, who had used declining rates of baptisms in the late 1970s as one lever to take control from moderates.

Beneath these statistics were deeply troubling trends. More than one in five Alabama Baptist churches baptized no one during 1992. In 1940 one of seven Alabamians was a Baptist; ten years later the figure was one in six; by 1970 it had reached one in four. After 1970 the figure remained constant through the mid-1990s. The denomination seemed to have developed a project mentality. Growth depended on special drives. Retention had become a real problem, with nearly as many members leaving as new ones joined. Between 1980 and 1985, ABSC churches enrolled 277,000 new members but had a net gain of only 47,000 because so many died, dropped out, or transferred to other denominations. In the mid-1980s, 468 (or 15 percent) of nearly 3,100 ABSC churches enrolled half of all white Baptists, baptized nearly half of all converts, generated 63 percent of all gifts, and gave 70 percent of all Cooperative Program contributions. Of 21,000 baptisms in 1987, some 12,500 were preschoolers, children, and teenagers who represented biological growth. Another 2,300 were Christians coming from other denominations. Some 2,300 were rebaptisms. That left only 3,900 who were unsaved adults from what one Baptist called the "pagan pool." The fact that 11 percent of SBC baptisms were formerly baptized Southern Baptists made many wonder whether the denomination had begun what was essentially "infant baptism" of children too young to understand the meaning of conversion.[157]

Plateaued and declining conditions were blamed on a multitude of factors. Fundamentalists blamed stagnant statistics on the lingering influence of theological liberalism that had eroded commitment to evangelism. Moderates (and even inerrantist Carl F. H. Henry) blamed denominational stagnation on continued controversy in the SBC that drained energy and resources and created negative public perceptions of the denomination. Repeatedly urged by fundamentalists to leave the SBC, many moderate Baptists finally did so. Others explained losses on transitions in evangelism from ineffective door-to-door visitation to life-style evangelism. Still others blamed the problem on demographics. There were simply fewer people in the key age groups that produced most baptisms. George Gallup and other surveyors reminded Southern Baptists that though their growth had flattened, at least the denomination was not declining, as were most main-line churches. In Alabama, for instance, membership in the North Alabama Conference of the United Methodist Church declined from 178,000 in 1983 to 168,000 in 1989.[158]

Increase in baptisms or membership was not the only way to judge congregations, though Baptists were stuck with their traditional ways of measuring progress. Most of the nearly 700 churches that seldom baptized anyone were dying churches located in stagnant communities. Ministering to overwhelmingly aging populations that had been deserted by young people was as central to the gospel as baptisms, though one would hardly believe that fact from the statistical mania of the convention. Faithful ministers who buried aging Baptists and congregations with dignity deserved more credit than they received.

Some areas of Alabama Baptist life experienced rapid growth. Ethnic churches multiplied as ministries to blacks, Hispanics, and Koreans bore fruit. Madison County started four new congregations on the same day in 1987, each in a rapidly growing and unserved area. A number of congregations were begun in the rapidly expanding suburbs south of Birmingham. Riverchase Baptist Church, begun in 1987 in a planned community near the Cahaba River, advertised itself as a liturgical church open to all races and with ordained women in leadership roles. Meadow Brook was also a new moderate church begun cooperatively by Mountain Brook and Brookwood churches. These kinds of churches served some of the sixty-four communities in Alabama that had no Baptist congregation in 1992. Progress could also be measured by eleven Alabama congregations that ranked in the top seventeen SBC churches in growth of worship attendance for 1986–1987 (including inerrantist churches like Dauphin Way and moderate churches like Dothan First Baptist).[159]

One area that did not stagnate was giving. Alabama regularly ranked among the top conventions in rate of growth in Cooperative Program gifts. While the percentage of CP giving of SBC churches was declining, Alabama churches remained constant. Between 1976 and 1994, CP gifts from Alabama increased by nearly 300 percent, highest of any of the fourteen "old line" state Baptist conventions. Denominational leaders attributed this increase to WMU support and less controversy within the state convention. Interestingly, seven of the top twenty-five churches (28 percent) in contributions to the 1992 Cooperative Program also supported the Cooperative Baptist Fellowship.[160] The denominational controversy did have some effect on contributions even in Alabama. A 1993 survey of twenty large churches that experienced declines in CP contributions the previous year revealed that 30 percent of the pastors attributed the decline partly or entirely to conflict within the SBC.[161]

Despite flattened growth, Alabama Baptists had no reason to feel that they had failed in their Christian mission, especially in comparative terms. More than half of all church members in Alabama in 1991 were either black or white Baptists. A majority of Alabamians believed the Bible was the infallible word of God, and 95 percent believed in some kind of hell. In 1992 Alabama tied for fourth as the most religiously saturated state in the nation. Three-quarters of the state's adults considered themselves "born again" in 1996 compared to a third nationally.[162]

Not only were churches being formed in new areas, but worship practices were changing. Contemporary music, praise songs, technologically produced music, informal worship services at nontraditional times (such as Saturday night), charismatic practices, use of liturgical calendars, and the Apostles' Creed all flourished. Many new suburban megachurches even began to omit "Baptist" from their name.[163]

New denominational leadership accompanied new forms of worship. More fundamentalist pastoral leadership seemed poised to take over the state's churches. Tom Corts, Michael A. Magnoli, and David Potts replaced Leslie Wright, William Weaver, and N. H. McCrummen as presidents of Samford, the University of Mobile (formerly Mobile College), and Judson. Beverly Sutton replaced Mary Essie Stephens as head of the state's WMU,

Samford University became one of the best endowed and most highly regarded regional universities under the presidencies of Leslie S. Wright and Thomas E. Corts. (Courtesy of Samford University Archives)

and Bob Terry replaced Hudson Baggett as editor of the *Alabama Baptist*. Few eras had produced so much change in such a brief period of time.

Denominational life also became more complicated. In 1945 the state board of missions employed a dozen people and the state WMU four more. By 1996 the staff numbered more than a hundred. The minutes and reports of the administration committee and board of missions for the years 1915 through 1927 could be contained in one volume. Reporting the records just for 1992 required eighteen volumes. In 1915 most members of the board of missions came from small churches. In 1981 fifty-one represented churches with more than 500 members, only twenty-five with fewer than that.

In other ways the problems faced by the convention were familiar. More than half the pastors of 3,175 Alabama Baptist churches in 1996 were bivocational ministers. Half the churches had fewer than 150 members, not nearly enough to afford a full-time pastor. The election of Leon Ballard as president of the ABSC in 1996 was belated recognition of their service. So

Jewett Hall (the "Judson Building") has become the physical symbol of Judson College. Twice destroyed by fire, this most recent incarnation of the primary academic building on campus was fashioned after the Governor's Palace in Williamsburg, Virginia. (Courtesy of Kristin Potts, Judson College)

Nestled among pines on a knoll overlooking the University of Mobile campus, historic Lyon Chapel exemplifies the university's Baptist heritage. The chapel, formerly First Baptist Church of Saint Stephens, was 104 years old when it was moved to the university campus in 1988 and renovated. Lyon Chapel was renamed in memory of Mrs. Willie Mae Lewis Lyon, a founding trustee of the University of Mobile. (Courtesy of University of Mobile Office of Public Relations)

was Samford University's selection of an annual bivocational pastor of the year. Rural churches continued to pose the most complex challenges to Alabama Baptists. Between 1971 and 1989, 234 Baptist congregations permanently closed their doors.[164] Had it not been for the faithful service of bivocational ministers, the figure would have been higher.

Nor were most pastors adequately compensated for such strenuous duties. A 1992 survey estimated that three-fourths of the state's Baptist pastors were underpaid according to national standards. Many aging pastors had no equity in a home and only minimal retirement programs. Even full-time churches seeking seminary graduates in 1992 offered pay packages between $15,000 and $20,000. The head of the minister-church relations department estimated that one-third of the state's ABSC ministers did not make a livable income. "There is still the concept that the pastor lives off hard bread and grace," he explained.[165] Such conditions, added to the stress of denominational controversy, reduced the number of ministerial students and made many pastors consider other professions.

As the twentieth century ended, Baptist life seemed in many ways to have come full circle. Debates over Calvinism, the authority of the Bible, creedalism, and the priesthood of the believer seemed as relevant in 1998 as they had in 1823. Internal controversies diverted time, money, and attention from more important causes. Bivocational ministers constituted more than half of all pastors. Despite the presence of large numbers of small churches, a few large urban congregations dominated denominational life. After a century of racial conflict, blacks composed an ever growing percentage of ABSC members. Arguments about whether ministers should use manuscripts or speak extemporaneously, use emotion or preach intellectually, continued as well.

In other ways, much had changed in the 175 years since Baptists met at Salem church in Greensboro. They no longer argued about missions. Support for the worldwide outreach of Baptists was in fact one of the few remaining hinges holding the denomination together. Political participation (which had never been as unusual as many thought) held a priority third only to evangelism and mission involvement. By 1998 political activity in some churches rivaled that of a political party. Having defined an entire range of public policy issues as "moral," white Alabama Baptists overwhelmingly voted Republican, something unheard of in the 1860s. Even in conservative churches, women had opportunities (through WMU) unparalleled before the 1880s. Discipline of members as a function of congregational life had ceased to exist. Venerable beliefs such as separation of church and state had little meaning to the new generation of Alabama Baptists who came of age after 1960.

Both fundamentalists and moderates were partly correct and partly wrong in their uses of the past. Strict Calvinism, creedalism, and inerrancy were more an Alabama Baptist legacy than moderates were willing to admit. And Baptists had tolerated much more diversity from their small liberal wing than fundamentalists believed. John W. Phillips, L. L. Gwaltney, and J. C. Stivender (all ABSC presidents) held theological views that would have disqualified them from leadership of the denomination at the end of the twentieth century. The social justice views of George B. Eager, Joshua Hill Foster, A. J. Dickinson, Charles A. Stakely, James H. Chapman, and James E. Dillard would not have been compatible either. The service of China missionaries Willie Kelly, Martha Foster Crawford, Addie Cox, and Irene Jeffers as preachers and deaconesses would not have been well received in 1998 despite their lifetime of self-sacrificing service.

Pessimism and gloom over the future of Alabama Baptists seemed exaggerated. There had been many controversies before, some that threatened the life of the denomination just as seriously (the antimission movement of the 1820s, the Landmark dispute of the late nineteenth century, the loss of more than half the membership in the decade after 1865). Membership had leveled out in the 1930s just as it did in the 1980s and 1990s.

In some ways, conditions were better in the 1990s. Never before had the ABSC been so affluent and powerful. Both its fundamentalist and moderate wings were closer to a genuinely egalitarian attitude toward race than at any time in history (though there were still miles to go to reach the standard of justice and equality that they proclaimed).

With power and affluence came responsibility. Baptists were better at defining what they opposed than articulating what they favored. They opposed legalizing liquor, gambling, and abortion. They were largely silent on how to generate adequate money for public schools or social services for children born into poor families. They took the leadership in abolishing the welfare system and insisted that families and churches would fill the void left by federal and state programs. But their historic rejection of the social gospel left them with neither a theology nor programs for the poor. Their ideal to solve the problems of poverty by converting the poor ignored the fact that most of the poor were already converted. But critics could not fault their sincerity or good intentions. If Alabama was the worst place to be a child or to be poor in terms of institutional programs, it was one of the easiest places to find individuals willing to help. Whether kindheartedness and private charity could cross racial and class barriers to fill the vast human needs of the state's poor remained to be seen.

Alabama Baptists had inhabited a wild frontier in 1823, and they had tamed it. No single group of people had a more profound impact on the state or left so enduring a legacy. Alexander Travis, Hosea Holcombe, and Julia Barron would have been proud if somehow they could have been transported from Greensboro in 1823 to Birmingham in 1998. There would have been much to disturb them and even more they would not have understood. But they would have recognized immediately that some of the seeds they had planted so carefully nearly two centuries earlier had fallen on fertile ground.

Notes

Chapter 1: Confronting the Frontier, 1800–1845

1. *Christian Index and South-Western Baptist,* May 9, 1872; *Alabama Baptist,* October 10, 1878.

2. *Alabama Baptist,* December 14, 1844, March 8, 1845.

3. Joel W. Martin, *Sacred Revolt: The Muskogees' Struggle for a New World* (Boston: Beacon Press, 1991), 114–35, 212.

4. Alabama Baptist State Convention Minutes, 1827, 11. The official minutes of the convention are located at ABSC headquarters in Montgomery.

5. Cemetery and Bible Records, Bledsoe-Kelly Collection, Samford University Archives, Birmingham.

6. Articles or Declaration of Faith, Church Covenant, Principles of Ruhama First, Huntsville (Enon), Eufaula, Mount Hebron, Big Creek, and Bethany Baptist Churches found in: Fanna K. Bee and Lee N. Allen, *Ruhama Baptist Church, 1819–1969* (Birmingham: Ruhama Baptist Church, 1969), 10–11; Mildred Burden Bobo and Catherine Ryan Johnson, *First Baptist Church of Huntsville, Alabama* (Huntsville: First Baptist Church, 1985), 1–2; Eufaula, Mount Hebron, Big Creek, and Bethany Baptist Church Minutes, all in Samford University Archives.

7. Bobo and Johnson, *First Baptist Church of Huntsville,* 2; Eufaula and Big Creek Baptist Church Minutes.

8. Eufaula and Mount Hebron Baptist Church Minutes.

9. Hosea Holcombe, *History of the Rise and Progress of the Baptists in Alabama* (Philadelphia: King and Baird Printers, 1840), 17.

10. Bethany Baptist Church Minutes.

11. *Alabama Baptist,* December 14, 1950.

12. Bobo and Johnson, *First Baptist Church of Huntsville,* 1.

13. Exact dating of the earliest Alabama Baptist churches is a matter of intense emotion and pride, so contenders are numerous. For a variety of opinions see: Davis C. Woolley, "Historic Baptist Churches of Alabama," "Notes from Flint River Association Minute Book," Davis C. Woolley Papers, Samford University Archives; "Old Churches," "Foundations and Frontiers in Alabama Churches," and press release to *Huntsville Times,* all in Woolley Papers; "Old Extinct Churches," "Inactive Alabama Baptist Churches," and "Active Alabama Baptist Churches," all in Leon M. Macon Papers, Samford University Archives; Holcombe's *History of the Baptists in Alabama* is the most reliable guide if for no other reason than this initial historian **625**

of Alabama Baptists established many of the churches himself and corresponded extensively with those who founded others.

14. *Alabama Baptist,* October 10, 1878; Holcombe, *History of the Baptists in Alabama,* 43.

15. *Alabama Baptist,* October 10, 1878.

16. Claudia Mae Huston, "A History of Early Baptist Churches in Alabama" (master's thesis, University of Alabama, 1960), 73–75; Joe D. Acker, "Baptist Beginnings in Alabama," *Alabama Baptist Historian* 15 (January 1979): 8–9; *Alabama Baptist,* February 21, 1844; John H. Jeffers, *The Auburn First Baptist Church, 1838–1988* (Auburn: Gnu's Room, 1990), 3.

17. Acker, "Baptist Beginnings in Alabama," 8–9; Lee N. Allen, "The Alabama Baptist Association: Years of Fulfillment, 1840–1860," *Alabama Baptist Historian* 16 (January 1980): 3.

18. Huston, "History of Early Baptist Churches in Alabama," 28–29.

19. James H. Chapman, "Alabama Baptist Biographies 1900–1925: Background and Foreground," James H. Chapman Papers, Southern Baptist Historical Library and Archives, Nashville, Tennessee (hereafter cited as Southern Baptist Archives).

20. *Alabama Baptist,* December 9, 1843; Allen, "Alabama Baptist Association, 1840–1860," 6–9.

21. *Alabama Baptist,* July 27, 1844.

22. Holcombe, *History of the Baptists in Alabama,* 44–45.

23. Bethany Baptist Church Minutes.

24. "Russellville First Baptist Church," ms., Samford University Archives; *Alabama Baptist,* September 20, 1973.

25. "Russellville First Baptist Church"; E. B. Teague, "An Outline of the Baptist Denomination in Alabama in Former Times," E. B. Teague Papers, Samford University Archives.

26. Samuel S. Hill, "Religion," in *The Encyclopedia of Southern Culture,* ed. Charles R. Wilson and William Ferris (Chapel Hill: University of North Carolina Press, 1989), 1271–73.

27. Holcombe, *History of the Baptists in Alabama,* 311–22.

28. F. Wilbur Helmbold, "Five More Pioneer Churches in Madison County," *Alabama Baptist Historian* 6 (July 1970): 31–32, 33–34; Huston, "History of Early Baptist Churches in Alabama," 99.

29. Jeffers, *Auburn First Baptist Church,* 2.

30. *Alabama Baptist,* July 27, 1844.

31. Lida Robertson Papers, Samford University Archives.

32. Daniel Fate Brooks, "The Mind of Wilcox County: An Antebellum History, 1819–1861" (master's thesis, Samford University, 1984), 55–61; *Alabama Baptist,* September 14, 1844.

33. Robert G. McLendon Jr., *George Granberry McLendon, 1807–1895: Pioneer Missionary Baptist Preacher* (n.p., 1990), 19, 24, 30.

34. *Alabama Baptist,* January 27, 1876, October 10, 1878, February 13, 1879; "Preachers, Bigbee Association," in Julia Praytor Killingsworth Papers, Samford University Archives.

35. *Alabama Baptist,* March 15, 1883.

36. "Preachers, Bigbee Association," Killingsworth Papers; James E. Dean, *Baptists in Greensboro, Alabama,* pamphlet published in 1938; *Alabama Baptist,* March 8, 1845; A. B. Moore, *History of Alabama and Her People,* vol. 3 (Chicago: American Historical Society, 1927), 772–73.

37. Jerry M. Windsor, "Preaching Up a Storm from 1839 to 1889," *Alabama Baptist Historian* 29 (January 1993): 13–20.

38. Lee N. Allen, *The First 150 Years, 1829–1979: First Baptist Church, Montgomery, Alabama* (Montgomery: First Baptist Church, 1979), 19–22.

39. Luther Q. Porch, *History of the First Baptist Church, Tuscaloosa, Alabama, 1818–1968* (Tuscaloosa: Drake Printers, 1968), 15–16.

40. Allen, *First 150 Years,* 22. One reason for DeVotie's prominence was his longevity and phenomenal record keeping. In a preaching career of nearly forty years, he preached 5,500 sermons, made an estimated 10,000 pastoral visits, and baptized 1,300; James Harvey DeVotie Papers, Samford University Archives.

41. Porch, *History of the First Baptist Church, Tuscaloosa*, 18–19.

42. The term "gentleman theologian" was coined by E. Brooks Holifield to qualify the stereotype of southern antebellum ministers as poorly educated emotional revivalists. "Gentlemen theologians" such as Manly were strongly influenced by Scottish "common sense realism," which offered a middle ground between sensationalism and idealism. This philosophy gave rise to a natural theology in which scientific investigation of the created order disclosed the existence and nature of God as creator. See E. Brooks Holifield, *The Gentlemen Theologians: American Theology in Southern Culture, 1795–1860* (Durham: Duke University Press, 1978), 22–23, 110–26.

43. Timothy George, " 'Faithful Shepherd, Beloved Minister': The Life and Legacy of Basil Manly, Sr.," *Alabama Baptist Historian* 27 (January 1991): 15.

44. Ibid., 14–22.

45. Ibid., 28–32.

46. Ibid., 26–31.

47. Ibid., 22, 25–26.

48. Irma Russell Cruse, "Hardin Edwards Taliaferro: Baptist Preacher-Editor, 1811–1875" (master's thesis, Samford University, 1984), 6–19, 35–37; *Alabama Baptist*, December 7, 1875; Walter Belt White, *History of the First Baptist Church, Talladega, Alabama: Its Pastors, People, and Programs Through One Hundred Fifty Years, 1835–1985* (Macon: Omni Press, 1985), 10–11.

49. *Alabama Baptist*, January 6, 1876; James Mallory Diary, Southern Historical Collection, University of North Carolina Library, Chapel Hill.

50. Cruse, "Hardin Edwards Taliaferro," 44–57, 83, 86–87, 143, 151; oral history with Margaret Taliaferro Ham, by Irma R. Cruse, June 2, 1983, in Samford University Archives.

51. *Christian Index and South-Western Baptist*, May 9, 1872; "Alexander Travis," ms. in box 1, Woolley Papers.

52. *Christian Index and South-Western Baptist*, May 9, 1872.

53. Acker, "Baptist Beginnings in Alabama," 10; Davis C. Woolley, "Hosea Holcombe: Pioneer Alabama Baptist Historian," ms. of speech presented to Alabama Historical Association, 1959, in box 1, Woolley Papers.

54. William Carey Crane to *Annals of the American Pulpit*, January 25, 1859, copy in box 1, Woolley Papers; *Alabama Baptist*, December 23, 1873.

55. E. Glenn Hinson, "Historical Patterns of Lay Leadership in Ministry in Local Baptist Churches," *Baptist History and Heritage* 13 (January 1978): 26–29; Acker, "Baptist Beginnings in Alabama," 8–10.

56. *Alabama Baptist*, March 16, 1844; Holcombe, *History of the Baptists in Alabama*, 305.

57. "Notes from Minutes of Enon Baptist Church," box 2, Woolley Papers; William Sep Love and Dorothy Clifton Bishop, *History of the First Baptist Church, Oxford, Alabama: 150 Years, 1836–1986* (n.p., 1985), 6; Karen A. Stone, *The History of First Baptist Church of Wetumpka, 1821–1996* (Montgomery: Brown Publishing Co., 1996), 11.

58. Holifield, *Gentlemen Theologians*, 186–87.

59. *Alabama Baptist*, June 26, July 3, 1930.

60. The topology of Baptist traditions (two of which originated in Charleston and Sandy Creek) has been most fully developed by Walter B. Shurden in the 1980–1981 Carver-Barnes Lectures, Southeastern Baptist Theological Seminary, Wake Forest, North Carolina. The first lecture was entitled "The Southern Baptist Synthesis: Is it Cracking?" For an interesting debate about Calvinist influence on Southern Baptists, see Thomas J. Nettles, "Southern Baptist Identity: Influenced by Calvinism," *Baptist History and Heritage* 31 (October 1996): 17–26, and W. Wiley Richards, "Southern Baptist Identity: Moving Away from Calvinism," in ibid., 27–35.

61. Holifield, *Gentlemen Theologians*, 189–92.

62. Teague, "Outline of the Baptist Denomination in Alabama."

63. *Alabama Baptist*, December 23, 1873.

64. Holcombe, *History of the Baptists in Alabama*, 50–51.

65. *Christian Index and South-Western Baptist,* September 24, 1868.

66. *Alabama Baptist,* April 27, 1849, November 17, 1859.

67. For an excellent survey of benevolence as a form of social control, see Lois W. Banner, "Religious Benevolence as Social Control: A Critique on an Interpretation," *Journal of American History* 60 (June 1973): 23–41. A recent essay by John W. Quest, "Slaveholding Operatives of the Benevolent Empire: Bible, Tract, and Sunday School Societies in Antebellum Tuscaloosa County, Alabama," *Journal of Southern History* 62 (August 1996): 481–526, disputes this conclusion and, while rejecting the social control thesis, argues that emphasis upon an orderly life, industry, and good government was an attempt to integrate marginal people into a market economy.

68. The best work on this subject has been done by John W. Kuykendall; see his "James Ely Welch: Baptist Home Missionary and Ecumenical Pioneer," *Quarterly Review* 42 (January– February–March 1982): 50–58, and *Southern Enterprize: The Work of National Evangelical Societies in the Antebellum South* (Westport, Conn.: Greenwood Press, 1982).

69. Quest, "Slaveholding Operatives of the Benevolent Empire," 487–88, 494, 511.

70. Ibid., 490, 497, 521, 522.

71. Holcombe, *History of the Baptists in Alabama,* 344–59, 369–70.

72. F. Wilbur Helmbold, "Alabama Baptist Bible Society," December 15, 1969, ms. in F. Wilbur Helmbold Papers, Samford University Archives.

73. Love and Bishop, *History of the First Baptist Church, Oxford, Alabama,* 6; *Alabama Baptist,* November 7, 1878.

74. *Alabama Baptist,* December 9, 1843, May 4, July 20, August 10, 1844.

75. The most influential arguments for a class-based antimission movement were advanced by Bertram Wyatt-Brown, "The Antimission Movement in the Jacksonian South: A Study in Regional Folk Culture," *Journal of Southern History* 36 (November 1970): 501–29; and Wyatt-Brown, "Religion and the Formation of Folk Culture: Poor Whites of the Old South," in *The Americanization of the Gulf Coast, 1803–1850,* ed. Lucius F. Ellsworth (Pensacola: Historic Pensacola Preservation Board, 1972), 20–33. Some historians rejected the Wyatt-Brown explanation for Kentucky, where Primitive Baptist leaders often held prominent positions (Larry Douglas Smith to Wayne Flynt, August 17, 1981), and the argument fits Alabama no better than Kentucky. Nor was antimissionism confined to Alabama, the Appalachian region, or even the South. See, for instance, Robert A. Baker, *The Southern Baptist Convention and Its People, 1607– 1972* (Nashville: Broadman Press, 1974), 121–50; T. Scott Miyakawa, *Protestants and Pioneers: Individualism and Conformity on the American Frontier* (Chicago: University of Chicago Press, 1964), 147–58.

76. F. Wilbur Helmbold, "The Initial Missionary Dispute in North Alabama," *Alabama Baptist Historian* 1 (June 1965): 12; Richard G. Crowe, "The Early Beginnings of the Colbert-Lauderdale Baptist Association, Alabama," *Alabama Baptist Historian* 19 (July 1983): 4.

77. Holcombe, *History of the Baptists in Alabama,* 88–105; Davis C. Woolley, "History of the Convention," 33–35, ms. in Woolley Papers; copy of "Non-Fellowship Resolutions," in box 2, Woolley Papers; Helmbold, "Initial Missionary Dispute," 12–13; Ed Ables, "A History of the DeKalb Baptist Association: Early Struggles and Growth" (master's thesis, Samford University, 1984), 9, 12–19; James H. Chapman, "Epochs of the Century of the Birmingham Baptist Association," *Alabama Baptist Historian* 2 (December 1965): 7–9; John H. Jeffers, *History of the Tuskegee-Lee Association* (n.p., 1992), 1.

78. *Alabama Baptist,* November 28, 1878, January 9, 16, 1879; Allen, "Alabama Baptist Association, 1840–1860," 3–6.

79. *Christian Index and South-Western Baptist,* November 3, 1870; *Alabama Baptist,* November 21, 1878.

80. Teague, "Outline of the Baptist Denomination in Alabama."

81. See comments from G. W. Wilcox (in *Alabama Baptist,* March 23, 1875) that in north

Alabama, Baptists still suffered from triple blows of financial chaos, Reconstruction, and antimission influence.

Chapter 2: Taming the Frontier, 1800–1845

1. The best study of such conflicting social values within early evangelicalism is found in Randy J. Sparks, *On Jordan's Stormy Banks: Evangelicalism in Mississippi, 1773–1876* (Athens: University of Georgia Press, 1994).

2. For excellent insights on the complex relationship of hierarchy, individualism, democracy, and community, see Miyakawa, *Protestants and Pioneers*, 3–5, and Donald G. Mathews, *Religion in the Old South* (Chicago: University of Chicago Press, 1977), 39–46.

3. Holcombe, *History of the Baptists in Alabama*, 58–59, 333–37.

4. For samples of early church discipline, see Huston, "History of Early Baptist Churches in Alabama," 85–100; White, *History of the First Baptist Church, Talladega*, 51–58; Wayne Flynt, " 'A Special Feeling of Closeness': Mt. Hebron Baptist Church, Leeds, Alabama," in *American Congregations*, vol. 1, *Portraits of Twelve Religious Communities*, ed. James P. Wind and James W. Lewis (Chicago: University of Chicago Press, 1994), 111–30.

5. Stone, *History of First Baptist Church of Wetumpka*, 22–23.

6. Eufaula Baptist Church Minutes.

7. See Barbara L. Epstein, *The Politics of Domesticity: Women, Evangelism, and Temperance in Nineteenth Century America* (Middletown, Conn.: Wesleyan University Press, 1981); Jean E. Friedman, *The Enclosed Garden: Women and Community in the Evangelical South, 1830–1900* (Chapel Hill: University of North Carolina Press, 1985); and Mathews, *Religion in the Old South*, for contrasting interpretations of gender and antebellum religion.

8. Stone, *History of First Baptist Church of Wetumpka*, 4–5; Hermione Dannelly Jackson and Mary Essie Stephens, *Women of Vision, Centennial Edition* (n.p.: Alabama Woman's Missionary Union, 1988), 10; Mount Hebron Baptist Church Minutes.

9. Mount Hebron Baptist Church Minutes.

10. Jackson and Stephens, *Women of Vision*, 10.

11. *Alabama Baptist*, July 1, 1843, September 7, November 2, 1844.

12. For the interaction of white and black religion, see Sparks, *On Jordan's Stormy Banks*, and Randy J. Sparks, "A Mingled Yarn: Race and Religion in Mississippi, 1800–1876" (Ph.D. diss., Rice University, 1988); Mechal Sobel, *Trabelin' On: The Slave Journey to an Afro-Baptist Faith* (Princeton: Princeton University Press, 1988).

13. Sean A. Flynt, "Lee Compere," ms. of paper presented to Alabama Historical Association, April 1994, ms. in author's possession; "Alabama," ms. in Woolley Papers; W. Calvin Dickinson, "Rev. Noah Parker: A Missionary Baptist Leader in South Alabama," *Alabama Baptist Historian* 21 (July 1985): 14; Allen, *First 150 Years*, 45; *Alabama Baptist*, July 12, 1956.

14. See David T. Bailey, *Shadow on the Church: Southwestern Evangelical Religion and the Issue of Slavery, 1783–1860* (Ithaca: Cornell University Press, 1985); and Thomas Virgil Peterson, *Ham and Japheth: The Mythic World of Whites in the Antebellum South* (Metuchen, N.J.: Scarecrow Press, 1978), quoted on 5.

15. John Boles, ed., *Masters and Slaves in the House of the Lord: Race and Religion in the American South, 1740–1870* (Lexington: University of Kentucky Press, 1988), 9–18.

16. Stone, *History of First Baptist Church of Wetumpka*, 10, 34–36; Eufaula Baptist Church Minutes; Allen, *First 150 Years*, 45–46.

17. Mallory Diary.

18. McDonald Hughes, *History of the First African Baptist Church, 1866–1986* (Tuscaloosa: n.p., 1986), 5; Porch, *History of the First Baptist Church, Tuscaloosa*, 7, 29–33.

19. *South-Western Baptist*, October 13, 1859; Mallory Diary.

20. *Alabama Baptist*, July 12, 1883.

21. Alabama Baptist State Convention Minutes, 1835.

22. Mount Hebron Baptist Church Minutes.

23. Edward R. Crowther, "Independent Black Baptist Congregations in Antebellum Alabama," *Journal of Negro History* 72 (Summer, Fall 1987): 68–70.

24. Ibid., 66–68.

25. Huston, "History of Early Baptist Churches in Alabama," 76–77.

26. For excellent discussions of the theological meaning of the great revivals, see: Paul V. Conkin, *Cane Ridge: America's Pentecost* (Madison: University of Wisconsin Press, 1990); John Boles, *The Great Revival, 1787–1805: The Origins of the Southern Evangelical Mind* (Lexington: University Press of Kentucky, 1972); Dickson D. Bruce Jr., *And They All Sang Hallelujah: Plain-Folk Camp-Meeting Religion, 1800–1845* (Knoxville: University of Tennessee Press, 1974); Bill J. Leonard, "Southern Baptist Confessions: Dogmatic Ambiguity," in *Southern Baptists and American Evangelicals,* ed. David S. Dockery (Nashville: Broadman and Holman Publishers, 1993); Hill, "Religion," 1269–73.

27. Teague, "Outline of the Baptist Denomination in Alabama."

28. Holcombe, *History of the Baptists in Alabama,* 45–46; Huston, "History of Early Baptist Churches in Alabama," 80.

29. Mallory Diary.

30. Holcombe, *History of the Baptists in Alabama,* 46–47.

31. *Alabama Baptist,* May 11, 18, October 19, 1844; Mallory Diary.

32. *Alabama Baptist,* June 15, 1844.

33. Daniel Dupre, "Barbeques and Pledges: Electioneering and the Rise of Democratic Politics in Alabama," *Journal of Southern History* 60 (August 1994): 479–87, 499–501; for a fuller discussion of the Jacksonian aspirations of Alabama's white masses, see J. Mills Thornton III, *Politics and Power in a Slave Society: Alabama, 1800–1860* (Baton Rouge: Louisiana State University Press, 1978).

34. Richard R. Beeman and Rhys Isaac, "Cultural Conflict and Social Change in the Revolutionary South: Lunenburg County, Virginia," *Journal of Southern History* 46 (November 1980): 534, 538–47, 550; Thomas E. Buckley, "After Disestablishment: Thomas Jefferson's Wall of Separation in Antebellum Virginia," *Journal of Southern History* 61 (August 1995): 449, 452, 457–59, 466, 472–80.

35. See Robert M. Calhoon, *Evangelicals and Conservatives in the Early South, 1740–1861* (Columbia: University of South Carolina Press, 1988), especially 8–9; Anne C. Loveland, *Southern Evangelicals and the Social Order, 1800–1860* (Baton Rouge: Louisiana State University Press, 1980), 38–53.

36. Teague, "Outline of the Baptist Denomination in Alabama"; Mrs. W. G. Lockard, "John Ellis Sumners—Baptist Pioneer," *Alabama Baptist Historian* 17 (January 1981): 17–18; *Alabama Baptist,* June 7, 1883, May 16, 1895.

37. Teague, "Outline of the Baptist Denomination in Alabama"; "Rev. Daniel P. Bestor," ms. in Robertson Papers; unidentified clipping in James H. DeVotie scrapbooks, DeVotie Papers.

38. *Alabama Baptist,* December 16, 1843, May 4, 25, December 7, 1844.

39. Ibid., August 10, 1844; Mallory Diary.

40. Mallory Diary; *Alabama Baptist,* December 8, 23, 30, 1843, March 23, October 12, 1844, February 1, 15, 1845.

41. *Alabama Baptist,* January 6, 1844.

42. James H. DeVotie Journal, 43–44, DeVotie Papers.

43. *Alabama Baptist,* March 2, 1844; Paul Terry and Verner Sims, *They Live on the Land: Life in an Open-Country Southern Community* (Tuscaloosa: Bureau of Educational Research, 1940), 9–11; Teague, "Outline of the Baptist Denomination in Alabama."

44. *Alabama Baptist,* January 6, 1844.

45. Mitchell B. Garrett, "Sixty Years of Howard College, 1842–1902," *Howard College Bulletin* 85 (October 1927): 7–17.

46. *Alabama Baptist*, September 9, 1926, January 13, 1927; see also Frances Dew Hamilton and Elizabeth Crabtree Wells, *Daughters of the Dream: Judson College, 1838–1988* (Marion: Judson College, 1989).

47. Ms. in Julia Ann Tarrant Barron Papers, Samford University Archives.

48. DeVotie Journal, 74–77; Marie Bankhead Owen, *History of Alabama and Dictionary of Biography* (Chicago: S. J. Clarke Co., 1921); Samuel S. Sherman to James H. DeVotie, December 6, 1841, DeVotie Papers; R. E. E. Harkness to James H. Chapman, January 24, 1946, Chapman Papers; *Alabama Baptist*, September 30, 1843.

49. Garrett, "Sixty Years of Howard College," 23; *Alabama Baptist*, June 24, 1843.

50. Garrett, "Sixty Years of Howard College," 25–26.

51. For the early Howard College curriculum, see James A. Pate, "The Development of the Instructional Program at Howard College, 1842–1957" (Ph.D. diss., University of Alabama, 1959).

52. *Alabama Baptist*, October 12, 14, 1844; Pate, "Development of the Instructional Program," 161–65, 170–71.

53. *Alabama Baptist*, July 15, 1843; Live W. Lawler to J. H. DeVotie, September 10, 1843, DeVotie Papers; see also a series of articles on Howard's original trustees: Chriss H. Doss, "The Original Fifteen Trustees of Howard College," serialized in four parts in *Alabama Baptist Historian* 28 (July 1992): 3–36; 29 (January 1993): 2–12; 29 (July 1993): 3–25; and 30 (January 1994): 3–25.

54. DeVotie Journal; *Alabama Baptist*, February 4, 1843, January 27, February 10, 1844. The two most useful sources on the early history of the paper are F. Wilbur Helmbold, "Baptist Periodicals in Alabama, 1843–1873," *Alabama Baptist Historian* 2 (July 1966): 2–12, and Randy B. Rosenberg, "John Davis Williams: Antebellum Southern Baptist Evangelical" (master's thesis, Auburn University, 1982).

55. Chapman, "Alabama Baptist Biographies"; Eufaula Baptist Church Minutes; *Alabama Baptist*, November 18, 1948.

56. Acker, "Baptist Beginnings in Alabama," 7, 14; Holcombe, *History of the Baptists in Alabama*, 40.

57. Dean, *Baptists in Greensboro*; Alabama Baptist State Convention Minutes, 1823.

58. Howard L. Holley, "Charles Crow, 1770–1845," *Alabama Baptist Historian* 1 (June 1965): 7; *Alabama Baptist*, November 7, 1935, November 8, 1973; Hermione Dannelly Jackson, *Women of Vision* (n.p.: Woman's Missionary Union, 1964), 1, 6; Alabama Baptist State Convention Minutes, 1823.

59. Huston, "History of Early Baptist Churches in Alabama," 48–52; Alabama Baptist State Convention Minutes, 1823.

60. Holcombe, *History of the Baptists in Alabama*, 66; Alabama Baptist State Convention Minutes, 1827, 1829, 1835; *Alabama Baptist*, March 9, 1844.

61. Huston, "History of Early Baptist Churches in Alabama," 54.

Chapter 3: The Work of the Gospel, 1845–1860

1. *Alabama Baptist*, September 18, 1846.

2. Edward R. Crowther, "Holy Honor: Sacred and Secular in the Old South," *Journal of Southern History* 58 (November 1992): 624; *Alabama Baptist*, September 20, 1845; U.S. Census Office, 8th Census, 1860, *Statistics of the United States in 1860* (New York: Norman Ross Publishers, 1990), 353.

3. *Alabama Baptist*, September 20, 1845; *South-Western Baptist*, July 9, October 15, 1851, August 5, 1858; Teague, "Outline of the Baptist Denomination in Alabama."

4. *South-Western Baptist,* October 2, 1850, November 5, 1851.

5. Ibid., November 26, 1851.

6. Ibid., July 3, October 16, 1850, March 18, 1853, September 7, 1854.

7. *Alabama Baptist,* August 16, 1845.

8. Ibid., August 8, 1846.

9. Ibid., August 1, 1849.

10. I. T. Tichenor Papers, Samford University Archives.

11. *South-Western Baptist,* January 14, 1852.

12. Ibid., January 14, February 4, 1852; Stone, *History of First Baptist Church of Wetumpka,* 45.

13. *Alabama Baptist,* April 12, 1883.

14. Ibid., January 11, 1845.

15. Ibid., March 2, 1849; *South-Western Baptist,* February 25, March 3, May 7, 1852.

16. Joseph Walker, "Mental Requisites of Pulpit Efficiency," *Baptist Preacher* 13 (October 1854): 166–81.

17. *South-Western Baptist,* April 15, 1853.

18. Ibid., April 28, 1852, August 24, 1854; *Alabama Baptist,* July 25, 1849.

19. *South-Western Baptist,* August 31, 1854, April 7, 1859.

20. Ibid., January 12, 1854.

21. *Alabama Baptist,* July 18, 1849; Walker, "Mental Requisites," 166–81.

22. *Alabama Baptist,* July 18, September 5, 1849.

23. Ibid., March 15, 1845, April 18, 1846; *South-Western Baptist,* August 24, 1854; Tichenor Diary; Jacob S. Dill, *Isaac Taylor Tichenor: The Home Mission Board Statesman* (Nashville: Sunday School Board, 1908), 25–26.

24. *South-Western Baptist,* November 5, 1857; *Alabama Baptist,* April 18, June 13, 1846, May 15, 1850; Teague, "Outline of the Baptist Denomination in Alabama."

25. *South-Western Baptist,* March 11, 1853, November 9, 30, December 7, 1854, January 4, 1855.

26. Ibid., May 24, August 30, 1860.

27. *Alabama Baptist,* July 4, 1849, May 15, 1850.

28. *South-Western Baptist,* January 5, December 11, 1850; Basil Manly Sr. to William Ashcraft, December 22, 1849, Basil Manly Sr. Papers, Southern Historical Collection.

29. *South-Western Baptist,* March 12, 1851.

30. *Alabama Baptist,* December 11, 1846.

31. Ibid., June 22, August 15, October 10, December 12, 1849; series of editorials in *South-Western Baptist,* March–April 1852, April 15, 1853, March 13, 1856; A. W. Chambliss, "The Consecration and Support of the Gospel Ministry," *Baptist Preacher* 7 (August 1848): 133–63.

32. A. T. M. Handey Papers, Samford University Archives; Basil Manly Sr. to his brother, January 10, 1850, Manly Papers.

33. *Alabama Baptist,* December 11, 1846; Eufaula Baptist Church Minutes.

34. For J. H. DeVotie's negotiations with a number of churches between 1852 and 1855 see: J. H. DeVotie to Brother Chase, October 9, 1852; DeVotie to Brother Sherman, September 28, 1853; DeVotie to Brother Edwards, September 28, 1853; S. C. Tutt to DeVotie, May 7, 1853; C. H. Judson to DeVotie, July 19, 1853; J. S. Mims to DeVotie, March 14, 1853; C. J. Elford to DeVotie, August 28, 1853; DeVotie to Brother Judson, September 27, 1853; DeVotie to Brethren, September 27, 1853; DeVotie to Congregation, July 13, 1853; Live W. Lawler to DeVotie, September 26, 1855; Lawler to DeVotie, October 13, 1855; all in DeVotie Papers.

35. *South-Western Baptist,* June 1, 1854, February 21, 1856.

36. *Alabama Baptist,* March 23, 1849; *South-Western Baptist,* November 4, 1853, June 26, 1856, January 13, 1859.

37. See *Alabama Baptist,* April 6, 13, May 4, 18, 25, June 1, 8, 22, 1849, September 18, 1846;

South-Western Baptist, October 26, 1854, January 4, 1855, February 1, 22, March 1, 22, 1855; series in October, November, December 1856.

38. *Alabama Baptist,* July 11, 1846.

39. Ibid., September 5, 12, 1846.

40. *South-Western Baptist,* series of articles in October, November, December 1858, especially November 3 and December 2.

41. See James H. DeVotie, "Scripture the Inspiration of God" and "The Word to be Spoken Faithfully," sermon notes, DeVotie Papers.

42. *Alabama Baptist,* February 15, 22, 1845.

43. Teague, "Outline of the Baptist Denomination in Alabama."

44. *South-Western Baptist,* April 19, 1855.

45. Ibid., April 16, September 3, 1851.

46. *South-Western Baptist,* August 4, 11, 25, September 29, November 3, 1852, February 18, 1853, January 4, February 1, April 5, 26, May 31, 1855.

47. *Alabama Baptist,* April 20, 1844, June 28, 1845, April 18, November 26, 1846, June 1, 1849.

48. Edward Baptist, "The Power of Man to Obey the Gospel," *Baptist Preacher* 10 (February 1851): 45–53.

49. James M. Watt, "The Covenant of Redemption," *Baptist Preacher* 8 (April 1849): 53–66; H. E. Taliaferro, "The Covenant of Redemption, the Soul of the Missionary Enterprise," *Baptist Preacher* 8 (January 1849): 1–18.

50. Thomas F. Curtis, "The Certainty of Divine Purposes and the Contingency of Second Causes," *Baptist Preacher* 10 (April 1851): 77–90.

51. C. F. Sturgis, "The Divine Scheme of Evangelization," *Baptist Preacher* 13 (August 1854): 127–51; *South-Western Baptist,* January 8, 1857. "Crispus" elaborated these arguments in a series of articles in January and February 1857.

52. *South-Western Baptist,* October 18, 1855, April 28, 1852, May 7, 21, 1851, January 8, 1851, August 18, 1852, February 8, 1855, September 21, 1854.

53. Ibid., September 29, 1852, May 3, 1855, January 17, 1856, January 6, 1859.

54. Ibid., July 20, 1854, January 4, 1855; Edward Baptist, "The Millennium," *Baptist Preacher* 8 (November 1849): 191–200.

55. *South-Western Baptist,* February 4, 1852, September 18, 1856.

56. *South-Western Baptist,* January 20, 1859; H. Clay Pless, "Historical Sketch of Lebanon Baptist Church," July 21, 1940, Samford University Archives; Mary Florence Arthur Word, *Big Springs: A History of a Church and a Community, Randolph County, Alabama* (LaGrange, Ga.: Family Tree, 1986), 11.

57. *Alabama Baptist,* September 19, November 21, 1849; J. H. DeVotie, "Prejudice," sermon ms. in vol. 4 of DeVotie Papers (although the sermon is undated, the context fits the Landmark controversy); *South-Western Baptist,* June 5, 1856. See also Marty G. Bell, "James Robinson Graves and the Rhetoric of Demagogy: Primitivism and Democracy in Old Landmarkism" (Ph.D. diss., Vanderbilt University, 1990).

58. William Terry Martin, "Samuel Henderson and His Response to J. R. Graves and Landmarkism Through the *South-Western Baptist,* 1857–1859" (master's thesis, Samford University, 1977), 1, 4–5, 7–8, 10–19, 22, 28–30, 53; for the all-consuming nature of this debate, see *South-Western Baptist,* March 4, April 1, 8, 22, May 13, 27, June 4, 19, 1858.

59. *South-Western Baptist,* January 6, 13, 27, April 7, 28, September 8, 15, 1859.

60. Ibid., October 27, 1859, June 7, 1860.

61. *Alabama Baptist,* August 29, 1849; Manly Papers.

62. *South-Western Baptist,* October 22, November 26, 1851, October 9, 1856.

63. Hamilton and Wells, *Daughters of the Dream,* 43–44, 52–54.

64. Jesse Hartwell to Milo P. Jewett, March 25, 1843; Samuel S. Sherman to "brother,"

October 22, 1850; both in DeVotie Papers; Henry Talbird to Basil Manly Sr., April 25, 1858, Manly Papers.

65. *Alabama Baptist*, September 12, 1846, December 5, 1849.

66. Garrett, "Sixty Years of Howard College," 28–43, 49–50.

67. J. H. DeVotie to Howard College President and Trustees, undated, but late 1850s, DeVotie Papers; *South-Western Baptist*, January 13, 1859.

68. Saranne Elizabeth Crabtree, "*South-Western Baptist*, 1850–1860: Defender of Southern Rights" (master's thesis, Auburn University, 1973), 22–23.

69. James T. Murfee, "Journalism of the Baptist Denomination in Alabama," in Washington B. Crumpton, *Our Baptist Centennials, 1808–1923* (n.p., 1923), 16; Helmbold, "Baptist Periodicals in Alabama," 5; Jon G. Appleton, "Samuel Henderson: Southern Minister, Editor, and Crusader, 1853–1866" (master's thesis, Auburn University, 1968), 19–21; *South-Western Baptist*, March 17, 1852, August 5, 1858.

70. *South-Western Baptist*, November 20, 1850, July 31, 1856, February 25, March 11, 1858, September 1, 1859; a series of thirteen parts beginning February 9, 1860.

71. A. W. Chambliss, "Public Offenses, or Church Discipline," pt. 1 in *Baptist Preacher* 4 (September 1845): 173–90; pt. 2 in ibid. (October 1845): 191–209. This advice became the standard practice in Alabama; see *South-Western Baptist*, February 5, 1851, for similar recommendations.

72. DeVotie Papers, 1856.

73. *Alabama Baptist*, May 10, 1845.

74. *South-Western Baptist*, August 18, 1859.

75. Eufaula Baptist Church Minutes; Stone, *History of First Baptist Church of Wetumpka*, 44; *South-Western Baptist*, August 4, 1852.

76. *South-Western Baptist*, October 1, 1857.

77. Ibid., June 2, 1859.

78. Ibid., March 6, 1850, March 15, 1855.

79. *Alabama Baptist*, March 14, 1846, November 28, 1849.

80. Teague, "Outline of the Baptist Denomination in Alabama."

81. *Alabama Baptist*, November 21, 1849; *South-Western Baptist*, November 13, 1850.

82. *Alabama Baptist*, May 31, June 7, 14, 21, 1845.

83. Teague, "Outline of the Baptist Denomination in Alabama."

84. *Alabama Baptist*, June 20, 27, July 11, 1846.

85. Ibid., August 22, October 23, 1846; Hamilton and Wells, *Daughters of the Dream*, 51; Thelma Wolfe Hall, *I Give Myself: The Story of J. Lewis Shuck and His Mission to the Chinese* (Richmond: privately published, 1983), 75; Wayne Flynt and Gerald W. Berkley, *Taking Christianity to China: Alabama Missionaries in the Middle Kingdom, 1850–1950* (Tuscaloosa: University of Alabama Press, 1997), 46–47.

86. Flynt and Berkley, *Taking Christianity to China*, 47–53; for a perceptive study of Foster's Alabama years, see Carol Ann Vaughn, "The Early Life of Martha Foster Crawford in Antebellum Alabama, 1830–1851" (master's thesis, Auburn University, 1994).

87. *Alabama Baptist*, August 29, April 18, December 4, 18, 1846.

88. Eufaula Baptist Church Minutes; J. H. DeVotie, "Sermon Notes," vol. 5, DeVotie Papers.

89. *South-Western Baptist*, January 28, 1853.

90. Ibid., February 3, 10, 1859.

91. See Ian R. Tyrell, "Drink and Temperance in the Antebellum South: An Overview and Interpretation," *Journal of Southern History* 48 (November 1982): 485–510.

92. *Alabama Baptist*, August 23, 1845; *South-Western Baptist*, October 28, November 3, 1852, February 18, April 1, 1853, January 6, 1859, May 31, 1860; Salem Baptist Church Minutes, Samford University Archives.

93. *Alabama Baptist*, November 21, 1849; *South-Western Baptist*, April 29, 1853.

94. *Alabama Baptist*, January 25, 1845, February 19, May 22, 1850; *South-Western Baptist*, March 1, 1855; Salem Baptist Church Minutes.

95. *Alabama Baptist*, August 29, 1849, January 15, 1851; *South-Western Baptist*, September 15, 1859.

96. *Alabama Baptist*, February 8, 22, 1845, March 14, 1846, August 16, 1860.

97. Ibid., January 4, 1845; *South-Western Baptist*, July 20, 1853.

98. *South-Western Baptist*, February 9, 16, 23, March 9, October 12, 1854, March 26, 1857; see Robert E. Hunt, "Home, Domesticity, and School Reform in Antebellum Alabama," *Alabama Review* 49 (October 1996): 253–75.

99. *South-Western Baptist*, July 31, 1850, March 3, 1852.

100. Ibid., March 15, August 2, 1860. For an excellent treatment of agrarian resistance to industrialization, see Thornton, *Politics and Power in a Slave Society*, 291–324, 431–32.

101. *Alabama Baptist*, March 14, 1849; *South-Western Baptist*, June 1, 1854, April 7, 1859; Stone, *History of First Baptist Church of Wetumpka*, 27–30; C. E. Smith to Alabama Baptist State Convention, October 25, 1851, in D. L. McCall Papers, Samford University Archives.

102. *South-Western Baptist*, September 3, 1857.

103. *Alabama Baptist*, December 5, 1849; *South-Western Baptist*, January 28, April 22, 1853, October 5, 12, 1854, March 5, 1857.

104. *South-Western Baptist*, August 13, 1851, October 12, 1854.

105. Martha Foster Crawford Diaries, May 27, 1850, Duke University Archives, Durham, North Carolina.

106. *Alabama Baptist*, May 3, June 14, 1845.

107. *South-Western Baptist*, February 4, 1858; Big Creek Baptist Church Minutes, December 1858.

108. *South-Western Baptist*, August 12, 1853.

109. Sermon text on women, DeVotie Papers.

110. Blake Touchstone, "Planters and Slave Religion in the Deep South," in Boles, *Masters and Slaves in the House of the Lord*, 109–17; see also Richard J. Carwardine, *Evangelicals and Politics in Antebellum America* (New Haven: Yale University Press, 1993), and Timothy L. Smith, *Revivalism and Social Reform in Mid-Nineteenth Century America* (Nashville: Abingdon Press, 1957).

111. *Alabama Baptist*, February 28, 1846.

112. Ibid., and November 20, 1846; Robert E. Praytor, "From Concern to Neglect: Alabama Baptists' Religious Relations to the Negro, 1823–1870" (master's thesis, Samford University, 1971), 10, 12, 13.

113. "Muscogee," writing in *South-Western Baptist*, March 2, 1854; Praytor, "From Concern to Neglect," 13.

114. *South-Western Baptist*, August 22, September 16, 1846, July 30, 1851, June 12, 1856.

115. *Alabama Baptist*, August 20, 1931; notes in Killingsworth Papers.

116. Quoted in Praytor, "From Concern to Neglect," 16.

117. *Alabama Baptist*, February 13, 1850; *South-Western Baptist*, January 12, 1854.

118. *Alabama Baptist*, December 20, 1845, December 4, 1846; *South-Western Baptist*, July 14, 1852, September 3, 1857; W. O. Perry to James H. Chapman, January 27, 1944, Chapman Papers.

119. *Alabama Baptist*, May 31, 1845; *South-Western Baptist*, March 26, 1851; Word, *Big Springs*, 11; W. O. Perry to James H. Chapman, February 7, 1944, Chapman Papers.

120. Tichenor Diary, November 24, December 14, 1850. Growing separation of the races was a common pattern in churches during the years 1845–1860. See Larry M. James, "Biracial Fellowship in Antebellum Baptist Churches," in Boles, *Masters and Slaves in the House of the Lord*, 54–58.

121. *South-Western Baptist*, April 9, 1857; *Alabama Baptist*, April 20, 1950; Eufaula Bap-

tist Church Minutes; Stone, *History of First Baptist Church of Wetumpka*, 34–37; Bessie Conner Brown, *A History of the First Baptist Church, Tuskegee, Alabama, 1839–1971* (Tuskegee: First Baptist Church, 1972), 9–10.

122. Hughes, *History of the First African Baptist Church*, 6–7.

123. *South-Western Baptist*, May 17, June 21, 1860.

124. Ibid., December 11, 1856, November 12, 1857; Eufaula Baptist Church Minutes.

125. Allen, *First 150 Years*, 89; Charles O. Boothe, *The Cyclopedia of the Colored Baptists of Alabama* (Birmingham: Alabama Publishing Co., 1895), 112–13.

126. Boothe, *Cyclopedia of the Colored Baptists*, 30–31.

127. *Alabama Baptist*, April 20, 1844.

128. Lotsey White to Elder Howard Montague, August 24, 1869, A. P. Montague Papers, Samford University Archives.

129. *Alabama Baptist*, April 12, 26, May 3, 1845.

130. Ibid., November 23, 1844.

131. Ibid., November 30, 1844, January 4, March 15, 22, 1845; Jesse Hartwell to Foreign Mission Board, March 22, 1845, DeVotie Papers.

132. *Alabama Baptist*, April 5, May 10, 1845, June 20, 1846; A. Hamilton Reid, *Baptists in Alabama: Their Organization and Witness* (Montgomery: Paragon Press, 1967), 69–75.

133. *Alabama Baptist*, December 6, 20, 1845.

134. Reid (*Baptists in Alabama*) concedes slavery was an issue but emphasizes other causes. Historian Robert A. Baker in *Southern Baptist Convention and Its People*, 171, concedes that there were other issues but identifies slavery as the central source for creation of the SBC.

135. *Alabama Baptist*, May 22, 1850; *South-Western Baptist*, October 2, 1856, October 15, 1857.

136. *Alabama Baptist*, September 3, 1848, May 8, August 28, 1850.

137. Ibid., February 13, 1850.

138. Ibid., May 1, 1850; *South-Western Baptist*, July 31, August 28, 1850; see also Crabtree, "South-Western Baptist," and Appleton, "Samuel Henderson."

139. *South-Western Baptist*, February 28, 1856, April 5, 1860.

140. See David B. Chesebrough, *God Ordained This War: Sermons on the Sectional Crisis, 1830–1865* (Columbia: University of South Carolina Press, 1991), 1–8; C. C. Goen, *Broken Churches, Broken Nation* (Macon: Mercer University Press, 1985); Carwardine, *Evangelicals and Politics in Antebellum America;* Crowther, "Holy Honor," 624, 630–35.

141. *Alabama Baptist*, May 22, July 31, 1850.

142. *South-Western Baptist*, March 16, April 13, September 28, 1854, May 31, 1855, August 7, 28, 1856; Appleton, "Samuel Henderson," 25, 34.

143. *South-Western Baptist*, November 3, December 22, 1859.

144. Ibid., February 16, September 5, November 1, 1860.

145. Ibid., November 22, 29, December 13, 1860.

146. Walter Belt White, "J. L. M. Curry: Alabamian" (master's thesis, Samford University, 1971), 152, 159, 170–77, 183–84; DeVotie Journal; Appleton, "Samuel Henderson," 8–10, 46.

147. Appleton, "Samuel Henderson," 46–49; *South-Western Baptist*, January 10, February 7, 1861.

Chapter 4: War and Reunion, 1860–1874

1. Alabama Baptist State Convention Minutes, 1860, 11–12.

2. Allen, *First 150 Years;* George, " 'Faithful Shepherd, Beloved Minister,' " 24.

3. Basil Manly Sr., "The Purpose of Calamities," sermon preached on February 28, 1862 ("Fast Day"), Manly Papers.

4. George, " 'Faithful Shepherd, Beloved Minister,' " 24–25.

5. *South-Western Baptist*, August 8, 1861, February 20, 27, 1862, January 28, 29, 1863.

6. Ibid., February 27, 1862; see also Appleton, "Samuel Henderson," 49–72.

7. *South-Western Baptist,* September 26, 1861, February 11, 1864.

8. Ibid., January 23, 1862.

9. Ibid., May 8, 1862, February 11, 1864; George L. Lee Papers, Samford University Archives.

10. *South-Western Baptist,* August 1, 1861, October 29, 1863.

11. Ibid., August 15, 1861.

12. Brooks, "Mind of Wilcox County," 54–55; *Alabama Baptist,* March 18, 1926; *South-Western Baptist,* July 11, August 29, 1861, March 26, 1863.

13. "John J. Bullington," Alabama Baptist Biography Files, Samford University Archives; DeVotie Journal; Arthur L. Walker Jr., "Three Alabama Baptist Chaplains, 1861–1865," *Alabama Review* 16 (July 1963): 174–84; *South-Western Baptist,* April 24, 1862.

14. Cecil Orion Sewell Jr., "The Carey Baptist Association of Alabama During the Civil War" (research paper, University of Alabama, 1963), copy in Samford University Archives.

15. *South-Western Baptist,* April 10, 17, 1862, July 2, 1863.

16. I. T. Tichenor Diary and Tichenor to the *Richmond Whig,* in Tichenor Papers; *South-Western Baptist,* May 1, 1862. This gory account became part of the Tichenor legend, mentioned prominently in all biographies of him; see, for instance, Dill, *Isaac Taylor Tichenor,* 27–28, and Willie Jean Stewart, *Heroes of Home Missions* (Atlanta: Home Mission Board, 1945), 39.

17. *South-Western Baptist,* January 22, 1863.

18. Ibid., October 1, 1863; J. J. D. Renfroe Papers, Samford University Archives.

19. For a sociological explanation of the 1863–1864 revivals, see Drew Gilpin Faust, "Christian Soldiers: The Meaning of Revivalism in the Confederate Army," *Journal of Southern History* 53 (February 1987): 63–90.

20. *South-Western Baptist,* May 28, October 15, 1863; John C. Bush, "J. J. D. Renfroe," in John C. Bush Papers, Samford University Archives.

21. William C. Jordan, *Some Events and Incidents During the Civil War* (Montgomery: Paragon Press, 1909), 87–89.

22. *South-Western Baptist,* October 12, 1863.

23. Renfroe Papers.

24. J. J. D. Renfroe, "John the Baptist Advising Soldiers" and "The Sin of Stealing," sermon mss. in ibid.

25. J. J. D. Renfroe, "Royal Business Demands Haste," sermon ms. in ibid.

26. J. J. D. Renfroe, "The Battle Is God's," sermon ms. in ibid.

27. J. J. D. Renfroe, "God Hath a Controversy with the Nations" and "Pure and Undefiled Religion," sermon mss. in ibid.

28. J. J. D. Renfroe, "Bitter Waters Made Sweet" and "Heaven," sermon mss. in ibid.

29. Bush, "J. J. D. Renfroe"; "William Carey Bledsoe," Alabama Baptist Biography Files; Faust, "Christian Soldiers," 88–90.

30. J. J. D. Renfroe to Hubbard Publishers, March 14, 1888, Renfroe Papers.

31. Ms. in Renfroe Papers.

32. White, "J. L. M. Curry," 225–26, 249, 288, 291, 294, 304, 306, 309; *Alabama Baptist,* June 21, 1883; Stone, *History of First Baptist Church of Wetumpka,* 52–53.

33. For the key role of evangelical Christianity in sustaining Confederate nationalism, see Drew Gilpin Faust, *The Creation of Confederate Nationalism: Ideology and Identity in the Civil War South* (Baton Rouge: Louisiana State University Press, 1988).

34. *Baptist Correspondent,* November 28, 1860, February 27, 1861.

35. *South-Western Baptist,* January 24, 31, April 18, May 9, 16, July 18, 25, 1861, January 23, 1862.

36. Ibid., January 31, May 30, June 13, 1861.

37. Ibid., July 24, October 9, 1862; *Richmond* (Va.) *Whig,* May 18, 1863.

38. *South-Western Baptist,* April 25, 1861.

39. Ibid., July 11, 1861.

40. Ibid., June 13, 1861, May 29, 1862, March 12, 1863. See also Old Liberty Baptist Church Minutes (Cleburne County), April 8, 10, 1864, Samford University Archives.

41. *South-Western Baptist*, January 31, 1861, October 9, 1862.

42. Ibid., April 10, 1862.

43. Ibid., September 5, 1861, May 1, 1862, January 14, February 25, 1864.

44. Ibid., February 26, 1863.

45. Ibid., September 25, 1862, September 10, 17, 24, 1863.

46. Ibid., April 28, 1864.

47. Ibid., March 31, April 7, 1864; Lee N. Allen, "The Alabama Baptist Association: Distress, Destitution, and Decline, 1861–1882," *Alabama Baptist Historian* 18 (January 1982): 8. For an excellent history of the state Baptist orphanage, see Cynthia A. Wise, *The Alabama Baptist Children's Home: The First One Hundred Years* (Montgomery: Brown Printing Co., 1991), especially 1–2.

48. *South-Western Baptist*, August 14, 1862.

49. Jordan, *Some Events During the Civil War*, 38–39.

50. *South-Western Baptist*, August 29, November 28, 1861.

51. Ibid., June 5, 1862, June 2, September 29, 1864; Walter L. Fleming, "The Churches of Alabama During the Civil War and Reconstruction," *Gulf States Historical Magazine* 1 (September 1902): 5; *Baptist Correspondent*, September 25, 1861.

52. *South-Western Baptist*, February 5, July 23, August 13, 1863.

53. Ibid., November 14, 1861, August 21, 1862, August 20, 27, October 22, November 5, 1863, February 4, June 9, 1864.

54. Ibid., December 24, 1863.

55. Historian James W. Silver writes that the church was the most effective propaganda agency in the Confederacy and the single most successful institution in building and maintaining Confederate morale. See James W. Silver, *Confederate Morale and Church Propaganda* (Tuscaloosa: University of Alabama Press, 1957).

56. Baker, *Southern Baptist Convention and Its People*, 227–28; Flynt and Berkley, *Taking Christianity to China*, 124, 239, 263–70.

57. *South-Western Baptist*, November 21, 1861; Davis C. Woolley, "Activities of Baptist Churches During the Civil War and Reconstruction," 4–7, ms. in Woolley Papers.

58. *South-Western Baptist*, November 20, 1862.

59. Ibid., September 26, 1861, October 2, 1862, September 2, November 5, 1863; Sewell, "Carey Baptist Association During the Civil War," 5–17.

60. Stone, *History of First Baptist Church of Wetumpka*, 53; Word, *Big Springs*, 11; Woolley, "Activities of Baptist Churches During the Civil War and Reconstruction," 17–18.

61. Mallory Diary.

62. *Christian Index and South-Western Baptist*, June 27, 1867, March 4, 11, 1869.

63. Elizabeth Rhodes Diary, Book 3, January 1–November 17, 1861, in author's possession.

64. *Baptist Correspondent*, November 13, 1861; *South-Western Baptist*, January 17, 1861, March 6, April 3, 1862, September 10, November 5, 1863, August 18, 1864.

65. Jon Appleton explores this episode fully in his biography of Henderson, "Samuel Henderson," 73–75.

66. James Dean Lancaster Jr., "Howard College During the Civil War and Reconstruction, 1860–1873" (master's thesis, Samford University, 1974), 33–46, 53–58.

67. Hamilton and Wells, *Daughters of the Dream*, 58–69; *Alabama Baptist*, July 6, 1882; "Sherman, Samuel S.," in M. Owen, *History of Alabama and Dictionary of Biography*.

68. *Christian Index and South-Western Baptist*, April 12, 1866, May 7, 1868, January 28, 1869.

69. Quoted in Praytor, "From Concern to Neglect," 48–53.

70. Ibid., 54–57, 61–63.

71. Ibid., 43–47, 67–72.

72. For a thorough treatment of northern white-black Baptist relations, see James M. Washington, *Frustrated Fellowship: The Baptist Quest for Social Power* (Macon: Mercer University Press, 1986).

73. Brown, *History of First Baptist Church, Tuskegee*, 11.

74. *Christian Index and South-Western Baptist*, July 12, 1866, September 30, 1869; Cruse, "Hardin Edwards Taliaferro," 151.

75. *Christian Index and South-Western Baptist*, May 30, June 13, 20, 1867, August 6, 13, October 1, 8, 22, 1868, April 8, 1869; Jeffers, *History of Tuskegee-Lee Association*, 16–17.

76. For a perceptive essay on the theological origins of black religious separatism, see Katharine Dvorak, "After Apocalypse, Moses," in Boles, *Masters and Slaves in the House of the Lord*, 173–91.

77. *Christian Index and South-Western Baptist*, June 11, 1868, February 18, 1869, September 29, 1870; Steve Tondera, "Presidential Address," Steve Tondera Papers, Samford University Archives.

78. Stone, *History of First Baptist Church of Wetumpka*, 64–66.

79. Hughes, *History of the First African Baptist Church*, 8–19.

80. Allen, "Alabama Baptist Association, 1861–1882," 8; Fleming, "Churches of Alabama During the Civil War," 20; *Christian Index and South-Western Baptist*, April 22, 1869, June 16, 1870.

81. Eufaula Baptist Church Minutes.

82. *Christian Index and South-Western Baptist*, September 2, October 21, 1869.

83. Mallory Diary.

84. *Christian Index and South-Western Baptist*, September 9, 1869.

85. Ibid., May 2, 30, 1867; *Alabama Baptist*, June 1, 1882.

86. Boothe, *Cyclopedia of the Colored Baptists*, 57, 112.

87. Charles A. Stakely, *The History of the First Baptist Church of Montgomery* (Montgomery: Paragon Press, 1930), 43, 68.

88. *Christian Index and South-Western Baptist*, October 21, 1869.

89. Mallory Diary.

90. Killingsworth Papers.

91. Gene L. Howard, *Death at Cross Plains: An Alabama Reconstruction Tragedy* (Tuscaloosa: University of Alabama Press, 1984), 62, 84.

92. B. F. Riley, *A Memorial History of the Baptists of Alabama* (Philadelphia: Judson Press, 1923), 166–67. Local Selma historians and Boothe (*Cyclopedia of the Colored Baptists*) dispute this account.

93. *Christian Index and South-Western Baptist*, January 17, 1867.

94. Henry Yates to Leon Macon, March 15, 1955, in "Churches—Historical Notes," Macon Papers.

95. David M. Reimers, *White Protestantism and the Negro* (New York: Oxford University Press, 1965), 25.

96. Baker, *Southern Baptist Convention and Its People*, 232.

97. Peter Kolchin, *First Freedom: The Responses of Alabama's Blacks to Emancipation* (New York: Greenwood Press, 1972), 87–121; see also Edward L. Wheeler, *Uplifting the Race: The Black Minister in the New South Movement, 1865–1902* (New York: University Press of America, 1986).

98. For the extent of Civil War and Reconstruction devastation in Alabama, see William W. Rogers et al., *Alabama: The History of a Deep South State* (Tuscaloosa: University of Alabama Press, 1994), 203–40; Wayne Flynt, *Poor But Proud: Alabama's Poor Whites* (Tuscaloosa: University of Alabama Press, 1989), 36–55.

99. *Christian Index and South-Western Baptist*, February 24, March 3, 1866.

100. J. J. D. Renfroe Sermons, Renfroe Papers.

101. Ibid.

102. *Christian Index and South-Western Baptist,* November 5, 1868; Stone, *History of First Baptist Church of Wetumpka,* 72–73.

103. *Christian Index and South-Western Baptist,* December 9, October 14, 1869, August 18, 1870, August 14, October 2, 1873; Brown, *History of the First Baptist Church, Tuskegee,* 13–14.

104. Word, *Big Springs,* 12–13, 53–54.

105. Fanny Chiltore to Basil Manly Sr., August 27, 1866, Manly Papers; *Christian Index and South-Western Baptist,* September 30, 1869.

106. *Christian Index and South-Western Baptist,* July 30, 1868, September 30, 1869, July 7, 1870.

107. Ibid., October 1, November 19, December 17, 1868.

108. Ibid., March 19, 1868, November 21, 1872, August 21, 1873, April 7, 1874.

109. Flynt, *Poor But Proud,* 50; *Christian Index and South-Western Baptist,* May 16, 1867, August 27, September 10, 1868, February 1, May 30, 1872, March 24, 1874.

110. Lee Diary; *Christian Index and South-Western Baptist,* March 7, 1867.

111. *Christian Index and South-Western Baptist,* March 26, June 11, 1868; Sarah R. Espy Diary, Alabama State Archives, Montgomery.

112. *Christian Index and South-Western Baptist,* February 6, 1868, March 18, 1869.

113. Ibid., July 8, 1869, May 2, 1872.

114. White, "J. L. M. Curry," 320–23, 348, 368; Lancaster, "Howard College During the Civil War," 64, 67–69, 79–81.

115. *Christian Index and South-Western Baptist,* January 2, 23, September 10, 1868; Lancaster, "Howard College During the Civil War," 83.

116. Lancaster, "Howard College During the Civil War," 99–112; Pate, "Development of the Instructional Program," 64–69.

117. Hamilton and Wells, *Daughters of the Dream,* 69–80.

118. Appleton, "Samuel Henderson," 81.

119. Ibid., 77; *Christian Index and South-Western Baptist,* March 5, 12, 1868.

120. Appleton, "Samuel Henderson," 88; Murfee, "Journalism of the Baptist Denomination," 16–19; *Alabama Baptist,* December 23, 1873, March 24, April 14, 1874, January 6, 1927.

121. *Christian Index and South-Western Baptist,* March 28, 1867.

122. C. W. Buckley to Henry Houghton [*sic*], June 13, 1865, Henry C. Hooten Papers, Samford University Archives; *Alabama Baptist,* July 22, 1892; Ables, "History of DeKalb Baptist Association," 34–35; "Bailey Bruce," clipping in Alabama Baptist Biography Files.

123. *Christian Index and South-Western Baptist,* July 11, August 1, 1867, July 1, 1869, September 8, 1874.

124. Ibid., December 7, 1871, January 25, 1872; *Alabama Baptist,* December 12, 1895.

125. *Christian Index and South-Western Baptist,* May 16, 1867, May 28, 1868, June 10, August 12, 1869.

126. Ibid., September 4, October 9, 1873; *Alabama Baptist,* July 14, September 15, 1874; Eufaula Baptist Church Minutes, 1870; Martha McGhee Glisson, "The Role of the Good Hope Baptist Church in the Community of Uchee, 1837–1987," *Alabama Review* 42 (July 1989): 227.

127. *Christian Index and South-Western Baptist,* July 1, September 16, 1869.

128. Ibid., June 21, 1866; *South-Western Baptist,* February 2, 1865; *Alabama Baptist,* March 31, April 14, 1874.

129. Renfroe Sermons; DeVotie Journal.

130. White, "J. L. M. Curry," 362; *Christian Index and South-Western Baptist,* June 6, 1867.

131. *Christian Index and South-Western Baptist,* April 9, 1868; *Baptist Correspondent,* February 29, 1860.

132. *Baptist Correspondent,* October 3, 1860, February 27, 1861; *Christian Index and South-Western Baptist,* February 13, 1868.

133. For a provocative exposition on gender relations in rural southern religion, see Ted

Ownby, *Subduing Satan: Religion, Recreation, and Manhood in the Rural South, 1865–1920* (Chapel Hill: University of North Carolina Press, 1990).

134. *Christian Index and South-Western Baptist*, June 13, 1869; Eufaula Baptist Church Minutes.

135. *Christian Index and South-Western Baptist*, October 23, 1873.

136. Ibid., February 10, March 17, 1870; Flynt and Berkley, *Taking Christianity to China*, 50.

137. *Alabama Baptist*, July 14, 1874; *Christian Index and South-Western Baptist*, January 13, 1866.

138. For particularly insightful generalizations on Southern Baptists, black and white, after 1860, see: Martin E. Marty, *Righteous Empire: The Protestant Experience in America* (New York: Dial Press, 1970); Samuel S. Hill Jr., *The South and the North in American Religion* (Athens: University of Georgia Press, 1980); Paul Harvey, "Southern Baptists and Southern Culture, 1865–1920" (Ph.D. diss., University of California at Berkeley, 1992).

Chapter 5: Building a New South, 1875–1890

1. *Alabama Baptist*, January 11, 18, 25, 1877.

2. Ibid., April 6, 1875, March 16, 1876, January 29, 1880, July 10, 1884, January 12, 1888.

3. Ibid., August 17, 31, October 19, 1875.

4. Harvey, "Southern Baptists and Southern Culture," 322–23; Lincoln Missionary Baptist Church "Articles of Agreement and Rules of Order, 1887," in J. D. Acker Papers, Samford University Archives; *Alabama Baptist*, October 24, 1878, February 7, 1889.

5. *Alabama Baptist*, July 20, 1875, July 27, 1876, January 4, June 28, 1877, September 26, 1878.

6. Ibid., March 9, 1875, January 14, 21, 1886, March 10, July 7, 1887.

7. Ibid., February 1, September 20, October 11, 1877.

8. Ibid., September 20, 1877, December 13, 1883, January 12, 1888.

9. Ibid., September 20, 1877, July 4, 1878, December 13, 1883, July 15, 1886, August 18, 1887.

10. Ibid., January 10, 1878, May 29, 1884, July 23, 1885, December 23, 1886, January 6, 1927.

11. Ibid., March 2, 1876, July 9, 1885, December 23, 1886, January 6, 1887.

12. Ibid., August 11, November 10, 1887.

13. Ibid., April 13, 1876, May 23, October 3, 1878, September 23, 1880, January 1, 1885.

14. Ibid., October 4, November 1, 1877, January 29, 1880, November 10, 1881, September 4, 1890, February 16, 1882.

15. Ibid., November 6, 1879, January 1, 1880, January 20, 1881; Lincoln Missionary Baptist Church Minutes, in Acker Papers.

16. *Alabama Baptist*, April 27, February 17, 1876, November 29, 1877, February 3, 1887.

17. Ibid., March 2, 1876, January 25, November 15, 1883.

18. Ibid., July 13, 1875, December 12, 1889.

19. David Edwin Harrell, "Religious Pluralism: Catholics, Jews, and Sectarians," in Charles R. Wilson, ed., *Religion in the South* (Jackson: University of Mississippi Press, 1985), 68–71; Stone, *History of First Baptist Church of Wetumpka*, 87–88. For Landmarkers, primitivism, and republicanism, see Harvey, "Southern Baptists and Southern Culture," 11, 157–70.

20. *Alabama Baptist*, March 30, October 5, 1876, July 12, August 30, 1877.

21. Ibid., January 24, 1878, July 24, 1884, February 16, 1888.

22. H. Shelton Smith et al., eds., *American Christianity: An Historical Interpretation with Representative Documents*, vol. 2 (New York: Charles Scribner's Sons, 1960), especially 255–60.

23. *Alabama Baptist*, September 18, October 2, 1879, October 19, 1882.

24. Ibid., October 23, 1879, December 23, 1880, April 21, September 29, 1881.

25. Ibid., November 25, December 2, 1880.

26. Ibid., May 9, 1878, January 6, 1881, April 20, 1876. The series on science ran in the fall of 1876.

27. Ibid., March 30, 1876, March 8, 1883.

28. Ibid., September 7, 1876, August 7, 1879, May 27, 1880.

29. Ibid., January 1, 8, 1885.

30. Ibid., June 19, 1879, June 10, February 12, 19, 1880, November 3, 1881, October 2, 1884.

31. Ibid., January 6, February 3, 1881, December 5, 1889.

32. Ibid., June 15, 1875, March 16, 1876, July 4, 1878, February 22, 1883; Nicholas B. Williams to H. A. Tupper, March 19, 1878, Nicholas B. Williams File, Foreign Mission Board Papers, Southern Baptist Historical Library and Archives.

33. *Alabama Baptist*, June 20, 1878, May 6, 1880.

34. For excellent discussions of biblical fundamentalism and premillennialism, see Ernest R. Sandeen, *The Roots of Fundamentalism: British and American Millennarianism, 1800–1930* (Chicago: University of Chicago Press, 1970), and Timothy P. Weber, *Living in the Shadow of the Second Coming: American Premillennialism, 1875–1925* (New York: Oxford University Press, 1979); *Alabama Baptist*, July 9, 1885.

35. David Hackett, "Gender and Religion in American Culture, 1870–1930, *"Religion and American Culture: A Journal of Interpretation* 5 (Summer 1995): 131–32; "William Carey Bledsoe," Alabama Baptist Biography Files; *Alabama Baptist*, February 12, 1880, August 2, 1888.

36. *Alabama Baptist*, September 7, 1875.

37. Ibid., November 16, 1875, May 6, 1880; Stone, *History of First Baptist Church of Wetumpka*, 85. Stone, in another church history, traces the origins of the Prattville WMU to interdenominational community work during the Civil War by the Prattville Ladies' Aid Society; Karen A. Stone, *Prattville First Baptist Church: Sharing Our Past with a Vision for the Future, 1838–1988* (Montgomery: Brown Printing Co., 1989), 28.

38. *Alabama Baptist*, August 3, 1875, September 13, 1877; Minutes of Ladies Benevolent Society, Ladies Aid Society, and Woman's Missionary Society, First Baptist Church, Huntsville, copy in Samford University Archives; "Willing Workers in Retrospect, Ninety-First Anniversary of Organized Woman's Work, First Baptist Church, Greenville, Alabama, 1872–1963," Samford University Archives.

39. "History of the Woman's Missionary Union of East Liberty Association," ms. in box 3, Denson Family Papers, Auburn University Archives, Auburn; Stone, *Prattville First Baptist Church*, 48.

40. *Alabama Baptist*, January 27, 1876.

41. Ibid., July 19, 1883, February 4, 1886, July 26, 1888; Jackson, *Women of Vision*, 12.

42. *Alabama Baptist*, January 9, 1879, June 2, 16, 23, 1881.

43. Ibid., June 16, July 7, 1881; Jeffers, *Auburn First Baptist Church*, 12, 18.

44. *Alabama Baptist*, December 14, 1882.

45. Ibid., March 23, 1882.

46. Ibid., June 6, 1878, March 9, 1882.

47. Ibid., August 26, 1886.

48. Ibid., July 11, 1889.

49. Ibid., September 2, 1876, December 21, 1882.

50. Ibid., March 4, 1886.

51. Ibid., March 25, May 13, 1886.

52. Ibid., February 17, 1887.

53. Ibid., October 19, November 2, December 21, 1882.

54. Ibid., September 11, 1884; Jackson, *Women of Vision*, 13–14.

55. Jackson, *Women of Vision*, 14; Reid, *Baptists in Alabama*, 141.

56. *Alabama Baptist*, January 9, 1879, July 7, 1887, July 5, 1888; Hamilton and Wells,

Daughters of the Dream, 87–90; Catherine B. Allen, *A Century to Celebrate: History of Woman's Missionary Union* (Birmingham: Woman's Missionary Union, 1987), 30–31.

57. *Alabama Baptist*, August 4, 1881.

58. Mrs. S. A. Chambers, "Woman's Work in the Church," Samford University Archives. This essay was also read at the Bigbe Association and perhaps at other associational meetings as well; *Alabama Baptist*, August 30, 1883.

59. Jackson, *Women of Vision*, 15–19; Reid, *Baptists in Alabama*, 141–42.

60. Jackson, *Women of Vision*, 20–27; Crumpton, *Our Baptist Centennials*, 79–82.

61. *Alabama Baptist*, March 29, November 15, 1883, October 25, 1888, January 3, 1889. For the progression of evangelical women from missionary society to temperance society to woman suffrage, see Anne Firor Scott, *The Southern Lady: From Pedestal to Politics, 1830–1930* (Chicago: University of Chicago Press, 1970).

62. *Alabama Baptist*, September 5, 1878, July 5, August 23, 1888.

63. Jackson, *Women of Vision*, 12; Flynt and Berkley, *Taking Christianity to China*, 234–36.

64. *Alabama Baptist*, April 5, 1877, October 19, 1882, July 23, 1885, August 9, September 12, 1888.

65. Ibid., January 3, 1889; *Minutes, Fourth Annual Session of the Evergreen Association* (Troy: John Post Printer, 1888), copy in Alabama State Archives.

66. *Alabama Baptist*, August 31, October 5, 1876, January 9, November 27, December 4, 1879, February 5, 1880, March 20, 1884.

67. Ibid., August 17, 24, 1876.

68. Ibid., June 10, August 5, 1880.

69. Ibid., June 6, 1878, June 10, 1886; see also Flynt and Berkley, *Taking Christianity to China*, especially 72–102.

70. *Alabama Baptist*, July 6, 1882, November 4, 1886.

71. Ibid., October 25, December 13, 1883, July 19, 1888, January 24, 1889.

72. Ibid., August 17, 1875, February 3, 1876, July 11, 1878, May 29, August 14, 1879, February 7, 1889. For attitudes of Alabama whites on black education, see Robert G. Sherer, *Subordination or Liberation? The Development and Conflicting Theories of Black Education in Nineteenth Century Alabama* (Tuscaloosa: University of Alabama Press, 1977).

73. *Alabama Baptist*, November 30, 1876, February 12, 1880.

74. Ibid., April 20, 1875, May 17, September 27, 1877, October 31, 1878.

75. Ibid., May 17, 1877, May 26, June 23, July 14, August 11, September 29, October 13, November 10, December 8, 22, 1881; for an excellent survey, see Edward R. Crowther, "Interracial Cooperative Missions Among Alabama Baptists, 1868–1882," *Journal of Negro History*, forthcoming.

76. *Alabama Baptist*, May 9, 1878, April 19, 1883, July 24, 1884, April 1, 1886, November 15, 1888, June 20, 1889.

77. Reid, *Baptists in Alabama*, 119–24.

78. *Alabama Baptist*, March 22, April 19, May 3, 1877, January 26, 1882.

79. Ibid., January 5, May 25, 1875, June 15, 1876, March 29, 1877, November 14, 1878, January 30, February 6, 1879, April 21, 1881, March 2, 1882, April 10, 1884, May 19, 1887, August 8, 1889.

80. Ibid., November 7, 1878, October 2, 1879, January 1, 1880, January 5, 1898.

81. Salem Baptist Church Minutes.

82. *Alabama Baptist*, March 18, 1926; "W. B. Crumpton, An Eminent Baptist Missionary, Reformer and Politician," in Samford University Archives; Washington B. Crumpton, *A Book of Memories, 1842–1920* (Montgomery: Baptist Mission Board, 1921), 188–90.

83. James Benson Sellers, *The Prohibition Movement in Alabama, 1702 to 1943* (Chapel Hill: University of North Carolina Press, 1943), 53–67; Crumpton, *Book of Memories*, 190–91; *Alabama Baptist*, January 8, March 4, April 15, 1880, July 20, 1882, November 15, 1883.

84. Sellers, *Prohibition Movement*, 73.

85. Reid, *Baptists in Alabama*, 131.

86. *Alabama Baptist*, July 6, 13, 1875; quoted in Sally G. McMillen, "To Train Up a Child: Southern Baptist Sunday Schools and the Socialization of Children, 1870–1900" (paper read at Southern Historical Association, 1986, copy in author's possession). I am grateful to Prof. McMillen for permission to use this early version of her excellent scholarship on the Sunday school in the South. See also Marty, *Righteous Empire*, 75–76.

87. *Alabama Baptist*, January 6, 20, 1876, March 22, 1877, April 24, 1884, December 6, 1888, February 7, 1889. For an insightful analysis of Curry, see Horace Mann Bond, *Negro Education in Alabama: A Study in Cotton and Steel* (1939; reprint, Tuscaloosa: University of Alabama Press, 1994), 198–203.

88. *Alabama Baptist*, March 30, 1876, September 18, 1879, October 16, 1884, January 20, 1887, October 24, 1889.

89. Ibid., April 6, 1875, February 1, 1877, August 23, 1883, August 22, 1889; "History of the Mud Creek Association," in box 1, Woolley Papers.

90. *Alabama Baptist*, February 1, 1877, July 7, 1881, April 16, 1885.

91. Ibid., August 3, 1875, March 1, April 5, July 5, 1883.

92. John Evan Barnes Jr., "My Autobiography as I Recall It," ms. in possession of Meg Stringer Lambert, Prattville, Alabama.

93. James M. Grant, "Alabama's Reaction to Late Nineteenth Century Revivalism" (honor's thesis, Samford University, 1968), 8, 11, 13, 30–31, 34, 36, 39, 40–44; *Alabama Baptist*, March 16, September 14, 1876, October 29, November 26, December 3, 1885.

94. Grant, "Alabama's Reaction to Revivalism," 46, 48–49, 50–51, 55–56. For accounts of revivals, see *Alabama Baptist*, January 6, 1876, September 18, 25, 1879, October 4, 1883.

95. *Alabama Baptist*, February 9, March 23, 1875, September 26, 1878, October 10, 1881.

96. Ibid., June 8, 1882, August 25, November 3, 1887.

97. The best treatment of late-nineteenth-century southern civil religion is Charles R. Wilson, *Baptized in Blood: The Religion of the Lost Cause, 1865–1920* (Athens: University of Georgia Press, 1980). See also Paul M. Gaston, *The New South Creed: A Study in Mythmaking* (New York: Alfred A. Knopf, 1970).

98. *Alabama Baptist*, May 10, August 30, 1877, July 3, 1879.

99. Ibid., October 5, 1899, March 18, April 22, 1926.

100. "The Confederate Soldier," James Hardy Curry Sermons, James Hardy Curry Papers, Samford University Archives.

101. "July 4th Sermon," Renfroe Sermons. See also Renfroe's sermon entitled "New South."

102. *Alabama Baptist*, July 10, 1890.

103. Ibid., June 22, 1875.

104. Ibid., August 21, 1875, January 6, 8, March 16, 1876, June 13, 1878, February 19, 1880, January 13, 1881.

105. Ibid., May 6, 1880, August 25, 1881, February 24, 1887, January 27, 1887, July 3, 10, 1890.

106. Ibid., September 6, 1877, May 23, 1878, January 18, 1883, February 10, 1887, January 17, 1889, July 10, 1890.

107. Ibid., April 7, 1887.

108. For an excellent survey of Alabama political thought during these years, see Daniel L. Cloyd, "Prelude to Reform: Political, Economic, and Social Thought of Alabama Baptists, 1877–1890," *Alabama Review* 31 (January 1978): 48–64.

109. *Alabama Baptist*, June 29, 1875.

110. Ibid., January 20, October 26, 1876, November 4, 1880.

111. Ibid., February 24, 1876, January 28, 1880.

112. Ibid., January 9, 1879, January 12, 1888, January 24, 1889; Stone, *History of First Baptist Church of Wetumpka*, 71–72.

113. *Alabama Baptist*, August 2, 1877, July 11, 1878, January 13, 1887.

114. For example, see ibid., April 4, 1887.

115. Ibid., August 23, 1877, August 7, 1890; Grace Hooten Gates, *The Model City of the New South: Anniston, Alabama, 1872–1900* (Huntsville: Strode Publishers, 1978), 197; Miriam Higginbotham and Ralph Higginbotham, *Upon This Rock I Will Build My Church: Parker Memorial Baptist Church, 1887–1987* (n.p.: Parker Memorial Baptist Church, 1987), 13, 29, 39, 50, 55–64; Harry M. Ayers, *Parker Memorial Baptist Church, Anniston, Alabama, 1887–1937* (n.p., 1937), 7, 12–22.

116. "Kirby Ward's Memories of Dr. Renfroe, October 5, 1952," John R. Sampey Papers, Samford University Archives.

117. Hinson, "Historical Patterns of Lay Leadership," 31–33; *Alabama Baptist*, July 3, 1879, January 5, 1888.

118. Ms. of speech to Sunday School State Convention; undated sermon ms.; J. H. Joiner to Caroline, August 1, 1881; Ermine McGaha to J. H. Joiner, undated; all in James Harvey Joiner Papers, Southern Historical Collection.

119. *Alabama Baptist*, January 10, December 19, 1878, March 6, 1879, March 11, 1880.

120. Ibid., October 4, 1877, July 31, 1882, January 15, 1885.

121. Ibid., July 19, 1877, May 30, 1878, February 5, March 4, May 27, July 8, 29, August 26, October 14, December 9, 1880, March 21, April 4, 11, 18, May 2, September 5, 19, 1889, March 20, April 10, 24, 1890.

122. Ibid., November 22, 1883; Biographical Sketch of E. T. Winkler, in E. T. Winkler Papers, Southern Baptist Archives.

123. E. T. Winkler, "Policy of Internal Improvements," undated, sermon ms. in Winkler Papers.

124. See Terry L. Jones, "Benjamin Franklin Riley: A Study of His Life and Work" (Ph.D. diss., Vanderbilt University, 1974); *Alabama Baptist*, March 1, 1883, January 26, 1888, May 13, 1926.

125. See B. F. Riley, *Alabama As It Is: The Immigrants and Capitalists Guide Book* (Atlanta: Constitution Publishing Co., 1888); Wayne Flynt, *Mine, Mill and Microchip: A Chronicle of Alabama Enterprise* (Northridge, Calif.: Windsor Publications, 1987), 103–4.

126. *Christian Index and South-Western Baptist*, March 21, 1872; *Alabama Baptist*, July 14, 1874; Tichenor Diary. See also Keith Harper, *The Quality of Mercy: Southern Baptists and Social Christianity, 1890–1920* (Tuscaloosa: University of Alabama Press, 1996), 37–45; Joel C. Watson, "Isaac Taylor Tichenor and the Administration of the Alabama Agricultural and Mechanical College, 1872–1882" (master's thesis, Auburn University, 1968); and Kimball Johnson, "Isaac Taylor Tichenor: A Biography" (Ph.D. diss., Southern Baptist Theological Seminary, 1955).

127. Stewart, *Heroes of Home Missions*, 39–43; Dill, *Isaac Taylor Tichenor*, 40–52; J. C. Bradley, "Profiles of Home Mission Board Executives," *Baptist History and Heritage* 30 (April 1995): 26–28; Glenn T. Miller, "Baptist Businessmen in Historical Perspective," *Baptist History and Heritage* 13 (January 1978): 58; Baker, *Southern Baptist Convention and Its People*, 242–44; Leon H. McBeth, *The Baptist Heritage: Four Centuries of Baptist Witness* (Nashville: Broadman Press, 1987), 427–32.

Chapter 6: Revolt at the Forks of the Creek, 1890–1900

1. William W. Rogers, *The One-Gallused Rebellion: Agrarianism in Alabama, 1865–1896* (Baton Rouge: Louisiana State University Press, 1970), 115, 133–34, 167, 171, 187, 189, 192, 206–7, 266, 297–308, 316, 323.

2. *Alabama Baptist*, December 7, 1882; W. Scott Morgan, *History of the Wheel and Alliance and the Impending Revolution*, reprint ed. (New York: Burt Franklin, 1968), 308–10.

3. Rogers, *One-Gallused Rebellion*, 99–101, 109–10, 115–20, 161–62, 167–85, 193–94, 201–5, 207–11, 272–91, 331.

4. For a description of the white descent into tenancy see Flynt, *Poor But Proud*, 59–91.

5. *Alabama Baptist*, June 26, 1890, June 2, 1892, June 13, July 4, September 5, 1895, August 13, 1896, January 14, 1897; W. B. Crumpton to Rev. Willingham, September 19, 1894, Foreign Mission Board Papers, Southern Baptist Archives.

6. C. Allyn Russell, "J. Frank Norris: Violent Fundamentalist," *Southwestern Historical Quarterly* 75 (January 1972): 272–73.

7. Mickey Crews, *The Church of God: A Social History* (Knoxville: University of Tennessee Press, 1990), 1–20; *Alabama Baptist*, September 9, 1897, December 1, 1898.

8. *Alabama Baptist*, November 14, 1889, November 27, 1890, March 19, 1891, March 7, 1895; Rosa Cilley Hunter, "History of the W.M.U. of Mobile Association," ms. in T. M. and R. M. Hunter Papers, Samford University Archives.

9. *Alabama Baptist*, September 24, 1885, September 3, 1891, February 4, 1892, October 19, 1893, July 4, 18, 25, August 8, 1895, January 2, 16, July 30, September 3, 24, 1896, May 27, 1897, March 14, 1898, July 6, 1899, February 9, 16, August 31, 1893.

10. Ibid., January 3, February 21, March 7, June 27, July 25, 1895, September 16, 1897, November 17, 1898; J. H. Curry, "Ministerial Education" and "The Church and Its Need," sermon mss. in Curry Papers.

11. Sellers, *Prohibition Movement*, 40–51.

12. Karl Rodabaugh, *The Farmers' Revolt in Alabama, 1890–1896* (n.p.: East Carolina University, 1977), 88.

13. *Alabama Baptist*, March 27, 1884.

14. Ibid., November 20, 1890; for examples of temperance articles and editorials, see ibid., March 3, April 7, 21, 1881, June 1, 22, 1882, August 2, 16, 1883, July 17, 24, 31, 1884.

15. Ibid., January 30, 1890, June 25, 1891.

16. "Temperance," sermon ms. in Curry Papers.

17. *Alabama Baptist*, November 26, 1892.

18. Ibid., September 18, 1890, March 19, October 29, 1896, October 27, 1898, August 21, 1890.

19. Ibid., January 3, 1884, June 18, 1891.

20. Ibid., March 20, 1884, January 7, 1886, November 13, 1890, January 29, 1891.

21. Carl D. English, "Ethical Emphases of Baptist Journals Published in the Southeastern Region of the United States, 1865–1915" (Ph.D. diss., Southern Baptist Theological Seminary, 1948), 8.

22. *Alabama Baptist*, January 17, February 7, April 3, 1884.

23. Ibid., July 24, 31, November 6, 1884.

24. Ibid., August 28, 1884, January 8, December 10, 1885, February 18, April 8, 1886, March 17, 1887, July 5, November 8, 1888; Sellers, *Prohibition Movement*, 80.

25. *Alabama Baptist*, June 24, July 15, 1886; Sellers, *Prohibition Movement*, 80–85.

26. *Alabama Baptist*, February 18, March 11, April 1, July 15, 1886.

27. Ibid., March 11, June 3, November 11, 1886.

28. Ibid., August 21, 1884, January 28, December 16, 1886, March 17, December 8, 1887, November 21, 1889.

29. Ibid., January 10, February 21, 28, March 7, 14, 1889.

30. Ibid., November 6, 1884, February 24, 1887, July 13, 1893.

31. Ibid., May 10, 17, 1888, January 20, March 17, 1889, February 20, 27, March 13, April 3, December 11, 1890, February 19, October 22, November 12, 19, December 3, 1891, June 16, 1892.

32. Ibid., May 29, 1890, May 7, 1891, February 11, 1892; Carl Harris, *Political Power in Birmingham, 1871–1921* (Knoxville: University of Tennessee Press, 1977), 63–81.

33. *Alabama Baptist*, December 13, 1894, January 10, 1895.

34. For an example of such conclusions, see Frederick A. Bode, "Religion and Class Hegemony: A Populist Critique in North Carolina," *Journal of Southern History* 37 (August 1971): 419–26.

35. Robert C. McMath Jr., "The Farmers' Alliance in the South: The Career of an Agrarian Institution" (Ph.D. diss., University of North Carolina, 1972), 266–89; see also Bruce E. Palmer, "The Rhetoric of Southern Populists: Metaphor and Imagery in the Language of Reform" (Ph.D. diss., Yale University, 1972); and Robert H. Craig, *Religion and Radical Politics: An Alternative Christian Tradition in the United States* (Philadelphia: Temple University Press, 1992).

36. *Alabama Baptist*, July 14, 1874; Henry P. Martin, "A History of Politics in Clay County During the Period of Populism from 1888–1896" (master's thesis, University of Alabama, 1936), 4, 9, 11; Samuel L. Webb, "From Independents to Populists to Progressive Republicans: The Case of Chilton County, Alabama, 1880–1920," *Journal of Southern History* 59 (November 1993): 715.

37. Richard C. Goode, "The Godly Insurrection in Limestone County: Social Gospel, Populism, and Southern Culture in the Late Nineteenth Century," *Religion and American Culture: A Journal of Interpretation* 3 (Summer 1993): 158–65.

38. *Alabama Baptist*, August 15, 29, 1889, March 6, July 10, August 7, 14, 21, 28, September 18, 1890, January 1, February 5, April 23, 1891.

39. Ibid., November 8, 1888, July 30, 1891.

40. Ibid., March 1, 1888.

41. Ibid., February 7, 1889, October 30, November 6, 20, 1890, January 1, 29, February 5, 19, May 2, 1891.

42. Ibid., March 6, July 16, September 25, 1890.

43. Rogers, *One-Gallused Rebellion*, 133, 276, 291, 296, 310, 313.

44. For three quite different interpretations of Samuel M. Adams as a reformer, see ibid., 133–34, 166–73, 210, 316–17, 295–99, 308–9; Sheldon Hackney, *Populism to Progressivism in Alabama* (Princeton: Princeton University Press, 1969), 45–46, 95, 118, 130–31; and Webb, "From Independents to Populists," 720. For Adams's revivals and defense of populism, see *Alabama Baptist*, May 9, 1889, May 21, November 19, 1891.

45. *Alabama Baptist*, March 17, 1892.

46. Ibid., March 24, 1892.

47. Ibid., January 7, April 14, 1892, December 14, 1893, July 19, 26, 1894.

48. Ibid., April 12, July 26, September 27, October 11, 1894, March 5, 12, 19, 1896.

49. Eufaula Baptist Church Minutes; Rogers, *One-Gallused Rebellion*, 99, 117–18; *Alabama Baptist*, August 16, January 12, May 31, 1888, June 20, August 29, September 12, 1889.

50. Cary C. Lloyd, "Separation of Church and State, Soul Liberty and Equality," sermon ms. in author's possession; Marilyn Davis Haln, *Butler County in the Nineteenth Century* (n.p., 1978), 156.

51. *Alabama Baptist*, September 4, 1890, January 8, June 18, 1891, September 7, 1893.

52. Ibid., March 19, May 7, 1891.

53. Ibid., February 14, 1889, October 1, 1891, November 10, 1909; George E. Sims, "Progress, Problems, and Promise: The Orrville Baptists, 1888–1959" (honors thesis, Samford University, 1976), 21–22; *Anniston Star*, January 5, 1954.

54. *Alabama Baptist*, August 28, 1890, December 10, 1891.

55. Ibid., February 11, 1892.

56. Ibid., March 31, July 21, 28, August 11, 25, 1892, August 10, 24, 1893.

57. Ibid., March 1, 8, 22, April 19, June 28, July 5, 12, August 2, 9, 23, October 11, 1894.

58. Ibid., February 14, 21, 1895, June 27, August 15, 1895.

59. Ibid., February 13, 20, March 19, April 30, August 6, September 3, 1896.

60. Ibid., October 26, 1893; Samuel M. Adams to Joseph F. Johnson, November 17, 1898,

January 26, April 28, May 25, 1899, February 17, 1900, Joseph F. Johnson Papers, Alabama State Archives; Dr. G. B. Crowe to O. D. Street, August 29, 1898, O. D. Street Papers, University of Alabama Archives, Tuscaloosa.

61. *Alabama Baptist,* April 23, May 7, 1896, November 17, 1898, January 22, December 14, 1899.

62. Ibid., August 17, 1899.

63. Ibid., January 5, 19, 1893, June 18, 1891, February 7, 1889, January 9, 1890, April 30, 1891, January 28, 1892, December 24, 1896, January 21, 1897, December 8, 1898.

64. Ibid., June 25, 1891, June 23, August 18, 1892, January 11, 18, 25, 1894, January 3, 1895.

65. Ibid., October 22, 1891; J. H. Curry, "Education, Schools and School Teachers," ms. of speech in Curry Papers.

66. *Alabama Baptist,* November 20, 1890, July 9, 1891, April 14, 1892, September 14, 1899.

67. Ibid., April 14, 1892.

68. Ibid., October 31, November 21, 1895, October 3, November 26, 1896, February 23, March 9, April 20, 27, 1899; "George Boardman Eager: An Appreciation of Life and Work," copy in George B. Eager Papers, Samford University Archives.

69. *Alabama Baptist,* October 10, 1895.

70. Ibid., August 7, 1890.

71. Ibid., June 19, 1890, August 10, 1893.

72. Ibid., November 20, 27, 1890, May 28, 1891, February 4, 1892.

73. Ibid., February 2, 1893.

74. Ibid., February 12, 1891, February 25, April 28, 1892.

75. Ibid., April 16, August 31, December 10, 1891, April 7, August 25, 1892, August 9, 1894.

76. Ibid., January 12, 1893, August 29, 1895.

77. Ibid., January 1, May 21, 1891, January 11, February 15, 1894, February 13, 1896, February 1, 1900.

78. Ibid., May 10, June 21, September 6, 1894.

79. Ibid., May 3, 10, 31, November 22, 1894.

80. Ibid., July 10, 1890, June 22, 1899; L. T. Reeves Diary, 1899, Samford University Archives.

81. *Alabama Baptist,* July 5, 1894, March 14, October 31, December 5, 1895.

82. Ibid., October 25, 1888.

83. Ibid., February 20, 1890, January 11, 18, 25, February 22, 1894.

84. Ibid., April 22, 1886.

85. Ibid., June 28, July 26, September 20, 1894.

86. Ibid., August 9, 1894.

87. *Birmingham News,* July 30, 1894; Ayers, *Parker Memorial Baptist Church, Anniston.*

88. *Alabama Baptist,* January 22, 1891, March 16, 1893, January 25, 1894, July 1, 1897.

89. Ibid., May 31, 1894, November 9, 1899.

90. Ibid., September 18, November 20, 1890, January 22, 1891, February 9, 1893, June 13, 1895.

91. For an excellent summary of race relations during these decades, see Terry L. Jones, "Attitudes of Alabama Baptists Toward Negroes, 1890–1914" (master's thesis, Samford University, 1968).

92. *Alabama Baptist,* February 18, June 2, 1892, January 5, 1893, November 14, 28, 1895, July 7, 1898.

93. Ibid., June 11, 1891, July 14, 1892, April 27, 1899.

94. Ibid., June 19, 1890, June 30, 1892.

95. Ibid., January 9, July 3, 1890, August 22, 1895.

96. Ibid., April 23, 1891.

97. Ibid., January 9, 1890, January 11, February 22, March 1, 1894, January 22, 1899; Jones, "Attitudes of Alabama Baptists Toward Negroes," 83–98.

98. *Alabama Baptist,* March 3, 1892, September 1, 1898.

99. Ibid., July 14, 1892, August 29, 1895.

100. Ibid., September 19, 1895, March 5, April 16, 1896.

101. Ibid., July 5, 1894; Flynt and Berkley, *Taking Christianity to China,* 125-28, 211-13, 221-31, 243-44.

102. *Alabama Baptist,* December 18, 1890, April 2, 1896.

103. Ibid., October 29, 1896, June 17, 1897, November 2, 1899; Brown, *History of First Baptist Church, Tuskegee,* 22-23; Bethany Baptist Church Minutes.

104. *Alabama Baptist,* March 21, 1940; Mrs. T. A. Hamilton, " 'Little Alabama' or Alabama's Contribution to the Woman's Missionary Union, Birmingham, 1914," in Records of Alabama WMU, 1909-1969, Samford University Archives.

105. Records of Alabama WMU.

106. Lura Harris Craighead, *History of the Alabama Federation of Women's Clubs,* vol. 1, *1895 to 1918* (Montgomery: Paragon Press, 1936), 11, 14, 15, 27-31, 72.

107. Hunter, "History of W.M.U. of Mobile Association." Rosa Cilley Hunter was for many years president of the Mobile Associational WMU. Like Annie Ashcraft, she was also a Judson College graduate.

108. *Alabama Baptist,* January 6, February 3, March 3, 1898.

109. Ibid., July 20, September 21, 1899.

110. Ibid., February 5, 28, 1895, January 23, 1896.

111. Ibid., March 3, 1892, May 23, July 4, 1895.

112. Ibid., July 13, 1899.

113. George B. Eager, "Bible Doctrine of Inspiration," ms. in Eager Papers.

114. James Clyde Harper, "A Study of Alabama Baptist Higher Education and Fundamentalism, 1890-1930" (Ph.D. diss., University of Alabama, 1977), 54-55.

115. Ibid., 56-58; *Alabama Baptist,* August 10, September 14, 1893, February 22, 1894, January 3, 10, 1895, April 27, May 18, 1899.

116. *Alabama Baptist,* October 15, 1891, August 4, 11, 1892, January 19, June 1, 1893, January 18, 1894, January 12, 1899.

117. For a summary of this controversy, see Walter B. Shurden, *Not a Silent People: Controversies That Have Shaped Southern Baptists* (Nashville: Broadman Press, 1972), 22-32; also see Harper, "Study of Higher Education and Fundamentalism," 50-52, 61-70.

118. *Alabama Baptist,* May 7, September 10, November 12, December 3, 1896.

119. For a detailed account of Haralson's role in the Whitsitt affair, see correspondence in Jonathan Haralson Papers, Alabama State Archives, especially letters to and from William E. Hatcher, e.g., Hatcher to Haralson, December 22, 1897.

120. Z. D. Roby to George B. Eager, December 20, 1897; Jonathan Haralson to Eager, December 13, 1897, January 20, 1898, in Haralson Papers.

121. *Alabama Baptist,* April 1, May 27, August 26, October 7, 14, November 4, 25, December 15, 23, 1897.

122. Ibid., May 26, June 2, 1898; J. B. Cranfill to Jonathan Haralson, December 8, 1898; Haralson to Cranfill, December 17, 1898; Charles L. Cocke to Haralson, April 23, 1898; O. F. Gregory to Haralson, March 18, 1898; J. J. Taylor to Haralson, October 18, 1898; all in Haralson Papers.

123. Jonathan Haralson to William E. Hatcher, February 18, 1899, ibid.

124. *Alabama Baptist,* May 21, June 29, July 6, 1899.

125. Ibid., January 5, 1899.

Chapter 7: Progressivism and Baptists, 1900–1920

1. C. Vann Woodward, *Origins of the New South: 1877-1913* (Baton Rouge: Louisiana State University Press, 1951), 450.

2. This survey was intended to result in three volumes of Alabama Baptist biographies as approved by the 1934 state convention. See Chapman Papers.

3. James R. Hobbs, "Morgan Marion Wood," copy in ibid.

4. James H. Chapman, "Doctor Alfred J. Dickinson," copy in ibid.; *Alabama Baptist,* September 27, 1923; John H. Burrows, "The Great Disturber: The Social Philosophy and Theology of Alfred James Dickinson" (master's thesis, Samford University, 1970), 96–102.

5. Chapman, "Doctor Alfred J. Dickinson"; Burrows, "Great Disturber," 47–48, 52–56.

6. Chapman, "Doctor Alfred J. Dickinson."

7. "Dempsey Wyatt Hodges," ms. in George W. Franklin Papers, Samford University Archives.

8. "Joseph William Phillips," ms. in George W. Franklin Papers, Samford University Archives.

9. Word, *Big Springs,* 58–60.

10. Grant, "Alabama's Reaction to Revivalism," 97–99; *Alabama Baptist,* August 25, 1915.

11. U.S. Bureau of the Census, *Religious Bodies: 1916* (Washington, D.C.: Government Printing Office, 1919), 103–4, 123; *Maloney's Birmingham 1900 City Directory,* vol. 15 (Atlanta: Maloney Directory Co., 1900), 47–54.

12. *Alabama Baptist,* October 2, 1912, November 26, 1913; *Alabama Baptist State Convention Annual, 1902,* 5, and *1913,* 15, Alabama State Convention, Montgomery.

13. *Alabama Baptist,* February 3, 1915, July 26, 1916, December 11, 1918.

14. *Birmingham News,* July 14, 1973; *Sixty Glorious Years: A Summary of the History of Progress in Mignon Baptist Church of Sylacauga, Alabama, 1902 to 1962* (n.p., 1962); oral history with Mrs. L. A. House, by Wayne Flynt, July 10, 1974; *Alabama Baptist,* April 12, 1911, May 7, 1913, October 18, 1916.

15. Bee and Allen, *Ruhama Baptist Church,* 129; Stone, *History of First Baptist Church of Wetumpka,* 99; *Alabama Baptist,* July 17, 1919; L. L. Gwaltney, "Rev. John W. Stewart," copy in Chapman Papers.

16. Reid, *Baptists in Alabama,* 202–4; Executive Board Minutes of the Alabama Baptist State Convention, December 6, 1915, to November 14, 1927; hereafter cited as Executive Board Minutes.

17. *Alabama Baptist,* August 4, 1915, May 16, June 6, 1917; Burrows, "Great Disturber," 75–77.

18. Murfee, "Journalism of the Baptist Denomination," 16–19; *Alabama Baptist,* April 18, 1906, September 4, 1918, January 23, 1919.

19. Ms. in L. L. Gwaltney Papers, Samford University Archives.

20. "P. V. Bomar" and "Andrew Philip Montague," in Chapman Papers.

21. *Alabama Baptist,* January 27, 1921; Jesse Cook Papers, Samford University Archives.

22. Stone, *History of First Baptist Church of Wetumpka,* 99, 114; interview with Renny Johnson, July 12, 1989.

23. *Anniston Star,* January 5, 1954; Fannie E. S. Heck, *In Royal Service: The Mission Work of Southern Baptist Women* (Richmond: Foreign Mission Board, 1915), 366–67; "Supplies for SBC Hospitals in China," Records of Alabama WMU. For a more complete study of Alabama Baptist missionaries in China, see Flynt and Berkley, *Taking Christianity to China.*

24. For a brief summary, see Burrows, "Great Disturber," 10–15.

25. Ibid., 97–98; Bee and Allen, *Ruhama Baptist Church,* 139; *Birmingham News,* October 28, 1969; *Alabama Baptist,* September 15, 22, 1915.

26. *Alabama Baptist,* April 2, 1902, August 16, 1916.

27. Ibid., August 8, 1901; "Sound Doctrine," sermon ms., A. G. Moseley Papers, Samford University Archives.

28. *Alabama Baptist,* June 13, July 18, November 21, 1906; "The Book of Jeremiah," ms. in A. J. Dickinson Papers, Samford University Archives.

29. For this exchange, see *Alabama Baptist*, February 5, 19, 26, March 19, 26, April 2, 23, 1913.

30. "John Walter Phillips," ms. in Chapman Papers; *Alabama Baptist*, September 8, 1938.

31. James H. Chapman, "Lesley [sic] Lee Gwaltney," Chapman Papers; L. L. Gwaltney, *Forty of the Twentieth or the First Forty Years of the Twentieth Century* (Birmingham: Birmingham Printing Co., 1940), 120–28; "The Truth of the Old Testament," "The New Testament," "The Ground of Our Faith," sermon mss. in Gwaltney Papers.

32. *Alabama Baptist*, March 31, 1915, January 3, 1917, November 27, December 11, 1918; "Is There a God?" and "God's Existence: In the Beginning God," sermon mss. in Gwaltney Papers.

33. "The Miracles of Christ" and "Pentecost," sermon mss. in Gwaltney Papers; Gwaltney, *Forty of the Twentieth*, 128.

34. *Alabama Baptist*, September 5, 1917.

35. "Lemuel Orah Dawson," ms. in Chapman Papers; Burrows, "Great Disturber," 31–33.

36. Clipping on "Frank Willis Barnett," in Alabama Baptist Biography Files.

37. *Alabama Baptist*, January 12, February 9, June 1, 1910, March 11, 1911, October 6, 1915.

38. Ibid., April 23, 1913, March 6, 1919; autobiography and sermon ms. in Cook Papers.

39. *Alabama Baptist*, March 28, 1902, June 1, 1910, September 11, 25, November 20, 1918, November 27, 1919.

40. Ibid., October 4, November 22, 1911, January 17, 1912.

41. Ibid., February 27, 1918, December 18, 1919, January 1, 1920; Burrows, "Great Disturber," 103–4.

42. For a brief survey of this debate, see: Marty, *Righteous Empire*, 204–8; Robert T. Handy, "The Social Gospel in Historical Perspective," *Andover Newton Quarterly* 9 (January 1969): 175–77; Winthrop S. Hudson, "Walter Rauschenbusch and the New Evangelicalism," *Religion in Life* 30 (Summer 1961): 412–30. Since the appearance of Woodward's *Origins of the New South*, many historians of southern progressivism have noted a much larger role for Protestant Christianity in the reforms of 1900–1920. See George B. Tindall, *Emergence of the New South: 1913–1945* (Baton Rouge: Louisiana State University Press, 1967), and Dewey W. Grantham, *Southern Progressivism: The Reconciliation of Progress and Tradition* (Knoxville: University of Tennessee Press, 1983). See also John Boles, "The Discovery of Southern Religious History," in *Interpreting Southern History: Historiographical Essays in Honor of Sanford W. Higginbotham*, ed. John Boles and Evelyn Thomas Nolen (Baton Rouge: Louisiana State University Press, 1987), especially 540–45. For the role of religion in Alabama progressivism, see Hackney, *Populism to Progressivism*, 213–14, 245–48.

43. For Southern Baptists and social Christianity see Allen, *Century to Celebrate*, and John L. Eighmy, *Churches in Cultural Captivity: A History of the Social Attitudes of Southern Baptists* (Knoxville: University of Tennessee Press, 1972); George D. Kelsey, "The Social Thought of Contemporary Southern Baptists" (Ph.D. diss., Yale University, 1946), 79–84; Bill Sumners, "The Social Attitudes of Southern Baptists Toward Certain Issues, 1910–1920" (master's thesis, University of Texas at Arlington, 1975); Harvey, "Southern Baptists and Southern Culture," especially 476–541.

44. "Washington Bryan Crumpton: Alabama's Foremost Citizen," ms. in Chapman Papers.

45. "God to the Rescue," sermon ms. in Gwaltney Papers.

46. "Strong Drink," and "Paul's Substitute for Wine," sermon mss. in Moseley Papers.

47. *Alabama Baptist*, September 26, 1906; *Alabama Baptist State Convention Annual, 1904*, 26–27, 45–46; *Alabama Baptist State Convention Annual, 1907*, 61; *Alabama Baptist State Convention Annual, 1911*, 49–50.

48. *Alabama Baptist*, March 16, 1910, July 3, 1913.

49. Ibid., August 7, 1907, October 13, 20, 1919; *Alabama Baptist State Convention Annual, 1907*.

50. *Alabama Baptist*, November 8, 1905, June 2, October 6, 1909, July 10, 1910, February 22, 1911.

51. Ibid., August 4, 1909, April 1, 1914, January 5, 20, 1915, July 31, 1918.

52. For additional ministerial vows to become politically active on behalf of prohibition, see ibid., February 24, 1904, July 21, 1909, November 23, 1910.

53. Ibid., April 19, May 3, 1900, June 18, July 30, August 13, 20, 1902, August 8, 1906.

54. Ibid., January 16, March 20, July 10, October 16, November 6, 1907.

55. Ibid., September 8, 1909, February 9, April 27, October 26, November 2, 1910, February 1, 1911; *Alabama Citizen* 3 (February 1 and May 1, 1908); see petitions from churches in container 9, folder 2, John H. Bankhead Papers, Alabama State Archives; "H. S. D. Mallory," box 1, Woolley Papers.

56. *Alabama Baptist*, March 11, 1914; Richard N. Sheldon, "Richmond Pearson Hobson as a Progressive Reformer," *Alabama Review* 25 (October 1972): 244–56; B. F. Riley Diaries, Southern Baptist Archives.

57. *Alabama Baptist*, December 11, 1919; for a more thorough study of the Baptist role in the 1920 Musgrove-Underwood election, see Wayne Flynt, "Organized Labor, Reform, and Alabama Politics, 1920," *Alabama Review* 23 (July 1970): 163–80.

58. For editorials involving "bucket shops" (speculation on cotton futures), see *Alabama Baptist*, August 15, 22, 29, 1906; for other issues of "civic righteousness," see ibid., October 12, 1904, June 19, 1912, June 18, 1913, August 30, 1916, January 31, 1917.

59. For the role of Birmingham Baptists in the city's moral crusades, see Martha C. Mitchell Bigelow, "Birmingham: Biography of a City of the New South" (Ph.D. diss., University of Chicago, 1946), 110–11; Harris, *Political Power in Birmingham*, 37, 55–56, 63, 71–72, 81–88. Unfortunately, Harris knew little about Dickinson and mistakenly identified him as a reactionary advocate of anti-Catholicism with a puritanical moral agenda. Hence, Harris's use of the confusing term "liberal element" to describe opposition to Dickinson.

60. *Alabama Baptist*, September 20, 1911, July 24, 1912; "Frank Willis Barnett," clipping in Alabama Baptist Biography Files.

61. *Alabama Baptist*, May 1, 1907, August 19, 1908, October 5, 1910, June 19, December 4, 1912, February 5, March 26, 1913, December 8, 1915, December 4, 1918; Hudson, "Walter Rauschenbusch," 415, 418–22, 430.

62. *Alabama Baptist*, October 9, November 6, 20, 1912, October 1, November 19, 1913.

63. Ibid., September 6, 1905, February 2, 1910, October 11, 1911, February 7, 14, June 19, July 10, 1912, April 2, November 20, 1913, January 27, March 24, 1915, November 1, 1916, July 25, 1917; for Charles Gardner, see Sumners, "Social Attitudes," 13.

64. *Alabama Baptist*, April 22, October 14, 1903, May 31, 1911.

65. Ibid., May 22, August 14, 1907, November 13, 1912, January 3, June 13, 1917; for Barnett's view of socialism, see ibid., June 2, 1909, July 24, 1912, August 2, October 4, 1916.

66. Ibid., January 15, 1908; Reid, *Baptists in Alabama*, 184.

67. Stone, *Prattville First Baptist Church*, 66–67; Chapman, "Lesley [*sic*] Lee Gwaltney."

68. Sermon mss., Gwaltney Papers; *Alabama Baptist*, October 28, 1908, August 18, 1915, November 6, 1918, October 16, 30, 1919.

69. Burrows, "The Great Disturber," 84, 88–91, 98–105; *Alabama Baptist*, July 20, 1904, April 4, 1906, May 15, 1919.

70. Sermons and other mss., A. C. Davidson Papers, Samford University Archives; *Alabama Baptist*, March 1, 15, 29, April 19, 1905; James F. Sulzby Jr., *Annals of the Southside Baptist Church, Birmingham, Alabama* (Birmingham: Birmingham Printing Co., 1947), 49–59; "Statistics—Southside Baptist Church," ms. in Chapman Papers.

71. Joshua Hill Foster, *Sixty-Four Years a Minister* (Wilmington, N.C.: First Baptist Church, 1948), 63–64; *Alabama Baptist State Convention Annual, 1909*; Crumpton, *Our Baptist Centennials*, 46; Ayers, *Parker Memorial Baptist Church, Anniston*, 3–4; *Birmingham News*, May 7, 1902.

72. "James Horton Chapman," *Alabama Baptist Historian* 2 (December 1965): 1–3; *Alabama Baptist,* January 3, February 14, 1917.

73. "Four Forces that Make for Character," sermon ms. in Moseley Papers; "The Believer to Do Greater Works than Christ," sermon ms. in Alexander T. Sims Papers, Samford University Archives.

74. Sermon ms. by Jesse A. Cook in Chapman Papers.

75. *Alabama Baptist State Convention Annual, 1912; Alabama Baptist,* November 7, 1917.

76. *Alabama Baptist,* April 23, 1913, June 5, November 20, 1919.

77. Ibid., February 9, 1910.

78. Ibid., August 27, October 8, 1902, January 28, 1903. Historian Sheldon Hackney calls the 1903 child labor law the most spectacular victory of progressivism in Alabama; see Hackney, *Populism to Progressivism,* 246–48.

79. *Alabama Baptist,* February 6, 13, July 3, 24, 1907.

80. Ibid., December 22, 1909, May 25, June 8, 1910, September 20, December 13, 1911, January 3, February 7, October 9, 1912, February 26, July 16, December 17, 1913, February 4, 1914, March 3, 1915, March 1, 1916.

81. Ibid., August 30, 1911, March 19, 1913, October 27, 1915, August 23, 1916, July 4, 1917, July 17, October 9, 1918.

82. Ibid., June 18, 1913.

83. Ibid., October 30, 1912.

84. Ibid., January 30, 1907, February 16, 23, June 1, September 21, 1910, September 18, October 23, November 6, 1912.

85. Ibid., June 26, 1919; Burrows, "Great Disturber," 101–2, 104–6.

86. *Alabama Baptist,* July 3, 1919.

87. Leah Rawls Atkins, "Early Efforts to Control Tuberculosis in Alabama: The Formation and Work of the Alabama Tuberculosis Association, 1908–1930" (master's thesis, Auburn University, 1960), 25, 53–54.

88. *Alabama Baptist,* August 20, 1902, June 14, 1905, September 30, 1908, August 4, 1915.

89. Ibid., February 21, 1901, July 25, 1906, August 19, 1908, June 2, 1909, March 2, 1910, September 13, October 11, 1916.

90. Ibid., June 4, 1902, June 6, 1906, June 26, 1919.

91. Ibid., March 21, 1906; also see Flynt and Berkley, *Taking Christianity to China.*

92. *Alabama Baptist,* September 12, 1901, February 7, September 18, 25, 1912.

93. Sermon ms. in Clay I. Hudson Papers, Samford University Archives; "Home Missions," sermon ms. in Sims Papers; speech ms. in T. M. and R. M. Hunter Papers.

94. *Alabama Baptist,* April 24, July 3, 1919; Records of Alabama WMU; Sulzby, *Annals of Southside Baptist Church,* 89.

95. Edwin S. Gaustad, *Historical Atlas of Religion in America* (New York: Harper and Row, 1962), 52; Executive Board Minutes, December 6, 1915, to November 14, 1927; *Birmingham City Directory, 1910* (n.p.: R. L. Polk and Co., 1911), 86–88.

96. *Alabama Baptist,* July 28, August 11, 1909, March 5, 1913.

97. Ibid., June 17, 1903, January 9, 1907, June 25, 1913, July 14, 1915, October 23, 1918.

98. *Alabama Baptist State Convention Annual, 1908,* 70; *Alabama Baptist,* June 11, July 16, 23, 1902, February 15, 22, May 3, 1905, August 25, 1909, September 21, December 14, 1910, August 14, 1912, August 16, 1916.

99. Mss. in Acker Papers and R. E. Pettus Papers, Samford University Archives.

100. Mabel Swartz Withoft, *Oak and Laurel: A Study of the Mountain Mission Schools of Southern Baptists* (Nashville: Sunday School Board of the Southern Baptist Convention, 1923), 16; Records of Alabama WMU; Leon Macon to A. H. Reid, February 20, 1956, in Hudson Baggett Papers, Samford University Archives; *Alabama Baptist,* December 6, 1916.

101. For a history of Newton Institute, see Elizabeth Barton, "The Baptist Collegiate Institute and Its First Principal, A. W. Tate" (master's thesis, University of Alabama, 1943); "The

Baptist Collegiate Institute," speech ms. by Mrs. R. M. Hunter, in T. M. and R. M. Hunter Papers.

102. *Alabama Baptist*, March 20, 1907.

103. Victor I. Masters, *Country Church in the South* (Atlanta: Publicity Department of the Home Mission Board of the Southern Baptist Convention, 1916), 94, 119, 174, Appendix D.

104. Ibid., 55; John W. Jent, *The Challenge of the Country Church* (Nashville: Sunday School Board, 1924); L. G. Wilson et al., "The Church and Landless Men," *University of North Carolina Extension Bulletin* 1 (March 1, 1922): 1–27.

105. James H. Madison, "Reformers and the Rural Church, 1900–1950," *Journal of American History* 73 (December 1986): 646–49, 655, 658. Ms. by Gary Farley, "Celebrating the Jubilee Year of the Rural Church Program," in author's possession. I acknowledge with gratitude this excellent survey by Farley and his willingness to share it with me.

106. See Jent, *Challenge of the Country Church*, for the influence of Warren Wilson and social gospel ideas.

107. Masters, *Country Church*, 19, 24–25, 27–28, 39–40, 58–59, 64–67, 75–76.

108. *Alabama Baptist*, June 1, July 13, 1910, March 1, 1911, August 14, 1912, September 10, 1913.

109. Ibid., June 21, August 9, 1916, February 28, 1917.

110. A. J. Dickinson, "Rural Church Problems and Ministry," *Home Field* 22 (December 1910): 12–14.

111. Until the 1920s, many churches had both Ladies Aid Societies and Women's Missionary Societies, reflecting confusion about gender roles as well as the function of women within churches.

112. Stone, *History of First Baptist Church of Wetumpka*, 100–101, 112.

113. Minutes of Ladies Benevolent Society, Ladies Aid Society, and Woman's Missionary Society, First Baptist Church, Huntsville.

114. Jeffers, *History of Tuskegee-Lee Association*, 27; Hunter, "History of W.M.U. of Mobile Association"; Records of Alabama WMU.

115. Allen, *Century to Celebrate*, 212–23; see also Judith Ann Trolander, *Professionalism and Social Change: From the Settlement House Movement to Neighborhood Centers, 1886 to the Present* (New York: Columbia University Press, 1987), and Gregory Vickers, "Southern Baptist Women and Social Concerns, 1910–1929," *Baptist History and Heritage* 23 (October 1988): 3–13.

116. Records of Alabama WMU.

117. Ibid.

118. *The Story of Alabama: A History of the State*, vol. 4 (New York: Lewis Historical Publishing Co., 1949), 20.

119. Records of Alabama WMU; Catherine B. Allen, *Laborers Together with God: 22 Great Women in Baptist Life* (Birmingham: Woman's Missionary Union, 1987), 182–84; Annie Wright Ussery, *The Story of Kathleen Mallory* (Nashville: Broadman Press, 1956), 8–9, 22, 32, 34–35, 38, 41, 138–41.

120. Allen, *Laborers Together with God*, 46–50; Jackson and Stephens, *Women of Vision*, 28–35.

121. Jackson and Stephens, *Women of Vision*, 36.

122. Ibid., 28; see Alabama WMU, *Report of Eighteenth Annual Session of the Woman's Missionary Union, November 7–9, 1911* (Montgomery: Paragon Press, 1911), copy in Records of Alabama WMU, 1909–1969.

123. Alabama WMU, *Report of Eighteenth Session*, 14; Allen, *Laborers Together with God*, 46–50.

124. Jackson and Stephens, *Women of Vision*, 42; *Baptist World*, July 29, 1909.

125. Bill Sumners, "Southern Baptists and Women's Role in the Church, 1910–1920," *Alabama Baptist Historian* 16 (July 1980): 4–10; *Baptist World*, August 1, 1912.

126. Records of Alabama WMU.

127. Mrs. J. E. Weeks to Hermione Jackson, June 19, 1963, in Hermione Jackson Papers, Samford University Archives.

128. Mrs. J. A. Cheney to Mrs. J. S. Wittmeier, February 15, 1916, Records of Alabama WMU.

129. Mrs. J. S. Wittmeier to Laura Lee Patrick, January 16, 1916; Mrs. T. E. Sullivan to Laura Patrick, April 7, 1916; both in Records of Alabama WMU.

130. Burrows, "Great Disturber," 86; Allen, *Century to Celebrate*, 235–36; Sumners, "Southern Baptists and Women's Role in the Church," 5; Bill Sumners, "Southern Baptists and Women's Right to Vote, 1910–1920," *Baptist History and Heritage* 12 (January 1977): 49–50.

131. W. B. Crumpton, "Questionnaire to the Alabama Solons," in Alabama Woman Suffrage Organization Papers, Alabama State Archives; *Alabama Baptist*, May 29, 1919.

132. "Woman in History and Service," and untitled speech, both mss. in Montague Papers.

133. For Maud McLure Kelly's remarkable life, see Cynthia Newman, *Maud McLure Kelly: Alabama's First Woman Lawyer* (Birmingham: Birmingham Printing and Publishing, 1984).

134. For an example of the anti-imperial attitudes of Alabama missionaries, see Flynt and Berkley, *Taking Christianity to China*, 300–303.

135. *Alabama Baptist*, May 3, 1905, October 31, 1906, August 7, 1907, October 11, 1910, May 31, 1911.

136. Ibid., November 23, 1904, March 21, 1906, November 18, 1908.

137. Ibid., June 17, 1903, November 29, 1911, April 14, 1915.

138. Ibid., August 5, 1914, January 13, April 7, June 3, September 22, October 27, 1915, January 19, September 20, 1916.

139. Ibid., January 6, July 28, November 3, 1915, October 14, 1917; *Baptist Biography*, vol. 3, ed. B. J. W. Graham (Atlanta: Index Printing Co., 1923), 429–33.

140. *Alabama Baptist*, May 6, 1917, January 16, August 28, September 29, October 23, November 6, 13, 1918.

141. Ibid., November 27, 1918, March 13, 27, April 10, 24, December 11, 1919.

142. Ibid., January 1, 1920.

143. Ibid., November 6, 1912, March 29, 1916; Edward P. Allen to Oscar W. Underwood, January 19, 1915, Oscar W. Underwood Papers, Alabama State Archives; Harris, *Political Power in Birmingham*, 163–64.

144. Glenn T. Eskew, "Demagoguery in Birmingham and the Building of Vestavia," *Alabama Review* 42 (July 1989): 200–205; Burrows, "Great Disturber," 95–96; also see Marvin Y. Whiting, " 'True Americans,' Pro and Con: Campaign Literature from the 1917 Race for the Presidency of the Birmingham City Commission," *Journal of the Birmingham Historical Society* 6 (July 1980): 11–23.

145. *Alabama Baptist*, April 24, 1919.

146. Ibid., October 24, 1901.

147. Ibid., April 26, May 17, 1900.

148. Ibid., April 23, 1902, August 12, 1903, March 24, April 21, June 30, 1909; T. M. Owen to John H. Bankhead, August 3, 1909, container 10, folder 1, Bankhead Papers; "Washington Bryan Crumpton."

149. Burrows, "Great Disturber," 78–81.

150. *Alabama Baptist*, October 24, November 7, 1901, February 19, June 11, October 22, 1902; "Religious Divisions—Or Types of Religious Beliefs," sermon ms., 1900, in Sermon Book of Sidney J. Catts, Samford University Archives.

151. *Alabama Baptist*, July 2, 1902, August 31, September 14, 21, 1904, January 16, 1907, April 8, 1914, January 2, September 18, 1918, March 6, 1919; Crumpton, *Our Baptist Centennials*, 53; *Alabama Baptist State Convention Annual*, 1901, 11, 1902, 5, 1904, 4.

152. *Alabama Baptist*, February 19, 1902, March 18, 1903; Minutes of the Ladies Benevo-

lent Society, Ladies Aid Society, and Woman's Missionary Society, First Baptist Church, Huntsville.

153. *Alabama Baptist,* May 18, September 21, 1904, April 10, 1907, October 9, 1919; Glenn Feldman, "Lynching in Alabama, 1889–1921," *Alabama Review* 48 (April 1995): 131–34.

154. *Alabama Baptist,* July 30, 1913, May 19, 26, 1915.

Chapter 8: The Ballyhoo Years Alabama-Style, the 1920s

1. See Larry V. Wells, "The 1928–39 Depression Years at First Baptist Church, Fort Payne, Alabama," March 11, 1985, research paper at Samford University Archives.

2. For excellent descriptions of these general patterns in southern and national religious life, see William A. Link, *The Paradox of Southern Progressivism, 1880–1930* (Chapel Hill: University of North Carolina Press, 1992); Ferenc M. Szasz, *The Divided Mind of Protestant America, 1880–1930* (Tuscaloosa: University of Alabama Press, 1982); and Marty, *Righteous Empire,* especially chaps. 20 and 21.

3. Bill J. Leonard, *God's Last and Only Hope: The Fragmentation of the Southern Baptist Convention* (Grand Rapids: Eerdmans Publishing Co., 1990), 6–8, 21, 120–28.

4. Robert A. Baker, "The Magnificent Years (1917–1931)," *Baptist History and Heritage* 8 (July 1973): 151; see Nancy Tatom Ammerman, *Southern Baptists Observed: Multiple Perspectives on a Changing Denomination* (Knoxville: University of Tennessee Press, 1993), especially essays by Samuel S. Hill, Arthur E. Farnsley II, David R. Norsworthy, Joe E. Barnhart, Ellen M. Rosenberg, and James L. Guth.

5. Eighmy, *Churches in Cultural Captivity,* 79–98.

6. The best study of SBC opinion during the 1920s is James J. Thompson Jr., *Tried as by Fire: Southern Baptists and the Religious Controversies of the 1920s* (Macon: Mercer University Press, 1982); see especially 44–58.

7. Ibid., 65–191.

8. *Alabama Baptist,* July 8, September 2, 1926.

9. Ibid., November 25, 1926, April 25, 1929.

10. Ibid., November 25, 1926; Executive Board Minutes, December 11, 1929, January 14, 1930.

11. Executive Board Minutes, December 14, 1927, December 9, 1941; *Alabama Baptist,* July 21, 1921, April 5, 1928, April 25, 1929.

12. *Alabama Baptist,* March 20, April 3, 1919, January 1, August 26, 1920, July 8, December 9, 1926.

13. Ibid., July 1, 1920, January 3, 1924; Earl Potts, "Shaping Alabama Baptists: The Cooperative Program," *Alabama Baptist Historian* 15 (July 1979): 4–6; Executive Board Minutes, December 10, 1923, June 3, 1926, December 14, 1927.

14. *Alabama Baptist,* August 5, 1920; "Financing Work of Alabama Baptists, 1910–1937," ms. in Gwaltney Papers.

15. *Alabama Baptist,* January 27, 1921, July 24, 1924; Higginbotham and Higginbotham, *Upon This Rock I Will Build My Church,* 72.

16. *Alabama Baptist,* October 10, 1929; Executive Board Minutes, May 24, December 12, 1928; D. F. Green to W. O. Carver, April 11, 1929, W. O. Carver Papers, Southern Baptist Archives.

17. *Alabama Baptist,* April 4, 1929.

18. Ibid., January 11, 1945; Thomas McAdory Owen, *History of Alabama and Dictionary of Alabama Biography,* vol. 3 (Chicago: S. J. Clarke Publishing Co., 1921), 699.

19. *Alabama Baptist,* September 2, 1920, January 20, 1921, June 21, 1928. These sources disagree over the number of pastorless churches in 1920–1921, one citing 200, the other 700. The latter figure, representing one-third of all white Baptist congregations, seems too high.

20. Ibid., January 3, 1929.

21. Ibid., September 26, 1940, April 23, 1942. These biographical data are based on my analysis of four of the Alabama Baptist Biography Files ("A," "Ba–Bo," "Br–Bz," and "Si–Sz"), Samford University Archives.

22. *Alabama Baptist*, November 28, 1929; Executive Board Minutes, December 14, 1927, to November 11, 1935.

23. Oral history with Brady R. Justice, by Ray M. Atchison, August 20, 1984, Samford University Archives.

24. "Historical Sketch," Chapman Papers; *Encyclopedia of Southern Baptists*, vol. 1 (Nashville: Broadman Press, 1958), 362.

25. *Alabama Baptist*, August 9, 1956.

26. "Autobiography of James Randolph Hobbs," ms. in Chapman Papers.

27. Hal D. Bennett, "An Inquiry into the Life and Works of Editor Leslie L. Gwaltney of Alabama" (Th.D. diss., New Orleans Baptist Theological Seminary, 1954), 7–12, 26; "Autobiography of L. L. Gwaltney," ms. in Chapman Papers.

28. "Autobiography of L. L. Gwaltney," and Chapman, "Lesley [sic] Lee Gwaltney."

29. Chapman, "Lesley [sic] Lee Gwaltney"; Bennett, "Life and Works of Editor Gwaltney," 15 and 26; oral history with Edward B. Warren, by George E. Sims, December 3, 1975.

30. Bennett, "Life and Works of Editor Gwaltney," 41, 109–11, 163–64.

31. Ibid., 31–33.

32. "Autobiography of L. L. Gwaltney."

33. Ibid.

34. Reid, *Baptists in Alabama*, 566–67; *Alabama Baptist*, July 10, 1930.

35. See Flynt and Berkley, *Taking Christianity to China*.

36. *Alabama Baptist*, April 8, September 9, 1920.

37. Ibid., June 22, September 14, 28, 1922, September 13, 1923, January 7, 1926.

38. Ibid., June 25, 1925, June 30, 1927, April 11, 1929.

39. Ibid., March 25, 1920, July 12, 1923.

40. Ibid., July 14, September 29, 1927.

41. Ibid., September 9, 1920.

42. U.S. Bureau of the Census, *Census of Religious Bodies, 1926*, vol. 2 (Washington, D.C.: Government Printing Office, 1927), 105–6.

43. Mrs. L. A. House oral history, July 10, 1974.

44. Executive Board Minutes, December 14, 1927, May 24, 1928, December 27, 1932.

45. *Alabama Baptist*, August 10, 1922.

46. Ibid., October 5, 1922.

47. Ibid., June 21, 1923, February 26, 1925.

48. Ibid., September 30, October 7, 1920, July 10, 1924.

49. Ibid., June 25, 1925, January 21, July 1, 1926, January 27, 1927, May 10, 1928.

50. For examples of rural church literature, see Jent, *Challenge of the Country Church*, and John W. Jent, *Rural Church Development: A Manual of Methods* (Shawnee: Oklahoma Baptist University Press, 1928).

51. Executive Board Minutes, July 5, December 11, 1922, April 28, 1925, December 14, 1927; *Alabama Baptist*, August 18, 1927, January 24, 1929.

52. *Alabama Baptist*, July 7, 1921, July 19, 1923, March 29, 1928.

53. Ibid., January 12, 1922, July 3, 31, 1924.

54. Ibid., February 21, 1924.

55. Ellin Sterne, "Prostitution in Birmingham, Alabama, 1890–1925" (master's thesis, Samford University, 1977), 125–26.

56. *Alabama Baptist*, September 22, October 20, 1921.

57. Ibid., May 19, 1921, February 16, 23, 1922.

58. Ibid., September 22, 29, 1927, July 11, 1929; Executive Board Minutes, December 8, 1924.

59. Notasulga First Baptist Church Minutes, December 17, 1922, Samford University Archives; Clarence Cason to Stringfellow Barr, August 18, 1931, Clarence Cason Papers, University of Virginia Archives, Charlottesville; David R. Goldfield, "The Urban South: A Regional Framework," *American Historical Review* 86 (December 1981): 1020–25. Goldfield overemphasizes evangelical resistance to change. As this section makes clear, many Alabama Baptist ministers endorsed a wide variety of changes designed to modernize urban life.

60. *Alabama Baptist,* February 12, 1920, February 10, 1921, July 13, 1922, July 17, August 14, 1924, September 3, 1925.

61. Ibid., January 24, 1929.

62. Ibid., November 11, September 2, 1920.

63. Ibid., October 14, 28, 1920, February 23, March 30, 1922.

64. Ibid., May 3, 1923, April 14, 1927.

65. Ibid., November 7, 1929.

66. "Pastoral Theology. Number III," ms. in Gwaltney Papers.

67. *Alabama Baptist,* March 21, 1929.

68. Ibid., December 23, 1926; Bureau of the Census, *Religious Bodies, 1926,* 2:105.

69. *Alabama Baptist,* May 19, 26, 1921, April 20, 1922; Kathleen Mallory to Ida M. Stallworth, September 17, 1924, Records of Alabama WMU.

70. Juliette Mather to Mrs. Samford, September 13, 1923; Hannah Reynolds to Juliette Mather, September 17, 1923; Mather to Reynolds, August 13, 1923; in Records of Alabama WMU.

71. Ida M. Stallworth to Kathleen Mallory, July 5, 1924; Mallory to Stallworth, July 21, 1924; Stallworth to Mallory, July 24, 1924; Berta Malone to Ida Stallworth, 1927; in ibid.

72. Records of Alabama WMU; Jackson and Stephens, *Women of Vision,* 52–53.

73. "Ida Mitchell Stallworth," Alabama Baptist Biography Files; Kathleen Mallory to friend, August 4, 1925, Records of Alabama WMU.

74. Executive Committee Minutes, November 12, 1929.

75. *Alabama Baptist,* November 25, 1920, December 23, 1926, April 5, 1928, January 10, 1929; Records of Alabama WMU.

76. Letter to Ida Stallworth, August 21, 1925; "WMU Scholarships for Session 1924–1924"; Ida Stallworth to M. M. Lackey, November 19, 1928; all in Records of Alabama WMU; *Alabama Baptist,* November 24, 1921.

77. Rosa Cilley Hunter Papers, 1924, Samford University Archives; *Alabama Baptist,* July 1, 1926, April 7, 1927.

78. *Alabama Baptist,* November 19, 1925; Alma Wright to Hannah E. Reynolds, September 20, 1923, and Report of Personal Service Committee, 1927, both in Records of Alabama WMU.

79. Lucille Loyd Papers, Samford University Archives.

80. Ibid. In 1958 Loyd was invited back to speak at the opening of a new BSU center at the University of Alabama, a chapter she had organized.

81. W. P. Wilks, *Biographical Dictionary of Alabama Baptists, 1920–1947* (Opelika: Post Publishing Co., n.d.).

82. Ibid.

83. *Alabama Baptist,* May 12, 1921, October 5, 1922, April 19, October 4, 1923, February 7, 1924.

84. "Pastoral Theology, Number III."

85. Gwaltney, *Forty of the Twentieth,* 125–28.

86. *Alabama Baptist,* July 5, 1923, January 12, 1928. The comparison between these two reports, one by the SBC committee, the other by Alabama's social service committee, is striking.

87. Ibid., June 15, 1922.

88. Wise, *Alabama Baptist Children's Home,* 52–55; John S. Ramond, *Among Southern Baptists,* vol. 1, *1936–1937* (Kansas City: Western Baptist Publishing, Co., 1936), 103–4.

89. *Alabama Baptist*, July 2, 1925; Una Roberts Lawrence, *Look Upon the Fields: A Study of Home Missions* (n.p., n.d.), and "Alabama Good Will Centers, 1927," both in Records of Alabama WMU; newspaper clipping in Una Roberts Lawrence Papers, Southern Baptist Archives.

90. *Alabama Baptist*, January 22, 29, 1920, December 1, 1921.

91. Ibid., September 23, October 7, 28, 1920, February 3, 1921, October 28, 1926.

92. Ibid., January 25, July 5, 1923; Elizabeth Boner Clark, "The Abolition of the Convict Lease System in Alabama, 1913–1928" (master's thesis, University of Alabama, 1949), 93–94.

93. *Alabama Baptist*, March 25, August 26, 1926; Susan Ingram Hunt Ray, *The Major: Harwell G. Davis, Alabama Statesman and Baptist Leader* (Birmingham: Samford University Press, 1996), 33–43.

94. *Alabama Baptist*, August 7, 21, September 4, 1924, September 30, 1926, November 3, 1927; Robert F. Crider, "The Social Philosophy of L. L. Gwaltney, 1919–1950" (master's thesis, Samford University, 1969), 86–90.

95. *Alabama Baptist*, August 7, October 23, 1924, February 26, 1925.

96. Ibid., May 20, 1920, August 25, November 24, December 21, 1921, May 17, 1923, January 10, February 4, 1924, April 16, 1925, January 18, 1926, February 23, 1928, May 9, August 22, 1929.

97. Sandeen, *Roots of Fundamentalism*, finds the origins of fundamentalism in theological conflict. George M. Marsden, *Fundamentalism and American Culture: The Shaping of Twentieth-Century Evangelicalism, 1870–1925* (New York: Oxford University Press, 1980), traces the origins to social upheaval.

98. Marsden, *Fundamentalism and American Culture*, especially 141–98; George M. Marsden, "Contemporary American Evangelicalism," in Dockery, *Southern Baptists and American Evangelicals*, 32.

99. See George E. Webb, *The Evolution Controversy in America* (Lexington: University Press of Kentucky, 1994), and Edward B. Davis, "Fundamentalism and Folk Science Between the Wars," *Religion and American Culture: A Journal of Interpretation* 5 (Summer 1995): 217–48.

100. Bennett, "Life and Works of Editor Gwaltney," 27–28; *Alabama Baptist*, June 8, 1922, July 2, 1925, February 7, 1929; "Autobiography of L. L. Gwaltney"; Harper, "Study of Higher Education and Fundamentalism," 81–98.

101. *Alabama Baptist*, August 7, 28, 1924, September 10, 1925, March 18, May 6, 1926.

102. Ibid., February 23, March 23, 1922, October 25, 1923, January 22, 1925.

103. Ibid., August 6, 1925; R. M. Hunter, "A Tract on Evolution," in T. M. and R. M. Hunter Papers.

104. *Alabama Baptist*, July 8, 1920, October 25, 1923, August 7, 1924, June 4, 1925; J. J. Taylor, *The Evolution Theory* (n.p., n.d.). For the controversy between W. O. Carver and Taylor, see a multitude of letters between October 14 and December 14, 1926, in Carver Papers. Also see Marsden, *Fundamentalism and American Culture*, 141–98.

105. *Alabama Baptist*, February 12, 1920, August 18, 1921, January 12, February 23, 1922, October 18, 1928, July 3, 1924, January 8, July 2, 16, 23, August 6, December 10, 1925, July 1, 1926, January 20, 1927, January 10, 1929. For criticism of Gwaltney, see ibid., January 19, February 2, 1922.

106. Crider, "Social Philosophy of Gwaltney," 36; C. H. Bolton to Hudson Baggett, May 13, 1966, Baggett Papers.

107. Gwaltney, *Forty of the Twentieth*, 135–37; Harper, "Study of Higher Education and Fundamentalism," 91.

108. *Alabama Baptist*, January 20, 1927.

109. "The Fifth Estate and the Sixth Estate," ms. in James C. Stivender Papers, Samford University Archives.

110. *Alabama Baptist*, November 12, 1925; Harper, "Study of Higher Education and Fundamentalism," 94–98.

111. *Alabama Baptist*, January 19, March 22, 1928.

112. Gwaltney, *Forty of the Twentieth*, 134; *Alabama Baptist*, December 14, 1922, December 11, 1924. For similar ambivalence within the denomination, see J. Thomas Meigs, "Southern Baptists and the Fundamentalist-Modernist Controversy of the 1920s," *Quarterly Review* 38 (October–November–December 1977): 54–67.

113. *Alabama Baptist*, April 1, 1920, July 22, 1926.

114. Ibid., December 23, 1920, February 9, July 6, August 10, 1922, February 8, 1923, January 24, 1924, August 27, 1925, September 12, November 7, 1929.

115. Ibid., April 7, 1921; "Autobiography of L. L. Gwaltney."

116. *Alabama Baptist*, October 5, 1922, February 5, 1925, July 8, 1926.

117. Ibid., October 6, 1927, November 29, 1928.

118. Ibid., December 19, 1929; James F. Sulzby Jr., *Toward a History of Samford University* (Birmingham: Samford University Press, 1986), 565–66.

119. *Alabama Baptist*, August 19, 1920, March 24, April 14, 1921, March 23, 30, April 6, 13, 20, 27, August 24, 1922, April 5, 12, 1923, May 1, 29, October 30, 1924, January 15, March 26, April 2, 30, May 21, 28, June 18, August 27, 1925, March 3, 17, 31, July 7, October 6, 1927, February 14, August 29, 1929.

120. Ibid., January 12, February 16, 1922, May 3, 1928.

121. Ibid., April 6, 1922, October 7, 1926.

122. Dwain Waldrep, "Fundamentalism, Interdenominationalism, and the Birmingham School of Religion, 1927–1941," *Alabama Review* 49 (January 1996): 29–54.

123. L. L. Gwaltney, *The World's Greatest Decade: The Times and the Baptists* (Birmingham: Birmingham Printing Co., 1947), 69–75; *Alabama Baptist*, November 3, 1921, November 8, 1923; for other examples see Sims, "Orrville Baptists"; *Alabama Baptist*, December 15, 1927.

124. Executive Board Minutes, December 21, 1920; Crider, "Social Philosophy of Gwaltney," 95–105; *Alabama Baptist*, September 30, 1920, January 13, 1921, January 12, 19, 1922, November 8, 1923, June 9, 1927.

125. *Alabama Baptist*, November 25, 1920, April 10, June 5, 1924, May 19, 1927.

126. Noble Y. Beall, "A Guide to the Study of Negro Life in America"; Noble Y. Beall, "The Front Line of Home Missions," 4–5, 10, 20–25, 51–52, 57–58, 64; Noble Y. Beall to James H. Chapman, January 23, 1935; all in Chapman Papers; Noble Y. Beall, *The Preacher and His Task* (Atlanta: Home Mission Board, 1939), 121–23; Ramond, *Among Southern Baptists*, 1:35–36.

127. *Alabama Baptist*, November 25, 1920, August 25, 1921, July 24, 1924.

128. Blaine A. Brownell, "The Urban Mind in the South: The Growth of Urban Consciousness in Southern Cities, 1920–1927" (Ph.D. diss., University of North Carolina, Chapel Hill, 1969), 19.

129. Liesl Deann Dees, "Anti-Catholicism Among Alabama Baptists, 1917–1928" (senior honors thesis, Samford University, 1989), 3–4, 78.

130. *Alabama Baptist*, March 17, August 11, 1921, January 11, 1923, July 3, 1924; Gwaltney, *Forty of the Twentieth*, 149.

131. William R. Snell, "The Ku Klux Klan in Jefferson County, Alabama, 1916–1930" (master's thesis, Samford University, 1967), 51–53, 121, 150, 161.

132. Ibid., 158; see Glenn A. Feldman, "The Ku Klux Klan in Alabama" (Ph.D. diss., Auburn University, 1996), for dozens of cases of Baptist involvement in the 1920s Klan and Klan acts of violence; Dean, *Baptists in Greensboro*, 17.

133. For national reaction to the murder, see Charles P. Sweeney, "Bigotry in the South," *Nation* 109 (November 24, 1920): 585–86, and Charles P. Sweeney, "Bigotry Turns to Murder," *Nation* 113 (August 31, 1921): 232–33; *Alabama Baptist*, August 18, September 22, October 27, 1921.

134. *Birmingham News*, July 24, 1927; *Birmingham Age-Herald*, July 24, 1927; see also Feldman, "Ku Klux Klan."

135. *Alabama Baptist*, July 28, August 18, September 1, 1927; Snell, "Ku Klux Klan," 161.

136. *Alabama Baptist,* July 21, 1927; *Birmingham Age-Herald,* July 11, 19, 24, 1927; see also Feldman, "Ku Klux Klan"; Snell, "Ku Klux Klan," 176.

137. Flynt, "Organized Labor, Reform, and Alabama Politics," 163–80.

138. Dees, "Anti-Catholicism," 17; *Alabama Baptist,* July 27, 1922.

139. Virginia Van der Veer Hamilton, *Lister Hill: Statesman from the South* (Chapel Hill: University of North Carolina Press, 1987), 44.

140. *Alabama Baptist,* July 15, 1926, July 7, 14, December 8, 1927, February 2, July 5, 1928.

141. *Alabama Baptist,* July 19, August 1, 9, 30, October 25, 1928; Ayers, *Parker Memorial Baptist Church, Anniston,* 31.

142. For an excellent study of Alabama Baptists in the 1928 campaign, see Jimmy R. McLeod, "Methodist and Baptist Reaction to the 1928 Presidential Campaign in Alabama" (master's thesis, Samford University, 1972).

143. *Alabama Baptist,* March 7, 1929.

144. Dees, "Anti-Catholicism," 34–43; Charles G. Dobbins, "Alabama Governors and Editors, 1930–1955: A Memoir," *Alabama Review* 29 (April 1976): 137, 154; interview with Charles G. Dobbins, by Wayne Flynt, Auburn, October 30, 1987.

Chapter 9: The Great Depression, 1930–1939

1. For the depression's impact on Alabama, see Rogers et al., *Alabama,* 465–509.

2. Letters to FDR from: Jonathan H. Darden, January 4, 1936; Bryant Sanders, undated; W. L. Sprayberry, November 8, 1935; W. J. H. Sasser, September 30, 1935; all in Clergy Letters, Alabama, 1935, box 4, President's Personal Files 21-A, Franklin Delano Roosevelt Papers, Franklin D. Roosevelt Library, Hyde Park, New York. Henceforth cited as PPF, FDR Papers.

3. Letters to FDR from J. W. B. Pannell, October 28, 1935, box 3, and Mrs. Roy R. Keathley, October 9, 1935, box 4, PPF, FDR Papers.

4. Roy Niager to FDR, undated; C. E. Raley to FDR, October 26, 1935; both in box 3, PPF, FDR Papers.

5. J. A. Francis to FDR, October 1, 1935, box 4, PPF, FDR Papers.

6. Jeff Ellis to FDR, October 4, 1935; Joseph W. Rucker to FDR, n.d., box 4, PPF, FDR Papers.

7. Charles R. Bell Jr. to FDR, October 3, 1935; J. L. Aders to FDR, September 28, 1935; both in box 4, PPF, FDR Papers.

8. *Alabama Baptist,* October 18, 1973.

9. Allen, *First 150 Years,* 178–79.

10. Wells, "Depression Years at First Baptist Church, Fort Payne."

11. *Alabama Baptist,* October 18, 1973.

12. "Financing Work of Alabama Baptists"; Executive Board Minutes, June 17, December 11, 1930, February 18, 1931, December 27, 1932.

13. *Alabama Baptist,* October 23, November 13, 27, 1930, April 20, 1939, October 18, 1973; Ray, *The Major,* 54–55.

14. *Alabama Baptist,* December 17, 1936, October 18, 1973.

15. Ibid., November 23, 1939; Reid, *Baptists in Alabama,* 573.

16. *Alabama Baptist,* October 2, 1930, February 11, 18, 25, August 19, 1937, January 13, March 3, 1938, March 9, 1939.

17. Ibid., July 1, 1973, November 17, 1938.

18. Ibid., March 6, August 7, 1930, April 16, 1931, April 1, 1937, March 10, 1938, January 12, 1939.

19. Ibid., April 3, May 22, 1930.

20. Ibid., June 24, 1937, February 10, August 25, 1938.

21. "Brief of Historical Address of M. M. Wood at Mount Olive Baptist Church, June 18, 1933," ms. in M. M. Wood Papers, Samford University Archives.

22. *Alabama Baptist,* July 31, 1930, August 12, 1937; "Home Missions in Alabama, 1933," and Letter to Dr. Lawrence, 1931, both in Records of Alabama WMU; Frank Joseph Fede, *Italians in the Deep South: Their Impact on Birmingham and the American Heritage* (Montgomery: Black Belt Press, 1994), 41–42.

23. *Alabama Baptist,* February 23, 1939.

24. Marona Pucciarelli Aprile, "The Lives of Arcangelo Pucciarelli and Alice Mae Dupree Pucciarelli," *Alabama Baptist Historian* 33 (January 1997): 24–29.

25. *Alabama Baptist,* September 24, 1936.

26. Ibid., January 28, 1937; Willie Kelly to friends, January 21, 1935, in Records of Alabama WMU.

27. *Alabama Baptist,* March 6, 1930; ms. of speech to Alabama WMU, Gwaltney Papers.

28. Alabama WMU, *Woman's Missionary Union of Alabama, 1930, Annual;* WMU Minutes, March 24, 1931; Executive Board Minutes, WMU, June 19, 1931; all in Records of Alabama WMU; Jackson and Stephens, *Women of Vision,* 64; *Alabama Baptist,* April 10, 1930.

29. Robert Bowling to Ida M. Stallworth, September 2, 1936; Stallworth to Bowling, September 5, 1936; Irene Curtis to Stallworth, September 16, 1936; all in Records of Alabama WMU.

30. Letters to Mr. Murphree and to Howard College Auxiliary, 1931, in ibid.

31. *Alabama Baptist,* April 10, 1930; Records of Alabama WMU. The eleven churches in order of contributions were: Southside (Birmingham), Birmingham First Baptist, Montgomery First Baptist, Mobile First Baptist, Parker Memorial (Anniston), Selma First Baptist, Woodlawn (Birmingham), Clayton Street (Montgomery), Troy First Baptist, Dauphin Way (Mobile), and Hunter Street (Birmingham).

32. Records of Alabama WMU; Jackson and Stephens, *Women of Vision,* 65.

33. Salem Baptist Church Minutes; Brown, *History of First Baptist Church, Tuskegee,* 61; Stone, *History of First Baptist Church of Wetumpka,* 128, 146, 148–49.

34. *Alabama Baptist,* September 25, 1930.

35. Ibid., April 20, 1939.

36. Ms. of speech by L. L. Gwaltney to Alabama WMU, in Gwaltney Papers; Mrs. E. K. Hanby to Personal Service Chairman, 1933, Records of Alabama WMU.

37. *Alabama Baptist,* May 8, 1930.

38. Lida Bestor Robertson to Baptist State Board of Missions, October 22, 1915; L. C. Kelly to Baptist State Board of Missions, October 28, 1915; both in Records of Alabama WMU.

39. Lida Robertson to Charles F. Kent, August 25, 1924; Robertson to M. E. Foster, November 14, 1928; Robertson to Dr. Van Ness, November 29, 1930; Robertson to Fred H. McDuff, May 31, 1933; all in Robertson Papers.

40. "Baptists and Social Reform"; Lida Robertson to Rev. William M. Fore, April 12, 1940; Robertson to Henry L. Anderton, October 23, 1938; Robertson to Paul de Launay, January 30, 1939; all in ibid.

41. *Alabama Baptist,* February 27, 1930; "Our Foundations," sermon ms. in Gwaltney Papers; Gwaltney, *Forty of the Twentieth,* 163.

42. *Alabama Baptist,* October 24, 1929, March 20, August 21, 1930, January 14, 1932.

43. Ibid., January 15, 29, March 19, 1931.

44. Ibid., March 17, 1932, December 2, 1937; "The Licensed Liquor Traffic and Its Bearing on Home Missions," sermon ms. in Gwaltney Papers.

45. *Alabama Baptist,* May 11, August 17, 1939.

46. Flynt, " 'A Special Feeling of Closeness,' " 138–40; Robin D. G. Kelly, *Hammer and Hoe: Alabama Communists During the Great Depression* (Chapel Hill: University of North Carolina Press, 1990), 196–97, 214.

47. *Alabama Baptist,* April 23, December 10, 1931.

48. "Home Missions, 1933"; Terry and Sims, *They Live on the Land,* 146–80.

49. Oral history with Evelyn L. Mims, by Ray M. Atchinson and Doris L. Atchinson, August 3, 1979, Samford University Archives.

50. *Alabama Baptist*, May 1, August 7, 1930; survey data in "Mountain Survey" file, Mountain Missions box, Home Mission Board Papers, Southern Baptist Archives.

51. *Alabama Baptist*, March 13, 1930, December 17, 1970.

52. Acker Papers.

53. Edward B. Warren oral history.

54. W. Albert Smith Diary, Samford University Archives.

55. Oral history with Andrew W. Oden, by Gilbert Burks, May 4, 1990, Samford University Archives.

56. For a perceptive biography of J. W. Lester, see Karen Stone, "J. W. Lester and the Southern Baptist Rural Church Movement, 1908–1983" (master's thesis, Auburn University, 1984).

57. *Alabama Baptist*, February 27, 1930, July 16, 1931; Executive Board Minutes, December 14, 1927, December 6, 1932, January 5, December 13, 1934.

58. *Alabama Baptist*, June 29, 1939.

59. See Augustus Evans Lanier essay on the SBC and aesthetics in "Christianity in Contemporary South" notes, in Chapman Papers.

60. *Alabama Baptist*, October 1, 1931, June 1, 1939.

61. Marty, *Righteous Empire*, 235–42; see also Robert F. Martin, "A Prophet's Pilgrimage: The Religious Radicalism of Howard Anderson Kester, 1921–1941," *Journal of Southern History* 48 (November 1982): 511–30.

62. L. L. Gwaltney to W. O. Carver, December 2, 1936, Carver Papers; *Alabama Baptist*, January 6, 1938; oral history with Sam Jones Ezell, by Rollin Armour, July 21, 1978, Samford University Archives.

63. Bennett, "Life and Works of Editor Gwaltney," 28, 163–64; *Alabama Baptist*, July 29, 1937, January 30, 1938.

64. *Alabama Baptist*, August 30, 1923, August 25, 1932, August 13, 1936.

65. Ibid., May 14, 1931.

66. Ibid., May 14, June 5, 25, 1931.

67. Ibid., July 2, 1931.

68. Ibid.

69. Ibid., September 17, 1931.

70. D. R. Price, "A Brief Account of the Discussion Group," 1937, in Minutes of Birmingham Ministers Discussion Group, Samford University Archives.

71. Charles R. Bell Jr. to Dr. and Mrs. W. O. Carver, November 29, 1933; George Washington Carver to Bell, October 26, 1932; Sam H. Franklin Jr. to Bell, July 20, 1937, and January 24, 1938; all in Charles R. Bell Jr. Papers, Samford University Archives; oral history with Charles R. Bell Jr., by Wayne Flynt, January 28, 1972, Samford University Archives; Kathryn H. Campbell, "Sojourn of a Southern Liberal: The Life and Ministry of Charles R. Bell Jr." (master's thesis, Auburn University, 1986); Higginbotham and Higginbotham, *Upon This Rock I Will Build My Church*, 86–96; oral history with Harry Edwin Dickinson, by W. S. Love, December 13, 1984, Samford University Archives; Wayne Flynt, "Growing Up Baptist in Anniston, Alabama: The Legacy of the Reverend Charles R. Bell Jr.," in *Clearings in the Thicket: An Alabama Humanities Reader*, ed. Jerry Elijah Brown (Macon: Mercer University Press, 1985), 147–82.

72. *Alabama Baptist*, January 21, 28, 1937.

73. *Alabama Baptist*, May 20, 1937; Charles R. Bell Jr. oral history; unidentified newspaper clipping, in Bell Papers.

74. G. B. Snoddy to W. O. Carver, March 24, 1937; Carver to Snoddy, March 27, 1937; Snoddy to Carver, March 29, 1937; Carver to Snoddy, April 3, 1937; Carver to Charles R. Bell, May 19, 1937; Bell to Carver, August 24, 1937; Carver to Bell, August 19, 1937; all in Carver Papers; Carver to Bell, September 9, 1937, in Bell Papers.

75. "Brief Sketch of Rev. James E. Dean," Samford University Archives; James E. Dean to Franklin D. Roosevelt, October 25, 1935, box 3, PPF, FDR Papers.

76. *Alabama Baptist*, March 21, 1935, April 30, May 11, 18, June 29, 1939.

77. John C. Slemp to W. O. Carver, October 4, December 14, 1937; Carver to Slemp, December 15, 1937; A. D. Zbinden to Carver, December 9, 13, 18, 1937, January 7, March 26, 1938; Carver to Zbinden, January 6, March 29, 1938; Zbinden to Slemp, January 7, 1938; all in Carver Papers.

78. *Alabama Baptist*, January 28, 1937; John H. Buchanan to W. O. Carver, June 22, 1939, Carver Papers.

79. Brown, *History of First Baptist Church, Tuskegee*, 61–62; Stone, *History of First Baptist Church of Wetumpka*, 147–56.

80. *Alabama Baptist*, October 13, November 3, 1938.

81. Ibid., October 23, 1930, March 5, 1931.

82. Ibid., September 30, 1937.

83. Ibid., May 6, August 12, 1937.

84. Ibid., November 19, 1936, February 11, 1937; Stone, *History of First Baptist Church of Wetumpka*, 137–38.

85. *Alabama Baptist*, November 26, 1936, July 27, 1939.

86. Edward J. Larson, *Sex, Race, and Science: Eugenics in the Deep South* (Baltimore: Johns Hopkins University Press, 1995), 18–19, 42–49, 54–55, 65–67, 81–84, 139–45, 157.

87. *Alabama Baptist*, November 9, 1922.

88. Ibid., June 4, 1931, July 4, 1935; Larson, *Sex, Race, and Science*, 167.

89. *Alabama Baptist*, September 18, 1930, January 22, 1931.

90. Ibid., October 9, 1931.

91. Ibid., July 17, 1930, January 8, 1931, January 27, 1938.

92. Ibid., April 8, 1937, April 7, 1938, April 13, 1939.

93. Executive Board Minutes, May 10, 1934; "Home Missions, 1933."

94. For the strength of New Deal economic liberalism in Alabama, see Rogers et al., *Alabama*, 494–509.

95. Gwaltney, *Forty of the Twentieth*, 168–77; *Alabama Baptist*, July 2, 1936.

96. *Alabama Baptist*, February 18, May 6, August 12, 1937, January 6, 1938.

97. Ibid., July 1, 1937, June 30, November 17, 1938, February 2, June 8, 1939.

98. Ibid., August 20, 1936; R. M. Hunter to FDR, September 28, 1935, Clergy Papers, box 4, PPF, FDR Papers.

99. *Alabama Baptist*, July 1, 1937, August 25, 1938.

100. A. C. Davidson Diary, 1933, in Davidson Papers.

101. For Alabama responses to the 1936 poll of clergy, see Monroe Billington, "The Alabama Clergy and the New Deal," *Alabama Review* 32 (July 1979): 214–25. For my computations, I identified 51 of the 327 clergymen from Alabama who responded.

102. Letters to FDR from: A. D. Zbinden, October 14, 1935; J. V. Dickinson, October 4, 1935; J. G. Dickinson, October 4, 1935; Charles A. Stakely, October 14, 1935; James Allen Smith, September 26, 1935; Charles F. Leek, October 9, 1935; L. L. Hearn, September 26, 1935; J. M. Thomas, October 8, 1935; John J. Milford, October 1, 1935; all in Clergy Papers, box 4, PPF; and from John E. Marion, November 7, 1935; Robert L. Motley, October 14, 1935; W. F. Yarborough, October 11, 1935; Oscar L. Minks, October 23, 1935; all in Clergy Papers, box 3, PPF, FDR Papers.

103. Letters to FDR from: J. Blanton, March 9, 1936; D. R. Wyatt, October 31, 1935; James E. Bird, November 4, 1935; all in Clergy Papers, box 3, PPF; and from H. C. Stephens, October 8, 1935; A. C. Stevenson, October 9, 1935; D. S. Ridgway, September 28, 1935; all in Clergy Papers, box 4, PPF, FDR Papers.

104. Letters to FDR from: W. B. Morgan, November 21, 1935; F. D. King, November 21, 1935; both in Clergy Papers, box 3, PPF; and from G. F. Campbell, undated; S. H. Jones, October

14, 1935; W. C. Kirk, undated; Lewis W. Dockery, October 9, 1935; all in Clergy Papers, box 4, PPF, FDR Papers.

105. Jimmy Harper, "Alabama Baptists and the Rise of Hitler and Fascism, 1930–1938," *Journal of Reform Judaism* (Spring 1985): 1–11; *Alabama Baptist*, March 6, April 3, 17, 1930, May 7, 1931.

106. *Alabama Baptist*, January 7, July 29, September 16, 1937, September 29, October 13, December 1, 22, 1938, January 12, April 6, June 22, 29, July 6, September 7, 1939.

107. Harper, "Alabama Baptists and the Rise of Hitler," 2–11.

108. *Alabama Baptist*, May 4, 1933, November 17, 1938.

109. Ibid., December 1, 1938, December 14, 1939.

110. Oral history with Leroy Richard Priest, by Cynthia A. Wise, April 19, 1990, Samford University Archives.

Chapter 10: War and Remembrance, 1940–1954

1. *Alabama Baptist*, February 17, 1994.

2. Numan V. Bartley, *The New South, 1945–1980* (Baton Rouge: Louisiana State University Press, 1995), 107, 112, 121, 123, 127, 134, 145–46.

3. See Ammerman, *Southern Baptists Observed*, especially essays by Timothy George, "Toward an Evangelical Future," 278–83, and Nancy Tatom Ammerman, "After the Battles: Emerging Organizational Forms," 305–13.

4. See Robert Wuthnow, *The Restructuring of American Religious Society Since World War II* (Princeton: Princeton University Press, 1988), and Ammerman, "After the Battles," 313.

5. Walter L. Knight, "Southern Baptists Nationwide," *Quarterly Review* 43 (April–May–June 1983): 61–67.

6. Samuel S. Hill, "The Story Before the Story: Southern Baptists Since W. W. II," in Ammerman, *Southern Baptists Observed*, 31–32.

7. *Alabama Baptist*, November 28, 1940, March 13, April 3, 10, 17, November 20, 1941.

8. Ibid., January 25, March 28, May 9, 16, June 6, September 12, 25, 1940, October 18, 1941; "Background of World Conditions," ms. of speech to Birmingham Civitan Club, [1941?], Gwaltney Papers; L. L. Gwaltney, *A Message for Today on the Chariots of Fire or the Triumph of the Spiritual* (Birmingham: Birmingham Printing Co., 1941), 21–26.

9. *Alabama Baptist*, July 4, 1940.

10. Ibid., December 11, 1941, January 1, August 13, September 3, 1942, June 3, 1943.

11. Ibid., January 1, 1942, November 18, 1943.

12. Ibid., December 4, 1941.

13. Ibid., April 24, May 1, 1941.

14. Juliette Mather to W. O. Carver, August 20, 1941; two other letters from Mather to Carver, both undated; all in Carver Papers.

15. Flynt, "Growing Up Baptist," 174–75.

16. *Alabama Baptist*, February 6, June 12, 1941.

17. L. L. Gwaltney to Charles R. Bell Jr., June 3, 1941, Bell Papers.

18. John H. Buchanan to Charles R. Bell Jr., June 13, 1941, February 4, 1942; Montague Cook to Bell, June 16, 1941; in ibid.

19. *Alabama Baptist*, March 19, 1942.

20. Flynt, "Growing Up Baptist," 177–78.

21. Anonymous letter to Charles R. Bell, June 13, 1944, Bell Papers.

22. John L. Cottrell to Bell, June 19, 1944; Alex and Nan Hall to Bell, June 21, 1944; W. B. Crabb to Bell, June 15, 1944; all in ibid.

23. S. J. Ezell to Bell, June 30, 1944; H. Ross Arnold to Bell, June 30, 1944; T. W. Ayers to Bell, October 4, 1944; John H. Buchanan to Edwin McNeill Poteat, July 3, 1944; Poteat to Buchanan, July 12, 1944; L. B. Moseley to Bell, August 6, 1944; all in ibid.

24. *Alabama Baptist*, October 19, 1944, January 20, 1949.

25. Executive Committee Minutes, January 21, 1944.

26. "Some Unusual Experiences in the Chaplain's Corps," ms. in Claude M. Haygood Papers, Samford University Archives.

27. George M. Marsden, "Contemporary American Evangelicalism," in Dockery, *Southern Baptists and American Evangelicals*, 32–35; David H. Watt, "The Private Hopes of American Fundamentalists and Evangelicals, 1925–1975," *Religion and American Culture: A Journal of Interpretation*, 1 (Summer 1991): 155–63.

28. Marsden, "Contemporary American Evangelicalism," 32, 34; see essays in the same volume by Leon McBeth, "Baptist or Evangelical?" and Joel Carpenter, "Is Evangelical a 'Yankee' Word?"

29. This list of topics comes from the agenda of thirty-minute papers presented by Baptist members of the discussion group, 1940–1955; see Minutes of Birmingham Ministers Discussion Group. Approximately one-third of the membership (limited to fifteen ministers) were Southern Baptists.

30. Sermon ms. by Jesse A. Cook, in Chapman Papers.

31. *Alabama Baptist*, April 4, 1940.

32. Ibid., May 7, 1942, June 3, July 22, 1948, May 4, 1950.

33. Ibid., March 28, 1946.

34. Ibid., January 5, 1950.

35. "This I Leave with You," ms. in Gwaltney Papers.

36. *Alabama Baptist*, January 31, April 11, 1946, November 16, 23, 1950.

37. Cynthia A. Wise, "Aspects of the Social Thought of Leon Macon, Editor of the *Alabama Baptist*, 1950–1965" (master's thesis, Samford University, 1970), 1–5.

38. *Alabama Baptist*, January 25, February 22, 1940, July 13, September 21, 1950, March 29, June 14, 1951, January 10, August 14, 1952, April 9, August 27, 1953, May 20, 1954; Wise, "Social Thought of Leon Macon," 43–52.

39. *Alabama Baptist*, August 10, 1950, August 5, 1954; ms. of lecture by Leon Macon, in Chapman Papers; also see Wise, "Social Thought of Leon Macon," 21–29.

40. Ms. of lecture by Claude M. Haygood, in Chapman Papers.

41. *Alabama Baptist*, February 25, 1943.

42. John H. Buchanan Papers in the Southern Baptist Archives detail this committee's work in detail. For examples, see: John H. Buchanan to W. O. Carver, February 15, 1940; Buchanan to Charles E. Maddry, February 15, 1940; Buchanan to L. R. Scarborough, February 27, 1940; Buchanan to A. J. Barton, February 27, 1940; Buchanan to Ellis A. Fuller, February 28, 1940; Arthur J. Barton to John Buchanan, March 1, 1940; Buchanan to W. O. Carver, March 14, 1940; "Suggested Reply to World Council of Churches"; all in box 2 of Buchanan Papers.

43. *Alabama Baptist*, May 11, 1944, April 26, 1945, August 21, October 2, 1947.

44. Annie G. Perry et al. to Charles Bell, September 19, 1943, in Bell Papers; *Alabama Baptist*, March 19, 1942.

45. *Alabama Baptist*, December 7, 1944, January 30, 1947, January 15, 1948, February 24, 1949, December 7, 1950; ms. reports of Social Service Commission to Alabama Baptist State Conventions in 1941, 1948, 1952, all in Stivender Papers.

46. Executive Committee Minutes, January 12, 1945; *Alabama Baptist*, April 26, 1945.

47. *Alabama Baptist*, December 12, 1940, January 25, 1945.

48. Ibid., April 11, December 12, 1940, September 3, December 31, 1942.

49. Ibid., August 21, 1947.

50. Ibid., December 7, 1950, October 4, 1951, December 11, 1952, June 25, 1953, August 12, 1954; also see Wise, "Social Thought of Leon Macon," 30–42.

51. *Alabama Baptist*, July 20, 1950, April 3, 1952.

52. Ibid., February 1, 1951.

53. Ibid., September 27, 1951, June 4, 1953, September 16, 1954, October 6, 1955.

54. Ibid., May 23, 1946.

55. Lerond Curry, *Protestant-Catholic Relations in America: World War I through Vatican II* (Lexington: University Press of Kentucky, 1972), 37–58, 62–68.

56. Edward L. Queen II, *In the South the Baptists Are the Center of Gravity: Southern Baptists and Social Change, 1930–1980* (Brooklyn: Carlson Publishing, 1991), 97–118.

57. *Alabama Baptist*, April 21, May 19, June 9, October 6, 1949, March 15, November 1, 1951, January 1, July 16, 1953, December 16, 1954.

58. James Swedenburg to O. C. Carmichael, August 30, 1954, in James Swedenburg Papers, Samford University Archives.

59. *Alabama Baptist*, November 28, 1940, February 27, March 6, 13, April 24, October 16, 1947, February 3, March 3, 10, April 28, May 12, July 28, 1949, July 23, 1953, February 18, 1954, February 6, 1958; Lister Hill to Leon Macon, August 3, 1953, in Baggett Papers; ms. report of 1948 Social Service Commission, in Stivender Papers.

60. *Alabama Baptist*, September 26, 1946, July 21, 1949, August 17, 1950; Ray, *The Major*, 79; Executive Board Minutes, December 4, 1950.

61. Hal D. Bennett to Lynn E. May Jr., October 16, 1972, copy in author's possession; Executive Board Minutes, November 15, 1948, October 20, 1949; Sam Jones Ezell oral history; *Alabama Baptist*, December 7, 1944.

62. L. L. Gwaltney, "A Discussion of the Hill-Burton Act as Related to Baptists," ms. in James H. Butler Papers, Samford University Archives.

63. *Alabama Baptist*, January 4, 1940.

64. Ibid., February 24, 1944, January 29, May 6, 1948.

65. Ibid., January 24, July 31, 1952, December 10, 1953, January 19, 1956, January 2, 1958.

66. Ibid., September 14, November 30, 1950, March 15, 1951.

67. Ibid., November 24, 1949.

68. "A Baptist Program of Higher Education in Alabama: A Study Report, October 1, 1945," copy in Gwaltney Papers; *Alabama Baptist*, April 3, May 1, October 30, November 6, 13, 1947, November 8, 1951, November 20, 1952; Harwell G. Davis to Harry M. Ayers, January 5, 1943, in box 138, Harry Mell Ayers Papers, University of Alabama Archives; L. L. Gwaltney to H. C. Pannell, October 24, 1945, box 2, Buchanan Papers; Ray, *The Major*, 82–88; Hamilton and Wells, *Daughters of the Dream*, 153–55, 160–68.

69. "The Baptist Philosophy of World Christian Movements"; and James H. Clark to James H. Chapman, September 12, 1951; both in Chapman Papers.

70. *Alabama Baptist*, June 8, 29, 1950.

71. Ibid., September 6, 1945, October 20, 1955.

72. Ibid., January 3, 1946.

73. Reid, *Baptists in Alabama*, 357–402; Executive Board Minutes, December 7, 1953.

74. Budget for November 1, 1948, through October 1949; Executive Board Minutes, November 10, 1947, December 5, 1950, December 5, 1949, through November 9, 1953, December 9, 1954, through November 12, 1956.

75. Executive Board Minutes, December 7, 1942, March 9, 1945, December 7, 1953; "Report of the Committee to Study Allocations for Associational Missions," in Samford University Archives.

76. C. E. Jones to Leon Macon, September 28, 1957; Murray Hall to Leon Macon, October 8, 1952; both in Macon Papers.

77. *Alabama Baptist*, August 14, October 2, 1952.

78. Ibid., April 9, 1942, June 21, 1945, May 27, 1954.

79. Carl A. Clark, *Southern Baptists and Rural Churches* (Fort Worth: Baptist Book Store, 1956), 6–9; *Book of Reports*, Southern Baptist Convention, 1949, 310.

80. *Alabama Baptist*, November 21, 1940, February 20, 1941; "Bethlehem East, Kent, Alabama, Rural Minister of the Year, 1949," file in J. W. Lester Papers, Auburn University Archives;

Royce A. Rose, "The Rural Church Movement," paper presented at Rural Church Conference, January 1996, at Home Mission Board, Atlanta, Georgia.

81. *Alabama Baptist,* October 7, 1948, April 12, 1951.

82. Executive Board Minutes, July 12, 1950; F. M. Barnes to W. P. Wilks, December 18, 1941, F. M. Barnes Papers, Samford University Archives.

83. E. H. Littlejohn to F. M. Barnes, February 21, 1942, Barnes Papers; biographical data sheets on Shelton D. Bartlett, Arthur Hurston Smith, and C. E. Arnold, all in Alabama Baptist Biography Files.

84. Oral history with Gordon C. Chandler, by W. S. Love, October 25, 1983, Samford University Archives.

85. Oral history with Hubert Williams, by A. M. Daugherty, June 16, 1987, Samford University Archives.

86. Oral history with Claude A. Crane, by Jim Nogalski, March 20, 1979, Samford University Archives.

87. Executive Board Minutes, December 7, 1942, December 6, 1943, December 4, 1944, January 12, 1945, May 1, August 6, 1951; *Alabama Baptist,* May 6, 1954.

88. *Alabama Baptist,* February 20, 1930, November 27, 1947; Reid, *Baptists in Alabama,* 384–86.

89. *Alabama Baptist,* January 9, 1946, November 27, 1947, May 13, 27, 1948, August 25, 1949, January 4, May 17, 1951; "Howard College Extension," Samford University Archives.

90. *Alabama Baptist,* January 6, 1949, July 2, 1953; Stone, "J. W. Lester," 63.

91. *Alabama Baptist,* July 9, 1953; "Soil Conservation Fighting Soil Erosion," sermon ms. in Lester Papers.

92. *Alabama Baptist,* June 2, July 7, 1949.

93. Ibid., February 1, 1940; "Temperance," in "SBC Encyclopedia," Samford University Archives.

94. *Alabama Baptist,* March 27, 1941; Executive Board Minutes, March 25, 1938, December 10, 1940.

95. Birmingham Baptist Association Report, copy in Butler Papers; *Alabama Baptist,* February 17, 1949, February 4, 1954.

96. John H. Buchanan to Ellis A. Fuller, March 1, 1940, Buchanan Papers; *Alabama Baptist,* March 23, 1950.

97. *Alabama Baptist,* July 4, 1946, April 5, 1951, July 10, 1952, May 13, 1953, September 2, October 14, 1954; "Revivals 1952," ms. in Butler Papers.

98. *Alabama Baptist,* January 10, 1946, December 18, 1947, November 18, 1948, July 1, 1954, December 8, 1955.

99. Reid, *Baptists in Alabama,* 568–69.

100. *Alabama Baptist,* May 16, October 3, 1940, July 13, 1944.

101. Ibid., April 5, 1945, January 14, 1954.

102. Ibid., February 24, 1944, August 21, 1947; for photographs of Baptist women in military service, see February/March 1944 issues of the paper.

103. John Bob Riddle to W. Cosby Hall, May 1, 1951, W. Cosby Hall Papers, Samford University Archives.

104. Jackson, *Women of Vision,* 78; Higginbotham and Higginbotham, *Upon This Rock I Will Build My Church,* 101.

105. *Alabama Baptist,* May 10, July 12, September 29, 1951, February 12, 1953.

106. Gordon C. Chandler oral history; F. L. Hacker to F. M. Barnes, July 27, 1942, Barnes Papers.

107. Annie Dopson Scrapbooks, Samford University Archives.

108. *Alabama Baptist,* December 14, 1950.

109. Records of Alabama WMU; Jackson, *Women of Vision,* 71–73.

110. Jackson and Stephens, *Women of Vision*, 71, 89; *Alabama Baptist*, March 20, 1941, March 19, 1942, March 25, 1954; Records of Alabama WMU.

111. Owen J. Perry to Mrs. Travis H. Wood, March 16, 1958; Nick O. Demus to WMU, November 16, 1958; both in Records of Alabama WMU.

112. Records of Alabama WMU; Alabama WMU Minutes, 1945, 29–31, and 1947, 31, in ibid.

113. Jackson, *Women of Vision*, 73, 85–86.

114. Ibid., 75–76; *Alabama Baptist*, March 23, 1950.

115. Executive Board Minutes, November 15, 1948, December 5, 1949, February 22, November 11, 1951, November–December 1989; Jackson, *Women of Vision*, 77.

116. Executive Board Minutes, December 9, 1952.

117. David Ray Norsworthy, "Rationalization and Reaction Among Southern Baptists," in Ammerman, *Southern Baptists Observed*, 75–76; Watt, "Private Hopes," 156, 164–69.

118. *Alabama Baptist*, July 5, 1945, July 29, September 30, 1954.

119. Ms. reports of the 1948 and 1952 Social Service Commissions, in Stivender Papers.

120. Ms. review of *Marriage for Moderns*; "The Church and the New Community," February 1, 1943; "Some Accentuated and Emerging Problems in the Ministry," April 1944; both mss. of papers presented to Birmingham Protestant Pastors' Union; "Some Modern Trends in Religion," ms. of paper; all in Stivender Papers.

121. *Alabama Baptist*, April 11, 1940, August 23, November 22, 1945; William David Stell Papers, Samford University Archives. Ellen M. Rosenberg, a perceptive historian of Southern Baptists, has noted the role of Baptist politicians in shaping southern politics and has urged historians to pay more attention to the subject (Ellen M. Rosenberg, "The Southern Baptist Response to the Newest South," in Ammerman, *Southern Baptists Observed*, 144).

122. *Alabama Baptist*, January 22, 1942.

123. Ibid., June 5, 1952; Wayne Pinegar, "John H. Buchanan Sr.," Samford University Archives; W. M. Beck to editor, December 11, 1950; B. Locke Davis to Leon Macon, December 14, 1950; both in Macon Papers.

124. *Alabama Baptist*, August 8, 1940, March 6, 1941, January 7, July 8, October 28, 1943, May 4, 1944, February 22, 1945, August 8, 1946.

125. Ibid., April 5, 19, September 6, 1945, July 11, 1946, January 16, April 24, September 18, 1947, January 1, November 11, 1948, January 25, April 20, 1950.

126. Ibid., August 16, 30, 1951, August 7, September 11, 1952, November 5, 1953.

127. Ibid., September 9, 1943, March 23, 1944, February 6, 1946, November 4, 1948.

128. Ibid., February 5, October 8, 1942, June 10, 24, August 5, 1943, June 29, July 13, 1944, January 4, June 21, July 5, 19, August 9, September 13, October 18, 1945, February 21, August 1, September 12, 1946, January 2, 1947, April 13, July 20, 1950; L. L. Gwaltney to P. D. Walter, March 11, 1946, Baggett Papers. For Gwaltney's compelling vision of the postwar world, see Gwaltney, *Message for Today*, 43.

129. Executive Board Minutes, July 12, 1950; Harry M. Ayers to B. Locke Davis, March 20, 1954, Ayers Papers.

130. *Alabama Baptist*, March 7, 1946, October 15, 1953.

131. Ibid., August 22, September 12, November 7, 1946, August 28, 1947, June 2, 1949, July 3, 1952; L. L. Gwaltney to Joseph Stalin, December 14, 1943, in Gwaltney Papers.

132. *Alabama Baptist*, January 18, May 24, 1945, June 16, 1949, August 24, 1950, February 15, 1951, January 31, 1952, November 26, 1953.

133. For southern civil religion, see Andrew M. Manis, *Southern Civil Religions in Conflict: Black and White Baptists and Civil Rights, 1947–1957* (Athens: University of Georgia Press, 1987).

134. *Alabama Baptist*, January 4, June 28, 1945.

135. Manis, *Southern Civil Religions in Conflict*, 73–77.

136. *Alabama Baptist*, January 16, 1941, August 8, 1946, June 24, 1948, July 7, 1949. Also see Feldman, "Ku Klux Klan."

137. Records of Alabama WMU; *Alabama Baptist,* October 30, 1952, June 24, 1954.

138. Executive Board Minutes, December 10, 1940, December 7, 1942, December 7, 1943, December 5, 1944, July 12, 1950, May 1, 1951; D. V. Jemison to F. M. Barnes, May 23, 1942, Barnes Papers; *Alabama Baptist,* August 15, 1946, October 16, 1947, February 12, 1948, September 13, 1951, July 2, 1953.

139. *Alabama Baptist,* March 5, 1942.

140. "Baptists and the Race Problem," ms. by Claude T. Ammerman, in Chapman Papers.

141. "Some Accentuated and Emerging Problems in the Ministry," ms. report of 1948 Social Service Commission; ms. report of 1952 (?) Social Service Commission, both in Stivender Papers.

142. *Alabama Baptist,* July 20, 1944, November 28, 1946.

143. *Birmingham Post-Herald,* March 16, 1953.

144. *Alabama Baptist,* October 30, 1941.

145. Ibid., December 15, 1949.

146. Ibid., March 7, 1940, April 16, August 6, 1942, June 10, 1943, August 10, March 2, 1944, April 4, 1946, January 23, November 13, 1947, February 12, 1948, October 13, 1949.

147. Ibid., February 5, 1948. For an excellent biography of Horace Wilkinson, see Glenn A. Feldman, *From Demagogue to Dixiecrat: Horace Wilkinson and the Politics of Race* (New York: University Press of America, 1995).

148. *Alabama Baptist,* February 19, February 26, March 4, 1948.

149. Ibid., September 25, 1952, June 25, 1953, March 11, 1954; Wise, "Social Thought of Leon Macon," 53–68.

150. *Alabama Baptist,* May 24, 1951, June 18, 1953.

151. John B. Atkins to Leon Macon, May 24, 1951; and newspaper clipping; both in Macon Papers.

Chapter 11: Racial Religion, 1955–1970

1. Rogers et al., *Alabama,* 546–47.

2. *Alabama Baptist,* July 4, 1957.

3. Ibid., November 7, 1957.

4. Ibid., January 19, 1967, September 19, 1968.

5. Ibid., January 26, February 9, March 2, 1967, February 15, September 19, October 3, 1968.

6. S. Jonathan Bass, "Bishop C. C. J. Carpenter: From Segregation to Integration," *Alabama Review* 45 (July 1992): 184–215; William J. Ward to Thomas J. Toolen, March 19, 1965, in Macon Papers; *Birmingham News Magazine,* December 7, 1969.

7. Bill J. Leonard, "A Theology for Racism: Southern Fundamentalists and the Civil Rights Movement," ms. of paper presented at Cambridge University, September 1995, in author's possession. I am grateful to Professor Leonard for sharing his paper with me.

8. James F. Findlay, "Religion and Politics in the Sixties: The Churches and the Civil Rights Act of 1964," *Journal of American History* 77 (June 1990): 66–92.

9. Mark Newman, "Getting Right with God: Southern Baptists and Race Relations, 1945–1980," ms. in author's possession; "A Statement Concerning the Crisis in Our Nation," resolution passed by SBC, June 5, 1968, copy in Samford University Archives; Rosenberg, "Southern Baptist Response," 156; Walter B. Shurden, "The Christian Life Commission: Evolved Conscience of the Southern Baptist Convention," *Quarterly Review* 42 (October–December 1981): 63–76; Leonard, *God's Last and Only Hope,* 14–19; *White Citizens' Council,* May 1958, copy in "Race Relations" file, A. C. Miller box, Christian Life Commission Records, Southern Baptist Archives.

10. Mark Newman, "Alabama Southern Baptists and the Black Quest for Equality, 1954–

1980," ms. of paper presented at conference on the Montgomery bus boycott, July 1996, University of Hull, United Kingdom; in author's possession. I am grateful to Professor Newman for sharing his excellent paper with me.

11. *Alabama Baptist,* May 27, 1954, March 8, May 3, 1956, August 20, 1959.

12. Leon Macon to J. Howard Williams, February 3, 1958; Williams to Macon, February 26, 1958; Alma Hunt to Macon, February 18, 1958; J. Wash Watts to Macon, February 12, 1958; A. C. Miller to Macon, February 19, 1958; all in Baggett Papers.

13. *Alabama Baptist,* June 14, August 13, 1959.

14. Ibid., July 27, August 10, September 21, 1961; George E. Bagley, *My Four Decades with Alabama Baptists: An Oral History Memoir* (Birmingham: Alabama Baptist Historical Commission, n.d.), 205–6; Leon Macon to J. Theodore Jackson, August 15, 1961, Macon Papers.

15. Leon Macon to Samuel Southard, July 13, 1962, Macon Papers.

16. *Alabama Baptist,* May 16, 1963.

17. Ibid., May 28, 1964.

18. Ibid., February 18, 1965; Leon Macon to W. G. Robertson, July 29, 1964; Macon to James L. Sullivan, September 10, 1964; both in Macon Papers.

19. *Alabama Baptist,* March 18, 25, April 15, 1965; Leon Macon to John R. Claypool, May 18, 1965; Claypool to Macon, May 28, 1965; both in Macon Papers.

20. *Alabama Baptist,* June 24, 1965; Leon Macon to Mrs. P. D. Gates, May 10, 1965; Macon to K. G. Purcell, February 9, 1965; both in Macon Papers; Bagley, *Four Decades with Alabama Baptists,* 204.

21. *Alabama Baptist,* May 30, June 20, 1968, January 9, 1969.

22. "Report to Administration Committee and Executive Board, Alabama Baptist State Convention, December 9–10, 1965," from Department of Special Missions, Samford University Archives.

23. Ibid.; *Alabama Baptist,* September 28, 1961, July 4, 1968.

24. "Report to Administration Committee and Executive Board," December 9–10, 1965; Administration Committee Minutes of the Alabama Baptist State Convention, August 16, 1955, December 8, 1958 (hereafter cited as Administration Committee Minutes); *Alabama Baptist,* October 10, 1963.

25. Jackson, *Women of Vision,* 92–93, 109–15.

26. *Alabama Baptist,* July 14, 1960, December 3, 1964.

27. Ibid., January 11, May 2, 1968; R. M. Harper to Leon Macon, June 7, 1954; John Hopper to Macon, 1956; Louis Rambo to Macon, 1957; Alfred P. Streety to Macon, May 17, 1964; S. J. Smith to Macon, 1964; W. M. Sides to Macon, 1964; all in Macon Papers.

28. Mrs. W. F. Schmidt to Leon Macon, July 16, 1964; Mrs. Jewell Price to Macon, August 31, 1964; Mrs. Ada Smith to Macon, 1964; Mrs. R. l. Freeze to Macon, September 1964; Mrs. Harvey Steele to Macon, April 15, 1965; Mrs. P. D. Gates to Macon, May 9, 1965; all in Macon Papers; *Alabama Baptist,* April 16, 1964, August 29, 1968.

29. See four articles by Walter B. Jones: "Is It Unchristian to Believe in Segregation?" *Alabama Bible Society Quarterly* 13 (October 1957): 2–9; "100 Things You Should Know about Communism and Religion," ibid., 12 (July 1956): 11–20; "A Challenge," ibid., 16 (July 1960): 68–70; and "The Struggle for Local Self-Government," ibid., 16 (October 1960): 76–84.

30. Henry L. Lyon Jr., "Is Racial Segregation Christian? What Is the Position of the Minister of the Gospel?" *Alabama Bible Society Quarterly* 14 (July 1958): 21–23; transcript of interview with Dr. Henry L. Lyon Jr. over WSFA-TV, November 3, 1957, copy in Baggett Papers.

31. Quoted in Thomas J. Gilliam, "The Second Folsom Administration: The Destruction of Alabama Liberalism, 1954–1958" (Ph.D. diss., Auburn University, 1975), 415; Henry L. Lyon Jr., "Racial Agitation in Montgomery," *Alabama Bible Society Quarterly* 17 (July 1961): 60–61.

32. Henry L. Lyon Jr. to Leon Macon, January 12, 1963, Macon Papers; Queen, *Baptists Are the Center of Gravity,* 88.

33. Quoted in Stephan Lesher, *George Wallace: American Populist* (New York: Addison-Wesley Publishing Co., 1994), 206; *Alabama Baptist,* June 17, 1965.

34. Herschel H. Hobbs to Leon Macon, April 14, 1965; Bob Marsh to *Christianity Today,* March 23, 1965; Sam S. Douglas to Don L. Bell, May 4, 1965; Bell to Douglas, 1965; Douglas to Macon, 1965; Sam S. Douglas, "An Open Letter to Martin Luther King and Associates"; all in Macon Papers.

35. James R. Swedenburg to Leon Macon, January 17, 1963, Macon Papers; *Alabama Baptist,* June 13, 1968.

36. Leon Macon to K. Owen White, September 10, 1964; Macon to Estelle Hall, October 28, 1963; Macon to Mr. and Mrs. G. S. King, April 20, 1964; all in Macon Papers; *Alabama Baptist,* October 10, 1957, May 14, 1964.

37. *Alabama Baptist,* August 11, 1960, July 6, 1961, February 14, May 23, 1963, August 19, 1965.

38. Ibid., October 3, 1957, October 11, 1962, April 2, 1964; Leon Macon to Mrs. V. S. Rice, April 2, 1964; Macon to Howard Rush, March 27, 1964; Macon to B. E. Reed, May 14, 1963; Macon to M. L. Rogers, April 23, 1964; all in Macon Papers.

39. Leon Macon to Mrs. Patricia W. Taylor, June 12, 1964; Macon to Governor George C. Wallace, August 20, 1965; both in Macon Papers.

40. *Alabama Baptist,* February 20, 1958, April 20, June 8, 1961, October 3, 24, November 7, 1963, July 23, 1964, April 1, 1965; Leon Macon to Gainer E. Bryan Jr., April 20, 1965, Macon Papers. For a more complete essay on Macon's racial views, see Wise, "Social Thought of Leon Macon," 53–68.

41. H. G Nettles Jr. to Leon Macon, December 17, 1957; J. R. Farneman to Macon, November 15, 1958; both in Macon Papers; resolution by Montgomery Ministerial Association, September 1, 1964, copy in Baggett Papers; Administration Committee Minutes, September 30, 1965; *Alabama Baptist,* November 28, 1957, November 22, 1962, March 2, 1967, March 14, 1968.

42. *Alabama Baptist,* July 8, 1965.

43. Ibid., May 23, 1968, November 13, 1969; Gilliam, "Second Folsom Administration," 516.

44. *Birmingham News,* April 8, 1969; Mrs. Cecil Thrasher, "Salem Baptist Church, Lawrence County," *Alabama Baptist Historian* 6 (July 1970): 43–45; Leon Macon to Theo Sommerkamp, July 12, 1963, Macon Papers; oral history with Mrs. Julian Newman, by Clyde Presley, July 29, 1981, Samford University Archives.

45. *Alabama Baptist,* April 1, 1965, July 25, 1968.

46. Oral history with Louis Wilhite, by Lee Hazelgrove, January 21, 1975, Samford University Archives; article from June 1974 *Home Mission* magazine, in Arlington Baptist Church Records, Samford University Archives.

47. Jeffers, *Auburn First Baptist Church,* 85–89; G. B. Phillips to Leon Macon, August 8, 1963, Macon Papers.

48. *Alabama Baptist,* April 2, 1964, January 5, 1967; Jeffers, *Auburn First Baptist Church,* 90–93.

49. Ms. by Fred Lackey, January 31, 1997, in author's possession.

50. Jerry L. Jumper to Leon Macon, January 11, 1963, Macon Papers.

51. *Alabama Baptist,* September 3, 24, 1964.

52. Ibid., April 15, 1965.

53. Ibid., April 25, July 25, 1968; Leon Macon to John Claypool, June 7, 1965, Macon Papers.

54. *Alabama Baptist,* August 16, 1962, June 25, 1964, March 7, June 27, 1968; copy of resolution adopted by Greensboro Baptist Church, February 9, 1958, in Baggett Papers; Harry K. Martin to Leon Macon, June 29, 1957, in Macon Papers; Bagley, *Four Decades with Alabama Baptists,* 205.

55. *Alabama Baptist,* April 22, 1965, November 28, 1968; Bagley, *Four Decades with Alabama Baptists,* 86–87.

56. Brown, *History of First Baptist Church, Tuskegee,* 67, 69, 78.

57. J. P. Abler to Leon Macon, November 11, 1954, in Baggett Papers; Louis G. Rambo to Leon Macon, 1957; Selma Baptist Association to Duke McCall, May 5, 1961; both in Macon Papers; *Alabama Baptist,* April 30, 1964.

58. Morris Dees and Steve Fiffer, *A Season For Justice: The Life and Times of Civil Rights Lawyer Morris Dees* (New York: Charles Scribner's Sons, 1991), 51, 77–78, 86–88, 91, 94–97, 136–37, 258, 273, 276–77, 333; Findlay, "Religion and Politics in the Sixties," 90.

59. *Alabama Baptist,* November 10, 1966.

60. Ibid., April 27, 1967, May 9, 1968.

61. Ibid., May 2, October 3, 1968; John A. Salmond, *A Southern Rebel: The Life and Times of Aubrey Willis Williams, 1890–1965* (Chapel Hill: University of North Carolina Press, 1983), 279.

62. *Alabama Baptist,* October 16, 1958, September 28, 1961, March 31, June 9, July 14, 1966, October 12, 1967; Leon Macon to Louis G. Rambo, April 19, 1964, in Macon Papers.

63. *Alabama Baptist,* June 30, 1955, March 29, August 2, 23, 30, 1956, October 17, 1957, June 12, September 18, 1958, December 31, 1959, January 7, 1960, May 4, 1961, August 20, 1964.

64. Ibid., November 1, 1956, June 20, December 12, 1957, March 19, 1959, November 24, 1960, November 9, 1961; "Alabama Legislature" file in George Bagley Papers, Samford University Archives.

65. *Alabama Baptist,* August 9, 1956, April 3, July 10, December 4, 1958, February 26, March 12, 1959; J. D. Douthit Jr. to Leon Macon, November 15, 1958; R. E. Ables Sr. to John Patterson, June 17, 1959; Leon Macon to John Patterson, 1959; all in Macon Papers.

66. For examples of 1960 anti-Catholic articles, see *Alabama Baptist,* June 16, 30, July 7, 21, 28, September 1, 8, 15, 22, October 6, 13, 20, 27, November 3; for examples of sermons against Kennedy's election, see ibid., July 7, 21, August 11, September 22, October 13, 20, 27, November 3; see also ibid., March 17, August 18, October 16, 1960; sermon ms. by H. O. Hester, "Let Freedom Ring," October 16, 1960, copy in Butler Papers.

67. Russell V. Jensen to Leon Macon, May 17, 1961; William A. Glenn to Macon, May 21, 1962; C. L. Hollingsworth to Macon, November 19, 1963; Mrs. Edwin C. Hand to Macon, May 17, 1962; all in Macon Papers.

68. Curry, *Protestant-Catholic Relations in America,* 62–85; *Alabama Baptist,* August 25, 1966.

69. Mrs. Orice Gaither to Leon Macon, May 14, 1964; George C. Wallace to Macon, October 22, 1964; Robert H. Garner to Macon, March 8, 1964; all in Macon Papers.

70. Leon Macon to Louis G. Rambo, July 25, 1962, in ibid.

71. *Alabama Baptist,* October 18, 1962, July 11, 1963, January 2, March 19, 26, April 9, 1964.

72. Leon Macon to Ralph H. Richardson, July 30, 1964; Charles V. Simpson to Leon Macon, August 12, 1965; Macon to Simpson, August 18, 1964; all in Macon Papers; *Alabama Baptist,* July 22, 1965.

73. *Alabama Baptist,* December 16, 1965, July 4, August 15, 1968, October 9, 1969.

74. Ibid., May 16, November 21, 1968, July 31, 1969, November 17, 1994; Bagley, *Four Decades with Alabama Baptists,* 214–16.

75. *Alabama Baptist,* January 18, 1968, January 23, September 11, 1969.

76. Ibid., July 14, 1955, July 19, 1962.

77. Ibid., September 20, 1956.

78. Administration Committee Minutes, January 25, 1955, January 29, 1957, July 23, 1963; "Report of Committee on Gadsden Hospital, December 5, 1963," in Administration Committee Minutes, July 23, 1963; *Alabama Baptist,* July 19, 1956, March 7, 14, 1957, November 2, 1967.

79. Leon Macon to Mrs. Henry C. Rogers, September 25, 1961, Macon Papers; *Alabama Baptist,* March 17, 1955, December 20, 1956, January 16, April 24, July 31, 1958, February 12, 1959, March 3, 1960, January 5, 1961. For a sample of Macon's prolific writing on the subject,

see *Alabama Baptist,* January 11, 24, February 14, 28, May 30, June 6, 13, 27, August 29, 1963, March 26, April 16, August 20, 1964.

80. *Alabama Baptist,* January 12, March 2, 9, 16, 30, June 29, July 20, August 3, 1961, March 19, 1964, February 25, 1965; Administration Committee Minutes, May 1, 1961; Executive Board Minutes, November 11, 1968.

81. Oral history with B. Locke Davis, by Wayne Flynt, January 22 and 26, 1976, Samford University Archives; B. Locke Davis to D. W. Burson, May 9, 1958; Davis to James D. Bailey, October 15, 1962; Davis to Editor, *Christian Century,* October 2 and November 24, 1947; all in B. Locke Davis Papers, Samford University Archives.

82. Mrs. John Chapman to B. Locke Davis, October 20, 1960; Davis to Chapman, October 22, 1960; *This Nation Under God,* pamphlet of sermon by B. Locke Davis; all in Davis Papers.

83. *Alabama Baptist,* July 5, 12, 26, September 27, 1962; Leon Macon to Clyde King, September 17, 1962, Macon Papers.

84. Leon Macon to W. K. Stephenson, July 1, 1963, Macon Papers.

85. Albert Rains to George E. Bagley, May 12, 1964; Darold H. Morgan to Bagley, May 14, 1964; H. H. Harwell to Bagley, May 10, 1964; Kenneth A. Roberts to Bagley, April 29, 1964; all in Bagley Papers; resolution by Oakman Baptist Church, copy in Macon Papers.

86. Jimmy C. Jones to Leon Macon, May 15, 1964; O. R. Williams to Macon, June 24, 1964; both in Macon Papers; *Alabama Baptist,* November 14, 1963, October 17, 1968.

87. *Alabama Baptist,* February 8, October 25, 1962, July 11, 1963.

88. Ibid., September 8, 1966, April 24, 1969.

89. Ibid., October 2, 1958, July 23, September 3, 1959, January 28, February 11, 18, May 27, August 12, 1965.

90. Ibid., November 1, 1956, October 22, 1959, August 11, November 10, 24, 1966, November 20, 1969.

91. Ibid., February 18, 1965.

92. Ibid., July 10, 17, August 14, 21, September 18, 1969.

93. I have relied primarily on the following theses and books about the SBC controversy: Jeff Kirk Walters, "Though the Heavens Fall: Liberal Theology and the Southern Baptist Theological Seminary, 1894–1925" (master's thesis, Auburn University, 1992); David T. Morgan, *The New Crusades, The New Holy Land: Conflict in the Southern Baptist Convention, 1969–1991* (Tuscaloosa: University of Alabama Press, 1996); Leonard, *God's Last and Only Hope;* Ammerman, *Southern Baptists Observed;* Ellen M. Rosenberg, *The Southern Baptists: A Subculture in Transition* (Knoxville: University of Tennessee Press, 1989); Dockery, *Southern Baptists and American Evangelicals.*

94. *Alabama Baptist,* December 12, 1957, May 8, 1958, July 5, 1962, February 7, 1963, December 31, 1964, November 25, 1965.

95. Ibid., November 14, 1963 (Macon's presidential speech to the 1963 state convention); Leon Macon to Mrs. B. H. Roberts, March 19, 1964, Macon Papers.

96. *Alabama Baptist,* January 20, March 10, August 11, 1955, May 31, 1956, July 3, 1958, June 15, 1961, July 2, September 10, 1964.

97. Ibid., October 4, 1956, August 1, 1957, September 25, 1958, October 15, 1959, July 27, August 17, 1961, April 19, August 9, 1962; Robert Shank to Leon Macon, March 21, 1961, Macon Papers. For Macon's additional denunciations of modernism/liberalism, particularly during Alabama's racial turmoil, see *Alabama Baptist,* January 9, 30, February 6, 13, 20, July 2, 16, August 6, 13, October 22, November 5, 1964, January 14, February 11, March 11, July 1, 22, August 12, 1965.

98. J. C. Blakeney to Leon Macon, December 16, 1955; Jack Moore to Macon, 1961; C. V. Beaseley to Macon, March 7, 1963; all in Macon Papers.

99. *Alabama Baptist,* February 4, April 21, July 14, 1960, August 3, 1961.

100. Ibid., December 1, 1960.

101. Ibid., January 11, February 1, 15, 22, May 3, 17, June 7, 14, September 20, November

8, 1963; Leon Macon to Mrs. B. H. Roberts, June 28, 1963; Macon to Jesse M. Rogers, April 4, 1963; Macon to K. Owen White, January 4, 1963; Macon to O. R. Williams Sr., June 26, 1964; all in Macon Papers.

102. Leon Macon to Robert G. Witty, August 12, 1964, Macon Papers; *Alabama Baptist*, January 14, 1965, March 20, April 24, May 29, June 26, August 7, 1969.

103. *Alabama Baptist*, May 5, 1955, April 12, 1956, February 21, 1963, May 14, 1964, February 4, July 7, 1965.

104. N. H. Owen to Leon Macon, May 25, 1965; Ken Purcell to Macon, 1965; both in Macon Papers.

105. Jesse L. Gann to Leon Macon, October 2, 1956, Macon Papers; *Alabama Baptist*, August 15, 1963, February 3, 1966, May 29, 1969.

106. *Alabama Baptist*, January 4, April 26, 1962, July 9, 23, 1964.

107. Ibid., October 5, 19, 1967, October 2, 30, December 11, 1969.

108. Ibid., July 6, 1967.

109. Ibid., January 7, 1965.

110. Ibid., November 23, December 7, 1961.

111. Howard M. Reaves to Leon Macon, October 3, 1962; Resolution of Mount Olive Baptist Church, 1962; Macon to Reaves, October 5, 1963; all in Macon Papers.

112. John C. Bush to Mack Douglas, March 15, 1962; Douglas to Bush, March 20, 1962; Bush to F. Paul Allison, January 9, 1962; Ralph Elliott to Bush, December 6, 1963; Bush to E. Mack Johnson Jr., March 6, 1964; Bill Bush to John Bush, September 1960; various undated letters; John Bush Diary; all in John C. Bush Papers, Samford University Archives.

113. *Alabama Baptist*, February 7, 1957, August 15, 1968.

114. Ibid., March 3, July 21, 1955, April 4, 1957, February 6, May 1, 22, June 5, 26, October 2, 30, November 27, 1958, July 2, 1959, January 7, 1960, February 15, March 1, April 12, 1962, August 1, December 5, 1963, July 16, 23, November 26, 1964; Leon Macon to Kenneth Crawford, August 11, 1965; Macon to Al Couch, May 21, 1965; both in Macon Papers.

115. T. L. Junkins to Leon Macon, March 22, 1965, Macon Papers.

116. *Alabama Baptist*, May 20, December 2, 1965.

117. Ibid., August 3, 1967, August 15, 1968, October 2, 1969.

118. George D. Lovett to Leon Macon, March 11, 1965; Russell J. Drake to Macon, August 4, 1965; both in Macon Papers; *Alabama Baptist*, September 19, 1968.

119. *Alabama Baptist*, June 15, 29, October 12, 1967, May 30, 1968.

120. Ibid., November 22, 1956, July 22, August 5, 1965, November 21, 1968; interview with John Jeffers, December 1, 1996.

121. *Alabama Baptist*, March 17, 1966.

122. Ibid., September 15, 1966, August 22, 1968, January 16, February 20, May 22, June 5, 1969.

123. Ibid., October 9, 1958, August 30, 1962, September 1, 1966, March 16, 1967; Administration Committee Minutes, September 3, 1968.

124. *Alabama Baptist*, August 1, 1957, March 12, 1959, January 7, 1960, February 2, 1961, January 14, 1965, November 10, 1966, January 26, October 12, 1967.

125. Ibid., February 28, 1957, January 7, 1960, October 19, 1961; "Alabama Baptist Statistics," Administration Committee Minutes, 1984, and "1952–1971 Statistics," Administration Committee Minutes, 1972.

126. *Alabama Baptist*, November 27, 1958, November 22, 1962; Potts, "Shaping Alabama Baptists," 3–10; "1952–1971 Statistics," Administration Committee Minutes, 1972; Bagley, *Four Decades with Alabama Baptists*, 123–24; Executive Board Minutes, July 26–27, 1965.

127. *Alabama Baptist*, February 12, 1959, July 28, 1966.

128. Ibid., November 27, 1958, March 30, 1961; Bagley, *Four Decades with Alabama Baptists*, 85, 165–67; Administration Committee Minutes, November 11, 1957, November 14, 1960, November 13, 1961.

129. *Alabama Baptist,* February 13, 1958, July 6, 1961; Executive Board Minutes, December 11, 1964, June 29, July 27, 1965.

130. *Alabama Baptist,* September 20, 1962, July 21, 1966.

131. Executive Board Minutes, July 26–27, 1965; "Baptist Higher Education," report in Executive Board Minutes, September 30, 1965.

132. Executive Board Minutes, December 11, 1964; "Progress Report of Special Study Committee," in Administration Committee Minutes, December 9, 1960, July 23, 1963.

133. Administration Committee Minutes, November 17, 1958, November 17, 1969; Executive Board Minutes, September 8, 1961.

134. *Alabama Baptist,* January 10, October 17, 1957, April 16, 1959, January 12, 1961.

135. Bagley, *Four Decades with Alabama Baptists,* 170–71.

136. *Alabama Baptist,* December 14, 1967.

137. Executive Board Minutes, May 2, June 25, 1963; Leon Macon to Brady Justice, January 11, 1963, Macon Papers.

138. *Alabama Baptist,* July 11, 1963; anonymous interview, August 6, 1996.

139. *Alabama Baptist,* April 28, June 9, July 28, 1966.

140. Ibid., May 10, December 20, 1956, July 27, 1961, May 4, 1967, February 1, 1968; Executive Board Minutes, January 25, 1955; Robert Rennier, "Rural Population and Rural SBC Trends, 1950–1990," *Research Report,* Home Mission Board, 1996, 19; *Crisis—Our Challenge: Rural-Urban Missions Colloquium,* pamphlet by Home Missions Board, 1970; L. S. Trotter to Cecil Murphy, August 18, 1965, Salem Baptist Church Minutes.

141. Bagley, *Four Decades with Alabama Baptists,* 152–56; *Alabama Baptist,* August 3, 1995.

142. *Alabama Baptist,* March 24, September 15, 1966, May 11, July 15, 1967, March 28, 1968; Bagley, *Four Decades with Alabama Baptists,* 200–201.

143. *Alabama Baptist,* September 29, 1955, December 12, 1957, July 17, 1958, January 5, February 24, May 4, 1961, September 29, 1966; *Birmingham News,* November 6, 1968.

144. *Alabama Baptist,* October 10, 1957, June 19, 1958, September 14, 1961, October 4, 1962, July 18, 1963.

145. Ibid., August 2, 1962, July 13, 1967.

146. W. Albert Smith to Harold Seever, April 24, 1965; Smith to Harold Proctor, December 22, 1965; Smith to James Holland, April 14, 16, 23, 26, 30, May 14, 1965; Smith to Mrs. Billy J. Hyatt, September 21, 1965; Smith to Gerald K. Eure, February 4, March 2, 1966; Smith to B. W. Allen, March 29, 1966; all in W. Albert Smith Papers, Samford University Archives.

147. *Alabama Baptist,* September 14, 1961, August 10, 1967; S. P. Wiggins Sr. to Leon Macon, April 11, 1964; Macon to Wiggins, April 20, 1964; Miss Jackie Ables to Macon, December 18, 1964; Macon to Glenn Bynum, May 3, 1965; all in Macon Papers.

148. Jackson, *Women of Vision,* 100–15; Hermione Jackson to Mary Essie Stephens, August 3, 1963, Records of Alabama WMU.

149. Oral history with Mary Essie Stephens, by C. Clyde Presley, September 23, 1985, Samford University Archives; interview with Camilla Lowry, January 3, 1997.

150. Executive Board Minutes, December 9, 1958; Administration Committee Minutes, December 9, 1965, November 13, 1967, December 5, 1968; "Report of Committee to Study Departments of Work of the Executive Board, December 5, 1968," and "Budget 1950's Forward," in Records of Alabama WMU.

151. *Alabama Baptist,* August 4, 1955, July 26, October 4, 1956, July 20, 1961.

152. Oral history with Lillie Falkenberry, by Nina Brice Gwin, May 25, 1985, Samford University Archives; Edward B. Warren oral history.

Chapter 12: Race and Politics during the 1970s

1. Wendell F. Wentz Diary; "It Happened in Alabama," ms. by Wendell F. Wentz; both in Wendell F. Wentz Papers, Samford University Archives. Earl Hall, who pastored the church during the 1970s, disputes some details of the incident described in Wentz's diary.

2. Walter L. Knight, "Race Relations," in Ammerman, *Southern Baptists Observed*, 166–78.

3. *Alabama Baptist*, October 6, 1966, January 8, 1970, January 6, February 10, 1972. For examples of 1970s SBC literature attacked by Southern Baptists, see Home Mission Board pamphlets, *Southern Baptist Home Mission Board Cooperation with National Baptists, Be Reconciled . . . Care!* and Christian Life Commission pamphlets, *What Christians Can Do About Race Relations* and Foy Valentine, *Southern Baptists and the Contemporary Racial Crisis*, all in Southern Baptist Archives.

4. J. Herbert Gilmore Jr., *They Chose to Live: The Racial Agony of an American Church* (Grand Rapids: Eerdmans Publishing Co., 1972); for the account of a staff member's wife, see Katherine Hillhouse Goss, "A Personal Account of the Conflict of the First Baptist Church, Birmingham, Alabama, and the Beginning of the Baptist Church of the Covenant, 1970," ms., Samford University Archives.

5. For the views of Gilmore's adversaries, see *Alabama Baptist*, March 11, 1971, and *Birmingham News*, February 26, 1971.

6. Goss, "Personal Account"; *Alabama Baptist*, July 16, 1970.

7. Goss, "Personal Account."

8. Ibid.; Wentz, "It Happened in Alabama," 60–62; *Alabama Baptist*, July 16, 1970, March 11, 1971.

9. Goss, "Personal Account."

10. *Birmingham Post-Herald*, July 21, 1973; Oley C. Kidd to Pastor, January 4, 1974, in author's possession; *Alabama Baptist*, July 29, October 15, 1971, January 27, June 1, 1972.

11. Wentz, "It Happened in Alabama," 11, 17–19, 30–31.

12. Quoted in ibid., 62.

13. Ibid., 9, 12, 36–38.

14. Ibid., 1–8, 12–16, 23–24, 27–39, 42–67; Wentz Diary.

15. *Alabama Baptist*, September 3, 1970; Wendell F. Wentz to Wayne Flynt, October 6, 1995, in author's possession.

16. Wentz Diary.

17. *Alabama Baptist*, October 22, 1970, October 21, 1971.

18. Ibid., October 10, 1974.

19. Ibid., March 5, April 6, 1970, July 22, August 26, 1971, August 12, 1972, June 20, 1974, May 19, 1977; O. E. Williams to Hudson Baggett, July 1, 1970; Mrs. Archie McIntyre to Baggett, April 17, 1970; both in Baggett Papers.

20. "Inner-City Survey Committee, Birmingham," Samford University Archives; *Alabama Baptist*, February 28, 1974.

21. *Alabama Baptist*, March 7, 1970, February 24, 1977.

22. Administration Committee Minutes, May 9, 1972; *Alabama Baptist*, April 11, 1974, June 16, September 29, 1977.

23. *Alabama Baptist*, July 29, 1971, February 28, April 11, 1974.

24. Betty Bock, "Consideration for Long-Term Planning," report to Birmingham Baptist Association, undated but probably 1973; report of Committee to Study Urban Churches in Transition, Birmingham Baptist Association; both in Samford University Archives.

25. *Alabama Baptist*, February 24, 1977; Jere Allen to George Bagley, April 14, 1977; Henry H. Cox to Jere Allen, April 11, 1977; both in Administration Committee Minutes, 1977; Wentz, "It Happened in Alabama," 39–40.

26. Wentz, "It Happened in Alabama," 21–22.

27. *Alabama Baptist*, April 2, 1970, May 20, 1971.

28. "Extremism: A Threat to Freedom," July 5, 1970; "Living with Diversity," August 23, 1970; "Selling One's Soul," August 30, 1970; sermon mss. in Abe G. Watson Papers, Samford University Archives.

29. Administration Committee Minutes, March 20, July 31, 1970, October 26, 1973, July 12, 1974; "Program Goal, Department of Special Missions," in 1972 Administration Committee Minutes; *Alabama Baptist*, April 14, 1977, March 22, 1979.

30. *Alabama Baptist,* November 4, 1976.

31. "Inter-Baptist Fellowship Committee and Human Relations Conference," copy in Earl Potts Papers, Samford University Archives.

32. *Alabama Baptist,* May 21, 1970, March 4, 1971, January 13, 1972, August 29, 1974, July 12, 1979.

33. Ibid., February 5, 19, March 12, 19, 1970, September 30, October 28, November 18, December 2, 1971, November 22, December 13, 1973, January 17, 1974, December 4, 18, 1975.

34. Ibid., January 22, 1970, July 22, 1971, August 18, September 15, November 24, December 8, 15, 1977.

35. Ibid., March 28, 1974, April 21, 1977, March 22, April 15, 1979.

36. Executive Board Minutes, July 25–26, 1974.

37. *Alabama Baptist,* August 1, 1974.

38. Ibid., February 5, 12, 19, 26, March 5, 19, 29, 1970; resolutions dated January 15, February 10, March 29, June 7, 1970; J. B. Snyder to James L. Sullivan, January 15, 1970; all in Baggett Papers.

39. *Alabama Baptist,* March 19, 26, April 2, 9, 16, 1970.

40. Ibid., March 19, 26, 1970.

41. Ibid., January 23, February 6, March 13, April 24, 1975, August 3, 1978.

42. Ibid., May 12, 1955, April 30, 1970, September 17, 1970.

43. Ibid., January 11, 1973, August 8, 1974.

44. Ibid., February 5, September 16, 1976, June 23, 1977.

45. Ibid., June 10, 1976, June 23, 1977.

46. Ibid., September 16, 1971, March 16, April 6, October 19, 1972, May 31, 1973; Sarah Frances Anders and Marilyn Metcalf-Whittaker, "Women as Lay Leaders and Clergy," in Ammerman, *Southern Baptists Observed,* 212.

47. *Alabama Baptist,* March 29, May 2, 1973, June 13, 1974, July 17, 1975, October 19, 1978; Anders and Metcalf-Whittaker, "Women as Lay Leaders," 204–6.

48. *Alabama Baptist,* March 16, April 27, May 4, June 1, 1978.

49. Ibid., September 25, 1958, April 1, 1976, October 5, 1978; Earl Potts to Orrin Morris, September 28, 1978; Potts to Catherine Allen, September 28, 1978; both in Potts Papers.

50. *Alabama Baptist,* November 23, 1972, June 6, 1974.

51. Ibid., April 20, June 29, 1972, January 18, February 8, 15, March 8, 29, April 5, 19, July 19, 1973, April 11, 1974, June 23, 1977, November 9, 16, 21, December 7, 1978.

52. Ibid., March 15, 1973, February 20, 1975, November 3, December 1, 1977; Administration Committee Minutes, 1977; minutes of meeting, "Resolution on Concern for the Christian Family"; Bill Tillman to Earl Potts, undated; Olivia Byrd to Sue McInnish, November 28, 1977; all in Potts Papers.

53. *Alabama Baptist,* December 7, 1972, February 8, 1973, July 14, 1977.

54. Ibid., August 9, 23, 1973, April 29, June 10, 1976.

55. Ibid., February 15, 1973.

56. Ruby Welsh Wilkins to Wayne Flynt, December 5, 13, 1991.

57. Oral history with Grace Philpot Nelson, by Irma R. Cruse, January 27, 1982, Samford University Archives; Lee N. Allen and Catherine B. Allen, *Outward Focus: The First Fifty Years of Mountain Brook Baptist Church, 1944–1994* (Mountain Brook: Mountain Brook Baptist Church, 1994), 174.

58. Leonard, *God's Last and Only Hope,* 22–24.

59. Watt, "Private Hopes," 165–69. I found only one article during the 1970s attacking Catholicism, and that one came not from convention officials or *Alabama Baptist* editors.

60. *Alabama Baptist,* June 11, 1970, January 7, 1971, January 11, 1973. For an excellent discussion of the prelude to what moderates call the 1979 "takeover" and what fundamentalists refer to as the "correction," see Morgan, *New Crusades.*

61. See Morgan, *New Crusades;* Leonard, *God's Last and Only Hope,* 135–38.

62. *Alabama Baptist,* June 21, 1979; *Birmingham News,* June 17, 1979.

63. *Alabama Baptist,* July 27, 1978; lectures by Martin Marty at Auburn University, April 9–10, 1978.

64. Leonard, *God's Last and Only Hope,* 6–8.

65. *Alabama Baptist,* January 1, July 16, 30, 1970, April 15, June 10, August 12, 26, 1971, May 24, 1973, August 21, 1975, February 9, 1978.

66. Ibid., January 14, 1971, February 5, 12, 19, 26, 1976, February 2, November 2, 1978.

67. Ibid., March 23, 1972, November 6, December 4, 1975, July 1, 1976.

68. Ibid., June 4, 1970, January 14, June 10, July 22, August 12, 1971, May 18, July 13, 1972, June 26, 1975, August 25, 1977, June 1, 1978.

69. Ibid., May 18, 1972, February 2, 1978, May 31, 1979.

70. Ibid., September 10, 24, November 12, December 17, 1970, January 14, February 4, 25, 1971, February 4, 1972, June 7, 14, 1979.

71. "The Rediscovery of the Bible," sermon ms. in Watson Papers.

72. Oral history with John Harvey Wiley Jr., by Irma R. Cruse, July 1, 1987, Samford University Archives.

73. Minutes of Birmingham Ministers Discussion Group.

74. *Alabama Baptist,* October 22, 1970, August 30, 1973, January 30, May 1, 15, June 12, 1975.

75. Ibid., January 8, 15, April 1, July 22, August 5, 19, 1976, November 24, December 8, 15, 1977, January 5, 1978.

76. Homer B. Coleman to Hudson Baggett, July 30, 1970, Baggett Papers.

77. *Alabama Baptist,* February 1, 1973.

78. Ibid., November 6, 1975.

79. Ibid., February 19, 1970.

80. "The Christian in Relationship to the Economic Order," October 1972, sermon ms. by Alvin H. Hopson, copy in Butler Papers.

81. *Alabama Baptist,* July 1, 1976.

82. Ibid., August 20, 1970, August 5, 1971, October 6, 1977; Administration Committee Minutes, 1972.

83. Christian Life and Ministries Fellowship Minutes, Auburn First Baptist Church, in author's possession.

84. Billy Nutt to George Bagley, May 3, 1976, in Administration Committee Minutes, 1976; notes on Ira Myers telephone conversation, October 5, 1971, in Administration Committee Minutes, 1971; see Administration Committee Minutes, 1972, for associations with Christian Social Ministries program.

85. *Alabama Baptist,* January 15, 1970, September 9, 1971.

86. Ibid., July 20, 1972, December 13, 1973, March 20, 1975, October 21, 1976, April 21, 1977, May 25, 1978; *Birmingham Post-Herald,* September 13, 1973.

87. *Birmingham News,* February 9, 1974.

88. *Alabama Baptist,* June 17, 1976.

89. Jimmie Lewis Franklin, *Back to Birmingham: Richard Arrington, Jr., and His Times* (Tuscaloosa: University of Alabama Press, 1989), 67–68, 159–60; *Alabama Baptist,* April 9, 1970.

90. *Alabama Baptist,* February 17, August 3, 1972, July 18, 1974, August 21, 1975.

91. Ibid., June 10, August 26, October 28, 1976, January 6, 1977, January 19, 1978.

92. Ibid., January 5, June 15, 1978; Mission Service Corps files in Potts Papers.

93. Ms. in Potts Papers.

94. *Alabama Baptist,* September 13, October 11, 1979.

95. J. R. White to Fellow Baptist, April 1970; Ewell R. Jernigan to *Alabama Baptist,* April 27, 1970; George Bagley to Dan Calloway, April 24, 1970; Mrs. Edward Hardin to Hudson Baggett, April 24, 1970; Baggett to L. E. Kelly, May 4, 1970; Kelly to Baggett, May 12, 1970; all in Baggett Papers.

96. *Alabama Baptist,* September 5, 1974.

97. Ibid., February 13, November 20, 1975, September 2, November 18, 1976.

98. Ibid., February 26, 1976, January 12, 1978, January 4, 1979, February 28, 1980.

99. Ibid., November 20, 1975, February 5, 1976; Executive Board Minutes, 1980.

100. *Alabama Baptist,* November 18, 1971, July 1, 1976, September 28, 1978; Executive Board Minutes, June 17, 1971.

101. *Alabama Baptist,* January 28, 1971, March 15, 1979; "Alabama Baptist Statistics," in Executive Board Minutes, 1980 and 1984; Douglas W. Johnson et al., eds., *Churches and Church Membership in the United States* (Atlanta: Glenmary Research Center, 1974), 15–19, 32–38.

102. *Alabama Baptist,* January 4, 1973, February 6, 1975, February 26, 1976; "Alabama Baptist Statistics," Executive Board Minutes, 1980.

103. Report on Listening Sessions, Administration Committee Minutes, 1972; *Alabama Baptist,* April 25, May 2, 23, 1974, September 9, 1976.

104. Executive Board Minutes, July 27–28, December 1, 1972; Administration Committee Minutes, March 8, 1974; *Alabama Baptist,* May 21, July 2, 1970.

105. *Alabama Baptist,* November 26, 1970, November 22, 1973, June 6, 1974, November 20, 1975, November 22, 1979.

106. Minutes of Task Force Meeting on Rural Church in Alabama, November 23, 1976, in Potts Papers; "Report of Task Force on Rural Churches," Administration Committee Minutes, 1977; "Task Force on Rural Churches in Alabama," 1978, in Potts Papers.

107. *Alabama Baptist,* May 23, 1974, April 10, 1975; "The Bi-Vocational Issue," 1978, in Potts Papers; "The Bi-vocational Pastor," *Home Missions* 48 (October 1977): 5–17.

108. "Report of Task Force on Rural Churches"; "Task Force on Rural Churches in Alabama," 1978; *Alabama Baptist,* January 22, 1970, December 16, 1976.

109. *Alabama Baptist,* March 9, 1972; George H. Jackson to Jere Allen, November 1, 1977, Potts Papers.

110. *Alabama Baptist,* March 7, 1974.

111. "Report of Layman's Committee on Pastors' Salaries, 1972," Administration Committee Minutes, 1972; *Alabama Baptist,* September 7, 1978.

112. *Alabama Baptist,* February 26, 1970.

113. Ibid., February 20, 1975.

Chapter 13: The Fundamentalist Controversy in Alabama, 1980–1998

1. Hudson Baggett to Frank Bledsoe, March 8, 1993, Baggett Papers.

2. See Wuthnow, *Restructuring American Religious Society.*

3. George H. Gallup Jr. and Robert Bezilla, "Importance of Religion Climbing Again, According to New Polls," *Baptists Today,* February 17, 1994.

4. *Birmingham Post-Herald,* August 4, 1990.

5. *New York Times,* March 14, 1982; Carpenter, "Is Evangelical a 'Yankee' Word?" 80–102. Dockery, *Southern Baptists and American Evangelicals,* contains a number of essays contrasting mainstream American evangelicalism and SBC fundamentalism.

6. *Montgomery Advertiser,* July 18, 1992.

7. Carpenter, "Is Evangelical a 'Yankee' Word?" 102, 106–8; John Newport, "Southern Baptist Responses to American Evangelicals," 116–26; Richard Mouw, "Theological and Ethical Dimensions of American Evangelicals," 40; all in Dockery, *Southern Baptists and American Evangelicals.*

8. Helen Lee Turner, "Myths: Stories of This World and the World to Come," in Ammerman, *Southern Baptists Observed,* 108–18.

9. Rosenberg, "Southern Baptist Response," 145–56; Knight, "Race Relations," 167–78.

10. Larry L. McSwain, "Swinging Pendulums: Reform, Resistance, and Institutional Change," in Ammerman, *Southern Baptists Observed,* 266–73; Leonard, *God's Last and Only Hope,*

91, 120–28. For additional discussions of the controversy during the 1980s and 1990s, see Morgan, *New Crusades*, 37–185; Arthur E. Farnsley II, *Southern Baptist Politics: Authority and Power in the Restructuring of an American Denomination* (University Park: Pennsylvania State University Press, 1994); for a balanced treatment by moderate and fundamentalist leaders, see "The Southern Baptist Convention, 1979–1993: What Happened and Why?" *Baptist History and Heritage* 28 (October 1993). For a fundamentalist interpretation that casts the controversy exclusively in theological terms, see L. Russ Bush and Tom J. Nettles, *Baptists and the Bible: The Baptist Doctrines of Biblical Inspiration and Religious Authority in Historical Perspective* (Chicago: Moody Press, 1980).

11. *Opelika-Auburn News*, June 12, 1988; clipping in Tondera Papers.

12. Dr. Carl Todd, ms. on Cottage Hill Baptist Church, in author's possession; oral history with Fred Wolfe, by Wayne Flynt, February 1, 1997, Samford University Archives.

13. *Alabama Baptist*, June 8, 1989, February 15, April 4, 1996.

14. Ibid., June 1, 1989; *Birmingham Post-Herald*, August 31, 1991.

15. *Alabama Baptist*, June 22, 1989.

16. Ibid., June 21, 1990; *Birmingham Post-Herald*, March 7, 1990.

17. *Alabama Baptist*, December 15, 1983.

18. Ibid., December 30, 1982, March 5, 1987; "Tally-Southern Baptist Alliance," in author's possession; "Is First Baptist a Liberal Church?" September 29, 1985, and "The Bible and Current Trends in Religion," undated, both sermon mss. by John H. Jeffers, preached at Auburn First Baptist Church, in author's possession.

19. *Alabama Baptist*, January 3, 17, 1980, October 29, November 5, 1987; Hudson Baggett to Jack Harwell, November 6, 1987, Baggett Papers.

20. *Alabama Baptist*, March 9, 16, 1989.

21. Ibid., April 23, 1987.

22. Ibid., May 31, 1990; *Birmingham Post-Herald*, August 28, 1990.

23. *Alabama Baptist*, May 24, 1990; Ron McKeever to Page H. Kelly, February 22, 1991; Hudson Baggett to Page Kelly, April 5, 1991; both in Baggett Papers.

24. *Alabama Baptist*, May 5, 1994.

25. Ibid., October 9, 1980.

26. Ibid., November 24, 1983; Administration Committee Minutes, March 1, August 13–14, November 12, 1984, June 11–13, 1985, January 26, 1987.

27. *Alabama Baptist*, August 22, 1991, November 23, 1995.

28. Ibid., March 17, 24, 1994.

29. Ibid., February 14, 1980, May 19, 1988, November 9, 1995.

30. Ibid., June 2, 1988, May 6, 1993.

31. "Memorandum" from Thomas E. Corts, January 27, 1988; Al Jackson to Thomas E. Corts, February 3, 1988; both in Tondera Papers.

32. Douglas E. Dutton to Thomas E. Corts, November 20, 1986; Ralph Langley to *Alabama Baptist*, November 19, 1987; Gary A. Enfinger to Thomas E. Corts and members of Board of Trustees, February 24, 1988; all in Tondera Papers.

33. Al Jackson to Harry B. Brock Jr., April 15, 1987; Calvin Kelly to Thomas Corts, March 25, 1987; Kelly to Steve Tondera, April 16, 1987; Dan Springfield to "Dear Brother," undated but 1987; Rev. Sidney W. Nichols to Trustee, April 16, 1987; Albert Lee Smith to Dear Brother, April 13, 1987; all in Tondera Papers; Hudson Baggett to "Friend," June 12, 1987; Rev. J. Derek Gentle and Rev. E. P. Wallen to William Hull, October 20, November 13, 1987; Baggett to Hull, August 30, 1988; all in Baggett Papers.

34. *Alabama Baptist*, May 7, 1987; memorandum from Thomas E. Corts to Board of Trustees, April 10, 1987; Harold D. Wicks to Friends of Samford, April 17, 1987; both in Tondera Papers.

35. Jonathan D. Reaves to Thomas E. Corts, January 23, 1991; Corts to Reaves, January 25, 1991; Lawrence G. Avery to Corts, July 6, 1992; all in Baggett Papers.

36. *Alabama Baptist,* November 22, 29, 1990; Executive Board Minutes, September 5–6, 1985.

37. Jonathan D. Reaves to Thomas E. Corts, December 6, 1990, Baggett Papers.

38. Drew J. Gunnells to Thomas E. Corts, February 17, 1988 (with handwritten postscript on Tondera's copy); Edwin J. Hayes to Corts, February 25, 1988; both in Tondera Papers; Hudson Baggett to Timothy George, May 8, 1989; Ralph Langley to Baggett, June 27, 1989; both in Baggett Papers.

39. *Alabama Baptist,* February 18, March 3, May 19, 1988; *Wall Street Journal,* August 14, 1996.

40. *Alabama Baptist,* November 26, 1987; *Birmingham News,* November 22, 1987; J. Derek Gentle and E. P. Wallen to William E. Hull, September 21, 1987; Hull to Gentle and Wallen, October 20, 1987; both in Tondera Papers; Wallen to Thomas E. Corts, February 18, August 1, 1988, November 22, 1989; William E. Hull to Wallen, December 7, 1989; all in Baggett Papers.

41. E. P. Wallen to Thomas E. Corts, February 15, 1993, Baggett Papers.

42. Wayne Dorsett to Thomas E. Corts, April 22, 1992; Corts to Dorsett, April 30, 1992; both in Baggett Papers; *Alabama Baptist,* November 26, 1992.

43. *Alabama Baptist,* November 21, 1991, September 22, 29, October 6, 1994; *Birmingham Post-Herald,* September 15, 1994; *Huntsville Times,* September 15, 1994; "Report to Alabama Baptists," September 13, 1994, in author's possession.

44. *Alabama Baptist,* September 14, 1995, May 23, 1996, May 8, 22, June 12, 1997; *Mobile Register,* April 30, May 1, 9, 13, 14, 20, 23, 24, 31, June 1, 3, 4, 5, 7, 8, 1997.

45. *Alabama Baptist,* March 7, July 25, 1996; *Birmingham Post-Herald,* February 9, 1989; "ALCAP And You!" report in Administration Committee Minutes, 1988.

46. *Alabama Baptist,* July 15, 1982, July 14, November 17, 1983, March 14, 1996.

47. Ibid., July 29, August 5, 1982, July 28, October 6, December 15, 1983.

48. Oral history with James (Jimmy) Moore, by A. M. Daugherty, January 9, 1986, Samford University Archives.

49. *Alabama Baptist,* November 27, 1980; motion by M. G. Daniels, copy in Baggett Papers.

50. *Alabama Baptist,* July 9, 1987; *Montgomery Advertiser,* December 7, 1983; *Birmingham Post-Herald,* May 10, 1984; *Opelika-Auburn Bulletin,* December 11, 1983.

51. *Mobile Register,* November 15, 1994.

52. *Alabama Baptist,* October 23, 1986; *New York Times,* October 17, 1986.

53. *Alabama Baptist,* October 16, 1986, September 3, 1987.

54. Ibid., September 14, 1989, August 29, 1991.

55. "Christian Sex Education," copy in State Board of Missions Minutes, 1989.

56. *Birmingham Post-Herald,* November 15, 1982; Board of Missions Minutes, September 17–18, 1987; Denise George to Hudson Baggett, July 21, 1990; Baggett to Mrs. Ramona Clark, November 20, 1987; both in Baggett Papers.

57. Michele Dillon, "Religion and Culture in Tension: The Abortion Discourses of the U.S. Catholic Bishops and the Southern Baptist Convention," *Religion and American Culture: A Journal of Interpretation* 5 (Summer 1995): 159–80; *Alabama Baptist,* September 4, November 20, 1980.

58. *Alabama Baptist,* July 20, 1989, May 3, 1990; Administration Committee Minutes, May 16, 1985, 1987.

59. *Alabama Baptist,* October 20, 1988, November 23, 1989, January 11, 18, 1990.

60. Ibid., January 18, February 1, April 19, May 3, 9, 1990, April 11, 1996.

61. Ibid., January 18, 1990.

62. Ibid., January 11, 18, March 8, 1990, April 2, 1993; "What Does It Mean to Be Pro-Life?" sermon ms. by James A. Auchmuty Jr., August 6, 1989, in author's possession; *Birmingham News,* October 30, 1989.

63. *Alabama Baptist,* November 26, 1981, January 7, 1982.

64. Ibid., May 21, June 4, 1992; Byrd Goodman to Hudson Baggett, June 28, 1993, Baggett Papers.

65. *Alabama Baptist*, November 1, 1984, September 10, 1987, August 10, 1989, July 25, 1996; "What Jesus Said About Divorce and Remarriage," sermon ms. by Howard W. Roberts, March 7, 1993, in author's possession.

66. *Birmingham Post-Herald*, March 11, 1989; *Alabama Baptist*, July 27, 1989.

67. *Alabama Baptist*, January 28, 1993, March 16, 1995, June 27, 1996; Wayne Martin and Gail Anderson to Dellanna W. O'Brien, April 13, 1993; Hudson Baggett to Mrs. Helen B. Newton, March 11, 1993; both in Baggett Papers.

68. Administration Committee Minutes, August 11–12, 1986, and 1989; Jackson and Stephens, *Women of Vision*, 128–30.

69. *Alabama Baptist*, May 29, 1980.

70. Ibid., April 22, 1982, October 27, November 17, December 1, 8, 22, 1983, January 26, 1984.

71. Ibid., November 10, 1983, February 9, 1984.

72. Ibid., March 12, 1981.

73. Ibid., June 23, 1983, June 21, 1984.

74. Ibid., July 19, October 11, December 20, 1984.

75. Beth Baldwin to editor, November 19, 1987, Tondera Papers.

76. Fay White to Steve Tondera, November 21, 1986, Tondera Papers.

77. *Alabama Baptist*, January 8, 1987; *Birmingham Post-Herald*, November 18, 19, 1987; George Bagley to Hudson Baggett, July 31, 1989, Baggett Papers.

78. *Birmingham Post-Herald*, October 17, 1989; *Alabama Baptist*, September 28, October 19, 26, November 16, December 14, 1989.

79. "Women in the Kingdom," sermon ms., November 18, 1990, in author's possession.

80. *Alabama Baptist*, March 14, August 8, 1991, August 19, 1993; *Birmingham News*, June 7, 1996.

81. Melvin G. Cooper to Hudson Baggett, February 15, 1990, Baggett Papers; *Alabama Baptist*, October 27, 1988, February 18, 1993.

82. See Todd A. Baker et al., eds., *Religion and Politics in the South: Mass and Elite Perspectives* (New York: Praeger Publishers, 1983); and Clyde Wilcox, "Religious Orientations and Political Attitudes: Variations Within the New Christian Right," *American Politics Quarterly* 15 (April 1987): 274–96; *Alabama Baptist*, September 13, 1984.

83. *Birmingham Post-Herald*, May 28, 1985; *Alabama Baptist*, March 28, 1996.

84. See Matthew C. Moen, *The Transformation of the Christian Right* (Tuscaloosa: University of Alabama Press, 1992).

85. *Birmingham News*, September 7, 1980.

86. Ibid.

87. *Alabama Baptist*, February 18, 1982.

88. *Opelika-Auburn News*, November 18, 1984.

89. Vernon G. Offord Sr. to Earl Potts et al., November 1, 1987, Tondera Papers; Anna Marie Cannon to Hudson Baggett, December 14, 1987, Baggett Papers.

90. *Alabama Baptist*, December 10, 1987, October 13, 1988.

91. Ibid., October 13, November 10, 1988.

92. Vernon G. Offord Sr. to Hudson Baggett, August 28, 1992; Baggett to Offord, August 31, 1992; Gail Hoecherl to Baggett, August 7, 1992; all in Baggett Papers; *Alabama Baptist*, May 9, 1991, February 25, 1993.

93. *New York Times*, July 31, 1980, January 3, 1985; *Alabama Baptist*, September 20, 1984, March 10, October 6, 1988; *Birmingham Post-Herald*, September 6, 1996; *Birmingham News*, September 13, 1996; Hudson Baggett to Frances A. Garner, October 8, 1990; Baggett to Dan Ivins, October 15, 1990; both in Baggett Papers.

94. *Alabama Baptist,* October 6, 1983, September 5, 1985.

95. *Birmingham News,* September 30, 1989; *Auburn Plainsman,* November 30, 1989; *Alabama Baptist,* March 15, 1990.

96. *Alabama Baptist,* December 1, 1994.

97. Ibid., August 16, 1990.

98. Ibid., August 7, 1980.

99. Ibid., March 15, 1990; *Birmingham News,* November 5, 1995.

100. *Alabama Baptist,* May 15, 1980, May 7, 1987, September 19, 1991, April 14, 1994; *Birmingham News,* March 25, 1984; Lee N. Allen, *Born for Missions: 150 Years, Birmingham Baptist Association, 1933–1983* (Birmingham: Birmingham Baptist Association, 1984), 104–5.

101. *Alabama Baptist,* November 3, 1988, August 1, 1991; *Birmingham Post-Herald,* April 1, 1981.

102. *Opelika-Auburn News,* July 17, 1978; *Alabama Baptist,* August 9, 1990, March 14, 1996; *Baptist Light,* January–March 1990, 5.

103. *Alabama Baptist,* February 28, 1980, May 12, 1983, March 15, 1984, March 21, 1996; Powell Brewton to Hudson Baggett, June 11, 1992, Baggett Papers.

104. *Alabama Baptist,* December 15, 1994; *Birmingham Post-Herald,* September 28, 1991.

105. Administration Committee Minutes, May 2, 1986, September 15, 1988; *Alabama Baptist,* December 2, 30, 1993, November 21, 1996.

106. *Birmingham News,* May 6, 1990; *Alabama Baptist,* February 8, 1996, January 16, 1997.

107. *Alabama Baptist,* June 29, 1995, January 4, 1996; *New York Times,* June 21, 1995.

108. *Opelika-Auburn News,* July 17, 1978; *Birmingham Post-Herald,* July 3, 1995.

109. *Alabama Baptist,* July 13, 1995.

110. *Baptist Light,* January–March 1990, 5; *Alabama Baptist,* November 9, 1989; *Birmingham Post-Herald,* September 28, 1991.

111. *Alabama Baptist,* January 4, September 26, 1996; Baptist Center for Ethics press release, March 3, 1992.

112. *Alabama Baptist,* October 22, 1987, June 6, 1996; *Birmingham Post-Herald,* September 30, 1989.

113. *Alabama Baptist,* March 28, April 18, 1996.

114. Ibid., July 15, August 26, 1982, September 20, 1984.

115. Ibid., November 16, 1995; *Birmingham Post-Herald,* April 26, 1986.

116. *Alabama Baptist,* November 7, 1991; *Alabama Baptist Network of Community Ministries,* 1994, 1995, 1996; Lee N. Allen, *The First Baptist Church of Montgomery, Alabama, 1980–1995* (Montgomery: First Baptist Church, 1996), 45–49.

117. See Dees and Fiffer, *Season for Justice; Birmingham News,* December 5, 1982.

118. *Alabama Baptist,* April 2, 1987; Administration Committee Minutes, March 16–17, 1987.

119. *Alabama Baptist,* December 3, 1987, November 17, 1988.

120. Ibid., March 15, 1990.

121. David T. Morgan, "Alabama Baptists and the Controversy in the Southern Baptist Convention, 1979–1991," *Alabama Review* 47 (October 1994): 269, 270–71, 283; Fred Wolfe oral history.

122. Administration Committee Minutes, September 8–9, 1983, April 19, 1984.

123. *Alabama Baptist,* May 24, 1984, November 23, 1989, August 16, 30, 1990.

124. Ibid., July 12, 1990.

125. Ibid., July 10, 1980, June 3, December 2, 1982, May 10, June 7, September 13, 1984, March 13, 1986, March 17, June 23, 1988, April 6, 1989, May 5, 1994; "The *Alabama Baptist,*" ms. in Baggett Papers.

126. *Alabama Baptist,* May 15, 1980; Hudson Baggett to W. A. Criswell, October 30, 1991; Criswell to Baggett, October 22, 1992; Baggett to William A. Baggett, March 28, 1990; Fred Wolfe to Hudson Baggett, October 6, 1993; Baggett to Junior Hill, January 5, 1989; Baggett to

Timothy George, February 3, 1993; Baggett to Stephen W. Anderson, February 3, 1993; all in Baggett Papers.

127. Praise for Baggett's fairness can be found in: Bob Curlee to Hudson Baggett, December 2, 1987; R. F. Adams to Baggett, July 19, 1988; William L. Dean to Baggett, June 19, 1986; Jean Beaird to Baggett, May 4, 1993; Charles E. Graham to Baggett, September 1, 1990; all in Baggett Papers.

128. David T. Morgan to Hudson Baggett, May 6, 1993; Baggett to Terry R. Mitchell, January 17, 1992; Baggett to Dr. and Mrs. C. R. Daly, March 14, 1989; Baggett to Mrs. Holt Cannon, June 19, 1990; Baggett to Max Thompson, October 9, 1992; Baggett to T. M. Hamby, January 9, 1991; Baggett to R. Inman Johnson, June 14, 1991; all in Baggett Papers.

129. Hudson Baggett to Herschel H. Hobbs, February 12, 1993; Susan L. Mackey to Baggett, May 5, 1992; Baggett to Mackey, May 6, 1992; Baggett to Dr. R. G. Puckett, December 11, 1992; Ross Arnold to Baggett, July 23, 1993; all in Baggett Papers.

130. Gary A. Enfinger to Hudson Baggett, May 29, 1991; Enfinger to Board of Directors, July 24, 1991; Charles W. Roe to Enfinger, July 30, 1991; Roe to Baggett, July 30, 1991; Catherine B. Allen to Baggett, January 10, 1991; Baggett to William E. Whitfield, June 19, 1992; Jay Gordon to Baggett, undated; Baggett to Gordon, May 8, 1992; David Dockery to Baggett, March 1992; all in Baggett Papers; *Alabama Baptist*, August 21, 1980.

131. *Alabama Baptist*, November 26, 1981; *Opelika-Auburn News*, November 19, 1981.

132. *Alabama Baptist*, October 9, 1980, November 24, 1983; *Birmingham Post-Herald*, March 17, 1984; oral history with Wallace B. Henley, by Irma R. Cruse, September 12, 1985, Samford University Archives.

133. *Alabama Baptist*, November 28, 1985.

134. Ibid., November 13, 1986; clippings in Tondera Papers; Dan W. Hollis to Steve Tondera, November 24, 1986, Tondera Papers.

135. Newspaper clipping, October 28, 1987, Tondera Papers.

136. Clippings from *Huntsville Times*, November 18, 1987; Keith Adams to Steve Tondera, February 18, 1987; Mark T. Long to Tondera, February 17, 1987; Burma Leggett to Tondera, November 20, 1986; Beverly Sutton to Tondera, November 16, 1988; Janet Little to Tondera, March 31, 1988; all in Tondera Papers.

137. Clipping from *Decatur Daily*, October 17, 1987, Tondera Papers; *Alabama Baptist*, November 12, 1987, November 10, 1988.

138. *Alabama Baptist*, May 2, 1985, November 8, 15, 1990; Executive Board Minutes, November 13, 1989; Hudson Baggett to Charles T. Carter, November 7, 1990, Baggett Papers.

139. *Birmingham Post-Herald*, August 27, 1990; *Birmingham News*, November 15, 1990; *Alabama Baptist*, November 14, 1991.

140. Crystal A. Haynes to Hudson Baggett, January 21 and February 1, 1991; Baggett to Haynes, January 23, 1991; Gary Forsyth to Baggett, July 9, 1990; Baggett to Forsyth, July 30, 1990; all in Baggett Papers.

141. For representative letters from Masons, see Paul M. Bearden to Hudson Baggett, undated; Margaret Bryan to Baggett, July 9, 1992; Larry Holly to Baggett, June 4, 1992; all in Baggett Papers.

142. Hudson Baggett to Julian Scott, June 22, 1992; Baggett to Vernon L. Lowe, June 17, 1992; Baggett to Mr. and Mrs. Edwin H. Lusk, October 27, 1993; all in Baggett Papers.

143. *Alabama Baptist*, November 26, 1992; Hudson Baggett to Fred Lackey, November 9, 1992, Baggett Papers.

144. Hudson Baggett to Fred Lackey, November 9, 1992, Baggett Papers; *Birmingham News*, November 17, 1994; *Alabama Baptist*, November 23, 1995.

145. *Birmingham News*, November 21, 1996; *Alabama Baptist*, November 28, 1996.

146. *Baptists Today* 11 (April 29, 1993): 19; *Birmingham News*, August 26, 1990; *Alabama Baptist*, May 27, 1993, March 3, 1994.

147. One survey discovered that lay persons wanted their pastors to excel in fourteen

separate categories. Hudson Baggett to Bryant Strain, September 29, 1993; unidentified author to Baggett, May 7, 1993; both in Baggett Papers.

148. *Alabama Baptist,* August 26, 1982, January 11, 1990, September 26, 1991.

149. Ibid., August 25, 1988; Arthur Hudson to author, April 1994.

150. Hudson Baggett to Mrs. Clyde Kinnaird, October 31, 1989; Baggett to Jim Holmes, March 23, 1990; both in Baggett Papers.

151. *Alabama Baptist,* May 24, 1984, April 28, May 12, 1988, November 30, 1989; Michael J. Brooks to Hudson Baggett, April 14, 1993, Baggett Papers.

152. See Administration Committee Minutes, 1985, for Bold Mission Thrust goals.

153. *Alabama Baptist,* April 13, 1995, April 4, May 2, 1996; *Annual Report to the Alabama Baptist State Convention, November 19–20, 1996,* 65, Samford University Archives.

154. Rheta Grimsley Johnson, "Alabama Baptists hoist upon their own press release," *Birmingham Post-Herald,* September 27, 1993.

155. Hudson Baggett to William Hobson, September 27, 1993; Baggett to Tommy Pirkle, October 8, 1993; both in Baggett Papers.

156. "Alabama Baptist Statistics," Administration Committee Minutes, 1984 and 1986; *Alabama Baptist,* February 20, 1986, February 19, 1987, February 18, 1988, February 23, 1989, February 22, 1990, February 18, 1993, April 25, 1996, May 15, 1997.

157. *Alabama Baptist,* November 22, 1990, February 3, 1994; Harry L. Poe, "Teenage Rebaptism: When Is It Manipulation?" *Home Life* (January 1990): 42–43; Administration Committee Minutes, 1981, January 23, 1984, August 12–13, 1985.

158. *Alabama Baptist,* February 11, April 14, 1988, August 24, 1989, January 17, 1991; *Birmingham News,* May 20, 1990.

159. *Alabama Baptist,* October 11, 1984, April 2, 1987, April 20, 1989, April 23, 1992; John F. Loftis to Hudson Baggett, August 24, 1989, Baggett Papers.

160. *Alabama Baptist,* April 14, 1988, December 14, 1989, May 27, 1993, June 8, 1995.

161. Survey conducted by author; survey data in his possession.

162. *Birmingham News,* April 12, 1991, July 17, 1992; *Birmingham Post-Herald,* June 13, 1995; *Wall Street Journal* (southeastern edition), August 14, 1996.

163. *Alabama Baptist,* September 22, 1988, May 11, August 24, 1989, October 4, 1990, June 20, October 31, 1991, July 29, 1993, February 29, 1996.

164. Ibid., July 9, 1981, March 17, 1983, October 22, 1987, January 7, 1988, October 11, 1990, April 18, 1991, February 22, 29, March 7, October 31, 1996.

165. Ibid., April 23, 1992; Board of Missions Minutes, September 17–18, 1987.

Bibliography

Manuscript Collections

Alabama Baptist State Convention, Montgomery, Alabama
    Administration Committee Minutes of the Alabama Baptist State Convention
    Alabama Baptist State Convention Minutes and Annuals, 1827–1997
    Executive Board Minutes of the Alabama Baptist State Convention
    State Board of Missions Minutes
Alabama State Archives, Montgomery, Alabama
    Alabama Woman Suffrage Organization Papers
    John H. Bankhead Papers
    Sarah R. Espy Diary
    Jonathan Haralson Papers
    Joseph F. Johnson Papers
    Minutes, Fourth Annual Session of the Evergreen Association. Troy: John Post Printer, 1888
    Oscar W. Underwood Papers
Auburn University Archives, Auburn, Alabama
    Denson Family Papers
    J. W. Lester Papers
Duke University Archives, Durham, North Carolina
    Martha Foster Crawford Diaries
Franklin D. Roosevelt Library, Hyde Park, New York
    Franklin Delano Roosevelt Papers
Mss. in author's possession, Auburn, Alabama
    James A. Auchmuty Jr. Sermon. "What Does It Mean to Be Pro-Life?" August 6, 1989
    John Evan Barnes Jr. "My Autobiography as I Recall It"
    Christian Life and Ministries Fellowship Minutes. Auburn First Baptist Church
    Gary Farley. "Celebrating the Jubilee Year of the Rural Church Program"
    Sean A. Flynt. "Lee Compere." Paper presented to Alabama Historical Association, April
        1994
    John H. Jeffers Sermons

Fred Lackey ms., January 31, 1997

Bill J. Leonard. "A Theology for Racism: Southern Fundamentalists and the Civil Rights Movement." Paper presented at Cambridge University, September 1995

Cary C. Lloyd. "Separation of Church and State, Soul Liberty and Equality"

Sally G. McMillen. "To Train Up a Child: Southern Baptist Sunday Schools and the Socialization of Children, 1870–1900." Paper presented to Southern Historical Association, 1986

Mark Newman. "Alabama Southern Baptists and the Black Quest for Equality, 1954–1980." Paper presented at conference on Montgomery bus boycott, University of Hull, United Kingdom, July 1996

——. "Getting Right with God: Southern Baptists and Race Relations, 1945–1980"

Elizabeth Rhodes Diary. Book 3

Howard W. Roberts Sermon. "What Jesus Said about Divorce and Remarriage"

Walter B. Shurden. "The Southern Baptist Synthesis: Is It Cracking?" Carver-Barnes Lectures, Southeastern Baptist Theological Seminary, Wake Forest, North Carolina

Carl Todd. Cottage Hill Baptist Church

Samford University Archives, Birmingham, Alabama

J. D. Acker Papers

Alabama Baptist Biography Files

Arlington Baptist Church Records

Hudson Baggett Papers

George Bagley Papers

F. M. Barnes Papers

Julia Ann Tarrant Barron Papers

Charles R. Bell Jr. Papers

Bethany Baptist Church Minutes

Big Creek Baptist Church Minutes

Bledsoe-Kelly Collection of Cemetery and Bible Records

John C. Bush Papers

James H. Butler Papers

Sermon Book of Sidney J. Catts

Mrs. S. A. Chambers. "Woman's Work in the Church"

Jesse A. Cook Papers

Irma R. Cruse. "A Sketch of the Religious Life of Paul H. Mabe As He Lived It," July 24, 1981

James Hardy Curry Papers

A. C. Davidson Papers

B. Locke Davis Papers

James Harvey DeVotie Papers

A. J. Dickinson Papers

Annie Dopson Scrapbooks

George B. Eager Papers

Eufaula Baptist Church Minutes

George Franklin Papers

Katherine Hillhouse Goss Papers

Clay I. Hudson Papers

L. L. Gwaltney Papers
W. Cosby Hall Papers
A. T. M. Handey Papers
Claude M. Haygood Papers
F. Wilbur Helmbold Papers
Henry C. Hooten Papers
"Howard College Extension" ms.
Rosa Cilley Hunter Papers
T. M. and R. M. Hunter Papers
John W. Inzer Papers
Hermione Jackson Papers
Julia Praytor Killingsworth Papers
George L. Lee Papers
Lucille Loyd Papers
D. L. McCall Papers
Leon M. Macon Papers
Minutes of Birmingham Ministers Discussion Group
Minutes of Ladies Benevolent Society, Ladies Aid Society, and Woman's Missionary Society, First Baptist Church, Huntsville
A. P. Montague Papers
A. G. Moseley Papers
Mount Hebron Baptist Church Minutes
Notasulga First Baptist Church Minutes
Old Liberty Baptist Church Minutes (Cleburne County)
R. E. Pettus Papers
Joseph W. Phillips Sermons
Wayne Pinegar. "John H. Buchanan, Sr."
H. Clay Pless. "Historical Sketch of Lebanon Baptist Church," July 21, 1940
Earl Potts Papers
Records of Alabama WMU, 1909–1969
"Records of Big Creek Baptist Church, Jefferson County, Alabama, June, 1847–October, 1885." Transcribed by Ned Johnston, 1989
L. T. Reeves Diary
J. J. D. Renfroe Papers
Lida Robertson Papers
"Russellville First Baptist Church"
Salem Baptist Church Minutes
John R. Sampey Papers
Alexander T. Sims Papers
W. Albert Smith Papers
William David Stell Papers
James C. Stivender Papers
James Swedenburg Papers
E. B. Teague Papers
I. T. Tichenor Papers
Steve Tondera Papers

Abe G. Watson Papers

Larry V. Wells. "The 1928–39 Depression Years at First Baptist Church, Fort Payne, Ala-
    bama," March 11, 1985

Wendell F. Wentz Papers

"Willing Workers in Retrospect, Ninety-First Anniversary of Organized Woman's Work,
    First Baptist Church, Greenville, Alabama, 1872–1963"

M. M. Wood Papers

Davis C. Woolley Papers

Southern Baptist Historical Library and Archives, Nashville, Tennessee

John H. Buchanan Papers

W. O. Carver Papers

James H. Chapman Papers

Christian Life Commission Records

Foreign Mission Board Papers

Home Mission Board Papers

Una Roberts Lawrence Papers

B. F. Riley Diaries

E. T. Winkler Papers

Southern Historical Collection, University of North Carolina Library, Chapel Hill, North
    Carolina

James Harvey Joiner Papers

James Mallory Diary

Basil Manly Sr. Papers

University of Alabama Archives, Tuscaloosa, Alabama

Harry Mell Ayers Papers

O. D. Street Papers

University of Virginia Archives, Charlottesville, Virginia

Clarence Cason Papers

Oral Histories and Interviews

Samford University Oral History Collection, Birmingham, Alabama

Oral Histories

M. Reynolds Baum by Irma R. Cruse, March 14, 1980

Charles R. Bell by Wayne Flynt, January 28, 1972

Jack E. Brymer Sr. by Irma R. Cruse, January 22, 1984

Gordon C. Chandler by W. S. Love, October 25, 1983

Claude A. Crane by Jim Nogalski, March 20, 1979

B. Locke Davis by Wayne Flynt, January 22 and 26, 1976

Oscar A. Davis and Mrs. Eunice L. Davis by Ray M. Atchinson and Doris T. Atchinson,
    February 17, 1984

Harry Edwin Dickinson by W. S. Love, December 13, 1984

Sam Jones Ezell by Rollin Armour, July 21, 1978

Lillie Falkenberry by Nina Brice Gwin, May 25, 1985

Samuel Andrew Granade by Nina Brice Gwin, March 20, 1991

Margaret Taliaferro Ham by Irma R. Cruse, June 2, 1983

Wallace B. Henley by Irma R. Cruse, September 12, 1985
Mrs. L. A. House by Wayne Flynt, July 10, 1974
Brady R. Justice by Ray M. Atchinson, August 20, 1984
Evelyn L. Mims by Ray M. Atchinson and Doris L. Atchinson, August 3, 1979
James (Jimmy) Moore by A. M. Daugherty, January 9, 1986
Grace Philpot Nelson by Irma R. Cruse, January 27, 1982
Mrs. Julian Newman by Clyde Presley, July 29, 1981
Andrew W. Oden by Gilbert Burks, May 4, 1990
Leroy Richard Priest by Cynthia A. Wise, April 19, 1990
Mary Essie Stephens by Clyde Presley, September 23, 1985
Edward B. Warren by George E. Sims, December 3, 1975
John Harvey Wiley Jr. by Irma R. Cruse, July 1, 1987
Louis Wilhite by Lee Hazelgrove, January 21, 1975
Hubert Williams by A. M. Daugherty, June 16, 1987
Hoyt R. Wilson by Irma R. Cruse, March 19, 1980
Fred Wolfe by Wayne Flynt, February 1, 1997

Interviews

Anonymous, August 6, 1996
Charles G. Dobbins, October 30, 1987
John Jeffers, December 1, 1996
Renny Johnson, July 12, 1989
Camilla Lowry, January 3, 1997

Articles

Acker, Joe D. "Baptist Beginnings in Alabama." *Alabama Baptist Historian* 15 (January 1979): 3–16.
Allen, Lee N. "The Alabama Baptist Association: Distress, Destitution, and Decline, 1861–1862." *Alabama Baptist Historian* 18 (January 1982): 3–14.
———. "The Alabama Baptist Association: Years of Fulfillment, 1840–1860." *Alabama Baptist Historian* 16 (January 1980): 3–14.
Aprile, Marona Pucciarelli. "The Lives of Arcangelo Pucciarelli and Alice Mae Dupree Pucciarelli." *Alabama Baptist Historian* 33 (January 1997): 24–29.
Baker, Robert A. "The Magnificent Years (1917–1931)." *Baptist History and Heritage* 8 (July 1973): 144–57.
Banner, Lois W. "Religious Benevolence as Social Control: A Critique on an Interpretation." *Journal of American History* 60 (June 1973): 23–41.
Baptist, Edward. "The Millennium." *Baptist Preacher* 8 (November 1849): 191–200.
———. "The Power of Man to Obey the Gospel." *Baptist Preacher* 10 (February 1851): 45–53.
Bass, S. Jonathan. "Bishop C. C. J. Carpenter: From Segregation to Integration." *Alabama Review* 45 (July 1992): 184–215.
Beeman, Richard R., and Rhys Isaac. "Cultural Conflict and Social Change in the Revolutionary South: Lunenburg County, Virginia." *Journal of Southern History* 46 (November 1980): 525–50.
Billington, Monroe. "The Alabama Clergy and the New Deal." *Alabama Review* 32 (July 1979): 214–25.

"The Bi-vocational Pastor." *Home Missions* 48 (October 1977): 5–17.

Bode, Frederick A. "Religion and Class Hegemony: A Populist Critique in North Carolina." *Journal of Southern History* 37 (August 1971): 417–38.

Bradley, J. C. "Profiles of Home Mission Board Executives." *Baptist History and Heritage* 30 (April 1995): 26–33.

Buckley, Thomas E. "After Disestablishment: Thomas Jefferson's Wall of Separation in Antebellum Virginia." *Journal of Southern History* 61 (August 1995): 445–80.

Chambliss, A. W. "The Consecration and Support of the Gospel Ministry." *Baptist Preacher* 7 (August 1848): 133–63.

———. "Public Offenses, or Church Discipline." Part 1. *Baptist Preacher* 4 (September 1845): 173–90. Part 2. *Baptist Preacher* 4 (October 1845): 191–209.

Chapman, James H. "Epochs of the Century of the Birmingham Baptist Association." *Alabama Baptist Historian* 2 (December 1965): 4–17.

Cloyd, Daniel L. "Prelude to Reform: Political, Economic, and Social Thought of Alabama Baptists, 1877–1890." *Alabama Review* 31 (January 1978): 48–64.

Crowe, Richard G. "The Early Beginnings of the Colbert-Lauderdale Baptist Association, Alabama." *Alabama Baptist Historian* 19 (July 1983): 2–9.

Crowther, Edward R. "Holy Honor: Sacred and Secular in the Old South." *Journal of Southern History* 58 (November 1992): 619–36.

———. "Independent Black Baptist Congregations in Antebellum Alabama." *Journal of Negro History* 72 (Summer, Fall 1987): 66–75.

———. "Interracial Cooperative Missions Among Alabama Baptists, 1868–1882." *Journal of Negro History*, forthcoming.

Curtis, Thomas F. "The Certainty of Divine Purposes and the Contingency of Second Causes." *Baptist Preacher* 10 (April 1851): 77–90.

Davis, Edward B. "Fundamentalism and Folk Science Between the Wars." *Religion and American Culture: A Journal of Interpretation* 5 (Summer 1995): 217–48.

Dickinson, A. J. "Rural Church Problems and Ministry." *Home Field* 22 (December 1910): 12–14.

Dickinson, W. Calvin. "Rev. Noah Parker: A Missionary Baptist Leader in South Alabama." *Alabama Baptist Historian* 21 (July 1985): 13–17.

Dillon, Michele. "Religion and Culture in Tension: The Abortion Discourses of the U.S. Catholic Bishops and the Southern Baptist Convention." *Religion and American Culture: A Journal of Interpretation* 5 (Summer 1995): 159–80.

Dobbins, Charles G. "Alabama Governors and Editors, 1930–1955: A Memoir." *Alabama Review* 29 (April 1976): 135–54.

Doss, Chriss H. "The Original Fifteen Trustees of Howard College." Four-part series in *Alabama Baptist Historian* 28 (July 1992): 3–36; 29 (January 1993): 2–12; 29 (July 1993): 3–25; 30 (January 1994): 3–25.

Dupre, Daniel. "Barbeques and Pledges: Electioneering and the Rise of Democratic Politics in Alabama." *Journal of Southern History* 60 (August 1994): 479–512.

Eskew, Glenn T. "Demagoguery in Birmingham and the Building of Vestavia." *Alabama Review* 42 (July 1989): 192–217.

Faust, Drew Gilpin. "Christian Soldiers: The Meaning of Revivalism in the Confederate Army." *Journal of Southern History* 53 (February 1987): 63–90.

Feldman, Glenn A. "Lynching in Alabama, 1889–1921." *Alabama Review* 48 (April 1995): 114–41.

Findlay, James F. "Religion and Politics in the Sixties: The Churches and the Civil Rights Act of 1964." *Journal of American History* 77 (June 1990): 66–92.

Fleming, Walter L. "The Churches of Alabama During the Civil War and Reconstruction." *Gulf States Historical Magazine* 1 (September 1902): 2–127.

Flynt, Wayne. "Organized Labor, Reform, and Alabama Politics, 1920." *Alabama Review* 23 (July 1970): 163–80.

——. " 'A Special Feeling of Closeness': Mt. Hebron Baptist Church, Leeds, Alabama." In *American Congregations,* vol. 1, *Portraits of Twelve Religious Communities,* edited by James P. Wind and James W. Lewis. Chicago: University of Chicago Press, 1994.

Garrett, Mitchell B. "Sixty Years of Howard College, 1842–1902." *Howard College Bulletin* 85 (October 1927): 1–165.

George, Timothy. " 'Faithful Shepherd, Beloved Minister': The Life and Legacy of Basil Manly, Sr." *Alabama Baptist Historian* 27 (January 1991): 14–33.

Glisson, Martha McGhee. "The Role of the Good Hope Baptist Church in the Community of Uchee, 1837–1987." *Alabama Review* 42 (July 1989): 218–28.

Goldfield, David R. "The Urban South: A Regional Framework." *American Historical Review* 86 (December 1981): 1009–34.

Goode, Richard C. "The Godly Insurrection in Limestone County: Social Gospel, Populism, and Southern Culture in the Late Nineteenth Century." *Religion and American Culture: A Journal of Interpretation* 3 (Summer 1993): 155–69.

Hackett, David. "Gender and Religion in American Culture, 1870–1930." *Religion and American Culture: A Journal of Interpretation* 5 (Summer 1995): 127–58.

Handy, Robert T. "The Social Gospel in Historical Perspective." *Andover Newton Quarterly* 9 (January 1969): 170–80.

Harper, Jimmy. "Alabama Baptists and the Rise of Hitler and Fascism, 1930–1938." *Journal of Reform Judaism* (Spring 1985): 1–11.

Helmbold, F. Wilbur. "Baptist Periodicals in Alabama, 1843–1873." *Alabama Baptist Historian* 2 (July 1966): 2–12.

——. "Five More Pioneer Churches in Madison County." *Alabama Baptist Historian* 6 (July 1970): 27–35.

——. "The Initial Missionary Dispute in North Alabama." *Alabama Baptist Historian* 1 (June 1965): 11–13.

Hill, Samuel S. Jr. "Religion." In *Encyclopedia of Southern Culture,* edited by Charles Reagan Wilson and William Ferris, 1269–75. Chapel Hill: University of North Carolina Press, 1989.

Hinson, E. Glenn. "Historical Patterns of Lay Leadership in Ministry in Local Baptist Churches." *Baptist History and Heritage* 13 (January 1978): 26–34.

Holley, Howard L. "Charles Crow, 1770–1845." *Alabama Baptist Historian* 1 (June 1965): 3–10.

Hudson, Winthrop S. "Walter Rauschenbusch and the New Evangelicalism." *Religion in Life* 30 (Summer 1961): 412–30.

Hunt, Robert E. "Home, Domesticity, and School Reform in Antebellum Alabama." *Alabama Review* 49 (October 1996): 253–75.

"James Horton Chapman." *Alabama Baptist Historian* 2 (December 1965): 1–3.

Jones, Walter B. "A Challenge." *Alabama Bible Society Quarterly* 16 (July 1960): 68–70.

——. "Is It Unchristian to Believe in Segregation?" *Alabama Bible Society Quarterly* 13 (October 1957): 2–9.

——. "100 Things You Should Know about Communism and Religion." *Alabama Bible Society Quarterly* 12 (July 1956): 11–20.

——. "The Struggle for Local Self-Government." *Alabama Bible Society Quarterly* 16 (October 1960): 76–84.

Knight, Walter L. "Southern Baptists Nationwide." *Quarterly Review* 43 (April–May–June 1983): 61–67.

Kuykendall, John W. "James Ely Welch: Baptist Home Missionary and Ecumenical Pioneer." *Quarterly Review* 42 (January–February–March 1982): 50–58.

Lockard, Mrs. W. G. "John Ellis Sumners—Baptist Pioneer." *Alabama Baptist Historian* 17 (January 1981): 17–18.

Lyon, Henry L. Jr. "Is Racial Segregation Christian? What Is the Position of the Minister of the Gospel?" *Alabama Bible Society Quarterly* 14 (July 1958): 21–23.

——. "Racial Agitation in Montgomery." *Alabama Bible Society Quarterly* 17 (July 1961): 60–61.

Madison, James H. "Reformers and the Rural Church, 1900–1950." *Journal of American History* 73 (December 1986): 645–68.

Martin, Robert F. "A Prophet's Pilgrimage: The Religious Radicalism of Howard Anderson Kester, 1921–1941." *Journal of Southern History* 48 (November 1982): 511–30.

Meigs, J. Thomas. "Southern Baptists and the Fundamentalist-Modernist Controversy of the 1920's." *Quarterly Review* 38 (October–November–December 1977): 54–67.

Miller, Glenn T. "Baptist Businessmen in Historical Perspective." *Baptist History and Heritage* 13 (January 1978): 55–62.

Morgan, David T. "Alabama Baptists and the Controversy in the Southern Baptist Convention, 1979–1991." *Alabama Review* 47 (October 1994): 267–84.

Nettles, Thomas J. "Southern Baptist Identity: Influenced by Calvinism." *Baptist History and Heritage* 31 (October 1996): 17–26.

Poe, Harry L. "Teenage Rebaptism: When Is It Manipulation?" *Home Life* (January 1990): 42–43.

Potts, Earl. "Shaping Alabama Baptists: The Cooperative Program." *Alabama Baptist Historian* 15 (July 1979): 3–10.

Quest, John W. "Slaveholding Operatives of the Benevolent Empire: Bible, Tract, and Sunday School Societies in Antebellum Tuscaloosa County, Alabama." *Journal of Southern History* 62 (August 1996): 481–526.

Richards, W. Wiley. "Southern Baptist Identity: Moving Away from Calvinism." *Baptist History and Heritage* 31 (October 1996): 27–35.

Russell, C. Allyn. "J. Frank Norris: Violent Fundamentalist." *Southwestern Historical Quarterly* 75 (January 1972): 271–302.

Sheldon, Richard N. "Richmond Pearson Hobson as a Progressive Reformer." *Alabama Review* 25 (October 1972): 243–61.

Shurden, Walter B. "The Christian Life Commission: Evolved Conscience of the Southern Baptist Convention." *Quarterly Review* 42 (October–November–December 1981): 63–76.

"The Southern Baptist Convention, 1979–1993: What Happened and Why?" *Baptist History and Heritage* 28 (October 1993): 2–54.

Sturgis, C. F. "The Divine Scheme of Evangelization." *Baptist Preacher* 13 (August 1854): 127–51.

Sumners, Bill. "Southern Baptists and Women's Right to Vote, 1910–1920." *Baptist History and Heritage* 12 (January 1977): 45–51.

——. "Southern Baptists and Women's Role in the Church, 1910–1920." *Alabama Baptist Historian* 16 (July 1980): 4–10.

Sweeney, Charles P. "Bigotry in the South." *Nation* 111 (November 24, 1920): 585–86.

——. "Bigotry Turns to Murder." *Nation* 113 (August 31, 1921): 232–33.

Taliaferro, H. E. "The Covenant of Redemption, the Soul of the Missionary Enterprise." *Baptist Preacher* 8 (January 1849): 1–18.

Thrasher, Mrs. Cecil. "Salem Baptist Church, Lawrence County." *Alabama Baptist Historian* 6 (July 1970): 43–45.

Tyrell, Ian R. "Drink and Temperance in the Antebellum South: An Overview and Interpretation." *Journal of Southern History* 48 (November 1982): 485–510.

Vickers, Gregory. "Southern Baptist Women and Social Concerns, 1910–1929." *Baptist History and Heritage* 23 (October 1988): 3–13.

Waldrep, Dwain. "Fundamentalism, Interdenominationalism, and the Birmingham School of Religion, 1927–1941." *Alabama Review* 49 (January 1996): 29–54.

Walker, Arthur L. Jr. "Three Alabama Baptist Chaplains, 1861–1865." *Alabama Review* 16 (July 1963): 174–84.

Walker, Joseph. "Mental Requisites of Pulpit Efficiency." *Baptist Preacher* 13 (October 1854): 166–81.

Watt, David H. "The Private Hopes of American Fundamentalists and Evangelicals, 1925–1975." *Religion and American Culture: A Journal of Interpretation* 1 (Summer 1991): 155–76.

Watt, James M. "The Covenant of Redemption." *Baptist Preacher* 8 (April 1849): 53–66.

Webb, Samuel L. "From Independents to Populists to Progressive Republicans: The Case of Chilton County, Alabama, 1880–1920." *Journal of Southern History* 59 (November 1993): 707–36.

Whiting, Marvin Y. " 'True Americans,' Pro and Con: Campaign Literature from the 1917 Race for the Presidency of the Birmingham City Commission." *Journal of the Birmingham Historical Society* 6 (July 1980): 11–23.

Wilcox, Clyde. "Religious Orientations and Political Attitudes: Variations Within the New Christian Right." *American Politics Quarterly* 15 (April 1987): 274–96.

Wilson, L. G. "The Church and Landless Men." *University of North Carolina Extension Bulletin* 1 (March 1, 1922): 1–27.

Windsor, Jerry M. "Preaching Up a Storm from 1839 to 1889." *Alabama Baptist Historian* 29 (January 1993): 13–24.

Wyatt-Brown, Bertram. "The Antimission Movement in the Jacksonian South: A Study in Regional Folk Culture." *Journal of Southern History* 36 (November 1970): 501–29.

Books

Allen, Catherine B. *A Century to Celebrate: History of Woman's Missionary Union.* Birmingham: Woman's Missionary Union, 1987.

——. *Laborers Together with God: 22 Great Women in Baptist Life.* Birmingham: Woman's Missionary Union, 1987.

Allen, Lee N. *Born for Missions: 150 Years, Birmingham Baptist Association, 1933–1983.* Birmingham: Birmingham Baptist Association, 1984.

——. *The First Baptist Church of Montgomery, Alabama, 1980–1995.* Montgomery: First Baptist Church, 1996.

——. *The First 150 Years, 1829–1979: First Baptist Church, Montgomery, Alabama.* Montgomery: First Baptist Church, 1979.

———. *Notable Past, Bright Future: First Baptist Church, Enterprise, Alabama, 1893–1993*. Enterprise: First Baptist Church, 1993.

Allen, Lee N., and Catherine B. Allen. *Outward Focus: The First Fifty Years of Mountain Brook Baptist Church, 1944–1994*. Mountain Brook: Mountain Brook Baptist Church, 1994.

Ammerman, Nancy Tatom. *Southern Baptists Observed: Multiple Perspectives on a Changing Denomination*. Knoxville: University of Tennessee Press, 1993.

Ayers, Harry M. *Parker Memorial Baptist Church, Anniston, Alabama, 1887–1937*. N.p., 1937.

Bagley, George E. *My Four Decades with Alabama Baptists: An Oral History Memoir*. Birmingham: Alabama Baptist Historical Commission, n.d.

Bailey, David T. *Shadow on the Church: Southwestern Evangelical Religion and the Issue of Slavery, 1783–1860*. Ithaca: Cornell University Press, 1985.

Baker, Robert A. *The Southern Baptist Convention and Its People, 1607–1972*. Nashville: Broadman Press, 1974.

Baker, Todd A. *Religion and Politics in the South: Mass and Elite Perspectives*. New York: Praeger Publishers, 1983.

Baptist Biography. Vol. 3, edited by B. J. W. Graham. Atlanta: Index Printing Co., 1923.

Bartley, Numan V. *The New South, 1945–1980*. Baton Rouge: Louisiana State University Press, 1995.

Beall, Noble Y. *The Preacher and His Task*. Atlanta: Home Mission Board, 1939.

Bee, Fanna K., and Lee N. Allen. *Ruhama Baptist Church, 1819–1969*. Birmingham: Ruhama Baptist Church, 1969.

Bobo, Mildred Burden, and Catherine Ryan Johnson. *First Baptist Church of Huntsville, Alabama*. Huntsville: First Baptist Church, 1985.

Boles, John. *The Great Revival, 1787–1805: The Origins of the Southern Evangelical Mind*. Lexington: University Press of Kentucky, 1972.

———, ed. *Masters and Slaves in the House of the Lord: Race and Religion in the American South, 1740–1870*. Lexington: University Press of Kentucky, 1988.

Boles, John, and Evelyn Thomas Nolen, eds. *Interpreting Southern History: Historiographical Essays in Honor of Sanford W. Higginbotham*. Baton Rouge: Louisiana State University Press, 1987.

Bond, Horace Mann. *Negro Education in Alabama: A Study in Cotton and Steel*. 1939. Reprint, Tuscaloosa: University of Alabama Press, 1994.

Boothe, Charles O. *The Cyclopedia of the Colored Baptists of Alabama*. Birmingham: Alabama Publishing Co., 1895.

Brown, Bessie Conner. *A History of the First Baptist Church, Tuskegee, Alabama, 1839–1971*. Tuskegee: First Baptist Church, 1972.

Brown, Jerry Elijah, ed. *Clearings in the Thicket: An Alabama Humanities Reader*. Macon: Mercer University Press, 1985.

Bruce, Dickson D. Jr. *And They All Sang Hallelujah: Plain-Folk Camp-Meeting Religion, 1800–1845*. Knoxville: University of Tennessee Press, 1974.

Bush, L. Russ, and Thomas J. Nettles. *Baptists and the Bible: The Baptist Doctrines of Biblical Inspiration and Religious Authority in Historical Perspective*. Chicago: Moody Press, 1980.

Calhoon, Robert M. *Evangelicals and Conservatives in the Early South, 1740–1861*. Columbia: University of South Carolina Press, 1988.

Carwardine, Richard J. *Evangelicals and Politics in Antebellum America*. New Haven: Yale University Press, 1993.

Chesebrough, David B. *God Ordained This War: Sermons on the Sectional Crisis, 1830–1865.* Columbia: University of South Carolina Press, 1991.

Clark, Carl A. *Southern Baptists and Rural Churches.* Fort Worth: Baptist Book Store, 1956.

Conkin, Paul V. *Cane Ridge: America's Pentecost.* Madison: University of Wisconsin Press, 1990.

Craig, Robert H. *Religion and Radical Politics: An Alternative Christian Tradition in the United States.* Philadelphia: Temple University Press, 1992.

Craighead, Lura Harris. *History of the Alabama Federation of Women's Clubs.* Vol. 1, *1895–1918.* Montgomery: Paragon Press, 1936.

Crews, Mickey. *The Church of God: A Social History.* Knoxville: University of Tennessee Press, 1990.

Crisis—Our Challenge: Rural-Urban Missions Colloquium. Atlanta: Home Mission Board, 1970.

Crumpton, Washington B. *A Book of Memories, 1842–1920.* Montgomery: Baptist Mission Board, 1921.

———. *Our Baptist Centennials, 1808–1923.* Montgomery: Paragon Press, 1923.

Curry, Lerond. *Protestant-Catholic Relations in America: World War I through Vatican II.* Lexington: University Press of Kentucky, 1972.

Dean, James E. *Baptists in Greensboro, Alabama.* N.p., 1938.

Dees, Morris, with Steve Fiffer. *A Season for Justice: The Life and Times of Civil Rights Lawyer Morris Dees.* New York: Charles Scribner's Sons, 1991.

Dill, Jacob S. *Isaac Taylor Tichenor: Home Mission Board Statesman.* Nashville: Sunday School Board, 1908.

Dockery, David S., ed. *Southern Baptists and American Evangelicals.* Nashville: Broadman and Holman Publishers, 1993.

Eighmy, John L. *Churches in Cultural Captivity: A History of the Social Attitudes of Southern Baptists.* Knoxville: University of Tennessee Press, 1972.

Ellsworth, Lucius F., ed. *The Americanization of the Gulf Coast, 1803–1850.* Pensacola: Historic Pensacola Preservation Board, 1972.

Encyclopedia of Southern Baptists. Vol. 1. Nashville: Broadman Press, 1958.

Epstein, Barbara L. *The Politics of Domesticity: Women, Evangelicalism, and Temperance in Nineteenth Century America.* Middletown, Conn.: Wesleyan University Press, 1981.

Farnsley, Arthur E. II. *Southern Baptist Politics: Authority and Power in the Restructuring of an American Denomination.* University Park: Pennsylvania State University Press, 1994.

Faust, Drew Gilpin. *The Creation of Confederate Nationalism: Ideology and Identity in the Civil War South.* Baton Rouge: Louisiana State University Press, 1988.

Fede, Frank Joseph. *Italians in the Deep South: Their Impact on Birmingham and the American Heritage.* Montgomery: Black Belt Press, 1994.

Feldman, Glenn A. *From Demagogue to Dixiecrat: Horace Wilkinson and the Politics of Race.* New York: University Press of America, 1995.

Flynt, Wayne. *Mine, Mill and Microchip: A Chronicle of Alabama Enterprise.* Northridge, Calif.: Windsor Publications, 1987.

———. *Poor But Proud: Alabama's Poor Whites.* Tuscaloosa: University of Alabama Press, 1989.

Flynt, Wayne, and Gerald W. Berkley. *Taking Christianity to China: Alabama Missionaries in the Middle Kingdom, 1850–1950.* Tuscaloosa: University of Alabama Press, 1997.

Foster, Joshua Hill. *Sixty-Four Years a Minister.* Wilmington, N.C.: First Baptist Church, 1948.

Franklin, Jimmie Lewis. *Back to Birmingham: Richard Arrington, Jr., and His Times.* Tuscaloosa: University of Alabama Press, 1989.

Friedman, Jean E. *The Enclosed Garden: Women and Community in the Evangelical South, 1830–1900*. Chapel Hill: University of North Carolina Press, 1985.

Gaston, Paul M. *The New South Creed: A Study in Mythmaking*. New York: Alfred A. Knopf, 1970.

Gates, Grace Hooten. *The Model City of the New South: Anniston, Alabama, 1872–1900*. Huntsville: Strode Publishers, 1978.

Gaustad, Edwin S. *Historical Atlas of Religion in America*. New York: Harper and Row, 1962.

George Boardman Eager: An Appreciation of Life and Work: A Memorial by His Associates, Family and Friends. N.p., n.d.

Gilmore, J. Herbert Jr. *They Chose to Live: The Racial Agony of an American Church*. Grand Rapids: Eerdmans Publishing Co., 1972.

Goen, C. C. *Broken Churches, Broken Nation*. Macon: Mercer University Press, 1985.

Grantham, Dewey W. *Southern Progressivism: The Reconciliation of Progress and Tradition*. Knoxville: University of Tennessee Press, 1983.

Gwaltney, L. L. *Forty of the Twentieth, or the First Forty Years of the Twentieth Century*. Birmingham: Birmingham Printing Co., 1940.

———. *A Message for Today on the Chariots of Fire or the Triumph of the Spiritual*. Birmingham: Birmingham Printing Co., 1941.

———. *The World's Greatest Decade: The Times and the Baptists*. Birmingham: Birmingham Printing Co., 1947.

Hackney, Sheldon. *Populism to Progressivism in Alabama*. Princeton: Princeton University Press, 1969.

Hall, Thelma Wolfe. *I Give Myself: The Story of J. Lewis Shuck and His Mission to the Chinese*. Richmond: Privately published, 1983.

Haln, Marilyn Davis. *Butler County in the Nineteenth Century*. N.p., 1978.

Hamilton, Frances Dew, and Elizabeth Crabtree Wells. *Daughters of the Dream: Judson College, 1838–1988*. Marion: Judson College, 1989.

Hamilton, Virginia Van der Veer. *Lister Hill: Statesman from the South*. Chapel Hill: University of North Carolina Press, 1987.

Harper, Keith. *The Quality of Mercy: Southern Baptists and Social Christianity, 1890–1920*. Tuscaloosa: University of Alabama Press, 1996.

Harris, Carl. *Political Power in Birmingham, 1871–1921*. Knoxville: University of Tennessee Press, 1977.

Heck, Fannie E. S. *In Royal Service: The Mission Work of Southern Baptist Women*. Richmond: Foreign Mission Board, 1915.

Higginbotham, Miriam, and Ralph Higginbotham. *Upon This Rock I Will Build My Church: Parker Memorial Baptist Church, 1887–1987*. N.p.: Parker Memorial Baptist Church, 1987.

Hill, Samuel S. Jr. *The South and the North in American Religion*. Athens: University of Georgia Press, 1980.

Holcombe, Hosea. *History of the Rise and Progress of the Baptists in Alabama*. Philadelphia: King and Baird Printers, 1840.

Holifield, E. Brooks. *The Gentlemen Theologians: American Theology in Southern Culture, 1795–1860*. Durham: Duke University Press, 1978.

Howard, Gene L. *Death at Cross Plains: An Alabama Reconstruction Tragedy*. Tuscaloosa: University of Alabama Press, 1984.

Hughes, McDonald. *History of the First African Baptist Church, 1866–1986*. Tuscaloosa: N.p., 1986.

Jackson, Hermione Dannelly. *Women of Vision*. N.p.: Woman's Missionary Union, 1964.

Jackson, Hermione Dannelly, and Mary Essie Stephens. *Women of Vision: Centennial Edition.* N.p.: Woman's Missionary Union, 1988.

Jeffers, John H. *The Auburn First Baptist Church, 1838–1988.* Auburn: Gnu's Room, 1990.

——. *History of the Tuskegee-Lee Association.* N.p., 1992.

Jent, John W. *The Challenge of the Country Church.* Nashville: Sunday School Board, 1924.

——. *Rural Church Development: A Manual of Methods.* Shawnee: Oklahoma Baptist University Press, 1928.

Johnson, Douglas W., ed. *Churches and Church Membership in the United States.* Washington, D.C.: Glenmary Research Center, 1974.

Jordan, William C. *Some Events and Incidents During the Civil War.* Montgomery: Paragon Press, 1909.

Kelly, Robin D. G. *Hammer and Hoe: Alabama Communists During the Great Depression.* Chapel Hill: University of North Carolina Press, 1990.

Kolchin, Peter. *First Freedom: The Responses of Alabama's Blacks to Emancipation.* New York: Greenwood Press, 1972.

Kuykendall, John W. *Southern Enterprize: The Work of National Evangelical Societies in the Antebellum South.* Westport, Conn.: Greenwood Press, 1982.

Larson, Edward J. *Sex, Race, and Science: Eugenics in the Deep South.* Baltimore: Johns Hopkins University Press, 1995.

Leonard, Bill J. *God's Last and Only Hope: The Fragmentation of the Southern Baptist Convention.* Grand Rapids: Eerdmans Publishing Co., 1990.

Lesher, Stephan. *George Wallace: American Populist.* New York: Addison-Wesley Publishing Co., 1994.

Link, William A. *The Paradox of Southern Progressivism, 1880–1930.* Chapel Hill: University of North Carolina Press, 1992.

Love, William Sep, and Dorothy Clifton Bishop. *History of the First Baptist Church, Oxford, Alabama: 150 Years, 1836–1986.* N.p., 1985.

Loveland, Anne C. *Southern Evangelicals and the Social Order, 1800–1860.* Baton Rouge: Louisiana State University Press, 1980.

McBeth, Leon H. *The Baptist Heritage: Four Centuries of Baptist Witness.* Nashville: Broadman Press, 1987.

McLendon, Robert G. Jr. *George Granberry McLendon, 1807–1895: Pioneer Missionary Baptist Preacher.* N.p., 1990.

Maloney's Birmingham 1900 City Directory. Vol. 15. Atlanta: Maloney Directory Co., 1900.

Manis, Andrew M. *Southern Civil Religions in Conflict: Black and White Baptists and Civil Rights, 1947–1957.* Athens: University of Georgia Press, 1987.

Marsden, George M. *Fundamentalism and American Culture: The Shaping of Twentieth-Century Evangelicalism, 1870–1925.* New York: Oxford University Press, 1980.

Martin, Joel W. *Sacred Revolt: The Muskogees' Struggle for a New World.* Boston: Beacon Press, 1991.

Marty, Martin E. *Righteous Empire: The Protestant Experience in America.* New York: Dial Press, 1970.

Masters, Victor I. *Country Church in the South.* Atlanta: Publicity Department of the Home Mission Board of the Southern Baptist Convention, 1916.

Mathews, Donald G. *Religion in the Old South.* Chicago: University of Chicago Press, 1977.

Miyakawa, T. Scott. *Protestants and Pioneers: Individualism and Conformity on the American Frontier.* Chicago: University of Chicago Press, 1964.

Moen, Matthew C. *The Transformation of the Christian Right.* Tuscaloosa: University of Alabama Press, 1992.

Moore, A. B. *History of Alabama and Her People.* Vol. 3. Chicago: American Historical Society, 1927.

Morgan, David T. *The New Crusades, The New Holy Land: Conflict in the Southern Baptist Convention, 1969–1991.* Tuscaloosa: University of Alabama Press, 1996.

Morgan, W. Scott. *History of the Wheel and Alliance and the Impending Revolution.* Reprint ed. New York: Burt Franklin, 1968.

Newman, Cynthia. *Maud McLure Kelly: Alabama's First Woman Lawyer.* Birmingham: Birmingham Printing and Publishing, 1984.

Owen, Marie Bankhead. *History of Alabama and Dictionary of Biography.* Chicago: S. J. Clarke Publishing Co., 1921.

Owen, Thomas McAdory. *History of Alabama and Dictionary of Alabama Biography.* Vol. 3. Chicago: S. J. Clarke Publishing Co., 1921.

Ownby, Ted. *Subduing Satan: Religion, Recreation, and Manhood in the Rural South, 1865–1920.* Chapel Hill: University of North Carolina Press, 1990.

Peterson, Thomas Virgil. *Ham and Japheth: The Mythic World of Whites in the Antebellum South.* Metuchen: Scarecrow Press, 1978.

Porch, Luther Q. *History of the First Baptist Church, Tuscaloosa, 1818–1968.* Tuscaloosa: Drake Printers, 1968.

Posey, Walter B. *The Baptist Church in the Lower Mississippi Valley, 1776–1845.* N.p., 1957.

Queen, Edward L. II. *In the South the Baptists Are the Center of Gravity: Southern Baptists and Social Change, 1930–1980.* Brooklyn: Carlson Publishing, 1991.

Ramond, John S. *Among Southern Baptists.* Vol. 1, *1936–1937.* Kansas City: Western Baptist Publishing Co., 1936.

Ray, Susan Ingram Hunt. *The Major: Harwell G. Davis, Alabama Statesman and Baptist Leader.* Birmingham: Samford University Press, 1996.

Reid, A. Hamilton. *Baptists in Alabama: Their Organization and Witness.* Montgomery: Paragon Press, 1967.

Reimers, David M. *White Protestantism and the Negro.* New York: Oxford University Press, 1965.

Rennier, Robert. "Rural Population and Rural SBC Trends, 1950–1990." *Research Report.* Atlanta: Home Mission Board, 1996.

Riley, B. F. *Alabama As It Is: The Immigrants and Capitalists Guide Book.* Atlanta: Constitution Publishing Co., 1888.

———. *A Memorial History of the Baptists of Alabama.* Philadelphia: Judson Press, 1923.

Rodabaugh, Karl. *The Farmers' Revolt in Alabama, 1890–1896.* N.p.: East Carolina University, 1977.

Rogers, William W. *The One-Gallused Rebellion: Agrarianism in Alabama, 1865–1896.* Baton Rouge: Louisiana State University Press, 1970.

Rogers, William W., Robert David Ward, Leah Rawls Atkins, and Wayne Flynt. *Alabama: The History of a Deep South State.* Tuscaloosa: University of Alabama Press, 1994.

Rosenberg, Ellen M. *The Southern Baptists: A Subculture in Transition.* Knoxville: University of Tennessee Press, 1989.

Salmond, John A. *A Southern Rebel: The Life and Times of Aubrey Willis Williams, 1890–1965.* Chapel Hill: University of North Carolina Press, 1983.

Sandeen, Ernest R. *The Roots of Fundamentalism: British and American Millennarianism, 1800–1930.* Chicago: University of Chicago Press, 1970.

Scott, Anne Firor. *The Southern Lady: From Pedestal to Politics, 1830–1930*. Chicago: University of Chicago Press, 1970.

Sellers, James Benson. *The Prohibition Movement in Alabama, 1702 to 1943*. Chapel Hill: University of North Carolina Press, 1943.

Sherer, Robert G. *Subordination or Liberation? The Development and Conflicting Theories of Black Education in Nineteenth Century Alabama*. Tuscaloosa: University of Alabama Press, 1977.

Shurden, Walter B. *Not a Silent People: Controversies That Have Shaped Southern Baptists*. Nashville: Broadman Press, 1972.

Silver, James W. *Confederate Morale and Church Propaganda*. Tuscaloosa: University of Alabama Press, 1957.

Sixty Glorious Years: A Summary of the History of Progress in the Mignon Baptist Church of Sylacauga, Alabama, 1902 to 1962. N.p., 1962.

Smith, H. Shelton, ed. *American Christianity: An Historical Interpretation with Representative Documents*. Vol. 2. New York: Charles Scribner's Sons, 1960.

Smith, Timothy L. *Revivalism and Social Reform in Mid–Nineteenth Century America*. Nashville: Abingdon Press, 1957.

Sobel, Mechal. *Trabelin' On: The Slave Journey to an Afro-Baptist Faith*. Princeton: Princeton University Press, 1988.

Sparks, Randy J. *On Jordan's Stormy Banks: Evangelicalism in Mississippi, 1773–1876*. Athens: University of Georgia Press, 1994.

Stakely, Charles A. *The History of the First Baptist Church of Montgomery*. Montgomery: Paragon Press, 1930.

Stewart, Willie Jean. *Heroes of Home Missions*. Atlanta: Home Mission Board, 1945.

Stone, Karen A. *The History of First Baptist Church of Wetumpka, 1821–1996*. Montgomery: Brown Printing Co., 1996.

———. *Prattville First Baptist Church: Sharing Our Past with a Vision for the Future, 1838–1988*. Montgomery: Brown Printing Co., 1989.

The Story of Alabama: A History of the State. Vol. 4. New York: Lewis Historical Publishing Co., 1949.

Sulzby, James F. Jr. *Annals of the Southside Baptist Church, Birmingham, Alabama*. Birmingham: Birmingham Printing Co., 1947.

———. *Toward a History of Samford University*. Birmingham: Samford University Press, 1986.

Szasz, Ferenc M. *The Divided Mind of Protestant America, 1880–1930*. Tuscaloosa: University of Alabama Press, 1982.

Terry, Paul, and Verner Sims. *They Live on the Land: Life in an Open-Country Southern Community*. Tuscaloosa: Bureau of Educational Research, 1940.

Thompson, James J. Jr. *Tried as by Fire: Southern Baptists and the Religious Controversies of the 1920s*. Macon: Mercer University Press, 1982.

Thornton, J. Mills III. *Politics and Power in a Slave Society: Alabama, 1800–1860*. Baton Rouge: Louisiana State University Press, 1978.

Tindall, George B. *Emergence of the New South: 1913–1945*. Baton Rouge: Louisiana State University Press, 1967.

Trolander, Judith Ann. *Professionalism and Social Change: From the Settlement House Movement to Neighborhood Centers, 1886 to the Present*. New York: Columbia University Press, 1987.

Ussery, Annie Wright. *The Story of Kathleen Mallory*. Nashville: Broadman Press, 1956.

Washington, James M. *Frustrated Fellowship: The Black Baptist Quest for Social Power*. Macon: Mercer University Press, 1986.

Webb, George E. *The Evolution Controversy in America*. Lexington: University Press of Kentucky, 1994.

Weber, Timothy R. *Living in the Shadow of the Second Coming: American Premillennialism, 1875–1925*. New York: Oxford University Press, 1979.

Wheeler, Edward L. *Uplifting the Race: The Black Minister in the New South Movement, 1865–1902*. New York: University Press of America, 1986.

White, Walter Belt. *History of the First Baptist Church, Talladega, Alabama: Its Pastors, People, and Programs Through One Hundred Fifty Years, 1835–1985*. Macon: Omni Press, 1985.

Wilks, W. P. *Biographical Dictionary of Alabama Baptists, 1920–1947*. Opelika, Ala.: Post Publishing Co., [1948].

Wilson, Charles R. *Baptized in Blood: The Religion of the Lost Cause, 1865–1920*. Athens: University of Georgia Press, 1980.

———, ed. *Religion in the South*. Jackson: University of Mississippi Press, 1985.

Wise, Cynthia A. *The Alabama Baptist Children's Home: The First One Hundred Years*. Montgomery: Brown Printing Co., 1991.

Withoft, Mabel Swartz. *Oak and Laurel: A Study of the Mountain Mission Schools of Southern Baptists*. Nashville: Sunday School Board of the Southern Baptist Convention, 1923.

Woodward, C. Vann. *Origins of the New South: 1877–1913*. Baton Rouge: Louisiana State University Press, 1951.

Word, Mary Florence Arthur. *Big Springs: A History of a Church and a Community, Randolph County, Alabama*. LaGrange, Ga.: Family Tree, 1986.

Wuthnow, Robert. *The Restructuring of American Religious Society Since World War II*. Princeton: Princeton University Press, 1988.

Wyatt-Brown, Bertram. "Religion and the Formation of Folk Culture: Poor Whites of the Old South." In *The Americanization of the Gulf Coast, 1803–1850*, edited by Lucius F. Ellsworth. Pensacola: Historic Pensacola Preservation Board, 1972.

Dissertations, Theses, Honors Papers

Ables, Ed. "A History of the DeKalb Baptist Association: Early Struggles and Growth." Master's thesis, Samford University, 1984.

Appleton, Jon G. "Samuel Henderson: Southern Minister, Editor, and Crusader, 1853–1866." Master's thesis, Auburn University, 1968.

Atkins, Leah Rawls. "Early Efforts to Control Tuberculosis in Alabama: The Formation and Work of the Alabama Tuberculosis Association, 1908–1930." Master's thesis, Auburn University, 1960.

Barton, Elizabeth. "The Baptist Collegiate Institute and Its First Principal, A. W. Tate." Master's thesis, University of Alabama, 1943.

Bell, Marty G. "James Robinson Graves and the Rhetoric of Demagogy: Primitivism and Democracy in Old Landmarkism." Ph.D. diss., Vanderbilt University, 1990.

Bennett, Hal D. "An Inquiry into the Life and Works of Editor Leslie L. Gwaltney of Alabama." Th.D. diss., New Orleans Baptist Theological Seminary, 1954.

Bigelow, Martha C. Mitchell. "Birmingham: Biography of a City of the New South." Ph.D. diss., University of Chicago, 1946.

Brooks, Daniel Fate. "The Mind of Wilcox County: An Antebellum History, 1819–1861." Master's thesis, Samford University, 1984.

Brownell, Blaine A. "The Urban Mind in the South: The Growth of Urban Consciousness in Southern Cities, 1920–1927." Ph.D. diss., University of North Carolina, Chapel Hill, 1969.

Burrows, John H. "The Great Disturber: The Social Philosophy and Theology of Alfred James Dickinson." Master's thesis, Samford University, 1970.

Campbell, Kathryn H. "Sojourn of a Southern Liberal: The Life and Ministry of Charles R. Bell, Jr." Master's thesis, Auburn University, 1986.

Clark, Elizabeth Boner. "The Abolition of the Convict Lease System in Alabama, 1913–1928." Master's thesis, University of Alabama, 1949.

Crabtree, Saranne Elizabeth. "*South-Western Baptist, 1850–1860*: Defender of Southern Rights." Master's thesis, Auburn University, 1973.

Crider, Robert F. "The Social Philosophy of L. L. Gwaltney, 1919–1950." Master's thesis, Samford University, 1969.

Cruse, Irma R. "Hardin Edwards Taliaferro: Baptist Preacher-Editor, 1811–1875." Master's thesis, Samford University, 1984.

Dees, Liesl Deann. "Anti-Catholicism Among Alabama Baptists, 1917–1928." Senior honors thesis, Samford University, 1989.

English, Carl D. "Ethical Emphases of Baptist Journals Published in the Southeastern Region of the United States, 1865–1915." Ph.D. diss., Southern Baptist Theological Seminary, 1948.

Feldman, Glenn A. "The Ku Klux Klan in Alabama." Ph.D. diss., Auburn University, 1996.

Gilliam, Thomas J. "The Second Folsom Administration: The Destruction of Alabama Liberalism, 1954–1958." Ph.D. diss., Auburn University, 1975.

Grant, James M. "Alabama's Reaction to Late Nineteenth Century Revivalism." Honors thesis, Samford University, 1968.

Harper, James Clyde. "A Study of Alabama Baptist Higher Education and Fundamentalism, 1890–1930." Ph.D. diss., University of Alabama, 1977.

Harvey, Paul. "Southern Baptists and Southern Culture, 1865–1920." Ph.D. diss., University of California at Berkeley, 1992.

Huston, Claudia Mae. "A History of Early Baptist Churches in Alabama." Master's thesis, University of Alabama, 1960.

Johnson, Kimball. "Isaac Taylor Tichenor: A Biography." Ph.D. diss., Southern Baptist Theological Seminary, 1955.

Jones, Terry L. "Attitudes of Alabama Baptists Toward Negroes, 1890–1914." Master's thesis, Samford University, 1968.

———. "Benjamin Franklin Riley: A Study of His Life and Work." Ph.D. diss., Vanderbilt University, 1974.

Kelsey, George D. "The Social Thought of Contemporary Southern Baptists." Ph.D. diss., Yale University, 1946.

Lancaster, James Dean Jr. "Howard College During the Civil War and Reconstruction, 1860–1873." Master's thesis, Samford University, 1974.

McLeod, Jimmy R. "Methodist and Baptist Reaction to the 1928 Presidential Campaign in Alabama." Master's thesis, Samford University, 1972.

McMath, Robert C. Jr. "The Farmers' Alliance in the South: The Career of an Agrarian Institution." Ph.D. diss., University of North Carolina, 1972.

Martin, Henry P. "A History of Politics in Clay County During the Period of Populism from 1888 to 1896." Master's thesis, University of Alabama, 1936.

Martin, William Terry. "Samuel Henderson and His Response to J. R. Graves and Landmarkism Through the *South-Western Baptist, 1857–1859*." Master's thesis, Samford University, 1977.

Palmer, Bruce E. "The Rhetoric of Southern Populists: Metaphor and Imagery in the Language of Reform." Ph.D. diss., Yale University, 1972.

Pate, James A. "The Development of the Instructional Program at Howard College, 1842–1957." Ph.D. diss., University of Alabama, 1959.

Praytor, Robert E. "From Concern to Neglect: Alabama Baptists' Religious Relations to the Negro, 1823–1870." Master's thesis, Samford University, 1971.

Rosenberg, Randy B. "John Davis Williams: Antebellum Southern Baptist Evangelical." Master's thesis, Auburn University, 1982.

Sewell, Cecil Orion. "The Carey Baptist Association of Alabama During the Civil War." Research paper, University of Alabama, 1963. Copy in Samford University Archives.

Sims, George E. "Progress, Problems, and Promise: The Orrville Baptists, 1888–1959." Honors thesis, Samford University, 1976.

Snell, William R. "The Ku Klux Klan in Jefferson County, Alabama, 1916–1930." Master's thesis, Samford University, 1967.

Sparks, Randy J. "A Mingled Yarn: Race and Religion in Mississippi, 1800–1876." Ph.D. diss., Rice University, 1988.

Sterne, Ellin. "Prostitution in Birmingham, Alabama, 1890–1925." Master's thesis, Samford University, 1977.

Stone, Karen A. "J. W. Lester and the Southern Baptist Rural Church Movement, 1908–1983." Master's thesis, Auburn University, 1984.

Sumners, Bill. "The Social Attitudes of Southern Baptists Towards Certain Issues, 1910–1920." Master's thesis, University of Texas at Arlington, 1975.

Vaughn, Carol Ann. "The Early Life of Martha Foster Crawford in Antebellum Alabama, 1830–1851." Master's thesis, Auburn University, 1994.

Walters, Jeff Kirk. " 'Though the Heavens Fall': Liberal Theology and the Southern Baptist Theological Seminary, 1894–1925." Master's thesis, Auburn University, 1992.

Watson, Joel C. "Isaac Taylor Tichenor and the Administration of the Alabama Agricultural and Mechanical College, 1872–1882." Master's thesis, Auburn University, 1968.

White, Walter Belt. "J. L. M. Curry: Alabamian." Master's thesis, Samford University, 1971.

Wise, Cynthia A. "Aspects of the Social Thought of Leon Macon, Editor of the *Alabama Baptist*, 1950–1965." Master's thesis, Samford University, 1970.

Government Publications

U.S. Bureau of the Census. *Religious Bodies: 1916.* Washington, D.C.: Government Printing Office, 1919.

———. *Census of Religious Bodies, 1926.* Vol. 2. Washington, D.C.: Government Printing Office, 1927.

U.S. Census Office, 8th Census, 1860. *Statistics of the United States in 1860.* Reprint. New York: Norman Ross Publishers, 1990.

Newspapers/Newsletters

Alabama Baptist, 1843–1865, 1873–1997 (also called *South-Western Baptist*, 1850–1865)
Alabama Baptist Network of Community Ministries Newsletter, 1994–1997

Alabama Citizen, 1908–1909
Anniston Star, 1954
Auburn Plainsman, 1989
Baptist Correspondent, 1860–1861
Baptist Light, 1994–1997
Baptist Observer, 1860–1861
Baptists Today, 1989–1997
Baptist World, 1909–1917
Birmingham News, 1894, 1902, 1927, 1965–1997
Birmingham Post-Herald, 1953, 1965–1997
Christian Index and South-Western Baptist, 1865–1874
New York Times, 1980, 1983–1986, 1990–1997
Opelika-Auburn News, 1977–1992

Index

Abbott, Joe Boone, 548

Abolitionism, 30, 43, 44, 45, 46, 52, 63, 84, 87, 94, 106, 108, 109. *See also* Slavery

Abortion, 483, 530, 531, 532, 534, 535, 552, 554, 568, 571, 575, 580, 581, 582, 591, 592, 599, 601, 608, 623

Abstracts of faith. *See* Articles of faith

Acipco Baptist Church (Birmingham), 435

Adams, Keith, 610

Adams, Samuel M., 205, 206, 207, 210, 211, 216, 219, 221, 222, 225, 227

Addison Baptist Church, 555

Aders, J. L., 362

African Americans, 35, 42, 43, 44, 45, 46, 47, 48, 49, 72, 99, 103, 108, 133, 134, 141, 180, 201, 208, 210, 219, 227, 237, 238, 239, 272, 282, 293, 303, 304, 336, 341, 353, 354, 362, 364, 373, 375, 379, 383, 385, 393, 395, 440, 449, 450, 455, 462, 464, 465, 469, 477, 479, 480, 481, 516, 517, 518, 519, 526, 527, 528, 529, 541, 548, 549, 553, 561, 565, 567, 593, 594, 595, 596, 597, 598. *See also* Race; Racism; Segregation; Slavery

African Baptist Church Cottonport, 49

African Huntsville Church, 49

Agriculture: Baptist attitudes toward, 61, 194, 206, 219, 220, 223, 228, 289, 290, 326, 327, 360, 364, 379, 385, 394, 429

AIDS, 580, 583, 600, 601, 606, 607, 609, 610

Alabama Anti-Saloon League, 115, 184, 269, 270, 272, 273, 319. *See also* Alabama Citizens Action Program; Alcoholic beverages; Prohibition; Prohibition Party; Temperance

Alabama Association, 7, 10, 11, 18, 33, 45, 66, 100, 128, 130, 138

Alabama Baptist, xvii, xix, xx, 10, 19, 22, 25, 31, 41, 51, 54, 56, 57, 58, 59, 60, 61, 66, 72, 74, 75, 76, 77, 79, 82, 84, 85, 86, 88, 89, 92, 94, 95, 97, 98, 107, 109, 110, 114, 116, 117, 123, 124, 126, 127, 128, 131, 132, 147, 148, 150, 159, 160, 162, 163, 165, 166, 167, 173, 175, 176, 177, 178, 179, 183, 187, 189, 192, 193, 195, 196, 197, 199, 200, 201, 207, 210, 211, 214, 215, 216, 217, 220, 221, 222, 223, 225, 226, 227, 228, 230, 231, 232, 234, 235, 236, 238, 239, 240, 241, 243, 244, 245, 246, 247, 248, 249, 250, 255, 256, 258, 259, 261, 264, 272, 274, 275, 278, 280, 281, 284, 286, 290, 297, 300, 301, 302, 304, 305, 310, 313, 316, 317, 318, 319, 322, 325, 328, 342, 345, 346, 350, 354, 358, 371, 372, 379, 380, 382, 385, 386, 391, 392, 394, 397, 403, 404, 414, 417, 418, 419, 421, 423, 425, 436, 440, 446, 447, 451, 452, 453, 456, 460, 462, 470, 472, 478, 480, 491, 498, 503, 504, 510, 521, 528, 531, 532, 534, 535, 539, 544, 548, 549, 550, 554, 559, 569, 570, 578, 581, 592, 605, 606, 608, 619

Alabama Baptist Bible Society, 19, 31, 75, 93

Alabama Baptist Children's Home, xx,

707

About the Author

Wayne Flynt is Distinguished University Professor at Auburn University. He received his A.B. from Howard College (now Samford University) and his M.S. and Ph.D. from Florida State University. From 1977 to 1985 he served as chairman of the Department of History, Auburn University. He is author of *Duncan Upshaw Fletcher: Dixie's Reluctant Progressive* (1971), *Cracker Messiah: Governor Sidney J. Catts of Florida* (1977), *Dixie's Forgotten People: The South's Poor Whites* (1979), *Montgomery: An Illustrated History* (1980), *Southern Poor Whites: A Selected Annotated Bibliography* (1981), *Mine, Mill, and Microchip: A Chronicle of Alabama Enterprise* (1987), and *Poor but Proud: Alabama's Poor Whites* (1989). He is coauthor of *Alabama: The History of a Deep South State* (1994) and *Taking Christianity to China: Alabama Missionaries in the Middle Kingdom* (1997). He has chaired both the Southern Baptist Historical Commission and the Alabama Baptist Historical Commission. He has also been active in Baptist institutional life worldwide as a visiting scholar at Hong Kong Baptist University and as lecturer at many Baptist-affiliated colleges and universities.